SOCIAL PSYCHOLOGY

An Introduction to the Study of Human Relations

S. STANSFELD SARGENT

CLINICAL PSYCHOLOGIST, PHOENIX, ARIZONA
FORMERLY ASSOCIATE PROFESSOR OF PSYCHOLOGY
BARNARD COLLEGE, COLUMBIA UNIVERSITY

ROBERT C. WILLIAMSON

DEPARTMENT OF PSYCHOLOGY
LOS ANGELES CITY COLLEGE

SECOND EDITION

THE RONALD PRESS COMPANY · NEW YORK

5

Library of Congress Catalog Card Number: 58-6658

PRINTED IN THE UNITED STATES OF AMERICA

Preface

This book is an introductory text in social psychology which can be used either in the intermediate courses given in psychology and sociology departments or in social science survey and "human relations" courses. That is, it may serve as an introduction to scientific social psychology or as an approach to more practical, applied studies. The first three sections emphasize the facts, principles, and theories of social psychology, while the last two sections deal with its interpretations and applications in the areas of social phenomena and social issues. Like the first edition, this book brings together contributions from psychology, sociology, anthropology, psychiatry, political science, and other specialties. Its central viewpoint is a "field" approach which involves personality variables, situational factors, and also persons' perceptions of social situations.

Social psychology has developed enormously in the last several years—in research, in theory, in applications. Much of this new material has been incorporated in the present volume. Footnote references to all sources are given and, in addition, each chapter has an annotated bibliography for those who wish to do more specialized reading or advanced study.

The senior author wishes to acknowledge his great debt to the late Willard Waller, sociologist and colleague, with whom he collaborated for two years in teaching the social psychology course at Barnard College. Others to whom he is similarly indebted are Professors Mirra Komarovsky, Conrad Arensberg, and John Useem. Thanks for more recent stimulating associations go to his colleagues in the Graduate Program in Social Psychology at Columbia University, notably Professors Otto Klineberg, Goodwin Watson, Herbert Hyman, Conrad Arensberg, and Hubert Bonner. He expresses gratitude also to Professors Muzafer Sherif, Eugene Hartley, and Gerhart Saenger, and to Dr. Marian W. Smith, for many friendly and productive contacts during the past several years. And finally, thanks are extended to many users of the first edition who took the authors' request seriously and made suggestions for improving the book.

iii

The junior author is deeply grateful to a number of social psychologists who have influenced his orientation, beginning with his first courses in social psychology taught by Professor Franklin Fearing and Professor Emory S. Bogardus. In his work on the text he was helped in clarifying his ideas by many conversations with Dr. Eugene Ziskind and Dr. Fay Berger Karpf. He appreciates especially the contact with his students in social psychology classes at Los Angeles City and State Colleges which has helped him crystallize his thinking. Able secretarial help was furnished by Miss Marjorie Allison and particularly by Mrs. Samuella Craiker DeGrood. And, above all, gratitude is expressed for the editorial assistance and understanding of his wife, Virginia Lorenzini Williamson.

Both authors feel particularly indebted to Professors Georgene and John Seward who first brought them together and encouraged their collaboration. They wish also to thank Professor Elliott M. McGinnies of the University of Maryland for many valuable suggestions.

S. Stansfeld Sargent
Robert C. Williamson

Phoenix, Arizona
Los Angeles, California
   February, 1958

Acknowledgments

For permission to include a number of quotations, tables, and charts, the authors express thanks to the following holders of copyrights:

American Psychological Association, Inc., and the following journals, for permission to quote from a monograph by O. Klineberg, No. 132 (1931) in the *Archives of Psychology,* and from an article by R. Dymond in the *Journal of Consulting Psychology,* 1950, Vol. 14.

American Sociological Society, for permission to quote from an article by L. S. Cottrell, Jr., in the *American Sociological Review,* 1942, Vol. 7.

Appleton-Century-Crofts, Inc., for permission to quote from R. Linton, *The Study of Man,* copyright, 1936, by D. Appleton-Century Co., Inc.; and from J. R. Hilgard, *Theories of Learning,* rev. ed., copyright, 1956.

University of Chicago Press, for permission to quote from L. L. Thurstone and E. J. Chave, *The Measurement of Attitude,* copyright, 1929.

Columbia University Press, for permission to quote from A. Kardiner's chapter in R. Linton (ed.), *The Science of Man in the World Crisis,* copyright, 1945; and for permission to reproduce the diagram on social classes from James West, *Plainville, U.S.A.,* copyright, 1945.

The Commonweal, New York, for permission to quote from an article by G. W. Allport in its issue of October 6, 1944, copyright, 1944.

The Free Press, Glencoe, Illinois, for permission to quote from T. Parsons, R. F. Bales, and E. A. Shils, *Working Papers in the Theory of Action,* copyright, 1953.

The Government Printing Office, U.S. Department of State, for permission to quote from B. L. Whorf, *Collected Papers on Metalinguistics,* copyright, 1952.

Harcourt, Brace & Co., Inc., for permission to quote from R. S. Lynd and H. M. Lynd, *Middletown,* copyright, 1929; from R. S. Lynd and H. M. Lynd, *Middletown in Transition,* copyright, 1937; and from S. I. Hayakawa, *Language in Action,* copyright, 1941.

Harper & Bros., for permission to quote from E. R. Guthrie, *Psychology of Human Conflict,* copyright, 1938; and from G. E. Simpson and J. M. Yinger, *Racial and Cultural Minorities,* copyright, 1953.

Harvard University Press, and the President and Fellows of Harvard College, for permission to quote from D. Leighton and C. Kluckhohn, *Children of the People,* copyright, 1947; and from an article by R. R. Sears in T. Parsons and E. A. Shils (eds.), *Toward a General Theory of Action,* copyright, 1951.

Henry Holt & Co., Inc., for permission to quote from G. W. Allport, *Personality*, copyright, 1937; and from O. Klineberg, *Social Psychology*, rev. ed., copyright, 1954.

Houghton Mifflin Co., for permission to quote from R. Benedict, *Patterns of Culture*, copyright, 1934, by Ruth Benedict; and from N. A. Cameron, *Psychology of Behavior Disorders*, copyright, 1947, by Norman A. Cameron; and from L. F. Shaffer and E. J. Shoben, *The Psychology of Adjustment*, 2d ed., copyright, 1956, by Laurance Frederick Shaffer and Edward Joseph Shoben, Jr.

University of Illinois Press, for permission to quote from G. W. Allport's article in *Tensions That Cause Wars*, edited by Hadley Cantril, copyright, 1950.

International Universities Press, Inc., for permission to quote from E. H. Erikson's article, "Childhood and Tradition in Two American Indian Tribes," in the *Psychoanalytic Study of the Child*, 1945, Vol. 1.

Alfred A. Knopf, Inc., for permission to quote from Karl Menninger, *The Human Mind*, copyright, 1930.

Alfred McClung Lee and Elizabeth Briant Lee, for permission to quote from their *Fine Art of Propaganda*, copyright, 1939, and published by Harcourt, Brace & Co., Inc., and the Institute for Propaganda Analysis; Alfred McClung Lee for permission to quote from his *How to Understand Propaganda*, copyright, 1952, and published by Rinehart & Co., Inc.

Life magazine, for permission to quote from an article on Elvis Presley, August 27, 1956.

Longmans, Green & Co., for permission to quote from R. J. Havighurst, *Human Development and Education*, copyright, 1953.

The Macmillan Company, for permission to quote from G. Hicks, *Small Town*, copyright, 1947, and from W. Lippmann, *Public Opinion*, copyright, 1922.

John P. Marquand, for permission to quote from *The Late George Apley*, copyright, 1937, and published by Little, Brown & Co.

McGraw-Hill Book Co., Inc., for permission to quote from R. Stagner, *Psychology of Personality*, 2d ed., copyright, 1948.

William Morrow & Co., Inc., for permission to quote from Margaret Mead, *And Keep Your Powder Dry*, copyright, 1942, by Margaret Mead.

New York Academy of Sciences and the author, for permission to quote from an article by J. W. Woodard in Series II, Vol. 6, 1944, of the *Transactions* of the Academy, copyright, 1944.

Oxford University Press, for permission to quote from Salvador de Madariaga, *Englishmen, Frenchmen and Spaniards*, copyright, 1928.

Princeton University Press, for permission to quote from Hadley Cantril, *The Invasion from Mars*, copyright, 1940; from Hadley Cantril, *Gauging Public Opinion*, copyright, 1944; and from Robert S. Lynd, *Knowledge For What?*, copyright, 1939.

Redbook magazine, for permission to quote from an article on James Dean, written by Joe Hyams, which appeared in the September, 1956, issue.

Social Science Research Council, for permission to quote from Bulletin No. 57 by Robin M. Williams, copyright, 1947; and from Bulletin No. 60 by F. Mosteller, H. Hyman, P. J. McCarthy, E. S. Marks, and D. B. Truman, copyright, 1949.

Society for the Psychological Study of Social Issues, for permission to quote from Arthur Kornhauser's chapter in G. W. Hartmann and T. M. Newcomb (eds.), *Industrial Conflict,* copyright, 1940, and published by the Cordon Co., Inc.

The Wenner-Gren Foundation for Anthropological Research (formerly The Viking Fund, Inc.), for permission to quote from an article by L. M. Hanks, Jr., in S. S. Sargent and M. W. Smith (eds.), *Culture and Personality,* copyright, 1949.

John Wiley & Sons, Inc., for permission to quote from Hadley Cantril, *The Psychology of Social Movements,* copyright, 1941; and from A. B. Hollingshead, *Elmtown's Youth,* copyright, 1949.

Yale University Press, for permission to quote from M. A. May, in the Preface to N. E. Miller and J. Dollard, *Social Learning and Imitation,* copyright, 1941; from J. M. W. Whiting, *Becoming a Kwoma,* copyright, 1941, and from J. M. W. Whiting, and I. L. Child, *Child Training and Personality,* copyright, 1953; and for permission to quote and to reproduce a diagram of class structure from W. L. Warner and P. S. Lunt, *The Social Life of a Modern Community,* copyright, 1941.

Contents

PART IV

UNDERSTANDING SOCIAL PHENOMENA

PART V

IMPROVING HUMAN RELATIONS

SOCIAL
PSYCHOLOGY

1

Introduction

Social psychology is the scientific study of persons as members of groups with emphasis on their social or interpersonal relationships. It focuses on the individual's behavior, as it affects, and is affected by, the behavior of others. The term "behavior" refers to both covert behavior (what the individual perceives, thinks, and feels) and to overt or observable behavior (what he reads, how he votes, whom he marries).

This approach differs chiefly in emphasis from that of the psychologist, sociologist, and anthropologist, all of whom are interested in human behavior. Psychologists study the individual's reactions to stimuli of any kind. In the past few decades they have made great progress in understanding behavioral processes like learning, remembering, perceiving, feeling, and even more inclusive aspects of the individual such as intelligence and personality. On the other hand, sociologists and anthropologists focus upon group behavior and its products rather than the individuals composing the groups. These social scientists have increased our knowledge of modern and primitive societies—their cultures, customs, values, and institutions. But neither psychologists nor social scientists, separately, have been able to describe or interpret human social behavior in an adequate fashion. Something more is needed. That something involves both the individual and group approaches, notably studying the group in terms of the persons who comprise it and describing social behavior via the participating individuals.

Ralph Linton, a leading cultural anthropologist, expresses the idea succinctly when he says:[1] "The individual has been assigned to

[1] Ralph Linton, *The cultural background of personality* (New York: Appleton-Century-Crofts, Inc., 1945), pp. 4-5.

3

Psychology, society to Sociology, and culture to Cultural Anthropology. . . . It is now becoming apparent that the integration between the individual, society and culture is so close and their interaction so continuous that the investigator who tries to work with any one of them without reference to the other two soon comes to a dead end." Linton predicts that "the next few years will witness the emergence of a science of human behavior which will synthesize the findings of Psychology, Sociology and Anthropology." [2] Social psychology is the generally accepted name for the area in which these three disciplines come together.

To show more concretely the approach of the social psychologist, consider a few random examples—a parent punishing a child, a teacher in her classroom, a husband and wife quarreling, a crowd cheering at a football game, strikers picketing a store, diplomats arguing at an international conference. Each of these situations involves two or more individuals interacting directly. But people may also interact more indirectly. When a man watches television or reads a newspaper, when he makes up his mind how to vote or wrestles with a moral problem, he is reacting in large part to the behavior of others as expressed in words or pictures, and in the values of his social group as he has learned them. Furthermore, he will respond, sooner or later, and will influence the behavior of others at the same time that he continues to be influenced by them.

Note that in every case we are dealing with individuals, each of whom perceives, thinks, feels, learns, and has a certain "personality." We shall treat personality later, but at this point we can say that it is inseparable from the social milieu in which the individual has developed. He is constantly reacting to other individuals. His behavior takes place in social settings; he is constantly engaged in perceiving and interpreting these situations. This process is affected both by his underlying personality trends and by his knowledge of the language, values, and customs of the social group.

Who can best interpret such social behavior? Obviously both the psychologist and the social scientist have something valuable to contribute. The danger is that either specialist, by himself, is likely to overstress his own interpretation. For example, in diagnosing an unhappy marriage, the psychologist may point to incompatibility of attitudes and interests of husband and wife. The sociologist maintains that the different religious and socioeconomic backgrounds of husband and wife prevent their developing satisfactory accommodations and reciprocal roles. The psychiatrist may

2 *Ibid.*, p. 5.

find a mother-fixation or emotional insecurity in one or both spouses caused by parental rejection in childhood. The anthropologist, perhaps, comments that such marital difficulties reflect certain accelerated social changes characterizing the American culture pattern.

One is reminded of the clinic in which a problem child was diagnosed by the pediatrician as a hypothyroid case, by the psychologist as borderline I.Q., by the social worker as a product of a broken home, and by the psychiatrist as a case of compensation for insecurity and inferiority! A well-known poem by John Godfrey Saxe seems a relevant commentary:

> It was six men of Indostan
> To learning much inclined,
> Who went to see the Elephant
> (Though all of them were blind),
> That each by observation
> Might satisfy his mind.
>
> The *First* approached the Elephant,
> And happening to fall
> Against his broad and sturdy side,
> At once began to bawl:
> "God bless me but the Elephant
> Is very like a wall!"
>
> The *Second*, feeling of the tusk
> Cried, "Ho! what have we here
> So very round and smooth and sharp?
> To me 'tis mighty clear
> This wonder of an Elephant
> Is very like a spear!"
>
> The *Third* approached the animal,
> And happening to take
> The squirming trunk within his hands,
> Thus boldly up and spake:
> "I see," quoth he, "the Elephant
> Is very like a snake!"
>
> The *Fourth* reached out his eager hand,
> And felt about the knee.
> "What most this wondrous beast is like
> Is very plain," quoth he;
> " 'Tis clear enough the Elephant
> Is very like a tree!"
>
> The *Fifth*, who chanced to touch the ear,
> Said: "E'en the blindest man
> Can tell what this resembles most;
> Deny the fact who can,
> This marvel of an Elephant
> Is very like a fan!"

The *Sixth* no sooner had begun
  About the beast to grope,
Than, seizing on the swinging tail
  That fell within his scope,
"I see," quoth he, "the Elephant
  Is very like a rope!"

And so these men of Indostan
  Disputed loud and long,
Each in his own opinion
  Exceeding stiff and strong,
Though each was partly in the right,
  And all were in the wrong! 3

The moral should not be construed to imply that the social psychologist is the great synthesizer who supersedes the more orthodox psychologists and social scientists! It suggests, rather, his goal of advancing a science of human social behavior designed to integrate the approaches of several related diciplines. This goal is comparable to that found in several "in-between" fields, such as biophysics, biochemistry, geophysics, neurophysiology, physiological psychology, economic history, and political geography.

But the task of the synthesizer is never easy. Those trained in an established field learn a specialized vocabulary and acquire particular ways of viewing and interpreting their data, which make intercommunication difficult. Social psychologists are usually trained as either psychologists or sociologists, or perhaps as anthropologists or psychiatrists. Some of them, indeed, insist that social psychology is definitely a branch of psychology, while others assert that it is a subdivision of sociology, which hardly facilitates the synthesis referred to above by Linton.

On the other hand a number of integrative efforts have been made in recent years. Some of these take the form of textbooks and books of readings in social psychology.4 In addition several confer-

---

3 J. G. Saxe, *Poetical works* (Boston: Houghton Mifflin Co., 1882), pp. 111-12.

4 Perhaps the best examples of such texts are those by H. Bonner (New York: American Book Co., 1953), E. L. Hartley and R. Hartley (New York: Alfred A. Knopf, Inc., 1952), O. Klineberg (rev. ed.; New York: Henry Holt & Co., Inc., 1954), R. T. LaPiere and P. R. Farnsworth (3d ed.; New York: McGraw-Hill Book Co., Inc., 1949), A. R. Lindesmith and A. R. Strauss, (rev. ed.; New York: The Dryden Press, Inc., 1956), T. M. Newcomb (New York: The Dryden Press, Inc., 1950), and Kimball Young (3d ed.; New York: Appleton-Century-Crofts, Inc., 1956). Maccoby, Newcomb, and Hartley (eds.), *Readings in social psychology* (3d ed.; New York: Henry Holt & Co., Inc., 1958) and G. Lindzey (ed.), *Handbook of social psychology* (Reading, Mass.: Addison-Wesley Pub. Co., Inc., 1954) contain contributions from psychologists, sociologists, anthropologists, psychiatrists, and others.

ences have been held with the explicit goal of furthering interdisciplinary understanding in social psychology.[5]

Before taking up methods and outlining our own approach, a brief historical survey is in order to show how social psychology came into existence and developed to its present position.

THE FORERUNNERS OF SOCIAL PSYCHOLOGY

The contemporary position of a field of study often bears little relation to its origins. Thus astronomy and chemistry, two of the oldest and most firmly established sciences, sprang from astrology and alchemy respectively. Psychology, located in the area between biology and the social sciences, owes its origin to philosophy and to nineteenth-century physiology.

Social psychology, lying in the borderland between psychology and the social sciences, has a complex genealogy comprising strains from many disciplines. It came on the scene about 1900, after the way had been prepared by at least four groups of scholars.

Social philosophers. Ancient, medieval, and modern philosophers included in their writings many speculations and miscellaneous observations about human nature, heredity, instincts, impulses, customs, and social relations. In Plato's *Republic,* in Aristotle's *Politics* and *Ethics,* and in the writings of Bodin, Montesquieu, Hobbes, Locke, Rousseau, and many others, we find the pre-nineteenth-century social philosophers speculating about major issues and problems of social living.[6] Some of their ideas were original and provocative; others we now find (from our twentieth-century position) were vague, unscientific, and contradictory. It is hardly strange that they failed to understand the subtle relationship between individual and society. (There is some doubt whether we do now!) Nor did these early thinkers realize the importance of studying the individual in his social milieu. But they did focus interest

5 See W. Dennis (ed.), *Current trends in social psychology* (Pittsburgh: University of Pittsburgh Press, 1947); J. E. Hulett and R. Stagner (eds.), *Problems in social psychology* (Urbana, Ill.: University of Illinois, 1952); J. G. Miller (ed.), *Experiments in social process* (New York: McGraw-Hill Book Co., Inc., 1950); J. H. Rohrer and M. Sherif (eds.), *Social psychology at the crossroads* (New York: Harper & Bros., 1951); M. Sherif and M. O. Wilson (eds.), *Group relations at the crossroads* (New York: Harper & Bros., 1953); J. Gillin (ed.), *For a science of social man* (New York: The Macmillan Co., 1954); M. Sherif and M. O. Wilson (eds.), *Emerging problems in social psychology* (Norman, Okla.: University of Oklahoma, 1957).

6 See J. P. Lichtenberger, *Development of social theory* (New York: Appleton-Century-Crofts, Inc., 1923) or Howard Becker and H. E. Barnes, *Social thought from lore to science* (Washington, D. C.: Harren Press, 1952), for a good short account of many such contributions.

on many important questions later taken up by men more specialized in their training and more scientific in their approach.

Pioneer anthropologists. In 1860 two German scholars, H. Steinthal and M. Lazarus, established a journal of *Folk Psychology*.[7] They hoped to discover the mental processes of primitive peoples by studying their language, mythology, religion, literature, and art. Actually, their work turned toward philosophy and mysticism as they became concerned with "group minds" and "folk souls." But they inspired Wilhelm Wundt, famous as the father of experimental psychology. He produced a ten-volume *Elements of Folk Psychology*.[8] Wundt felt that higher social processes could not be explored in the laboratory, though they had to be investigated by way of individual minds. This was one of the first protests against the ancient doctrine that a group may have a mind, soul, or psyche over and above the minds of the individuals in the group. But Wundt could not stick to his individualized approach; like most of his contemporaries, he dealt with collective minds and made grand generalizations about the evolution of culture. Nonetheless, Steinthal, Lazarus, and Wundt brought anthropology and psychology within speaking distance of each other.

British evolutionists. One sometimes forgets that Charles Darwin made a tremendous contribution to social as well as to biological science. His proof of the theory of evolution, given in *The Origin of Species* (1859), changed the course of scientific thinking and stimulated Spencer, Bagehot, Karl Marx, and others to apply the laws of natural selection to social development.

Darwin contributed even more directly to social study. In his *Descent of Man* (1871) he traced human development from lower to higher forms, stressing the importance of cultural products such as language and inventions, and of processes like cooperation, sympathy, and sensitivity to praise and blame. Darwin indicated that man's survival depends less on natural selection in a biological sense than in a psychological and social sense. He insisted that natural selection operates on the intellectual, moral, and social plane just as it does at the organic level.[9]

[7] The best references on the nineteenth-century background of social psychology are F. B. Karpf, *American social psychology* (New York: McGraw-Hill Book Co., Inc., 1932) and G. W. Allport, The historical background of modern social psychology, in G. Lindzey (ed.), *Handbook of social psychology* (Reading, Mass.: Addison-Wesley Pub. Co., Inc., 1954), Vol. I, pp. 3-56.

[8] Translated into English by E. L. Schaub (New York: The Macmillan Co., 1916).

[9] C. Darwin, *Descent of man* (New York: Appleton-Century-Crofts, Inc., 1906), pp. 128-32.

Herbert Spencer, Darwin's contemporary, is even better known for applying evolutionary concepts to social life. He wrote on both psychology and sociology, stressing scientific method in studying human behavior (though his own methods were not always strictly scientific). His great contributions to social psychology were his insistence that life is a process of continual adjustment of internal to external relations (the latter including society),[10] and his emphasis on study of the social environment. He foresaw a "Social Science" which studies how the individual becomes an organic part of his group and how the group (consisting of individuals) becomes an organic unity.[11] Spencer did not develop these ideas very far, but his prestige helped focus the attention of others on them.

Early sociologists. Auguste Comte, nineteenth-century author of *Positive Philosophy* (1830), a comprehensive philosophy of the sciences, is considered the founder of sociology and the first genuine social scientist. Like Aristotle and other social philosophers, he found that society and social institutions originate in human nature. But he realized clearly that the human mind can develop only through society; the individual must be considered always in his social setting. In addition, Comte was one of the first to discuss the existence and importance of social change, though he overestimated the role of reason in producing it.

Another pioneer French sociologist important to social psychology was Emile Durkheim. His well-known theory of "collective representations" stressed the significance of group experience even more than Comte had done. Collective representations are images or memories of group experiences found in every individual. They evidence and symbolize the common social life.[12] Unfortunately Durkheim went on to propose that a "collective mind" develops— i.e., that the group thinks, feels, and acts differently from individuals—thus furthering the so-called "group mind fallacy."

Although his adherents have tended to overrate him, the Italian sociologist Vilfredo Pareto stimulated the emerging social psychology. For one thing, he proposed the "logico-experimental method" by which he hoped to classify all human events without *a priori* judgment or bias. Unfortunately, more than occasionally, he for-

10 H. Spencer, *Principles of biology* (New York: Appleton-Century-Crofts, Inc., 1900), Vol. I, p. 97; *Principles of psychology* (New York: Appleton-Century-Crofts, Inc., 1903), Vol. I, p. 293.

11 H. Spencer, *The study of sociology* (New York: Appleton-Century-Crofts, Inc., 1893), pp. 52-53.

12 See E. Durkheim, *The elementary forms of religious life*, trans. J. W. Swain (New York: The Macmillan Co., 1915).

got his precept. His theory of motivation has a contemporary ring. In his analysis of human action he distinguished between two classes of motives: the inner motives, which he labeled "residues," and their outer expression, known as "derivations." Whatever the limitations of his theory, his laborious *Trattado di Sociologia Generale* (translated as *The Mind and Society* [13]), published in 1916, was a milestone in the prescientific phase of social psychology.

In Germany Max Weber was a sociologist-economist-historian who influenced later social psychologists, both directly and indirectly, in terms of those who took sides for and against him. He defended the use of the historical method, believing that valid analyses could be made of social phenomena for a time or place removed from one's own context. He utilized the "ideal-type," a concept or hypothetical construct, for the purpose of testing or comparing similar social events. For example, his analysis of bureaucracy in government and business organization, of the effects of Protestantism on economic processes, and his studies of comparative religions have affected the research of present-day sociologists and social psychologists.[14]

THE FOUNDERS OF SOCIAL PSYCHOLOGY

The social philosphers and social scientists we have mentioned helped pave the way for social psychology, but none of them can, strictly speaking, be called a social psychologist. They did not focus their primary attention on the individual and the processes making him a social being; nor did they study systematically the interaction between the individual and his fellow beings. We now turn to four men who may be called "founders" of social psychology because each did one or both of these things.

Gabriel Tarde (1843-1904) was a French lawyer and judge. His studies of crime led him to conclude that imitation is the fundamental social process and the key to the mystery of social life.[15] Earlier writers, notably the Englishman Walter Bagehot, in his *Physics and Politics* (1884), had played up the importance of imitation. But Tarde went further. "Society," he said in 1890, "is imitation." Actually he admitted two elementary social acts, invention and imitation, but the former he found quite rare. Not only social intercourse but social evolution proceeds by imitation, which he considered a kind of hypnotic state.

13 (New York: Harcourt, Brace & Co., Inc., 1935.)

14 A good example of his writings is found in *From Max Weber, essays in sociology,* trans. H. A. Gerth and C. Wright Mills (New York: Oxford University Press, 1946).

15 G. Tarde, *The laws of imitation,* trans. E. C. Parsons (New York: Henry Holt & Co., Inc., 1903).

In Tarde's hands the concept of imitation was stretched too far, and his treatment is often naive and oversimplified. But his contribution is great because he explored a basic social process that is rooted in individual action. He was one of the first writers to probe exhaustively into what is often called "social interaction."

In 1895 Gustave Le Bon (1841-1931) published *The Crowd,* the first of many studies of crowd psychology. He was greatly influenced by contemporary French psychiatry, with its concern over suggestibility as the leading characteristic of hysteria. In crowds, said Le Bon, intelligence is overshadowed and the unconscious is dominant. Suggestibility, contagion, impulsiveness, emotionality, and credulity are rampant. The crowd has a collective mind inferior to the minds of the individuals in it.

Like Tarde, Le Bon used his terms too broadly. For him "crowds" meant all kinds of groups, whether physically gathered together or not. His treatment was dogmatic and biased and was colored by an aristocratic fear of a new era of crowds and an age of socialism. Yet his observations on crowd behavior (except the collective mind interpretation) were very penetrating and have been essentially confirmed by later students. Probably Le Bon's major contribution to social psychology was inaugurating the use of psychiatric concepts to explain group behavior.

In 1908 two books appeared, both using "social psychology" in their titles. These were *Social Psychology* by Edward A. Ross (1866-1951), professor of sociology at the University of Wisconsin, and *Introduction to Social Psychology* by William McDougall (1871-1938) of Oxford and Cambridge. (Later McDougall taught in this country at Harvard and Duke.) Both volumes were designed as texts and attempted comprehensive treatment of the subject.[16]

Ross had already defined social psychology as "the branch of knowledge that deals with the psychic interplay between man and his environing society." [17] More specifically, it studies psychic planes and currents.[18] Planes, as Ross uses the term, are uniformities in behavior, such as religion, diet, dress, pastimes, and moral ideas. Currents are not agreements, but "agitations" like the spread of the lynching spirit, the contagion of panic, or epidemics of religious emotion.

Ross followed the suggestion-imitation thesis of Tarde, to whom he paid tribute. He elaborated on suggestibility and imitation and

16 E. A. Ross, *Social psychology* (New York: The Macmillan Co., 1908); W. Mc-Dougall, *Introduction to social psychology* (Boston: John W. Luce & Co., 1908).

17 E. A. Ross, *Social control* (New York: The Macmillan Co., 1901), p. vii.

18 E. A. Ross, *Social psychology, op. cit.,* p. 1.

used these processes to interpret such matters as crowds, crazes and fads, fashions, conventionality, custom, conflict, compromise, and public opinion. The book has a wealth of lively illustrations from past and present: for example, the Children's Crusade, the Dutch tulip mania, ancient Greek customs, schools of art, and the case of Emperor Joseph II of Austria.

A psychology that minimized social influences Ross felt to be inadequate. Without social interaction, he pointed out, "the psychic development of the child would be arrested at a stage not far above idiocy." [19] However, his book contributed little or nothing to the crucial problem of how the individual is molded by social forces. Ross's value to social psychology lies in applying the suggestibility-imitation thesis to a variety of social phenomena.

In contrast to Ross, William McDougall centered his social psychology squarely in the individual. He posited a number of instincts as the basis of social life and social interaction. All human social activities have their foundation in certain deep springs and motive powers, which are innate, inherited tendencies. He classified these into seven principal instincts, each with an associated emotional state: flight–fear, repulsion–disgust, curiosity–wonder, pugnacity–anger, self-abasement–subjection, self-assertion–elation, and parental–tender emotion. As major instincts without clear associated emotions we have reproduction, gregariousness, acquisitiveness, and construction. He threw in for good measure, as "general or nonspecific innate tendencies," suggestion, imitation, sympathy, and a few others.

Directly or indirectly, said McDougall, instincts are the prime movers of all activity. "Take away these instinctive dispositions with their powerful impulses and the organism would become incapable of activity of any kind; it would lie inert and motionless like a wonderful clockwork whose mainspring had been removed or a steam-engine whose fires had been drawn. These impulses are the mental forces that maintain and shape all the life of individuals and societies, and in them we are confronted with the central mystery of life and mind and will." [20]

McDougall's views appealed not only to psychologists but to many philosophers and other scholars, largely because the time was ripe for an authoritative statement of instinct doctrines, already made popular by William James and others. At the same time McDougall's emphasis on instincts was distasteful to John Dewey and to the sociologists G. H. Mead and C. H. Cooley, whose views

[19] *Ibid.*, p. 12.
[20] McDougall, *op. cit.* (15th ed.; 1923), pp. 45-46.

we shall describe later. Dewey's functional views of behavior had focused attention on the social environment with which man continually interacts. Dewey had, in fact, developed the thesis that habits, not instincts, are the key to social psychology—habits "which are formed in the interaction of biological aptitudes with a social environment." [21] Mead and Cooley emphasized development of the "social self," pointing out how the maturing of human personality depends upon continuous social interaction.[22] In fact, Cooley, perhaps more than any other individual in America, influenced American social psychology in the direction of motivation, communication, and group participation.

SOCIOLOGICAL VS. PSYCHOLOGICAL APPROACHES

Many sociologists published books and articles in the 1920's which established a sociological brand of social psychology.[23] They stressed the significance of group life—of customs, mores, institutions, and social interstimulation—on human personality or "human nature." They did not overlook the presence of various innate and biological factors, but they were more impressed with the fact that these are socially conditioned from the moment of birth. They emphasized the actual processes of socialization, discussing rather fully the part played by language and gesture, by suggestion, imitation, and the like. Attitudes, values, social roles, social control, and social change were taken up at some length. In a word, the sociologists started with their specialty, man's psychosocial environment, and explored its effects on human development and human behavior.

In 1924 a psychologist, Floyd H. Allport, injected a new viewpoint.[24] Social psychology, he said, can be dealt with only in terms of individual psychology; it simply studies individual behavior in regard to that section of man's environment comprised by his fellows. He vigorously attacked the "group mind fallacy"—the theory held by some philosophers and social scientists, notably Durkheim and Le Bon, that the group has a mind of its own, apart from the minds of the individuals composing the group. Within the individual organism, insisted Allport, are all the mechanisms necessary to explain social behavior, which is primarily a means to satisfy

[21] J. Dewey, *Human nature and conduct* (New York: Henry Holt & Co., Inc., 1922), Preface. The implications of Dewey's ideas for social psychology had been worked out as early as 1901 by the sociologist C. A. Ellwood in his *Prolegomena to social psychology* (Chicago: University of Chicago Press, 1901).

[22] See Chapter 9, below.

[23] For example, W. I. Thomas, Ellsworth Faris, R. E. Park, E. W. Burgess, L. L. Bernard, and E. S. Bogardus.

[24] F. H. Allport, *Social psychology* (Boston Houghton Mifflin Co., 1924).

man's biological needs. These needs he interpreted not as instincts but as "prepotent reflexes" which are considerably modified through social conditioning. Allport's view influenced other psychologists who were turning toward the field of social psychology.

It is important to note this divergence between sociological and psychological interpretations, because it persisted through the 1920's and 1930's and, to a lesser extent, right down to the present time.[25] What are the major points of difference between the two approaches?

The psychologist says in effect: "Anything calling itself psychology must start with the individual. This individual is born with certain biologically based needs and potentialities which are the essence of his humanness. However, it is true that these needs and potentialities are continuously affected and modified by the social environment, through the process of learning." The psychologist usually is more interested in describing the mechanism of this learning process than in discussing the social environment which serves as the stimulus or model for learning.

The sociologist, on the other hand, is impressed with our social heritage of customs, institutions, and modes of social behavior into which each individual is born. He describes these rather fully and implies—if he does not say so explicitly—that this social heritage has more effect on human nature or personality than do man's innate and biological tendencies. Like the psychologist, he is vitally interested in learning, but he pays less attention to the process, the "how," of learning than he does to the "what," the content or finished product of the learning process.

Another important contrast may be noted. Most sociologists and cultural anthropologists are impressed with the uniformities or similarities of human social behavior found within a group. In accounting for these uniformities they focus, naturally enough, on those aspects of the cultural pattern which are widely shared. The psychologist is interested in uniformities but is also impressed with individual differences in personality and social behavior. He may try to account for these differences in terms of variations in biological equipment as well as by the varying constellations of social in-

[25] A study of social psychology textbooks written by sociologists and psychologists between 1926 and 1940 showed a striking contrast in that the great majority of sources cited by the former were sociologists and by the latter were psychologists. This trend does not hold true for texts written since 1945; these more recent authors, whatever their training, draw rather similarly upon psychological and sociological sources. See S. S. Sargent, Interdisciplinary contributions and cooperation in the development of social psychology, in J. E. Hulett and R. Stagner (eds.), *Problems in social psychology* (Urbana, Ill.: University of Illinois, 1952).

fluences (family, school, community, etc.) operating on each child within the broader cultural pattern.

The above characterization of differing viewpoints in social psychology is no doubt oversimplified, but one has the uncomfortable feeling that psychologists and sociologists, without realizing it, have been examining opposite sides of the same coin! Nonetheless, in recent years these differently oriented social psychologists, as indicated earlier, have shown encouraging signs of *rapprochement*. This has resulted, in part, from developments in their own work and in part from contributions made by other disciplines, notably anthropology and psychiatry.

Perhaps the interdisciplinary nature of social psychology can be demonstrated in Figure 1, oversimplified though it is. No social

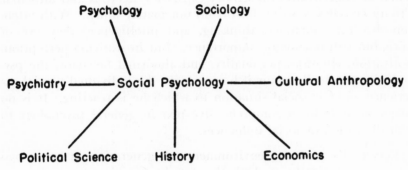

Fig. 1. The Interdisciplinary Nature of Social Psychology.

science can be isolated from any other; nor can any priority be conferred on a social science. Each of these studies or disciplines approaches a problem, such as the causation of war (or, perhaps more cautiously, the causes of a specific war), with its special techniques. The sociologist would, among other things, analyze some of the institutional aspects of international conflict; the anthropologist and historian might compare military conduct at different times and places; the social psychologist would analyze the motives and attitudes of individuals and groups. Likewise, the economist and political scientist would offer their services. In view of the complexity of social phenomena, it is not surprising that a number of universities, especially at the graduate levels, are conducting social research in interdepartmental groupings.

RECENT DEVELOPMENTS

As they progressed with their scientific studies, psychologists gradually became aware of the effects of social influences on individual behavior. These influences often were considered downright disturbing. It made a difference in a child's performance whether he took an intelligence test alone or with other children present, competing with him. (One really needed two different sets of norms— one for the individual and one for the social situation!) Both acquiring and expressing emotional reactions seemed greatly affected by one's experience with other people. In animals as well as humans, motivation was found to be not only a matter of physiological changes and bodily needs; knowledge of social experiences and present social stimuli was essential. Case histories of personality development, to be complete and useful, required full data on social influences past and present, direct and indirect.[26]

Of course, the significance of social factors was found to vary considerably with the kind of behavior the psychologist studies. When he concentrates on sensory capacities, nervous and muscular activity or reflexes, social factors do not matter much. With attention, learning, memory, thinking, and intelligence, they are of more, but still not major, importance. But in studying perception, motivation, emotion, personality, and abnormal behavior, the psychologist goes badly astray if he overlooks the individual's social experience and the social situation to which he is reacting. It is no longer possible for a comprehensive text in general psychology to omit discussion of social influences.

Personality and the environment. A generation or more ago sociologists typically studied the family, marriage and divorce, mores, taboos, laws, institutions, social conflicts, crime, and delinquency without tying any of them to the behavior and personality of the individual. Such social phenomena were treated, customarily, as though they existed independently from the lives of the individuals composing a society. But this approach began to change soon after 1920, largely because of the influence of W. I. Thomas and F. Znaniecki's *The Polish Peasant in Europe and America.* Sociologists became more oriented toward the individual and saw in case studies and personal documents an important if not essential research tool.[27]

A good example is furnished by Clifford Shaw, whose *Delinquency Areas,* a completely statistical study, was followed in the

[26] See O. Klineberg, *Social psychology* (rev. ed.: New York: Henry Holt & Co., Inc., 1954), for a good résumé of cultural influences upon motives and other psychological processes.

[27] See H. Blumer, An appraisal of Thomas and Znaniecki's "The Polish peasant in Europe and America," *Soc. sci. Res. Council Bull.,* XLIV (1939). Also L. Gottschalk, C. Kluckhohn, and R. Angell, The use of personal documents in history, anthropology and sociology, *Soc. sci. Res. Council Bull.,* LIII (1945), 117–232.

next decade by three quite extensive case studies of delinquents.[28] Many of the current texts in sociology reveal this newer psychological orientation, stressing how mores, values, and other aspects of culture are built into the growing individual and thus manifested as part of human nature or personality.[29]

Starting from society and culture, the sociologist has begun to discover the individual, much as the psychologist, starting with the individual, has begun to appreciate the significance of social and cultural forces.

Increasing *rapprochement* between psychological and sociological viewpoints in social psychology has also been furthered by several recent contributions of which we shall mention just a few.

Cultural anthropologists (often called ethnologists) have published more and more studies of primitive culture groups. Their accumulating data show clearly that "human nature," which seems to cover both personality and social behavior, is greatly affected—in fact, importantly determined—by the culture pattern in which a person is born and reared. Not only customs, institutions, and values are socially determined, but also attitudes, interests, habits, and the prevalent patterns of social interaction. The ethnological studies show that even motives, emotions, personality traits, and sex roles are affected considerably by the various social influences characterizing each broad culture pattern. The studies of Ruth Benedict and Margaret Mead are probably the best known of these contributions. The relation of culture and personality is a major concern of many social psychologists; we shall discuss it in Chapter 3.

Psychoanalysts and psychiatrists are coming to emphasize the part played by social influences in producing maladjustment and mental disease. Though Freud in his earlier writings did not say so explicitly, he was vitally concerned with personality development as affected by a primary social influence, the family. His later publications show increasing awareness that other social factors act as causes of conflicts and neuroses.[30] Many of his followers placed

28 C. R. Shaw, *Delinquency areas* (1929); *The jack-roller* (1930); *The natural history of a delinquent career* (1931); and *Brothers in crime* (1938), all published in Chicago by The University of Chicago Press.

29 L. Broom and P. Selznick, *Sociology* (Evanston, Ill.: Row, Peterson & Co., 1955); J. F. Cuber, *Sociology* (New York: Appleton-Century-Crofts, 1955); A. W. Green, *Sociology* (New York: McGraw-Hill Book Co., Inc., 1956); W. F. Ogburn and M. F. Nimkoff, *Sociology* (rev. ed.; Boston: Houghton Mifflin Co., 1950); A. M. Rose, *Sociology* (New York: Alfred A. Knopf, Inc., 1956); F. E. Merrill, *Society and culture* (rev. ed.; Englewood Cliffs, N. J.: Prentice-Hall, Inc., 1957).

30 E.g., *The future of an illusion* (London: Hogarth Press, Ltd., 1928); *Civilization and its discontents* (New York: Jonathan Cape and Harrison Smith, 1930).

particular emphasis on the cultural origins of personality and personality disorders; for example, Horney and Fromm.

Field theory and sociometry. A very productive conceptualization for social psychology is the *field approach*. The term derives from physics and has also been used in biology and sociology. In psychology it was first stressed by Kurt Lewin in his "topological psychology" [31] and by J. F. Brown.[32] In essence, field theorists insist that situations confronting an individual are always Gestalten or complex wholes, which the individual perceives and interprets for himself. Hence, we must understand not only the *objective* characteristics of a situation but even more importantly the person's *subjective* interpretation of it. This is done partly in terms of the dynamic aspects of the situation itself and partly in terms of the individual's experience and personality characteristics. The authors believe that the "field" approach lies at the heart of systematic social psychology; we shall discuss it further in Chapter 15.

Lewin originated "group dynamics," by which the interaction and the reactions of group members to internal and external pressures are analyzed. The Research Center for Group Dynamics, first at the Massachusetts Institute of Technology, and now at the University of Michigan, was founded by Kurt Lewin.

Equally important are sociometry and psychodrama initiated by J. L. Moreno.[33] Here the emphasis is on interpersonal relations, roles, and group structure. Except for terminology and certain research techniques, sociometry has much in common with group dynamics. Psychodrama has served to focus on the social context of adjustment problems, and the complexity of a person's social roles. (The important topic of social roles will be taken up later in Chapter 13.)

Community and stratification. Much has been contributed by the sociologist in his studies over the last decade or two in social structure, particularly the urban community. In a sense, the movement commenced with Robert and Helen Lynd in their now classic works, *Middletown* [34] and *Middletown in Transition*,[35] the analysis of social life in a midwestern small city. The most exhaustive of the community studies was the *Yankee City* series of Lloyd Warner

[31] K. Lewin, *Principles of topological psychology* (New York: McGraw-Hill Book Co., Inc., 1936).

[32] J. F. Brown, *Psychology and the social order* (New York: McGraw-Hill Book Co., Inc., 1936).

[33] J. Moreno, *Who shall survive?* (New York: Beacon House, Inc., 1934).

[34] R. S. and H. M. Lynd (New York: Harcourt, Brace & Co., Inc., 1929).

[35] R. S. and H. M. Lynd (New York: Harcourt, Brace & Co., Inc., 1937).

and his associates,[36] which portrayed the occupational, ethnic, and other aspects of the American status system as revealed in a historic New England town of 17,000. In addition, a number of other surveys of communities in different parts of the country have been made, particularly with respect to stratification and social class, which will be discussed later. From this research it appears that one of the most important determinants of one's perspective on the world is the class position he occupies. This hypothesis will be examined at greater length in Chapter 5.

Communication analysis, public opinion, and polls. Another development of the last twenty years is the investigation of mass media—the press, radio, television, and motion pictures. This field of activity is largely in the province of social psychology, since the media of communication are primary determinants of attitudes as well as increasingly important means of social interaction in themselves. Analysis may be directed to the source or communicator, to the medium or content, or to the recipient. The second of these, content analysis, is on the way to becoming a systematic, empirical, quantitative procedure by which attitudes, motives, and other trends may be assayed. Thus certain biases or prejudices, for example, may be disclosed in movies, magazine articles, newspaper columns, comics, and the like.

In the area of public opinion the most striking development has been the public opinion polls. In 1935 George Gallup established the American Institute of Public Opinion, whose best known activity came to be known as the "Gallup Poll." Although commercially and journalistically oriented, this and similar organizations have demonstrated the possibility of predicting political behavior. We shall return to this subject in Chapter 15.

Human relations. Perhaps the greatest amount of recent activity in social psychology is found in the area of human relations, especially as applied to industrial problems. Some of the previously mentioned topics, notably group dynamics and sociometry, are concerned with this. "Small group" research studies have focused on questions of labor morale, productivity, turnover, and absenteeism. The pioneer studies of Roethlisberger and Dickson [37] led to a variety of investigations within the laboratory and in industry which has helped significantly in improving industrial relations during the last decade. As with other developments we have noted, human

36 See W. L. Warner and P. S. Lunt, *The social life of a modern community* (New Haven, Conn.: Yale University, 1941).

37 F. J. Roethlisberger and W. J. Dickson, *Management and the worker* (Cambridge: Harvard University Press, 1934).

relations depends on various disciplines and is not the exclusive province of the psychologist and sociologist.

It seems clear that social psychology is making increasingly valuable contributions to the understanding of social behavior. We may also conclude that *rapprochement* in social psychology is on the way, though synthesis has by no means arrived. We need continuing efforts to integrate the ever increasing contributions made by sociologists, anthropologists, psychologists, psychiatrists, and others. We must understand what the individual is like at birth, what potentialities he has, how he is affected by his social group, and how he acquires its culture in order to describe adequately his personality and social behavior. We must know *how* the individual learns, and *what* he learns; both are significant. The persons in any society show *uniformities* in behavior and *differences* in behavior; who is to say which is more important? We need to know the nature and extent of both as we search for their causes and correlates. Social behavior manifests both constancy and variability; they are equally interesting to the student of social psychology. Anthropological, psychiatric, and "field theory" contributions are all valuable to the social psychologist in helping to describe and explain the individual's behavior in society.

RESEARCH METHODS IN SOCIAL PSYCHOLOGY

The social psychologist's task, as we see, is to describe and interpret social behavior in terms of the individuals participating in it. To achieve this he needs new facts, new data; that is, like any scientist, he has to do research. His motivation for this research may run the gamut from mere curiosity to the most practical of concerns. He may be interested in general laws governing interpersonal relations or in the most specific factors imaginable. In any event, he tries to identify the major variables determining relationships between individuals whether he is concerned with a marriage, a committee, a college class, a social movement, a national election, or international relations.

What research methods shall he use? Early social psychologists such as Tarde, Le Bon, Ross, and McDougall showed little concern with method, and, like most early social scientists, can hardly be considered research-oriented at all.[38] Their generalizations about

[38] This is not to imply that being *research-oriented* represents the supreme goal in science or scholarship. One well-known social scientist was heard to comment about one of his colleagues that he was never willing to say anything unless he could cite (in footnotes) at least five or ten others who had said it first! Similarly it has sometimes been commented that, with all its tremendous emphasis on research methodology, few really germinal or creative ideas have come out of American social science, in comparison with less scientifically advanced Europe.

imitation, suggestion, instinct, and the like actually were based on speculation and more or less uncontrolled observation. Their findings have naturally been questioned by those using more careful methods of investigation. It is important to describe and evaluate the procedures which may be used by social psychologists today.[39]

Research methods used by social psychologists, as by any scientist, depend on both the objective and the kinds of data available. Psychologists utilize different techniques to study imagination, speed of muscular reactions, and the origins of emotional crises. Sociologists' methods vary according to whether they are investigating the effects of urbanization on personality, the causes of crime and delinquency, or comparative trends in divorce rates.

There are many ways of classifying research methods. They may, for example, be divided into *subjective* and *objective, qualitative* and *quantitative,* or sorted into categories such as case history, field study, experimental or statistical techniques. Our own preference is for four broad categories of method which differ in degree of objectivity and in the investigator's control of variables. After describing these we shall turn briefly to several more specific research techniques used in social psychology today.

Introspection. When one introspects, he "looks within" and reports on some aspect of his own present and past experience.[40] Thus one may introspect about his aches and pains and his feelings, or about his attitudes or his reasons for joining a certain social group. Whenever a person reports on his subjective experiences, he is introspecting. Rating scales, questionnaires, and public opinion polls are based on introspection, since the respondents are asked to describe their private views.

Both advantages and disadvantages of introspection are obvious. The method is useful for yielding data on thoughts, feelings, hopes, wishes, attitudes, etc., which are peculiarly private and which we cannot easily study by other methods. But the data we thus obtain may be inaccurate if our respondent is careless or ignorant, or if he has reason to conceal his true reactions. Introspective methods are reasonably valid when the task required is not very complicated and the matter being investigated is not taboo or highly controversial. Thus asking a person whether he likes "rock 'n' roll" or

[39] Important references on methodology for social psychology and related fields are M. Jahoda, M. Deutsch, and S. W. Cook, *Research methods in social relations,* 2 vols. (New York: The Dryden Press, Inc., 1951); L. Festinger, and D. Katz (eds.), *Research methods in the behavioral sciences* (New York: The Dryden Press, Inc., 1953).

[40] E. B. Titchener used "introspection" in a more limited sense to refer to a person's description of his sensory processes. See E. B. Titchener, *Experimental psychology, qualitative, student's manual* (New York: The Macmillan Co., 1915), pp. xiii ff.

which political candidate he favors will probably bring a frank and honest response; but asking a person his attitude toward premarital sexual intercourse or if he thinks the Soviet system is superior to the American system in any respect might not. Many persons, hesitating to respond frankly, would give a report at variance with their beliefs and feelings. We shall discuss attitude and opinion measurement at some length in Chapters 8 and 16.

Though psychologists today seem to consider introspection a questionable method, it will probably continue to have a place of some importance in psychological research. It has already survived several decades of attack from "behaviorists" and other proponents of objective methods. One of the reasons, undoubtedly, is that each of us (including behaviorists!) has an inner mental life and is conscious of it. We are forced to agree with Descartes that "I think, therefore I am." Hence, it seems entirely proper to report our thoughts and feelings to others and to expect them to reciprocate. A danger, of course, lurks in the common tendency to assume that others' implicit reactions are similar to ours and that therefore we may generalize from our own subjective experience.

Cooley and a few other sociologists hoped to utilize the advantages of introspection and avoid its pitfalls by the method of "sympathetic penetration." [41] Here the investigator trains himself to use "empathy"; he learns to identify himself with others and "feel himself into" their conscious states, about which he can then report via his own introspections.[42] The usefulness of such a method depends on the breadth and richness of an investigator's experience, coupled with his ability to interpret cues such as facial expressions, gestures, and tone and inflection of the voice. Like all introspection, it is open to obvious errors. It may, however, furnish good hypotheses that can be followed up by more exacting methods.

Uncontrolled observation. Everyone, including the scholar and scientist, draws on his observations of people to answer psychological questions. If he has observed carefully and if he avoids generalizing without sufficient data, his conclusions may be exceedingly valuable. Plato, Descartes, Hobbes, Locke, and William James, not to mention Shakespeare, Goethe, Voltaire, Dickens, and other literary figures, were keen observers of their fellow human beings. Many, though by no means all, of their interpretations have held good.

Observing people's behavior is naturally a more objective procedure than asking them what they think and feel. The great de-

41 See C. H. Cooley, Roots of social knowledge, *Amer. J. Sociol.*, XXXII (1926), 59-79.
42 This technique, of course, is widely used in our daily living, though without training and with little effort to check the validity of our impressions.

fect of most such observation is its unsystematic nature. The persons observed may be a highly unrepresentative group, seen at odd times and in a variety of situations. Generalizations based on casual contacts are susceptible to error. In addition, such reports may be affected by inaccuracies of memory and by the reporter's unconscious bias. For example, during the 1930's numerous observers reported on the state of affairs in the Soviet Union. One traveler would comment on the happiness, security, and prosperity which he, with his own eyes, saw there. Another visitor would report widespread pessimism, fear, insecurity, and poverty. The conflicting reports might be explained, in part, by the somewhat differing experiences any two travelers might have. But a more significant factor in such cases is the previously existing favorable or unfavorable attitudes which can, as we shall see, color indelibly a person's experiences and interpretations. Even today visitors to the Soviet Union differ considerably in their observations, depending on their views of science, education, military strategy, economics, and the like, as well as on their basic attitudes and values.

However, uncontrolled observation is not necessarily capricious and without value. Historical research, for example, by its very nature precludes control. So does "participant observation" in which the researcher is intimately involved with a group and its activities, like a member of Alcoholics Anonymous who records his impressions and experiences.[43]

As with introspection, everyone makes random observations; only the most scientifically minded refrain from indulging in unwarranted generalizations. But if observations are reported *as observations,* they may furnish valuable "hunches" or hypotheses that can be tested by more careful methods.

Systematic observation. The difference between uncontrolled and controlled or systematic observation is one of degree. The student of public opinion cannot afford to rely on chance impressions; he surveys a representative sample of the population. Researchers into the social behavior of children observe youngsters systematically in a variety of situations. Frequently they do their observing behind a one-way screen so that their presence will not affect the naturalness of the children's behavior. Investigators of a social movement such as Moral Rearmament will attend meetings and talk with several leaders and followers. Indeed, a trained observer

[43] For a discussion of uncontrolled observation see P. V. Young, *Scientific social surveys and research* (3d ed.; Englewood Cliffs, N. J.: Prentice-Hall, Inc., 1956), pp. 139-64.

may go further. He may discover not only the political preferences or attitudes of respondents, but also their age, religion, education, socioeconomic status, and favorite newspapers, TV and radio programs, etc., so that he can look for correlations between opinions and background factors. The nursery school researcher may similarly study the relationship between the child's behavior in school and various home influences. The field study is basically a controlled type of observation within a particular community or social situation, though it may also involve surveys or experiments.[44]

In the category of systematic observation we shall include the *developmental* and *case history* techniques. A developmental (sometimes called "genetic") study focuses on the changes occurring in an individual over a period of time. Essentially, it is a matter of careful observation, though it may well include various kinds of measurement and experimentation. In the California Growth Study, for example, many children were studied from birth to twenty years of age.[45] The aim of the case history method is to discover significant influences, past and present, that operate on an individual. In making a case history all kinds of data are used: subjective reactions (such as the individual's comments on his own childhood), objective information (records of diseases, school attendance and grades, dates and kinds of employment, etc.), and ratings and evaluations by friends, relatives, neighbors, teachers, employers, and others who know the individual. The person who constructs a case history must be highly trained in order to know where to get information, what questions to ask, what data to include as real evidence, what to include as opinion, and what to exclude as irrelevant. Case histories are a specialty of psychiatric social workers, though psychiatrists, clinically trained psychologists, and social scientists often prepare them. The case study is essentially a *qualitative* record, though it usually includes *quantitative* data. Constructing a case history demands great skill; interpreting one is even more difficult. Years of training are needed before one has the requisite clinical insight. Fortunately the barriers between psychiatry, clinical psychology, and social psychology are breaking down. Before long, clinical experience may well be an integral part of the social psychologist's research training.[46]

44 See Festinger and Katz, *op. cit.*, chaps. ii and iii, by D. Katz and J. R. P. French.

45 See H. E. Jones, The California adolescent growth study, *J. educ. Res.*, XXXI (1938), 561-67.

46 See D. W. MacKinnon, The use of clinical methods in social psychology, *J. soc. Issues*, II (1946), 4, 47-54.

Experimental social psychology. Since the 1920's many hundreds of experimental studies in social psychology have been made, almost exclusively by psychologists. Very deep differences of opinion exist among social psychologists about experimentation, the fourth and last method we shall describe.

The distinction between observation and experimentation is more than a difference in degree. In a valid experiment variables are controlled in a way that is not possible when one merely observes social phenomena. The essence of experiment in any field is to set the stage so that whatever happens can be interpreted meaningfully. All variables must be kept constant except the one under consideration. A valid experiment is hard to perform; indeed, in many areas of social psychology it is practically impossible—as, for example, in studying riots or panics. However, in other areas, it can be done. When properly carried out, experimentation yields the greatest accuracy and predictability.

Let us sketch an experimental approach to the question of how much opinions are influenced by propaganda. A good-sized group of persons, such as a high school or college class, a woman's club, or a union meeting, is given a standardized opinion scale on current issues. Shortly after, without explaining why, the experimenter divides the group into two equal parts. One is subjected to some kind of propaganda—a movie, radio talk, or public lecture—presenting forcefully one side of the issues involved. The other half is not exposed to propaganda. Afterward both sections are brought together and given the same opinion test or a test known to be equivalent to the first. If the *experimental* group—the group subjected to the propaganda—shows more shift in opinion than the *control* group, we have a measure of the propaganda's effects. The control group's purpose, of course, is to indicate opinion changes that might occur as a result of influences other than the propaganda arranged for by the experimenter.

However, the experimenter cannot yet conclude that opinions are (or are not) greatly affected by propaganda, because he has used only a small and unrepresentative sample of the population. He must now repeat the experiment with other groups differing in age, intelligence, sex, socioeconomic background, geographic location, and the like. If similar findings occur in all groups, his evidence begins to look conclusive, at least within the nation or culture studied.

Despite the difficulties encountered in performing experimentation, this method may have certain real advantages over other procedures.

First, it goes furthest toward preventing the intrusion of personal bias on the part of the investigator; in this sense it is the most objective of methods.

Second, through experimentation—and only through experimentation—one can study the operation of one variable at a time. In studying the effects of propaganda, for example, several devices have been used to accomplish this end, such as the before-and-after tests and the use of a control group for comparative purposes.

Third, the use of quantitative techniques (in this case, opinion test scores) makes it possible to assess not only the existence and direction but also the *amount* of opinion shift resulting from propaganda.[47] This is very important, as a change of opinion may be slight or may be a complete reversal of viewpoint.

On the other hand, many social psychologists, especially those trained in sociology, believe the experimental method has important limitations. They say that many experiments are artificial, that they do not get at genuine social behavior, and hence cannot reach valid conclusions. How, for instance, might we criticize the experiment just described?

1. *Use of a scale or test.* Some investigators doubt that opinions are given accurately in tests. They question also whether subtle qualitative differences in opinions can be expressed in a numerical score.

2. *Effects of various social situations upon individual behavior.* For example, the group situation typically influences individual members toward conventionality, especially in the area of controversial issues.

3. *Changes of opinion.* Giving people an opinion test, or asking them about their opinions, may make them rethink and change the opinions as they state them.

4. *Attitudes toward the experimenter.* Some subject may be highly cooperative and anxious to please the experimenter; others may resent being "guinea pigs," hence fail to cooperate.

5. *Sophistication of subjects.* Some may "catch on" to the purpose of the experiment; others may not. If they do, they may be anxious not to change their opinions lest they be considered suggestible or "weak-minded."

6. *Incidental variables.* Subjects in the experimental group react unpredictably to extraneous factors such as the voice, clothing, or appearance of a speaker or the vocal inflections of a radio commentator. Their responses may be affected by existing attitudes

[47] The use of quantitative techniques, of course, is not limited to experimentation; various kinds of measurements may be used in observational studies. However, they are almost always used in experimental work. Statistics have to do not with the gathering of data but with the treatment of quantified data by means of averaging, correlation, etc.

toward the person, newspaper, radio, or other medium by which the propaganda is conveyed.

7. *Extraneous social factors.* Some persons may be affected by the smiles, frowns, yawns, whispers, etc., of others as they attend to the propaganda material.

Such criticisms should give pause to the ardent experimenter. How can they be answered?

Errors of experimentation center around failure to prevent the intrusion of unwanted variables, such as those just listed. The use of a carefully equated control group goes far toward removing difficulties connected with the use of tests or with the conventionalizing influence of a group, since these conditions hold true for both the experimental and control groups. Attitudes toward the experimenter may be controlled somewhat by care in giving instructions to the subjects, or by using as experimenter some one unknown to the group. Occasionally, indeed, it is possible to prevent subjects from knowing they are taking part in an experiment. Repetition of an experiment is always advisable and often extremely valuable. For example, if we obtain the same results with a sophisticated as with a naive group, we can be fairly sure that sophistication had little to do with the outcome. Other variables can often be pinned down. For instance, comparison may be made of propaganda effects on large groups, small groups, and isolated individuals, or on groups where the members know each other well and where the members are not acquainted with each other.

Actually, we already know that some of the above variables are seldom important. For example, subjects nearly always will cooperate with an experimenter and generally will refrain from laughing, whispering, and otherwise influencing their neighbors. But we know less about the possible effects of other variables. The experimenter must be aware of them and must try to control them by changing the design of his experiment, by repeating it, or by making other improvements.

We still have methodological extremists in social psychology. On the one hand are ardent experimentalists who are convinced that experimentation is the only genuinely scientific method. Others believe that experimentation never can have much value, since it introduces artificiality and is bound to overlook variables that may be very significant.

Each view seems biased. The anti-experimentalist forgets that real life situations, by whatever method studied, contain many uncontrolled variables. The experimenter goes farther than the observer toward isolating and controlling his variables. On the other hand, the experimentalist may forget that many social phenomena are difficult if not impossible to produce at will. One cannot (or at least dare not try) to produce a riot, panic, lynching mob, craze, or social movement. One might attempt to produce a fad or a new fashion, but the chances of its being successfully done are slight. The social psychologist must be ready for these when they occur and study them by the best observational methods at his command.

In recent years several social psychologists have shown ingenuity in extending experimental methods to the study of complex social phenomena. Hartmann compared the relative strength of rational and emotional appeals to voters in a real election campaign.[48] Kurt Lewin and his colleagues studied the effects of democratic and authoritarian leadership in boys' club groups.[49] Or, to choose an example outside our immediate culture, one may profitably investigate the relationship of movie attendance, religious devoutness, and social level in selected Arab countries.[50] In fact, psychologists have shown concern for some of the problems of interplanetary communication, such as attitudes of the public toward this new phenomenon, as well as the procurement, training, outfitting, and protection of the space traveler.[51]

Of course, the research methods to be used depend in part on the question asked. As pointed out by Jahoda, Deutsch, and Cook, social research is concerned with two kinds of questions—the discovery of general laws and the diagnosis of specific situations; these they call *descriptive* and *diagnostic* studies. The latter are more directly concerned with causal relationships and with implications for action. In the author's words, "A descriptive study is oriented toward finding out *what* is occurring; a diagnostic study is directed toward discovering not only *what* is occurring but *why* it is occurring and *what can be done about it.*"[52] Obviously these differing purposes may make a difference in methods. For example, case histories are more likely to be involved where one is searching for causal relationships.

The contrast between two methods—field studies and laboratory experiments—was brought out in a seminar sponsored by the Social

---

[48] See Chapter 17.

[49] See Chapter 14.

[50] P. Kendall and E. Katz, *Communications behavior and political attitudes in four Arabic countries: a quantitative comparison* (New York: Bureau of Applied Social Research, Columbia University, 1952), as reported in H. Hyman, *Survey design and analysis* (Glencoe, Ill.: Free Press, 1955), pp. 303-5.

[51] D. N. Michael, Man-into-space: a tool and program for research in the social sciences, *Amer. Psychologist*, XII (1957), 324-28.

[52] Jahoda, Deutsch, and Cook, *op. cit.*, pp. 53-58.

Science Research Council in 1954.[53] Experiments, it was concluded, are conducted usually to test a theory, whereas field studies typically arise from a desire to understand a problem of social or practical importance. This difference in goal often results in a lack of correspondence of the findings; conclusions from experiments are likely to be abstract and general, whereas those from field studies are likely to be specific and conditional. This makes for a lack of communication between workers in the two areas, though there are signs that the gap between field studies and laboratory experiments is narrowing, the report concludes.

In short, the best method to apply in social psychology depends on the kind of social behavior studied, the situations in which it occurs, and the kind of data we wish to obtain. If we want people's subjective reactions (as in attitude or opinion studies), we shall need some kind of introspective method. If we wish to trace the influence of social pressures on personality, we shall need case study techniques. For complex social activities we shall need refined observation and, if possible, experimentation. Where data are quantifiable, we may use statistics to compile and interpret results. Often two or more methods may be used and checked against each other.

Social psychology is too new and deals with matters too complex for us to be dogmatic about methods. We must be adaptable and eclectic, but always critical!

A FINAL NOTE ON METHODOLOGY

The purpose of scientific studies in social psychology is to arrive at valid laws and principles—at generalizations that will help us understand, predict, and control human social behavior. The social psychologist's first task is to study and describe the significant variables that interact to determine social behavior. Some he will find in individual personalities, for example, deep-seated attitudes, motives, and frustrations. Other influences arise from the type of interactional processes operating—e.g., competition, cooperation, imitation. Still other determinants inhere in the nature of the particular social situation—e.g., a group that is large or small, noisy or quiet, standing, sitting, drinking, eating, etc. However, the *objective* social situation does not exist as such; the important factor is the *subjective* situation, the way the individual perceives and interprets it.

The social psychologist uses one or another scientific method to discover the major determinants of social behavior and to depict

[53] From SSRC Items, *Soc. sci. Res. Council Bull.,* VIII (December, 1954), 4.

their interrelationships. His studies always are done in a fairly specific setting. As examples of this, the 1956 voting behavior of residents in a certain county; the effects of certain types of written and oral propaganda on members of a woman's club, a high school class, a labor union, or a luncheon club; and the extent of prejudice among students in a particular college can be cited. But always the social psychologist thinks beyond the group he studies, seeking principles and relationships of far wider scope and generality. Though his methods now are better than formerly, he still faces the task of drawing significant conclusions not generalized beyond what his data justify.

Overgeneralization is a constant danger, for both layman and scientist. There are many degrees of generalization. Suppose a mother sees her younger child following the older one about, imitating many of his actions. If she reports this fact, there is no generalization. If she says, "My younger child imitates his brother," she has generalized to a slight degree. If she says, "Younger children imitate older ones" or "Children imitate each other," she is utilizing successively higher orders of generalization which are progressively less justified by the facts observed.

The publications of psychologists and social scientists often contain invalid generalizations, both stated and implied. The psychologist who many years ago did a study of his wife and himself and reported it in terms of "individual and sex differences" is an example, though an extreme one, of overgeneralization. When an investigator studies the social behavior of college students, nursery school children, suburban housewives, businessmen, or farmers, he must remember that, logically and scientifically, his conclusions hold only for the group studied, and only for the particular time and place at which the study was done. To arrive at more interesting general conclusions about *people,* about *human nature,* about *personality* or *social behavior,* a researcher must repeat his observations or experiments on representative samples of persons varying in age, sex, educational status, social status, geographical location, and cultural background. If the same phenomena occur in all groups studied, then—and only then—is he justified in stating generalized conclusions.

Findings on socioeconomic differences in social behavior suggest that it is dangerous to generalize from one class to another. Political preferences diverged along class lines during the administration of Franklin D. Roosevelt. Davis and others have shown that the pattern of child training in lower-class homes differs from that in

middle- and upper-class homes.[54] Kinsey has reported striking differences in the sexual behavior of lower- and upper-class males.[55]

In practice, it is often impossible for the social psychologist
to repeat his studies on varying groups to test the validity of his
generalizations. Sometimes a previous study shows that intergroup
variation is slight, making it unnecessary to repeat the study with
other groups. In any event, he can state that his findings hold true
for "middle-class urban housewives," for "a large group of midwestern college students," or for whatever group he has sampled. His conclusions then became a hypothesis to be tested later for more general
validity. Only by testing and retesting conclusions can the social
psychologist arrive at the body of generalization toward which every
scientist strives.[56]

SUMMARY; SYNOPSIS OF THE BOOK

Social psychology deals with individual behavior as it affects and
is affected by the behavior of others. It draws heavily on contributions from psychology, sociology, cultural anthropology, and psychiatry, but its emphasis differs from that of each of these subjects.

Traces of a social psychological orientation can be found in the
writings of many social philosophers, early sociologists, anthropologists, and psychologists. It is fairly well agreed that social psychology
as such emerged between 1890 and 1910, chiefly through the writings of Tarde, Le Bon, Ross, and McDougall.

Contemporary social psychology is marked by a certain divergence between those trained in psychology and those trained in
sociology or anthropology. Psychologists tend to emphasize the individual personality and its development, as affected by various
aspects of the social environment. They are interested in the
processes of social learning and in individual differences in social
behavior. In general, they favor experimental and quantitative
methods of research. Those with an orientation in sociology and
anthropology stress primarily and describe most thoroughly the
features of man's social heritage that mold his personality and social
behavior. Usually they focus attention on the content or product
of social learning rather than on the processes by which it occurs.
They stress uniformities rather than differences in social behavior

54 A. Davis, Child training and social class, chap. xxxiv, in R. G. Barker, J. S. Kounin,
and H. F. Wright (eds.), *Child behavior and development* (New York: McGraw-Hill
Book Co., Inc., 1943). See Chapter 5, below.

55 A. C. Kinsey, W. B. Pomeroy, and C. E. Martin, *Sexual behavior in the human
male* (Philadelphia: W. B. Saunders Co., 1948), chap. x.

56 The integrative tendency in our social sciences is illustrated in R. R. Grinker,
Toward a unified theory of human behavior (New York: Basic Books, Inc., 1956).

and prefer introspective and observational methods (with or with-out quantification) instead of experimentation.

Recent years have seen increasing tendencies toward integration in social psychology. Several recent contributions have furthered it, notably ethnological data showing effects of culture on personality, psychiatric emphasis upon social determinants of mental disorder, and "field theory," arising from Gestalt psychology.

Discussion of methods used in social psychology leads to the con-clusion that introspection, controlled observation, and experimen-tation are all useful, depending on the phenomena studied and the kind of data desired. Each method has certain advantages and drawbacks. Each should be evaluated critically and supplemented and checked by other methods, if possible. Like all scientists, the social psychologist must exercise great caution in generalizing from his findings.

The authors, trained in both psychology and sociology, are try-ing to present an integrated and practical approach to social psy-chology. By "integrated" we mean bringing together psychological, sociological, anthropological, and psychiatric techniques and find-ings. The term "practical" refers to our interest in human rela-tions, which is primarily the application of social psychology to the solution of social problems.

Part I of the book is concerned with the cultural and social forces that shape personality development. Part II, relating also to socialization, focuses on dynamic and cognitive processes such as motivation, learning, and perceiving, together with their end-products—attitudes, social norms, and ego-structures.

In Part III, "Communication and Interpersonal Relations," we widen our focus to take in social interaction, and investigate lan-guage, social groups, roles, and leadership. Part IV centers about important social phenomena, like public opinion, mass behavior, and social change. The final section, "Improving Human Rela-tions," covers applications of social psychology in problem areas.

SUPPLEMENTARY READINGS
Books of Readings

BRITT, S. H. (ed.). *Selected readings in social psychology.* New York: Rinehart & Co., Inc., 1950.

Britt, S. H., Past and present trends in the methods and subject matter of social psy-chology.

Young, K., Statistical methods in personality study.

LINDZEY, G. (ed.). *Handbook of social psychology.* Reading, Mass.: Addison-Wesley Pub. Co., Inc., 1954. Vol. I.

Allport, G. W., The historical background of modern social psychology.
Heyns, R. W., and Lippitt, R. Systematic observational techniques.

The three books of readings from which passages will be frequently cited are:

E. E. Maccoby, T. M. Newcomb, and E. L. Hartley (eds.), *Readings in social psychology* (3d ed.; New York: Henry Holt & Co., Inc., 1958).

S. H. Britt (ed.), *Selected readings in social psychology* (New York: Rinehart & Co., Inc., 1950).

G. Lindzey (ed.), *Handbook of social psychology* (2 vols.; Reading, Mass.: Addison-Wesley Pub. Co., Inc., 1954).

Other References

BECKER, H., AND BARNES, H. E. *Social thought from lore to science,* 2d ed. Washington, D. C.: Harren Press, 1952, Vol. II.
This work, the most complete history of sociology, contains interesting comments on the beginnings of social psychology in the nineteenth and twentieth centuries.

FESTINGER, L., AND KATZ, D. (eds.). *Research methods in the behavioral sciences.* New York: The Dryden Press, Inc., 1953.
A compilation of readings on the use of research tools.

JAHODA, M., DEUTSCH, M., AND COOK, S. W. *Research methods in social relations.* 2 vols. New York: The Dryden Press, Inc., 1951.
An informative methodological treatment valuable for social psychology and related fields.

KARPF, F. B. *American social psychology.* New York: McGraw-Hill Book Co., Inc., 1932.
The only book in its field, this volume contains thorough accounts of the work of Comte, Durkheim, James, Mead, Cooley, and the other early social psychologists up to about 1920.

LAZARSFELD, P. F., AND ROSENBERG, M. (eds.). *The language of social research.* Glencoe, Ill.: Free Press, 1955.
An outstanding compendium of research studies in social psychology and sociology, which constitutes an introduction to methodology for the advanced student.

MURPHY, G. *Historical introduction to modern psychology.* New York: Harcourt, Brace & Co., Inc., 1949. Chapter xxvii especially.
This enables the reader to see social psychology in relation to other developing fields of psychology.

MURPHY, G., MURPHY, L. B., AND NEWCOMB, T. M. *Experimental social psychology.* New York: Harper & Bros., 1937. Pp. 3-24 especially, The field and methods of social psychology.
Though now out of date, this book shows how far and how fast social psychology had developed a generation ago.

NEWCOMB, T. M. Studying social behavior, in T. G. Andrews (ed.). *Methods of psychology.* New York: John Wiley & Sons, Inc., 1948, pp. 664-94.

———. *Social psychology.* New York: The Dryden Press, Inc., 1950. Chap. i, Asking and answering questions about social influence.
These two discussions, by an outstanding social psychologist, center about the aims and methods of research.

Part I

SOCIALIZATION, THE MATRIX
OF PERSONALITY

As a behavioral science, social psychology fulfills an integrative function in bringing closer together its related disciplines: psychology, sociology, and anthropology. As with other social sciences, social psychology is committed to empirical methods that will yield increasing knowledge and prediction of human behavior. In launching this task, the logical point of departure appears to be the investigation of the personality itself in its social setting. In order to understand social processes we must commence by analyzing the humanization of the individual within his group, or, as the problem is more frequently stated, the process of socialization.

Basic in this analysis are the biological factors of personality. What contribution can the social psychologist make to the perennially confusing question of heredity versus environment? Moreover, there are the cultural variables which have an important effect on personality. Social scientists have leaned rather heavily on the anthropologist for enlightenment in this area. The impact of anthropology has had almost as much influence on understanding personality dynamics as the contribution of, say, psychoanalysis. In fact, as mentioned in Chapter 1, there has been a merging of these two techniques in the investigation of culture and personality.

After examining a number of other cultures, we shall turn to our own society for the specific institutional framework that has provided texture and direction to personality: the influence of the home, the school, and the neighborhood. Not least in this Gestalt of social influences are social class and ethnic status, which will be treated in some detail in Chapter 5.

2

Biological and Cultural Backgrounds

College students sometimes groan when they come across still another discussion of heredity and environment. They may have been
introduced to the problem in biology, psychology, sociology, education, or philosophy. The relationship, however, is of particular
concern to social psychologists and, as Otto Klineberg points out,
the issues are by no means settled.[1] He believes, as do the present
authors, that the topic requires continuing attention.

The matter of hereditary-environmental relationships cannot be
sidestepped. Confused and erroneous assumptions are made constantly, more often tacitly than consciously, in daily life, in literary
productions, and even in scientific treatises. It is essential for both
theoretical and practical reasons to have a fairly clear understanding of the interaction of heredity and environment.

Consider the following random but not unusual examples:

1. A young woman worries incessantly about going insane because
   her grandfather died in a mental hospital and an aunt was recently
   committed.
2. A newspaper editorial urges that no more immigrants from Asia
   and Africa be admitted to the United States "because (much as
   we hate to say it) they are backward culturally and of poor stock,
   biologically speaking."
3. A legislator introduces a bill into the legislature designed to rid
   his state of crime by sterilizing criminal and insane persons.

[1] O. Klineberg, *Social psychology* (rev. ed.; New York: Henry Holt & Co., Inc., 1954),
pp. 232 ff.

37

4. A businessman states, in a dinner-table conversation: "Prejudice is natural because we instinctively distrust and dislike people of other nations and races."
5. A Southerner insists that segregation should not be ended because, in the last analysis, the white and Negro peoples "are basically different" (i.e., the Negro is inferior).
6. An editorial recommends compulsory military training, and concludes with these words: "After all, international war can never be abolished because pugnacity and aggressiveness are inherent in human nature."

All these cases show a misunderstanding of hereditary-environmental relationships, overstressing the potency of hereditary influences.

One may also find examples placing too much credence in environmental factors:

1. A lad had difficulty graduating from high school, but his father is having him intensively tutored so he can enter the liberal arts course at Harvard.
2. An ad: "You too can become a powerful personality—a social success—the president of your firm. Send one dollar for our booklet, etc., etc. . . ."
3. The perfectly normal parents of a mentally defective child feel sure their child's condition is due to the diphtheria he had when a year old.
4. A successful concert pianist says in a newspaper interview: "Perseverance and good training are the whole secret of musical genius."

Such confusion can only result in unfortunate consequences to individuals or to society or both. Our first task is to get the facts; when we have them, certain implications are clear. For example, where we find that hereditary determinants predominate, as with physical characteristics and certain diseases, we can do little about it except, possibly, through some long-range eugenics program. On the other hand, where environmental influences play an important role, we can exercise control through such means as education, clinical treatment, and social legislation.

INTERACTION OF HEREDITY AND ENVIRONMENT

Few college students have not engaged in heated arguments over the question, "Which is more important—heredity or environment?" Yet the same persons would see the fallacy in a comparable question: "Which is more important in an automobile, the gasoline or the engine?" Why are so many acrimonious words wasted over heredity and environment?

In part, the difficulty lies in our failure to define terms. Many persons think heredity means "resemblance to parents." Environment may signify, for them, only climatic and geographic factors like temperature, altitude, and humidity. In part, confusion arises because people think of this kind of interaction in terms of the interaction between an object and a force, as in physics. Again, people often assume that a particular form of hereditary-environmental interaction is similar for all aspects of "human nature"—physical characteristics, abilities, knowledge, personality, and social behavior. This assumption may be made whether one is a "hereditarian" or an "environmentalist."

"Heredity" means neither "similarity to parents" nor "characteristics present at birth." It simply means the pattern of characteristics determined by the genes. A human's heredity is established at the moment the male sperm fertilizes the female ovum. Just which genes from male and female unite is a matter of "chance." That is to say, we do not know all the factors causing this particular event. Since any individual's genetic patterns are tremendously complex, we can predict the characteristics of offspring only in terms of probability.[2] However, physical characteristics are "determined by heredity" in the sense that the *differences* between a straight, aquiline, and snub nose or between white, brown, and yellow skin color are correlated with differences in gene combinations. In addition, genetic factors continue to function in determining the individual's maturation—that is, the direction and rate of his development. Maturation may, however, be accelerated or retarded by a number of environmental factors, such as diet, climate, drugs, exercise, and training.

"Environment" refers to any nongenetic factors affecting the organism, starting from the moment of conception. Prenatal environment is quite constant from one human organism to another, including nourishment, temperature, pressure, and other physico-chemical conditions. However, bacteria, poisons, or injuries may harm the embryo or fetus and produce some sort of "congenital" defect—i.e., a nongenetic defect, though present at birth. Thus a newborn child's abnormality may be either genetic or congenital, or a combination of the two.

[2] Mendel's Law is the classic statement of such probabilities, but this law is of questionable value in predicting human characteristics. The genetic structure of even simple traits like eye color or hair color is so complex that it is not yet fully understood. Among the theories of inherited factors in human intelligence, one posits five genes in varying combinations which might account for the normal distribution found. See J. B. Hill and H. D. Hill, *Genetics and human heredity* (New York: McGraw-Hill Book Co., Inc., 1955), pp. 508-9.

The environmental variables operating before birth are relatively small in range compared to those occurring after birth. A "normal" pregnancy means the absence of upsetting conditions in the fetal environment. But what is a "normal" post-natal environment? Consider the tremendous variations in climate, diet, care, training, and social setting among babies born to Eskimos in Baffin Bay, to a professional couple in Philadelphia, and to natives of a tropical isle in Polynesia! These widely differing physical and social environments, always interoperating with heredity, influence many aspects of the child's development and help to determine the kind of person he becomes.

We already have hinted at the most important thing about heredity and environment—their constant and continuous interaction. Can one imagine a human being without a heredity? Or one who developed without an environment? Lindesmith and Strauss present an answer:

> The question itself does not make sense. Both are important and necessary. But to say that both are necessary is not to say that both determine behavior in the same way. Biologists point out that in the activities of the simplest organisms the connection between behavior and structure is relatively direct and stable, although even here a relatively constant environment is always necessarily presupposed. As organisms become more complex and specialized, the relationship between biological structures and forms of behavior become less direct, less stable, more variable. Moreover, as organisms grow more complex they have a tendency to be increasingly influenced by that part of their environment which is constituted by the presence and actions of other organisms.[3]

The psychologist, through no virtue of his own, happens to be in a favorable position to evaluate hereditary-environmental relationships, since psychology reaches from the domain of biology on the one side to that of the social sciences on the other. Despite considerable controversy among psychologists, hundreds of fruitful research studies have been made, and the outlines of a comprehensive interpretation are beginning to emerge.

METHODS OF STUDY

As already noted, many people speak of "heredity *versus* environment" or "heredity *plus* environment" as if the two existed independently of each other. If we must have a formula, it is better, as Woodworth suggests, to speak of "heredity *times* environ-

[3] Reprinted from *Social psychology*, the revised edition, by Alfred R. Lindesmith and Anselm L. Strauss, by permission of The Dryden Press, Inc. Copyright 1956 by The Dryden Press.

ment," thus stressing that the individual is always a product of the two.[4]

From the moment of conception, the new organism develops as a result of internal maturation and response to environment. Male and female germ cells unite and subdivide within a cellular environment. The embryo and fetus develop within the uterine environment. Certainly exercise, and probably learning, occurs in the fetus, particularly after the fifth month. By the time the child is born he has well-specialized sensory equipment, a number of ready patterns of response (reflexes), and, because of his flexible and modifiable nervous system, a strong tendency to respond and to learn from his experience. Development is a dynamic relationship between the internal states of the individual and the changing external environment.

However, despite the continuous interaction of hereditary and environmental variables, it is possible to differentiate and discover something of their precise functioning. As suggested above, this may be done by noting to what degree *variations* in the heredity of individuals or *variations* in their environment correlate with *differences* between the individuals. This can only be done, of course, when one factor—heredity or environment—is constant. There are several situations where this holds true:

(1) Identical twins can be assumed to have identical heredities, since monozygotic twins result from an additional division of the germ cells. When identical twins are separated early in life, we have constant heredity and variable environment. Later study of such twins reveals considerable differences in attitudes, traits, and other aspects of personality but practically no differences in eye-color, shape of nose, or height.[5] Thus variations in environment are correlated with (and presumably cause) changes in personality but not changes in physique.

(2) We may study individuals who exemplify *different* heredities but identical (or at least similar) environments. Leahy, for one, did this, when she studied nearly 200 adopted children, each matched with an "own" child in the same home.[6] (The adopted children were all placed before they were six months old and were

4 See his *Psychology* (4th ed.; New York: Henry Holt & Co., Inc., 1940); also R. S. Woodworth and D. G. Marquis, *Psychology* (5th ed.; New York: Henry Holt & Co., Inc., 1947).

5 See the account later in this chapter of Newman, Freeman, and Holzinger's study of twins.

6 A. M. Leahy, Nature-nurture and intelligence, *Genet. Psychol. Monogr.,* XVII (1935), 235-308.

not tested until they were five years or more of age.) Leahy found that variations in heredity were much more closely correlated with variations in intelligence than were variations in environment with I.Q.'s. Specifically, the "own" children's I.Q.'s correlated .60 with those of their parents, while the coefficient for adopted children and the parents was .18. (Incidentally, Leahy concluded, from somewhat scant evidence, that differences in personality traits were "accounted for less by variation in heredity than by variations in environment.")

(3) When a considerable change in a person's environment takes place (e.g., being put in a new home or moving to a locality which is quite different in culture), we may discover concomitant modifications of behavior and of personality. Here heredity is of course constant, since we are dealing with the same individual; the major variable is the environmental change.

(4) We may compare the behavior of two large physically similar groups of people brought up in different cultures. Clear differences in behavior we may attribute to their contrasting social environments, since the hereditary potentialities of the two groups can be considered equal, on the average.

So much for methodology. Let us now consider the evidence from research studies, then attempt an interpretation which will be useful to the social psychologist.

The geneticist's approach. What is clearly inherited? This question would be more accurate if we used the cumbersome form, "In what areas do differences in heredity clearly correlate with existing differences in structure and function?"

Before reviewing the findings, we note that some studies must be discounted because they have failed to control variables adequately. For example, most of the "family tree" studies or genealogies, starting with Galton's *Hereditary Genius* of 1869, are invalid because they slight the role played by environment in the lives of their subjects.[7] Even some contemporary researchers are careless about controlling variables. Several studies which have concluded that mental disease is inherited fail to rule out the possibility of environmental influences. This could be done by comparing the incidence of mental disease among children brought up by their mentally diseased parents with the disease rate among children separated early from their mentally diseased parents. The former group might, quite conceivably, show a higher incidence of men-

[7] H. H. Goddard's *Kallikak family* (New York: The Macmillan Co., 1912) is a well-known example.

tal disease than the latter; the difference in the two figures would give some idea of the significance of environmental influences. Similarly, social scientists sometimes overlook the possible significance of hereditary and physiological factors as determinants of mental disorder and social maladjustment. Such determinants seem to operate in the case of a small number of individuals in any culture, along with various social determinants, and should be taken into account.

One example may be given of the difficulties encountered in research and interpretation. Kallmann studied the inheritance of schizophrenia, our most prevalent form of psychosis, and found that 68 per cent of children having two schizophrenic parents were schizophrenic themselves.[8] For children having one schizophrenic parent the figure dropped to 16.4 per cent. The comparative incidence for the normal population, with no schizophrenic parents, was only 0.85 per cent. While the evidence for hereditary causation seems overwhelming, a number of pertinent criticisms can be made.[9] Those relating to possible effects of environmental influences were partially answered in a later study by Kallmann in which he reported on identical twins.[10] In 85.8 per cent of cases where one twin was schizophrenic, the other was found to be likewise. When the twins were reared in the same environment, the figure was 91.5 per cent; if they developed in different environments it dropped to 77.6 per cent. (Comparable figures for fraternal twins and ordinary siblings were between 14 and 15 per cent.) Thus environmental factors play at least a small part in the picture. It is probably safest to conclude with Weinberg that schizophrenia results from many factors including constitutional changes, personality reactions, innate predisposition, and social experience, whether or not we agree with this author that social experience is decisive in determining whether the psychosis will occur.[11]

The studies that contribute to our understanding of hereditary-environmental relationships hold constant hereditary variables where environmental influences are studied and control environmental variables where hereditary factors are studied. Moreover, the best studies do not deal with "human behavior" or "human nature" in general, but select definable aspects, such as certain physi-

8 F. J. Kallmann, *The genetics of schizophrenia* (New York: Augustin, 1938).

9 N. Pastore, The genetics of schizophrenia, *Psychol. Bull.*, XLVI (1949), 285-302.

10 F. J. Kallmann, The genetic theory of schizophrenia, *Amer. J. Psychiat.*, III (1946), 309-22.

11 S. K. Weinberg, *Society and personality disorders* (Englewood Cliffs, N. J.: Prentice-Hall, Inc., 1952), pp. 20-21.

cal characteristics or diseases, I.Q., aptitudes, personality traits, attitudes, or social behavior.

The geneticists' contribution concerns mainly inheritance of physical characteristics and diseases. We shall summarize their findings, without going into details of genetic research, which is outside our province.

Hereditary differentials, say geneticists,[12] are clearly responsible for structural differences, including color of skin, hair, and eyes; basic shape of hair and eye, and to a lesser extent of nose, ears, and mouth; height and body build. Several physical abnormalities trace to unusual gene patterns; for example, stub fingers, extra fingers, and some kinds of birthmarks and dwarfism. Under sex-linked hereditary determinants are found hemophilia and most cases of color-blindness and baldness. The only diseases known at present to have a clear-cut genetic basis are diabetes mellitus (common type), some uncommon forms of cancer, certain rare types of idiocy, cerebral sclerosis, albinism, anosmia (deficient sense of smell), progressive muscular dystrophy, and the rare form of nervous system disintegration called Huntington's chorea.[13]

Medical and genetic researchers are still in some doubt about the role of heredity in determining the common types of physical and mental disease such as cancer, heart disease, tuberculosis, epilepsy, and schizophrenia. Untangling the skeins of heredity and environment turns out to be extremely complicated. The most prevalent view is that hereditary factors are present in some form as latent "predisposing" causes; the disease is "precipitated" if and when supporting environmental conditions occur.

The psychologist's contribution. Psychological studies of heredity and environment in relation to human personality and behavior have concentrated on the I.Q., as intelligence tests are a generally accepted and fairly valid type of mental measurement.

Until well in to the 1920's most psychologists assumed that general intelligence is fixed by one's heredity. An individual's I.Q. seldom varied more than five or six points from one age to another or from one test to another.[14] But enough exceptions accumulated

---

12 This summary is based chiefly upon data from Amram Scheinfeld's *The new you and heredity* (Philadelphia: J. B. Lippincott Co., 1950), a nontechnical but authoritative discussion of almost every aspect of heredity. The genetic sections of this book were edited by Dr. Morton D. Schweitzer.

13 The "black genes" causing such conditions are sometimes dominant and sometimes recessive. Scheinfeld's book, chap. xxxi, describes the diseases and defects for which there is proof of a greater or lesser degree of hereditary determination.

14 Unless the tests were of different types, such as "verbal" compared with "performance" tests, which sample different abilities.

that many psychologists began to wonder whether I.Q. "constancy" could not be partially explained by the fact that most individuals stay in a fairly constant environment from year to year. If this were true, then radical changes in environment might raise or lower the I.Q. considerably.

Several investigators, notably in Chicago and Iowa, undertook extensive research studies. Within twenty years hundreds of articles and monographs appeared discussing the effect of environment on I.Q. We shall not describe these studies in detail, since many are already familiar to psychology students.[15] The conclusions, however, can be stated rather simply:

Nearly all studies agree that environmental changes raise or lower a child's I.Q., though not more than five or ten points in most cases. But where really striking changes in a child's environment occur, the increment or decrement in I.Q. is greater and may reach as much as thirty, forty, or more points. On the other hand, these environmentally produced changes in I.Q., important though they may be, are small compared to the variations caused by genetic factors. The disparity between an idiot (I.Q. 20) and a highly gifted child (I.Q. 180) is predominantly genetic in origin. Even the most extreme environmental changes do not account for more than a quarter or a third as much variation. Hilgard, for example, says that studies of foster children show an average gain of 10 or more I.Q. points "over predictions based on the true mother's intelligence level." [16] Some psychologists might be more generous in their estimate of the I.Q. gain resulting from transfer to a superior foster home.

A number of psychologists have investigated nature-nurture relationships with respect to motor development. The best known of these have studied maturation and training.[17] Arnold Gesell's many studies at Yale have underscored the importance of maturation in a child's muscular development and motor control.[18] Dennis discovered that Hopi Indian children, bound to a board nearly all their first year of life, walk at the same age as other Indian chil-

15 See *Intelligence: its nature and nurture,* 39th Yearb. Nat. Soc. Stud. Educ., 1940; also R. S. Woodworth, Heredity and environment, *Soc. sci. Res. Council Bull.,* 1941, No. 47.

16 E. R. Hilgard, *Introduction to psychology* (2d ed.; New York: Harcourt, Brace & Co., Inc., 1957), p. 468.

17 Maturation refers to the growth of muscles, glands, nervous system, and other organic structures. Training covers exercise and all kinds of learning.

18 See A. Gesell, The ontogenesis of infant behavior, chap. vi in L. Carmichael (ed.), *Manual of child psychology* (2d ed.; New York: John Wiley & Sons, Inc., 1954).

dren and only a few days later, on the average, than American children.[19]

Perhaps the best-known research in this area is McGraw's study of the twins, Johnny and Jimmy, over several years.[20] Johnny was given intensive early training in various motor activities to see whether it improved them, as compared with the "normal"—i.e., untrained—Jimmy. McGraw found that training had little or no effect on what she called "phylogenetic activities," such as reflexes, crawling, creeping, sitting, standing, and walking. These activities she interpreted as infracortical and essential to normal human functioning, hence fairly independent of training. Other activities she called "ontogenetic"; these depend on higher brain centers and may or may not be acquired by the individual. Examples are skating, swimming, jumping, and climbing. In these activities training produced amazing results. Johnny learned to swim alone at fourteen months and to dive from a five-foot board at fifteen months. He learned to skate quite proficiently at one year. Without special training, Jimmy swam and skated much later. Some of the impact of this study was lost when it was discovered that the twins were nonidentical; nevertheless, it suggests the major importance of maturation in certain basic activities.

TRAINING AND DEVELOPMENT

Impressed by the significance of hereditary determinants as shown in studies of both motor and intellectual development, many psychologists have assumed that other aspects of human development proceed similarly. This emphasis is reflected in a 1947 symposium on heredity and environment in which all five of the participating psychologists stressed the role of heredity in determining behavior.[21] Carmichael, for example, commented that it is hard to find any facts, biological or psychological, which refute a famous biologist's statement that "we are perhaps about nine-tenths inborn and one-tenth acquired." [22]

In opposition to this viewpoint the present authors insist that the relative roles of heredity and environment, of maturation and training, *vary greatly depending upon which aspects of behavior we are studying*. In other words, because sensory, motor, and intellectual

19 W. Dennis, Does culture appreciably affect patterns of infant behavior? *J. soc. Psychol.*, XII (1940), 305-17. Reprinted in Swanson *et al., Readings* (2d ed.), pp. 369-75.
20 M. McGraw, *Growth; a study of Johnny and Jimmy* (New York: Appleton-Century-Crofts, Inc., 1935).
21 *Psychol. Rev.*, LIV (1947), 297-352.
22 L. Carmichael, The growth of sensory control of behavior before birth, *Psychol. Rev.*, LIV (1947), 316.

development is strongly influenced by heredity, it does not follow that language, perception, emotion, skills, personality traits, and social behavior are affected by heredity to the same degree. In fact there is good reason to believe that they are not.

Most studies of heredity and environment are concerned with only one dimension of the person, such as physique, intelligence, or disease. A notable exception is the research on twins, done by Newman, Freeman, and Holzinger, which compared physique, intelligence, achievement, and personality.[23] Nineteen pairs of separated twins who had spent most of their lives in different environments were found to differ only three-quarters of an inch in height and eight points in I.Q. But clinical and test evidence indicated that environment had affected achievement and personality a good deal. Freeman presents some conclusions on this point.[24] In one twin pair, the sister from the better environment was poised, affable, and self-confident; the other awkward, diffident, and restrained. Twin boys, similar in appearance and temperament, differed greatly in character. One was steady, industrious, and responsible, while the other, who had worked only very briefly, and then as a laborer, often ran afoul of the law. Freeman notes that these differences correspond to the standards of their foster homes. In another case one twin, raised on a farm, became rugged, energetic, bold, and mannish; the other, reared in an urban home, was delicate, languorous, and feminine. Newman, Freeman, and Holzinger [25] felt justified in concluding that physical differences are least affected by environmental influences, intelligence somewhat more, educational achievement still more, and personality most.

This finding may seem obvious, but many psychologists have failed to make the point clearly. The explanation for differing patterns of hereditary-environmental interaction, depending on the characteristics studied, is suggested by analyzing various behavioral processes.

A child's ability to talk, for example, depends on both vocalization (ability to utter sounds) and knowing the meaning of words. Vocalization occurs from the moment of birth and increases in range and complexity as neuromuscular mechanisms mature. But language or "talking" is more than making sounds; it signifies understanding and producing socially meaningful sounds, which depend on experience. A child with certain organic defects cannot talk

[23] H. H. Newman, F. N. Freeman, and K. J. Holzinger, *Twins—a study of heredity and environment* (Chicago: University of Chicago Press, 1937).

[24] F. N. Freeman, Heredity and environment in regard to twins, *Sci. Mon.*, XLIV (1937), 13-19.

[25] *Op. cit.*, p. 353.

because he cannot vocalize, yet he may understand many words spoken to him. A child isolated from human contacts cannot talk either, but for very different reasons; he can vocalize but has learned no socially sanctioned meanings. Thus maturation and training participate more equally and essentially in speech development than in motor behavior.

Consider another illustration. Much controversy has centered about maturation and training effects in emotional development. The disputants usually fail to note that emotion is a complex process whose various aspects may be quite differently affected by nature and nurture. A complete emotional reaction involves at least five steps: (1) perception of a stimulus situation, which is (2) interpreted in such a way that there results (3) an organic or visceral reaction, (4) a feeling-state (predominantly pleasant or unpleasant), and probably (5) some outward expression of muscular or gland-ular activity, like smiles or tears.

Now physiological maturation undoubtedly affects all stages of an emotional reaction. As an organism grows and develops, more refined cerebral, visceral, and motor reactions become possible. But learning also is involved, particularly in steps (2) and (5) above. As the child lives he learns about his environment and comes to perceive and interpret stimuli as beneficial or harmful. He learns to modify his vocal, gestural, and glandular responses in socially acceptable directions. When psychologists fail to specify which aspects of emotion they have in mind as maturing or as learned, it is not surprising that fruitless controversy ensues. Both matura-tion and training play essential parts in determining the whole emotional reaction.

Other data suggest the necessity for specifying the kind of behavior under consideration when hereditary-environmental rela-tionships are described. A comparison of "intelligence," "achieve-ment," and "personality" is instructive.

We have already seen that the major I.Q. differences between individuals are a function of genetic variations. Yet studies have shown that environmental changes can produce sizable increases or decreases in intelligence test performance. How is this possible?

As interpreted by the psychologist, intelligence means adapta-bility, flexibility, learning ability, or ability to adjust to new situa-tions. Intelligent behavior depends definitely on the quality of sensory, neural, and reactive mechanisms, particularly the brain. However, this physiological and neurological efficiency cannot be measured as such. It can be judged only by performance or be-havior as indicated on standardized tests. Tests necessarily involve language, pictures, colors, forms, or other materials with which a child is familiar. Since children differ in their familiarity with such materials, experience plays some part in the test score and the I.Q. In addition, a child must be motivated to do his best, and must have rapport with the tester—two more areas in which his learning operates.

In order to get as accurate an index of "native ability" as possible, psychologists have constructed tests using materials with which all children have had approximately the same experience (e.g., building with blocks, naming objects like a button, key, chair, or fork, drawing a man, copying a square, counting objects, tying a knot, folding and cutting paper, and the like). Hence the major variable operating to determine differences in I.Q. is not experience or training but, presumably, native ability.

Now compare "achievement" with "intelligence." Achievement tests measure knowledge, information, or skill possessed by an individual, whatever may be the combination of ability, training, and personality factors that produced the manifested achievement. The main requisite for achievement is experience—knowledge of literature or history, or training in typing, carpentry, or whatever the test covers. Naturally achievement cannot come without some ability, or without a modicum of motivation in the learner. But achievement tests never show to what extent such factors are involved. A person of mediocre ability may be intensively trained and perform better than a very "able" person with less training. For this reason achievement is much more clearly affected by environmental influences, especially education, than is intelligence.

PERSONALITY AND SOCIAL BEHAVIOR

Hereditary-environmental relationships become more complicated when we turn to personality and social behavior. We shall be concerned with personality in the balance of this chapter and in the several succeeding chapters. We shall be focusing on social behavior in Part III on Interpersonal Relations and in the rest of the book. Because the relation between personality and social behavior is sometimes confusing, let us briefly discuss it here.

Psychologists often imply that social behavior, like any other kind of behavior, is the outcome of organismic trends in the individual (motives, attitudes, etc.), since these determine the way he responds to stimuli. Thus, since no two persons are exactly alike, individual differences in behavior are explained. But the sociologist and anthropologist, on the other hand, see the relationship differently; in fact, rather than seeing social behavior as the *outcome* of personality they would be more inclined to put it the other way around and view personality trends as the result of social influences. How can this disparity occur?

Part of the trouble lies, of course, in the starting point. The psychologist works from the individual outward; the social scientist from the social forces in toward the person. Furthermore, psychologists focus more naturally on *individual differences* rather than *uniformities* of behavior. Then too, social scientists think of personality more in terms of patterns of attitudes and values, while psychologists emphasize traits and, perhaps, temperament.

This relationship between personality and behavior is actually one of the most complex matters with which psychologists and social scientists have to deal. We shall return to the topic in Chapter 15. Let us be satisfied, at the moment, by saying that personality is importantly affected if not determined by cultural and social influences, though it depends on which aspects of personality one is concerned with. On the other hand, social behavior may be greatly affected by, if not determined by, personality factors, particularly when the social behavior is not very highly structured—that is, not strictly controlled by mores, conventions, and other social norms. At an evening reception social behavior follows accepted forms of etiquette, and everyone conforms whether he be extrovert or introvert, neurotic or normal. But when the very same persons leave the reception, they may decide to drink, go to a folk dance, gamble, take in an art exhibit, argue about politics, look at television, or go to bed. Now there is scope for personality trends, and people act in accordance with dominant interests, attitudes, motives, and frustrations.

The concept of personality. Let us turn now to examine in more detail what we mean by personality. Regardless of how it is analyzed, there are certain postulates about personality that are almost universally accepted among social psychologists: (1) Personality is an organized whole or Gestalt; otherwise the individual would have no integrity, meaning, or continuity. In fact, schizophrenia and most psychoses constitute a far-reaching break in the person's mental structure. (2) Personality appears to be organized into patterns variously known as traits, panels, or complexes. These are persistent and to some degree observable and measurable. (3) Although there is a biological basis (glands, motor capacity, etc.) to personality, the specific development is a product of social and cultural environment. The patterning of personality depends on social interaction, with emphasis on early influences, the role of parents and other family members. (4) There are both the superficial aspects (handwriting or attitude toward chess) and the deeper core in personality (religious sentiments or temperamental tendencies). It is generally with this deeper core that the psychologist is concerned. In other words, personality is a continuous, persistent structure. (5) Composed as it is of both individual and social motives, personality, as Newcomb indicates, involves both "common and unique factors." [26] Individual personalities differ within a society and among societies; however, there is no small degree of similarity between human beings over a large part of the world.

The concept "personality" presents the psychologist with a paradox. On the one hand he needs such a term to denote the total, "Gestalted" quality of a person's characteristics and tendencies.[27] On the other hand it is very difficult to maintain the "whole" quality of personality and to deal meaningfully and consistently with such a complex Gestalt. The result is that, while paying lip-service to the wholeness of personality, biologists, psychologists, psychiatrists, social scientists, and others have developed their own favorite meanings of "personality." To some the word seems to mean underlying emotional tone or energy level; to others, characteristic traits or habit-patterns; to still others, moral and ethical qualities, "ego-structure," attitudes and values, or the pattern of typical social behavior. Much more than with most psychological terms, the connotations of "personality" are disconcertingly variable.

One thing, however, is clear: whether or not we can maintain the totality aspect of personality as a working concept, we shall get nowhere if we try to study hereditary-environmental relationships in regard to personality as a whole. We saw earlier that different aspects of intelligence, language, and emotion are variously affected by nature and nurture. Some kind of analysis is even more essential in studying the determinants of the greater psychological complexity, personality.

An analogy may help to make the point clear. An automobile is a whole; it functions as a well-integrated unit. Yet it is possible and often necessary to focus our attention on the battery, gears, differential, fan, carburetor, or spark-plugs, or to contrast the engine and the body. Attending to the parts does not preclude our understanding the whole; indeed the latter is facilitated if we make an effort to comprehend the structure and function of the parts, singly and in relation to the whole.

[26] T. M. Newcomb, *Social psychology* (New York: The Dryden Press, Inc., 1950), p. 339.

[27] Gardner Murphy's *Personality* (New York: Harper & Bros., 1947) seeks to portray personality as a whole—as a biosocial organism always operating within a field.

In a similar vein, Stagner suggests that analysis of personality is legitimate if the methods used are appropriate. "Water can be studied with regard to such variables as temperature, color, rate of flow, volume, or pressure, without destroying it. If proper units of analysis are employed, personality can also be analyzed without doing violence to its unique totality." [28]

Aspects of personality. What analytical scheme shall we employ? Some, like Stagner, prefer to think of various levels in personality, such as the behavioral, the perceptual, and the motivational. The authors' preference, in relation to determinants at least, is to distinguish between broad aspects of personality, such as *temperament, traits,* and *attitudes.* These three categories by no means include all of personality; one thinks of motives, aptitudes, skills, and many other components which can be described and studied. However, psychologists agree that temperament, traits, and attitudes are three discriminable aspects of personality, and furthermore they agree reasonably well as to the meaning of each. Let us describe them briefly, then discuss how they are determined.

From the days of Hippocrates, about 400 B.C., "temperament" has nearly always signified dispositions or behavior-tendencies rooted in physiological states. Hippocrates proposed four human temperaments: sanguine, melancholic, choleric, and phlegmatic, corresponding to four bodily "humors": red blood, black bile, yellow bile, and phlegm, respectively. We now think of temperament in terms of variables like energy level, alertness, speed of reaction, and emotional tone or mood. These qualities of behavior depend primarily on the nature of the biochemical organism—on sensory and nervous equipment, on muscles and glands, and on organic processes like metabolism and digestion. As Allport puts it: "The more anchored a disposition is in native constitutional soil the more likely it is to be spoken of as temperament." [29]

Unfortunately, however, very little research on temperamental attributes has been done. Allport cites the study of a child showing considerable consistency over the period from birth to nine years in readiness to laugh, activity level, sensitivity to rhythm, adaptability, and the like. [30] Others who use the term "temperament" divide it up entirely differently. [31] For example, some South African

[28] From *Psychology of personality,* by R. Stagner, copyright 1937, 1948, p. 10; courtesy McGraw-Hill Book Co., Inc., New York.

[29] G. W. Allport, *Personality* (New York: Henry Holt & Co., Inc., 1937), p. 53. A good discussion of the temperament and other approaches is found in C. S. Hall and G. Lindzey, *Theories of personality* (New York: John Wiley & Sons, Inc., 1957).

[30] *Ibid.,* pp. 121-28.

[31] See, e.g., C. J. C. Earl, Some methods of assessing temperament and personality, in Brand, H. (ed.), *The study of personality* (New York: John Wiley & Sons, Inc., 1954).

psychologists use three major dimensions of temperament: impulsive-cautious, restless-calm, and variability-steadiness.[32]   So far studies of basic temperamental components such as energy, speed, and mood have not been done upon children systematically over a period of years.

In any event, temperament seems a pervasive influence, affecting the quality of all one's behavior. It has a great deal to do with the *how* of behavior, but not with the content or *what* of behavior—the precise character of the acts performed. Put in another way, temperament determines whether one behaves energetically, slowly, cheerfully, and the like, but it has nothing to do, per se, with whether the acts so performed are arguments for socialism, typing a poem, reading Sinclair Lewis, driving a car, or playing with a baby. Temperamental differences, rooted as they are in the physiology of the organism, are affected greatly by hereditary determinants and, so far as we know, relatively little by social and other environmental influences.

Traits represent another aspect of personality—the one most emphasized by psychologists in their tests. Some, like Murphy, define the word "trait" broadly as "anything by means of which one person may be distinguished from another." [33] Stagner is more specific: "[A trait is] a generalized tendency to evaluate situations in a predictable manner and to act accordingly." [34] Most psychologists consider a personality trait a more or less enduring tendency to react in a definable way—particularly with reference to other people. Dominance or submission, extroversion or introversion, sociability, persistence, self-sufficiency, and neuroticism are favorite trait categories used by personality testers, though they do not agree upon a list of fundamental traits. It is assumed that individuals differ in the degree to which they exemplify each trait and that a person manifests the trait fairly consistently in various situations.[35]

Various distinctions can be made between temperament and traits. Temperament affects the *how* of behavior without having much to do with the *what*, as we have seen. Knowing a person is alert or energetic or cheerful aids us in understanding his *manner* of behaving but tells us little or nothing as to the *content* of his behavior. Traits, however, indicate something about both manner and content. For example, sociability, submissiveness, or neuroti-

32 H. Reuning and E. J. Rosen, in *J. national inst. personnel res.* (Johannesburg), v (1953), 77-84.

33 G. Murphy, *op. cit.*, p. 999.

34 R. Stagner, *op. cit.*, p. 143.

35 The validity of this assumption will be discussed in Chapter 13 in connection with roles.

cism suggests both a manner of behaving toward others and the nature of the behavior pattern itself. However, a trait is not related to specific behavioral content in the same way that a habit is.

Whereas temperament depends on hereditary and physiological factors, we are not sure how much traits are thus influenced. Some studies show a degree of consistency of personality traits, which suggests a physiological basis. Others indicate that personality traits can be changed somewhat by environmental modification. McKinnon, for example, studied conformity, cautiousness, invasiveness, and withdrawal over a five-year period in nursery-school children. She found a trend toward consistency rather than toward change, but a definite tendency away from "invasiveness" and toward conformity in all the youngsters.[36] Another study, of twenty-five women over several years, found that the percentages of persisting traits varied from 26 to 85, with an average close to 60 per cent.[37]

On the other hand, clinical evidence shows that many aspects of a child's personality change when he is removed from a subnormal environment and placed in a satisfactory foster home. Unfortunately, most such findings are stated qualitatively in terms of "adjustment," making it difficult to tell which aspects of personality are most and which least affected by the changed social setting.[38]

An interesting case is cited by Guthrie, suggesting that personality traits can be modified even in the late teens:

> A small group of college men . . . agreed to cooperate in establishing a shy and inept girl as a social favorite. They saw to it . . . that she was invited to college affairs that were considered important and that she always had dancing partners. They treated her by agreement as though she were the reigning college favorite. Before the year was over she had developed an easy manner and a confident assumption that she was popular. These habits continued her social success after the experiment was completed and the men involved had ceased to make efforts in her behalf. They themselves had accepted her as a success. What her college career would have been if the experiment had not been made is impossible to say, of course, but it is fairly certain that she would have resigned all social ambitions and would have found interests compatible with her social ineptitude.[39]

George Kelly describes an interesting clinical technique, "fixed-role therapy," in which a new role is presented to a client for him

[36] K. M. McKinnon, *Consistency and change in behavior manifestations* (Child Develop. Monogr., 1942, No. 30).

[37] K. E. Roberts and V. V. Fleming, *Persistency and change in personality patterns* (Monogr. Soc. Res. Child Developm., 1943, No. 36).

[38] See Chapter 4 below and C. R. Rogers, *Clinical treatment of the problem child* (Boston: Houghton Mifflin Co., 1939).

[39] E. R. Guthrie, *The psychology of human conflict* (New York: Harper & Bros., 1938), p. 128.

to enact; he is encouraged to think, feel, and act like the new person.[40] While the technique is still in the experimental stage, it seems to have real possibilities for producing personality changes, at least in certain kinds of people.

Thus traits represent an aspect of personality different from temperament and seem to be more influenced by environmental forces than is temperament.

Attitudes confront us with still another aspect of personality. An attitude is considered a tendency to react in a characteristically favorable or unfavorable way toward persons, objects, or situations. (The concept of attitude is closely related to interests and values.) Attitudes may be specific or generalized; one may speak of attitudes toward Mr. O'Flaherty, toward Irishmen, toward foreigners, or toward people. A person may favor or oppose simplified spelling, reform of education, our system of government, or social change in general.

Whereas temperament colors all of one's behavior, attitudes are latent and segmental. The part they play in social behavior depends largely upon whether they are evoked by social situations. Mr. A, for example, is interested in birds and in golf but dislikes college professors and theoretical matters. These attitudes do not pervade his social behavior, but they are significant in determining how he will react if someone proposes a bird walk, a trip to the country club, or a discussion of existentialism.

Often it is difficult to distinguish between personality traits and generalized attitudes. But attitudes are more situationally linked than traits. Even the most elaborate trait analysis of an individual does not indicate how he feels about world government, modern art, or television, or whether he is interested in science, football, or stamp-collecting.

The evidence indicates clearly that attitudes are learned. Allport has suggested that they may arise out of one's daily experience, or from a single dramatic instance, or they may be taken over ready-made from parents, playmates, and others.[41] Sherif and Sherif maintain that attitudes are formed in relation to situations, persons, or groups with which the individual comes into contact in the course of his development.[42] Several studies confirm the finding that at-

[40] G. A. Kelly, *The psychology of personal constructs* (New York: W. W. Norton & Co., Inc., 1955), Vol. I, chap. viii.

[41] G. W. Allport, Attitudes, in C. Murchison (ed.), *Handbook of social psychology* (Worcester, Mass.: Clark University Press, 1935). A more complete discussion of attitudes will be found in Chapter 8 below.

[42] M. Sherif and C. W. Sherif, *An outline of social psychology* (rev. ed.; New York: Harper & Bros., 1956), p. 490.

titudes depend more upon social influences than do personality traits. For example, correlations between parents and children for neurotic tendency, self-sufficiency, and dominance average about .25 or .30. For attitudes, the correlations average about .50 to .60, suggesting the greater impact of family influence in this area.[43] Developmental evidence is also relevant. In the above-mentioned study of persistence and change in personality, 60 per cent of the traits persisted over the years but only 15 to 20 per cent of the attitudes. Similarly, Crook compared the decline in consistency, over a period of several years, of intelligence, neuroticism, and attitude scores.[44]

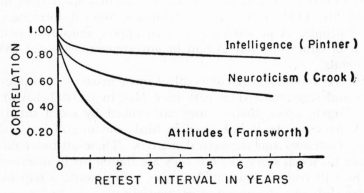

FIG. 2.—Chart showing relative consistency of intelligence, neuroticism, and attitudes over a period of years.

Intelligence is quite constant, neuroticism less so, and attitudes least of all. As Stagner remarks:

These findings are in harmony with what we should expect. Intelligence is determined to a substantial degree by hereditary factors, hence should show little inconsistency; attitudes are virtually pure effects of environment, hence are easily modified. Emotional instability is probably dependent upon both heredity and environment.[45]

CONCLUSIONS

Such evidence, though incomplete, shows that the pattern of hereditary-environmental influences differs considerably for various aspects of behavior and personality. Specifically, it indicates that differences in temperament and intelligence are largely a function of heredity, while differences in skills, attitudes, and, of course,

43 See Stagner, *op. cit.*, pp. 353-54.
44 M. N. Crook, Retest correlations in neuroticism. *J. genet. Psychol.*, XXIV (1941), 173-82.
45 Stagner, *op. cit.*, p. 162.

habits depend primarily upon environment and training. Personality "traits" seem to fall somewhere between these two extremes.

Newman, Freeman, and Holzinger, toward the conclusion of their study of twins, note that "personality" is too broad a term to have concrete meaning.

> The union of these different forms under the same term is doubtless a matter of practical convenience rather than strict psychological nature. General observation suggests that some of these forms are more fundamental and more permanent and stable than others. A sharp controversy rages as to whether personality is innate or acquired. Perhaps the opponents in this debate would not be so far apart if a distinction were drawn between features of personality, some of which are more and others less modifiable.[46]

In this chapter, three of many possible aspects of personality were compared—temperament, traits, and attitudes. These are by no means the major components of personality; they are simply three of its more distinguishable features. Actually some such analysis of personality is often implicit in the writings and research of psychologists or social scientists, though seldom made explicit. Sometimes one aspect is stressed to the exclusion of others. When an endocrinologist speaks of "glands regulating personality," or when an anatomist finds a relationship between constitutional type and personality, he is generally thinking of *temperament*. When the psychologist prepares a personality test, he usually centers it about one or more *traits*. When the ethnologist studies the effect of a primitive culture upon personality, he is concerned primarily with *attitudes* and *values*—or perhaps with a broader Gestalt of attitudes, values, and social norms. It may well be, as some have suggested, that the term "personality" has become so diffuse and confused that it has lost its usefulness!

On the other hand, we need a term to denote an individual's whole pattern of characteristics and tendencies. If we threw out "personality," another word would soon take its place. Perhaps we shall avoid semantic pitfalls if we specify, whenever we use the word, whether we mean personality in the sense of a comprehensive Gestalt or with a more restricted meaning. If the latter, we should make clear which aspect or aspects we emphasize.

Our discussion of hereditary-environmental relationships sets the stage for an examination, in the next chapters, of the major cultural and social forces which shape and mold the developing human child. (Hereditary or biological influences will not be elaborated here; these are taken up elsewhere, in developmental psychology or the psychology of personality.) It is not so much the *potentiality* or

[46] Newman, Freeman, and Holzinger, *op. cit.*, p. 332.

ability (e.g., temperament and intelligence) which will concern us in social psychology as it is the *content* side—the attitudes, values, interests, beliefs, roles, and habits. All of these have a fairly specific nature and direction which results from the individual's interaction with his social matrix. His motives and personality traits are also affected to some extent, as we shall see.

SUPPLEMENTARY READINGS

Books of Readings

MACCOBY, E. E., NEWCOMB, T. M., AND HARTLEY, E. L. (eds.). *Readings in social psychology*, 3d ed. New York: Henry Holt & Co., Inc., 1958.
Hebb, D. O. The mammal and his environment.

BRITT, S. H. (ed.). *Selected readings in social psychology*. New York: Rinehart & Co., Inc., 1950.
Murphy, G., The interdependence of outer and inner pressures.

Other References

ANASTASI, A., AND FOLEY, J. P. *Differential psychology*, rev. ed. New York: The Macmillan Co., 1949.
Chaps. iii (individual differences), iv (heredity and environment), and v (biological factors) are the most pertinent.

BOYD, W. C. *Genetics and races of man*. Boston: Little, Brown & Co., 1953.
An introduction to some of the latest developments in the principles of heredity.

DEWEY, R., AND HUMBER, W. J. *The development of human behavior*. New York: The Macmillan Co., 1951.
Chaps. ii-v present the essence of the environmental and hereditary viewpoints in the framework of a social psychology text.

DOBZHANSKY, T. *Evolution, genetics, and man*. New York: John Wiley & Sons, Inc., 1955.
A scholarly but readable approach. The first four chapters and the last two chapters are possibly most relevant for the student of social psychology.

FULLER, J. L. *Nature and Nurture*. Garden City; New York: Doubleday & Co., Inc., 1954.
An ably written account of the now almost ancient controversy.

HALL, C. S., AND LINDZEY, G., *Theories of Personality*. New York: John Wiley & Sons, Inc., 1957.
Chap. iv is entitled "Social psychological theories"; chaps. v-vii on Murray, Lewin, and Allport are also pertinent. Chap. xiii presents Murphy's biosocial theory.

MUNN, N. L. *Evolution and growth of human behavior*. Boston: Houghton Mifflin Co., 1955.
Developmental psychology with attention to animal as well as human studies.

SCHEINFELD, A. *The new you and heredity*. Philadelphia: J. B. Lippincott Co., 1950.
———. *The human heredity handbook*. Philadelphia: J. B. Lippincott Co., 1956.
Popular but well-documented surveys of the subject.

WOODWORTH, R. S. Heredity and environment: A critical survey of recently published material on twins and foster children. New York: *Social Science Research Council Bull.*, 1941, No. 47.
A summary of some of the research studies of the thirties.

YOUNG, K. *Personality and problems of adjustment,* 2d ed. New York: Appleton-Century-Crofts, Inc., 1952.
Chap. ii offers sound material on organic and environmental factors.

ZUBECK, J., AND SOLBERG, P. *Human development.* New York: McGraw-Hill Book Co., Inc., 1954.
A recent and fairly complete statement on background variables in the unfolding of mental and physical traits.

3

Culture and Personality

Our task in this and the following chapter is to describe the major social influences affecting personality and to depict their impact upon personality. We shall start with the broadest of these influences, culture, which has been studied extensively by the anthropologists.

WHAT IS CULTURE?

According to Kroeber, culture is the mass of learned and transmitted motor reactions, habits, techniques, ideas, and values and the behavior they induce.[1] It is the special and exclusive product of men; it is what we learn from others and what we add to it.[2] Culture rests on our biological heritage, says Goldschmidt, but is not merely a response to biological needs. The culture of any people is a unique set of solutions to biological and social needs in general. He defines culture as

. . . the pattern of learned behavior shared by the members of a society. It includes not only the way of making things and doing things, but the pattern of relationships among people, the attitudes they foster, the beliefs and ideas they have, and even the feelings with which they respond. Culture is not merely customs—though customs are a part of culture. For culture is the patterned whole of responses, the more or less consistent unity that links the many diverse elements of living into a way of life.[3]

In this sense culture includes institutions like state, church, and family, mores and customs of all sorts, and ideas of right and wrong.

1 A. L. Kroeber, *Anthropology* (New York: Harcourt, Brace & Co., Inc., 1948), p. 8.
2 *Ibid.*, p. 253.
3 W. Goldschmidt (ed.), *Ways of mankind* (Boston: Beacon Press, Inc., 1954), p. 6.

Often it is referred to as our "social heritage." Culture is not passed on intact, like an heirloom, from one generation to another without changing. It changes constantly, but the changes are slow enough that the basic features remain constant for at least a generation and usually considerably longer.

People commonly minimize the influence of culture on their behavior and personalities. On the other hand, they habitually overestimate the effects of heredity. The chief reason for this probably is that our culture is much like the air we breathe—so close, so natural, so much a part of us that we take it for granted and fail to note its influence.

Linton once remarked that the last creature in the world to discover water would be the fish, precisely because he is always immersed in it! Similarly, human beings begin to think about their cultural envelope only when they observe persons from different cultures—or better still when they get "culture shock" by visiting or otherwise coming into close contact with a people very different from themselves. Even at that, if the strange people are of a different race, they often attribute their "unusual" behavior to heredity rather than to cultural background. A recent humorous description of the American people, by Dr. Horace Miner of the University of Michigan, suggests the perspective with which we might be viewed by a visitor from afar: [4]

Nacirema culture is characterized by a highly developed market economy . . . ; a large part of the fruits of these labors and a considerable portion of the day are spent in ritual activity, the focus of which is the human body, the appearance and health of which loom as a dominant concern in the ethos of the people.

The daily body ritual performed by everyone includes a mouth-rite. Despite the fact that these people are so punctilious about care of the mouth, this rite involves a practice which strikes the uninitiated stranger as revolting. . . . The ritual consists of inserting a small bundle of hog hairs into the mouth, along with certain magical powders, and then moving the bundle in a highly formalized series of gestures.

In addition to the private mouth-rite, the people seek out a holy-mouth-man once or twice a year. These practitioners have an impressive set of paraphernalia, consisting of a variety of augers, awls, probes and prods. The use of these objects in the exorcism of the evils of the mouth involves almost unbelievable ritual torture of the client . . .

CULTURE IN PERSONALITY FORMATION

The findings of anthropology. Anthropologists, particularly ethnologists (cultural anthropologists), have always been interested in the customs, institutions, and behavior of primitive peoples.

[4] As reported in *The New York Times,* June 10, 1956.

Only recently, however, have they concerned themselves with personality. Following leads given by Boas, Malinowski, Radcliffe-Brown, Sapir, and other pioneers, several investigators set out in the late 1920's to study and compare the personalities of members of different cultures. Perhaps the best-known are Margaret Mead and the late Ruth Benedict, both former students of Boas.

Mead's studies in Samoa and New Guinea are now so well known to students they need not be described in detail. Briefly, she found that adolescence in Samoa was not a period of stress, and that Samoans were well-adjusted individuals, due chiefly to the large family groups, the liberal attitude toward sex, and freedom from pressure upon youth.[5] Among the Manus of New Guinea, by contrast, personality was marked by strong ego-drive and self-assertiveness; industry, physical prowess, and respect for authority were primary goals.[6] Sex was repressed and adolescence involved more strain than in Samoa.[7]

In a third study Mead investigated sex differences.[8] She wanted to find out to what degree "temperamental" differences between the sexes were innate and to what extent culturally determined, and to discover what kinds of training were involved. She chose three primitive groups in New Guinea—the Arapesh, Mundugumor, and Tchambuli—who were racially similar and lived in the same general area of the island.

The Arapesh were a cooperative society, emphasizing gentleness, responsiveness, and mutual aid. They accepted human nature as good and minimized age and sex differences. The deviants in this society were the violent and aggressive people, male or female. The Arapesh ideal was men and women who were maternal, gentle, responsive, and unaggressive.

The Mundugumor, formerly a cannibal tribe, were quarrelsome and hostile. They placed a premium on violence and physical courage. Babies were treated roughly and given Spartan training. The Mundugumor ideal was identical for both sexes: "men and women ... [were] expected to be violent, competitive, aggressively sexed,

[5] M. Mead, *Coming of age in Samoa* (New York: William Morrow & Co., Inc., 1928).

[6] M. Mead, *Growing up in New Guinea* (New York: William Morrow & Co., Inc., 1930). These and other studies by Margaret Mead have been reprinted in inexpensive paper editions.

[7] In *New lives for old* (New York: William Morrow & Co., Inc., 1956), Mead describes the effects of recent social changes in Manus; they have gone from the Stone Age to the Atomic Age in 25 years. She reports they are more relaxed and happy now, largely as a result of contacts with Australians, Americans, and others during and after World War II.

[8] M. Mead, *Sex and temperament in three primitive societies* (New York: William Morrow & Co., Inc., 1935). Copyright 1935 by Margaret Mead.

jealous and ready to see and avenge insult, delighting in display, in action, in fighting." [9] Meek, easy-going people were discounted socially, for they were against the tradition "where both men and women were expected to be proud, harsh and violent, and where the tenderer sentiments were felt to be as inappropriate in one sex as in the other." [10]

The third group, the lake-dwelling Tchambuli, had an elaborate artistic culture in which tribal ceremonies were very significant. Each man was skilled in many arts. In contrast to the Arapesh and Mundugumor, the Tchambuli had clearly defined roles for men and for women. Men did the acting and received the recognition, but women had the real power; they fished, manufactured, and controlled the trading. Women made the advances in courting and were tolerant and appreciative of the men's games and theatricals. Men had their own clubs and were quarrelsome, coquettish, sly, and suspicious.

Mead summarized the approved personalities for each sex in these three primitive societies. For the Arapesh the ideal was essentially feminine: cooperative, unaggressive, and responsive; the mild, responsive man married to the mild, responsive woman. The Mundugumor expected both men and women to be ruthless, aggressive, and positively sexed; this conception was of a violent masculine character. In Tchambuli, said Mead, we had a "genuine reversal of the sex-attitudes of our own culture, with the woman the dominant, impersonal managing partner, the man the less responsible and emotionally dependent person." [11] Naturally, Mead concluded that our beliefs about innate male and female characteristics are erroneous. Human nature, in this as in other respects, seems extremely malleable, primarily affected by cultural molding during early infancy.

Mead, with several collaborators, also studied cooperation and competition in primitive cultures.[12] While no culture was simple to analyze, and no society was exclusively cooperative or competitive, the survey revealed clear differences. The Kwakiutl were "grossly competitive," the Bathonga "grossly cooperative," and the Ojibwa "grossly individualistic"—i.e., characterized by the individual striving for his goals without much reference to other persons. These differences are not solely a result of geography, climate, food supply, or general culture area. Rather, cooperativeness or com-

9 *Ibid.*, p. 225.

10 *Ibid.*, p. 233.

11 *Ibid.*, p. 279.

12 M. Mead (ed.), *Cooperation and competition among primitive peoples* (New York: McGraw-Hill Book Co., Inc., 1937).

petitiveness or individualism is a function of the whole social pattern—"the way the structure of society is built up." This can be
studied in the educational system and in the ways certain types of
character are favored or rewarded by the culture. Key points in
character formation seem to be ego-development and strength of
the sense of security. In general, in competitive societies the ego
is highly developed; in cooperative societies a sense of security is
outstanding.

Important to the study of personality and culture is Ruth Benedict's *Patterns of Culture*.[13] Like Mead, she stressed the power of
culture in shaping human behavior.

> The life history of the individual is first and foremost an accommodation to
> the patterns and standards traditionally handed down in his community. From
> the moment of his birth the customs into which he is born shape his experience
> and behavior. By the time he can talk, he is the little creature of his culture, and
> by the time he is grown and able to take part in its activities, its habits are his
> habits, its beliefs his beliefs, its impossibilities his impossibilities. Every child
> that is born into his group will share them with him . . .[14]

Though cultures are amazingly diverse, said Benedict, each has
a certain pattern or integration. Each human society has somehow
selected certain segments of the great range of possible interests
and types of behavior. This is its culture pattern and represents
a coherent organization of behavior. She analyzed in detail three
cultures: the Zuñi of New Mexico, the Dobuans of New Guinea,
and the Kwakiutl of Vancouver Island on the Pacific Coast.

The Zuñi, a Pueblo Indian group stressing ritualistic ceremony,
were conventional to the point of suppressing individual initiative.
Their ideal was a dignified, affable, conventional person who
avoided deviation, or even leadership. Moderation, mildness, and
sobriety were the order of the day, with little conflict or sense of
guilt. Benedict characterized the Zuñi as an "Apollonian" culture,
in contrast to the neighboring "Dionysian" Indian cultures with
their violence and sanctioned sensual excesses. Formality, sobriety,
and "nothing to excess" were Zuñi watchwords and the outstanding
characteristics of the Zuñi group.

The Dobu of New Guinea, on the other hand, were violent, competitive, suspicious, and treacherous. They cheated and they believed in magic. Each person and each village seemed to be hostile
to the others. A girl's mother arranged her daughter's marriage
by trapping the boy she found sleeping with her daughter. A hus-

---

[13] R. Benedict, *Patterns of culture* (Boston: Houghton Mifflin Co., 1934); reprinted
in a pocket edition by Penguin Books, 1946.
[14] *Ibid.*, p. 2.

band had to spend alternate years in the village of his wife, during which time he was humiliated as an outsider. The wife suffered similarly the next year when she resided in the husband's village. Economic activities were highly competitive. "All existence is cut-throat competition, and every advantage is gained at the expense of a defeated rival." It was secret and treacherous; "the good man, the successful man, is he who has cheated another out of his place." There was widespread belief in magic—in incantations, passwords, and malevolent charms. Suspicion attached to practically all social relations, including those between husband and wife. Puritanical ideas and promiscuity went together in this society. Benedict concluded as follows:

> The Dobuan, therefore, is dour, prudish, and passionate, consumed with jealousy and suspicion and resentment. Every moment of prosperity he conceives himself to have wrung from a malicious world by a conflict in which he has worsted his opponent. The good man is the one who has many such conflicts to his credit, as anyone can see from the fact that he has survived with a measure of prosperity. It is taken for granted that he has thieved, killed children and his close associates by sorcery, cheated whenever he dared. As we have seen, theft and adultery are the object of the valued charms of the valued men of the community. . . . Sorcery and witchcraft are by no means criminal. A valued man could not exist without them. The bad man, on the other hand, is the one who has been injured in fortune or in limb by the conflicts in which others have gained their supremacy. . . .[15]

> Life in Dobu fosters extreme forms of animosity and malignancy which most societies have minimized by their institutions. Dobuan institutions, on the other hand, exalt them to the highest degree. The Dobuan lives out without repression man's worst nightmares of the ill-will of the universe, and according to his view of life virtue consists in selecting a victim upon whom he can vent the malignancy he attributes alike to human society and to the powers of nature. All existence appears to him as a cut-throat struggle in which deadly antagonists are pitted against one another in a contest for each one of the goods of life. Suspicion and cruelty are his trusted weapons in the strife and he gives no mercy, as he asks none.[16]

The Kwakiutl Indians of the Pacific Northwest were termed by Benedict a Dionysian culture, because of such features as their former cannibalism and their frenzied dances. Highly individualistic and competitive, they carried private ownership to the extreme of dividing up not only land but also the shore, deep sea areas, and even songs, myths, and titles. Acquiring status and shaming rivals was a primary aim in this society. It was signified by a "potlatch" or feast at which blankets, canoes, copper, and valuable oil were distributed or destroyed. If distributed, it was understood that the

[15] *Ibid.,* pp. 155-56.
[16] *Ibid.,* p. 159.

goods were to be returned later at usury—often a rate too high for the recipient to manage. Either distribution or destruction of goods added to the prestige of the host.

The main theme of Kwakiutl culture was the will to superiority, to self-glorification. "The relations between the sexes, religion, and even misfortune were elaborated in this culture in proportion as they offered occasion for demonstrating superiority by the distribution and destruction of property." [17] Gibes and insults played a great part in the process. The Kwakiutl recognized "only one gamut of emotion, that which swings between victory and shame. It was in terms of affronts given and received that economic exchange, marriage, political life, and the practice of religion were carried on." [18] Even accidents were an occasion for shame. "A man whose axe slipped so that his foot was injured had immediately to wipe out the shame which had been put upon him. A man whose canoe had capsized had similarly to 'wipe his body' of the insult. People must at all costs be prevented from laughing at the incident. The universal means to which they resorted was, of course, the distribution of property." [19]

Benedict emphasized that cultures are not heterogeneous assortments of acts and beliefs. They are organized and patterned around goals which their institutions are designed to further. The Kwakiutl pattern was bent to the service of an obsession. We consider it abnormal, "a megalomanic paranoid trend"; yet it was made the essential attribute of the ideal man in Kwakiutl society.

Neither Mead nor Benedict maintained that personality is fashioned completely by culture. Each recognized hereditarily and physiologically grounded individual differences in temperament; no culture eradicates these differences. They noted however, that a culture emphasizes and selects certain traits as desirable or undesirable; aggressiveness, dominance, or competitiveness—or their opposites—may be stressed so that one or more become the norm for a whole society. Social usage may also define the norms for the behavior and personality of some segment of its people, such as for men and for women. According to Mead and Benedict, customs and culture patterns cannot be understood solely through psychology; they must be interpreted historically as well. Abundant evidence indicates that situations shape people in ways that represent only a small part of the great arc of potential human purposes and motivations.

[17] *Ibid.*, p. 186.
[18] *Ibid.*, pp. 198-99.
[19] *Ibid.*, p. 199.

These pioneer studies by Mead and Benedict have been criticized on several counts. For example, it is said that Mead oversimplified her contrasts between the Arapesh, Mundugumor, and Tchambuli, and that Benedict made too sharp a dichotomy between Apollonian and Dionysian Indian cultures. Psychologists have suggested [20] that better sampling methods could reveal interesting and significant variations in attitudes and behavior within a given culture pattern. Anthropologists usually have replied that they are interested primarily in obtaining a composite picture of personality in each culture so that cross-cultural comparisons can be made. We shall discuss such criticisms later.

The theory of "basic personality." In 1937 a psychoanalyst, Abram Kardiner, and an anthropologist, Ralph Linton, collaborated in a different approach to culture and personality. They felt that existing studies fell short in two major ways. First, the studies did not show how culture affects an individual's dynamic tendencies, his "action systems" or "integrative systems"—what Freud would have called "instincts." Second, despite the evidence that culture and personality are interrelated, Kardiner and Linton believed that the earlier studies did not provide any well-defined technique for investigating and comparing the interaction of personality and culture in several societies. After surveying all possible techniques, Kardiner and Linton concluded that the only useful psychological method for the purpose is psychoanalysis, or "psychodynamics."

They proposed a central concept—"basic personality structure" or "basic personality type." This means the "constellation of personality characteristics which would appear to be congenial with the total range of institutions comprised within a given culture." [21] Or, in a later formulation: "that personality configuration found in any society which is shared by the bulk of the society's members as a result of the early experiences which they have in common." [22] "Basic personality structure," in other words, does not refer to the total personality of a given individual, but rather to those aspects which he has in common with his fellows, and which distinguish him and his fellows from the members of a different culture.

[20] See, for example, O. Klineberg, *Social psychology* (rev. ed.; New York: Henry Holt & Co., Inc., 1954), chaps. xiii, xiv.

[21] R. Linton, Foreword, in A. Kardiner, *The individual and his society* (New York: Columbia University Press, 1939), p. vi.

[22] R. Linton in A. Kardiner, *Psychological frontiers of society* (New York: Columbia University Press, 1945). See also R. Linton (ed.), *Science of man in the world crisis* (New York: Columbia University Press, 1945) and R. Linton, *Cultural background of personality* (New York: Appleton-Century-Crofts, Inc., 1945).

Study of several cultures convinced Kardiner that basic personality structure grows out of the child-care disciplines found in a society, i.e., the kind of maternal care, affectional relations with parents, kind of discipline or lack of it, and relationships with siblings. These influences determine the child's basic attitudes, which through the process of projection account for secondary institutions like religion, folklore, art, etc. The latter, which Kardiner calls "projective systems," in turn determine the "reality systems," that is, beliefs about cause-and-effect relationships, interpretations of the universe, and the like. Interpreting the Tanala and Marquesan cultures (studied by Linton), Kardiner found the religious systems to be replicas of the child's experiences with parental discipline. In the Tanala culture the child was forced to be obedient, and the religion stressed obedience to ancestral gods. In the Marquesas, obedience played no special role either in the family or in religion.

Kardiner and Linton regarded their concept of basic personality structure as an unproved hypothesis until they obtained thorough personality studies of many individuals from a given culture. They came upon the desired material when Cora Du Bois brought back from Alor both field data and eight rather detailed biographies, a number of Porteus intelligence test results, children's drawings, and thirty-seven Rorschach test records.[23] Kardiner found that his interpretation of the field report agreed well with the analysis of the biographies. He was even more impressed with the agreement between all these data and the Rorschach interpretations, which were made independently by an expert.[24]

From these materials the basic personality structure in Alor was found to be insecure, anxious, suspicious, lacking in confidence, with no interest in the outer world. Tensions had no adequate means of discharge; hence personality "is filled with repressed hatred and free floating aggression over which constant vigilance must be exercised." No action systems exist for manifesting mastery and constructiveness.

The basic cause for this kind of personality structure, according to Kardiner, lies in the maternal neglect fostered by a system in

---

[23] The Rorschach is the leading "projective" test of personality. A subject reports what he sees in each of ten rather elaborate ink blots, some of which are in color. Personality structure is determined by analyzing the responses in terms of wholeness, movement, form, color, and other variables.

[24] For the report on Alor, see A. Kardiner, *Psychological frontiers of society, op. cit.*, chaps. v to ix. The Rorschach analysis was done by Dr. Emil Oberholzer.

which the mother worked in the fields all day. The child was left in the hands of older siblings, relatives, or friends.

The consistency of the discipline was therefore destroyed; the image of the parent as a persistent and solicitous helper in case of need was not built up. The ego was feeble in development and filled with anxiety. . . . Although we find in the projective systems the concept of a deity, there is no effort at idealization of the divine image and the Alorese perform their religious rituals only under the pressure of urgent circumstances, and then in a reluctant manner. The interpersonal tensions within a society run high, distrust is universal, and the emotional development retarded and filled with anxiety.[25]

It is difficult as yet to evaluate properly Kardiner's contribution to the study of culture and personality. His emphasis on the dynamics of personality, notably on "integrative systems" and "projective systems," is very important, as is his attention to child-rearing techniques. His main sequence, child discipline→basic personality structure→projective systems→reality systems, is a productive idea which should stimulate further research and encourage deep rather than surface interpretations. Also his ambitious comparative study of a dozen or more whole culture patterns is noteworthy.

Critics of Kardiner's work object to his emphasis on child-rearing practices as the main determinant of personality structure, since family behavior patterns themselves result from complex cultural influences.[26] Many studies indicate that other social factors besides the family influence personality formation; for example, roles assigned according to age, sex, and status.[27] Despite the undeniable value of many "psychodynamic" concepts, probably it is not the only fruitful dynamic approach. The existence of many conflicting varieties of psychoanalysis and psychiatric interpretation suggests caution in accepting any one until we have more evidence.

Other psychiatric approaches. It is interesting to compare Kardiner's essentially Freudian approach with another psychiatric interpretation made by Erich Fromm. Where Kardiner regards the family situation as the matrix for basic personality structure, Fromm insists that "social character" is shaped by the adaptation of human needs to the plastic mode of existence of a society.[28] A society's way of life, says Fromm, results from a complex of historical, economic,

<hr/>

[25] Kardiner's chapter on The concept of basic personality structure, in Linton's *Science of man in the world crisis, op. cit.,* pp. 115-16.

[26] See the discussion of Fromm, below.

[27] See Chapters 5 and 13 below.

[28] E. Fromm, *Escape from freedom* (New York: Rinehart & Co., Inc., 1941). Fromm's "social character" is similar to Kardiner's "basic personality structure"; it means "the essential nucleus of the character structure of most members of a group which has developed as the result of the basic experiences and mode of life common to that group" (p. 277).

social, and psychological factors. This mode of existence manifests itself in ideas and attitudes which shape child personality via the family and the educative processes. Parents reflect in their personalities, behavior, and treatment of the child the dominant ideas (i.e., social character) of the society, modified by their class or other subculture status within it. Thus the family is "the psychological agent of society" and is the effect as well as the cause of social character. Fromm's interpretation, while it does not propose concrete research procedures, seems more congruent with recent psychological and sociological research than does Kardiner's.

Karen Horney was another influential "neo-psychoanalyst." Though chiefly concerned with neurosis rather than personality structure in general, Horney's views are relevant to interpretations of culture and personality. Like Benedict, she found neurosis rooted in the cultural pattern.[29] Feelings of anxiety, hostility, and alienation, which are basic to neurosis, arise from an individual's adopting or "introjecting" the conflicting values found in a culture. Some of these arise from inconsistencies between teachings and practices. For example, in our culture we teach a child to be generous, sympathetic, and cooperative; he learns from experience with our system that success depends on his being competitive, assertive, and aggressive. A normal person can cope with such a conflict without serious effects, but not the neurotic. As Horney concluded: "It seems that the person who is likely to become neurotic is the one who has experienced the culturally determined difficulties in accentuated form, mostly through the medium of his childhood experiences, and who consequently has been unable to solve them, or has solved them only at great cost to his personality. We might call him a stepchild of our culture."[30] Like Fromm, Horney sees basic personality trends stemming from highly ramified tendencies in culture, not solely from family disciplines.

Recently the term "modal personality" has been coming to the fore in preference to "basic personality," "social character," and the like. *Modal personality* refers to the most frequent or characteristic patterns appearing among members of a cultural group. One anthropologist says that it is largely socially derived, and represents the shared elements of personality, ranging from activities like eating, smoking, or games to highly generalized views of life.[31]

[29] K. Horney, *The neurotic personality of our time* (New York: W. W. Norton & Co., Inc., 1937).

[30] *Ibid.*, p. 290. A provocative account of the conflict between American business ethics and our Judeo-Christian moral values is found in Margaret Halsey, *The folks at home* (New York: Simon & Schuster, Inc., 1952).

[31] J. J. Honigmann, *Culture and personality* (New York: Harper & Bros., 1954), p. 30.

PERSONALITY STRUCTURE IN SIMPLE SOCIETIES

The Hopi personality. Of American Indian cultures, the Hopi and Navaho have been subjected to personality studies of considerable scope. The Hopi are a Pueblo Indian group, living in the semi-arid mesas of northern Arizona.[32] They are agricultural and pastoral, governed by a strict code of life called the "Hopi Way," to which individuals are induced to conform through sanctions like gossip and ridicule. Outstanding features of Hopi behavior were found to be lack of aggressiveness and of prestige-seeking. The authors of *The Hopi Way* gave various kinds of tests to many Hopi children and compared the results with those from a group of midwestern white youngsters. Results showed several clear-cut differences. For example, the Hopi children found more pleasure in meeting social expectations than did the white children, and much less pleasure in individual achievement. The Hopi were more likely to be ashamed of being embarrassed or aggressive than the white children, but much less ashamed of "bad behavior." Hopi fears centered about supernatural or subjective dangers rather than objective dangers. The typical Hopi child, the investigators concluded, was intelligent (average I.Q. 110-117 on performance scales—which suggests an atypical sample), industrious, and considerate. He became sad and angry at aggression and condemned individual efforts to rise above the group by bullying or fighting. While aware of his abilities, he did not admit or openly desire outstanding personal achievement which would separate him from his group. This personality pattern came about largely through the permissive training by which the Hopi child gradually learned the group purposes and became indoctrinated with the Hopi way. A price was paid in repression of spontaneity and a tendency toward rigidity, but this kind of training and its resultant personality pattern seem to have facilitated the survival of the Hopi in his rather unfavorable environment.

Recent evidence indicates that the Hopi has some degree of introjected aggression, though on the whole members of the culture have acquired a balance between duress and flexibility.[33] No doubt the distinction between the *biological* mother, who gives birth to the child, and the *social* mother (the mother's sister) may cause some conflict in the child's affection. In addition, there is care by the

[32] L. Thompson and A. Joseph, *The Hopi way* (Chicago: University of Chicago Press, 1947); W. Dennis, *The Hopi child* (New York: Appleton-Century-Crofts, Inc., 1940).

[33] D. Eggan, The general problem of Hopi adjustment, in C. Kluckhohn *et al.*, *Personality in nature, society and culture* (New York: Alfred A. Knopf, Inc., 1953), pp. 276-91. Also L. Thompson, *Culture in crisis* (New York: Harper & Bros., 1950), pp. 90-120.

older sister who plays the role of his mother. However, it would seem that whatever conflicts in loyalty may exist, the tightly knit family group provides the individual with a sense of security. Furthermore, the minimal sex repression, allowing some freedom for both heterosexual and homosexual play, from childhood through adolescence, probably has reduced Hopi anxiety.

It is significant that personality differences were revealed by emotion and attitude tests given at different parts of the reservation. The First Mesa boys were relatively spontaneous and outgoing, while those of Oraibi were definitely constricted and troubled by vague anxiety.[34] On the other hand, the girls of the First Mesa appeared more constricted than those of the Third Mesa. These findings point to the dangers of overgeneralization about a cultural group, as noted by the earlier students of personality and culture.

The Hopi personality of today may be the product as much of broad environmental determinants as of infantile sexual components or of affectional relations within the family. The Hopi has gradually adapted himself to the harsh desert environment of sand, heat, drought, and wind. His ability to grow crops in a setting that baffled the Department of Agriculture gave to the Hopi a sense of achievement that contributed to his security and interpersonal cooperation. In recent decades this pride has been threatened by the role of the United States government agencies which has reduced him to a relation of dependency with its well-meant program of economic assistance.

The Navaho personality. Leighton and Kluckhohn reported on Navaho personality in a book sponsored by the Indian Education Research Project.[35] On the basis of considerable interviewing, testing, and case study, the authors characterized the Navaho thus:

As to the chief personality traits to be found among The People, one might say first that Navahos are pre-eminently a practical folk. This has become apparent in so many connections that it seems almost axiomatic. A second striking trait is their respect for individuality, which allows each person a measure of free choice of action within the limits set by society and assigns a nearly equal place to men and women. Perhaps the third quality that should be mentioned is their activity, freedom of movement, and general air of alertness and interest in the world around them. White strangers might miss this because of the Navaho capacity for control of behavior in a strange situation, but those who know them well have a strong impression of their energy, vitality, and curiosity. Even their language emphasizes varieties of action rather than more static values. Although they maintain an outward poise and control under most circumstances, inwardly

[34] L. Thompson, *op. cit.*, p. 97.

[35] D. Leighton and C. Kluckhohn, *Children of the people* (Cambridge, Mass.: Harvard University Press, 1947).

they may be in turmoil. They are sensitive to criticism and ridicule by other people, but not prone to feel guilty over undiscovered misdeeds. Their imaginative capacities seem to find expression in adapting the inventions and methods of others to their way of living, in the artistic embellishment of themselves, their horses, and the designs of their jewelry and weaving, and in the music and poetry of their ceremonials. Although they are moody at times, they seem, on the whole, to enjoy life and have a keen sense of humor which delights in subtle puns and the frailty of human nature.[36]

While this personality pattern is interpreted in terms of child training and other aspects of the Navaho culture, the authors suggest that the Navahos may be born with temperamental potentialities which differ from those of other groups of people. Unfortunately, this possibility is difficult to prove.

The Ojibwa personality. Another psychologically oriented study of American Indians is found in Hallowell's investigations of the Ojibwa and the related Saulteaux.[37] Here was a culture which exhibited a considerable degree of anxiety. It was Hallowell's hypothesis that the mild and stoical outward personality was a façade beneath which existed hostility and ambivalence in interpersonal relations. As with other cultures, the taboo on overt aggression meant that other outlets must be found, such as gossip, sorcery, and magic. Illness and misfortune were explained by magic on the part of another individual. Dreams, folklore, and other aspects of fantasy life were caught up in suspicion and belief in the aggression of others. Another study of Wisconsin Ojibwa children, using the Thematic Apperception Test, revealed their inability to identify with any member of the group.[38] Each individual appeared to be completely self-sufficient, and disinterested in any personal ties, whether affectionate or hostile. (Even seventeenth-century observers had noted this tendency toward isolation.) One might argue that the anxiety of these people was due in part to their physical isolation. Close social ties were prevented in winter and only the fleeting contacts of the trading post occurred in summer. Even at the trading post individuals frequently appeared withdrawn and seclusive. The principal occupation of the Ojibwa male, hunting, required that he should isolate himself from social contacts, for he was expected to exert supernatural influences against other hunters and warriors. It is significant that the relative isolation and self-reliance of the Ojibwa occurred in a less harsh environment than

[36] *Ibid.*, p. 234.

[37] See A. I. Hallowell, *Culture and experience* (Philadelphia: University of Pennsylvania Press, 1955), for a collection of reports on the Ojibwa and Saulteaux.

[38] W. Caudill, Psychological characteristics of acculturated Wisconsin Ojibwa children, *Amer. Anthrop.*, LI (1949), 409-27.

that of the Eskimo, where the extreme scarcity of the food supply demanded cooperation and community solidarity in order to insure survival. Thus the physical environment as well as culture acts to condition personality.

One consequence of this social atomism was a relatively higher incidence of mental disturbances. Anthropologists have described the "windigo" psychosis among the Ojibwa and related tribes which, among other symptoms, involves attempted cannibalism, or at least a desire for human flesh.[39] Whether this was aggravated by interpersonal frustration, or a result of other pressures, is a matter of speculation. However, it appears that there is a connection between social isolation, sorcery, and strongly deviant behavior.

Acculturation among Indians has not had an entirely beneficial effect. The introduction to Western culture has deprived the Ojibwa men of their older traditional motivating values.[40] As with the Hopis, they no longer have the economic activities which once sustained them. For example, the return of the men from the Armed Services signified a dependence on such government aids as unemployment insurance. On the other hand, women secure employment more easily than ever before, which has affected the psychological welfare of both husbands and children. Interpersonal aggression is now more acute than under aboriginal conditions. The only means of effective social control are the legal and penal institutions of the dominant white group. Consequently, the earlier form of social organization, whatever the stresses and strains it may place on the individual, may produce a more integrated personality than the disorganization that follows cultural conflict and acculturation.

Other anthropological studies. Many anthropologists have studied personality patterns in "primitive" cultures. One investigator, for example, reported on Bali.[41] She was impressed by the great poise, relaxation, and happy temper of the people. Balinese society was highly stratified and the traditional code of manners strictly observed. As an escape from the measured tempo of daily living and from the rigid code, frequent festivals and ceremonials occurred, often eventuating in frenzy and trancelike states. A few years later Bateson and Mead did an ambitious study of the Balinese, including a comprehensive photographic analysis.[42] Their out-

39 See R. Landes, The abnormal among the Ojibwa Indians, *J. abnorm. soc. Psychol.*, XXXIII (1938), 14-33.

40 Hallowell, *op. cit.*, pp. 364-66.

41 J. Belo, The Balinese temper, *Character & Pers.*, IV (1935), 120-46.

42 G. Bateson and M. Mead, *The Balinese character* (New York: New York Academy of Sciences, 1942).

standing impression was of a schizoid or split-personality structure, marked by withdrawal and inattention. This they attributed chiefly to the child-rearing method of indulgence in the early years followed by teasing and rejection as the child became older. He learned a dreamy, dissociated kind of reaction as a way of meeting frustration, though some of his aggressiveness was displaced into the dances and other group ceremonials.

Another anthropologist studied a primitive New Guinea group, the Kwoma, a relatively aggressive, insecure, and superstitious people.[43] He traced these characteristics to early indulgence of the child followed by teasing, ridicule, and severe punishment by the parents. This society placed a premium on aggressiveness, some of which went into prestige-yielding activities and head-hunting.

The Negroes of St. Thomas in the Virgin Islands were also studied.[44] Insecure, suspicious, sensitive, egocentric behavior was found to be typical, particularly among the lower class. Much indirect aggression was apparent, such as argumentation, ridicule, gossip, profanity, and social discrimination. This personality pattern the investigator attributed to various aspects of the rather strict and animistic home training and a caste status lower than that of the Americans or the Danes on the island. But, in addition, notable class differences were present, which made generalizations difficult for the society as a whole.

Recent years have seen the development and elaboration of techniques to supplement the more usual field study methods of the anthropologist. One book lists several main techniques available to research workers in culture and personality: sampling, observation of behavior in its natural setting, interviewing (including passive and active interviews, life histories, and dream recording), testing, thematic and product analysis, empathy, and the mapping of physical and human relationships.[45] Although the quest for "culture-free" intelligence tests continues, researchers are convinced by now that it is impossible to measure ability and aptitude apart from and unaffected by cultural and social influences.[46] Anthropologists see more possibilities in projective tests of personality, notably Rorschach and the Thematic Apperception Test. Cora Du Bois pioneered in the 1930's by using Rorschach tests in her study of the

[43] J. W. M. Whiting, *Becoming a Kwoma* (New Haven, Conn.: Yale University Press, 1941).

[44] A. A. Campbell, St. Thomas Negroes, *Psychol. Monogr.,* LV (1943), 5.

[45] J. J. Honigmann, *Culture and personality* (New York: Harper & Bros., 1954), chap. vi.

[46] See O. Klineberg, *Social psychology* (rev. ed.; New York: Henry Holt & Co., Inc., 1954), pp. 304 ff., and A. Anastasi and J. P. Foley, *Differential psychology* (rev. ed.; New York: The Macmillan Co., 1949), chaps. xxi, xxii.

Alorese.[47] Hallowell has discussed the achievements, limitations, and potentialities of the Rorschach technique in anthropological research.[48] Sapir, Kluckhohn, and others have used biographies, autobiographies, and personal documents.[49] The camera's value, both motion picture and still, is demonstrated in Bateson and Mead's *Balinese Character*. Phonographic recordings on records, wire, or tape are beginning to be used more extensively by ethnologists. The more general question of psychological approaches valuable to the anthropologist has been discussed by Hallowell and others.[50]

Surveying studies of personality in so-called "primitive" cultures, we may say that a good beginning has been made. Investigators do not fully agree, however, on how to describe personality, what are the best techniques to disclose it, and how to discover what determines personality. The great need is for cooperative, interdisciplinary research teams and for increasing communication between the anthropologists, psychologists, sociologists, and psychiatrists interested in studying culture and personality.

PERSONALITY STRUCTURE IN MODERN SOCIETIES

The problems that arise in studying personality in rather com-pact primitive cultures become formidable when one studies a sprawling modern society like our own, or a nation in Europe or Asia. Yet, as Otto Klineberg has indicated very clearly, there is a great need for such study.[51] Knowledge about the nature of other peoples is essential in war or in peace; it provides the only lasting basis for international understanding and cooperation.

Reluctant scientists may be spurred to the difficult task by noting how our literature and conversation abound with references to the "fighting Irish," "emotional Italians," "stolid Swedes," "inscru-

47 See above, page 68.

48 A. I. Hallowell, The Rorschach test in personality and culture studies, in A. I. Hallowell, *Culture and experience* (Philadelphia: University of Pennsylvania Press, 1955), pp. 32-74.

49 See C. Kluckhohn, *The personal document in anthropological science* (Soc. sci. Res. Council Bull., 1945, No. 53); also C. Kluckhohn, Needed refinements in the biographical approach, in S. S. Sargent and M. W. Smith (eds.), *Culture and personality* (New York: Viking Fund, Inc., 1949).

50 A. I. Hallowell, Psychological leads for ethnological field workers, in D. G. Haring (ed.), *Personal character and cultural milieu* (Syracuse, N. Y.: Syracuse University Bookstore, 1948); also H. A. Murray, Research planning: a few proposals, in Sargent and Smith, *op. cit.*

51 See O. Klineberg, The UNESCO project on international tensions, *Int. soc. sci. Bull.*, 1949, Vol. I, pp. 11-21; also Psychological aspects of international relations, in A. H. Stanton and S. E. Perry (eds.), *Personality and political crisis*, (Glencoe, Ill.: Free Press, 1951), pp. 228-260, and M. L. Farber (ed.), New directions in the study of national character, *J. soc. Issues*, XI (1955).

table Orientals," "shiftless Negroes," "grasping Jews," and the like. Where such stereotyped ideas are not completely erroneous, they are much less than half-truths; worse still, such statements usually rest on the assumption that the characteristics mentioned are innate, inherited tendencies!

Stereotypes change with situations. When, in the late nineteenth century, Chinese laborers were needed in California, they were described as thrifty, sober, and law-abiding. Later when the Chinese were no longer needed they became "filthy and loathsome in their habits, unassimilable, clannish, dangerous, inferior mentally and morally." [52] In a study made in 1935, Americans described the Japanese as "intelligent" and "industrious"; in 1942, after the war had started, they had become "sly" and "treacherous"—two traits which had not been mentioned among the first dozen adjectives in the earlier study.[53]

Travelers, journalists, and essayists try to describe the "national character" of peoples. While their insights often are keen, they usually have some personal bias that colors their impressions. Their acquaintance with various classes and sections of a country may not be adequate. They may lack knowledge of social science. These factors make their contributions of doubtful value. For example, the Spanish writer and statesman Salvador de Madariaga published a book in 1928 titled *Englishmen, Frenchmen and Spaniards*. He says his essay is based on firsthand knowledge and intuition; it is not a "scientific" work based on statistics, comparative study of sources, and "facts." He speaks of observing the three peoples to note "their instinctive attitudes towards everyday life." The psychological keynote of the Englishman, de Madariaga concludes, is "fair play"; of the Frenchman, "le droit"; and of the Spaniard, "el honor." Admitting that he oversimplifies, the author presents this hypothesis:

The psychological centre of gravity of each of our three peoples is placed respectively:
for the English people, in the body-will;
for the French people, in the intellect;
for the Spanish people, in the soul;
and that the natural reaction toward life in each of these three peoples is:
for the Englishman, action;
for the Frenchman, thought;
for the Spaniard, passion.[54]

[52] See B. Schrieke, *Alien Americans* (New York: The Viking Press, Inc., 1936).
[53] M. Meenes, A comparison of racial stereotypes, *J. soc. Psychol.*, XVII (1943), 327-36.
[54] S. de Madariaga, *Englishmen, Frenchmen and Spaniards* (New York: Oxford University Press, 1928), p. 8.

In a second section, de Madariaga discusses with great skill the social and political structure, historical development, language, and literature of the three nations. But his introductory pages distress the social scientist, for he says:

> The main lines of this parallel between the English, French, and Spanish characters once established, it is possible to verify the conclusions thus reached *a priori* by direct observation of the individual and collective life of our three peoples.[55]

De Madariaga openly rejects the empirical approach and relies on impressionistic intuitive methods. Other writers are impressionistic without being as frank about it. Social scientists can only regard conclusions reached in this way as interesting hypotheses to be checked by scientific procedures.

Japanese culture and personality. Several attempts to describe Japanese national character have been made by anthropologists, historians, political scientists, and others. Ethnologists Gorer,[56] Benedict,[57] and Haring[58] and the veteran journalist Otto Tolischus[59] agreed fairly well in their interpretations. They found the Japanese code of behavior rigid, involving veneration for the Emperor, loyalty, obedience, conformity, sense of duty, and "taking one's own station." Self-discipline was important, with its strong sanction of shame and ridicule summed up in the concept "face-saving." Strong nationalistic and antiforeign attitudes have been noted due in part to the influence of the semiofficial Shinto religion.[60] Family loyalty, patriotism, and self-discipline have been consistently reported, with ambition, imperturbability, pride, honor, and initiative also mentioned by students of Japanese personality and culture.[61]

Japanese children were brought up rather indulgently, but with early stress on cleanliness, etiquette, and reverence for authority. Sex roles were differentiated early. Boys were encouraged to be proud, dominant, and aggressive. Girls were taught to be passive and affectionate. Status was greatly emphasized and enforced by fear of ridicule and mockery.

[55] *Ibid.*, p. 123.

[56] G. Gorer, Themes in Japanese culture, *Trans. N. Y. Acad. Sci.*, 1943, Sec. 2, V, 106-24.

[57] R. Benedict, *The chrysanthemum and the sword* (Boston: Houghton Mifflin Co., 1946).

[58] D. G. Haring, Aspects of personal character in Japan, *Far Eastern Quarterly*, VI (1946), 12-22.

[59] O. Tolischus, *Tokyo record* (New York: Reynal & Hitchcock, 1943).

[60] A. Menefee, in G. Murphy (ed.), *Human nature and enduring peace* (Boston: Houghton Mifflin Co., 1945), pp. 114-18.

[61] P. Hopkins, in Murphy, *op. cit.*, pp. 124-30.

Benedict has interpreted the acquiescent behavior of the Japanese since their defeat in 1945—a puzzling phenomenon to Occidentals. This attitude resulted only partially, she found, from obedience to the Emperor. More basically it sprang from the Japanese "ethic of alternatives." They tried war, and they lost. "That course, now, they can discard, because their whole training has conditioned them to possible changes of direction. Nations with a more absolutist ethic must convince themselves that they are fighting for principles. When they surrender to the victors, they say 'Right was lost when we were defeated,' and their self-respect demands that they work to make this 'right' win next time. Or they can beat their breasts and confess their guilt. The Japanese need do neither." [62] The Japanese were willing to accept as natural the consequences of defeat (such as demilitarization and indemnities), but they could not accept ridicule or humiliation. If the latter were avoided, concluded Benedict, the period of occupation would be relatively simple and successful.

A very different approach to the study of Japanese culture (and to other cultures as well) has been undertaken by UNESCO.[63] A research team with opinion questionnaires and related instruments, administered largely in 1951-52, obtained results rather different from those reported by Gorer and Benedict. (Actually, it is difficult to know whether the differences found are due to improved methodology or to postwar changes in the Japanese people.) It was found that youth generally, and educated adults under fifty, were more flexible than had appeared in the previous studies. Relative equality between the sexes was becoming evident in some of the urban sample. Choice of a spouse was no longer exclusively under the jurisdiction of the parents. While loyalty to Japan was expressed by practically all respondents, regardless of age, 58 per cent desired to "know all that goes on abroad." For respondents under twenty-five years of age the percentage was 73. Traditional morality, or *giri*, received less emphasis and was largely omitted from the school curriculum. There was growing disinterest in Shintoism, the divinity of the state, and its ruler. Pacifistic tendencies were demonstrated in a number of ways: for example, when asked what was the worst thing that could happen to them, 55 per cent of the men and 39 per cent of the women answered "war." There was an expression of passivity, inferiority, insecurity, and

[62] R. Benedict, *op. cit.*, p. 304.

[63] Jean Stoetzel, *Without the chrysanthemum and the sword* (New York: Columbia University Press, 1955). See also A. S. Quigley and J. E. Turner, *The new Japan* (Minneapolis: University of Minnesota Press, 1956).

escapism on the part of a sufficient number to indicate that the rigidity revealed in earlier studies would not apply today. Both Japanese culture and personality seem to be undergoing considerable change.

German character structure. German national character is difficult to study, partly because modern Germany is varied and complex, and partly because several major social and political changes have occurred since 1870. Between the two World Wars, German character structure seemed somewhere between that of Japan and that of the United States. Psychologists,[64] a psychiatrist,[65] a political scientist,[66] and others agree upon several items: strong obedience and respect for authority, intense nationalistic attitudes and willingness to sacrifice for the fatherland, deep-seated feelings of inferiority and insecurity (from defeat in 1918, from inflation and depression), and a compensatory drive for power and prestige which Brickner likened to paranoid megalomania.

In Germany before World War II the father administered strict discipline, and boys tended to identify themselves with him. Later they transferred their identification to those in positions of wider authority. Group and national solidarity was encouraged in youngsters, along with a lack of sympathy, if not actual hostility, toward outsiders. Romantic, sentimental tendencies also could be noted. The educational system contained little training in individual responsibility or democratic living. Nationalistic and authoritarian trends in German character were intensified by the Nazis; anti-intellectual, anti-Semitic, and anti-Christian emphases were added, along with glorification of racial superiority.[67]

An American psychiatrist who in 1946 worked with the American Military Government in Germany, found the German character structure rooted in the authoritarian family pattern.[68] The German child was trained to respect and fear authority, and he learned the value of duty, discipline, orderliness, cleanliness, and manliness. Hitler's Nazi party provided "a model of a state based upon the same principles as the authoritarian family" [69] and appealed to the basic values inculcated in the family. That typically German tendencies existed is shown by McGranahan's careful com-

64 E. Fromm, *Escape from freedom* (New York: Rinehart & Co., Inc., 1941); C. J. Leuba, in G. Murphy (ed.), *Human nature and enduring peace* (Boston: Houghton Mifflin Co., 1945), pp. 82-92.

65 R. M. Brickner, *Is Germany incurable?* (Philadelphia: J. B. Lippincott Co., 1943).

66 F. Schuman, *The Nazi dictatorship* (New York: Alfred A. Knopf, Inc., 1936).

67 See Leuba, *op. cit.*, p. 91.

68 B. Schaffner, *Fatherland* (New York: Columbia University Press, 1948).

69 *Ibid.*, p. 73.

parison of social and ethical attitudes of German and American youth.[70] Obedience, honor, and loyalty to the state were valued much more highly by the former, who also showed stronger belief in national superiority and greater contempt for the "average person" than did the Americans.

Some studies of Germans have suggested little change in personality structure as a result of their defeat in World War II. An anthropologist reported the same reverence for authority and willingness to follow a Führer as before. Instead of guilt feelings over Nazi extermination of millions of Jews and Slavs in gas chambers, Germans showed predominantly a reaction of self-pity.[71] Surveys made in 1947 and 1948 discovered intense nationalism and anti-Semitism.[72] The 1947 poll, using German interviewers, disclosed that 80 per cent of a cross-section of Germans in the U. S. zone were either ardent or potential anti-Semites. One study showed the same trend still operating several years later: prevalence of fascist-type attitudes was higher in the German sample than in any other national group studied.[73]

But the over-all picture of a nation's attitudes is not simple. In 1948-49, when Germany was still subject to acute deprivation, a UNESCO survey was directed toward attitudes regarding international relations.[74] One of the findings was that 84 per cent (higher than any other country surveyed) of the individuals interviewed thought that human nature can be changed. In the same vein, 58 per cent thought that peace was possible and favored a world government. On the other hand, 59 per cent replied that their national characteristics (which had been revealed to be favorable) were inborn, possibly a hangover of the Nazi ideology. Yet their evaluations of other national groups (such as Americans, French, and Russians) were not very different from the reactions to foreigners given by respondents in other nations.

Moreover, some evidence indicates that the German family is no longer the patriarchal structure that was pictured by prewar and wartime analyses. Baumert, for example, found in his survey of the middle-sized city of Darmstadt that the majority of responses

[70] D. V. McGranahan, Comparison of social attitudes among American and German youth, *J. abnorm. soc. Psychol.*, XLI (1946), 245-57.

[71] D. Rodnick, *Postwar Germans* (New Haven, Conn.: Yale University Press, 1948).

[72] By Opinion Surveys Hdqrs. of the U. S. Military Government, as reported in *PM*, New York, February 1, 1948, and by the International Committee for the Study of European Questions, as reported in *The New York Times*, June 11, 1948.

[73] T. S. Cohn and H. Carsch, Administration of the F scale to a sample of Germans, *J. abnorm. soc. Psychol.*, XLIX (1954), 471.

[74] W. Buchanan and H. Cantril, *How nations see each other* (Urbana, Ill.: University of Illinois Press, 1953), pp. 73-75.

pointed to maternal dominance in the home.[75] One of the authors of this text recently conducted informal interviews with some dozens of Germans and finds it difficult to arrive at any consistent generalization about *the* German modal personality. Both patriarchal and matriarchal families can be found; autocratically and democratically oriented schools; internationalists and nationalists.

The "German problem" is a complex one indeed. How much of the confused pattern of German attitudes has arisen from cultural rigidity and aggressiveness, and how much has been a reflection of the frustration and bitterness deriving from the war and from defeat and partition of their country is not clear. As Lowie indicates in a recent book, the tendency in German personality toward flexibility, democratic processes, and humanitarianism has been intermittently expressed from the time of Kant to the present and espoused by a constantly growing minority.[76] We have no reason to assume that neo-Nazism is a dominant viewpoint in Germany today; it is only too easy for observers to perceive events in the light of their hopes and fears, which applies equally to those who see hopeful and those who see discouraging trends.

Russian character structure. Several recent studies have been done, not only of the Soviet Union, its economy and social system, but also of the Russian individual's personality structure. Many of these are impressionistic, partly because investigators have not been admitted to the Soviet Union. For example, Dicks attributes variable moods to the Russian, including passivity and individual helplessness in the face of harsh authority figures, which are remote though omnipresent.[77] Interpersonal relations range from acts of kindness to cruelty. The personality structure is basically oral (as opposed to anal), implying intense needs for affectional protection and security.[78] There is an emphasis on physical pleasure, although there can be a strong interest in the mystical. The Russian personality system developed in agrarian and village life on the margin of Europe, and distant from more urban controls that characterized Western European life. For the average Russian there was a minimum of Western traits, such as orderliness, neatness, punctuality, protocol, sanitation, and privacy. It is Dicks' thesis that following the Russian Revolution it was necessary to introduce typically

---

75 G. Baumert, *Schule und Jugend in einer ausgebombten Stadt* (Darmstadt: Roether Verlag, 1952), p. 79.

76 R. H. Lowie, *Toward understanding Germany* (Chicago: University of Chicago Press, 1954).

77 H. V. Dicks, Observations on contemporary Russian behavior, *Human Relations,* V (1952), 111-75.

78 Psychoanalytic terms will be explained in Chapters 6 and 9.

Western notions into the personality system; for example, regularity in living habits and submission to bureaucratic authority—in other words, the "anal" components. Those citizens who could make this transition most readily became the preferred or ideal personality.

Most interpretive and philosophical of the Russian studies is that of Gorer and Rickman.[79] They make a great deal of the theory of infant swaddling, which places restraint on the infant's gross muscular movement, thus explaining the individual's acceptance of later restraints. This swaddling makes the child impervious to physical aspects and channels his concentration on the emotions, say the authors. Consequently there is indifference to physical pain, either one's own or another's. On the other hand, the Russian vocabulary regarding emotions, if not actually richer than ours, at least suggests different kinds of emotional experience. Except for this swaddling, the life of the child is not particularly constrained; sexual taboos are relatively few.

Margaret Mead's study remains closer to what might be called empirical facts, though it is also interpretive.[80] She maintains that there are three orientations to the Russian character; one, the traditional Russian personality, as delineated in history and literature, and as already analyzed psychologically; two, the Bolshevik idealized character, as presented by doctrinaire writers of the early Soviet period, and accounts of certain of the leaders; and three, a present generation, based on the above two and produced by Soviet institutions. She notes the interchangeability of love and hate, of good and evil; consequently, a lack of trust between individuals. Like other observers, she sees a vague, pervasive sense of guilt, which is considered to be roughly equal for all people and hence not a necessary source of anxiety. She also finds scant individual attention to planning, to self-control, or to the steps necessary to carry out action. Individuals are not held directly responsible for their actions in the sense that Anglo-Saxon culture defines rational responsibility.

The fair agreement between investigators on at least some findings suggests there may be a modal personality for national groups such as Japan and Germany at a given historical period. In the case of Russia, information is scanty because of the impossibility of doing field studies in the Soviet Union. More data will have to

79 G. Gorer and J. Rickman, *The people of Great Russia, a psychological study* (London: Cresset Press, Ltd., 1949).

80 M. Mead, *Soviet attitudes toward authority* (New York: McGraw-Hill Book Co., Inc., 1951).

be gathered on current child-rearing practices and the family environment generally, and on the influence of various institutions, including the Communist bureaucracy. Also, we should know considerably more about individual and subcultural variations at all age levels. The Russian Research Center at Harvard University has been investigating some of these questions with a sample of Russian refugees and expellees.[81] Naturally, there are questions about the validity of such a sample, but on the whole this type of investigation seems safer than nonempirical and nonquantitative studies like that of Gorer and Rickman.

American national character. It is probably easier to describe the outstanding personality patterns in an authoritarian state such as Japan or Germany than in a democracy like England or the United States. Democracies permit divergent trends in social behavior, education, and family life. In addition, the vastness of the United States, with its striking sectional differences and some relatively unassimilated immigrant groups, makes analysis doubly difficult. Only a few social scientists have tried to delineate British or American personality structure.

One of these, Margaret Mead, in *And Keep Your Powder Dry,* written in 1942, found that probably our essential themes are the drive for success and for conformity through economic achievement. She sums up her analysis as follows:

We have a certain kind of character, the American character, which has developed in the New World and taken a shape all its own; a character which is geared to success and to movement, invigorated by obstacles and difficulties, but plunged into guilt and despair by catastrophic failure or a wholesale alteration in the upward and onward pace; a character in which aggressiveness is uncertain and undefined, to which readiness to fight anyone who starts a fight and unreadiness to engage in violence have both been held up as virtues; a character which measures its successes and failures only against near contemporaries and engages in various quantitative devices for reducing every contemporary to its own stature; a character which sees success as the reward of virtue and failure as the stigma for not being good enough; a character which is uninterested in the past, except when ancestry can be used to make points against other people in the success game; a character oriented towards an unknown future, ambivalent towards other cultures, which are regarded with a sense of inferiority as more coherent than our own and with a sense of superiority because newcomers in America display the strongest mark of other cultural membership in the form of foreignness. . . .[82]

[81] See R. A. Bauer, A. Inkeles, and C. Kluckhohn, *How the Soviet system works* (Cambridge, Mass.: Harvard University Press, 1956); this is one of the studies published by the Center.

[82] M. Mead, *And keep your powder dry* (New York: William Morrow & Co., Inc., 1942), pp. 193-94. Copyright 1942 by Margaret Mead.

In 1948, an English anthropologist, Geoffrey Gorer, followed up Mead's study with a book called *The American People*.[83] He specified several major themes in American character: for example, rejection of authority, mother and female dominance, the child's fear of being considered "sissy," and the tendency for children, rather than one or both parents, to take the center of the stage. The American child, says Gorer, becomes insatiable for signs of love and attention, which is reflected in our interest in winning friends and influencing people, and in our treating personality as a commodity to be exploited, like other raw materials. The individual takes pleasure in machines and enjoys competing for *things*, his goal being to approximate his neighbor's standards—and be a little better. "Americanism" is believed in and affirmed loudly; we favor other nations according to the degree to which they approximate our form of government.

A notable summary of some of the characterizations of the American personality structure was made by sociologist Robin Williams, who defines what he calls the "major value-orientations in America" as follows: [84]

1. *Personal achievement* as demonstrated by the "success story," expansionism, mastery, and an ever higher standard of living.
2. *Activity and work*—the belief, largely inherited from our Puritan past, that idleness is evil.
3. *Moral orientation*—the tendency to view action in terms of ethical judgments in contrast to, say, the Russian's sense of irresponsibility of human behavior. Often our moralizations become split between theory and necessity, resulting in hypocrisy and empty "lip-service."
4. *Humanitarianism*—that complex of values, such as charity and helping the "underdog." One could recite evidence to the contrary (wars, lynching, treatment of the American Indian); yet there is a national norm of generosity—a trait that has brought us status abroad.
5. *Efficiency and practicality*—reverence for the technical, for quantity and standardization.
6. *Progress*—the concept of change and forward movement.
7. *Material comfort*—this contradicts to some degree "activity and work"—more specifically, today's emphasis is shifting from production to consumption. Content analysis reveals that mass media and popular literature increasingly stress themes of gratification, luxury, and leisure activities.

83 G. Gorer, *The American people* (New York: W. W. Norton & Co., Inc., 1948).
84 R. M. Williams, *American society, a sociological interpretation* (New York: Alfred A. Knopf, Inc., 1951), pp. 388-442.

8. *Equality*—a value that developed out of the political and social thought of the eighteenth century, together with the kind of migration and frontier situation that has characterized most of our history.
9. *Freedom,* often difficult to reconcile with equality, refers to the individual's independence from outside constraint.
10. *External conformity*—the sensitivity to group pressure on the part of the individual American. Although absent in no culture, this value seems more natural in American than in, say, British or French culture.

Other value-orientations that Williams mentions are *science, patriotism, democracy, individual personality,* and *racism* or *"group-superiority themes."* These concepts, although not altogether consistent, express the complexity of American personality. We are directed toward active mastery rather than passive acceptance; we show a restlessness and unwillingness to accept the status quo as unalterable. The American tends to be oriented toward the "external world" rather than the "contemplative." He tends to view other individuals in a "horizontal" fashion (peer-relations) rather than "vertical" (superordinate-subordinate); he is more comfortable with equality than with hierarchy.[85]

Riesman, in *The Lonely Crowd,* analyzes character structure in modern societies, particularly the American.[86] He finds three major types; first, *tradition direction,* which characterizes primitive societies with their rigid adherence to custom; only a few tradition-directed islands survive in the U. S. The second type is *inner direction,* which comes about through the implanting by parents and teachers of goals and ideals which guarantee social conformity through a kind of internalized gyroscope. Most Americans, says Riesman, are inner directed, even the working class. More recently, especially in urban United States, the third mode or *other direction* has developed—a depending upon others for approval and guidance. Where the inner-directed man depends largely on rational and authoritative ideals, the other-directed focuses on his peers and associates to insure his success. Instead of a gyroscope, the other directed man has something like a sensitive radar set to keep him in touch with his world. This type of character, says Riesman, "seems to be emerging in very recent years in the upper middle class of our larger cities: more prominent in New York than in Boston, in Los Angeles than Spokane, in Cincinnati

85 *Ibid.,* pp. 441-42.
86 D. Riesman, *The lonely crowd* (New Haven: Yale University Press, 1950).

than in Chillicothe." [87] Inner-direction was typical of the older middle class—the banker, tradesman, small entrepreneur, technically oriented engineer—while other-direction typified the newer middle class—the bureaucrat and salaried business employee. Riesman goes on to make an interesting comparison among his three types; for example, the sanction for the tradition-directed person is *shame;* for the inner-directed it is *guilt;* and for the other-directed (though shame and guilt controls are present), a prime lever is a diffuse *anxiety.*[88]

The studies of these four national cultures—Japanese, German, Russian, and American—are only a few of those which have appeared in this general area, though they are certainly some of the outstanding ones. Many other national groups have been evaluated. For example, recent interpretations of Chinese and British character structure have appeared.[89] The first of these is a comparison of the American and Chinese ways of life by an anthropologist who knows both well, through observation and reading. The other study, by an anthropologist-psychologist, utilized mass observation and questionnaires covering many phases of British interests, attitudes, and behavior.

PROBLEM AREAS IN CULTURE AND PERSONALITY STUDIES

We have described several outstanding investigations of personality in both primitive and modern cultures. These researches have shown that personality or character structure is, in considerable measure, a function of the culture in which a person lives. In conceptualization and in methodology they have improved on the older approaches.

What remains to be done? What further improvements can be made? Let us suggest a few relating to method, technique, and interpretation.

In future research, facts must be collected still more carefully. If one studies a whole culture, primitive or modern, the data used should be *generally* true of that culture. If variations occur (as they usually do) in section, class, caste, and the like, they should be specified.

Klineberg asks some pertinent questions:

When an anthropologist tells us about a culture pattern and its relation to individual behavior, we also would like to know . . . does *everybody* do this? Is this the sort of thing people *should* do or what they *actually* do? Do *you* do this?

[87] *Ibid.,* p. 19.
[88] *Ibid.,* pp. 25-26.
[89] F. L. K. Hsu, *Americans and Chinese* (New York: Henry Schuman, Inc., 1953); G. Gorer, *Exploring English character* (New York: Criterion Books, Inc., 1955).

Do you *always* do this? Do you *usually* do it? What would happen if you didn't do it? In other words, if the anthropologist asked the informant a whole series of questions, perhaps the answers would enable more psychologically oriented persons to find value in the material and gain insight into how it touches the individual.[90]

Klineberg also, following others, insists that we need more detailed information about the informants—their age, sex, and class as well as data on their agreements and differences. If we have similar groups of informants for each culture, and if we request of them the same kind of information, cross-cultural comparisons will be the more meaningful.[91]

More attention should be directed to research procedures. What hypotheses did the investigator have at the start? Did he guard against being unduly influenced by these hypotheses as he collected his data? Did he rely chiefly on impressions and intuitions or on directed observations? To what did he direct his observations—institutional behavior, interpersonal relations, official statements, biographies, myths, dreams, humor, press, radio, comics? Were tests or other relatively objective techniques used? If so, what evidence shows they were valid for the culture studied?

In interpreting, we must think carefully about the meaning of "culture" and "personality," and about their relationship. Recently some social scientists have tended to merge the two concepts. Spiro, for example, says that personality and culture should not be viewed as contradictory or conflicting processes but rather as a unified process developed by individuals for the purpose of biological adaptation, social adjustment, and personal integration. "The dichotomy that is held to obtain between them," he suggests, "is a function of our own highly disorganized cultural heritage." [92]

In the view of the authors, it is more productive to maintain some distinction in the meaning of culture and of personality. Thus culture should refer to the ways of behaving, thinking, and feeling shared by all or almost all of the members of a given society and should be contrasted with behavior arising either from physiological sources or from "subcultural" influences. The latter Kimball Young calls "personal-social" conditioning, meaning effects of social contacts other than those determined by the broad culture

---

[90] O. Klineberg, Recent studies of national character, in Sargent and Smith, *op. cit.,* pp. 135-36.

[91] Cf. G. P. Murdock, The cross-cultural survey, *Amer. sociol. Rev.,* V (1940), 361-70.

[92] M. E. Spiro, Culture and personality: the natural history of a false dichotomy. *Psychiatry,* XIV (1951), 19-46.

pattern.[93] "Culture" loses its essential meaning if we make it synonymous with total behavior or with all environmental influences.

Equally important is the clarifying of "personality." A distinction between social behavior and personality is necessary, as already mentioned earlier. If anthropologists study a people, and report on their institutions, customs, social groupings, child care, and sanctioned behavior in general, they are not *ipso facto* describing personality, as has been pointed out.[94] Linton makes much the same point when he excludes from the concept of personality overt behavior, physical structure, and physiological processes.[95]

Personality is a unique pattern which is never the same for any two individuals. Yet we can analyze personality in various ways which permit us to understand how it is affected by culture and other determinants. Kluckhohn and Mowrer, for example, suggest that personality includes a "universal" component (physiological influences and behavior accepted in all societies), a "communal" component (like basic personality structure—that which is uniform or common in a culture), a "role" component (depending on age, sex, and other subcultural factors), and an "idiosyncratic" component (peculiar only to the individual).[96] Similarly, Linton believes there is a basic personality type common to the members of a society, upon which are superimposed "status personalities," which become integrated with the basic personality type. The two together make up the nucleus of personality, which Linton thinks of as a configuration developed out of an individual's experience, though affected by various innate qualities.[97]

These approaches analyze personality according to determinants. Another possibility is to analyze it according to identifiable characteristics—e.g., temperament, traits, attitudes, etc., as mentioned in the last chapter. Psychologists, social scientists, and others commonly emphasize a particular aspect of personality. Thus psychologists usually deal with personality in terms of traits.[98] So-

---

[93] K. Young, *Personality and problems of adjustment* (2d ed.; New York: Appleton-Century-Crofts, Inc., 1952), pp. 124-25. We shall return to this topic in Chapters 4 and 5.

[94] M. Ginsburg, National character, *Brit. J. Psychol.*, XXXII (1942), 183-205.

[95] R. Linton, *Cultural background of personality* (New York: Appleton-Century-Crofts, Inc., 1945), p. 84.

[96] C. Kluckhohn and O. H. Mowrer, Culture and personality—a conceptual scheme, *Amer. Anthrop.*, XLVI (1944), 1-29.

[97] R. Linton, *op. cit.*, pp. 129 ff.

[98] See R. B. Cattell, *Personality* (New York: McGraw-Hill Book Co., Inc., 1950) for an elaborate trait analysis of personality.

ciologists and anthropologists, interested in the effects of social influences, stress values, attitudes, and habits.[99]

One's unstated emphases often make agreement difficult. The social scientist, studying "basic personality structure" or "national character," seeks commonalities or likenesses of personality. The psychologist, interested in individual differences, tries to understand the uniqueness of each personality. It is to be hoped that agreement can be reached upon a concept of personality which is meaningful yet flexible enough to be useful to the many specialists concerned with it.

Social psychologists are curious about the ways by which "culture" becomes transformed into "personality." (In Chapter 7 we shall deal with social learning at some length.) Unfortunately, anthropological field workers have not been able to follow the day-by-day training of a number of children over a period of several years, in order to study the whole process of socialization.[100] Valuable hypotheses, however, have been advanced. Following the lead of both anthropologists and psychiatrists, Kimball Young has classified the basic categories of child training and control which must be examined in each culture—primitive or modern—if we are to understand how an individual becomes a "participating member of his group," i.e., a socialized personality.[101] These include:

1. Regulation and degree of rigidity in training (nursing, weaning, elimination, walking)
2. Handling of frustration, aggression, and fear
3. Love, sympathy, indulgence, cooperation
4. Sanctions and moral controls
5. Education, knowledge, skills
6. Self-development (growth of ego, goals, security, rights, duties)
7. Maladjustments, problems, deviance

Focusing upon these fairly specific areas of child training facilitates intercultural comparisons, as Young shows by presenting data from eight primitive societies.

[99] This viewpoint is expressed by a number of authors, e.g., K. Young, *Social psychology* (3d ed.; New York: Appleton-Century-Crofts, Inc., 1956), chap. iv; and A. W. Green, *Sociology* (rev. ed.; New York: McGraw-Hill Book Co., Inc., 1956), chaps. viii and ix. In this connection, however, Maslow has suggested that it is the mark of intelligent and creative people to resist acculturation and maintain "a certain inner detachment from the culture in which they were immersed." This would not only make them more autonomous but also more like members-at-large of the human species. See Maslow, A. H., Resistance to acculturation, *J. soc. Issues,* VII:4 (1951), 26-29.

[100] The California Growth Study, conducted by J. W. MacFarlane and others, is attempting to do this for American children.

[101] K. Young, *Social Psychology* (2d ed.; Appleton-Century-Crofts, Inc., 1944), chap. iii.

One of the most critical studies of child-training practices has been performed by Whiting and Child.[102] They examine in detail a number of cultures on nursing, toilet training, and particularly affectional relations. They maintain that there has been a great deal of confusion surrounding the setting up of hypotheses as to whether certain personality traits are due to culturally imposed behavioral forms. These hypotheses should find a coherence between the antecedent (child rearing practice, for example) and the consequent (adult personality trait). Three principles are relevant in determining this coherence:

1. A suitable sample of cases are studied, rather than a single case, and statistical techniques may be applied to determine whether the apparent connection between antecedent and consequent is a true or dependable connection, rather than their association being due to accidental concomitance in one or a few individual cases.
2. Since the occurrence or non-occurrence of the supposed antecedent is produced by the arbitrary action of the experimenter, rather than by previous characteristics of the cases studied, it is possible to insure that the connection between antecedent and consequent is genuinely that of antecedent and consequent.
3. Evidence for the connection between antecedent and consequent is obtained by objective procedures which can be described and repeated by other investigators with the same outcome, rather than being dependent upon an intuitive judgment of relevance and coherence with which other investigators may legitimately disagree.[103]

Such categories or "frames of reference" are necessary when cultural studies are attempted. Child-rearing practices, gestures, language, and other forms of social behavior are frequently compared, with no necessary equivalence from one culture to another. This is illustrated by Gorer's discussion of swaddling as having certain effects on the child in Russian culture, when he is not certain of its consequences in our Western European society or, say, among the Hopis. The whole question of relating infant care patterns to adult personality expression has been raised by Orlansky.[104] For one thing, he questions whether infant treatment and training are as important as the regime of childhood and adolescence. In fact, it is on this point that the psychoanalytically oriented anthropologists differ from the neo-Freudian school.[105] The latter believe that

102 J. W. Whiting and I. L. Child, *Child training and personality: a cross-cultural study* (New Haven: Yale University Press, 1953).
103 Whiting and Child, *op. cit.*, pp. 19-20.
104 H. Orlansky, Infant care and personality, *Psychol. Bull.*, XLVI (1949), pp. 1-48.
105 See the discussion of Kardiner, Fromm, and Horney earlier in this chapter.

post-infancy experiences can be more critical than the events of the first three or four years in shaping personality.

Another problem is the search for motives, which will be dealt with in another chapter. Many of the writers in culture and personality tend to ascribe motives on the basis of flimsy evidence. In an extremely critical article, two sociologists allude to this weakness in the cultural school by saying: "The search for the 'real' motives, the 'deep inner core,' the 'authentic individual,' conceived as something separate from behavior leads to circularity of proof and immunity to negative evidence." [106]

SUMMARY

Anthropological evidence shows that culture affects personality most significantly. Broad differences are found between the personalities found in various primitive cultures, between those in primitive and modern cultures, and, less clearly perhaps, between those in modern cultures. Culture produces a modal personality—a core or nucleus shared by the members of a society—which has been called "basic personality structure," "social character," or "national character."

Ethnologists differ somewhat among themselves as to research methods and interpretations of data. Recent years have seen greater interest in the use of personal documents, projective techniques, and motion picture and sound recordings. Greater use is now made of psychiatric interpretations than formerly. Stimulated by social psychologists, sociologists, and psychiatrists, anthropologists continually explore the meaning of culture and of personality and of the relationship between them.

Anthropologists seek to study a culture pattern as a whole and to discover the uniformities it produces in the personalities of those living within it. Other investigators, notably sociologists and social psychologists, focus upon "subcultural" factors—i.e., variations within the broad culture pattern—and the differential effects they have upon personality. We turn to these studies in the next two chapters.

SUPPLEMENTARY READINGS

Books of Readings

Maccoby, E. E., Newcomb, T. M., and Hartley, E. L. (eds.). *Readings in social psychology*, 3d ed. New York: Henry Holt & Co., Inc., 1958.
Mead, M. Adolescence in primitive and modern society.
Whiting, J. W. M., Kluckhohn, F. R., and Anthony, A. The function of male initiation ceremonies at puberty.

[106] A. R. Lindesmith and A. L. Strauss, A critique of culture-personality writings, *Amer. sociol. Rev.*, XV (1950), 587-600.

BRITT, S. H. (ed.). *Selected readings in social psychology*. New York: Rinehart & Co., Inc., 1950.

LaBarre, W. The cultural basis of emotions and gestures.

Maslow, A. H. Personality and patterns of culture.

McGranahan, D. V. A comparison of social attitudes among American and German youth.

LINDZEY, G. (ed.). *Handbook of social psychology*, Vol. II. Reading, Mass.: Addison-Wesley Pub. Co., Inc., 1954.

Inkeles, A., and Levinson, D. National character: the study of modal personality and sociocultural systems.

Kluckhohn, C. Culture and behavior.

Other References

BATESON, G. Cultural determinants of personality, chap. xxiii in J. McV. Hunt (ed.), *Personality and the behavior disorders*. New York: The Ronald Press Co., 1944.

GERTH, H., AND MILLS, C. W. *Character and social structure*. New York: Harcourt, Brace & Co., Inc., 1953.

The role of the individual in Western culture written by two history-oriented sociologists.

GRAHAM, S. *American culture: an analysis of its development and present characteristics*. New York: Harper & Bros., 1957.

A very readable text on some of the leading value-orientations of our culture.

HALLOWELL, A. I. *Culture and experience*. Philadelphia: University of Pennsylvania Press, 1955.

A study of the more intricate problems of the effects of culture on a given society, the Ojibwa.

HARING, D. G. (ed.). *Personal character and cultural milieu*. Ann Arbor, Mich.: J. W. Edwards, 1948.

Selected research studies.

HONIGMANN, J. J. *Culture and personality*. New York: Harper & Bros., 1954.

Possibly the best interpretation of culture and personality and widely used as a text.

HSU, F. L. K. *Aspects of culture and personality*. New York: Abelard-Schuman, Ltd., 1954.

General interdisciplinary discussions of the subject are included.

KLUCKHOHN, C., MURRAY, H. A., AND SCHNEIDER, D. M. (eds.). *Personality in nature, society and culture*, rev. ed. New York: Alfred A. Knopf, Inc., 1953.

A much used compilation of readings on the subject.

LINTON, R. *The cultural background of personality*. New York: Appleton-Century-Crofts, Inc., 1945.

General discussions of culture and personality by an anthropologist.

SARGENT, S. S., AND SMITH, M. W. (eds.). *Culture and personality*. New York: Viking Fund, Inc., 1949.

The proceedings of an interdisciplinary conference are presented.

SHAW, F. J. *Personal adjustment in the American culture*. New York: Harper & Bros., 1953.

An excellent work on the adaptation of the personality to the culture system.

WILLIAMS, R. M. *American society, a sociological interpretation*. New York: Alfred A. Knopf, Inc., 1951.

An outstanding work on the American culture.

WOLFENSTEIN, M., AND LEITES, N. *Movies—a psychological study*. Glencoe, Ill.: Free Press, 1950.

Analysis of themes common to American movies; a technique for studying culture and personality.

4

Subculture: Family, School, and Peer Group

Anthropologists have shown that the culture in which one lives tends to produce a core of personality structure common to the members of the group. This is a real contribution to the story of human socialization, the process by which an individual becomes a functioning member of his society. But the social psychologist, working at a somewhat different level from the anthropologist, needs to interpret both the *uniformities* and the *differences* in social behavior among the persons of a given culture.

In this chapter we investigate various influences within the immediate environment of the child which have much to do with determining his later reactions to other individuals. These so-called "subcultural" factors include the home, the school, and the childhood and adolescent play associations which are known as "peer groups." In every society these agencies or institutions operate, formally or informally, to condition the younger members of the community to behave in accordance with certain norms.

ATYPICAL ENVIRONMENTS

Isolate cases. A good starting point is to ask, What happens when a really unusual social environment occurs such as, say, a non-human one? There are many tales and occasional wisps of evidence about "feral children"—i.e., wild or untamed children reared by wild animals like wolves or bears. Unfortunately for science, only 30 or 40 such cases have come to light, and of these only two, the

"Wild Boy of Aveyron" and the "Wolf Children" of India, have been reported in any detail.[1] The retarded and "unhuman" characteristics of these children have been attributed by some to the denial of early human experience. Others insist the data are too scanty to rule out the possibility of mental or organic defect.[2]

Somewhat more evidence exists in cases of isolated children, of which the best-known is Caspar Hauser.[3] This child, for reasons political or otherwise, was kept in a small cell until he was sixteen and never allowed to see his attendant. When set free, according to his biographer, he could walk only with great difficulty, could understand no human speech, and was socially helpless. Under friendly guidance he learned rapidly and later wrote the story of his experiences.

Kingsley Davis, a sociologist, has reported on two cases of isolated children, both born in 1932.[4] Anna, kept alone several years in an upper room of a farmhouse, appeared to be mentally defective. After two years of training she showed only meager comprehension, which led the examining psychologist to diagnose her condition as "congenital mental deficiency."[5] The other girl, Isabelle, was isolated with her deaf-mute mother in a dark room for six and a half years. When discovered, she too seemed unhuman and mentally defective. However, intensive training produced amazing results; in two years she could talk well and her I.Q. had tripled. At age fourteen she had completed the sixth grade and behaved like a normal child. Thus, in a child of normal endowment isolation produced a condition resembling mental deficiency, and later socialization restored her to normality.

In a few rare cases, then, it seems that a potentially normal child was rendered unhuman by a socially abnormal environment. This is hardly surprising, since parents everywhere spend years training their children in language and other habits, and in the forms of emotional and social behavior approved by their culture. Effects

[1] The best general reference on feral and isolated children is J. A. L. Singh and R. M. Zingg, *Wolf child and feral man* (New York: Harper & Bros., 1942). It contains reports on all known cases.

[2] See, for example, W. Dennis, The significance of feral man, *Amer. J. Psychol.*, LIV (1941), 425-32; D. G. Mandelbaum, Wolf-child histories from India, *J. soc. Psychol.*, XVII (1943), 25-44.

[3] In A. Feuerbach, *Casper Hauser*, trans. F. Lieber (1833); reprinted in Singh and Zingg, *op. cit.*, pp. 277-365.

[4] K. Davis, Extreme social isolation of a child, *Amer. J. Sociol.*, XLV (1940), 554-65; Final note on a case of extreme isolation, *Amer. J. Sociol.*, LII (1947), 432-37. See also the clinical report on these cases by F. N. Maxfield in Singh and Zingg, *op. cit.*, pp. 249-50.

[5] Davis noted that Anna's poor recovery was partly due to inadequate education.

of the absence of such training are strikingly illustrated in the rare and unusual cases such as those described above.

Animals in human environments. Humanitarian considerations prevent overenthusiastic scientists from entrusting human infants to the care of animals in order to collect more accurate data on feral children. However, the reverse is possible; animals can be brought up in a human environment.

W. N. and L. A. Kellogg, both psychologists, reared a young female ape, named Gua, with their infant son, Donald, for nearly a year. Gua was seven and a half months old and Donald ten months old when the experiment began. The Kelloggs were very careful to treat the two just alike, so that they could tell how far the animal could be humanized by its unusual environment. The procedures and results of this novel experiment are related in the Kelloggs' book; [6] we can give here only a few high points from the findings.

First, the ape was limited in what it could learn by its different physiological and neurological structure, as anyone would expect. Within these limits, however, considerable social learning appeared. The ape did not learn to talk, but its passive language achievement was remarkable. By the time Gua was sixteen months old, as the experiment terminated, it had learned to respond correctly to no less than fifty-eight verbal phrases, such as, "Don't do that," "Give it to me," "Show me your nose," and "Close the drawer." The slightly older Donald understood sixty-eight similar commands. Gua learned to walk upright, to skip, to open and close doors and drawers, to switch lights on and off, to eat with a spoon, and to drink from a glass and cup. She mastered bladder and bowel control easily. Tests of mental growth showed ape and child equal in their progress.

Furthermore, the ape learned cooperative play, including a game of tag and rolling a ball back and forth. Gua and Donald became very affectionate toward each other. The animal showed pronounced reactions of loyalty, jealousy, docility, and cooperation. Like the child, Gua learned obedience to the experimenter; also sly and mischievous behavior. Sometimes it showed tantrums, negativism, and what looked like disappointment and anxious behavior.

Unfortunately it was not possible to continue this study long enough to test the upper limits of the animal's capacities, or to make possible later comparisons of ape and child. Nor were com-

[6] W. N. and L. A. Kellogg, *The ape and the child* (New York: McGraw-Hill Book Co., Inc., 1933).

parative studies made of the humanized ape and apes reared in the normal simian environment. Hence one cannot be sure how many of Gua's achievements were the result specifically of the human social influences. Some obviously were, notably understanding spoken commands.

In a more recent experiment, Keith and Cathy Hayes reared a chimpanzee as a child for over three years.[7] As with Gua, their Vicki learned to respond to several dozen sounds, though her motor comprehension far exceeded that of the average child. Her degree of comprehension depended on the situation and the tone of voice in which the commands were uttered. More remarkable as compared to Gua, she learned to utter three words, "mama," "papa," and "cup," and apparently used them with meaning. For example, on her third birthday, Vicki drank her cup of coffee and when it was empty asked Mrs. Hayes for a refill by holding the cup up to the coffee pot saying: "Mama!" and then "Cup!" [8] To most lay and professional observers it appeared that Vicki's behavior was like that of the human being with the exception of the slowness to acquire language. Her perceptions of new objects, mirrors, manipulative situations, etc., were practically normal. Perhaps it might be said that she functioned like a "language defective" child who had not been exposed to sufficient normal stimulation.

In any event, the Kellogg and Hayes studies indicate that a human social environment can produce significant effects in the behavior of an organism having a much narrower range of potentialities than a human child. Thus they attest the molding and modifying power of human contacts in early life.

THE INFLUENCE OF HOME AND FAMILY

We may now turn to the child reared in a normal social setting. What aspects of his home environment have significant effects upon his personality? It is noteworthy to find agreement among specialists—psychologists, psychiatrists, sociologists, anthropologists, and social workers—that a child's earliest family experiences are the most important formative social influences in his development. As to the aspects of the child's personality affected by the family, we think first of security or emotional stability. Directly related to this is his self-esteem and his ego—both close to the core of personality. In addition to the basic ego-structure of the child's personality is the

[7] C. Hayes, *The ape in our house* (New York: Harper & Bros., 1951); K. J. and C. Hayes, The intellectual development of a home-raised chimpanzee, *Proc. Amer. Phil. Soc.*, XCV (1951), 105-9.

[8] C. Hayes, *op. cit.,* p. 191.

emergence of specific traits: attitudes, values, and habits. Specialists do not agree so well, however, as to which phases of personality and behavior are most affected, or as to which aspects of home and family are most significant. Thorpe suggests that the major influences of family life have to do with fulfilling the fundamental needs of the child: physical well-being, self or ego-security, emotional stability, and development of social maturity.[9]

Recent changes in the family. During the last hundred years a number of changes have occurred in family life, meaning that the sociopsychological functions have been tremendously altered:

1. The family has shrunk in size so that its members are interacting on a more intensive basis.
2. The functions of the family have shifted from a primarily biological continuing of the race to the providing of affectional and attitudinal security. The passing of home production and other primary economic bases of the family made for a more tenuous existence, and shifted the attention to psychological, rather than institutional, functions. This change has had far-reaching effects in patterns of child rearing.[10]
3. Due to a number of shifts in roles, especially in the status of women, marriage has moved from the patriarchal form to a system based on equalitarian relations. This has emphasized the companionship aspects of marriage. Children, too, may have equal rights in the family structure.
4. With mobility, urbanization, and the high standards set for marriage partners, there has been increasing instability and dissolution of family life. Divorce is associated with a number of variables, not least of which are the demand for affectional satisfaction in marriage and the belief that personal happiness is an end in itself. While divorce brings a number of severe problems for the individuals concerned, an unhappy marriage is coming to be considered by many Americans a satisfactory reason for terminating the relationship.

In view of these changes in the family structure, it is not surprising that socialization should be a changing phenomenon. The child no longer has the completely subordinate role he once had. Furthermore, as Parsons points out, the child must go further in socialization efforts with the present restricted size of the family.[11] In other words, the fact that he has only one sibling, or perhaps

9 L. P. Thorpe, *Child development* (2d ed.; New York: The Ronald Press Co., 1955), p. 385.

10 T. Parsons and R. Bales, *Family, socialization and interaction process* (Glencoe, Ill.: Free Press, 1955).

11 *Ibid.*, pp. 19-20.

none, means relatively more self-awareness. It is less likely he will have the opportunity to identify with other children. However, with our present-day mental hygiene emphasis, socialization has proceeded more smoothly, and with more sophistication on the part of parents.

To summarize these changes, we may quote Burgess, who pointed out some years ago that the family is a "unity of interacting personalities." [12] In fact, the family is becoming more and more a companionship rather than an institution; "its unity inheres less and less in community pressures and more and more in such interpersonal relations as the mutual affection, the sympathetic understanding, and the comradeship of its members." [13]

INTERACTION ASPECTS OF THE FAMILY

We shall now consider in turn the three important interactional aspects of the family: (1) relations between parents; (2) relations between parent and child; and (3) relations among children. Later we shall discuss the effects on the child of removal to a new family and shall compare nonfamily or institutional environments with the family setting.

Relations between parents. The quality of a marriage and of a family depends in large part on the degree to which the personal needs of each partner are satisfied. Levy and Munroe [14] found two differing need patterns on the part of spouses: one, the need for love, adoration, and protection, and two, the need for independence, self-fulfillment, and prestige. The satisfaction or frustration of these needs has much to do with whether the marriage is happy or unhappy.

Without going farther into the clinical or psychiatric aspects of marital adjustment, let us begin by noting that practically every study finds that harmonious relations between parents are essential to the development of a stable and well-integrated personality in a child. Constant dissension between parents is clearly one of the most upsetting experiences a child can have. Usually he loves and

[12] E. W. Burgess, The family as a unity of interacting personalities, *Family,* VII (1926), 3-9.

[13] E. W. Burgess and H. J. Locke, *The family* (2d ed.; New York: American Book Co., 1953), p. 7. Another influential sociological contribution to the family, by Waller, centers about personal interaction within the middle-class American family. See W. W. Waller and R. Hill, *The family—a dynamic interpretation* (2d ed.; New York: The Dryden Press, Inc., 1951). Equally concerned with psychodynamics is C. Kirkpatrick, *The family: As process and institution* (New York: The Ronald Press Co., 1955).

[14] J. Levy and R. Munroe, *The happy family* (New York: Alfred A. Knopf, Inc. 1938), pp. 240-319.

admires each parent and identifies himself with each; conflict between them becomes localized as conflict within him. He may run to his room and hide his head under a pillow when the dissension breaks out, but he cannot easily escape the disturbing emotional effects of the disharmonious home. His thwarted needs for love and emotional security lead to emotional tensions which in turn may lead to compensatory aggressive and even antisocial behavior, as in the case of B., a study made by one of the authors.

B., eight years old, was a constant problem in his home, school, and community. He was very intelligent but behaved incorrigibly in the classroom. He enjoyed pushing little girls downstairs and jumping in the paths of automobiles "to hear their brakes squeak when they stop." He once walked around a stone parapet at the edge of his apartment house roof, six stories above the ground. Yet B. was a likable child when approached in the right way.

B.'s mother was a somewhat neurotic woman in her late thirties, and his father was a bit older. They spent a great deal of time arguing, swearing at each other, screaming, and actually fighting. After a time the father left home, but the quarreling continued over the phone or when he returned to visit the children, as he did frequently. The parents were well educated and lived in a good neighborhood; their constant bickering was the only seriously unfavorable aspect of their family situation.

The interpretation is fairly obvious. Denied security and stability at home, B. turned to dramatic compensatory, aggressive, attention-getting devices. Another child might have resorted to daydreaming, masturbation, or other escapist activities. If B. had been older, he might have run away from home or become a juvenile delinquent, depending partly on other factors.

Probably this case is extreme. But serious disorganizing effects of the emotionally fractured home upon child personality are revealed typically in case studies. Consider two excerpts from psychological autobiographies written by former students of the authors:

Despite their unhappy life together, I believe my father and mother still love each other. They are very much alike—quick-tempered, impulsive, irrational yet highly intelligent. Their first year of marriage was spent in bickering over trivialities, weeks of living together without saying a word or cooing in the fashion of newlyweds. It ended in Dad's leaving for Canada where he joined the British army and was sent to the Near East.

Probably Mother would have divorced him had not an aunt intervened. The latter succeeded in convincing Mother that a divorce would label her as notorious, so when Dad returned he was quite warmly received. Mother is a creature of passion and love, and the lonely life did not appeal to her.

Her life with Dad after his return did not change and has not changed since. They are still quarreling and still making up. . . . When Mother and Dad argued I would always secretly take Mother's side of the argument. Dad sensed this and became more antagonistic toward me instead of trying to win me over to him. . . . Looking back, I find my immediate family really meant next to nothing to me. The people to whom I really gave affection were my aunt and her daughter. The aunt was a mother and the cousin a sister to me.

At school I was very shy, very silent and always daydreaming. . . .

During this period between 11 and 16 my attitude toward my Dad became openly hostile; we stopped talking to each other. My aunt lost favor in my eyes; I found her to be narrow and tyrannical. . . . I became conscious of the struggle between the classes and joined the radical movement, only to drop out because of definite class distinctions among members. Then I went to live with a very interesting woman, an intelligent, modern, Hungarian Jewess. I immediately adopted her as my ideal woman, for she was clever, beautiful, poised, charming. The veneer wore off after some months, and I spent two months with Mother again. I became more convinced than ever that I could not live at home. I found I was incapable of bearing the perpetual squabbling, the dominance over me and Mother's psychopathic moods.

I was tired of my existence, tired of the futility of life. I saw no reason for any hope that I might attain a definite goal. I had no faith in mankind, and I looked for no response. I was starved for affection but I felt it would be a responsibility I could not bear. I lived only in anticipation of new experiences, new amusements. . . .

The first disruption of my family involved me (says the second student), as did many subsequent clashes. I was beaten severely and unfairly by my father, especially when he had been drinking. . . .

Once he went away for three days, having been drunk, I suppose. His defense was that he had to get away from Mother's nagging. This was the first quarrel of which I can remember details, but occurrences like it became more frequent. I have never been able to decide whether Father drank because Mother nagged or Mother nagged because Father drank. Everything would go well for a couple of months and then they would quarrel. My brother and I would stay as far away as possible and shut our ears. . . . Gradually my brother's views leaned toward Mother and I rather favored Father. These feelings became intensified as the years went on, raising a barrier between my brother and me which remains to this day.

I started to read when I was eight or nine and it became almost an obsession. I would curl up with a book and become so absorbed I heard nothing that went on around me. When quarrels or scoldings threatened my peace of mind I retreated behind a book and actually lived in the book with the characters of the plot rather than in the actual world. Naturally Mother was against this; she could not tolerate such indifference to her suffering. When I was young I never outwardly rebelled, but said nothing and moved to another spot and went on reading. Later I grew bolder and said "Shut Up!" or "Let me alone." In fact the whole theme of my adolescence consisted of one phrase—muttered, spoken or screamed, "Let me alone!"

Systematic studies also reveal the unfortunate effects of disharmonious relations between parents. Hattwick used a group of 335 nursery school children in her search for relationships between social behavior and various factors in home backgrounds.[15] She found sizable positive correlations (.42 to .65) between tension in the home and forms of child behavior like jealousy, selfishness, fears, emotional upsets, and quarreling, all of which may be considered signs of emotional insecurity or instability. It is not surprising therefore that people often ask whether it is better to terminate a marriage torn by friction, which means divorce, or to continue the disharmonious marriage for the sake of the children. Nye recently showed in a study of several hundred high school students that divorce of the parents was apparently followed by fewer psychosomatic problems, less delinquent behavior, and generally better relations with parents than was true for those who remained in unbroken but unhappy homes.[16]

Conversely, as might be expected, an important background factor for stable personality is good parental relations. Interesting confirmation for this was found in two extensive studies of marriage. Terman concludes that the best recipe for happy marriage is emotional stability on the part of both husband and wife; the most important single cause of this is happily married parents.[17] Burgess and Cottrell, in their more sociological approach to marriage, arrived at the same conclusion.[18] Where parents of both spouses were rated as happily married, nearly three-quarters of the couples had good adjustment and only 12 per cent poor adjustment. Where the parents of the spouses were rated as average or unhappy in their marriages, 38 per cent had poor, and only 28 per cent good, marital adjustment. Again the implication is clear that harmony between parents is important to a child's emotional security and social adjustment.

Further evidence on this point was found in the Locke study which compared a group of happily married individuals with a divorced sample. He found that the husbands more than the wives enjoyed happiness scores if the marriage of the parents was happy. Moreover, a lack of divorces among close relatives was a favorable factor. The Locke study also showed that one's marital happiness

[15] B. W. Hattwick, in *Child Developm.*, VII (1936), 200-226.

[16] F. I. Nye, Child adjustment in broken and unhappy unbroken homes, *Marr. fam. liv.*, XIX (1957), 356-61. Similarly, widowed and separated mothers found as much difficulty, psychologically speaking, in rearing their children as did the divorced. But they all found that remarriage was followed by an improved relationship on the part of the children. See W. J. Goode, *After divorce* (Glencoe, Ill.: Free Press, 1956), pp. 329-30.

[17] L. M. Terman *et al., Psychological factors in marital happiness* (New York: McGraw-Hill Book Co., Inc., 1938).

[18] E. W. Burgess and L. S. Cottrell, *Predicting success or failure in marriage* (Englewood Cliffs, N. J.: Prentice-Hall, Inc., 1939).

was dependent on the attainment of some degree of independence as a child.[19]

Parent-child relationships. The kind of interaction between parent and child is obviously important to personality development; they very properly form a basic theme for Parent-Teachers' Association meetings and mental hygiene programs. Recent years have seen lively controversy between those favoring permissiveness and expression of affection versus those calling for firmness and strict discipline. One school of thought, sparked by the behaviorists, has maintained that development is largely a matter of conditioning, which can be applied scientifically and objectively without affectional demonstration.[20] This viewpoint had considerable vogue for a time. Then it changed: "From the depersonalized, highly scheduled regime prescribed in the early behaviorist paradigm for child care, Americans have returned to less regimented feeding schedules and to more permissive and accepting methods of dealing with their infants. These practices are derived most recently from psychoanalytic orientations and, more remotely, from the way grandmothers or great-grandmothers of the present parent generation handled their babies." [21] A good example of the changed emphasis is Dr. Benjamin Spock's popular "Pocket Book of Baby and Child Care," a modified psychoanalytic approach, which has sold hundreds of thousands of copies. The 1957 edition of the Spock manual, even more than the 1946 version, stresses permissiveness for the parents and the value of "trusting yourself." However, a countercurrent may also be discerned—a certain reaction against permissiveness and toward firmness and discipline—both in scientific and popular journals.

In this connection Martha Wolfenstein has compared child training concepts as revealed in publications of the Children's Bureau over a thirty-five year period.[22] In the 1914 edition the child was portrayed as having dangerous impulses, such as thumbsucking and masturbation, which the parents must vigilantly control. Parents were warned not to indulge in too much play with the child lest it make him irritable and restless. By the 1940's the infant had become veritably harmless; thumbsucking and autoeroticism were

19 H. J. Locke, *Predicting adjustment in marriage* (New York: Henry Holt & Co., Inc., 1951), pp. 106-24.

20 J. B. Watson, *Psychological care of infant and child* (New York: W. W. Norton & Co., Inc., 1928).

21 B. R. McCandless, in L. A. Pennington and I. A. Berg, *An introduction to clinical psychology* (2d ed.; New York: The Ronald Press Co., 1954), p. 227.

22 M. Wolfenstein, The emergence of fun morality, *J. soc. Issues,* VII (1951), 15-25.

seen as normal phases of development. In this more contemporary period parents were encouraged to play with and enjoy the child, an example of what Wolfenstein calls the "emergence of fun morality" in the United States. It is not inconceivable that in another decade or two the trend may reverse itself. Already we have seen some stiffening of the formal instruction program in American schools.

Until recently, in popular parlance, the worst type of parent-child relationship was "spoiling." Now we hear a great deal about different varieties of relationships—*rejection, overprotection, permissiveness,* and *overindulgence.* One writer speaks of two kinds of rejecting behavior in parents: one, the actively hostile; and two, the passive-neglectful. Even emotionally involved, warm parental attitudes may take the form of possessiveness. With more emotional detachment parents may achieve a kind of warm democracy, which makes for real acceptance and security on the part of the child.[23]

The relationship between parental behavior and child personality has been summarized (in a somewhat simplified form) as follows: [24]

Parent behavior	Commonest effects produced in child
Rejection	Aggressiveness, feelings of insecurity, and "nervousness"
Overprotection	Infantile behavior, submissiveness, insecurity feelings, anxiety
Submissiveness and permissiveness	Aggressiveness, carelessness, disobedience, independence, self-confidence
Disharmony	Aggressiveness, jealousy, delinquency

One type of parental behavior, *maternal overprotectiveness,* has come in for more than its fair share of notice. David Levy first drew scientific attention to it,[25] but Strecker's term "momism" caught popular fancy, especially since it had been made the central theme of Philip Wylie's commentary on American life, *Generation of Vipers.*[26] Both Strecker and Wylie found "momism" very prevalent in the United States; the former spoke of it as follows: "The seed which is productive of the most prolific and serious immaturity in adult life is the one which consists of the mother uncon-

[23] A. L. Baldwin, *Behavior and development in childhood* (New York: The Dryden Press, Inc., 1955), chap. xx.

[24] M. J. Radke, *The relation of parental authority to children's behavior and attitudes* (Minneapolis: University of Minnesota Press, 1946), and Baldwin, *op. cit.,* pp. 534 ff. Another reference is P. M. Symonds, *Psychology of parent-child relationships* (New York: Appleton-Century-Crofts, Inc., 1939).

[25] D. M. Levy, *Maternal overprotection* (New York: Columbia University Press, 1943).

[26] P. Wylie, *Generation of vipers* (New York: Rinehart & Co., Inc., 1942).

sciously but selfishly hanging on to her offspring and refusing to grant her sons and daughters emotional emancipation. For want of a better word I have used the word "Mom" to describe the maternal parent who fails in the elementary function of weaning her offspring emotionally as well as physically." [27]

Recently Wylie has revised his earlier position. He believes that the mother of the mid-fifties has become aware of the dangers of overindulgence and disguised egocentricity. She realizes the dangerous possibilities of training the child to overconsider mother. Whereas formerly mothers spoiled their children so that the latter might spoil them in later years, emphasis is now placed on self-reliance and a psychologically sound equalitarianism. [28]

In our own day a large number of parents have become increasingly aware that *rejection* of the child is the cardinal sin in the parents handbook. But, as Bettelheim notes in his *Love Is Not Enough*, it must be supplemented by constructive effort on the part of parents. [29] Frequently, love becomes indulgence or overprotection, instead of a genuine affectional relationship. It is not sufficient to follow the rules; rather "it must also be done with emotions that belong to the act." An example might be the mother who takes a permissive attitude toward her child's enuresis, but has a bullying attitude, or internal conflict, about the matter of laundering the sheets. In either case there are likely to be guilt feelings on her part which will make the relationship with the child unsatisfactory.

One might well wonder why parental rejection is so common. A number of the studies of marital adjustment find that there is considerable tension and ambivalence with respect to the child or children. Terman, Burgess and Cottrell, Locke, and Williamson found that, contrary to expectation, children did *not* contribute toward marital happiness; in fact, higher scores were frequently found in those marriages that were childless. [30] However, the *desire* for children was favorable toward marital adjustment. This may be a reflection of the financial strain of the early years of marriage, but it also points to the psychological tension associated with rearing children, whatever compensations may be involved. It is likely that unconscious, if not conscious, rejection of the child grows out of the frustrations associated with child rearing.

27 E. A. Strecker, The seeds of immaturity, *Penna. med. J.*, L (1947), p. 377.

28 P. Wylie, What's happened to "Mom"? *This Week Magazine*, May 13, 1956.

29 B. Bettelheim, *Love is not enough* (Glencoe, Ill.: Free Press, 1950).

30 Terman, *op. cit.*, pp. 171-73; Burgess and Cottrell, *op. cit.*, pp. 258-60; Locke, *op. cit.*, pp. 158-70. R. C. Williamson, Selected urban factors in marital adjustment, *Research Studies*, State College of Washington, 1953, pp. 237-41.

Thus parental rejection, or overprotection, often cause insecurity feelings with associated aggressiveness, submissiveness, or other compensatory reactions. In their early studies the Gluecks reported that bad parent-child relations are present in three-fourths or more cases of delinquency.[31] A later investigation compared 500 delinquent boys with the same number of nondelinquents; far more hostility, indifference, and overprotectiveness on the part of parents was found in the case of the former group. The control exercised tended to be lax, erratic, or overstrict rather than firm and kindly, with physical punishment the typical method of control.[32] Students of truancy, aberrant sexual behavior, and other juvenile problems find much the same thing. Each of the studies of marriage mentioned above [33] finds that close affectional ties with parents and absence of conflict with them are significant factors in determining a youngster's later marital adjustment.

Broken homes. What about the "broken home"—the family from which one parent has been removed by death, divorce, or separation? A dozen or more surveys [34] agree that nearly 50 per cent of juvenile delinquents come from broken homes. When control groups of nondelinquents were studied, the proportion of broken homes was found to be about 25 per cent. It would seem that death, divorce, or separation of one parent is an important factor in producing delinquency.

Of course, some doubt exists that control groups studied have been comparable to delinquents in all respects save tangling with the law. Shaw and McKay compared 1,675 delinquent boys with over 7,000 schoolboys of the same age, nationality, and neighborhood. Here the differences were much smaller—42.5 per cent of broken homes for the delinquents and 36 per cent for the school group.[35] Presumably the broken home has a bad effect on the child,

---

[31] S. and E. T. Glueck, *One thousand juvenile delinquents* (Cambridge, Mass.: Harvard University Press, 1934). Not only is there ample evidence of the effects of parental rejection, but it has also been suggested that the rejection of the parent by the child and adolescent is associated with delinquency, at least as revealed in a questionnaire study of a random high school sample. See F. I. Nye, The rejected parent and delinquency, *Marr. fam. liv.*, XVIII (1956), 291-300.

[32] See S. and E. T. Glueck, *Criminal careers in retrospect* (New York: Commonwealth Fund, 1943) and *Unraveling juvenile delinquency* (Cambridge, Mass.: Harvard University Press, 1950).

[33] Terman *et al.*, *op. cit.* pp. 212-19: Burgess and Cottrell, *op. cit.* pp. 92-98.

[34] Many of these are summarized in C. M. Louttit, *Clinical psychology of children's behavior problems* (New York: Harper & Bros., 1947), and in R. S. Cavan, *The family* (New York: The Thomas Crowell Co., 1942).

[35] C. R. Shaw and H. D. McKay, Social factors in juvenile delinquency, in Natl. Com. Law Observance and Enforcement, *Report on causes of crime* (1931), II, No. 13.

but other factors may be more important in the etiology of delinquency.

Some of these factors are suggested by other statistical studies. For example, the bad influence of a broken home is felt most strongly when children are younger—say eight or ten—rather than when they are sixteen. If one compares the percentages of delinquents and of controls whose parents (one or both) are dead, one finds no differences. However, where the rates of those having divorced or separated parents are compared, higher percentages occur among delinquents. This suggests that dissension or conflict (which undoubtedly preceded the divorce or separation) plays a more significant part than the absence or loss of a parent per se.

Some students have taken a more psychological approach to the problem of what a broken home does to child personality. Cavan, for example, compared neurotic inventory scores made by children from broken and unbroken homes.[36] About 10 per cent more children from the former showed instability. According to teachers' ratings children from the unbroken homes had somewhat better habits (e.g., honesty, courtesy, obedience). Wallenstein, matching children from broken and unbroken homes in regard to age, sex, nationality, mental age, and socioeconomic status, found a slight tendency toward better personality adjustment among the latter group.[37]

Most studies of broken homes are largely statistical, hence fail to reveal the subtle patterns of variables operating in the "psychological atmosphere" of the home. Actually, an unbroken home with continual parental dissension can be more harmful to a child than a broken home. Only careful case study techniques can reveal the salient family pattern features that affect, for better or for worse, the child's developing personality. Generalizing from the conclusions of many investigators, we may say that a broken home usually involves one or more of the following types of strain upon the child:

1. Discord or conflict between parents in the period preceding separation or divorce
2. Tension during visits to or from the separated parent
3. The problem of adjusting to a step parent if the child's own remaining parent remarries

36 R. S. Cavan, *The adolescent in the family* ("White House Conference on Child Health and Protection" [New York: Appleton-Century-Crofts, Inc., 1934]), pp. 117-18.
37 N. Wallenstein, *Character and personality of children from broken homes* (New York: Teach. Coll. Contrib. Educ., Columbia University, 1937, No. 721).

4. Loss of affectional contact and interaction with the departed parent (the father, in about 70 per cent of the cases) and difficulty of adjusting exclusively to the other parent
5. Degeneration of parental supervision when one parent has to assume the whole burden. (If the mother has to work, the whole pattern of parental responsibility breaks down.)
6. Increased responsibilities for the children, especially the older ones, which means little time for recreation, and possibly leaving school and going to work
7. Feeling of children from a broken home that they are different from, usually inferior to, children from normal homes, which accentuates feelings of inferiority and insecurity

Nearly always broken homes involve a strain both upon children and upon the remaining parent. But we must not forget that most children from broken homes are neither delinquent nor seriously maladjusted. A lone parent, if intelligent and devoted, can make up for the stresses of the unusual family situation so that the children do not suffer unduly. We need careful studies of how this is done, to compare with the more dramatic studies of maladjustment.

Sibling relationships. We have seen that statistical studies of broken homes fail to get at the heart of the psychological problems involved. This is even more true for studies of child personality as affected by birth-order, or position in the family.

Alfred Adler popularized the idea that younger children develop inferiorities and compensate by striving for superiority over their older brothers and sisters. He believed that ordinal position in the family has much to do with a child's personality.[38] Other writers maintain that an only child tends to be spoiled, and that the best-adjusted children are likely to be found in large families.

Using such theories as hypotheses, many investigators have studied the personalities of older, younger, middle, and only children. Murphy, Murphy, and Newcomb have summarized fifty studies made before 1938. The findings are quite inconclusive. Usually no differences are discovered; where they do appear, they are not statistically significant and may or may not be in the expected direction. The reason, as these authors suggest, is that ordinal family position has little to do with the much more significant "psychological position." The latter depends on whether or not the child

[38] See Alfred Adler, *The neurotic constitution* (New York: Moffat, Yard & Co., 1917); H. L. and R. R. Ansbacher (eds.), *The individual psychology of Alfred Adler* (New York: Basic Books, Inc., 1956).

feels accepted and loved, on his emotional relationship with parents and siblings, and on various other factors.[39]

Family position may, of course, affect a child's behavior in certain ways, especially at the younger ages. Jealousy typically occurs in a child when a new baby brother or sister arrives and usurps his place as the center of attention. "Only" children of four or five years are less socialized in their play activities than children of the same age who have brothers and sisters. Usually these are temporary conditions that change as the child gets older and comes into daily contact with other children in school or at the playground.

On the other hand, position in the family may be important as one feature in a pattern of several factors. For example, two brothers or two sisters, close in age, may be competitive toward each other, especially if competitiveness is countenanced or encouraged by the parents. Here the idea of "beating out my brother" may become a primary motive. But where the two children are farther apart in age, of different sexes, and where parents discourage competitiveness, the birth order as such may have no particular significance for personality development.

SPECIAL PROBLEMS IN ENVIRONMENT

Removal to a new family. What happens to a child's personality when he changes to another home and set of parents? Follow-up studies of children placed in adoptive or foster homes agree that about two-thirds of the youngsters get over their behavior and personality problems! [40] When a child is quite young and without organic defects, he makes a particularly good adjustment to his new home. Actually, this means that his personality changes in the new social situation, though we are seldom told by the investigators precisely what changes have taken place; the change usually is noted in broad terms of "adjustment."

One study involved one hundred problem children whose family backgrounds comprised broken homes, neurotic or psychotic parents, bad discipline, parental friction, infidelity, drunkenness, abuse, poverty, etc. Two-thirds of the group were placed in foster homes; 72 per cent of these children made a successful adjustment after two

---

[39] G. Murphy et al., Experimental social psychology (New York: Harper & Bros., 1938), pp. 348-63.

[40] C. R. Rogers, Clinical treatment of the problem child (Boston: Houghton Mifflin Co., 1939); S. Theis, How foster children turn out (Albany, N. Y.: New York State Charities Aid, 1924); W. Healy et al., Reconstructing behavior in youth (New York: Alfred A. Knopf, Inc., 1929); C. C. Hopkins and A. R. Haines, Study of 100 problem children, Amer. J. Orthopsychiat., I (1931), 107-28.

or three years. The investigators could find no type of behavior, from faulty habits to delinquency, that could not be modified in a foster home. Of the one-third not placed in foster homes, only 9 per cent adjusted successfully.[41]

An interesting and rather unusual case came to the attention of one of the authors a few years ago; it illustrates many aspects of family influence upon personality.

Peter was an illegitimate child whose father deserted the mother as soon as he learned she was pregnant. The birth was a difficult one, and the mother treated little Peter very badly, deserting him at intervals and placing him in a succession of boarding homes. Peter's insecurity led to continuous enuresis and to more aggressive compensatory reactions such as running away, stealing, lying and fire-setting even before he was six. A social agency became interested in him, and after diligent search found a good suburban foster home where the child could be loved and made the center of attention; he entered the home when he was 7 or 8. For several months his problem behavior continued but the foster parents persevered and gradual improvement occurred. By the third year of his stay he had made remarkable progress and was no longer considered a problem in the home, the school or the community.

Then Peter's mother came back into the picture. She had married a man several years younger than she and they decided to take Peter home with them. The new stepfather was an immature person and neither he nor the mother really loved the boy. Consequently, shortly after Peter returned to his own home all his old problems reappeared, along with some new ones, principally homosexual practices. Matters came to a head when he and a companion were caught stealing blankets from a department store so they could sleep out in the parks at night. Peter was sent to the detention home, then to a foster home where it was hoped he might improve enough so he could be saved from the last resort, the reformatory. At last reports he was showing improvement, but the reformatory and a delinquent career still loomed as a possibility for the future.

Here we see the successive effects of the rejecting and accepting types of family environment. Dramatic as it may seem, this case differs only in degree from thousands of cases seen every year in child guidance clinics and family welfare centers.

Institutional situations. Effects of orphanages, hospitalization, and other such settings have been studied. One researcher found that institutionalized infants who lived in some degree of social and emotional isolation showed aggression and other forms of un-socialized behavior and had little tolerance of frustration.[42] Spitz has done a series of studies on the effects of "hospitalism" on infant development. He finds, in general, that this kind of setting deprives the child of emotional interchange, particularly af-

[41] Hopkins and Haines, *op. cit.*

[42] L. G. Lowrey, Personality distortion and early institutional care., *Amer. J. Orthopsychiat.*, X (1940), 576-85.

fection between child and mother, and that this constitutes a serious handicap to personality development.[43]

It seems likely that the impersonal atmosphere of an institution inhibits a child's emotional and social development, somewhat like the cases of isolated children described above. The more an institution can approximate the warm social relationships of a good home, the more it will produce normal emotional development and better social adjustment.

LEARNING IN THE FAMILY

So far we have considered family influences as they affect a child's security and emotional stability, which are basic to personality and social behavior. Home influence has other important aspects, notably those relating to learning. Stagner refers to the parents' role in a child's development:

> They give affection and dispense discipline. They reward and punish. They encourage certain traits and discourage others, acting either on personal prejudice or as agents of the culture, indoctrinating the values of the larger group. Furthermore, they serve as models which the child imitates. When there is a discrepancy between parental instruction and parental behavior, the child is prone to follow the latter. Thus the parents are major determinants of the hopes, fears, and expectancies of the child.[44]

Obviously the family teaches language, early knowledge, habits, and skills. Several studies show how fears, attitudes, prejudices, and values are communicated from parent to child. Jersild, for example, found many children afraid of the supernatural, death, animals, strangeness, darkness, ghosts, robbers, and kidnapers.[45] Most of these fears traced directly or indirectly to their parents. Newcomb and Svehla found correlations between parents' and children's attitudes as follows: attitude toward the church, .63; toward war, .44; toward communism, .56. They also discovered consistencies in whole patterns of parental attitudes reflected in their children.[46]

[43] See R. A. Spitz, Hospitalism, *Psychoanal. Stud. Child.*, I (1945), 53-74; II (1946), 113-17. Spitz' studies were severely criticized by S. R. Pinneau in *Psychol. Bull.*, LII (1955), 429 ff., and a reply given by Spitz. A recent study showed that traumatic effects of institutional experience can be counteracted by proper foster home placement. Frequently therapy for both the child and the new parents must be initiated in order to provide a happy relationship. See L. K. Kaplan and L. L. Turitz, Treatment of severely emotionally traumatized young children of a foster home setting, *Amer. J. Orthopsychiat.*, XXVII (1957), 271-85.

[44] R. Stagner, *Psychology of personality* (2d ed.; New York: McGraw-Hill Book Co., Inc., 1948), p. 345.

[45] A. T. Jersild et al., *Children's fears, dreams, wishes* . . . (Child Developm. Monogr., 1933, No. 12).

[46] T. M. Newcomb and G. Svehla, Intra-family relationship in attitude, *Sociometry*, I (1937), 180-205.

The Horowitzes studied origins of racial prejudice among rural white children in Tennessee.[47] The learning pattern was clear; in most cases parents, reflecting regional and community practices, tell their children not to play with colored youngsters. The child's attitude toward Negroes, to quote the authors, "seems to have its origins with the child's parents. Apparently parents give direct instruction in these attitudes and cannot recall having done so. . . ." [48] The subtlety of this kind of learning in the family is suggested further by the Horowitzes' finding that toward adolescence the children also forget the origins of the attitudes and devise various kinds of rationalizations to support and maintain them.

As we shall see in Chapter 9, the family is a sort of social matrix, from which a child's "ego" or concept of self—the innermost core of his personality—emerges. Most interpreters of the self agree that it develops from the child's earliest social relationships, which occur in the family.

The family, then, influences significantly a child's emotional security, particularly through the quality of relationship between parents, between parents and children, and, to a lesser extent, between the children themselves. In addition, the parents serve as models for the child's learning of information, skills, habits, fears, attitudes, and prejudices, and as the primary source from which develops the child's ego or self.

THE SCHOOL AND PERSONALITY DEVELOPMENT

While family influences are paramount, other social institutions make their mark, great or small, on the child. Probably the foremost of these is the school.

Psychologically speaking, education advances the processes of intellectual, emotional, and social development already begun in the home. When the five-year-old enters kindergarten, he already is a personality in the making. Physically active and well coordinated, he has learned many habits and skills and is eager for new experiences. He is socialized to the point of communicating with others, of playing cooperatively, of showing sympathy, and otherwise beginning to recognize the rights of others. He has learned some control over infantile emotional outbursts.

When a child begins school, he enters a society very different from his home. He is placed with a number of children of his own age, usually both boys and girls. No longer is he at the center of

---

[47] E. L. and R. E. Horowitz, Development of social attitudes in children, *Sociometry*, I (1938), 301-38.

[48] *Ibid.*, p. 336.

the stage; he gets little personal attention and recognition. He must conform to new rules and regulations that hinder his self-expression. For the first time he is expected to engage in activities that may not interest him. In fact, when one considers the newness and strangeness of the school situation for the entering five-year-old, it seems remarkable that children adjust to school as well as they do.

Psychological studies of the effects of schooling usually stress mental and physical development, which do not very much concern the social psychologist. However, some researchers have tried to determine the impact of schools on the pupil's personality and social behavior. We present a few of their findings.

The role of the deviant. In general, children at the two extremes of ability have a bad time of it in school. The dull children experience repeated failure and frustration if kept in regular classes, or suffer social stigma if placed in ungraded, retarded, or "dumb-bell" classes. One study compared a large number of slow-progress children with a group of normals. Boys in the retarded group tended to be unfriendly, bullying, quarrelsome, selfish, and boastful. Retarded girls showed inattention, daydreaming, and discouragement. In other words, the boys showed an aggressive and the girls a withdrawing reaction to their frustration in school.[49] Conversely, bright children in regular classes find their work too easy, which often encourages laziness, boredom, fantasy, or aggressive forms of mischief making.

Children with personality or behavior problems also have difficulties in school. Usually teachers have too many pupils and too many teaching hours to give problem youngsters the individual attention they need. Even where teachers have the time, many do not understand clinical procedures well enough to do an effective job. Wickman compared the attitudes of a large group of teachers with those of clinical psychologists. The teachers considered sex offenses, lying, cheating, impertinence, and truancy the most serious of their pupils' problems. They found seclusiveness and withdrawal rather inconsequential. The clinicians, on the other hand, found children's unsocial behavior more serious and symptomatic of maladjustment than their aggressive behavior.[50] One can understand the teachers' attitudes; they must keep order in the classrooms. But the psychological implications of their attitudes are unfortunate.

[49] A. A. Sandin, *Social and emotional adjustments of regularly promoted and non-promoted pupils* (Child Developm. Monogr., 1944, No. 32).

[50] E. K. Wickman, *Children's problems and teachers' attitudes* (New York: Commonwealth Fund, 1928).

This discouraging picture is not universal. Teachers' colleges continually improve their clinical training programs. Almost any school system includes some fine teachers who inspire their pupils and manage somehow to give at least a bit of guidance to the youngsters who need it most. In the most modern schools the teachers are very carefully selected and are given time to work with pupils individually. Goals commensurate with a child's ability are set. The teacher, often aided by a school psychologist, identifies a child's problems and enlists the parents' help in resolving them. This newer viewpoint is to treat each child as an individual, unique personality.

Influence of the teacher. In addition, of course, the teacher can affect the values of the child in her choice of activities in the classroom. Here she is influenced to a large extent by the school administration, though she still has considerable latitude in most school systems within which to operate. Many schools are oriented toward what has been called, and still is called, "progressive education." According to its tenets the curriculum is directed toward the needs of the individual child—his affectional and ego needs as well as the attainment of intellectual and social skills. Progressivists maintain that effective learning takes place only when the individual child acquires a desire to learn. There are many variations of this philosophy, and a number of the practices have moved away from the views of John Dewey.[51] The way in which a child-centered curriculum is carried on reflects the needs of time and place. Opposed to this kind of educational orientation is the viewpoint of "formal discipline," by which all pupils are taught a number of skills and it is assumed that these will carry over or generalize to any kind of situation they may meet. Concentration on skill learning is likely to point up individual differences in the classroom and leave the less capable students with anxiety or feelings of inadequacy. If the teacher is aware of the needs of individual pupils, however, she may be able to structure the classroom situation so that a minimum of frustration is experienced by the pupils.

Another way in which the teacher influences the child's adjustment and social relations is in the formation or choice of the peer group.[52] She may determine the youngster's playmates or friends

51 J. Dewey, *Democracy and education* (New York: The Macmillan Co., 1916). A recent summary and discussion of progressivism and other philosophies is found in Theodore Brameld's *Philosophies of education in cultural perspective* (New York: The Dryden Press, Inc., 1955).

52 R. J. Havighurst, *Human development and education* (New York: Longmans, Green & Co., Inc., 1953), pp. 64-76.

to a considerable extent by placing him at a certain spot in the class-room or otherwise helping him select the proper group. A teacher can often help an isolated or diffident child to make friends and to become part of a group. Or she can experiment with friendship patterns by asking the child or adolescent to list his friends in order of preference; through rearrangement within the groups and among the groups she can facilitate better social relationships in the class-room and on the playground.

Status of the teacher. Many difficulties stem from the fact that in the United States the teaching profession is not held in very high esteem. Salaries are low, and teachers are unbelievably restricted, especially in small towns. One study showed community disapproval of the following out-of-school behavior: dating a student, drinking, smoking in public, making a political speech, running for political office, playing billiards, not attending church, and playing cards.[53] It is hardly surprising that the most intelligent, independent, and energetic college graduates generally choose professions other than teaching!

Besides, several studies show that many teachers have serious frustrations, complexes, and personality problems that militate against effective teaching, let alone helping pupils with their personal problems.[54]

In a recent survey of the teaching profession in an Eastern city it was found, among other things, that a high proportion of women teachers are living with elderly parents or with another unmarried woman. In a survey of their attitudes it was found that 62 per cent of the teachers were willing, after roughly five years of college training, to go to work at a wage lower than was being paid to unskilled and semiskilled workers; and 54 per cent stated they would accept as a maximum salary an amount less than was already being paid by the school system's prevailing contract and well below what the teachers' organization was striving for. Only 32 per cent considered themselves to have status in the community. Approximately 70 per cent thought that the public expected some sort of different or superior conduct on the part of teaching personnel than from other occupational groups. Half of the sample approved of this discrimination. On the whole, the study implied that teachers were detached from normalcy in living, largely due to their fail-

[53] L. A. Cook, R. B. Almack, and F. Greenhoe, Teacher and community relations, *Amer. sociol. Rev.*, III (1938), 167-74.

[54] See, e.g., W. W. Waller, *Sociology of teaching* (New York: John Wiley & Sons, Inc., 1932), Part V; R. C. Challman, Mental health of the teacher, in A. I. Gates *et al.*, *Educational psychology* (3d ed.; New York: The Macmillan Co., 1948).

ure to attain marriage, and showed they were subjected to a number of political barriers and pressures.[55] These frustrations and insecurities could hardly fail to affect the quality of instruction and prevent teachers from being interested in and honest with their students.

Indirect influence of the school. In a broad sociological sense, the school's function in any society is to transmit the social heritage —the language, essential skills and information, and the sanctioned attitudes, values, and ways of behaving. Much of this is imparted consciously. In our country we try to teach not only the three R's, but also obedience, politeness, patriotism, honesty, and, recently, tolerance toward those of different races and religions.

Psychologists are interested also in what schools may teach without conscious intent. It has been noted that in a widely used arithmetic book over 600 problems stressed profit and loss, interest rates, and other aspects of our capitalist economy. These problems, said the investigator, "place stress on commercial transactions in which monetary gain was ever the motive." [56] Others cite history books that indoctrinate students in militaristic and nationalistic directions, presumably without propagandistic intent on the writer's part.

Again, pupils are influenced by the atmosphere in which schools operate. Many schools have an authoritarian rather than a democratic pattern. As Lewin and his colleagues showed, an authoritarian group structure gets immediate results, but it promotes aggression and retards the development of initiative and independence in the group members.[57] Anderson has studied what he calls "dominative" and "integrative" social behavior in the classroom.[58] He discovered much more dominative than integrative behavior in teachers; dominative behavior, he found, produces resistive and aggressive reactions in others rather than cooperative, democratic behavior. Most school children experience democratic behavior neither in school nor at home, which seems poor preparation, to say the least, for life in a political democracy!

The American youngster learns in school much more than is furnished by the formal curriculum.[59] He learns respect for ma-

55 F. W. Terrien, The occupational roles of teachers, *J. educ. Sociol.*, XXIX:1 (1955), 14-20.

56 E. Freeman, *Social psychology* (New York: Henry Holt & Co., Inc., 1936), pp. 264-65.

57 See R. Lippitt and R. K. White, An experimental study of leadership and group life, in Swanson *et al.*, *Readings* (2d ed.), pp. 340-55.

58 H. H. Anderson, Studies in dominative and socially integrative behavior, *Amer. J. Orthopsychiat.*, XV (1945), 133-39.

59 See K. Young, *Personality and problems of adjustment* (2d ed.; New York: Appleton-Century-Crofts, Inc., 1952), chap. xv.

terial progress, for making money, for working rather than loafing. He realizes that one should be ambitious and set high goals and ideals for oneself. He comes to believe that the United States is the greatest country in the world. Very likely he learns to distrust persons who seek reforms or changes in our way of living. From emphasis on grades and scholastic honors, and from contests on the school playground or athletic field, he is sure to learn that competitiveness is tremendously important. Such values and attitudes are picked up from day-to-day school experience which reflects in large measure the values of the community and of the culture as a whole.

The conscious and unconscious imparting to the child of our dominant values and attitudes is natural and, indeed, inevitable. Unfortunately, the child also absorbs many conflicting values, as Karen Horney pointed out.[60] This culturally minded psychiatrist noted that the child in America learns to compete for success and to be assertive and aggressive in the process. At the same time he is imbued in church and school with Christian ideals of brotherly love and humility. The child is told that he is free and independent, that he can get what he wants if he is efficient and energetic. Actually, these possibilities are greatly limited, as he later realizes. Contradictions like these are embedded in our culture and form a potent source of neurotic conflicts, concluded Horney.

Thus the school transmits the social heritage to children and helps shape their personalities and social behavior. Bright and dull children and those with adjustment problems probably will be affected adversely by their school experience, partly because teachers have neither the time nor the training to help them effectively. In school, children gain knowledge and skills; they learn also a variety of values and attitudes. Some are taught intentionally. Others the youngsters pick up from the general atmosphere of the school. Unfortunately for the child, he learns certain incompatible values, such as aggressiveness and brotherly love, that may be the basis for neurotic conflicts. Though the school influence is secondary to that of the family, we may agree that "few get over the effects of a poor school or lose the benefits of a good one." [61]

PEER GROUPS AND PERSONALITY DEVELOPMENT

Along with family and school, peer groups account for a large share of the child's social, emotional, and attitudinal development.

60 K. Horney, *The neurotic personality of our time* (New York: W. W. Norton & Co., Inc., 1937), chap. xv. See also M. Halsey, *The folks at home* (New York: Simon & Schuster, Inc., 1952).

61 J. Tiffin, F. B. Knight, and C. C. Josey, *The psychology of normal people* (Boston: D. C. Heath & Co., 1940), p. 128.

The peer group may be defined as that constellation of associates of similar age and interest. It is perhaps the most effective determinant of the child and adolescent's attitudes—which may or may not correspond with the parents' outlook. Peer groups become effective at an early age and, according to Havighurst, have a number of functions: [62] (1) getting along with age mates; (2) developing sensitivity to values; (3) acquiring appropriate social attitudes and roles; and (4) arriving at a level of personal independence. The child is markedly influenced by his play contacts in attaining sociability, in achieving normality by avoiding behavior that might be labeled eccentric, and in acquiring attitudes on religion, ethnic relations, economic values, and various social issues.

By transferring allegiance from parental standards of dress and language and reading material to peer standards he has not necessarily become either more independent or more dependent. In the course of this transfer he may free himself somewhat from dependence upon his parents and discover a way of mutual interdependence with age-mates; or, he may learn to take the lead in the peer group, or to be a follower. There are a number of social roles available in the peer group, which can be described by such names as *clarifier, maintainer, supporter, complier, disruptor, stranger, permission giver,* and *scapegoat.* In our studies of boys and girls moving through middle childhood and adolescence, some of the most popular and successful children in the peer group created for themselves positions of independence, both of parents and peers.[63]

Most American youngsters are in school between nine and three o'clock. After school, on Saturdays and Sundays, and during vacations they spend much of their time with neighborhood companions, on the street, on the playground, in a gang, or in other groups. How do these social contacts affect personality?

Peer groups and delinquency. A great deal of research has gone to verify the fact that bad neighborhoods and companions are the most important causes of delinquency. The studies of the late Clifford Shaw and other Chicago sociologists are well known.[64] Shaw found high delinquency rates in Chicago's poorer sections, in what he called "interstitial areas" or areas in transition. Here gangs flourished and youngsters spent most of their time in the streets, in vacant lots, abandoned buildings, railroad yards, down by the river. In better residential areas, the delinquency rate dropped. In good suburban residential neighborhoods the rate fell almost to zero. Obviously factors other than neighborhood were involved, especially

[62] R. J. Havighurst, *Human development and education* (New York: Longmans, Green & Co., Inc., 1953), pp. 42-63.

[63] *Ibid.*, p. 56.

[64] C. R. Shaw, *Delinquency areas* (1929); *The jack-roller* (1930); *Brothers in crime* (1938). All published in Chicago by The University of Chicago Press.

different kinds of family control and supervision. But the type of neighborhood, Shaw found, was more important than national background or racial or religious factors. He located certain areas where ethnic composition had changed completely over a generation but where the delinquency rates had remained remarkably constant.

Other researchers confirm Shaw's findings. Thrasher studied more than a thousand gangs in Chicago [65] and reported that the type of gang, depending a good deal on the neighborhood, is a most important factor predisposing a boy toward delinquency. One psychologist concluded that delinquent associates are the strongest factor determining whether a youth will or will not commit a crime and what kind of crime it will be.[66]

However, the single-factor emphasis of Shaw and Thrasher has been questioned. According to one study, delinquent adolescents may be of two general categories: first, those who acquired their behavior in gangs, frequently emerging from interracial, lower class areas with substandard housing. In these cases there were many reports of disorganization, such as alcoholism on the part of the father. Second were the "non-gang" delinquents, who came from average neighborhoods but from unhappy family situations, with parents separated or deceased, with children hostile toward the mother, and the like. Family life was more strained than with the gang boys.[67]

Thus it may be that delinquency is only indirectly the product of gangs. The chief causative factors may well be previous experiences resulting in great emotional tension, direct contact with or observation of delinquent practices and techniques on the part of others, and to a lesser extent the effects of movies, TV, and comics. However, the effects of the neighborhood peer group cannot be ignored, if only because delinquents, like all adolescents, enjoy the companionship of others. Studies have shown that as many as two-thirds of misdemeanors occur in gangs, whether these are of the loosely knit, more integrated, or fully institutionalized type.[68]

Juvenile delinquency, then, results from a whole pattern of unfortunate social, economic, and psychological conditions which characterize certain urban areas, particularly in parts of very large cities. Remedying this situation involves large-scale social planning,

---

65 F. M. Thrasher, *The gang* (Chicago: University of Chicago Press, 1927).

66 V. Jones, Character development in children, chap. xiii in L. Carmichael (ed.), *Manual of child psychology* (2d ed.; New York: John Wiley & Sons, Inc., 1954).

67 W. W. Wattenberg and J. J. Balistrieri, Gang membership and juvenile misconduct, *Amer. sociol. Rev.*, XV (1950), 744-52.

68 M. L. Barron, *The juvenile in delinquent society* (New York: Alfred A. Knopf, Inc., 1954).

which is very difficult to bring about. On a smaller scale, however, juvenile delinquency has been reduced by substituting socially constructive programs for the destructive ones in the adolescents' peer groups. Athletic and social activities have been brought into gangs in Chicago, New York, and other metropolitan areas, which generally brings about some reduction in the delinquency rate. Similarly, the Boy Scouts and Girl Scouts, the Campfire Girls, the YMCA and YWCA, and other groups may help by giving a sense of belongingness and status to their members and by directing their activities into constructive channels. Undoubtedly more empirical study is needed in assessing the effect of community resources in solving the problem of delinquency.

Exactly how such groups as these affect the personality of their members is hard to determine. Some studies cast doubt on their effectiveness in character-building or shaping personality in socially desirable directions.[69] Others show that when a child becomes intensely interested in a group, as at a summer camp, the personality improvement may be considerable.[70] Clinical and anthropological data also indicate that one's peer groups are significant to personality development, particularly in the preadolescent and adolescent periods.[71]

Mere membership in a group does not guarantee attitude and behavior changes. Sherif points out that the degree to which a youngster takes over the attitudes, values, and norms of a social group depends on the extent to which he identifies himself with it.[72] This, in turn, depends on his need for affiliation or belongingness. These factors must be considered to understand the effects of peer groups on the personalities of children and adolescents.

SUMMARY AND CONCLUSIONS

Of the major "subcultural" influences shaping a child's personality development, the family is most significant. Relations between parents and between parent and child are particularly important for emotional security. With the many changes in family life have gone changes in ideas of rearing the young, seeking a middle course between permissiveness or overindulgence on the one hand, and

[69] E.g., H. Hartshorne and M. A. May, *Studies in deceit* (New York: The Macmillan Co., 1928).

[70] See, e.g., H. Dimock and C. Hendry, *Camping and character* (New York: Association Press, 1929).

[71] See J. B. Patrick, *The role of intimate groups in the personality development of selected college men* (U. of So. Calif. Res. Studies, 1935, No. 6).

[72] M. and C. W. Sherif, *Outline of Social Psychology* (rev. ed.; New York: Harper & Bros., 1956), chaps. vi and vii. See also their *Groups in harmony and tension* (New York: Harper & Bros., 1953).

rigidity (either overprotection or rejection) on the other. Possibly we in the United States are closer to that middle course now than we have been before. Parents also serve as models for the child's early learning of information, habits, skills and attitudes. Removal of a young child to a new family may gradually bring about profound and lasting personality changes. Recent evidence seems to suggest that the effects of institutionalization upon child personality are unfortunate.

The impact of school and peer group upon child and adolescent is, generally speaking, less significant than the effect of the family, but in certain respects and at certain stages of development the influence of school or of companions may be crucial.

SUPPLEMENTARY READINGS

Books of Readings

MACCOBY, E. E., NEWCOMB, T. M., AND HARTLEY, E. L. (eds.). *Readings in social psychology,* 3d ed. New York: Henry Holt & Co., Inc., 1958.
  Sears, R. R., Maccoby, E. E., and Levin, H. The socialization of aggression.
BRITT, S. H. (ed.). *Selected readings in social psychology.* New York: Rinehart & Co., Inc., 1950.
  Cole, L. Characteristics of a "delinquent environment."
  Gates, A. I. The curriculum.
  Johnson, C. S. Personality profile.
  Morgan, J. J. B. Effect of parental behavior on child's social development.

Other References

BOSSARD, J. H. *The sociology of child development,* rev. ed. New York: Harper & Bros., 1954.
  Perhaps the most complete statement on the relation of the child to the family setting.
BROOM, L., AND SELZNICK, P. *Sociology.* Evanston, Ill.: Row, Peterson & Co., 1955.
  Chap. iv (Socialization) and chap. x (The family) are most relevant to social influences on the child and adolescent.
BURGESS, E. W., AND LOCKE, H. J. *The family,* rev. ed. New York: American Book Co., 1953.
  A standard text that gives considerable space to the problem of socialization and family integration.
EISENSTEIN, V. W. (ed.). *Neurotic interaction in marriage.* New York: Basic Books, Inc., 1956.
ERIKSON, E. H. *Childhood and society.* New York: W. W. Norton & Co., Inc., 1950.
  A neo-Freudian presents his views on the unfolding of the child's ego.
GANS, R., STENDLER, C. B., AND ALMY, M. *Teaching young children.* New York: World Book Co., 1952.
HAYES, C. *The ape in our house.* New York: Harper & Bros., 1951.
  An entertaining account of a couple's attempt to rear a chimpanzee as their child.
HAVIGHURST, R. J., AND TABA, H. *Adolescent character and personality.* New York: John Wiley & Sons, Inc., 1949.
  The report of a number of studies, with interpretations, of family relationships, the school, and the peer group.

KIRKPATRICK, C., *The family: As process and institution.* New York: The Ronald Press Co., 1955.

Outstanding for its analysis of parent-child and parent-adolescent relationships and of family roles in general.

LEVY, J., AND MUNROE, R. *The happy family.* New York: Alfred A. Knopf, Inc., 1938.

A penetrating discussion by two counsellors on the dynamics of marital and family adjustment.

LOUTTIT, C. M. *Clinical psychology of exceptional children,* 3d ed. New York: Harper & Bros., 1957.

Chapters viii, ix, and x are particularly relevant for the problem of emotional conflicts.

MURPHY, L. B. Childhood experience in relation to personality development, chap. xxi in J. McV. Hunt (ed.), *Personality and the behavior disorders* (New York: The Ronald Press Co., 1944).

RIESMAN, D. *The lonely crowd.* New Haven, Conn.: Yale University Press, 1950.

An introduction to the peer group as it influences American character.

SINGH, J. A. L., AND ZINGG, R. M. Wolf child and feral man. New York: Harper & Bros., 1942.

The most complete source on feral cases.

THORPE, L. *Child development.* New York: The Ronald Press Co., 1956.

Excellent chapters on personality development in childhood.

WINCH, R. F. *The modern family.* New York: Henry Holt & Co., Inc., 1953.

Winch presents a moderately psychoanalytic interpretation of infancy and later life.

5

Subculture: Community, Social Class, and Ethnic Status

In the preceding chapter we have seen the primary agencies of socialization. The family remains in all societies the most potent factor in shaping the personality of the individual. In the schools, society initiates more formal control of the attitudes and value orientations of its members. In this chapter we turn to the more indirect but more pervasive influences of the wider society. Every individual is born and nurtured in a community, a class system, and an ethnocentric group. Even the family and school are part of this broad solid structure. In this context we are concerned with some of the factors and values in the community. Later there will be an analysis of the processes by which they are derived.

THE COMMUNITY

The term "community" has a variety of meanings. It can refer to a relatively wide area, such as the "world community," or to as narrow a framework as the neighborhood. In this discussion the emphasis will be on the more proximate type, the neighborhood—a segment of the larger urban unit, an ecological unit within the city, town, or village, inasmuch as the individual is most directly affected by social influences within this more restricted milieu.

Community studies have become increasingly important in sociology, anthropology, and social psychology. They provide a convenient framework in which to study attitudes, values, and behavior patterns within the larger social setting. In the United States, studies have focused to a large extent on the class structure, although that is only one aspect of the community fabric. Out of the many communities described we will select a few to show the ways in which personality development is affected by these diversified social settings.

Backward and submerged communities. Sherman and Henry investigated the people living in five neighboring Virginia communities that varied greatly in cultural and social level.[1] The most backward and isolated of these, Colvin Hollow, had no church, store, movie, or monetary system. Its children averaged only one and a half months of school a year and had a low mental level. Children under seven seemed normal, but older youngsters were dull and retarded. This suggests that cultural stimulation plays an essential role in normal mental development. The personalities of the children and adults appeared undeveloped. They lacked initiative, competitiveness, and responsiveness. However, interestingly enough, they lacked some of the conflicts and frustrations which apparently existed in individuals living in the more advanced neighboring communities.

Somewhat later, Claudia Lewis compared children in a rural Tennessee county with a group of New York youngsters of middle-class and professional background.[2] She found the Tennessee children more placid, easy-going, and untroubled, but at the same time less rebellious and less creative than the city youngsters. Why? Lewis believes the different ways of rearing children in the two areas account mainly for their different personality types. The Tennessee highlands child had a long babyhood, was accepted by parents and relatives, and was subject to few demands or restrictions compared to the middle-class city child. His life went on rather simply and placidly, with little frustration and little stimulation. He had a definite place in the family and in the community, but his parents had no rigid standards and aspirations for him. Life was calmer but less challenging, and his personality reflected this condition.

The agricultural frontier community. Compared to Colvin Hollow there is the less submerged community, as illustrated in Goldschmidt's "As You Sow"—a study of an agricultural community of

[1] M. Sherman and T. R. Henry, *The Hollow folk* (New York: The Thomas Crowell Co., 1933).

[2] C. Lewis, *Children of the Cumberland* (New York: Columbia University Press, 1946).

several thousand displaced midwesterners in the Central Valley of California.[3] This investigation, made at the end of the Depression, reflects the struggle for economic survival among farm tenants and seasonal workers in what may be called "industrialized agriculture." The community influences on the individual varied according to the group to which he belonged. A considerable degree of stratification was apparent—a contrast between the sedentary and "substantial" people who owned houses and farms, and the more unstable group, mostly outsiders who might be migrants from Oklahoma or seasonal Mexican laborers. With the growth of the "factories in the fields" [4] stratification had proceeded so far that whole communities had become lower status, in terms of social and economic position. This schism affected church identification, club membership, and social participation generally. About the only integrating force of any consequence was the schools.

Evon Vogt's *Modern Homesteaders* describes a group of Texas migrants who, during the Depression, moved to the arid, western portion of New Mexico.[5] In this relatively homogeneous community there was an insularism oriented about such frontier values as "mastery over nature." Optimistic and religious, the Homesteaders tended to live for future gratification. Another characteristic was a deep-seated individualism which did not exclude occasional "feuding" between the settlers. There was also a strong community solidarity; in fact, an ethnocentrism was exhibited in the feeling of hostility toward Navahos, Mexicans, and, to some extent, Mormons. There was some distinction in the community, however, between the Presbyterians, who might be compared to a lower middle class, and Baptists, who could be labeled as the upper lower class.

Despite the usual demands toward conformity that one finds in any small community, the marginal and isolated situation of these Homesteaders seemed to allow for variation in expression: two of the members were actually identified as atheists. It is interesting to note the extent to which the individual was attached to the community and returned to it after an absence. It would be safe to say that in the case of the Homesteaders, their local allegiance was more apparent than their identification with the larger American culture. Through the schools the younger generation acquired the proper civic attitudes, as well as a whole series of norms regarding status and roles which transcended the several hundred people and the

3 W. Goldschmidt, *As you sow* (New York: Harcourt, Brace & Co., Inc., 1947).
4 C. McWilliams, *Factories in the field* (Boston: Little, Brown & Co., 1939).
5 E. Vogt, *Modern Homesteaders* (Cambridge, Mass.: Harvard University Press, 1955).

plains of western New Mexico. Nonetheless, after more than three decades, the attachment to their own community goals and ideals was still uppermost in the value system of this erstwhile frontier community.

Middletown. Not the first, but probably the most significant, early community research by social scientists was "Middletown," studied by Robert and Helen Lynd in the mid-1920's, and again after a few years to see what the Depression had done.[6] "Middletown" was Muncie, Indiana, chosen because it seemed a typical middle-sized American city near the geographical and population center of the country. The Lynds trained their microscope on six aspects of community life: earning a living, making a home, training the young, using leisure, engaging in religious practices, and participation in community activities. One of the main conclusions of their survey had to do with the far-reaching effects of economic activity and economic status. In the Lynds' own words:

It is after all this division into working class and business class that constitutes the outstanding cleavage in Middletown. The mere fact of being born upon one or the other side of the watershed roughly formed by these two groups is the most significant single cultural factor tending to influence what one does all day long throughout one's life; whom one marries; when one gets up in the morning; whether one belongs to the Holy Roller or Presbyterian church; or drives a Ford or a Buick; whether or not one's daughter makes the desirable high school Violet Club; or one's wife meets with the Sew We Do Club or with the Art Students' League; whether one belongs to the Odd Fellows or to the Masonic Shrine; whether one sits about evenings with one's necktie off; and so on indefinitely throughout the daily comings and goings of a Middletown man, woman, or child.[7]

In their later study *Middletown in Transition* the Lynds presented a more psychological interpretation in a chapter describing the dominant values and attitudes found in that city.[8] This "Middletown Spirit" included such items as being honest, friendly, and successful; having common sense, being courageous and a good sport; beliefs that "radicals" would wreck our civilization, that good will solves most problems, that "American ways" are better than "foreign ways," that Negroes are inferior, that competition makes for progress, that labor organization is unwise and un-American, and that Christianity is the final and most superior form of religion.

The "design for living" of that central figure, the Middletown businessman, was found to be as described in the quotation which follows:

[6] R. S. and H. M. Lynd, *Middletown* (New York: Harcourt, Brace & Co., Inc., 1929).
[7] *Ibid.*, pp. 23-24.
[8] R. S. and H. M. Lynd, *Middletown in transition* (New York: Harcourt, Brace & Co., Inc., 1937), chap. xii.

He embodies the central beliefs and qualities recognized locally as desirable and American. He is essentially moderate, a middle-of-the-roader. He may have some unusual traits or abilities—a hobby, private enthusiasms for cultivated things most Middletown men know little about—provided they are not too exceptional and do not "distort" him. He must be active in trying to "get on" in the world. The quality of his life is measured in terms of tangible success, achievement, "something to show for it," ability to "produce the goods," but this success is mistrusted unless it is won by hard work, common sense, and careful planning. Hard work is more valued than "living by one's wits," common sense more than theory. He is the kind of person to whom many things may be "all right in theory, but not in practice." He should be married, have children, and be a church member, a lodge man, (though he need not go often to church or lodge meetings), and a member of a civic club, and be active in the Community Fund drive and other civic activities. He is a person who is practical and positive, not a dreamer or questioner; one who is genial, friendly, "one of us." And he must share Middletown's essential civic loyalty and optimism.[9]

Suburbia. Although there are many variations in Middletown and in what the sociologist calls the "ecological" areas of Metropolis, one of the most interesting and newest forms of community structure is "suburbia." In 1954 the editors of *Fortune* estimated that 9 million people had moved to the suburbs of American cities since 1947. It was estimated that there were some 30 million suburbanites in the United States—almost a fifth of the population.[10] The popularity of suburban life is due to dissatisfaction with living in the big city. Fairfield County, Connecticut, one of the more desirable suburbs of New York City, was described as follows:

It is a dream, a hope, a goal, a symbol. A comparative few have been born and have lived their lives here. But most have come from South and North and West, mostly by way of Manhattan canyons, looking for a pleasant place to spend their city-earned money and leisure, looking for smalltown roots without smalltown disadvantages. They want to be near the source of their often considerable income; they want the picture window views; they want super-colossal schools for their children; they want restrained neighbors. They want to belong without being bored.[11]

It is the young married, status conscious, upwardly mobile type of resident who is attracted to the suburbs. There is a similarity in the educational level and economic status of suburbanites. In one well-to-do suburb of New York, for example, a survey of the parents of public school children showed that 78 per cent were white collar (i.e. business and professional) and only 22 per cent manual workers. This kind of segregation by income level is increasingly apparent in the newer suburban communities.

9 *Ibid.*, pp. 419-21.
10 F. L. Allen, The big change in suburbia, *Harper's Magazine*, September and October, 1954.
11 Jo Matthews, in *Fairfield Co.* (Conn.) *Fair*, March 4, 1954.

In an article in *Harper's Magazine,* Frederick Lewis Allen discusses the "Big Change in Suburbia." The rise in number of commuters produces, in effect, a matriarchy in the suburbs during the day; the wife "busies herself furiously in organizations of all sorts, as if to rid herself of the frustrating feeling that the place where things are really going on is somewhere else, and that meanwhile she is condemned to play the part of a conscientious and hard-working waiting-room attendant." Furthermore, there is a shortage of unmarried men in suburbia; in Scarsdale and Bronxville, New York, for example, women between 20 and 45 outnumbered men in the same age group by three to two, according to 1950 census figures. Added to all this is the problem of constant and continuous change that occurs in the suburbs. "So frustrating is this process to dreams of rural peace," says Allen, "that most suburbanites hate to look ahead and envision the future; they can hardly help wishing that time would stand still. (Is it possible that the political conservatism of most suburban communities is related to this fear of what the future may bring?)" [12] In a word, suburbia epitomizes the desperate attempt of Americans to enjoy the advantages of both rural and urban living. Their success becomes increasingly frustrated as the suburbs spread further into the hinterland and the suburb of today becomes part of the centralized area of tomorrow.

In surveying some of the types of communities it is apparent that a number of other types have been omitted. One of these might be the "Gold Coast" of large cities with its apartment-house living, cocktail parties, avoidance of family entanglements, engagements, and higher than average marital instability. There are other derivations within this highly urbanized pattern, one example being Skid Row and its many examples of social disorganization; or artists' centers like Greenwich Village, characterized by unconventionality of its residents in tastes, vocational choices, and sex mores. There are also variations in middle and working class patterns of occupational levels, ethnic backgrounds, clubs, and associations that give color and character to each specific community. For example, it was conspicuous in Middletown that the lodges and social clubs were the fulcrum of attitudes and public opinion. Although the community is composed of a multiplicity of institutions and associations, and is expressed through family, church, economic functions, government agencies, education, and recreation, it patterns the values and aspirations of its members, and has a definite character of its own.

12 Allen, *loc. cit.,* p. 50.

SOCIAL CLASS

We have seen that a child's personality is shaped by direct social contacts in the family, school, and community. A more subtle but very significant influence is exerted by social class, which develops from the individual's "socioeconomic status." (Again, we refer primarily to children growing up in the United States, since the concept of social class is somewhat different in Europe.)

Socioeconomic status covers a great deal of ground. It overlaps not only class but education, occupation, income, and many other factors. "Low socioeconomic status" usually denotes a consistent pattern: little education, unskilled or semiskilled work, lower class social status, small income, and a poor residential area. "High socioeconomic status" connotes the opposite pattern.

His socioeconomic status limits and defines the social contacts a child will have. It affects mainly the aspects of his personality that develop through social interaction—namely, attitudes, interests, values, and habits. Before a child is born, his socioeconomic status is pretty clearly defined by the position which his parents hold in society.

Until the 1930's scant attention was given to the effects of socioeconomic status on personality. Sociologists had studied class, unemployment, social status, and the like, but seldom focused on individuals. Psychologists had measured I.Q.'s and devised personality questionnaires instead of investigating the social forces affecting personality. Researchers now tend to stress the more psychological effects of socioeconomic status. Several important studies have been done.

The Warner studies. W. Lloyd Warner, an anthropologist and sociologist at the University of Chicago, is more responsible than any one else for stimulating research into social class in America and for producing a six-fold scale of class which has become widely known and used in this country. With the aid of a number of collaborators, Warner studied an old New England community (Newburyport, Massachusetts) which was called "Yankee City." [13] Class, for these investigators, meant "two or more orders of people who are believed to be, and are accordingly ranked by the members of the community, in socially superior and inferior positions." [14] They found the natives of Yankee City had little difficulty in categorizing their fellow-townsmen as to social status. Many criteria were used, including wealth, occupation, social affiliations, area of residence, genealogy, and morals. The authors divided the population into

13 W. L. Warner and P. S. Lunt, *The social life of a modern community* (New Haven: Yale University Press, 1941).
14 *Ibid.,* p. 82.

upper, middle, and lower classes, each of which was subdivided into an upper and a lower part. Percentagewise, the class structure of Yankee City is shown in Figure 3.

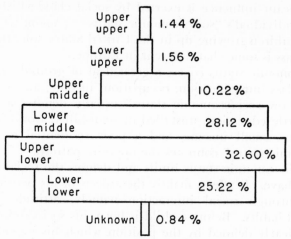

FIG. 3. Class Structure in "Yankee City."

SOURCE: Adapted from W. L. Warner and P. S. Lunt, *The Social Life of a Modern Community* (New Haven: Yale University Press, 1941), p. 88.

Besides describing the ethnic composition, economic behavior, and group affiliations of each class and subclass, the authors generalize as follows about the major values of each group:

The upper-upper class believes in the efficacy of birth and breeding, and the individuals of that class possess each in varying degrees and with proportionate feelings of security. Money is important, but its chief importance is to allow one to live properly.

The lower-upper class also believes in birth and breeding. They cannot use their money to buy birth, but they can spend it to acquire the proper upper-class secular rituals which they hope will secure them the high rank they seek. Money is very important to them, but they are willing to spend large portions of it to secure proper recognition for themselves or their children and to marry their children into the class above them.

The upper-middle class believes in money, but many of them also believe in what they call comfort. Some of them know that money is not enough to be at the top. Nevertheless, most try to get more money to gain higher status. More money is always important. Many of them want money for its own sake and because its mere accumulation has value.

The lower-middle class also wants more money and more comfort. They believe that money and morals are the keys to all of their problems. They are more secure, however, than the two lower classes, and most of them have greater psychological security than the people of the upper-middle class.

Individuals in the upper-lower class tend to be ambitious. They want money, but they are trying to acquire the symbols of higher status such as "nice furniture," "pretty yards," and "a good education." Such things differentiate them from the class below and make them more like the people who are just above them. They are much nearer the bare struggle for existence than the lower-middle class, but they utilize their money for neat-looking clothes, good magazines, and to "give our children a better education than we had."

The lower-lower class cares little for education. Money is important because it shuts the door on the ever-present wolf of want, but it is not of such importance that a parent would force his children to go to school that they might acquire an education in order to get better jobs. Money is to be spent and not saved.[15]

Davis and the Gardners made the same kind of sixfold division of social classes among the white inhabitants of "Old City" in the South.[16] They found that the three major classes illustrate general patterns of behavior. "The past is of prime importance to the upper class. Wealth and 'morality' mark the aspirations of the middle class, as well as concern with making themselves and the community 'better.' Poverty, lack of formal organization, and isolation from the other classes distinguish the lower class. . . ." [17] The authors stressed the "social perspectives" of each class, particularly their attitudes toward their own and other classes. The members of each class "think of themselves as a group and have a certain unity of outlook . . . ," with a "common set of beliefs, a common pattern of overt behavior, and other traits which function as symbols of status." [18] The authors note, however, that there is no strict uniformity within a class; it is rather a certain range of behavior and "modal average." They also discovered less social distance between an individual's own and adjacent classes than between classes farther from him on the social scale. The white inhabitants of Old City tended to minimize the differences between themselves and those above them, partly because of a tendency to identify themselves with their superiors.[19]

The significance of social class in the United States is suggested by Warner in a later publication in which he says:

. . . recent scientific studies of social class in the several regions of the United States demonstrate that it is a major determinant of individual decisions and social actions; that every major area of American life is directly and indirectly influenced by our class order; and that the major decisions of most individuals are partly controlled by it.[20]

15 *Ibid.*, p. 200.
16 A. Davis, B. B. Gardner, and M. R. Gardner, *Deep South* (Chicago: University of Chicago Press, 1941).
17 *Ibid.*, p. 83.
18 *Ibid.*, p. 71.
19 *Ibid.*, pp. 72-73.
20 From *Social class in America* by W. Lloyd Warner, Marchia Meeker, and Kenneth Eells. Copyright, 1949, by Science Research Associates, Inc. Reprinted by permission.

Thus Warner not only outlines a six-class system and describes the characteristics of persons at each level, but he also implies that social class is important all over the United States, though it varies somewhat from community to community.

Other analyses of class. A number of social scientists would differ with Warner as to the generality of social class in American communities and as to its significance in people's lives. The Useems and Tangent, for example, in a midwestern prairie town of 3500, found only two distinct strata, called locally the "Tops" and the "Bottoms," names deriving from the residential areas of the two groups. These classes seem to have developed within a couple of generations from the pioneering farm residents of the community, with stratification promising to increase rather than the reverse.[21] West published a rather complete study of a small cross-roads village of about 275 persons in the southern midwest area.[22] Along with the loafing and gossip groups in "Plainville" he found a class organization which

might well be called a "superorganization," because it provides for every person living there a master pattern for arranging according to relative rank every other individual, and every family, clique, lodge, club, church, and other organization or association in Plainville society. It provides also a set of patterns for expected behavior according to class, and a way of judging all norms and deviations from these norms in individual behavior.[23]

Yet, curiously enough, West found that many if not most Plainvillers completely denied the existence of class in their community. They would say with pride: "This is *one* place where ever'body is equal. You don't find no classes here."

Basically, Plainville was a two-class system, each comprising about half the population. The upper class was described as "good, honest, self-respecting, average, everyday working people," or perhaps as "nice, refined, better class people," or "people who are all right." The others were "good lower class people," except some who were a "lower element" and a small group at the bottom "who live like animals." Moving from one of these classes to the other was unusual, though not impossible.[24]

Thus in two smallish midwestern communities fairly definite two-class systems appeared. Other American rural communities

21 J. Useem, P. Tangent, and R. Useem, Stratification in a prairie town, *Amer. sociol. Rev.*, VII (1942), 331-42.
22 J. West, *Plainville, USA* (New York: Columbia University Press, 1945).
23 *Ibid.*, p. 115.
24 *Ibid.*, chap. iii.

studied about the same time, however, showed a great deal of variation in the patterns of stratification discovered.

The Bureau of Agricultural Economics of the United States Department of Agriculture sponsored sociological studies of six

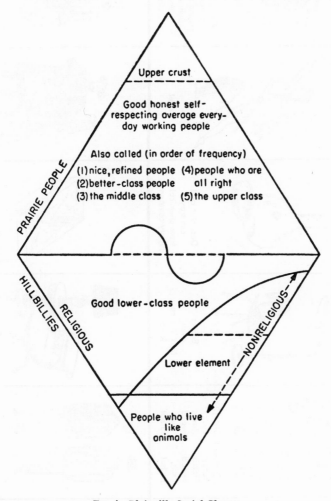

FIG. 4. Plainville Social Classes.

SOURCE: J. West, *Plainville, USA* (New York: Columbia University Press, 1945), p. 117.

communities which differed greatly in their stability.[25] One of
them, a New Hampshire farming community was found to have
four distinct strata: farm owners, tenants, laborers, and "floaters" or

[25] C. C. Taylor (ed.), Culture of a contemporary rural community, *Rural Life Studies*,
Nos. 1-6 (Washington, D. C.: U. S. Bureau of Agricultural Economics, 1942).

	CLOTHES	FURNITURE	USEFUL OBJECTS	ENTERTAINMENT	SALADS
HIGH-BROW	TOWN Fuzzy Harris tweed suit, no hat — COUNTRY Fuzzy Harris tweed suit, no hat	Eames chair, Kurt Versen lamp	Decanter and ash tray from chemical supply company	Ballet	Greens, olive oil, wine vinegar, ground salt, ground pepper, garlic, unwashed salad bowl
UPPER MIDDLE-BROW	TOWN Brooks suit, regimental tie, felt hat — COUNTRY Quiet tweed jacket, knitted tie	Empire chair, converted sculpture lamp	Silver cigaret box with wedding ushers' signatures	Theater	Same as high-brow but with tomatoes, avocado. Roquefort cheese added

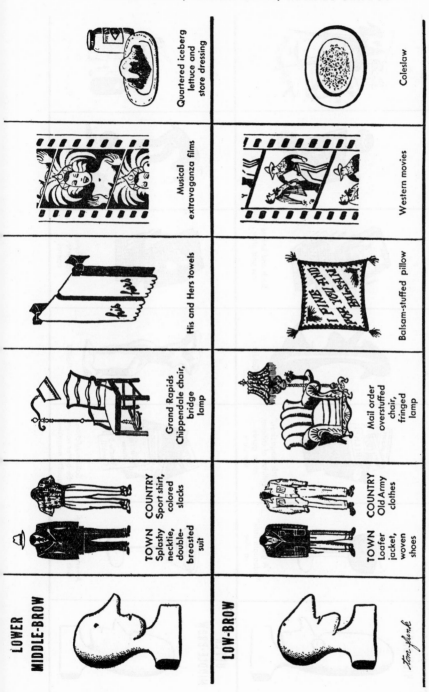

Fig. 5. Everyday Tastes from High-Brow to Low-Brow Are Classified on Chart. Although Somewhat Facetious, This Chart Implies That There Are Definite Values and Codes Prescribed in These Four None-Too-Well Defined Forms of Social Behavior.

(Continued on following pages.)

Source: Russell Lynes, in *Life*, April, 1949. Used by permission of the author.

	DRINKS	READING	SCULPTURE	RECORDS	GAMES	CAUSES
HIGH-BROW	A glass of "adequate little" red wine	"Little magazines," criticism of criticism, avant garde literature	Calder	Bach and before Ives and after	Go	Art
UPPER MIDDLE-BROW	A very dry Martini with lemon peel	Solid nonfiction, the better novels quality magazines	Maillol	Symphonies, concertos, operas	The Game	Planned parenthood

FIG. 5. (Concluded.)

migrant workers. In Irwin, Iowa, and among the white farmers of Harmony, Georgia, some differentiation between owners and tenants was found, but hardly a class distinction. In another community, situated in the Kansas Dustbowl, the division into Mennonites and "white men" (non-Mennonites) was "about the only example found of any grouping of which the people are keenly conscious." Businessmen and farmers had about the same income and working hours, and the population was extremely mobile, which tended to prevent the formation of classes and to foster a tendency to judge and rate each person individually. As the author puts it:

> The community does not consider everyone the equal of everyone else. Some individuals are considered less desirable or even worthless, but they are considered as individuals rather than as members of a group or class, and are characterized as personalities.[26]

The observations made by Granville Hicks in *Small Town* are relevant at this point. Here is an analysis by a sensitive and observant literary man who settled down in a small upstate New York town and participated actively in its life.[27] Hicks found only two classes, an upper and a lower, with no criteria being very satisfactory as differentiators between them. On the whole, it seemed to him that class divisions were essentially subjective—that a person belonged to the class he wanted to belong to. Class distinctions were recognized, and people had no difficulty in determining the status of a particular family. Hicks' conclusions, however, are penetrating, and probably hold true for class and status relationships in many a small town:

> When all is said and done, however, the situations in which class lines matter are less numerous than those in which they don't count. People meet more often in the stores, the drinking joints, and the barber shop than anywhere else. They meet and they talk, and class lines, so far as I can see, make little difference. People of the lower class come to square dances as well as people of the upper class, and often they dance in the same sets . . . Perhaps some lower class persons deliberately avoid church suppers, but others come and eat without embarrassment. Once in a long time a political contest seems to align one class against the other, but in general class has little to do with politics. . . .
>
> The truth is that in nine situations out of ten the class structure is overshadowed by a basic social equality that results from the smallness of the community and the sense of a common past. . . . In Roxborough almost everyone dresses alike . . . and . . . talks alike. Everyone knows everyone else and speaks to everyone else. . . . It is no wonder that for all the more important affairs of life Roxborough is a classless society.[28]

26 *Ibid., Rural Life Studies*, No. 2 by E. H. Bell.
27 G. Hicks, *Small town* (New York: The Macmillan Co., 1947).
28 *Ibid.*, pp. 97-98.

The viewpoint of Hicks, however, would not be accepted by most sociologists as applicable to communities in general. They find anywhere from two to six major class groups in all sizable American communities, and agree that these class differentiations have much to do with the patterning of social behavior. Further evidence as to the effects of class differences is given in the Kinsey report.[29] Judging "social level" both in terms of education and occupation, Kinsey found great variation in sexual behavior between lower- and upper-class men. For example, between the ages of sixteen and twenty, masturbation and petting to climax was much more frequent in upper- than in lower-class males, while premarital intercourse and homosexual outlet were much less frequent. Considerable differences were also found in attitudes toward nudity and in patterns of erotic arousal. Kinsey comments succinctly: "Each social level is convinced that its pattern is the best of all patterns; but each level rationalizes its behavior in its own way." [30]

Thus, in recent years, a number of sociologists have studied the effects of socioeconomic status, especially class membership, on social behavior. To some extent, they have studied also its effects upon the values and attitudes of individuals. Their findings are of great interest to social psychologists.

The social psychologist, however, would like to go still further. He would like to know the extent to which socioeconomic status affects personality and social behavior, as compared with the influence of family, school, and other institutions. He would like to know which areas of behavior and personality are affected and which are unaffected. He would like to explore the psychological processes by which the effects are produced in the child and adolescent. He would also like to explore individual differences, and the reasons for them, among members of each class.

INFLUENCE OF CLASS ON PERSONALITY

Several studies have focused more specifically upon the effects of class on the personalities and behavior of its membership. Hollingshead, for example, investigated the relation between adolescents' social behavior and their class position in a midwestern community of 10,000.[31] He found that upper- and middle-class children are taught not to be aggressive, to have good manners, to study hard, to attend Sunday school, and to avoid making friends with lower-class chil-

---

[29] A. C. Kinsey, W. B. Pomeroy, and C. E. Martin, *Sexual behavior in the human male* (Philadelphia: W. B. Saunders Co., 1948), chap. x.

[30] *Ibid.*, p. 384.

[31] A. B. Hollingshead, *Elmtown's youth* (New York: John Wiley & Sons, Inc., 1949).

dren. By contrast, the child in the lowest class learns that he and his family are held in contempt by boys and girls in the higher classes. Frequently he comes to resent his family and his dependence upon it for food, clothing, and shelter. But he has little family supervision and becomes quite independent by the time of adolescence. He is greatly influenced by other lower-class youths in the cliques and other groups to which he belongs.[32]

Hollingshead concluded that class values and patterns of behavior, working through the family and neighborhood subcultures "not only set the stage upon which the child acts, but they also provide him with ways of acting and definitions of action. In addition, they make him realize that he will be rewarded for some kinds of behavior and punished for others. They provide him with roles, teach him how to play them, and accord him different status positions as he plays such roles as child in the family, pupil in the school, and little boy on the street. As he participates in successive social situations, he learns to act in certain ways, to regard himself as a valued member of the group or as an unwanted person. Unconsciously, he is being molded into a personality that is simultaneously a creature of his experiences and a creator of new situations in which he will act as a molder of conduct." [33]

Allison Davis has described the way social class membership affects personality.[34] Using data from both white and Negro studies, he showed how behavior is defined according to class standards—modified, of course, by the interpretation given by the child's own family. He found that class membership patterns a child's roles, his goals, ethical codes, and other values. Class defines and limits the way he eats, his choice of playmates, selection of an occupation, the time and place of recreation, the chores he has to do, the rooms and articles he may use, his clothing, his studying, his use of money, and his conceptions of right and wrong. Davis presented thorough data on contrasting value systems and methods of child training in the lower-middle and lower classes of Negro society in two southern cities.

Ericson showed that child-rearing practices differed in middle- and lower-class white families.[35] Fewer middle-class children were breast-fed. They were weaned earlier from either breast or bottle. Three times as many middle-class children were thumbsuckers!

---

32 *Ibid.*, pp. 443-44.

33 *Ibid.*, p. 445.

34 A. Davis, Child training and social class, chap. xxxiv in R. Barker *et al.* (eds.), *Child behavior and development* (New York: McGraw-Hill Book Co., Inc., 1943).

35 M. C. Ericson, Social status and child-rearing practices, *Amer. J. Sociol.*, LII (1946), 190-92.

Middle-class parents taught bowel and bladder control earlier, but it was achieved no sooner than with lower-class children. Lower-class families were more lenient in their training and in their demands that a child assume responsibility, contrary to what has been popularly supposed. This delay seemed to make learning easier and to prevent frustrations and anxieties.

Unfortunately Ericson's study did not compare directly the personalities of children reared under these different training systems, which was an important check to make.[36] When children older than Ericson's subjects (maximum age seven) were studied, the personality adjustment of those in the middle class was found to be better. Brown discovered that differences in the emotional stability of 1,650 children between nine and fifteen were much more significantly related to socioeconomic status than to religion or geographic location.[37] Emotional instability rose significantly as socioeconomic status fell. The work of Springer confirms that of Brown.[38] Springer compared 415 children aged six to twelve from poor neighborhoods with a like number of middle-class children, the two groups being equated for age and intelligence. He found significantly more problem tendencies and emotional instability in the lower-class children.

The apparent inconsistency between Ericson's and the last two studies might be explained thus: the middle-class training, with its emphasis on supervision and assuming responsibility, arouses more early anxiety and frustration but at the same time prepares the child for adjusting to the fairly strict regulations of school life and of adult life in general. The lower-class child, more independent and less frustrated in his early years, is less well prepared for supervision and conformity. This hypothesis seems reasonable in view of evidence that teachers in America "represent middle-class attitudes and enforce middle-class values and manners."[39] Small wonder that the lower-class child has difficulty adjusting to standards of the essentially middle-class elementary and high school!

Lower- and middle-class values. More recent studies of social class differences in early childhood training find less distinction than

36 The personality contrast found by Lewis between Tennessee and New York City children is relevant here. See above, page 124.

37 F. Brown, A comparative study of the influence of race and locale upon emotional stability of children, *J. genet. Psychol.*, XLIX (1936), 325-42.

38 N. N. Springer, Influence of general social status on emotional stability of children, *J. genet. Psychol.*, LIII (1938), 321-28; Influence of general social status on school children's behavior, *J. educ. Res.*, XXXII (1939), 583-91.

39 W. L. Warner, R. J. Havighurst, and M. B. Loeb, *Who shall be educated?* (New York: Harper & Bros., 1944).

formerly between lower- and middle-class methods. For example, while lower-class parents are more severe in punishment and in toilet-training demands, and while middle-class parents have higher education expectations for their children, no differences were found in display of aggression in the home, or in the amount of attention given children by the father.[40]

Some of these results may be due to the mobility of lower-class members up the status scale. Others may result from difficulties or errors involved in interviewing; for example, middle-class mothers may play down their severity, or lower-class mothers may be embarrassed about uncleanliness or aggression. In any event, it seems that the middle-class child or adolescent is strongly affected by taboos on free sex experience and aggression; certainly the lower-class child is permitted more physical activity in fist fights. According to Warner, the middle class is oriented toward restraint, deferred goals, and achievement of various skills. In the lower class there is less incentive for this kind of planning and symbolic gratification. Anxiety centers about physical necessities rather than social approval and other indirect forms of satisfaction.[41]

It may well be, however, that the results reported are more affected by time, place, and special conditions than the investigators thought. A 1955 study, for example, reports some rather different findings in this area.[42] Middle-class mothers permitted more aggression against parents, were less severe in toilet-training, and were more responsive to the baby's crying. Middle-class mothers wanted their children to be "well adjusted," while working-class mothers wanted theirs to be "good" or "nice." Middle-class children did more thumbsucking and working-class children more nailbiting. White suggests that there is no fixed relation between social class and child-rearing practices, and that our current ideas may have to be revised.

Kornhauser made an extensive study of the psychological bases of class divisions in American society.[43] He concluded that a continuous selective factor operates which "tends to bring to the upper

40 R. J. Havighurst and A. Davis, Social class differences in child rearing, *Amer. sociol. Rev.,* XX (1955), 438-42.

41 W. L. Warner, *American life—dream and reality* (Chicago: University of Chicago Press, 1953), pp. 86-92.

42 M. S. White, Effects of social class position on child-rearing practices and child behavior, *Amer. Psychologist,* X (1955), 440.

43 A. W. Kornhauser, Analysis of "class" structure of contemporary American society, chap. xi in G. W. Hartmann and T. M. Newcomb (eds.), *Industrial conflict* (New York: The Cordon Co., Inc., 1939).

levels those persons who have greater mental ability, longer school-ing, and such personal qualities as self-confidence, energy, ambition, forcefulness, hard-headedness, and willingness to 'play the game.' The middle-class positions go more largely to persons of moderate abilities and education, with personality traits like industry, loyalty, orderliness, and modest ambitions, playing a more prominent role. To the lower levels are left those of less intellectual competence and training, on the average, and those less characterized by the qualities conducive to 'success.' The constant sifting tends to create groups and classes which differ in their average understanding of social problems and in the personal aims and orientations in terms of which they take their stands toward public issues, leaders, and sym-bols." [44]

These differences, Kornhauser added, are accentuated by the dif-ferential training given in the higher and lower classes. As to attitudes, he found large differences between upper and lower economic groups with respect to the New Deal, labor unions, gov-ernmental control of industry, and distribution of wealth. He also found large differences in personal satisfaction—in feelings about opportunity to enjoy life, about pay, job security, and chance to get ahead. Kornhauser, however, found no clear dividing lines between classes, and he found considerable variability within each income and occupational group. He concluded that his findings support neither speculative theories of conflicting class attitudes and class antago-nisms nor theories postulating complete harmony of interests among different segments of the American population. [45]

Differences in the values and attitudes of middle- and working-class members have been found in later studies, but the most clear-cut differences tend to be found in fairly restricted areas such as the value of a college education or the importance of congeniality in a job. [46] For example; the percentages recommending a college edu-cation for young people were as follows:

Professional people	74%
White-collar workers	65
Business and proprietors	62
Skilled labor	53
Semiskilled	49
Domestic and personal service workers	42

[44] *Ibid.*, pp. 258-59.
[45] *Ibid.*, p. 258.
[46] H. H. Hyman, The value systems of different classes, in R. Bendix and S. M. Lipset (eds.), *Class, status and power* (Glencoe, Ill.: Free Press, 1953).

Or again, with respect to the criteria to be considered in choosing an occupation:

	Per cent mentioning	
Males between 14-20	Congeniality	Economic benefit
Wealthy or prosperous	61%	15%
Middle class	57%	17%
Lower class	42%	29%

These differences are in the expected direction: professional and business people value college education more highly than working people. But the differences are not very great: about two-thirds of the former recommend a college education, but so do nearly half the manual workers.

In a recent study of a western community by one of the authors, many of the expected differences in political attitude were found between white-collar and manual-worker groups. Also there were differences in some activities; for example, manual workers were less likely to play bridge, use the library, or learn a musical instrument. On the other hand, in many places where one might expect to find differences, they did not materialize. In answer to the question, "If someone made you a gift of $10,000 tomorrow, what would you do with it?" there were no significant differences between the responses of economic groups, though there were between men and women. Similarly white-collar and manual workers showed no important differences in description of their greatest worries, in their favorite radio and TV programs, in newspaper and magazine preferences, in type and number of hobbies, or in classes and courses taken in the junior college extension division or elsewhere. Conceivably this lack of differentiation might be due to the more equalitarian nature of a newer western, as compared with an older eastern community. To make a test, a similar study was done in a New England community comparable in census characteristics. Generally speaking, the same lack of differences was found, with the exception of magazine preferences and courses taken. In all probability this fact is to be explained by recent social changes, which will be discussed in a later chapter.

CONSCIOUSNESS OF CLASS

One difficulty in studying socioeconomic status is to find valid criteria by which to differentiate social or economic classes. Income, occupation, and education are used as criteria for class, but no one of them seems satisfactory. Hyman showed that subjective status also is important—"a person's conception of his own position relative to other individuals." [47] Hyman's findings suggested a reason for

---

[47] H. H. Hyman, *The psychology of status* (Arch. Psychol., No. 269, 1942), p. 5.

discrepancy between objective and subjective status. "Individuals operate for the most part in small groups within the total society, and the total population may have little relevance for them. Far more important are their friends, people they work with. Consequently, objective measures will very likely differ from subjective measures if total population is the basis for the determination of objective status." [48] Hyman set up a scale to measure subjective status, but found the relationship between subjective status and radicalism of attitude is not clear, though differences were in the expected direction. [49]

Centers went further than Hyman, making "class" a strictly psychological phenomenon. [50] Stratification, he said, is objective, deriving from the prevailing economic system. But "classes are psycho-social groupings, . . . essentially subjective in character, dependent upon class consciousness (i.e., a feeling of group membership), and class lines of cleavage may or may not conform to what seem to social scientists to be logical lines of cleavage in the objective or stratification sense." [51]

Interviewing 1,100 persons, a national cross-section of the adult male population, Centers found in 1945 the following percentages [52] identifying themselves with each social class:

Upper class 3%
Middle class 43%
Working class 51%
Lower class 1%

Queries as to the basis for affiliating oneself with a certain class showed that occupation was most important. Nearly three-quarters of business, professional, and clerical people identified themselves with the middle or upper classes; 79 per cent of manual workers identified themselves with the working and lower classes. Centers discovered class identification was most intense in the upper and the working classes and less strong in the middle class. Furthermore, there was a marked linkage between the individual's occupational affiliation and his expressed class position. For instance, within the middle class the higher the rating of the occupation by an individual, the more he considered himself a member of the middle class. Likewise within the lower or working class the lower

48 *Ibid.*, p. 24.
49 *Ibid.*, pp. 76-79.
50 R. Centers, *The psychology of social classes* (Princeton, N. J.: Princeton University Press, 1949).
51 *Ibid.*, p. 27.
52 *Ibid.*, p. 77. This distribution has larger percentages in the two higher categories than do distributions based on economic or educational criteria.

the occupational rating, the more potent was the working class identification.[53]

Centers also found that while a person's occupational status is a
better index to his attitudes than subjective class affiliation, the latter also is important. He showed that when people of a given occupation differ in class membership, they also differ in attitude.
Conversely, "if people's class identifications are the same, their attitudes tend to be similar even though their objective occupational
positions are different." [54] Centers concluded that objective and
subjective data together enable us to predict attitudes better than
either criterion separately.

Many sociologists dislike defining class subjectively. Lynd, for
example, criticized Centers for dodging "the fact of objective class
membership based squarely on occupation and resulting wealth"
which "enables him to bypass the objective power relations of class,
to see class struggle as a cloud as yet little larger than a man's
hand. . . ." [55]

These differences of opinion, it seems to the authors, stem from
differences in orientation. Lynd was interested in the ramifications
of class stratification for social cleavage, social change, and power
relationships in society. Working at this level, he was not particularly concerned with the individual and his attitudes. Centers and
Hyman, as social psychologists, dealt with attitudes and individual
differences. Hence their finding that subjective status differs somewhat from objectively determined status is important. It helps us
understand the case of a poverty-stricken old family whose attitudes
and values are those of the community's aristocrats, or of a well-to-do
professional man who is an active member of a radical political
party.

Related to the above considerations is the matter of awareness or
salience of class in people's thinking. Most investigators have assumed a high degree of conscious awareness of class position on the
part of their respondents. It seemed to one of the authors that a

53 R. Centers, The intensity dimension of class consciousness and some social and
psychological correlates, *J. soc. Psychol.*, XLIV (1956), 101-14.

54 R. Centers, The American class structure, in Swanson *et al.*, *Readings* (2d ed.),
pp. 299-311.

55 R. S. Lynd, Tiptoeing around class, *New Republic*, July 25, 1949, pp. 17-18. A recent study compares five methods (index of status characteristics, education, occupation,
Centers' subjective questions, and an open-end questionnaire) with a number of behavioral items (membership in voluntary organizations, religious behavior, political
preferences, listening and reading habits, travel experience, etc.). Results indicated
that the objective measurements were the best predictors and subjective indices the
worst. The index of status characteristics was the most reliable tool of the five. See
J. L. Haer, Predictive utility of five indices of social stratification, *Amer. sociol. Rev.*,
XXII (1957), 541-46.

necessary first step is to discover whether or not class is a significant variable in people's thinking. So the following open-ended question was devised, and given to a sample of the residents of Ventura, California.[56]

What would you say are the most important *differences* found among the people of Ventura? That is, how do you divide them up in your mind?

Responses were classified as follows:

Class or status	14%
Economic	17
Occupational	14
Old-timers vs. newcomers	9
Religious	9
Ethnic	8
Attitudinal	6
Residential area	3
Miscellaneous	9
"There are no differences"	2
Don't know	2
No answer	7
	100%

The class or status answers (e.g., upper, middle, and lower) and the economic (e.g., the rich and the poor) together make up 31 per cent of the total. Some of the occupational classifications also lean toward class or economic categories, while others do not. Altogether about 35–40 per cent of the answers are oriented toward socio-economic status, and somewhat more—say 40–50 per cent—are not so oriented.

When the identical open-ended, projective-type question was used in a similar study of a cross-section of a 200-year-old New England community, the results were almost exactly the same.[57] These studies tend to challenge the assumption so often made that class and status are at the forefront of people's consciousness, though they do not deny the very real effects of socioeconomic influences upon personality.

Another bit of evidence of the same sort came to light in the confusion and doubt on the part of respondents when later questions on social class were asked. About a quarter to a third of the respondents seemed unfamiliar with or puzzled about the concept of class.[58] The same thing was found in a study of a much larger community, Minneapolis, where over a third of the respondents said

[56] S. S. Sargent, Class and class consciousness in a California town, *Social Problems,* I (1953), 22-27.

[57] S. S. Sargent, Unpublished study.

[58] Sargent, Class and class consciousness in a California town, *op. cit.*

they belonged to no class, didn't know, or refused to answer.[59] This kind of evidence parallels the finding of Mills and others as to the lack of class consciousness in the United States.[60] In all probability the great degree of social mobility and social change, especially since World War II, has considerably changed the picture of stratification in our country.[61] We shall return to this topic in a later chapter.

Summarizing, we see that class, as an aspect of socioeconomic status, is a significant determinant of a child's patterns of social behavior, his values and attitudes, and perhaps other aspects of personality. Research on class does not provide perfect agreement as to the number of classes found in the United States or as to the specific effects upon personality and behavior. Class has been defined either by objective criteria, such as income, occupation, or education, or subjectively, according to a person's group identifications or conception of his relative position. For most persons objective and subjective criteria agree, though exceptions occur. Some recent evidence casts doubt on the assumption that Americans are continually aware of class and class differentiation.[62]

ETHNIC STATUS

Another broad social factor which may affect child personality development is "ethnic status," a term covering differences in race, religion, nationality, language, and culture. Generally speaking, if he belongs to the accepted racial, national, and religious groups, his ethnic status is not a significant influence, as compared with family, school, community, and socioeconomic factors. But if he is Negro or Mongolian, Jewish or Catholic, or of foreign extraction, his minority group status may have important effects upon his personality.

---

[59] N. Gross, Social class identification in the urban community, *Amer. sociol. Rev.,* XVIII (1953), 398-404.

[60] C. W. Mills, *White collar* (New York: Oxford University Press, 1951), chap. xv.

[61] Cf. K. B. Mayer, *Class and society* (Garden City, N. Y.: Doubleday & Co., Inc., 1955), chaps. iv and viii.

[62] Space has permitted only a partial discussion of the various effects of class position on behavior patterns in American life. For example, there is the effect of class on religion (T. F. Hoult, Economic class consciousness in American Protestantism, *Amer. sociol. Rev.,* XV [1950], 97-100); on marriage adjustment (J. Roth and R. F. Peck, Social class and social mobility factors related to marital adjustment, *Amer. sociol. Rev.,* XVI [1951], 478-86, or R. C. Williamson, Socio-economic factors in marital adjustment in an urban setting, *Amer. sociol. Rev.,* XIX [1954], 213-16). The effect of class on attitudes will be discussed in Chapter 8. It is regrettable that space confines our discussion of the class system to American culture. Typical of some of the analyses of class factors in other national cultures are A. Inkeles and P. H. Rossi, National comparisons of occupational prestige, *Amer. J. Sociol.,* LXI (1956), 329-39; or A. Inkeles, Social stratification and mobility in the Soviet Union, pp. 609-22, in R. Bendix and S. M. Lipset (eds.), *Class, status and power* (Glencoe, Ill., Free Press, 1953).

In the United States there are many ethnic minority groups against whom discrimination is directed. First by far is the Negro, who, as Dollard and Myrdal have shown,[63] belongs to a definite lower caste in the South and who is the recipient of economic and social discrimination all over the country. Next in order comes the Jew. But other minority groups have felt the whiplash of prejudice from time to time Orientals in the Far West, Mexicans and Spaniards in the Southwest, French Canadians in the Northeast, and Poles or Italians in many parts of the East and Middle West are good examples.

Growing up in the shadow of race. Probably the best studies of the effects of minority group status upon personality have been sponsored and published by the American Council on Education. A number of noted scholars collected and interpreted data on Negro personality development in the rural South, the urban South, the middle states, and in a northern city.[64] They combined statistical, observational, and case study approaches in answering the question, "How does the fact of being born a Negro affect the developing personality of a boy or girl?"

Their answer is clear. The American Negro child grows up in the "shadow of race." Gradually or suddenly he learns he is a member of a race considered inferior and assigned to an unfavorable status within the American culture pattern. The effects of this lower caste status are apparent in almost every Negro personality, though it is not necessarily the most important personality determinant.

The point was driven home with great clarity in the Supreme Court decision banning racial segregation in the schools of our country, promulgated on May 17, 1954. This unanimous decision read in part as follows:

[Referring to children in grade and high schools] To separate them from others of similar age and qualifications solely because of their race generates a feeling of inferiority as to their status in the community that may affect their hearts and minds in a way unlikely ever to be undone.

[63] J. Dollard, *Caste and class in a southern town* (New Haven: Yale University Press, 1937); G. Myrdal, *An American dilemma* (New York: Harper & Bros., 1944).

[64] C. S. Johnson, *Growing up in the black belt* (Washington, D. C.: American Council on Education, 1941); A. Davis and J. Dollard, *Children of bondage* (Washington, D. C.: American Council on Education, 1940); E. F. Frazier, *Negro youth at the crossways* (Washington, D. C.: American Council on Education, 1940); W. L. Warner, B. H. Junker, and W. A. Adams, *Color and human nature* (Washington, D. C.: American Council on Education, 1941); R. L. Sutherland, *Color, class and personality* (Washington, D. C.: American Council on Education, 1942).

The Supreme Court decision quoted with approval a finding in a relevant Kansas case:

Segregation of white and colored children in public schools has a detrimental effect upon the colored children. The impact is greater when it has the sanction of the law; for the policy of separating the races is usually interpreted as denoting the inferiority of the Negro group. A sense of inferiority affects the motivation of a child to learn. Segregation with the sanction of law, therefore, has a tendency to retard the educational and mental development of Negro children and to deprive them of some of the benefits they would receive in a racially integrated school system.

Reactions to discrimination. The 1954 Court decision derived in large part from a brief on the effects of segregation which had been signed by a large group of social scientists. Among other things, this report noted that Negro children of lower socioeconomic status "may react by overt aggressions and hostility directed toward their own group or members of the dominant group." On the other hand, middle and upper class members are more likely to "react to their racial frustrations and conflicts by withdrawal and submissive behavior."

"Minority group children of all social and economic classes," the report said, "often react with a generally defeatist attitude and a lowering of personal ambitions." It added that segregation was bad for the majority group children too; they had been taught principles of equality but now were encouraged to think of whole groups of people as inferior, which set up emotional conflicts.

The volume summarizing the American Council on Education findings noted that the Negro youth typically adopts one or another of four ways of reacting to his inferior minority status: [65]

1. He may attempt to dodge the castelike barrier by "passing over"— i.e., passing for white, if his features are light enough, or he may simply avoid contacts with white persons.
2. He may compensate by showing pride in the Negro race, praising and defending its virtues and achievements.
3. He may strike back, through direct or sublimated forms of aggressive behavior.
4. He may adopt an outwardly servile or submissive demeanor consistent with his subordinate social status.

The particular pattern adopted by an individual depends upon many factors, notably the attitudes and teachings of his family.

"Learning how to be colored in a white world is a difficult task," concluded Sutherland. "Conditions of discrimination vary in different localities; they vary to some extent according to social class; and

[65] Sutherland, *op. cit.*

they often vary in their effects upon different personalities. Some youth make the adjustment easily, while for others the problem remains a constant source of conflict." [66]

Other types of reactions to the discrimination that minority group members experience are described by Gordon Allport: [67]

1. Clowning, as in the hyperdevelopment by some Negroes of their drawl and other stereotypes. This behavior elicits a patronizing sympathy on the part of some of the dominant group—a few coins may be dropped into his hand.

2. Clannishness or the "strengthening of in-group ties." This may involve joining organizations, such as the National Association for the Advancement of Colored People, or drifting into a state of aloofness. Some minority group members insist that it is better to live apart and feel a minimum of anguish than attempt the more painful course of integration. Undoubtedly, a number of southern Negroes prefer the segregated schools they have at present to bi-racial institutions they may have in the future. Parents in minority groups debate in their own minds whether it is better to tell their children about the world outside and thus prepare them psychologically for the shocks, or let them have a few untroubled years before reality rears its ugly head. The Jew in the Bronx, or the Negro in rural Alabama, generally has less personality conflict than either would have in Hilltown, Iowa.

3. There is shyness and cunning, especially when survival depends on dishonesty. It is doubtful that the Jews could have survived persecutions in Eastern Europe if they had not resorted to cunning. "Sneaky" traits are found among our southern Negro, such as taking food home from the master's kitchen, not only for economic reasons, but for petty revenge.

4. The rejection of his group may be sufficiently intense to stimulate self-hate in the Negro or some form of aggressive behavior toward his fellow minority group members. This may be expressed by the "passing," mentioned above, or by a neurotic kind of self-depreciation. There are, of course, wide variations in personality manifestations among members of minority groups just as there are among members of the in-group. Consider the North Italian's depreciation of the Sicilian or Calabrian, the attitude of the German Jew toward Polish Jew, or the sharp class distinctions among our American Negroes.

5. There is the trait of sympathy not infrequently found among minority group members. They can readily identify with members of other out-groups. It is no accident that Julius Rosenwald contributed heavily to the betterment of the Negro.

66 *Ibid.*, p. 59.
67 G. W. Allport, *The nature of prejudice* (Reading, Mass.: Addison-Wesley Pub. Co., Inc., 1954).

One might summarize Allport's thesis that frustration resulting from discrimination leads to two general reaction tendencies: one, outward blame or recrimination toward the dominant group; two, self-blame or inferiority feelings.[68] The first is demonstrated in militancy or aggressiveness, slyness and cunning, persecution complexes, and "enhanced" striving—the tendency to do better than the majority group, as often seen among the study habits of American Jews. The second disposition has a number of patterns: seclusion and passivity, clowning, neuroticism, self-hate, and "symbolic status striving"—the pride some individuals have in their success, even though it fits the stereotype with which they have been labeled, as shown by the Negro soldier's pride in his shiny brass buckle or his impeccable uniform. Naturally, these tendencies may or may not develop in any given individual. One can hardly emphasize too frequently the necessity of avoiding stereotypes in classifying reactions of minority group members. The particular pattern adopted by an individual depends upon many factors: who are his playmates, what happens at school, the varieties of contacts he has with individuals of the other group, and most important, the attitudes and teachings of his family.

Jews are a religious rather than a racial minority in American society; they are subjected to but a fraction of the discrimination visited upon the Negro. Nonetheless, anti-Semitism is considerable in many parts of the United States. Typically, a Jewish child learns rather early in life that he belongs to a group considered different, if not inferior. If the prejudice and discrimination present in the child's community are great, or if the child is very sensitive, he is likely to develop some degree of conflict and to show one or another compensatory defense mechanism. Clinicians often report that a major or minor factor in a Jewish person's maladjustment is his reaction to his unfavorable ethnic status.

To a lesser degree, minority group status may affect the personalities of Catholics, Poles, Italians, and persons in other ethnic groups.[69] Probably the more intelligent and sensitive persons feel the prejudice most, but many of them adopt efficacious ways of dealing with the problem. As we shall indicate later,[70] a substantial fraction of our population suffers or has suffered frustration and emotional strain solely because of prejudice directed toward those of different racial, national, or religious membership.

[68] *Ibid.*, pp. 142-64.
[69] See, e.g., I. L. Child, *Italian or American?* (New Haven: Yale University Press, 1943).
[70] See Chapter 22 below.

The factors which influence the behavior of ethnic minorities have been summarized by two sociologists: [71]

Nature of parental advice and training with regard to the dominant group; level of education; income; occupational status; temperament of the individual; amount of minority-majority contact (contrast the experience of the North European immigrant, for example, with that of the American Indian in terms of the kind of contact they had with the dominant group); region of the country; nature of surrounding group support or opposition to prejudice; age; extent of experience with other intergroup patterns (for example, the Jamaican-born Negro in Harlem will see the situation differently from the way the native-born New Yorker sees it, and to both it will look different from the way the migrant from Georgia sees it); color variations *within* the minority group. (There is ample evidence that a light-skinned Negro and a dark-skinned Negro have, in many ways, significantly different experiences.)

The role of culture conflict. A related aspect of minority group status is the situation called "culture conflict." This means frustration and conflict on the part of an individual caught between the demands of two different cultures. The person most subject to culture conflicts is the child born in this country of immigrant parents, since many immigrants strive to bring up their children in the ways of the old country while at the same time the children are being Americanized in their school and community. It has often been said that the children of immigrants are a difficult lot, more likely than native American children to manifest behavior problems and delinquency. At least one study, however, casts doubt on such a generalization.[72]

Probably the interpretation is similar to the one given in the case of broken homes: the elements of strain are not necessarily brought to light by statistical studies. Case studies and autobiographies, however, reveal the significance of culture conflict situations when parents insist upon rigid conformity to the customs of the old country and oppose the natural tendency of their children to become Americanized.

The problem of culture conflict and its effects on personality is studied by Georgene Seward in her book *Psychotherapy and Culture Conflict*.[73] One area where she finds cultural conflict most acute is with the Jew who has a heritage which is not readily acceptable to the prevailing culture pattern. Among the mechanisms by which the Jew tends to resolve the conflict he experiences is overconformity. This reaction tendency is exemplified by the case of Eli, an

---

[71] G. E. Simpson and J. M. Yinger, *Racial and cultural minorities* (New York: Harper & Bros., 1953), pp. 166-67.

[72] E. T. Glueck, Culture conflict and delinquency, *Men. Hygiene*, XXII (1937), 46-66.

[73] G. Seward, *Psychotherapy and culture conflict* (New York: The Ronald Press Co., 1956).

adolescent boy, who insisted on arising early to make daily visits to the rabbi. This extremely devout practice may have been in reality a rejection of his orthodox parents, who were sufficiently disturbed and inconvenienced by this behavior to demand that he discontinue it. Two, rebellion is another outlet, which is the converse of over-conformity. Three, there is rejection of both cultures, the embracing of some extremist ideology or social movement, atheism or communism. Four, the development of a marginal culture is probably the most satisfactory method of solving the conflict. The present tendency to fuse Hanukkah and Christmas in some areas is an example.

In the case of the Negro, on the other hand, the conflict becomes more a matter of solving the anxiety that accompanies his inferior position.

Unfortunately for the Negro American, there is no adequate solution for his problem. Whichever way he turns, he remains in conflict because of his double identity in this black-and-white society. If he throws in his lot with the black, he cannot escape the demands of the white society around him; if he tries to identify with this white society he cannot escape his blackness.[74]

There is increasing evidence that the Negro has personality conflicts that grow out of his inferior status. This is manifested by, among other things, his high delinquency rate, his tendency to join bizarre religious and social movements, as, for example, the Father Divine movement. As the southern, rural Negro has moved to northern, urban centers the number of psychosomatic illnesses reported is evidence of the conflict. Peptic ulcer, since it appeared so rarely in the Negro, was at one time believed to be absent constitutionally from him. But this is no longer the case. The emergence of this individual into the middle class with all of the striving and mobility has induced more personality conflict. It is not surprising that a fair ratio of the tension is converted into skin disorders. High blood pressure, which may stem from the necessity to inhibit hostility, is not infrequent. As the largest racial group, and a minority surrounded by the most barriers, the Negro is subject to tremendous personality stresses.

SUMMARY AND CONCLUSIONS

This chapter has continued the account of important environmental influences upon the individual. First, the community is a determinant that provides him with major orientations, attitudes, and behavior patterns. In the various types of American commu-

[74] *Ibid.*, p. 141.

nities there is wide diversity; yet there are many features that remain constant, such as basic agreement as to the value of morality, humanitarianism, democratic individualism, and the like.

Social class membership has far-reaching effects on the individual's attitudes and behavior—his speech, choice of friends, and sex behavior, to mention a few. On the other hand, there may be important differences in the amount and the type of stratification in different parts of our country, and according to changes brought about by time. It is not surprising that social scientists are devoting attention to this relatively new area of interest.

Belonging to a minority group may also influence personality importantly, especially if the group is one against which discrimination is directed, in which case personality conflicts are very likely to occur. The efforts being made to study and solve these problems will be discussed in a later chapter.

The cultural and subcultural social forces by no means determine the whole pattern of personality. A child's heredity furnishes him with various potentialities, each having a certain range. The function of social environment is to sketch in the details of the "finished portrait" of personality. These are mainly habits, interests, attitudes, and values, and they are salient determinants of social behavior.

The significance of social experience, however, must not lead us to assume that individuals are mere passive recipients of environmental influences. Human organisms are active and selective. They differ one from another, because of varying native endowments and early experiences. Therefore they react differently to, and are affected differently by, the social situations they encounter. How the individual acquires the various reaction patterns is brought out in the next chapters on motivation and frustration, perception and learning.

SUPPLEMENTARY READINGS

Books of Readings

MACCOBY, E. E., NEWCOMB, T. M., AND HARTLEY, E. L. (eds.). *Readings in social psychology*, 3d ed. New York: Henry Holt & Co., Inc., 1958.
Bronfenbrenner, U. Socialization and social class through time and space.
Converse, P. E. The shifting role of class in political attitudes and behavior.
Davis, A., *et al.* The class system of the white caste.
Hollingshead, A. B. Factors associated with the prevalence of mental illness.
Strodtbeck, F. L., James, R. M., and Hawkins, C. H. Social status in jury deliberations.

BRITT, S. H. (ed.). *Selected readings in social psychology*. New York: Rinehart & Co., Inc., 1950.
Warner, W. L., *et al.* Class among New England Yankees.

Other References

BARBER, B. *Social stratification: a comparative analysis of structure and process.* New York: Harcourt, Brace & Co., Inc., 1957.
A thorough analysis of the literature, with some theoretical interpretation as well as historical data on certain European status systems.

BENDIX, R., AND LIPSET, S. M. (eds.). *Class, status and power.* Glencoe, Ill.: Free Press, 1953.
A reader in social stratification.

CENTERS, R. *The psychology of social classes.* Princeton, N. J.: Princeton University Press, 1949.
A large scale social psychological approach to class in America.

DAVIS, A., GARDNER, B. B., AND GARDNER, M. R. *Deep South.* Chicago: University of Chicago Press, 1941.
A penetrating study of the dual class structure in a southern community.

DRAKE, ST. CLAIR, AND CAYTON, H. R. *Black metropolis.* New York: Harcourt, Brace & Co., Inc., 1945.
The culture, including the class structure, of Chicago's Negro south side is revealed.

HOLLINGSHEAD, A. B. *Elmtown's youth.* New York: John Wiley & Sons, Inc., 1949.
How the class system affects behavior patterns in a Midwestern town.

KAHL, J. A. *The American class structure.* New York: Rinehart & Co., Inc., 1957.
A readable text on the class system, its styles of life, and the problem of vertical mobility. Chap. viii deals with ethnic groups.

KOMAROVSKY, M., AND SARGENT, S. S., Research into subcultural influences upon personality, in SARGENT, S. S., AND SMITH, M. W. (eds.), *Culture and personality.* New York: Viking Fund, 1949.

LYND, R. S., AND H. M. *Middletown.* New York: Harcourt, Brace & Co., Inc., 1929.

———. *Middletown in transition.* New York: Harcourt, Brace & Co., Inc., 1937.
The Middlewestern city of the twenties and of the depression is a classic study of institutional life.

MAYER, K. B. *Class and society.* New York: Doubleday & Co., Inc., 1955.
A bird's-eye view of class in America.

McDONAGH, E. C., AND RICHARDS, E. S. *Ethnic relations in the United States.* New York: Appleton-Century-Crofts, Inc., 1953.
A popular text on the position of our minorities.

MILLS, C. W. *White collar.* New York: Oxford University Press, 1951.
A lively sociologist writes both subjectively and empirically of upward mobility and the new middle class.

NEUMEYER, M. H. *Juvenile delinquency in modern society,* 2d ed. New York: D. Van Nostrand Co., Inc., 1955.
An introduction, among other things, into some of the community aspects of delinquency.

SEWARD, G. *Psychotherapy and culture conflict.* New York: The Ronald Press Co., 1956.
A discussion of the neurotic tendencies that may accompany minority status.

SIMPSON, G. G., AND YINGER, J. M. *Racial and culture minorities.* New York: Harper & Bros., 1953.
An unusually complete statement on psychology and sociology of ethnic relations.

WARNER, W. L.   *American life, dream and reality*. Chicago: University of Chicago Press, 1953.
A stimulating discussion of the effects of class on American culture.

WARNER, W. L., AND LUNT, P. S. *The social life of a modern community*. New Haven: Yale University Press, 1941.
Yankee City is the prototype of class analyses in sociology.

WARNER, W. L., *et al. Democracy in Jonesville*. New York: Harper & Bros., 1949.
An excellent survey of a community in terms of its class structure, its associational life, and its institutions.

WARNER, W. L., MEEKER, M., AND EELLS, K. *Social class in America*. Chicago: Science Research Associates, Inc., 1949.
A good summary of data on class and stratification.

ZORBAUGH, H. *The Gold Coast and the slum*. Chicago: University of Chicago Press, 1929.
One of the first ecological studies of class.

Part II

SOCIALIZATION— ITS PROCESSES AND PRODUCTS

Up to this point we have discussed the biological and sociocultural background of the individual. Personality represents a unique interrelationship of hereditary and environmental components that elude disentangling. The preponderant evidence has indicated that the sociocultural world structures personality, but no one can assess the subtle relationship between heredity and environment, between obscure temperamental tendencies and the operation of the family, the neighborhood play group, or the first-grade teacher in the developing personality. Most important, we want to examine the role of motives in the dynamics of personality. Frequently there has been the danger of ignoring complex interactional factors that are involved in growth. Personality development is not a one-sided process. The individual must actively select the most relevant of the stimuli that surround him. In the chapters ahead we will examine the development of motives, urges, and strivings, as well as personal defenses, reactions to frustration, and thwarting of our motives.

In addition, there are cognitive processes which are never separable from motivation. Cognition includes perceiving, symbolizing, and learning. These functions cannot be detached from motives, for no one aspect of our behavior can be isolated from any other part. The man on the street is not aware that he represents a Gestalt of motives and cognitions interacting in a dynamic fashion to determine his constantly changing behavior. But the social psychologist is especially interested in attitudes which are both the product and the determinant of this interplay of cognition and motivation. Social attitudes, values, and norms provide feeling tone, consistency, and meaning to our behavior.

Still another phase of this dynamic interrelationship is the evolvement of the self and the ego. The self is a unique structure that gives integration and direction to the personality. The interrelation and functioning of motives, cognitions, attitudes, and the ego constitute the subject matter of the following four chapters.

6

Motives, Conflicts, and Defenses

In many ways motivation is the fundamental problem in psychology. For one thing, it is concerned with causation; motives are in a sense causes. Why do we drink water, why do we read this book, why do we marry—these are questions having to do with determination or causation of behavior. This search for causes, though difficult and baffling, is the central task of any science and can hardly be ignored in social psychology. Our major concerns, such as attitudes, leadership, social change, group dynamics, all are involved with and depend upon this quest for motives or causes. It is not surprising that a psychologist, when introduced to Mr. A or Mrs. B at a luncheon, P.-T.A. meeting, or cocktail party, is immediately asked, "Doctor, why does my Junior do so-and-so?" or "What makes me feel such-and-such?"

INSTINCTS, DRIVES, AND MOTIVES

Theories of instinct. Up to about 1920 it was easy to answer "why?" questions in psychology. "Why are people sociable—why do they seek the company of others?" The answer seemed obvious — "because they are *instinctively* gregarious." Instincts of acquisitiveness, competitiveness, and pugnacity were invoked to explain possession of goods, business practices, and war. Instinct theorists, including James, McDougall, and Thorndike, drew up long lists of instincts which purported to explain practically every human activity, from sex to stamp-collecting. In 1924 the sociologist L. L. Bernard reported a survey of some 400 instinct theories and found that, among them, almost 6,000 human urges or activities had been called "instincts" or "instinctive!" [1]

[1] L. L. Bernard, *Instinct* (New York: Henry Holt & Co., Inc., 1924).

Shortly after 1920 the instinct theories became badly discredited. For one thing, it was becoming clear that positing instincts was like arguing in a circle: "People are sociable because they have an innate tendency to be sociable," which is at best dubious reasoning. More important, anthropologists were accumulating considerable data to show that different culture patterns produce great variations in human behavior or "human nature." Psychologists and sociologists were demonstrating that much of the behavior considered innate is actually learned. Since the word "instinct," from its very derivation, has to mean "innate" and "inherited," it was a misnomer when applied to behavior or behavior tendencies based on experience. Since so little human behavior is clearly inherited, unaffected by training, and universal to the human species, the term "instinct" began to drop out of the vocabulary of the psychologist and social scientist.[2] It is currently used, of course, for fairly complex patterns of animal behavior which are clearly innate, unlearned, and universal to a species (for instance, the web-spinning of the spider, nest-building in birds, honeycomb construction in bees, etc.).

The concept of drive. Abandoning the instinct theories left an uncomfortable gap—how was the psychologist to explain the needs, urges, and desires of human beings?

One answer was provided by the researches of physiologists and comparative psychologists. They began to speak of physiological tensions like hunger, thirst, and sex as "drives" which impelled the organism toward satisfaction of its tissue needs. They discovered physiological bases for these tensions in muscular and glandular activities of the organism. These conditions, they found, activate the organism to seek food, water, or a member of the opposite sex. In other words, tissue needs very definitely "motivate" the organism, in the sense of initiating activity directed toward satisfaction.

Investigators studying physiological needs agree upon many basic drives: hunger, thirst, sex, activity or exercise, sleep, evacuation of waste products, and needs for oxygen and for fairly constant temperature and barometric pressure. Some would include play, avoidance of danger, maternal drive, esthetic drives, and the like.[3] Various classifications have been suggested. Tolman divided drives into appetites (e.g., hunger, thirst, sex) and aversions (e.g., injury-avoidance). Murphy has posited four broad groups of drives: visceral, such as hunger and thirst; activity drives, like restlessness and

2 In popular usage, the terms "instinct" and "instinctive" are still very common, and help to perpetuate confusion.

3 E. C. Tolman, *Drives toward war* (New York: Appleton-Century-Crofts, Inc., 1942), pp. 9-10.

curiosity; sensory drives, such as sights, sounds, smells, etc., and emergency responses, like fear, rage, and disgust.[4] In an exhaustive study of man's wants, an economist classified drives according to temporal effect: continuous, recurrent, and sporadic.[5] All interpreters agree that these drives are essentially biological and are found in all human beings irrespective of training, though the way they are aroused, and their mode of expression, are affected by experience.

Classifications of motives. A number of psychologists and social scientists did not believe that the source of all human motivation could be found in organic tissue needs. They prepared lists of motives, wishes, needs, or urges irrespective of their physiological or social origin. In 1923 the sociologist W. I. Thomas posited four "fundamental wishes": security, response (both sexual and social), recognition, and new experience.[6] This short list became very popular, especially with social scientists. Some classifications were even simpler. Freud in his earlier writings referred to sex and hunger, but later changed his basic motives to the life and death instincts.[7] Kurt Goldstein had the simplest scheme of all: he proposed one primary and all-inclusive motive— "self-actualization." [8]

Others attempted to distinguish between physiological drives and socially acquired motives. One author, for example, speaks of "biological needs" and "psychological needs" (security, adequacy, affection, social approval, self-esteem, and curiosity-exploration).[9] Then he mentions "society's needs" which are over and above the needs of the individual (e.g., fighting of wars, obedience to the law, and going to school).[10] Perhaps the best-known current list, however, is Murray's twenty-odd "viscerogenic" and "psychogenic" needs, including activity, nurturance, succorance, harm-avoidance, autonomy, acquisition, affiliation, cognizance, construction, deference, dominance, recognition, achievement, and blame-avoidance.[11]

4 G. Murphy, Social motivation, in G. Lindzey (ed.), *Handbook of social psychology* (Reading, Mass.: Addison-Wesley Pub. Co., Inc., 1954), Vol. II, pp. 608-9.

5 C. R. Noyes, *Economic man in relation to his natural environment* (New York: Columbia University Press, 1948), Vol. I, p. 183.

6 W. I. Thomas, *The unadjusted girl* (Boston: Little, Brown & Co., 1923).

7 W. Healy *et al.*, *Structure and meaning of psychoanalysis* (New York: Alfred A. Knopf, Inc., 1930), pp. 70-72.

8 K. Goldstein, *The organism* (New York: American Book Co., 1939).

9 J. C. Coleman, *Abnormal psychology and modern life* (Chicago: Scott, Foresman & Co., 1950), pp. 65-68.

10 M. Sherif and C. W. Sherif, in *Outline of social psychology* (rev. ed.; New York: Harper & Bros., 1956), propose the terms "biogenic" and "sociogenic" for these categories.

11 H. A. Murray, *Explorations in personality* (New York: Oxford University Press, 1938).

The above-mentioned motives are classified according to their nature or content. Klineberg has suggested a different method; he posits four broad categories of motives according to their origin:

1. Motives which are absolutely dependable, have a definite physiological basis, and admit of no exceptions. Social factors play a part in their manifestations but do not determine their existence. These include hunger, thirst, the need for rest and sleep, the elimination of waste products from the body, and similar organic requirements; also activity drives and "esthetic" drives.
2. Motives which have a definite physiological basis, are found in all societies, but admit of exceptions in the case of individuals. Social factors not only determine the manner of their expression but may also in certain circumstances cause them not to appear. These include sex, post-maternal behavior, and possibly also self-preservation.
3. Motives which have an indirect physiological basis and occur with great frequency but admit of exceptions both in groups and in individuals. These include aggressiveness, flight, and probably also self-assertiveness.
4. Motives which have no known physiological basis but which occur with some frequency either because of social factors common to the majority of human communities or as a means to the satisfaction of practical interests. They are primarily means to an end, but may come to function as ends in themselves. These include gregariousness, the paternal motive, the pre-maternal motive, the filial motive, acquisitiveness, and self-submission.[12]

Maslow proposes a hierarchical theory of human motivation, with five "basic needs" arranged into an order or prepotency.[13] Those listed here first are the strongest and most dominant; by and large, says Maslow, each of these motives emerges only when the one above it in the list is satisfied.

1. Physiological needs—hunger, thirst, sex, physical activity, and related needs
2. Safety needs—security from physical and even psychological deprivation
3. Belongingness and love needs—the wide category of response, affection, and affiliative relationships
4. Esteem needs—desire of all people in our society for "a stable, firmly based, usually high evaluation of themselves, for self-respect" and for the esteem of others. On one side is the need for achievement, freedom and independence, and on the other is desire for prestige.

[12] O. Klineberg, Social psychology (rev. ed.; New York: Henry Holt & Co., Inc., 1954), p. 164.

[13] A. H. Maslow, Motivation and personality (New York: Harper & Bros., 1954), chap. v.

5. Self-actualization [14]—in part this is the fusion or culmination of the other needs; however, it is also the desire for self-realization or fulfilment, the need to become everything that one is capable of becoming.

PRINCIPLES OF MOTIVATION

Problems in studying motives. Before going further, let us consider some of the difficulties and problems in this confused area of motivation.

1. Motivation is difficult, first of all, because it is primarily concerned with the "whys" rather than the "hows" or "whats" of behavior. That is, it is concerned with *explanation* rather than *description*. And, as any scientist or philosopher knows only too well, the search for causes is one of his most puzzling and frustrating activities—at the same time that it is fascinating and important.

2. Motives are never directly observable, in the sense that emotions, learning, memory, or even intelligence are observable. Motives are always inferred or hypothesized from behavior. If an individual seeks out people and seems to enjoy being with them, we say he has a sociability or affiliation motive. If he persistently amasses goods and wealth, we posit an "acquisitive drive."

The trouble is, people sometimes do the same thing for different reasons. Of five people attending church, one is devoutly religious, another wishes to show off her new spring outfit, another hopes to make good business connections, another is escaping from a noisy household, and still another seeks enjoyment in the music. Conversely, persons similarly motivated may behave differently. Two individuals each intent upon recognition may seek it in widely different ways—one through boasting, let us say, and the other through writing or scientific research.

Perhaps, of course, we should not hypothesize motives at all. But psychologists seem forced to do so for both theoretical and practical reasons.

3. Psychologists and other students of motivation are unclear as to the meaning of terms they use. Is a motive an "inner push," like an instinct? Or is it in some measure a response to external stimuli? Do motives operate all the time, or do they come into play only at certain times or in certain situations? Should we think of motives as broad dynamic tendencies like "prestige-seeking" and "gregariousness"? Or are they more specific, like "seeking prestige in my community" and "wanting to be with my old friends"? Again, are motives separate from, or do they overlap, attitudes, habits, in-

14 This term was first used by Kurt Goldstein in *The organism* (New York: American Book Co., 1939).

terests, emotions, and other processes? Agreement will have to be reached on such matters before real progress can be made.

Despite this array of difficulties, the social psychologist refuses to be discouraged. He realizes that social behavior cannot be understood and predicted on the basis of motives alone—even if he were sure he had accurate data on them. But, equally, he knows that one cannot interpret social behavior realistically without taking into account the dynamic, energetic, goal-seeking behavior of individuals. Like the educator, the clinician, the advertiser, the newspaper editor, and the politician, the social psychologist cannot understand, predict, or influence human behavior without a fairly adequate knowledge of motives. And the social psychologist, as a scientist, has the even more difficult job of trying to present a systematic theory of motivation.

Behavior and motive. Perhaps we can advance our understanding of motives by going back a bit and asking a few questions about behavior. First, under what conditions does behavior occur?

Behavior is, of course, the response of an organism to some kind of stimulation. We are interested in the kind of stimuli known as social situations. Now, what determines how an individual reacts? Sensory acuity, nerves, and muscles are involved; attention and conditions like fatigue, illness, anxiety, and the like; also past experiences which influence the meaning and significance of the situation for him. Any one of these factors could be crucial in determining his reaction.

But we have not finished our inventory. Another significant variable of the organism is made up of his "sets" and needs, or broadly speaking, motives. These are tensions, or as Woodworth says, "activity in progress," and involve readiness or preparation for certain kinds of behavior.[15] Suppose the individual has not eaten for five or six hours. His physiological tensions—rhythmic contractions of the stomach wall—make up a need and provide a "set" which orients him toward food. Under these conditions food is an incentive or goal. If sexually deprived, he will be very favorably oriented toward an attractive female. Similarly, as we shall see, he may have needs or sets orienting him toward or away from association with people, toward or against conformity to social norms, toward mastery over others, toward prestige, or toward helping others.

This relationship between behavior and motive is well summed up in one psychologist's definition of need as "tension within the

15 R. S. Woodworth and D. G. Marquis, *Psychology* (5th ed.; New York: Henry Holt & Co., Inc., 1947), p. 306.

organism which tends to organize the field of the organism in regard to certain incentives or goals and to excite activity directed toward their attainment." [16] Or again, another analysis states that to identify a motive, one must "specify the *need* or *situation* that gives rise to it, the *drive* or tension that operates, the behaviors or *mechanisms* that result, and the *adjustment* that will bring the sequence to a close. Any motive involves all of these more elementary concepts. *Motive,* then, is a complex, socially learned pattern involving situation, drive, mechanism, and end result." [17]

The role of incentives. Since the days of instinct theories, psychologists have stressed the "inner push" aspect of motivation rather than the relationship between inner tension and external stimulus. Lewin made his colleagues aware of the importance of the "field." [18] He distinguished between the *physical field,* the objective stimulus situation, and the *psychological field,* referring to the situation as perceived, interpreted, and given meaning by the individual. Objects, persons, and activities, according to Lewin, have *positive valence* for the individual if they attract him, and *negative valence* if they repel him. The main determinant of valence, of course, is the person's favorable or unfavorable experience with the stimulus in question. Thus, to a hungry American a hamburger sandwich has positive valence; seal blubber does not. To a hungry Eskimo the reverse might be true. Valences or incentive values change as tension-states change in the individual. After a person eats heartily, food temporarily loses its positive valence.

This seems fairly simple. Actually the relationship between tension-states and incentives is rather complicated. Not only does a tension-state influence the valence of an incentive, but the incentive affects the tension-state. This can be seen best when the need or tension-state is latent—not conscious or operating to produce overt activity. Though not consciously hungry, we can suddenly become so about 11 A.M. if we happen to smell a broiling steak. A change in either the motive (internal) or the goal (external) will affect the other. If a young man finds that the girl he wants to marry does not share his rhapsodic attachment, his whole motivational structure —his sexual and emotional needs—will undergo change. On the

[16] D. W. MacKinnon, in E. G. Boring, H. S. Langfeld, and H. P. Weld, *Foundations of psychology* (3d ed.; New York: John Wiley & Sons, Inc., 1948), p. 126.

[17] L. F. Shaffer and E. J. Shoben, *The psychology of adjustment* (2d ed.; New York: Houghton Mifflin Co., 1956), p. 85.

[18] K. Lewin, *Dynamic theory of personality* (New York: McGraw-Hill Book Co., Inc., 1935), and *Principles of topological psychology* (New York: McGraw-Hill Book Co., Inc., 1936).

other hand, if his marital ardor cools, the young lady will seem less attractive than before.

Often people speak of behavior as if it were a function exclusively of "inner pushes" of some sort. Why did Mr. Brown run off with Mrs. Jones? Because he or she is "oversexed." Smith never speaks up because he's such a "conformist," that is, he has such a strong conformity drive. Louise talks all the time because she "just has to be the center of attention." Mrs. Blank wears those daring clothes because she likes to be talked about. And so on.

The point is not to suggest that inner pushes are insignificant; they are very important. But in organized societies they are typically latent, becoming active in response to outside stimuli. They seldom act like all-compelling energizers which drive a person hither and yon to seek his satisfactions. Normally, behavior results from the energizing or activating of latent sets by external stimuli, social or otherwise. Hence, for a complete picture of human motivation we need to know about tensions and needs and also about the stimulus situations or incentives which touch them off. In a word, study of motives apart from social settings is fruitless if not actually misleading.

Consider sex, which like hunger has a clear organic basis. Sometimes so much energy is generated by a pent-up sex urge that it dominates behavior. Perhaps a sailor returning to port or a forest ranger coming back to civilization exemplifies this. But here again, as with hunger, sexual activity (in the broad sense, including romance and love) results from a latent set being stimulated by an incentive. What else is "falling in love"? A young man meets a young lady and perceives or interprets her as "the one" for him (for reasons not entirely clear to the young man, psychologists, or anyone else!). The resultant changes in his behavior are considerable. He did not fall in love because there was a sudden change in his endocrines but because he met a girl who evoked certain already existing latent tendencies in him.

A meaningful account of motivation, then, requires knowledge of tension-states or needs, which is to be found partly in human physiology and partly in an individual's experience. It requires also understanding of incentives, which involves knowing the material and social stimuli of a person's environment and their valence for him.

Patterning of motives. Motives exist as Gestalten or "motive patterns," as Newcomb suggests.[19] They may be considered *molar*

19 T. M. Newcomb, *Social psychology* (New York: The Dryden Press, Inc., 1950), p. 97.

rather than *molecular*, to use Tolman's distinction. The term "molar" refers to units of behavior which are not reducible to elements, whereas "molecular" behavior is defined in terms of underlying physical and physiological details.[20] Motives may be relatively simple or complex, but they are difficult to disentangle. Examine, for example, the complexity of motives in your reading of this page. Some of them are explained by the concept of *deferred gratification* —such as the prospect of an "A" grade at the end of the semester. Others may involve high scholarship standards or obtaining an impressive transcript, which could mean a better position after graduation or assured entrance to a chosen professional school. And there are other reasons why you are reading this page: you do not have money for a show tonight or you are staying around waiting for an important telephone call. Or perhaps you are at least vaguely interested in the subject and there is a test next week or tomorrow. All the above, in turn, depend on your being in college, which itself is related to many factors and determinants. Hence, a relatively simple act may involve a great number of motives.

Social and cultural factors in motivation. Despite certain unanswered physiological questions, the motivating character of drives or *biogenic* motives is relatively easy to understand. Our great difficulty is in explaining the learned or *sociogenic* motives. Here we can find no evidence of tissue needs; yet motives which we call "prestige-seeking," "sociability," "mastery," "conformity," and the like, may outweigh physiological drives. How do sociogenic motives come into being?

Actually, of course, the specific patterning of motives is always social. Whether it is satisfaction of the hunger drive, choice of a friend or an occupation, or purchase of furniture or an automobile, cultural conditioning has played a major role in the selective process. In Western culture, for example, our preference is for certain foods; only under acute starvation is an individual likely to eat grasshoppers or live worms. While members of a few subcultures in our larger society may favor rattlesnake meat over hamburger or filet mignon, this only demonstrates the power and sanctity of the broad cultural norms. Presumably, in prehistoric and early historical periods when culture changed slowly, motives remained fairly constant. As cultural change has come to occur at an accelerated pace in the twentieth century, patterns of motivation have become diversified and altered.[21]

[20] M. Scheerer, Cognitive theory, in G. Lindzey (ed.), *Handbook of social psychology*, (Reading, Mass.: Addison-Wesley Pub. Co., Inc., 1954), Vol. I, pp. 94-97.

[21] See Chapter 3 on culture and personality, and Chapter 19 on social change.

Almost no developmental studies have been made of the changing motivation in a child. We may, however, venture interpretation from various clinical and observational data.

The newborn child's needs are primarily biological—food, warmth, dryness, activity, etc. As the infant's mother satisfies these needs, she acquires positive value in his eyes.[22] As father, brothers, and sisters care for and amuse the baby, they too acquire positive value. Out of such satisfaction with people, including later experience with playmates, arises a more generalized set which may be called "sociability." Contrariwise, out of unfavorable experiences with people come unsocial or misanthropic tendencies. Or again, in our culture the basis of recognition- and prestige-seeking is found in the rewards given a child by parents and society for winning contests or doing something outstanding. Likewise the child may learn there are rewards for being masterful, powerful, or pugnacious. Or he is encouraged to collect things, to acquire money and other possessions, and this behavior is reinforced by members of his family and community. The rewards he receives are in terms of satisfying biological drives (for instance, through ice cream cones or candy bars) or already learned sociogenic motives, such as recognition.

Thus each child continues to acquire certain "sets" or tendencies according to the way his behavior has been rewarded through satisfying existing needs and drives. These dynamic patterns differ from individual to individual. One child is rewarded for being pugnacious or acquisitive and hence develops these tendencies; another is punished for such behavior, hence does not learn to behave in these ways. Cultural differences likewise occur, as has already been mentioned. The American child is rewarded for being competitive and outstanding; the Zuñi child is not. The German child's masterful and aggressive behavior may be reinforced; such tendencies in an Eskimo child are punished. Anthropological studies are rich in examples of this type of cultural patterning.[23]

In this, as in all types of learning, certain principles can be discerned, such as reinforcement, generalization, canalization, and the like. Since these will be described in the next chapter, we shall merely summarize here by saying that certain kinds of behavior on the part of parents and others, originally devoted to the satisfaction of a child's bodily needs, come to acquire positive valence. They come to be valued and responded to in their own right if experience with them is favorable.

[22] This process has been called "cross-conditioning." See E. B. Holt, *Animal drive and the learning process* (New York: Henry Holt & Co., Inc., 1931), chap. xx.

[23] See O. Klineberg, *Social psychology* (rev. ed.; New York: Henry Holt and Co., Inc., 1954), chaps. v and vi, for a good summary of this material.

Some unsettled questions about motives. Several objections and questions may be raised about the interpretation of sociogenic motives just given. One might ask whether a generalized motive of superiority, sociability, mastery, etc., could arise from one or a few satisfying experiences. The point is a good one; highly generalized sets usually do develop only where one has had reinforcement in a variety of situations. Others believe the generalization is one we make for convenience. MacKinnon says, for example: "We do not have a general need to be superior, but rather a special need to be superior in a particular way in a specific situation . . . yet it is often helpful . . . to conceptualize general needs of which any given behavior trait is but a specific and concrete expression." [24]

The answer seems to be that acquired motives like need for affiliation or superiority do generalize to some extent, but by no means to the point of covering all situations. When one describes motivation by using a concept like "need for affiliation," he implies a degree of generality which may not accord with the facts.

Other questions have to do with the physiological basis of motives. Let us start by saying that all motives can be considered *tensions,* which suggests a neuromuscular condition. In amoeba or in man the organism moves from one tension to another; it alternates between quiescence and tension. All animals, including man, pursue the goal of stabilization or freedom from tension. The term *homeostasis* is used to denote the tendency of organisms to maintain their equilibrium amid the tensions that arise, whether due to organic changes or environmental stresses. In the human being tensions are more elaborate, more variable, are subject to symbolization, and are oriented to social goals and values. Pangs of hunger remind us of breakfast; subtler tensions impel us to study or go to the office and cause us to worry about whether or not we will have a date for Saturday night.

But the question still remains, Is there a physiological basis for each fairly specific motive? The answer usually given is that the sociogenic motives operate like physiological drives in that both involve release of energy directed toward a goal, whether or not they have any identifiable physiological basis. Morgan, however, once proposed a "central motive state"—a persistent condition in the nervous system—which underlies all motivated behavior. Though its nature is not clear, Morgan suggested that this central motive state, once initiated, tends to continue, that it evokes both general activity and certain kinds of specific behavior, and that it involves a set or potentiality for certain patterns of behavior when the right

[24] D. W. MacKinnon, *op. cit.,* p. 126.

stimulus occurs. Morgan called this last one a "priming" function and believed it is what makes motivated behavior seem clearly purposive. If Morgan's hypothesis is found to be valid, it puts sociogenic motives on much firmer ground.[25]

Another unsettled matter is whether or not to include with the motives several other psychological processes which have dynamic aspects. Attitudes, for example, have motivational character, since they are sets having a favorable or unfavorable emotional tone directed toward persons, objects, and situations. Interests, similarly, are favorable sets based upon rewarding experiences. Values too, as we shall see, orient the individual to respond positively in some directions, negatively in others. "Sentiments," defined as generalized patterns or complexes of values and attitudes, should also be included as having motivational character.

"A purpose can be the most definite of motives and the most powerful." [26] Purposes are consciously formulated goals to which the individual has committed himself. A "level of aspiration" constitutes one kind of conscious goal which arises in a specific situation and influences behavior demonstrably. Furthermore, as will be indicated in Chapter 9, one's "ego-ideal" or "concept of self" has great driving force.

Psychologists have suggested from time to time that emotions, too, have motivational character. Leeper makes the point clearly.[27] He criticizes the usual psychological interpretation—that emotions are disorganized or disorganizing responses—and insists that they are primarily motives, since they are processes "which arouse, sustain and direct activity." [28] He states further that "emotional processes are one of the fundamental means of motivation in the higher animals—a kind of motivation which rests on relatively complex neural activities rather than primarily on definite chemical states or definite receptor stimulations, as in the case of bodily drives. . . ." [29] Thus—and the authors agree with Leeper—fear, anger, elation, and other emotional states serve as motives in the sense that they arouse and organize activity and channel it in a particular direction.

The psychological processes just mentioned have motivational character because they serve to activate or energize the individual.

[25] C. T. Morgan, *Physiological psychology* (New York: McGraw-Hill Book Co., Inc., 1943), pp. 460 ff. It may be significant, however, that the 1950 edition (written with E. Stellar) does not mention the "central motive state," nor is it found in Morgan's recent *Introduction to psychology* (New York: McGraw-Hill Book Co., Inc., 1956).

[26] Woodworth and Marquis, *op. cit.*, p. 325.

[27] R. W. Leeper, A motivational theory of emotion, *Psychol. Rev.*, LV (1948), 5-21.

[28] *Ibid.*, p. 17.

[29] *Ibid.*, p. 19.

Incentives and appeals, on the other hand, cannot be considered motives, since they are basically external to the organism. Their function in arousing latent motivational tendencies has already been discussed.

THEORIES OF MOTIVATION

Freud: the libido and the unconscious. We turn now to consider a few of the important theories of motivation which have been proposed. Foremost is that of Sigmund Freud. The first point to note is that his orientation is largely biological. The basis of motivation, according to Freud, is found in the various instincts—sex, hunger, thirst, and aggressiveness. Most important of these is the sex instinct, or *libido*. Practically all social and emotional behavior and experience of the human being is rooted in this striving, pulsating, amorphous force, which is largely unconscious in origin. Second, there is a rigid determinism in that all motivation is directly or indirectly connected with the sex libido. Every act, every idea, every dream, "slips of the tongue"—all are somehow caused by this unconscious impulse. Third, ambivalence is strategic to motivation and conflict. There is the life instinct (which is identified largely with the libido) and the death instinct. The former represents the positive, constructive tendencies in opposition to the latter destructive forces. There is love against hate, life against death, and the individual is constantly caught in the warfare of these vast instinctual forces. Fourth, Freud had a unique conception of the conservation, or in his case, transformation of energy. What he called psychic energy could be changed into muscular and mechanical energy. This shift in the form of energy becomes thinking (psychic energy) followed by action (muscular energy). Consequently, the libido expresses itself in a number of distinct fashions and will find devious ways of controlling thought and behavior. In fact, for Freud the major problem in motives is the concealment of the genuine urges.

In evaluating Freud's theory it would be difficult to overestimate the enormous contribution he made in opening up a new forbidden territory. Up to his time, sex as a motivational factor had been ignored, or more exactly, had been driven underground. Even more important was his discovery of the unconscious as a potent force in the dynamics of adjustment. There are weaknesses, however, in his system. For one, his terminology was vague and not verified empirically. In some cases the misunderstanding over terms was due to errors in translation. His unfortunate use of our term "instinct," which had come into disfavor in American psychology by 1920, was contrary to the leading trend in American psychology. In addition, his unicausational viewpoint and frequent dogmatism oversimplified and led to considerable revision on the part of later psychoanalysts. It is unlikely that any one factor, whether sex in classical psychoanalysis, or economics in Marxian theory, can be the central cause of most of our actions, either personal or social. Human behavior is sufficiently complex that only a multicausational viewpoint is relevant.

Functional approaches to motivation. How shall we explain sociogenic or learned motives which are sometimes as dynamic, compelling, and intense as tissue needs like hunger, thirst and sex?

Many years ago John Dewey proposed that habits are dynamic. "All habits are demands for certain kinds of activity; and they constitute the self. In any intelligible sense of the word will, they *are* will. They form our effective desires and they furnish us with our working capacities. They rule our thoughts, determining which shall appear and be strong and which shall pass from light into obscurity." [30] Woodworth developed much the same idea in his *Dynamic Psychology* when he stated that a mechanism (i.e., habit) becomes a drive. Originally the mechanisms are instrumental behavior, but they become ends in themselves and acquire true motivational character.[31]

The more recent interpretation of E. C. Tolman is similar.[32] Man, like other gregarious animals, develops what he calls "social techniques"—types of social behavior which insure more food, drink, and sexual satisfactions. Broadly he classifies these techniques as the self-assertive (e.g., dominance, competitive acquisition), self-abasive (e.g., submitting), collective (e.g., imitation, cooperation), and collective-assertive (e.g., loyalty to group). Tolman implies that these learned social techniques are as dynamic and impelling as physiological drives.

Because many psychologists regard habits as skills or "passive tools waiting to be called into action from without," [33] they find it difficult to accept the thesis that habits are inherently motivational. "Bad" habits like smoking or drinking are recognized as dynamic, because of their physiological basis. But most habits, particularly

30 J. Dewey, *Human nature and conduct* (New York: Henry Holt & Co., Inc., 1922), p. 25.

31 R. S. Woodworth, *Dynamic psychology* (New York: Columbia University Press, 1918).

32 E. C. Tolman, *Drives toward war* (New York: Appleton-Century-Crofts, Inc., 1942), chaps. iii, iv.

33 Dewey, *op. cit.*, p. 24.

motor habits like walking, typing, driving a car, or machine-tending, do not have deep-seated motivational foundations.

Gordon Allport has made an ingenious attempt to explain why all habits and skills do not develop into drives.[34] He concludes that it is not the perfected talent or automatic habit that has driving power but the imperfect talent and habit-in-the-making. The child who is *just learning* to speak, to walk, or to dress is likely to engage in these activities for their own sake, as does the adult with an unfinished task in hand. Motor skills are often perfected, whereas art, science, religion, and love are not, which accounts for their ongoing dynamic quality, Allport concludes.

A more comprehensive contribution is Allport's theory of *functional autonomy* of motives, which proposes that adult motives are "infinitely varied . . . self-sustaining, *contemporary* systems, growing out of antecedent systems, but functionally independent of them." [35] That is to say, purposive activities proceed under their own steam, no matter how they originated. Thus, says Allport, the ex-sailor yearns for the sea, or a businessman "long since secure economically, works himself into ill-health, and sometimes even back into poverty, for the sake of carrying on his plans. What was once an instrumental technique becomes a master motive." [36]

Allport's ingenious theory has aroused no little controversy.[37] One of the criticisms that may be made is that "autonomous" motives may actually be latent rather than active. Or, if they are active, they may be serving other motives. Thus, the businessman's devotion to his work may serve primarily to bring him to his friends and to get him away from a nagging wife. In a word, the theory of functional autonomy is unclear in its relation to learning, perception, frustration, and other psychological processes.

A TENTATIVE ORGANIZATION OF IMPORTANT SOCIAL MOTIVES

Despite the difficulties in identifying and classifying motives, it is possible and feasible to draw up a workable schema of the chief social motives, as in Figure 6.

It can be seen that the items in the left column of Figure 6 represent an active kind of individual-centered striving, for goods and power chiefly. Those in the middle column center about social relationships, but still with an egocentric emphasis. The third col-

[34] G. W. Allport, *Personality* (New York: Henry Holt & Co., Inc., 1937), pp. 204-5.
[35] *Ibid.*, p. 194.
[36] *Ibid.*, p. 196.
[37] See, e.g., P. A. Bertocci, A critique of G. W. Allport's theory of motivation, *Psychol. Rev.*, XLVII (1940), 501-32.

umn contains the more integrative, truly interpersonal, and less individualistic needs and urges.

The clustering and combining of motives is indicated not only by the columns but also by the spacing, which suggests the grouping in a narrower fashion. Further interrelationships are suggested

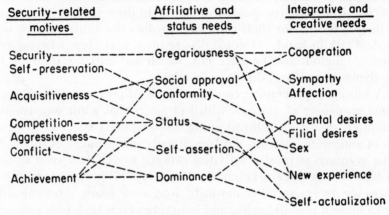

FIG. 6. Schema of Some Major Social Motives.

by the horizontal and diagonal lines between columns. All of this, however, is only tentative; the complex relations between motives and motivational patterns is far too intricate to be portrayed accurately in such a schema.

Furthermore, although social motives are found in all societies of the world, their patterning differs greatly. Also, they may become practically nonoperative when existence itself is in jeopardy, as suggested in Maslow's hierarchical theory.[38] That is, status, social approval, and even sex hardly function if one is threatened with starvation. In our society, however, the drives and basic physical needs are seldom critical, because of our inventions and social arrangements which protect us against the rigors of climate and the depredations of man and beast. This means that the role of social motives is highlighted, and that the major choices are made between motives, such as status and achievement, or security and new experience, rather than between hunger or thirst or temperature maintenance and a supposedly inconsistent social motive.

Security. What, then, are some of the clusters of social motives? Security may serve to illustrate their complexity. Actually, there is more than one form of security. Most important is *physical* security, since that includes satisfaction of biological needs like food and

38 See pp. 164-65 above.

temperature maintenance. Next, *financial* security or *economic* security derives from our socioeconomic order and is instrumental to our physical security. (Some psychologists call this kind of drive "secondary.") Third, there is *psychological* security, based upon the first two types, and involving other personality needs. Psychological security is basically a feeling of well-being, whether or not it harmonizes with relatively objective criteria of stability and tension reduction.

There is a close connection between psychological security and physical security. Failure to receive adequate nutrition and fulfillment of other biological needs in the early years leaves the individual with adolescent and adult anxiety. Material deprivation can be a crucial factor, though in our culture the opposite kind of situation—material gratification in lieu of affectional warmth—is more serious and more prevalent. As mentioned in Chapter 4, rejection, whether physical or affectional, is the greatest enemy of psychological security, that primary motive of them all.

Associated with security are several other motives, which may become as important as security itself in the psychological structure of the individual. Acquisitiveness, for example, covers quite a range, from a mild degree of property-consciousness at one extreme to pathological hoarding at the other. Conflict seems to be found in some degree in all societies, although the situations which elicit it and the ways in which it is expressed vary enormously.[39]

Affiliative and status needs. The cluster of motives that surround gregariousness, sociability, or the "wish for response," as Thomas called it, covers an enormous range of behavior. At one extreme are the mild social tendencies exemplified by enjoying the knowledge that other people are living in the house down the road even though we are not acquainted with them. Or the increased responsiveness one feels in attending a movie, as compared with sitting alone before a television set. At the other end of the range of affiliative needs is the deep relationship of affection, love, and sexual response. Somewhere between these extremes are the tendencies to association and friendship which operate in most of our social contacts. As pointed out earlier in the chapter, these sociable tendencies are very greatly affected by, if not determined by, social experience.

In every society there is some status patterning which comes to act as a kind of motive. Within an open class system, for example, there is a widely distributed drive for upward mobility. In our

[39] See Chapter 11.

society the varieties of prestige—occupational, financial, educational, residential, ethnic, esthetic—help make up a complex of motives which differs somewhat for every individual. For one, the goal may be prowess on the football team; for another, a Cadillac; for the criminal, the joy of eluding the law. One's peer group, or reference group, has most to do with setting his goals.

As with sociability, the antecedents of the status motive are found well below the level of mammals in the animal world. A pecking order exists among chickens by which a dominance hierarchy is established; within many animal groups some of the males are consistently dominant over less vigorous competitors. Among the world's cultures there are wide variations in stratification. At one extreme is the Australian Bushman with his relative absence of status, while at the other some African tribes exhibit a system of royalty and nobility reminiscent of eighteenth-century Europe. In our own society, the debutante party or the annual excitement over our ever faster, ever larger, multicolored and multifinned automobiles serves as a ritualistic display of status-seeking behavior.

Integrative and creative motives. For most people in all societies of the world, motivation involves more than the need for security, affiliation, and approval. The urge to work and play with other human beings, to enter into deep affectional relationships, to marry and have children, and to create things of lasting value—all these are characteristically human.

Cooperation is universal, for social life would not be possible without some degree of interdependence. In fact, there is a biological basis for this social motive: sex relations, the nursing of the infant, and symbiosis (biological interdependence) among animals, for example. However, there is conclusive evidence showing that the motive of cooperation depends upon learning. Dependence of the infant upon the adult for his needs is one of the initiating phases of cooperation. Play with siblings and neighborhood children helps it along. Conditioning and other mechanisms of learning rather than hormic theory or instinct doctrine account for the development of this motive, as we shall observe in the next chapter.

Considerable variation in competition and cooperation has been found among and within cultures. The study of Utopian colonies has produced material which has been cited as evidence both for and against cooperation as an inherent drive. The enduring desire through the ages for a community based on brotherhood and equality has raised the question whether cooperativeness is a primary, but socially repressed, drive. On the other hand, the historical fact that nearly all of these experiments have been short lived has led to the view that man is basically competitive and aggressive. Actually, both these arguments rest on hypotheses that have not been critically tested.

Sympathy involves feeling and identification with others and ability to comprehend emotional situations. As with other social motives, the particular background of the individual is important, especially his childhood experience. There is no small degree of variation among Western cultures in the development of this motive; even greater variations appear among non-Western groups. Judeo-Christian tradition has emphasized sympathy and cooperation, though it was not until the nineteenth century that humanitarian movements diverted European culture in the direction of reforms in the care of the downtrodden and unfortunate.

Parental desires seemed to be one of the clearest of the instincts, particularly the maternal drive, which was found to have a hormonal basis. However, wide variations in both the pre-maternal and the post-maternal drives argue against a simple inborn determination.[40] In the United States, for example, nearly 10 per cent of married women of childbearing age apparently dislike the idea of motherhood. The many cases in which rejection occurs in mothers of legitimate as well as illegitimate children leads us to question the existence of a maternal instinct. Forces prompting married persons to have children involve other social motives and a number of economic and psychological considerations.

ADJUSTMENT AND DEFENSE MECHANISMS

The dynamics of social behavior deals with the effects of individuals' tension-states upon interpersonal behavior and social adjustment. In describing motives we have said nothing about their fulfilment. Ordinarily a motive initiates behavior which results in satisfaction and reduction of tension. But what happens if the fulfilment is blocked—if the individual is "frustrated"?

The answer is clear. When frustrated by the blocking or thwarting of a strong motive, the individual becomes emotional (e.g., angry or fearful). Emotions are particularly dynamic and lead to striving in one or another direction until some degree of satisfaction is achieved. This behavior may be overt and direct, like attacking the person who caused the frustration. But more often, owing to social pressures, we resort to substitute forms of expression. These reactions, following Freud, are called "mechanisms," "de-

[40] The pre-maternal drive means the desire for children; the post-maternal drive refers to the desire to protect and care for one's offspring. See Klineberg, *op. cit.,* pp. 79 and 164.

fense mechanisms," "dynamisms," or just "defenses." Thus one regresses, displaces, rationalizes, projects, or compensates in response to frustration.[41] We shall describe first the common defense mechanisms and their social implications and will present later a systematic treatment of reaction to frustration.

The concept of mechanism comes from psychoanalysis and has been used almost exclusively in clinical studies like psychiatry, mental hygiene, and abnormal and clinical psychology. Actually, it is a most important concept for the social psychologist, as we shall see. By "mechanism" Freud meant a device adopted by the ego to defend itself against unwanted urges coming from the id.[42] His fertile and original mind identified and named most of the mechanisms we know today: repression, sublimation, displacement, projection, rationalization, regression, identification, and others.

Most of these terms have been taken over by clinicians, whether or not their views are psychoanalytic, and in recent years there has been a great proliferation of new terms.[43] Clinicians generally treat mechanisms as ways of reacting to frustration, or as ways of defending the ego against anxiety. They agree that these defenses are habits, learned usually in childhood. They are nearly always unconscious; persons seldom are aware that they are regressing, displacing, rationalizing, etc. We shall describe briefly the nature of each defense mechanism, then discuss its social origins and some of its effects upon social behavior.

Repression. According to psychoanalysis, repression is the most basic mechanism of all. It arises from conflict between the *superego* (conscience or moral ideas) and the *id* (man's primitive or animal nature); it represents an unconscious kind of pushing back, or holding operation, performed by the *ego*, which has become the battleground for the conflict. It is widely agreed now that the matrix of repression is social—stemming from the taboos of society. Parents, teachers, and others disapprove and punish in children those

41 Most psychologists now use "frustration" in a sense broad enough to include "conflict," which implies the incompatibility of two motives rather than the external blocking of a motive. The reactions caused by frustration and conflict are similar, so we shall use the term "frustration" to cover both.

42 The handiest source for explanation of psychoanalytic terms is C. S. Hall's *Primer of Freudian psychology* (Cleveland: World Publishing Co., 1954); it is also published in a paper edition. Some of the psychoanalytic concepts will be described later, in Chapter 9.

43 We shall stick to the more widely used concepts. For psychoanalytic treatment of the subject, see Otto Fenichel, *The psychoanalytic theory of neurosis* (New York: W. W. Norton & Co., Inc., 1945); and Anna Freud, *The ego and mechanisms of defense* (London: Hogarth Press, Ltd., 1937). A more psychological approach is found in chaps. iv–x of L. F. Shaffer & E. J. Shoben, *The psychology of adjustment* (2d ed.; Boston: Houghton Mifflin Co., 1956).

types of behavior considered "wrong" in their society—for instance, sex and aggression. The child then inhibits his behavior and re presses his thoughts and feelings in these areas because he fears pun ishment and loss of his parents' love.[44] While some effects of repression result in socialized behavior, in harmony with the mores of society, repression in the case of severe conflicts is usually inade quate and results in some form of neurotic behavior.

Repression often occurs in our primary group relationships. When we have suspicions or jealous thoughts about friends and loved ones, we generally repress them as unworthy of us. The young husband inhibits criticism of his wife's cooking, and the wife represses anger provoked by the husband's late hours. Thus repression keeps social relations pleasant on the surface but at the same time prevents solution of the problem. If the repression is in tense and continuous, it is likely to lead to an explosion of some kind, or to other defense mechanisms such as rationalization, pro jection, or fantasy.

In areas of social conflict like race and labor relations, "accom modations" or compromise working relationships are established (e.g., Negro segregation; agreements between employers and their employees). When minor infractions of these arrangements occur, recognition of the fact is often repressed in order to preserve good social relations. But such repression generates increasing tensions and furnishes the dynamics for aggression and violence, which may be precipitated by some apparently trivial incident. Study of the background conditions of race riots, lynchings, and bloody strikes often indicates that a considerable amount of such repression has occurred. Many other factors operate, of course, in producing social conflicts. But violent incidents always trace back to tensions and frustrations in the participating individuals, many of which have been repressed over a long period of time.

Culturally sanctioned repression of strong motives has tremen dous implications for social behavior. For example, in Western cultures generally and in our society in particular, premarital and extramarital sexual experiences are taboo. That is to say, consid erable repression of sexual tendencies occurs, despite marked nonobservance of the taboo. This repression has much to do with neurosis, as psychoanalysts have stressed, and with the storm and stress of adolescence. It is probably basic also to our emphasis on romantic love, our interest in dancing, and the prevalence of neck ing and petting. Some would add prostitution to the list as another

44 P. M. Symonds, *Dynamics of human adjustment* (New York: Appleton-Century- Crofts, Inc., 1946), p. 230.

outcome of sexual repression. Similarly, one might trace many kinds of social behavior to the taboo upon direct expression of hostile impulses.

A related aspect of repression is a denial, an unwillingness to admit, that anything is wrong with ourselves or our community. "We have no problem in this town," and "That could never happen here," are frequent comments in regard to minority group problems. As one kindly South African lady put it: "It's awful in Johannesburg, but we have a nice kind of apartheid [segregation] here in Durban."

Rationalization. In his original formulation of rationalization, Freud noted that it results from partial failure of repression. He saw it as a tendency of the ego to justify and defend id impulses to oneself and to others. The term has become widely used by clinicians in the sense of explaining and justifying the acts and urges we feel do not have full social approval. It means "explaining" (i.e., justifying) our behavior by giving *good* rather than *true* reasons for it.

Rationalization is likely to occur whenever a questionable reason or possibly uncomplimentary explanation might come up. Ask someone why he is a Republican or Democrat. The answer is seldom "because my relatives are Republicans—or Democrats"—which is one of the commonest causes for party preference.[45] Or ask someone why he is a Methodist, why he lives in Suburbia, or why he sends his child to a select private school, and you will receive an answer which is at best only partially true. Much of the time the respondent does not know he is rationalizing—he is merely giving an interpretation which seems reasonable and which is socially acceptable.

Rationalizations are largely social in origin. They are a sop to reason and logic; they apparently occur only in cultures where logic and science are stressed. Furthermore, rationalizations are in line with the kinds of explanations which are approved in the society. In fact, the process is socially approved. We look askance, in our society, at someone who fails to rationalize. We are surprised and shocked if Mr. B. says: "I didn't hit back because I was afraid A. would beat me up!" Or if the young lady says, "I bought this car because I want to show off and make that Smith woman jealous!" "No, no!" we protest, "wasn't it because . . . ?"—then we furnish the rationalization!

45 See P. Lazarsfeld, B. Berelson, and H. Gaudet, *The people's choice* (2d ed.; New York: Columbia University Press, 1948), pp. 140-45.

Indeed, our society's approval of the process of rationalization is shown by widely but unconsciously accepted patterns of rationalization. Professor Waller noted that we drink to celebrate a victory, or to "drown our sorrows." We drink because we are with friends, and we drink because we are lonely. In the winter we take a drink to "warm up"; in the summer to "cool off." Seldom if ever does one admit drinking because he is bored, because he has acquired a thirst for liquor, or because he just likes the effect of it.

The recent attempts to defend segregated schools in the South, to label individuals with different political viewpoints as "Communists," and to defend colonialism as an ethical necessity or as the "white man's burden" are basically rationalizations. It is not to say that those who support the opposing viewpoints on these and other issues are necessarily free of rationalization or other forms of defensiveness; however, it is more difficult to get objective and scientific support for some positions than for others. The close relationship between desire and belief is almost sure to make for some distortion.

It has been said that much of our religion and philosophy represents a rationalization of the status quo. While this is a broad statement, it seems to fit where (1) an assumption is made that our world, country, culture, economic system, etc., is practically perfect, and where (2) explanations are given showing why this is so. In such cases, science and logic go by the board in favor of fixed assumptions and biased reasoning.

Like all mechanisms, rationalization has utility for the individual—as a person and as a member of society. It makes him feel comfortable by helping avoid unpalatable explanations and by justifying his own behavior and existing social practices and attitudes. Hence rationalization functions as one of the major obstacles to social change.

Displacement. Displacement means the expressing of emotional reactions in a situation other than the one which aroused them. It is a shift of feelings or attitudes away from a person or situation where they cannot or should not be expressed to a person or situation where they can be. A child, punished by his parent, goes over to his sister and strikes her. An emotion, aroused but unexpressed, finds outlet in the first appropriate situation. One indicator of displacement is excessiveness of the emotional reaction, far beyond that normally shown at such a time or place.

Any emotional reaction may be displaced. A good example is the "rebound" phenomenon: a jilted young lady promptly falls in

love with her next suitor. But the commonest instances, and those
with most obvious social significance, are anger, hate, and fear.
This is partly because they are strong emotions and partly because
social situations so often militate against their expression.

Displacement is common and often disconcerting in everyday
social contacts. But it becomes a serious matter, socially speaking,
when it assumes the form known as "scapegoating." A scapegoat,
in the Bible, was an animal sacrificed to atone for the sins of all.
In the modern sense scapegoating means the displacing of anger or
hostility upon an innocent victim. Scapegoating may be defined as:

... a phenomenon wherein some of the aggressive energies of a person or group
are focused upon another individual, group or object; the amount of aggression
and blame being either partly or wholly unwarranted.[46]

The best large-scale example of a scapegoat was the Jews in Nazi
Germany, who were blamed for every real or imagined ill suffered
by the country—from military defeat in 1918 to the economic depression of the 1930's.

The social implications of scapegoating are tremendous. A political party, a social group, or an ethnic minority are handy
scapegoats against whom may be focused the anger and hostility
generated from all sorts of deep-seated frustrations. A study of
political behavior in the dustbowl area furnishes an interesting
example. It was found that during periods when rainfall was below
average the political party in power was usually turned out of office
at the next election.[47] When rainfall was above average, people
generally voted to continue the party in office. Apparently the hostile and aggressive reactions arising from economic frustrations
were leveled against politicians as the most available scapegoat.
Another study reports a negative correlation between the price of
cotton and number of lynchings in the South [48]—again, economic
frustration generates hostility, which in this case is directed against
members of an ethnic minority group. Studies of hate groups—
fascist-minded organizations like the Ku Klux Klan, etc.—have
shown that increase in their membership is correlated positively
with severity of economic depression.[49]

[46] G. W. Allport, *ABC's of scapegoating* (rev. ed.; New York: Anti-Defamation
League, 1948), p. 13.

[47] S. Rice and J. D. Barnhart, Rainfall and the Populist Party in Nebraska, *Amer.
pol. Sci. Rev.*, XIX (1925), 527-40.

[48] C. Hovland and R. R. Sears, Correlation of lynchings with economic indices,
J. Psychol., IX (1940), 301-10.

[49] See, e.g., D. S. Strong, *Organized anti-Semitism in America* (Washington, D. C.:
American Council on Public Affairs, 1941).

Five main types of "scapegoaters" have been identified: [50]

1. The compulsive scapegoater, characterized by obsessional and delusional beliefs
2. The thwarted scapegoater, who cannot cope with his problems realistically and "takes it out" on an innocent victim
3. The conventionalist scapegoater, who, lacking self-knowledge, blames Negroes, Jews, or other out-groups for the difficulties and inconveniences he encounters
4. The conforming scapegoater, who is not frustrated but who follows the crowd rather than take an unpopular stand against scapegoating
5. The calculating scapegoater, like certain demagogues, who exploits people's scapegoating tendencies to his own financial or political advantage

The first three types of reaction clearly depend upon frustration, while the last two involve following or manipulating frustrated scapegoaters.

During war the enemy, or certain enemy leaders, are made scapegoats against whom the wrath of a whole nation is directed. This process of focusing hatred upon the enemy is commonly looked upon as one of the chief ingredients of morale-building [51] and as a means of eliminating domestic conflicts. During periods of economic and social strain, powerful propagandists seek to provide scapegoats for poignantly felt but ill-understood frustrations. Among our most prominent potential scapegoats are Jews, Negroes, Catholics, foreigners, Communists, labor, "Wall Street," capitalists, and "international bankers." At the present "the Reds" are our foremost scapegoat in regard to both domestic and international difficulties.

There is danger, however, in implying that scapegoating is at the bottom of all our prejudice against minority groups.[52] Many other forces play a part in producing prejudices, notably the traditional attitudes found within a society. We shall return to this subject in a later chapter on prejudice.

We conclude that when frustrations engender strong feelings of anger and hostility, displacement is very likely to occur. From a social standpoint the problem is to prevent aggressive behavior from being directed toward a scapegoat—an innocent victim. Various means have been suggested for channeling aggression. A few

[50] Allport, *op. cit.*, pp. 37-41.

[51] Cf. G. Watson, Five factors in morale, in G. Watson (ed.), *Civilian morale* (Boston: Houghton Mifflin Co., 1942), pp. 34-35.

[52] See B. Zawadzki, Limitations of the scapegoat theory of prejudice, *J. abnorm. soc. Psychol.*, XLIII (1948), 127-41.

years ago a department store advertised cheap china gewgaws which could be smashed against the floor or wall when a person felt violently angry. Some primitive peoples have socially sanctioned ways of expressing aggression—as by striking rocks or singing sarcastic songs instead of taking it out on people.[53] So far, little effort has been expended in civilized societies to devise ways of channeling aggressive reactions away from innocent persons or social groups. Are we slowly coming to realize that the surest way to eliminate scapegoating is to prevent the frustrations which engender it?

Projection. As a mechanism, projection is primarily a way of defending oneself against anxiety and guilt—through ascribing his unwanted or rejected urges to others.[54] One avoids blame by attributing his faults to other people. Thus a youth who has been suspected of delinquent behavior seems prone to accuse others of various delinquencies. A lady with a reputation as a gossip is often the first to criticize others for gossiping. Frequently the person who suspects others of moral shortcomings is the one whose own record is not above reproach.

Projection is a subtle mechanism and one of the most difficult to identify accurately. Is a teacher revealing projection, for example, when he announces there was considerable cheating in a recent examination? Or when a visitor to a small town remarks on the prevalence of gossip there? Clear evidence may exist to back up these statements.

As with other mechanisms, projection is partly social in origin and definitely social in its effects. The mores and folkways determine which kinds of behavior are reprehensible; the individual feels anxious or guilty about them because of social sanctions. A person in whom projection is a strong tendency causes many confusions and misunderstandings in his social group. Extreme forms of projection are akin to paranoia—"old maid's delusion," for example, in which an aging female suspects sexual attacks from every male. Delusions of persecution are essentially projectional.

Three types of projection have been identified.[55]

1. *Direct projection* is attributing to another person or group motives or feelings that the subject himself has. One of the best

53 See O. Klineberg, *Social psychology* (rev. ed.; New York: Henry Holt & Co., Inc., 1954), chap. v.

54 "Projection" is also used in the broader sense of interpreting the external world via one's own ideas, attitudes, motives, emotions, etc. In this sense it comes close to what we call "perceiving the situation." Projective techniques like the Rorschach Test depend upon projection in this broader sense.

55 G. W. Allport, *The nature of prejudice* (Reading, Mass.: Addison-Wesley Pub. Co., Inc., 1954), pp. 380-92.

examples was the Nazi leaders, many of whom projected their guilt complexes to the Jews.[56]

2. *Mote-beam projection* is the exaggeration of a given characteristic in another person or group, although in both the subject and object the characteristic is present. The labeling of the Japanese as "aggressive," of Roman Catholics as "fanatical," of the French as "indifferent," are a few cases in point.

3. *Complementary projection* is the justification of one's own anxiety by attributing imaginary motives and actions to others. It is most often a reaction to fear and, therefore, prevalent in times of crisis. The chauvinist who imagines that foreigners are arming on the border is an example of this type of projection. Or the individual who is frightened of a minority group will read aggressive motives into their action; and the disturbed person who has stomach difficulties (largely due to emotional conflicts) believes someone is poisoning him.

Regression. Freud interpreted regression as a retreat of the libido to an earlier and lower level of development. Clinicians use the term similarly, meaning recurrence of a more infantile mode of adjustment to frustration or conflict. Regression is commonly observed in children. When a new baby brother or sister appears, the older child often reverts to bed-wetting or temper tantrums. When the responsibilities of adult status are too much for the adolescent, he may burst into tears. In our culture an adult male may throw things and become aggressive; an adult female may pout or stamp her foot when intensely frustrated. In certain abnormal cases the regression may be so pronounced that an adult resumes the complete role of a child. Such reactions are more likely where a person has had a protected, carefree childhood which seems heavenly compared to the harsh responsiblities of the present.

Regression is observable in many broader social contexts. It is apparent in the "old-time religion" which sings of a heaven with golden streets and a benevolent father-type God who takes all our cares on his shoulders. Regressive tendencies are apparent in literature which centers about the "good old days" of the past, and in songs like "The Old Oaken Bucket" or "The Church in the Wildwood."

Much clearly regressive behavior is socially sanctioned in our culture. At many parties, at baseball and football games, at alumni gatherings, and most of all at American Legion and political conventions, a great deal of juvenile behavior is expected and condoned.

[56] G. M. Gilbert, *Psychology of dictatorship* (New York: The Ronald Press Co., 1950).

Sometimes large groups, even whole nations indulge in regressive fantasies, especially when they face economic, diplomatic, or military decline. The French in the mid-nineteenth century revived the Napoleonic legend; fascist Italy talked of restoring the Roman empire. Recent enthusiastic display of Confederate flags and trappings in parts of our South is another example. Sometimes such regressions are harmless or comic and actually tension-reducing; in other cases they may be pathetic or even lead to tragic consequences.

Psychologists have shown that regressive behavior can be produced experimentally. Barker, Dembo, and Lewin frustrated thirty children by preventing them from playing with desirable toys.[57] The investigators found that under frustration the children regressed a year and a half in their behavior, on the average, as shown by a scale for constructiveness of play. There were, of course, wide individual differences, but the general regressive trend was clear and unmistakable. This study points the way to systematic investigations which may indicate situations in which regression occurs and the extent to which it occurs.

Fantasy. Another common reaction to frustration is fantasy, or flight into fancy and unreality. It is an escapist or withdrawal method of reacting to difficulties. It is probably best exemplified in daydreaming, which has been studied by several clinicians. Wish-fulfilment is the keynote; in the daydream, frustrations disappear and one becomes a conquering hero, a professional success, a millionaire, the husband of one's romantic ideal.

Fantasy is natural in childhood, and occasional daydreaming is common in adolescents and adults.[58] For some people it becomes a characteristic reaction to unhappiness, failure, and frustration. Fantasy arises predominantly from frustrations which are social, like being snubbed or rejected, or failing to gain recognition from others. The chief effect of fantasy, of course, is to decrease rather than increase direct social participation.

The widespread occurrence of fantasy reactions, however, is of great social consequence. For example, a sizable percentage of our fiction and drama deals with exciting and satisfying situations which serve as manufactured fantasies for frustrated persons. Through "empathy" (identifying with the hero or heroine) the reader or auditor achieves vicarious satisfaction; he "rides with Autry, fights with

---

[57] R. G. Barker, T. Dembo, and K. Lewin, *Frustration and regression* (Univ. Ia. Stud. Child Welf., 1941, No. 1).

[58] L. Cole, *Psychology of adolescence* (4th ed.; New York: Rinehart & Co., Inc., 1954).

Gable, loves with Garbo." [59]   Of course people differ greatly in the satisfactions they get from such borrowed fantasies. For some persons, generally the least frustrated, an occasional bit of escapist literature suffices. For others, like an unhappy machine operator, clerk, or stenographer, the movies, pulp magazines, and radio dramas are a daily diet.

Folklore represents a richly developed social fantasy in the form of myths and legends about natural and human events. The more the degree of crisis, the greater the tendency toward mythical transformation. History and tradition are embellished by the exploits of leaders and folk-heroes. Group identifications are made more secure by the idealized behavior of great men. [60]

Sublimation. In the Freudian sense sublimation refers to the socially sanctioned expression of urges which are not, per se, approved. Sublimation is a substitution for the original or natural expression of an impulse or wish—a substitution which is harmonious with the wish and also socially acceptable. [61] It serves as a kind of compensatory outlet for urges like sex or power-seeking. When a person is unmarried and thus denied approved sexual gratification, he or she may turn to activities which involve love and affection without sex. Thus a spinster or widow lavishes affection on her cat or other pets, on her relatives, or on small children. Sublimation is also a means of releasing socially disapproved feelings, particularly hostility. Thus football, boxing, and other sports permit us to express aggression, directly through participation, or vicariously through identifying ourselves with others who are expressing it.

It is very difficult to estimate accurately how much social behavior derives from sublimation. Undoubtedly much dammed-up hostility is expressed in aggressive sports and contests of various kinds. It may well be that sublimated hostility also accounts for the tremendous popular interest in crime fiction and drama. As to sex, there is more difference of opinion. Some social behavior is pretty clearly based on sublimation of sex, e.g., dancing or kissing games. Other activities, such as caring for children, and various kinds of humanitarian or charitable work may represent sublimation for one person but not for another. It is difficult to accept at

[59] L. Rosten, *Hollywood* (New York: Harcourt, Brace & Co., Inc., 1941), p. 11. See also M. Wolfenstein and N. Leites, *Movies—a psychological study* (Glencoe, Ill.: Free Press, 1950).

[60] For a discussion of mythology, see K. Young, *Social psychology* (3d ed.; New York: Appleton-Century-Crofts, Inc., 1956), pp. 196-216.

[61] P. M. Symonds, *op. cit.,* p. 405.

face value the psychoanalytic theories that art, religion, and science are essentially sublimation. Such theories are stated in very general terms and lack supporting evidence. It would seem that the satisfactions obtained through creative work are wide and varied. One artist's work may furnish vicarious satisfaction for the frustrations incurred in an unhappy love life. Another artist—equally good or bad—may have fine sexual adjustment; for him his painting represents the most complete expression of all his ideas and feelings.

Compensation. Compensation is a defense mechanism which traces not to Freud but to Alfred Adler, who described it as a reaction to feelings of inferiority. The inferiority feeling may be based on a real or fancied defect, physical or otherwise, and compensation is an attempt to overcome or neutralize the defect.[62]

Since frustration occurs primarily in a social matrix, we may say that compensation is largely social in origin. This is true even where the felt inferiority or insecurity centers about organic defect. For it is seldom the organic defect, per se, which causes the frustration, but rather the unfavorable comparison of oneself with others. If everyone stuttered, had a club foot, a large head, or short stature, then possession of these characteristics would be normal and would not result in feelings of inferiority.

It is very difficult to estimate how much social behavior is a function of compensatory mechanisms. Each case must be analyzed in terms of the individual involved. For one, going to college may be a form of compensation; for another it may not be. Dancing, athletics, joining the D.A.R., or wearing the latest fashions may or may not have compensatory value for a given person; a mechanism cannot be identified from a single item of behavior. The clinician identifies a mechanism only when he knows a good deal about the personality of the individual.

A possible exception to the above statements is furnished by *overcompensation*. Definitely boastful or attention-getting behavior almost certainly represents an attempt to compensate for felt inferiority. Most of us have met minor officials whose talk runs like this: "Just yesterday I was talking with the Governor, and he said to me, 'Joe, you can help us. . . .' " Or the former movie extra who stresses her intimate contacts with stars of the screen, or the small, cocky man who "talks big."

---

62 A. Adler, *Study of organ inferiority and its psychical compensation* (Nerv. Ment. Dis. Monogr. Ser., 1917, No. 24). See also Adler's later books, such as *Understanding human nature* (New York: Greenberg, Publisher, 1927).

Without doubt compensation operates widely as a determinant of various kinds of social behavior. But care must be exercised in identifying it. Amateur psychologizing is dangerous!

Reaction formation. This defense mechanism is a kind of overcompensation by which one strives to maintain equilibrium by expressing outwardly the opposite of what he actually feels. It is an unconscious adoption of behavior and attitudes which are antithetical to one's own tendencies when the latter are socially disapproved. Thus the overscrupulous person, honest down to the last penny, may be expressing anxiety about his own dishonesty. A kindly and ingratiating social role, with excessive cordiality and cooperativeness, may mask a basically hostile and aggressive personality. Or a blustering and boastful demeanor may well cloak an underlying timidity. Reaction formation is akin to the concept of the "persona," or mask, in Jungian analysis which one wears to hide his true self. It is a means of adjusting to the social world and at the same time protecting one against recognizing his unwanted impulses and wishes.

Other mechanisms. Many other ways of dealing with frustration have been described by psychoanalysts and other clinicians. Some are minor and segmental, some overlap with mechanisms already discussed. We shall describe only a few.

In Freudian terminology "identification" refers to the molding of a person's ego after a model, as if to bolster up one's own weakness. It may function in social situations as different as hero-worship, testimonial advertising, and empathy with a movie star or society leader. In its function it is similar to compensation.

Many other mechanisms have been suggested.[63] "Attention-getting" and "withdrawal" are too obvious to explain. "Criticism" means lowering another's prestige because of anxiety about one's own deficiencies. Those who seem to enjoy picking flaws in eminent people exemplify this mechanism—which overlaps with compensation and displacement. "Sympathism" means seeking the sympathy of others to avoid facing one's own problems. "Nobody loves me!" "I have *such* a hard life," and similar statements illustrate this tendency, which has something in common with rationalization. "Egocentrism" has been suggested as a term to cover

[63] See K. A. Menninger, *The human mind* (3d ed.; New York: Alfred A. Knopf, Inc., 1945) for description of many of these defenses. Good accounts are also found in L. F. Shaffer and E. J. Shoben, *The psychology of adjustment* (2d ed.; Boston: Houghton Mifflin Co., 1956), Part II; in G. F. Lehner and E. Kube, *The dynamics of personal adjustment* (Englewood Cliffs, N. J.: Prentice-Hall, Inc., 1955), chap. vi; and in E. Ziskind, *Psychophysiologic medicine* (Philadelphia: Lea & Febiger, 1954), chap. xvi.

attention-seeking behavior of a compensatory sort. "Extroversion" can be considered a mechanism, according to Strecker and Appel,[64] when it involves a round of excessive activity which prevents the individual from facing his difficulties squarely. Similarly, they note a tendency they call "segregation"—a schizoid-like mechanism which produces water-tight compartments in the personality and prevents us from realizing our inconsistencies. In more extreme form this becomes "dissociation," a symptom found in hysteria and other neuroses.

REACTION TO FRUSTRATION

We have just described some of the defense mechanisms best known to the clinician and have noted their significance for a dynamic type of social psychology. But we must not overstress their role in social behavior. Where we have a large number of frustrated persons and a handy scapegoat, as in Nazi Germany, mechanisms like displacement and projection may be the most important determinants of social behavior. On the other hand, in much of the customary, institutionalized behavior in any society, the function of mechanisms may be negligible. Between these extremes we find many social situations where defense mechanisms may be significant, depending largely on the personalities of the participating individuals.

The four major steps. As noted earlier, defense mechanisms are called into play when a strong motive is thwarted or frustrated. When we analyze the situation further, we find that frustration produces behavior whose chief steps are fourfold: *frustration, emotion, habit or mechanism,* and *overt behavior.* Each stage of the process is determined largely by interaction of two factors: the individual's past experience and the present situation as he perceives it. Let us consider an example.[65]

An individual intent upon a promotion in his business or profession learns that the advancement has gone to another person, which produces real frustration. What happens? First of all, a pronounced emotional reaction, probably anger. But if he knows, or thinks he knows, whose efforts defeated him, the emotion will take the more specific form of hostility or hatred, possibly with components of jealousy.

Let us assume that our hero has no detailed information about the events leading up to the loss of his expected promotion and

[64] E. A. Strecker and K. E. Appel, *Discovering ourselves* (2d ed.; New York: The Macmillan Co., 1943).

[65] This thesis is developed at greater length in S. S. Sargent, Reaction to frustration —a critique and hypothesis, *Psychol. Rev.*, LV (1948), 108-14.

that, therefore, he is in a state of generalized anger. Then what? If he characteristically expresses emotion in an uninhibited way, he may throw things, kick chairs around, and curse vehemently. But he is less likely to do this if persons whose opinions he values are present. If they are, he might rather engage in some substitute type of expression, such as rationalizing or seeking sympathy.

On the other hand, he may be the kind of person who seldom gives free vent to his emotions. He may then displace his anger upon his wife and children if they are present. He might kick the dog or cat, or "take it out" on a clumsy delivery boy, depending upon who is present at the time and what his relationship to them happens to be. Or if he were a person of violent prejudices, he might displace his anger upon "the Jews," "the Reds," "the Catholics," or some other handy scapegoat. Again, he might regress; if his mother were present, he might burst into tears and put his face in her lap as he always did when a child. Or he might engage in one or another kind of comforting fantasy.

Actually he would probably utilize more than one kind of defense mechanism. Seldom does one type of response relieve all of one's strong emotional tensions. An immediate emotional outburst might well be followed by rationalizing, fantasy, or some kind of compensatory behavior. Clinical data suggest that as children most of us acquire quite a repertory of forms of substitute expression. Hence the particular one or ones we employ depends in large measure upon the social situation as we interpret it.

Another possibility is that, because of past training and/or a very stringent social situation, an individual inhibits or represses nearly all overt behavior. If so, we would expect some sort of delayed overt expression, possibly in disguised form, as in dreams or physical symptoms of illness.

Frustration and aggression. Interest in the social implications of frustration was stimulated by the publication, in 1939, of a book called *Frustration and Aggression* by a group of Yale psychologists. Their thesis was that frustration leads to aggression, and that the occurrence of aggression presupposes frustration.[66]

These two general conclusions are hard to defend, though certainly frustration typically produces anger of some sort and often leads to behavior which is *aggressive,* in the sense of an attack directed against someone—which seems to be the best meaning of the term aggressive. But this does not prove that "frustration *always* leads to aggression" as the authors stated in the preface to their

[66] J. Dollard, L. W. Doob, N. E. Miller, O. H. Mowrer, and R. R. Sears, *Frustration and aggression* (New Haven, Conn.: Yale University Press, 1939).

book. Probably they arrived at their sweeping conclusion because the cases they considered were more dramatic, anger-producing types of frustration rather than those which involve fear or anxiety, with mechanisms like fantasy and identification, which seem not to lead to aggression. For example, a rejected child's emotional reaction is one of general anxiety or insecurity (i.e., fear rather than anger). How does he react? Depending on his training and perception of the situation, he may compensate in the form of bullying or boasting or other kinds of aggressive behavior. But on the other hand, he may identify with the teacher or with an older boy or girl. He may join a social group with prestige value. If he withdraws and daydreams, his fantasies may or may not be of an aggressive sort. In other words, aggression is not necessarily the outcome.

Hilgard points out that the reaction to frustration may assume the form of apathy, implying withdrawal, indifference, and sometimes fantasy. Another variation in the individual's reaction to frustration is *stereotypy*—i.e., responding in an irrational, repetitive, fixated manner.[67] The businessmen's club in a Texas town which reacts to the announcement of federally enforced school integration by saluting the Lone Star banner exemplifies a form of stereotyping. In this age of man-made satellites and intercontinental ballistic missiles, stereotypes like "Texas first" or "America first" seem not only outmoded but downright dangerous, with their flavor of rigidity and aggressiveness.

Of course, whether or not frustration results in aggression, it has unfortunate effects upon personality adjustment and social behavior. Many students of child development are greatly concerned over childhood frustration. L. K. Frank, for example, is shocked at the way cultural patterns are imposed upon the child without regard to his fundamental needs. Such enforcing of social conformity engenders, says Frank, a variety of frustrations, anxieties, and hostilities which often eventuate in neurotic and antisocial behavior.[68] The influential psychiatric and pediatric emphasis of such child specialists as Ribble and Spock centers about establishing an affectionate and permissive parent-child relationship which prevents frustration and promotes emotional security.[69] The studies of childhood

[67] E. R. Hilgard, *Introduction to psychology* (2d ed.; New York: Harcourt, Brace & Co., Inc., 1957), pp. 184-88.

[68] L. K. Frank, The fundamental needs of the child, *Ment. Hyg.*, XXII (1938), 353-79.

[69] M. A. Ribble, *The rights of infants* (New York: Columbia University Press, 1943); B. Spock, *Baby and child care* (rev. ed.; New York: Pocket Books, Inc., 1957). Orlansky has criticized Ribble and others for overstressing the child's need for "mothering" and sucking. See H. Orlansky, Infant care and personality, *Psychol. Bull.*, XLVI (1949), 1-48.

social experience by Lois Murphy draw upon a wide variety of psychological, sociological, and psychiatric data.[70] She is chiefly concerned with the child's emotional security as determined by the satisfactions and frustrations arising out of family, school, and community experience. The importance of emotional security and lack of frustration is suggested in the following paragraph:

> The capacity to participate in democratic government, as compared with the need to achieve power and wield it fascistically, will be the result of the whole complex social experience of the individual, of frustration or happiness in the family group, feeling of respected membership, or being excluded from school and neighborhood groups, as well as feelings of respect for the rights of others and sympathy for others which are experienced and fostered as the accepted mores of the group.[71]

SUMMARY

It is difficult to treat motivation in a way which is satisfying to the scientist, though we have made progress since the days of instinct doctrines. Scientists are fairly well agreed as to the tissue needs of the human organism and their function in producing activity. Furthermore, in satisfying his bodily drives, a child acquires a number of "sets" toward people, things, and activities which may be called "sociogenic motives" (e.g., affiliation, prestige-seeking, acquisitiveness, etc.). These sets are or become more or less generalized, and energize behavior when evoked by appropriate incentives. No known physiological basis for sociogenic motives exists, though one may, of course, be discovered in the future.

The motives operating in our daily lives seem to be typically latent rather than internally compelling, though theories of motivation are not in agreement on this—or on other—aspects of this complex topic.

For a number of reasons it is difficult to draw up a satisfactory classification of human motives. The authors, however, present a tentative schema of leading social motives and discuss their origins, their functions, and their interrelationships. This organization centers about security-related needs, affiliative and status needs, and integrative and creative needs.

We then described the "defense mechanisms" which serve to guide and channel behavior arising from frustration and conflict.

[70] L. B. Murphy (ed.), Childhood experience in relation to personality development, chap. xxi in J. McV. Hunt (ed.), *Personality and the behavior disorders* (New York: The Ronald Press Co., 1944). See also L. B. Murphy, *Personality in young children*, 2 vols. (New York: Basic Books, Inc., 1956).

[71] L. B. Murphy, Social factors in child development, in T. M. Newcomb and E. L. Hartley (eds.), *Readings in social psychology* (New York: Henry Holt & Co., Inc., 1947), p. 136.

The major mechanisms—repression, rationalization, displacement, projection, regression, fantasy, identification, compensation, sublimation—are learned in social contexts and produce behavior which is primarily social. To some extent, also, they are perpetuated by social influences. For example, in our society, people are expected to rationalize. Demagogues encourage displacement by suggesting scapegoats upon whom our anger and hostility can be vented. Social taboos upon sex and aggression facilitate repression, which in turn often leads to other kinds of mechanisms.

An interpretation of reaction to frustration is proposed, involving the sequence: frustration, emotion, mechanism, overt behavior. The part played by experience and by perception of the immediate social situation is discussed. The frustration-aggression hypothesis is criticized as too general, though frustration may typically lead to some kind of aggressive reaction. The origins of much neurotic and antisocial behavior are found in the intense and prolonged frustrations which sometimes occur during infancy.

SUPPLEMENTARY READINGS

Books of Readings

BRITT, S. H. (ed.). *Selected readings in social psychology.* New York: Rinehart & Co., Inc., 1950.
  Guthrie, E. R., Motives.
  Sears, R. R., Experimental studies of projection.
  Wright, M. E., Constructiveness of play as affected by group organization and frustration.
LINDZEY, G. (ed.). *Handbook of social psychology.* Reading, Mass.: Addison-Wesley Pub. Co., Inc., 1954. Vol. II.
  Murphy, G., Social motivation.

Other References

ALLPORT, G. W. *The nature of prejudice.* Reading, Mass.: Addison-Wesley Pub. Co., Inc., 1954.
  A most readable account enriched by a profound knowledge of history and psychology of the mechanisms involved in discrimination.
DOLLARD, J., *et al. Frustration and aggression.* New Haven, Conn.: Yale University Press, 1939.
  This classical study by the Yale group is still worth reading although some of its findings have been superseded by more recent research.
HEALY, W., BRONNER, A. F., AND BOWERS, A. M. *The structure and meaning of psychoanalysis.* New York: Alfred A. Knopf, Inc., 1930. Sec. 5.
  A basic treatment in Freud's theory of dynamics.
KLEIN, D. B. *Mental hygiene,* rev. ed. New York: Henry Holt & Co., Inc., 1956.
  Chap. xv, Coping with reality, is an enlightening discussion of adjustive mechanisms and the nature of prejudice.
KLINEBERG, O. *Social psychology,* rev. ed. New York: Henry Holt & Co., Inc., 1954.
  An excellent discussion of motives with both psychological and anthropological evidence.

LEWIN, K. *Field theory in social science,* D. Cartwright, ed. New York: Harper & Bros., 1951.
A review of some of Lewin's work in motivation and other areas of psychology; includes an interesting study of regression.

MAIER, N. R. *Frustration.* New York: McGraw-Hill Book Co., Inc., 1949.
Both laboratory and clinical aspects of the problem.

MASLOW, A. H. *Motivation and personality.* New York: Harper & Bros., 1954.
A theory of motives and the role they play in adjustment.

MAY, R. *The meaning of anxiety.* New York: The Ronald Press Co., 1950.
One of the best accounts of the subject for the general and professional student.

McCLELLAND, D. C. *Personality and motivation.* New York: The Dryden Press, Inc., 1951.
Theoretical and empirical study of motives in personality.

MUNROE, R. L. *Schools of psychoanalytical thought.* New York: The Dryden Press. Inc., 1955.
A profound work for the advanced student.

NEWCOMB, T. M. *Social psychology.* New York: The Dryden Press, Inc., 1950. Chaps. ii and iii.
Some original and insightful generalizations about motives.

OLDS, J. *The growth and structure of motives.* Glencoe, Ill.: Free Press, 1956.
A brilliant attempt to integrate sociological and psychological theory. For the advanced student who has a foundation in learning theory.

PATTY, W. L., AND JOHNSON, L. S. *Personality and adjustment.* New York: McGraw-Hill Book Co., Inc., 1953.
One of several good texts on the subject of the individual's adjustment to social and emotional problems.

ROSENZWEIG, S. Outline of frustration theory, in J. McV. Hunt (ed.) , *Personality and the behavior disorders.* New York: The Ronald Press Co., 1944.
This is only one of the excellent selections of the book that bear on adjustment.

SHAFFER, L. F., AND SHOBEN, E. J. *Psychology of adjustment,* rev. ed. Boston: Houghton Mifflin Co., 1956.
Informative chapters on motivation and adjustive mechanisms.

YOUNG, K. *Personality and problems of adjustment,* rev. ed. New York: Appleton-Century-Crofts, Inc., 1952.
Treats almost all aspects of adjustment, especially in regard to age and vocational areas, and presents a theoretical background.

7

Cognitive Processes: Perceiving and Learning

In the last few chapters we have been surveying the social-cultural framework in which we live and the kinds of motives we acquire. In this chapter we want to raise some questions about cognition, particularly the perceptual and learning processes by which human beings orient themselves to the world and become members of society. Perception as a process appears even before learning in the individual's attempt to organize his behavior. His sensations gradually become structured into meaningful relationships, which are the essence of perception. No less fundamental to cognition is learning, which has been the subject of most extensive experimentation and theorizing in psychology. We shall first turn our attention to perception.

PERCEIVING OUR WORLD

A major determinant in our social behavior is the kind and quality of communication we have with the outside world. This problem of how we come to know our universe and what knowledge we really have of our world has preoccupied philosophers from the time of the ancient Greeks. While social scientists are not directly concerned with these more ultimate questions, the basic problem of perception as a kind of "reality testing" is of concern to him. In the interchange of energy between the organism and the environment only partial communication occurs. We only know the world outside as our limited sense organs permit us to experience a narrow range of light waves, sound frequencies, and a few other physical modalities. The degree to which we are dependent on sense modalities is nowhere better portrayed than in the case of the blind and deaf Helen Keller, who had to employ other senses, particularly touch, to communicate with the world. The tenuous quality of our perceptions is further complicated by the peculiar language and thought structure that our culture imposes on us, a problem that we will examine in Chapter 10.

The psychological environment. Less agreement is reached on another point. Psychologists generally assume that stimuli or stimulus situations have objective existence. From this comes the unconscious assumption that a given stimulus is interpreted or *perceived* in the same way by different individuals, although they may respond differently to it. This assumption has been criticized vigorously by Kurt Lewin and others interested in social psychology, clinical psychology, and personality.[1] According to them, a given situation, particularly a social one, never is *psychologically* identical for different persons. Each individual perceives and interprets a situation via his sensory capacities, attention, past experience, motives, attitudes, expectations, and the like—i.e., in terms of his unique pattern of experience and personality. Thus a speaker's words may seem amusing to one person, boring to another, crude to another, and insulting to a fourth person. A newcomer to a social group is considered most attractive by one member, rather conventional by another, and actually obnoxious by a third.

The authors believe this "phenomenological" viewpoint is crucially important to social psychology. When we use terms like "cue" or "stimulus situation," we must beware of assuming they imply objectivity and constancy. We need a term to denote the process of apprehending and interpreting which always occurs. W. I. Thomas suggested the phrase "defining the situation."[2] He used this to designate both perceptual and adjustive processes—both assigning meaning and interpreting one's relationship to the situation (i.e., his "role" in it). Rather than adopt Thomas' term, however, it seems preferable to call the process "perceiving the situation," remembering that "perceiving" is used in a broad sense.

[1] Kurt Lewin, *Dynamic theory of personality* (New York: McGraw-Hill Book Co., Inc., 1935), chap. iii. See also C. R. Rogers, Some observations on the organization of personality, *Amer. Psychologist,* II (1947), 358-68; R. B. MacLeod, The phenomenological approach to social psychology, *Psychol. Rev.,* LIV (1947), 193-210; D. Snygg and A. W. Combs, *Individual behavior* (New York: Harper & Bros., 1949).

[2] W. I. Thomas, *The unadjusted girl* (Boston: Little, Brown & Co., 1923), pp. 42 ff.

This subjective or phenomenological view does not mean that the "objective" properties of stimulus situations are unimportant. Obviously the number of persons present, their movements, speech, laughter, etc., are significant. But these objective actions (objective in the sense that they could be recorded by motion picture and phonograph) *never determine completely the observer's interpretation*. Objective actions always are perceived in a context of personal experiences and tendencies, past and present. As Lewin puts it, the objective or physical environment, interpreted by the individual, makes up his "behavioral" or "psychological" environment. And it is this psychological environment with which we must deal to understand learning or any other form of social behavior.

Basic determinants of perception. The fundamental problem of perception, as with all mental and physical processes, is the maintenance of equilibrium and stabilty. In this sense, perception is one of the several behaviors by which the organism achieves homeostasis. From birth on, the infant strives to make adjustments to the outside world. He learns to coordinate his eye muscles, to distinguish the variety of sights and sounds that signify the objects constituting his complex physical and social world.

The Gestalt psychologists, in particular, have been interested in this problem and have formulated some principles regarding perceptual processes. These principles refer to the "structural" properties of the organism, or at least universal forms of perceiving which cut across all cultures. A few of these principles are:

1. *Figure-ground* refers to the tendency to perceive an object or entity against a neutral background. There is a central stimulus that stands out in comparison with the peripheral stimuli in the broader perceptual field. The racing enthusiast sees *his* horse on the track to the neglect of all others; the professor focuses on the students in his class rather than the walls or windows that form the background. The southerner who wanders into a strange neighborhood may find his gaze fixated on the residence which he learns is occupied by a non-white.

2. *Grouping* is another characteristic inherent in the perceptual process. The individual perceives events in nuclei, groups, or classes. These may be based on similarity or contrast, nearness or farness, or any other direct or indirect means of grouping. Whether concerned with musical notes or the manufacture of automobiles, one perceives objects with some degree of clustering.

3. *Closure* is the tendency to complete an experience even where there are unfinished areas or gaps in the stimulus situation. One tends to think of a square as complete, although one of the sides or a corner may be broken. This need for closure is sufficiently in-

tense that we fill in missing letters to complete a word or the missing features of a face or figure without realizing we have done so.

4. *Prägnanz* ("pregnance"), which is related to closure, refers to the process of organizing our perceptions into meaningful wholes. The constant, recurring barrages of stimuli are structured into coherent relationships. There is no situation confronting a human being which he does not perceive with some degree of significance. He endows with meaning all his experiences. These meanings correspond to his motives, feelings, and attitudes of the moment, or to his more lasting predispositions. Closure is apparently more frequent when there is ambiguity or anxiety or some strong need is present. Experiments on rumor have found that subjects assimilate their stimulus field in conformity with their motives and attitudes, as with the American tourist to the Mediterranean who perceives the vague figure in the hotel patio as an Arab, who by definition must be a thief!

These factors operate to provide clarity and stability in our perceptual world. Presumably they develop out of the nature of neural processes, though their content and the areas within which they operate are largely determined by social forces.

DEVELOPMENT OF PERCEPTION; MOTIVES AND LEARNING

As we have already noted, a distinction can be made between *objective* and *subjective* aspects of perceptions. If the properties of the outside situation are clearly structured, there is relatively little cognitive regrouping or distortion. On the other hand, complex intellectual or social situations allow for a great deal more interpretation on the part of the subject. Cognition at the human level is characterized by an elaborateness that is made possible by the enormous complexity of nerve connections. The higher the organism in neural complexity, the more flexible is its behavior, including the range of its perceptions.

According to Bruner, there are three phases in the perceptual process: [3]

1. There is a hypothesis, or kind of expectancy, which prepares the individual for perceiving in a particular fashion. We consciously or unconsciously assume a *set* to look for a given experience. At a football game one person may be intent upon the rooting section, another is trying to get the attention of the hot-dog dispenser, another is looking for her boy friend, while most of the spectators are probably interested in what is happening on the

[3] J. S. Bruner, Personality dynamics and the process of perceiving, in R. R. Blake and G. V. Ramsey, *Perception, an approach to personality* (New York: The Ronald Press Co., 1951), pp. 124-25.

field. Even for the latter, however, the *perceptual set* will vary from time to time.

2. The "input of information from the environment" is the next— the objective phase of perception. What information the individual accepts or rejects will depend on the kind of hypothesis he has set up.

3. The hypothesis must now be tested or confirmed. The information that he has "taken" in from the outside world must now be subjected to a test of coherence. How does this perception harmonize with previous information and with earlier hypotheses that have been to some degree, at least, tested in the past? Do the present perceptual data support or contradict the total pattern? To return to our football scene, a reference to the behavior of the right guard of the other team as unsportsmanlike or "illegal" is the result of many variables dependent on both present and past perception. Undoubtedly cognitions occur in our young man that are different from those of the fans on the other side of the field. If the player's name should be foreign-sounding, there is further structuring of the perceptual data in line with current prejudices. It is not unlikely that our spectator can more readily recognize, say, a Pole, if he has trained himself in this capacity. In fact, an experiment indicated that among a group of college subjects (to whom a racial attitude scale had been administered), the anti-Semitic were more accurate than the nonprejudiced in the identification of Jewish and non-Jewish faces.[4]

No area of cognition, then, is unaffected by the relevant constellation of experiences the individual has had. In the categorization of our experiences, hypotheses are posed and acted upon, however unaware the individual may be of the perceptual tests he makes. We may refer to the ordering and codification of these experiences as the acquiring of *significances*.[5] There are several types of significances that occur in the development of perception:

1. *"Thing" significance* is the kind of perceptual hypothesis we attach to objects or people. For example, we have learned that there is a certain "size constancy" between two buildings regardless of the distance separating them. For example, the visitor in Washington, D. C., who looks from the Capitol to the Washington Monument finds that the latter appears large despite its small retinal image. Again to our football spectator, the Pole has certain fixed characteristics whether of the market place or the gridiron.

[4] G. W. Allport and B. M. Kramer, Some roots of prejudice, *J. Psychol.*, XXII (1946), 9-39.

[5] W. H. Ittelson and H. Cantril, *Perception, a transactional approach* (Garden City, N. Y.: Doubleday & Co., Inc., 1954), pp. 19-22. The "significances" listed below are an adaptation of their system.

2. *Sequential significance* derives from the temporal arrangement of items by which the repeated patterns of events become a basis of our perceptions. The routines and rituals of life, whether the change of the season, the infant's feeding schedule, or the Sunday morning church service, remind the individual of the continuity of his universe and of his place in it.

3. *Action significances* are those perceptual situations where we enter actively into the events that follow. The child touches the hot stove and finds that this action has a dire outcome; the worker finds economic motivation a main determiner of his daily endeavor.

4. *Social emotional significance* refers to the meaning associated with interpersonal relations on the primary group level. Perceptual events are almost continually fraught with emotions; however, some actions assume an intense affective response. Love, anger, fear, serve as perceptual activators, as in making love or learning to fight.

5. *Evaluative significances* are the weighing of alternatives. The school boy asks: Shall I play truant or report to school? The decision on this spring morning is not only the resultant of a number of previous actions and other significances, but may play a role in future perceptions.

6. *Intellectual significances* refer to the more exclusively symbolic perceptions of a highly conceptualized level. The child solving his arithmetic problem, the formation of a political party platform, the theorizing of the scientist—all represent an intellectualization of a given problem but involve perception, in both the dependence of present thinking on past perceptions, and the entertainment of visual or other kind of images. It may be added that symbols themselves may be regarded as a high order of perceiving.

These "significances," or what might be termed categories of perceptual analysis, are suggestive rather than a complete treatment of the bases of perception. They indicate the complexity of communicating with the outside world. The problems of how perception develops revolves around the role of learning and motivation. In addition to the more explicit motives that may be operative in our perceptions (hunger, the lure of bright lights, or the desire to be President of the United States), there may also be subtler motives; perhaps curiosity itself may be a motive of far reaching consequences. In other words, organisms may be born with, or acquire early in life, a motive toward exploring the world, whether through perception or some other aspect of cognition, namely learning. In this connection it is interesting to note Harlow's experiment on the learning capacity of rats.[6] A rat can be

6 H. F. Harlow, The formation of learning, *Psychol. Rev.*, LXV (1949), 51-56.

trained to choose food under a circular disk. If the food should be placed under a square figure, he will look there, and continue to do so on the next trial. In other words, he has learned to change his set; "he has learned how to learn." In a sense, he has acquired a kind of "evaluative significance." The relationship of learning and perception is reciprocal. Moreover, the ability to shift perceptual sets is a matter of learning and motivation. One can only repeat that perception is a kind of selective process that depends on trial and error, conditioning, reinforcement, and other learning factors.

Social and cultural factors in perception. There is a growing volume of research dealing with the reciprocal relations of perception and of social attitudes and behavior.

One of the classic experiments in this area was performed by Zillig, who divided a group of classroom children on the basis of a sociometric test into a popular and nonpopular group. She then instructed the nonpopular group to do calisthenic exercises with no mistakes, whereas the popular group was instructed to make mistakes. When the class was asked to indicate which group had performed more adequately, the popular group was rated higher.[7] Perception, then, is influenced by the feelings, attitudes, and mental set of the subject. In other words, one literally "sees" the world as he wishes; the distortion is usually not deliberate, but unconscious. In an experiment to be described more fully in the next chapter, Sherif showed that judgments of length were primarily determined by social standards or "norms." [8]

Cantril and his associates have for some time been interested in the problem of space perception as it is affected by social experience. They have performed a number of experiments which show that it is the past rather than the present that determines our perceptions:

All of this may be obvious enough when considered intellectually, but comparatively few people have learned as yet to think and act accordingly in everyday living. Most people tend to think and act as though the characteristics of those things or people *irrespective of* the function served in carrying out their purposes. People forget that a baseball or a cigarette or a house is seen by them as being of a certain constant "size" because they have built up through past experience with such objects certain assumptions that they are the size they are. The constancy of the size of objects, the fact that we do not see a man changing his size as he approaches us on the sidewalk, is due to an assumption we have built up in our past experience with other men.[9]

7 M. Zillig. Einstellung and Ausage, Z. *Psychol.*, CVI (1928), 58-106.
8 M. Sherif, A study of some social factors in perception, *Arch. Psychol.*, 1935, No. 187.
9 H. Cantril, *The "why" of man's experience* (New York: The Macmillan Co., 1950), p. 71.

Another study of social factors in perception showed that the average person tends to perceive in others of his class or affiliation his own attitude to an exaggerated degree.[10] Within a given sample of factory workers, less than 36 per cent voted for Eisenhower in 1952. Yet 60 per cent of Republican supporters in the working class contended that more than half of their fellow workers preferred "Ike." Also there was more accuracy in perceiving the attitudes of others in a primary group situation such as one's own shop or club as opposed to judging the views of one's social class or other secondary group. In an ambiguous situation it appears that there is more opportunity to perceive in accordance with one's own motivational system or frame of reference.

In shaping one's perceptions, the cultural pattern, particularly language, plays a crucial role. The structure and content of a language provides the means and standards by which we apprehend our environment. For instance, the fact that verb forms are so important in Western language acts as both cause and effect in molding behavior toward temporal values, whereas Hopi language contains no reference to time, either explicit or implicit.[11]

Likewise, the technical vocabulary of our system of communication only serves to form and refine our perceptions of the intricacy of our tools and machines. The cultural traits within a society themselves are, of course, a crucial determinant of what one sees or hears. Even the perception of color reflects the repertory of objects within the culture. For example, the inabilty to make valid distinctions in the blue-green area has been mentioned by a number of anthropologists. Some observers have insisted that certain races or primitive societies are anatomically or neurologically deficient in color receptivity, but at present all evidence leads one to believe that the naming or identifying of spectral values is culturally determined. Within our society subcultures affect the individual's perceptions. Women, for example, are better able to distinguish and name colors than are men. They prefer colors that men do not; they will be able to describe how a given person was dressed, to mention only a few perceptual differences. Likewise, intelligence, education, occupation, religion, geographic background, are all conditioning influences in the interpretation of reality. It is not particularly imaginative to suggest that an architect, painter, anthro-

[10] M. Monk and T. M. Newcomb, Perceived consensus and occupational classes, *Amer. sociol. Rev.*, XXI (1956), 71-79.

[11] B. L. Whorf, An American Indian model of the universe, *Int. J. Amer. Linguistics*, XVI (1950), pp. 67-72 as reported in G. Lindzey (ed.), *Handbook of Social Psychology* (Reading, Mass.: Addison-Wesley Pub. Co., Inc., 1954), Vol. II, p. 933.

pologist, social worker, housewife, and tax appraiser could all visit
an orphanage and each perceive it in a different way.

Perceptual variables in personality organization. There has
been in recent years considerable interest in the ways by which perception affects the core of personality. Likewise, psychologists are
engaged in research to determine the effect of his personality structure on an individual's perceptual processes. After all, it is through
one's interpretation of his sense experiences, namely, perception,
that one maintains his identity and self-pride. The ego must be
kept intact from the thoughts and events that constantly arise to
threaten one's picture of the self and the world, which is the function
of defense mechanisms.

One development in this area has centered in an aspect of personality dynamics called *perceptual defense.*[12] One phase of this
problem is the struggle for perceptual clarity on the part of the
individual. For probably all human beings, but especially for the
neurotically inclined, there exists the necessity of integrating one's
feelings of insecurity into a more stable structure. Homeostasis is
demonstrated in perceptual processes as it is in other psychological
functions. Apparently, anxiety intensifies the need for clarifying
one's perceptions. In an ambiguous situation, the individual re-
solves his tension by imposing closure and *prägnanz.* Various experiments have noted the tendency of the perceiver to restructure or
redefine a given situation (such as naming pictures, identifying
the value of words or phrases, identifying perceptual figures) in order
to lessen ambiguity or ward off some perceived threat.[13]

Many projections and displacements grow out of the individual's
anxiety and self-depreciations. His ego-enhancement is ensured by
his perceiving the out-group member as an inferior being. The
adaptability of perceptions, or the ability to change mental set, is
more restricted in the case of the maladjusted as opposed to the
more normal person. Certainly the kinds of hypotheses with which
one approaches his perceptual world reflect his ego strength, as well
as his general value orientation. In other words, one's relations to
other people depend largely on their perceived images. For example, one study showed that a group of subjects (to whom had been

[12] L. Postman, J. S. Bruner, and E. McGinnies, Personal values as selective factors in
perception, *J. abnorm. soc. Psychol.*, XLIII (1948), 142-54. Also pp. 375-83 in Swanson
et al., Readings (2d ed.).

[13] A good example of this type of experiment is E. Frenkel-Brunswik, Intolerance of
ambiguity as an emotional and perceptual personality variable, *J. Pers.*, XVIII
(1949), 108-43. Much of this experimental research is found in chapters by E. R. Hilgard, J. S. Bruner, U. Bronfenbrenner, N. Cameron, G. S. Klein, and E. Frenkel-
Brunswick in R. R. Blake and G. V. Ramsey, *op. cit.*

administered the Allport-Vernon value test) preferred individuals among a series of pictures who resembled their own value systems.[14]

THEORIES AND MECHANISMS OF LEARNING

Human beings differ from each other in terms of three fundamental processes: motivation, perception, and learning. We have already described the multiplicity of motives that characterize the individual and account for much of human activity. Yet, important as motivation is, if one were to ask what the most significant variable distinguishing human beings is, most psychologists would probably say "learning." Certainly the differences in learning ability among individuals are of great importance, to say nothing of the enormous difference in learning capacity between other organisms and man. Also, we have seen how varied are the products of man's learning— the *what* as compared with the *how* of learning. Various cultures and subcultures offer the individual widely differentiated behavior patterns, traits, goals, and values that he may acquire.

In the psychological approach to the problem of learning there have been two general classes of theories. One viewpoint, represented by Thorndike, Watson, Skinner, and Hull, emphasizes mechanistic concepts, with discrete behavorial units like the conditioned response. In this atomistic approach, trial and error, exercise, and the elimination of faulty responses are the principal means of learning, although in recent theories a whole new jargon, including "operants," "reaction potentials," etc., have taken the place of the earlier vocabulary. Primarily, this behaviorist approach, whether classical or new, is unified on one point: they regard the learning process as fundamentally a mechanistic type of habit formation.

The other broad viewpoint maintains that learning is a purposive, dynamic process. In this group are men like Köhler, Tolman, and Lewin. Terms such as "Gestalt," "signs," "latent," "goal orientations," and particularly "insight," are familiar in their writings. Fundamentally, this group of theorists maintains that learning is a form of cognition or understanding, rather than a mechanical behavior sequence. They regard learning as totalistic or molar, rather than segmental or molecular.

The reader probably suspects that this latter viewpoint will contribute more to the understanding of social learning; yet we must

14 H. Fensterheim and M. E. Tresselt, The influence of value systems on the perception of people, *J. abnorm. soc. Psychol.*, XLVIII (1953), 93-98. See also E. McGinnies and W. Bowles, Personal values as determinants of perceptual fixation, *J. Pers.*, XVIII (1949), 224-35. The experimental literature on how needs and values affect our perceptions becomes increasingly great. A recent example is J. Luft, Monetary value and the perception of persons, *J. soc. Psychol.*, XLIV (1957), 245-51.

still ask what the earlier behaviorist theories have been able to offer social psychologists. Our discussion will remain fairly simple, as the more recent learning theorists have tended to be preoccupied with abstractions which are very remote for the general student. Furthermore, the fact that most theoretical advances have been made in animal research means that the applications to human behavior lose some scientific validity, and may have little significance for social learning. As Hilgard has pointed out in his discussion of Skinner, who is by no means a narrow theorist:

The generality of Skinner's approach to problems of behavior is suggested by the titles chosen for his books: *The behavior of organisms* (1938) and *Science and human behavior* (1953). Neither title betrays that the precise data derive largely from experiments on rats and pigeons. Although the data are now being supplemented by experiments with human subjects, both children and adults, normal and disturbed, in these books the extension of the theory is by analogy rather than by experimentation. From a scientific point of view (using the word "science" as Skinner uses it) the extensions merely explore the kinds of variables which may eventually be brought under scientific control. The ultimate possibilities, as Skinner envisages them, are boundless: one chapter he includes is entitled "Designing a culture." [15]

Although there is no doubt that investigation into the fundamental nature of the learning process is crucial to the science of psychology, it appears that it may take some time before theories and concepts are developed which are adequate to explain human social behavior.

Learning as conditioning. In classical behaviorism, learning has been oriented around conditioning concepts for the last half-century. The conditioned reflex traces to the research of Ivan Pavlov beginning in 1906. Let us examine a few of the more important conditioning concepts.

1. *Extinction* is the tendency for a response to disappear when the original stimulus is not present, as the salivation of Pavlov's dog stopped when the meat powder was removed. A human example— bearing in mind the danger of transplanting laboratory concepts to the human everyday world—would be the clerk whose boss has just been retired and who stops saying "Good morning" to the boss's wife.

2. *Reinforcement* is the stamping-in process associated with the reward. The dog's salivation "depended" on the satisfaction of hunger. Reinforcement has become a central concept in most conditioning theories and has replaced, or become almost identical with, the older "law of effect." It refers to satisfaction as a means of fixating given behavior. The child will learn to conform to the

[15] Ernest R. Hilgard, *Theories of Learning* (2d ed.; New York: Appleton-Century-Crofts, Inc., 1956), p. 106.

parent's request to acquire proper table manners if he is rewarded with positive responses, i.e., smiles, affectional gestures, more food, etc.

3. *Spontaneous recovery* is the tendency to reacquire suddenly behavior that was apparently lost or forgotten. For example, after months of using an automatic gear shift, a man suddenly reverts to his former manual approach. In a more social context, there is the husband who finds himself thinking of an old sweetheart, or the woman who throws a temper tantrum, which she had not done since her childhood thirty years ago.

4. *Generalization* has been a central pivot of the conditioning theory. In fact, the term "stimulus generalization" has been frequently employed as synonymous with classical conditioning. More specifically, Pavlov used the term to refer to the dog's tendency to salivate for the entire range of vibration frequencies similar to the sound of the conditioned stimulus. In our social context an example would be the individual who has had two or three unpleasant business contacts with Chinese persons and arrives at the generalization that "the Chinese" are dishonest. This kind of faulty thinking is a primary basis of our stereotyped judging of other people.

5. *Discrimination* refers to the situation where the laboratory dog perceives with sufficient training the difference between one cycle or pitch that means food and another cycle that indicates no food. Similarly, and irrespective of the facts, our friend may have learned that Northern Chinese have a healthy integrity, whereas, the Southern Chinese are a treacherous lot. One can already see the confusion and invalidity arising from applying experimental generalizations to both the human and infrahuman level. Even within the laboratory framework there is considerable disagreement regarding stimulus generalization and its limits.[16]

6. *Experimental neurosis* refers to the fact that when discrimination between stimuli becomes sufficiently baffling, the organism experiences a number of maladjustive symptoms. Pavlov found that there was a tendency for the animal to "break down" when he was subjected to irreconcilable stimuli. From this came the theory that neurosis is substantially a conflict situation: the inability to decide between two courses of action, to accept one feeling state as opposed to another. The man who is torn between loving and hating his mother, between marrying or remaining single, between two attrac-

---

[16] W. W. Lambert, Stimulus response contiguity and reinforcement theory in social psychology, in G. Lindzey, *Handbook of social psychology* (Reading, Mass.: Addison-Wesley Pub. Co., Inc., 1954), Vol. I, pp. 59-63.

tive jobs, will find this neurotic kind of conflict and indecision very wearing and painful.

7. *Higher order conditioning* is the ability of the dog, and even more of the primate, to substitute another stimulus for the already conditioned stimulus. In other words, a light is now equivalent to the bell in eliciting salivation. For the behaviorist, most of human symbolization and thinking is based upon this capacity for multiple conditioning.

Although our summary of mechanistic learning principles has been oversimplified, it is apparent that their application to social learning leads to certain difficulties. Here are some of the cautions that must be considered: [17]

1. The concepts are laboratory products derived primarily from animals, and the applications that have been made to human events are not entirely justified. The examples of social learning mentioned above were several stages removed from the original Pavlovian experiment.

2. A great part of the scientific status of the theory rests on quantification of time intervals and, in one instance, the flow of saliva. The attempt to duplicate such precise methodology in the human area has not been successful. This does not imply, however, that learning theorists may not at some later time be able to refine their techniques, and integrate these results into a more comprehensive and practical theory.

3. Finally, and most important, these learning theories have developed from study of organisms reared in *isolation*.

The distinction has been made by Gibson in an article contrasting *proper* learning, which is the socialized cognitive type of learning in human beings, with the *expedient* learning of the animal with his more stereotyped responses and more limited nervous system. Specifically, the animal, as viewed by the learning theories to date, has been concerned with need satisfaction, i.e., organic drives. Gibson maintains that human beings express a less primitive hedonism. Much of our learning is not in the direction of economy but rather the reverse: we learn to put on clothes in the summer or we go out of our way to help other people.[18] The analysis of social motives in the last chapter showed that needs are frequently in opposition to biological urges. In this connection, the importance that many theorists have attached to the animal's search for the shortest path between two points within the maze does not apply to social

17 J. J. Gibson, The implications of learning theory for social psychology, in J. G. Miller (ed.), *Experiments in social process* (New York: McGraw-Hill Book Co., Inc., 1950), pp. 147-68.
18 *Ibid.*

behavior. Human action or learning is more frequently deferred, symbolic, and in the nature of a detour, or what might be termed a higher level in the search for economy of action.

The role of motives in learning. In formulating a theory of human learning we can agree that we are dealing with intricate variables in a complex social environment. Furthermore, the individual forms a distinct unity with that environment. Most important, no learning can take place without motivation, whether the various motives are conscious or unconscious or a combination of both.

The role of motivation in learning has been debated since the psychology of learning began. In Thorndike, it was the "law of effect"; in Hull, "need satisfaction"; among certain Gestaltists, "goal gradients"; and in Skinner, "reinforcement." As useful as these concepts have been, they have not adequately answered the problem of motivation and learning at the human level. The motives in any given learning situation are dynamic and intermeshed. The question as to how the child acquires speech may be explained in terms of material reward—he may receive larger and more appetizing portions of food as a result of his attempts at language acquisition. Or his attempts may be due to a simple desire to communicate with the world about himself. On the other hand, at least in the early stages of attempted speech, we are dealing with imitative reactions with probably no specific motivation involved. As another example of how motives affect learning, the reader's interest in acquiring knowledge may be ascribed to a variety of motives. It would not be difficult for you to give a half dozen reasons why you are reading this book at the present moment.

The concept of latent learning only serves to emphasize the significance of motives. Typical of latent learning is the experiment in which rats ran a maze for several days with no reward at the end of the maze and with no improvement. On the eighth day when a food reward was introduced they showed a precipitous drop in the error curve. In other words, there had been a hidden learning, whose presence was not recorded until later.[19] Likewise the student who enrolls in a course with no interest in either the subject matter or the grades may find that his interest develops in spite of himself.

[19] H. C. Blodgett, The effect of the introduction of reward upon the maze performance of rats, *Univer. Calif. publ. psychol.*, IV (1929), 113-14. There is some difference of opinion among learning theorists whether this is a case of latent learning or whether pure latent learning exists. The rat may receive secondary reinforcement in the laboratory situation. However, there is in the literature evidence of at least quasi-latent learning.

Test scores sometimes indicate that learning has taken place as a result of his physical presence in the room and his exposure to the lectures even though he has no conscious interest in the course.

Reward and punishment as conditions of learning. A never-ending subject of controversy both in tabloid newspapers and in technical and professional journals has been the contribution of reward and of punishment to the learning process. The "law of effect" was a general statement of the operation of these two factors. If there is any point of agreement between the conditioning theorists and those who emphasize cognition and insight, it is that acquisition or fixation of the learning must somehow be related to satisfying-ness. Even Freud accepted the notion that learning is related to the pleasure principle. There is considerable recent literature on the subject of satisfyingness and reinforcement. For one thing, it has been suggested that there are two types of *reinforcement*: (1) *internal,* where the individual specifically experiences an event as having value for him, and (2) *external* reinforcement, as when society or the culture pattern provides a predictable assurance that the item is of value. The former is reinforcement as interpreted by the subject; the latter is more objective as judged by the experimenter or observer. There is a close but not inevitable similarity between the two.[20] In other words, the child may enjoy painting for its own sake, but it is not until the parents provide a reward that he derives full satisfaction from the task. In this same connection rewards may be *intrinsic* or *extrinsic*. If the child enjoys a game for the activity and satisfaction it offers, one speaks of intrinsic rewards; if the child plays the game for medals or for ice cream that has been promised, the reward is extrinsic.

Reinforcement or reward takes on a variety of forms, and learning theories have varied as to the importance they attach to reward. The significance of reward depends to some extent on the experimental framing of the learning situation. In "instrumental" conditioning experiments, the response serves to bring about the reward directly, as when the animal lifts his right leg in order to avoid an electric shock. In contrast, in the original Pavlovian conditioning experiments, there is a more "natural" response, such as salivation. Many of our responses in the family, in school, and in other social settings are anxiety-relieving, hence function directly or indirectly as a reward.

[20] J. B. Rotter, *Social learning and clinical psychology* (Englewood Cliffs, N. J.: Prentice-Hall, Inc., 1954), pp. 112-13.

In maze-learning, there has been evidence for *goal gradients* in which correct turns were more easily learned when close to the goal than at the beginning of the maze. More than study habits are involved when college students show relative ease in mastering their senior courses as compared with the difficulties of the freshman year. Whether the college student or the rat is involved, relief of tension is equivalent to reward.

It is significant that in our complex society, there is a multiplicity of rewards by which learning is stimulated: social approval, status, money, power—in addition to the sense of accomplishment and creativity it provides. Undoubtedly, many extrinsic rewards for learning and other behaviors have been in the nature of bribes. The teacher often wishes that students might enjoy knowledge more as an end in itself. Perhaps this is reminiscent of the employer who regrets that the laborer cannot look at company policy in a different perspective, and the employee who urges that wage needs receive the same degree of attention as the desires of the stockholders. However, the nature of Western society is geared to individual rewards, and this does not exclude the learning situation.

Punishment is the twin factor along with reward in the motivation of learning. Generally punishment has not been found to be as effective a motivator as reward. Experiments with both animal and human learning have resulted in fewer errors when the organism was rewarded for correct responses, rather than being punished for errors. In addition, the vast literature in child psychology has generally stressed the superiority of positive, as opposed to negative, approaches to training. Some of the reasons for this preference are: (1) Punishment introduces emotional conflicts; anxiety or fear may be attached to the learning situation. The individual's behavior is oriented toward escape from the situation which may inhibit the acquisition of new responses. (2) Punishment is less predictable than reward in fixating the learning process. In the confusion or anxiety the wrong response may be acquired. A child may perform the opposite behavior pattern of what the parent desires. (3) There is the possibility of developing a number of unfortunate by-products. The child who is punished by the teacher for inadequate memorization may begin to dislike school, may develop inferiority feelings, and become hostile to more successful competitors. In other words, the teacher may insure better learning and more favorable personality tendencies on the part of the students by encouraging positive and intelligently chosen rewards.

The average person engages in behavior that is approved by his parents or society at large. The fear of loss of approval acts as a potential punishment. In view of the sharp difference between individuals and the way they view a situation, it is not always clear whether a given stimulus or response should be labeled approach or avoidance. It may be added that most parents evolve through trial and error an equilibrium between reward and punishment.[21]

THE LEARNING SEQUENCE IN SOCIAL SITUATIONS

In general, psychologists and social scientists emphasize different aspects of learning. Psychologists are more interested in the processes than in the content—in *how* the individual learns rather than *what* he learns. They discuss conditioning, trial and error, reinforcement, canalization, generalization, and related concepts. Sociologists and ethnologists, on the other hand, are concerned with the product or content of learning and do not care very much how the learning took place. They emphasize the folkways, mores, conventions, roles, and other aspects of the social heritage that pattern and modify a person's behavior in every society.

Social psychologists believe both these emphases are essential to understanding learning or socialization. The two approaches are like the warp and woof of the complete fabric. For theoretical and practical reasons we need to understand both the how and the what of social learning. This point was well expressed by Mark May, Director of the Yale Institute of Human Relations, when he said that "those who work with the principles of learning (psychologists, social psychologists) cannot evolve a theory of social behavior without understanding the social order which sets the conditions for human learning. Conversely, technicians in the social sciences must consent to take some account of the principles governing that long learning experience which fits any individual for participation in the social order. From psychology, then, are derived the fundamental principles of learning, and from social science its prime conditions. Sooner or later the twain must meet." [22]

We have described several learning theories and mechanisms and have used them for a few piecemeal interpretations of social behavior. Let us turn now to the more systematic work of Neal Miller, a psychologist, and John Dollard, a social anthropologist.[23] Inspired by Hull, these men elaborated his learning concepts to fit the requirements of social psychology. They start out by analyzing the learning process into four basic factors: *drive, cue, response,*

---

[21] For a discussion of the experimental evidence on reward and punishment, see D. C. McClelland, *Personality* (New York: The Dryden Press, Inc., 1951), pp. 458-75.

[22] M. A. May, in the Preface to N. E. Miller and J. Dollard, *Social learning and imitation* (New Haven, Conn.: Yale University Press, 1941), p. vii.

[23] Miller and Dollard, *op. cit.*

and *reward*. An organism "wants something," "sees something," "does something," and "gets something."

For them, drive means "a strong stimulus which impels action." It may be *primary*, or innate, such as pain, hunger, or thirst. It may be *secondary*, or acquired, like ambition and desire for approval or money. "Without drives, either primary or acquired, the organism does not behave and hence does not learn."

If drive impels a person to respond, "cues determine when he will respond, where he will respond, and which response he will make." The cues or social stimuli vary quantitatively and qualitatively. They have a certain drive value, say Miller and Dollard, depending on strength, and a certain cue value, depending on distinctiveness. Learning fails to occur when drive is absent, and it fails if cues are absent or too obscure to be perceived.

Before real learning can occur, continue Miller and Dollard, a response must be made. The response of a bashful boy at his first dance depends on the immediate drive, on the cue, on his past experience, and on other factors like anticipation. Random behavior may occur. The learner may be guided by verbal instructions, or he may imitate another's responses.

Assuming a proper response is made, however it happens, it will not be repeated—i.e., actually learned—unless reinforced; that is to say, rewarded. Reward means pleasant consequences for the individual. It satisfies him and reduces the drive; hence the response bringing the reward tends to become a habit. Without reward, particularly when punishment results, the act tends to disappear. Punishment causes one to learn, *not* to respond.

What Miller and Dollard have done is to describe four crucial aspects of all learning. No learning can be described well unless we take into account the individual's motives, the stimulus situation, and how the response is made and reinforced. We shall modify slightly the Miller-Dollard categories as we describe and illustrate social learning under the headings:

1. Initiating action
2. Perceiving the situation
3. Making the new response
4. Learning the response; forming a habit

Initiating action. Woodworth and Marquis describe four general factors which work together in producing a response: "the permanent characteristics of the individual, his internal state, his goal or activity in progress, and the stimulus reaching him at the moment. The response depends on all four, sometimes more clearly on one and sometimes on another." They give an illustration: "What response will a young woman make to the advances of a young man? It depends on the young woman, on her temperament and character, on her habits and past experiences. It depends on her physiological and emotional state at the time. It depends on what she is doing at the time. And it depends on the young man and his 'appeal.' Evidently it is impossible to give a general answer to the question, Which of the four factors is most potent and compelling? Sometimes one dominates, sometimes another." [24]

This quotation describes briefly what is involved in Miller and Dollard's "drive" and "cue," or in our "initiating action" and "perceiving the situation." Behavior depends on both organism and stimulus, on the nature of the individual and the nature of the situation. A stimulus does not itself lead automatically to a predictable response, as the behaviorists once fondly thought. Nor does a person's drive, goal, or internal state, per se, determine behavior. Behavior results from a functional relationship between individual and situation.

Perceiving the situation. Having noted several aspects of the individual which initiate activity, we turn to the stimulus, or better, "stimulus situation," to which and within which he responds.

Obviously real life situations seldom are as simple as favorite laboratory stimuli like buzzes, clicks, flashing lights, or mild electric shocks. Stimuli, particularly social stimuli, are complex patterns or Gestalten. We respond to a whole field or situation rather than to a single isolable item. This point, emphasized by the Gestalt school, is well agreed upon.

Furthermore, as already mentioned earlier in this chapter, the subjective aspect of perceptions is extremely significant. Knowing how a situation is defined or interpreted by an individual is more important, psychologically, than having the most objective description and measurement of the stimulus situation. Ideally, of course, we should have both, but if we must choose, the former is one step closer to "explaining" behavior.

Let us illustrate "initiating action" and "perceiving situations." At a party of adolescents, the hostess rolls back the carpet and says, "Let's dance." The dancing begins, but one boy holds back; he doesn't know how to dance. A girl comes up and says, "Come on, George; I'll teach you." He hesitates for a few seconds, then starts out on the dance floor with her.

[24] R. S. Woodworth and D. G. Marquis, *Psychology* (5th ed.; New York: Henry Holt & Co., Inc., 1947), p. 210.

Here is a social learning situation of medium complexity. On the organismic side we have George's desire to learn to dance and thus conform to the accepted pattern of his social group, along with the fear that he may make a fool of himself. His perception of the situation includes awareness of the rhythmic music, of the ease with which others are dancing, a feeling that he is being regarded as a wallflower, and a favorable reaction toward the girl who offers to teach him—all of which eventuate in his starting out on the dance floor. A difference in any of these salient features might alter his behavior radically. For example, if he cared little about the opinion of the others present, if he thought they might not notice him standing on the side lines, if he did not like the girl, he might well have declined to dance. Thus whether or not the initial response necessary for this kind of social learning (dancing) will be made at all depends on George's major dynamic tendencies and the way he perceives the situation.

Making the new response. Unless a response is made and then reinforced, learning does not take place. A response is a person's behavior in a situation, as he perceives and defines it, under given conditions of motivation and "set." It may be chiefly muscular, as in dancing or playing tennis, verbal, as in learning a new language, or emotional, as in learning to fear rattlesnakes or to get over one's timidity toward the opposite sex. Usually a new social response involves motor, verbal, emotional, and ideational components. An example is learning to speak in public or to behave properly at a formal social function.

Much of our learning difficulty, as Miller and Dollard point out, centers about making the *first correct response*. These authors state that the initial tendency for a stimulus situation to evoke a response is very important. "In order to describe this factor," they continue, "one may arrange the responses in the order of their probability of occurrence and call this the *initial hierarchy* of responses." Some responses would be high up or dominant in this hierarchy; others would be weaker and less likely to occur. The learning process, by rewarding certain responses and not rewarding or punishing others, produces a new *resultant hierarchy* of responses. After learning, a different reaction to the given stimulus situation occurs, since new responses have become dominant.[25]

Sometimes the first correct response comes about in a random or "trial-and-error" fashion, as nonrewarded responses high in the initial hierarchy give way to weaker responses, one of which finally

[25] Miller and Dollard, *op. cit.,* pp. 24-25.

is rewarded. This process can be short-circuited by imitating a proper model, if the individual already knows the imitation technique. Conditioning and insight, say Miller and Dollard, are mechanisms that enable the individual to respond correctly on the first trial. When a child touches a hot radiator, the pain causes immediate withdrawal, the dominant response in his hierarchy. The withdrawal is rewarded by escape from pain, and the first trial succeeds without errors. Reasoning and insight produce a response that might not have been made otherwise or produce an appropriate response more quickly. If the response is rewarded, it will be learned. "Insight, the conditioning technique, imitation and verbal instruction are different ways of producing responses likely to be rewarded." [26]

The various ways of making social responses are illustrated in real life situations. An adolescent girl from a lower middle-class family is invited to a rather formal dinner at the home of a well-to-do classmate. Three kinds of spoons lie beside her plate. Bouillon cups are brought in; which spoon does she use? Perhaps she makes a random response and uses any of the three without thinking about it. Unless she notices that other guests are using a different spoon, learning may not occur at all. Or she may watch the hostess, intending to imitate her. Or she may, almost automatically, pick up the outside spoon and be rewarded by noting that everyone else does the same. This would be a sort of conditioning, since a dominant response is reinforced in one trial. She may, on the other hand, respond correctly because her mother instructed her in table etiquette beforehand. Or she may employ reasoning: not the teaspoon or that queer-looking long-handled spoon but probably the little round one would be correct for a cup of bouillon!

Reinforcing the response—forming a habit. However a new social response is made, it is not actually *learned* unless it brings the individual satisfaction through reward. Once rewarded, the response is reinforced or strengthened to some extent, and continued reinforcements produce a well-integrated habit. If, instead of reward, punishment occurs, the response tends to disappear or at least remain latent. Let us give a few examples of responding and reinforcing.

Returning to the young man just launched on the dance floor, we find he does badly at first. He does not keep time, steps on his partner's foot, and the like—but he keeps at it. Finally he takes

[26] *Ibid.*, p. 27.

four or five good steps across the floor in perfect time. His partner smiles and says, "That's it! You're getting it." This reinforces those correct responses. Then our hero, George, looks at Jack, a good dancer, and notices how he holds his partner and what kinds of steps and turns he takes and tries to imitate him. If George succeeds, his partner compliments him again. His responses will be further reinforced insofar as he becomes aware that he is succeeding—that he is achieving his desire to dance and keep up with his social crowd.

The principles of social learning were neatly demonstrated in a public speaking class. The teacher, who acted as a sort of master of ceremonies, asked four people to come up to the front and face the rest of the class. Then he asked one of the four to give his name and tell why he was present. The man did so and was vigorously applauded by the teacher and class. This broke the ice for the others, who followed in turn, each being applauded heartily as he finished.

Analyzing this bit of social learning, we see that motivation was strong. Each student wanted to learn to speak in public or he would not have spent money to take the course. Probably some or all had failed at public speaking formerly and were apprehensive about facing an audience. The teacher took care of this by arranging that each would-be speaker should perceive the situation in most favorable terms. The room was small—just large enough for the twenty-five or thirty persons present. When a student came forward to speak, he did not stand alone but with three others like himself. His assigned task was easy and natural—merely to give his name and briefly tell his purpose in joining the class. Thus the response to be made was not entirely new; instead it involved carrying over already learned verbal behavior into a new social situation. Any response in the new situation was reinforced immediately by applause and encouragement. The applause given one speaker heartened all who followed. Additional reinforcement came from the individual's satisfaction at actually having spoken in public. The writer heard one student exclaim jubilantly: "I never thought I could do it, but I really did speak in public!"

Returning now to learning in the child, we find the same principles exemplified. Various motives are present, notably a tendency to gain approval. Parents and teachers furnish models for the child and reward him when he makes the desired response. Consider, for example, how parents teach a child to say "thank you." They help him to perceive the appropriate situation by saying, "When someone gives you a present" or "when somebody does something nice for you." They stress the appropriate response: "We say 'thank you.'" When the child sizes up the situation correctly—when Uncle Ben, say, brings him a squirt gun—and the child says "thank you," we then praise him, give him a piece of candy, or otherwise reinforce the response. On the other hand, if the child fails to say "thank you," we disapprove or, perhaps, punish him, which also strengthens the correct response and makes it more likely to occur the next time.

Where the most efficient and rapid learning occurs, we usually can account for it in terms of drive, cue, response, and reward. The parents, let us say, are amazed at Junior's progress as a Boy Scout. He is anxious to be accepted and to win prestige among his age-mates. He admires his patrol leader. The social situation facilitates his learning to pass tests and advance from a "tenderfoot" to a "second-class" and "first-class" Scout; "all the kids are doing it." Models are provided; the patrol leader instructs him. He is rewarded for his efforts by the award of buttons and badges and by the approval of his peers.

Of course much of a child's learning is "unconscious." He picks up new words, gestures, knowledge, attitudes, and habits. But if we look closely, we can track down at least some basic principles of learning. Whiting, an anthropologist, attempted to do this when he analyzed the socialization of Kwoma children according to the Miller-Dollard fourfold schema:

Kwoma infants when they are hungry turn toward their mother's breast and suckle. In this case the drive is hunger; the response is turning toward the mother's breast and suckling; the cues are the sight of the mother and her breast, and the feeling of contact with her; and the reward is the ingestion of milk. From many repetitions of this sequence an infant learns the habit of turning toward the mother's breast and suckling when he is hungry in the presence of the mother. During the weaning period a Kwoma child learns not to cling to his mother. In this case the drive is pain from being pushed away and the fear of being scolded, the response is staying away from the mother, the cues are the presence of the mother, and the reward is escape from pain and reduction of fear.

During childhood a Kwoma boy learns to avoid the house tamberan while ceremonies are being held. The drive in this case is anxiety (he is warned that he would die if he did so); the response is avoiding the house tamberan; the cues are the sound of the gong rhythms, the statements of others that a ceremony is being held, the sight of his father, uncles, and older brothers decorating themselves; the reward is escape from anxiety. In adolescence a boy learns to carry on secret love affairs with adolescent girls. The drives are sex, sex appetite, and anxiety (sex impels him to seek girls, sex appetite leads him to choose a girl culturally defined as attractive, and anxiety impels him to do so secretly); the response is the complex of behavior which leads to and includes sexual intercourse in the bush; the cues are the sight of an attractive girl, verbal permission from her, the environmental scene which has both public and secluded spots, etc.; the reward is sexual orgasm, satisfaction of sex appetite, and anxiety reduction.[27]

"Thus," concludes Whiting, "although the habits become more and more complex as the individual matures, the four essentials of learning and performance pertain to the behavior of individuals of all ages." [28]

We must emphasize again that learning theory is a highly controversial subject among psychologists. By no means all of them would endorse the simple schema furnished by Miller and Dollard. On the other hand, motivation, perception, response, and reinforcement undeniably are significant, and categorizing them thus helps us interpret the process of learning in social situations.

SUMMARY

Perceiving and learning are the two major cognitive processes involved in social behavior. Perceiving depends upon the quality of our sense modalities and upon certain structural processes, though its content is determined largely by social experience. It is through perception that our world takes on meaning, and a consistent frame of reference is provided. Misinterpretations and distortions in perception become the basis of maladaptive social attitudes. In "perceptual defense" the individual may derive some variety of ego expansion and reduce his inner tensions, with the chain of rationalizations and projections so familiar in the clinical area.

Learning for many remains the single most important variable in human cognition and behavior generally. Although the social psychologist has not profited as much as he had hoped from the learning theorist, both the neo-behaviorist and particularly the neo-Gestalt approaches have offered explanations for some of the mechanisms in social learning. Learning is closely related to motivation as no psychological process can be detached from another. Reward and punishment function as important conditioners of learning. Essential aspects of social learning are summed up in the "drive," "cue," "response," and "reward." We discussed each one under the headings "initiating action," "perceiving the situation," "making the new response," and "reinforcing the response." This

27 J. W. M. Whiting, *Becoming a Kwoma* (New Haven, Conn.: Yale University Press, 1941), pp. 176-77.
28 *Ibid.*, p. 177.

type of analysis provides common ground for psychologists, primarily interested in the processes of learning, and sociologists and anthropologists oriented toward the content or product of learning.

SUPPLEMENTARY READINGS

Books of Readings

Maccoby, E. E., Newcomb, T. M., and Hartley, E. L. (eds.). *Readings in social psychology*, 3d ed. New York: Henry Holt & Co., Inc., 1958.
Bartlett, F. C., Social factors in recall.
Bruner, J. S., Social psychology and perception.
Jones, E. E., and deCharms, R., Changes in social perception as a function of the personal relevance of behavior.
Levine, J. M., and Murphy, G., The learning and forgetting of controversial material.
Tagiuri, R., Bruner, J. S., and Blake, R. R., On the relation between feelings and the perception of feelings among members of small groups.
Thibaut, J. W., and Riecken, H. W., Some determinants and consequences of the perception of social causality.

Britt, S. H. (ed.). *Selected readings in social psychology*. New York: Rinehart & Co., Inc., 1950.
Allport, G. W., The ability to judge people.
Hanawalt, N. G., and Ruttiger, K. F., The effect of an audience on remembering.
Linton, R., Personality.
Postman, L. and Bruner, J. S., Perception under stress.

Lindzey, G. *Handbook of social psychology*. Reading, Mass.: Addison-Wesley Pub. Co., Inc., 1954.
Lambert, W. W., Stimulus-response contiguity and reinforcement theory in social psychology. Vol. I.
Scheerer, M., Cognitive theory. Vol. I.
Bruner, J. S., and Tagiuri, R., The perception of people. Vol. II.

Other References

Berrien, F. K., and Bash, W. H. *Human relations: comments and cases,* rev. ed. New York: Harper & Bros., 1957.
Chaps. iii and iv are most pertinent to the present discussion. Part I is a good exposition of social psychology.

Blake, R. R., and Ramsey, G. V. *Perception, an approach to personality.* New York: The Ronald Press Co., 1951.
Probably the most complete statement regarding perception and its relationships to personality, language, learning, and psychological processes in general.

Bartlett, F. C. *Remembering.* Cambridge, Eng.: Cambridge University Press, 1932.
A now classic study of experiments on the social factors in memory.

Cantril, H. *The "why" of man's experience.* New York: The Macmillan Co., 1950.
A very well written study of perception and other aspects of cognition in their relation to society and the self.

Dollard, J., and Miller, N. E. *Personality and psychotherapy, an analysis in learning, thinking, and culture.* New York: McGraw-Hill Book Co., Inc., 1950.
The authors present some corrections of their hypothesis of frustration and aggression. It is well documented with clinical material.

Hilgard, E. R. *Theories of learning,* rev. ed. New York: Appleton-Century-Crofts, Inc., 1956.
An excellent synthesis of learning theories, both classical and contemporary, presented in a readable style.

KLINEBERG, O. *Social psychology,* rev. ed. New York: Henry Holt & Co., Inc., 1954.
Chap. viii, Social factors in memory and perception, presents a résumé of some experiments in this area.

KRECH, D., AND CRUTCHFIELD, R. S. *Theory and problems of social psychology.* New York: McGraw-Hill Book Co., Inc., 1948.
Chap. iii, Perceiving the world; and chap. iv, Reorganizing our perceptions. Outstanding in their presentation of the Gestalt approach as applied to social phenomena.

LEWIN, K. *Field theory in social science,* ed. D. Cartwright. New York: Harper & Bros., 1951.
Some brilliant papers dealing with cognition and other topics in connection with group dynamics.

MILLER, N. E., AND DOLLARD, J. *Social learning and imitation.* New Haven, Conn.: Yale University Press, 1941.
This offers one of the best approaches to learning in its social setting.

MOWRER, O. H. *Learning theory and personality dynamics.* New York: The Ronald Press Co., 1950.
A work for the more advanced student; among other things, an interesting analysis of Edgar Allen Poe's work from a semi-Freudian viewpoint.

ROTTER, J. B. *Social learning and clinical psychology.* Englewood Cliffs, N. J.: Prentice-Hall, Inc., 1954.
A systematic work that attempts to integrate learning and cognitive theory with the psychology of personality.

SHERIF, M., AND WILSON, M. O. (eds.). *Group relations at the crossroads.* Norman, Okla.: University of Oklahoma Press, 1953.
Contains some interesting papers on social perception.

SKINNER, B. F. *Science and human behavior.* New York: The Macmillan Co., 1953.
A prominent learning theorist discusses some of the human applications of his "operant behavior" approach.

8

Social Attitudes, Norms, and Values

The introduction to motivation and cognitive processes, together with the cultural bases, has led us to a central area of social psychology, namely, attitudes and values. A great part of socialization assumes the shape of attitudes. How does the child come to feel about the Negro family down the street? How does the Iowa farmer, the New York waiter, or the Louisiana Creole react to the idea of the United Nations? Under what conditions will he go to war or change his views of the Federal administration? What are the reactions of the child and parent toward the teacher or the doctor? What ideas or commodities in the world are worth struggling for? It is apparent in most of these questions that we are focusing on concepts more basic and deeper than opinion. Opinion tends to be specific and ephemeral, whereas attitudes and values are usually more general and enduring.

THE NATURE OF ATTITUDES

Some would describe attitudes as the flywheel of social psychology. Probably no single area in social psychology has been the subject of so much experimentation. In its emphasis on the individual as a member of society, our discipline stresses attitudes as indicating how the person feels and thinks about his social situation. Attitudes are one of the most dynamic factors in social behavior, since they are linked with those key processes: motivation, learning, and perception. The range of attitudes is practically unlimited: what does one think of the foods he eats or of the place of the deity in the universe? How does he react to a symphony orchestra or to the Negro who sits next to him on the street car? It is primarily, although not exclusively, with *social* attitudes we are concerned. We have positive, or negative, attitudes toward food, music, or the deity, each of which has social overtones. However, attitude surveys have been concerned chiefly with politics, international and ethnic relations, or aspects of social change. Yet there is no item or subject— dress, music, or religion—that can be removed from its social and cultural context.

Thus we may think of an attitude as a fairly consistent learned tendency to behave in a certain way (generally positively or negatively) toward persons, objects, or situations; attitudes are dynamic and tend to pass over into behavior. Probably the most frequently cited definition is that of Gordon Allport: "An attitude is a mental and neural state of readiness, organized through experience, exerting a directive or dynamic influence upon the individual's response to all objects and situations with which it is related." [1] It is in attitudes, together with values and norms, that one's orientation to the social world is structured.

There are certain implications from this definition of attitudes that should be made clear.

First, an attitude defines one's *position* toward a given aspect of his perceptual world. An attitude is either *for* or *against* an object, situation, person, or group. It is doubtful that a neutral position can ever be called an attitude. It is unlikely that you have an attitude toward mathematical concepts ($2\times2=4$, for example), for they are inherent in the universe, and, as constructs, are remote to human events and hardly subject to public controversy. On the other hand, it is not inconceivable that you have an attitude regarding a food, like potatoes. You are vaguely fond of them, although there may be some fear attached because of their high caloric value. To a person in another culture the only relevant fact is that they are a cheap food supply, without which no meal would be complete. Unusual experiences, of course, may influence one's attitudes: One might have been forced by a famine condition to live on potatoes for an extended period of time. Or one's favorable attitude might be attributed to the fact that the family fortune was made in the marketing of this commodity.

The discussion of this common vegetable only illustrates that attitudes can be formed about relatively neutral objects, although the attitude itself is not neutral. In the case of social and emotional

[1] G. W. Allport, Attitudes, in C. Murchison (ed.), *Handbook of social psychology* (Worcester, Mass.: Clark University Press, 1935).

situations, as, for example, what one thinks of other people, or of the possibility of war, the cognitive process and social-emotional resultants are much more complicated.

Second, attitudes are rooted in *motivation* and *emotion* and exist as a continual potential toward *behavior,* as implied by Allport in his term "state of readiness." A teacher's favorable or unfavorable attitude toward foreigners will affect, probably unconsciously, her grading of essay tests written by foreign students. She may also fail to speak, except perfunctorily, to the Lithuanian janitor. Attitudes provide the emotional basis of most of our interpersonal relations and identification with groups and social movements. They have a driving force which impels toward action. It is attitudes that lead man to vote, fight wars, engage in labor strikes, or contribute to alleviate suffering in a foreign land. Whether attitudes are overt and well verbalized, or implicit and nonexpressed, they operate as motives and initiators of behavior.

Third, attitudes are integrated into an organized system, although this does not exclude the possibility of contradictions in the totality of attitudes and opinions. Also, they are close to the core of personality, as we mentioned in an earlier chapter. They are relatively persistent and enduring; yet like any aspect of the self they are subject to change. This problem of persistence and change is a central one in the measurement of attitudes.

THE MEASUREMENT OF ATTITUDES

There are several dimensions or properties of attitudes which are important to the problem of measurement.

1. *Direction* refers to the positive or negative, the "like" or "dislike," aspects of attitude—its "for" or "against" quality—whether the attitudes involved relate to quiz shows, a high school bond issue, disarmament, euthanasia, or the possibility of interplanetary travel.

2. *Degree* denotes the amount of favorableness or unfavorableness an attitude possesses. I do, or do not, like politicians, proletarians, or Poles—but to what extent? Attitudes imply a continuum along which the positive or negative feeling can be measured.

3. *Strength or intensity.* Attitudes are at different levels of intensity. The tourist abroad may like Frenchmen, but he may prefer Englishmen. To what extent can an attitude become a basis of action? How strong is a belief compared to other beliefs? The motivational and emotional aspects of the problem dominate this dimension.

4. *"Salience"* has been used to refer to the freedom with which one gives vent to his attitudes. It is closely related to intensity. For example, one's anti-Negro feelings might be more overtly expressed in Alabama than in Connecticut. The reactions of Germans to Jews demonstrated more salience under Hitler than under the Weimar Republic, although the attitude may have been of approximately equal strength in both periods. Salience in a sense may refer to the centrality the attitude has within the individual as well as to the spontaneity with which it is manifested. Salience is affected not only by cultural permissiveness but by many internal factors conditioning the outer behavior of the individual. Some individuals find it difficult to give outer expression to their attitudes, and not infrequently an individual is unaware what his attitude may be.

5. *Coherence* or *consistency* is the ordering or integration of attitudes. How does the individual maintain his attitude under different situations? If I believe in civil rights, do I extend it to all races and classes?

Not all of these characteristics are measured satisfactorily to the same extent. The first three—direction, degree, and strength—are more conveniently incorporated into a scale than salience or consistency. Nor can we say that this group of five exhausts the possible list.[2] The measurement of these latter categories will likely prove to be a challenging research area in future years.

Attitude scales. Even before the principles and methods of public opinion polling had been worked out, a number of psychologists and social scientists had developed scales for the measurement of attitude. Most of these investigators conceived of attitude as a fairly broad or generalized tendency to respond in a characteristic way (favorably or unfavorably) toward certain classes of objects, persons, or situations. Examples are tests for radicalism-conservatism, pacifism-militarism, and internationalism-prejudice toward foreign and minority groups. The early scales were little more than collections of statements presumably related to the attitude being studied.[3] Students taking the test noted their approval or disapproval of the statements made or checked the item most nearly approximating their own attitude. Each item was scored in some fashion (e.g., strong disapproval = —2, mild disapproval = —1, no opinion = 0, etc.), and a total for the test was computed.

[2] Others have been suggested such as importance, specificity, and verifiability. A good discussion of some of these other dimensions is found in D. Krech and R. S. Crutchfield, *Theories and problems of social psychology* (New York: McGraw-Hill Book Co., Inc., 1948), pp. 160-67.

[3] Bogardus' social distance test is an exception to this statement; it will be discussed later in connection with prejudice.

Objecting to these crude methods, Thurstone set about devising a more scientific procedure for the construction of attitude measures. He maintained that an attitude score could have meaning only if the weight given each item were empirically determined. In one study, he and Chave asked three hundred judges to sort each of 130 miscellaneous opinions about the church into eleven piles, which extended from the extremely favorable end (pile #1) to the extremely unfavorable (pile #11).[4] The median position of each item, as judged, determined its scale value. (Only those items on which the judges' agreement was fairly close were selected for the final attitude scale, however.) The forty-five items chosen to make up the test represented different gradations along the total scale from 1 to 11. A few illustrative items are:

Scale value:
.5   I feel the church is the greatest agency for the uplift of the world.
3.0 There is much wrong in my church, but I feel it is so important that it is my duty to help improve it.
4.2 I am sympathetic toward the church, but I am not active in its work.
5.5 Sometimes I feel the church is worth while, and sometimes I doubt it.
7.2 I believe that the church is losing ground as education advances.
8.6 The church deals in platitudes and is afraid to follow the logic of truth.
10.6 I regard the church as a parasite on society.

In such scales the items are presented in random order and subjects are asked to check every statement with which they agree. An average or median of the scale values of the items checked yields a score for the test. Thurstone and various associates have prepared attitude scales in a number of areas by the use of their judging technique: e.g., attitude toward war, prohibition, birth control, the Negro, censorship, treatment of criminals, and the like. High reliability was reported, and the tests have been widely used.

Likert, however, soon insisted that the Thurstone judging technique is laborious and that an arbitrary assignment of scores to the questionnaire items is just as satisfactory.[5] He proposed an alternative method. A large number of statements relating to a subject (e.g., internationalism, the Negro) are collected. These are presented to groups of persons who are instructed to indicate their approval or disapproval on a five-point scale. Strong approval counts 5, approval 4, undecided 3, disapproval 2, and strong disapproval 1. The value of a given item is determined by discovering whether or not it correlates highly with the rest of the list. For example, if

[4] See L. L. Thurstone and E. J. Chave, *The measurement of attitudes* (Chicago: University of Chicago Press, 1929).

[5] R. Likert, A technique for the measurement of attitudes, *Arch. Psychol.,* 1932, No. 140.

those who favor segregating the Negro receive consistently higher scores on the rest of the list, and those who favor nonsegregation receive consistently lower scores on the rest of the test, it seems as if the segregation question is a good one for inclusion.

Considerable controversy has occurred over the relative merits of the Thurstone and Likert methods, much of which is rather technical.[6] Each has been used as the model for a number of attitude tests. Actually there is a high correlation between scales prepared by the two methods, which suggests they are measuring much the same thing.[7]

Various improved procedures have been suggested. Guttmann, for example, has developed a "scale analysis" technique, which selects about ten to twelve consistent items and arranges them along a single dimension. A person's rank on the continuum then shows fairly accurately how he answered the questions both above and below.[8] Edwards later proposed a somewhat complicated "scale-discrimination" method which attempts to combine the better points of the Thurstone, Likert, and Guttmann techniques.[9] However, it is too early to comment on the validity and general efficiency of the Guttmann and Edwards scales. Lazarsfeld has contributed a rather complex "latent structure analysis" which was used, along with the Guttmann method, in studying the attitudes of servicemen during World War II.[10]

Other measuring techniques. There are, of course, other ways of measuring attitudes. One is the *behavioral* test, namely, observing what the individual does in taking a seat on the bus (whether or not he sits next to a Negro) or what kinds of complaint reach the personnel department from employees of a factory that employs ethnic minorities, or some cultural and subcultural comparisons in verbal and overt patterns of social relations (tipping of the hat in passing a woman may reflect a more chivalrous attitude in the South, for example, than in other parts of the country). A varia-

[6] For brief discussions, see A. L. Edwards and K. C. Kenney, A comparison of the Thurstone and Likert techniques . . . , *J. appl. Psychol.*, XXX (1946), 72-83; also Q. McNemar, Opinion-attitude methodology, *Psychol. Bull.*, XLIII (1946), 300-308, and Krech and Crutchfield, *op. cit.*, pp. 214-20.

[7] Edwards and Kenney, *op. cit.*

[8] L. Guttmann, A basis for scaling qualitative data, *Amer. sociol. Rev.*, IX (1944), 139-50. See also Guttmann's contributions in S. A. Stouffer *et al.*, *Measurement and prediction* (Princeton, N. J.: Princeton University Press, 1950).

[9] A. L. Edwards and F. P. Kilpatrick, A technique for the construction of attitude scales, *J. appl. Psychol.*, XXXII (1948), 374-84.

[10] See M. Rosenberg, W. Thielens, and P. F. Lazarsfeld, The panel study, and S. A. Stouffer, Scaling concepts and scaling theory, in M. Jahoda, M. Deutsch, and S. W. Cook, *Research methods in social relations* (New York: The Dryden Press, Inc., 1951), Vol. II.

tion of this technique was used in selecting personnel for the OSS during World War II, where a variety of behavioral personality tests were tried out. Some investigators prefer to use more indirect approaches to attitudes, because of various inconsistencies between cognitive states and actual behavior. One interesting version is the *projective* technique used by Proshansky in his pictures of social conflict. Ambiguous figures were described and labeled in a way which revealed a pro- or anti-labor attitude on the part of respondents. Here are two examples; both are reactions to the same picture: [11]

1. Home of a man on relief—shabby—dresses poorly. Scene is probably of a shack down South. Also might be the home of some *unemployed* laborer. Horrible housing conditions. Why don't the government provide for these people? The ordinary workers is always forgotten and allowed to rot.

2. Picture of one room, very messy, stove in center, woman on the left, man standing next to stove, couple of children near them. This is a room of what we call "poor people." They seem to be messy, sloppy people, who seem to enjoy dwelling in their own trash.

Another indirect approach is Hammond's "error choice" test which presents alternative items on a given social attitude.[12] The subjects are to mark which of two statements is the correct item although both are equally distorted. The direction of the error reveals the individual's attitude, as compared with a judge's rating or with a control group.

In evaluating the measurement of attitudes it is evident that all of these approaches have some degree of *validity*, though critics differ as to just how much. It will be recalled that validity refers to the ability of the instrument to measure what it purports to measure. In other words, will the respondents genuinely feel and demonstrate in their action the characteristics indicated by their performance on the attitude scale? In general, validity is improved by such techniques as combining the Thurstone equal-appearing intervals with the Likert summated rating, i.e., the five-point scale, or through development of projective and other indirect techniques. However, the discrepancy between the attitude and action is a somewhat broader question than validity. In other words, one might have a verbalized hostile feeling toward a minority group and yet not display it in his treatment of that group. In fact, one sociologist que-

11 H. Proshansky, A projective method for the study of attitudes, *J. abnorm. soc. Psychol.*, XXXVIII (1943), 393-95.

12 K. Hammond, Measuring attitudes by error choice, an indirect method, *J. abnorm. soc. Psychol.*, XLIII (1948), 38-48. See also R. E. Bernberg, The direction of perception technique of attitude measurement, *Int. J. Opin. and Attitude Res.*, V (1951), 397-407. This method has been employed in the study of employee morale.

ried by mail a number of hotel managers and innkeepers as to whether they would accept Oriental guests. Overwhelmingly the responses were negative. However, when he and his wife traveled across the country with a young Chinese couple, they were accepted for lodging, with but one or two exceptions.[13] In a more recent study a letter was sent to restaurants asking whether a small dinner party of whites and Negroes might be permitted to dine in the establishment. Practically all proprietors refused, were evasive, or did not respond. Some who replied they did not accept reservations, apparently as a means of avoiding the issue, still accepted the reservations when a member of the party made them without identifying the nature of the group. In any case the group was allowed to dine when it appeared at the restaurant.[14]

It is not altogether simple to offer explanations for this discontinuity of verbalization and behavior. The proprietor will discriminate on a verbal level at a safe distance by refusing to acknowledge a letter or giving a negative response to a telephone call. Yet when a Negro appears on the spot it would seem inappropriate or inhuman to refuse service. Perhaps an increasing sense of democracy has forced many people to drive underground a number of their prejudicial or antisocial attitudes. Undoubtedly in this case the economic motive is relevant: the manager would be reluctant to go on record in favor of discrimination. In any case, it is an interesting contrast to the individual who voices liberal attitudes but is conservative in action.

This discussion illustrates the complexity of measuring and analyzing social attitudes. It is usually difficult to provide for behavioral tests, so the hope lies in a combination of conventional verbal scales with projective techniques. Although the latter have the advantage of depth, and tap to some degree unconscious factors, there is a problem of standardization in the testing instrument.[15]

THE PATTERNING OF SOCIAL ATTITUDES

Having defined the nature of attitudes, we may explore the formation, persistence, and change of attitudes. These questions are, of course, not confined to any one area of social psychology. In our discussion of motivation, perception, and learning, reference was

[13] R. T. LaPiere, Attitudes vs. actions, *Soc. Forces*, XIV (1934), 230-37.

[14] B. Kutner, C. Wilkings, and P. R. Yarrow, Verbal attitudes and overt behavior involving racial prejudice, *J. abnorm. soc. Psychol.*, XLVII (1952), 649-52.

[15] For further discussion of this problem see T. M. Newcomb, *Social psychology* (New York: The Dryden Press, Inc., 1950), pp. 147-93, and B. Green, Attitude measurement, in G. Lindzey (ed.), *Handbook of social psychology* (Reading, Mass.: Addison-Wesley Pub. Co., Inc., 1954), Vol. I, pp. 335-69.

made to the development of attitudes. As attitudes play a central role in personality and social functioning, we will observe their significance in our investigation of communication, group processes, and role patterns.

The formation and structure of attitudes. Foremost in the crystalization of attitudes is the cultural pattern in its various institutional groupings. First of all, the cultural situation sets limits to the shaping and expression of attitudes. For example, one compares the rigidity of thinking and speech in a totalitarian regime with the situation of a relatively free democracy. And within these two general forms of government there are almost infinite gradations. During a trip through certain Iron Curtain countries in 1949, one of the authors noted marked variations in communication and access to information. In Czechoslovakia, for example, there appeared to be more freedom of speech and locomotion than in Poland, which may be explained by a number of factors, such as higher standard of living, history of civil rights, and closer access to Western norms.

In Chapter 3, "Culture and Personality," we examined the bases on which the individual's needs are structured, namely, the early relations of the individual to his family and larger group. The Russian's acceptance of inevitability and harshness of the physical and social world may or may not be related to infant swaddling. The American's predisposition toward certain, but not other, forms of delinquency may be a result of individualism rooted in the history of an open frontier, varied political institutions, and ethnic pluralism. Actually we are not able to discover dependable continuities between cultural patterns and the individual's social attitudes. Yet there is little reason to doubt that attitudes are related in various ways to the cultural framework. Indoctrination or enculturation may be by formal or informal means. Attitudes may be deliberately cultivated, as in the school or church, or they may be acquired in noninstitutionalized fashion through the primary group. Probably the greater part of teen-age attitudes develops from contact with the peer group rather than with the family.

In addition to the cultural conditioning of attitudes, there is, then, the influence of group identifications and norms. Group loyalties will determine what outlook the individual will accept, or reject, or in what frame of reference he will express his attitudes. Charters and Newcomb investigated this problem in terms of religious identifications. A sample of college students, who had previously identified themselves as Catholic, Jewish, and Protestant, were subjected to a religious attitude scale. Each religious group had also been divided into three groups (two control and one experimental): Group A, attending class in a normal fashion; Group B, a religious group separated from the others but not identified as being of a given religion; Group C, the experimental group, being informed that the test would include items relevant to their particular faith. The control groups were unaware of their religious identity; for them religion did not become a reference group. It was found that the experimental group in the case of the Catholics (though not for the Jews and Protestants) had what might be called a "pro-Catholic" score in comparison with the control groups. In other words, when the group was identified as Catholic, their attitudes displayed increased "membership group potency." On the other hand, scores of the two Catholic control groups resembled those of the Protestants and Jews more closely than that of the experimental Catholic group. The authors suggest that the reason results were not obtained for the other two religions is that there was "salience of religious membership" in the Catholic. Possibly the non-Catholics regard religion more as a negative reference group. Certainly for all of the subjects in this study, other influences were operating, such as membership in student activities.[16]

Another study pointing to the importance of the group was that of Kelley and Volkart dealing with a Boy Scout group. An outside speaker presented the idea that woodcraft and nature study were less desirable in the Scout program than performing civic tasks in the community. This viewpoint was not popular with any of the group but was most emphatically rejected by those Scouts who were most identified with the organization. Again, heightened group belongingness sharpens one's attitude in line with the group's norms. The greater the members' desire for status in the group, the less they could be influenced by deviant ideas.[17]

Change in attitudes. Attitudes are in a constant equilibrium involving both rigidity and fluidity. Society and culture are in continual process of change, and attitudes reflect the relation of the individual to his inconstant world. Social change will be treated in a later chapter; at this point we are concerned with the problem of how attitudes can be reformed.

There are a number of factors that operate toward stability and mobility in one's attitudes: family background, age, intelligence,

16 W. W. Charters, Jr., and T. M. Newcomb, Some attitudinal effects of experimentally increased salience of a membership group, in Swanson *et al., Readings* (2d ed.), pp. 415-20.

17 H. H. Kelley and E. H. Volkart, The resistance to change of group-anchored attitudes, *Amer. sociol. Rev.,* XVII (1952), 453-65.

education, class, occupation, and geography. Considerable research has centered on this aspect of attitudes. Typical of this approach is the study of Newcomb and Svehla mentioned earlier, who found a high correlation between children's and parents' attitudes. The coefficients were for war, .44; communism, .56; religion, .63.[18] In other words the most decisive influence upon attitudes, at least early in life, is the parents' orientation. Newcomb also discovered that during college a student's attitudes shift away from the more conservative parental position. Over a four-year period, 1935-1939, it was found that a sample of college students moved consistently toward a more "liberal" attitude regarding certain New Deal issues. The effects were significantly more evident for those remaining in college three or four years in contrast to those having a shorter residence there. The latter tended to revert to their less liberal pre-college viewpoint.[19] Hovland found that in the presentation of orientation films, such as "The Battle of Britain" and "Prelude to War," to service personnel during World War II, the effectiveness was in part a function of the subject's educational level. This may be a matter of intelligence, namely, those with lower I.Q.'s were less capable of perceiving the relationships involved.[20] At the same time, studies have indicated that above average intelligence may operate to prevent an audience from being influenced by obvious propaganda, especially of many war materials. In other words, intelligence and education generally appear to favor attitudinal change, particularly when the change is in the direction of improved social relationships.

The changing of attitudes in the area of ethnic relationships depends not only on acquiring information but on the experience of personal conduct, as we shall see in Chapter 22. Individuals modify what may be neutral or negative attitudes in a positive direction when they have associated with members of a given group over a period of time. Demonstrations of this type of change have been evident in the armed forces, work groups in industry, housing projects, education, and religion. Social scientists feel that, for instance, school integration, once established in the South, will proceed reasonably smoothly, since shared experiences, when initiated, lead toward acceptance. However, growing familiarity of ethnic

[18] T. M. Newcomb and G. Svehla, Intra-family relationships in attitude, *Sociometry*, I (1937), 180-205.

[19] T. M. Newcomb, *Personality and social change* (2d ed.; New York: The Dryden Press, Inc., 1957).

[20] C. I. Hovland, A. A. Lumsdaine, F. D. Sheffield, *Experiments on mass communication* (Princeton, N. J.: Princeton University Press, 1949).

groups, whether on the French-German border or in the Gulf States, will not *necessarily* bring favorable attitudes.

At the same time, most studies have pointed out that there is a tendency toward acceptance through wider knowledge and inter-action, as shown by the experiment of F. T. Smith on graduate students and their reactions to Harlem, the Negro community in New York City. From a group of 354 graduate students, mostly in education, who were administered an ethnic distance scale, 46 participated in a large scale visit to Harlem social welfare facilities, a tea, and interviews with prominent community members. Though there was no initial difference in the scores of the volunteer group and the control group, the former were consistently higher at the end of the project. The sample now accepted a number of social relationships with Negroes that were previously nonacceptable to them: dining at the same table, sharing a room, accepting as a friend, to mention a few. On retesting after a year, the high scores were retained on the part of most subjects.[21]

Brophy's study, with a markedly different type of population, revealed a basic change in anti-Negro feeling among a merchant marine sample. He found that 33 per cent of those with no experience of having shipped with Negroes were rated as unprejudiced. There was an increase to 46 per cent if they had shipped once with Negroes; 62 per cent and 82 per cent after second and third shippings, respectively. The extreme favorableness of the score can probably be attributed in part to the fact that the sample was derived from the National Maritime Union, which has traditionally had a more favorable racial policy than most other unions.[22] Likewise, Harding and Hogrefe found that department store employees who had worked with Negroes were more willing to continue that relationship than those who had not been accustomed to interracial work groups.[23]

Research on the improvement of interracial attitudes is not entirely consistent; increased contacts make a higher tolerance score likely but do not guarantee the attitude change is permanent. Studies frequently exhibit some bias, which has further complicated the problem. Undoubtedly, much of the success of educational and shared experience projects in this area depends on the frame of reference of the individual subject. The frame of reference is a

21 F. T. Smith, *An experiment in modifying attitudes toward the Negro* (New York: Columbia University, Teachers College Contributions to Education, No. 887, 1943).

22 I. N. Brophy, The luxury of anti-Negro prejudice, *Pub. Opin. Quart.,* IX (1946), 456-66.

23 J. Harding and R. Hogrefe, Attitudes of white department store employees toward Negro co-workers, *J. soc Issues,* VIII (1952), 18-28.

determinant of one's attitudes in that attitudes incorporate a large share of the total experience one has had to date. Selective perception becomes a critical part of this frame of reference, and certainly no attitudes can be isolated from other prevailing beliefs. One "sees" in a social situation data that are in harmony with one's prior set of attitudes.[24]

Changes of attitude also depend on the type of communication involved. This was demonstrated in an experiment by Lumsdaine and Janis who presented to a high school group an argument that the Soviet Union would be unable to produce any sizable amount of atomic bombs for a five-year period. Another group was lectured to on a more objective basis but reached largely the same conclusions. The audience was convinced in both cases, but the students who had heard both sides were less easily influenced by opposing arguments.[25] Attitudes tend to be relatively objective if there has been a "nonloaded" communication.

In a greater sense, attitudes reflect the ego or self-involvement of the individual. Hence, change is likely to occur only where there has been a lack of defensiveness. The individual who has definite religious and political convictions with a long history of emotional conditioning is not likely to change. Many attitudes involve cherished economic and prestige goals. The young man who wants to become manager of the local bank would scarcely commit suicide by overtly questioning individualism, capitalism, and private enterprise. During his first few months on the job he might cling to "liberal" or "radical" views which he had acquired from a nonconformist high school or college teacher, but the prevalence of more orthodox attitudes on the part of his colleagues would probably bring about a more subdued evaluation of the social scene.

[24] A recent study showed the effects of linking an attitude change with other cognitive and value areas. The issue of allowing Negroes to move into white neighborhoods was related to four goals: American prestige in other countries, security of property values, equality of opportunity for personal development, and sophistication in judgment. While there was some change after the communication and discussion phase, there was not sufficient change in either the markedly unprejudiced and the extremely prejudiced to confirm, at a significant statistical level, the hypothesis that changes in one attitude or value context could affect measurably another attitudinal area. E. R. Carlson, Attitude change through modification of attitude structure, *J. abnorm. soc. Psychol.*, LII (1956), 256-61.

[25] A. A. Lumsdaine and I. L. Janis, Resistance to "counterpropaganda" produced by one-sided and two-sided "propaganda presentations," *Pub. Opin. Quart.*, XVII (1953), 311-18. Reprinted in E. E. Maccoby, T. M. Newcomb, and E. L. Hartley, *Readings in social psychology* (3d ed.; New York: Henry Holt & Co., Inc., 1958). See also C. I. Hovland, O. J. Harvey, and M. Sherif, Assimilation contrast effects in reactions to communication and attitude change, *J. abnorm. soc. Psychol.*, LV (1957), 244-52, for a discussion of change as related to respondents' distance from the position advocated in the communication.

Again, attitude change is difficult when the new attitude would be in conflict with the individual's deep-seated motives.

Stereotypes. Through the processes of communication, and in accord with human tendencies to conceptualize, attitudes and opinions become "stereotyped." The term "stereotype" was introduced by Walter Lippmann, who used it in the sense of a rigid and standardized "picture in our head." Modern life, he pointed out, is hurried and often impersonal, with little time or opportunity for intimate acquaintance. "Instead we notice a trait which marks a well known type, and fill in the rest of the picture by means of the stereotypes we carry about in our heads. He is an agitator. That much we notice, or are told. Well, an agitator is this sort of person, and so *he* is this sort of person. He is an intellectual. He is a plutocrat. He is a foreigner. He is a 'South European.' He is from Back Bay. He is a Harvard Man. How different from the statement: he is a Yale Man. He is a regular fellow. He is a West Pointer. He is an old army sergeant. He is a Greenwich Villager: what don't we know about him then, and about her? He is an international banker. He is from Main Street." [26]

Furthermore, added Lippmann, stereotypes persist because they often provide us with a consistent picture of the world in which we come to feel at home. Any disturbance of our stereotypes becomes an attack upon the foundations of *our* universe, particularly because they become emotionally charged. We resist mightily any threat to our stereotypes. [27]

A few years later, Stuart Rice showed that people have fairly consistent stereotyped notions about the characteristics of members of various professions. [28] He cut out pictures from a newspaper which included a bootlegger, a European prime minister, a Bolshevik, a United States senator, a labor leader, an editor-politician, two manufacturers, and a financier. The pictures and the occupational names were presented in mixed order to a large number of college students, who were asked to match picture and occupation. Over half the students identified the bootlegger correctly; his outdoor costume, turned-up collar, and cigar seemed to fit their stereotype. But over half the group identified the premier, Herriot, as a Bolshevik, and almost as many chose the Soviet envoy, Krassin, as a

26 W. Lippmann, *Public opinion* (New York: Harcourt, Brace & Co., Inc., 1922), p. 89.
27 *Ibid.*, pp. 95-96.
28 S. A. Rice, Stereotypes; a source of error in judging human character, *J. Person. Res.*, V (1926), 267-76; also S. A. Rice and W. W. Waller, Stereotypes, *Pub. Amer. Sociol. Soc.*, XXII (1928), 180-85.

European premier! In these cases the subjects had stereotyped concepts which led them astray.

Confusion as to the meaning of the term led Edwards to propose that stereotypes have four dimensions, which he found displayed by political stereotypes:

1. Uniformity, indicating the extent to which an individual's response agrees with responses of others
2. Direction—whether a response is favorable or unfavorable
3. Intensity—the degree of favorableness or unfavorableness
4. Quality—the content of the response [29]

Edwards found a correlation between uniformity and intensity. In his experiments, those who strongly opposed communism agreed better on the characteristics of democracy than did those who favored communism; those who favored communism agreed better as to its nature than did those who opposed it.[30] However, Schoenfeld, in a later study using two other types of material, failed to discover a relationship between uniformity and intensity, though he agreed with the fourfold classification proposed by Edwards.[31]

In any event, studies of stereotypes demonstrate how attitudes and opinions, based on varying individual experience, come to form rigid patterns often highly standardized for the members of a group. The existence of stereotypes facilitates the consensus which is basic to public opinion.

THE SOCIAL HERITAGE AND SOCIAL NORMS

The most important influence patterning a child's socialization, according to social scientists, is his social heritage—i.e., the customs and values handed down from generation to generation within his culture group. But the social heritage by no means determines the whole content of a child's social learning. What he learns depends considerably on his family, school, community, social class, and ethnic group, in each of which many deviations and differences occur. Yet a common pattern of approved customs and values comes to characterize the personality and behavior of all individuals who have grown up in a given culture. This common core of values and

29 A. L. Edwards, Four dimensions in political stereotypes, *J. abnorm. soc. Psychol.,* XXXV (1940), 566-72.

30 A. L. Edwards, Studies of stereotypes: I. The directionality and uniformity of responses to stereotype, *J. soc. Psychol.,* XII (1940), 357-66.

31 W. N. Schoenfeld, An experimental study of some problems relating to stereotypes, *Arch. Psychol.,* 1942, No. 270. Other attributes of stereotypes have recently been discussed; see W. E. Vinacke, Stereotypes as social concepts, *J. soc. Psychol.,* XLVI (1957), 229-46.

habits Kardiner and Linton call "basic personality structure" and Fromm calls "social character." [32]

Now the customs or the "folkways and mores" making up the social heritage manifest themselves in human behavior as habits and attitudes. As such they are models to be learned by children and adolescents. Furthermore, children are rewarded for learning to behave in a "customary" and "moral" manner—i.e., according to the customs and mores of the group—and punished for responding differently.

Social scientists note, however, that customs have different degrees of importance. It is not very serious to flout some customs, but failure to conform to others is considered downright shocking and immoral. Woodard makes this point clear in a fivefold classification of socially sanctioned forms of behavior,[33] which we simplify in the three following sections.

Folkways and usages. Folkways and usages are approved forms of behavior for specific situations. Examples from our culture are shaking hands with a new acquaintance, tipping one's hat to a lady, drinking coffee at breakfast, saying "hello" when answering the phone, and eating peas with the fork rather than knife or spoon. Such practices commonly are observed within our culture. But, since nonobservance is not a vital matter, social sanctions are relatively mild. Violations are not punished severely; they are met rather with a lifted eyebrow, a smile, or expressions of moderate surprise.

Conventions. Conventions are rules regulating more significant social behavior—being polite to other people, for instance, or wearing clothes in public, attending to one's bodily functions in private, courtship and engagement practices, or using knife, fork, and spoon rather than one's fingers in eating. Parents generally do not care to leave such learning to chance; they instruct their children in the conventions (though often they cannot explain *why* the child must conform!). Conventions are violated less often than folkways or usages, and the sanctions are more severe: ridicule, "shock," strong disapproval, and gossip, for example. As Woodard points out, the necessity for conformity produces "fictions":

The directly false "as if" of the conventions may be illustrated by the type-example of a guest leaving a party which he hasn't enjoyed. Let us assume that he didn't want to go in the first place, but it was his boss who was giving the party, and his boss is a great bore socially. They played bridge, which he de-

---

[32] See Chapter 3 above.
[33] J. W. Woodard, in *Trans. N. Y. Acad. Sci.*, VI (1944), sec. 2, 311-44.

tests; his partner kept trumping his aces; the wine was flat, the jokes corney, and the sandwiches mouldy; and the hostess had halitosis. Now, he is at the door, saying goodnight. What *must* he say? Explicitly or implicitly, he must carry out the directly false fiction that he had a lovely time, is glad he came, and hopes to come again soon. And, though the host only invited him for conventional rather than spontaneous reasons and was himself bored stiff by the whole affair, he must respond in kind, "I'm so glad you could come. It was a pleasure to have you. Do come again soon." And if he hopes never to see the guest again, he just might add, "Don't wait for an invitation. Come any time." [34]

Mores, taboos, and institutional roles. Mores ("Thou shalt") and taboos ("Thou shalt not") center about our most touchy and vital social relationships. They make up the moral standards of a group and are considered essential to social preservation. The mores are not to be questioned, as Sumner pointed out in his pioneer study, *Folkways*.[35] Examples of mores in our culture are feminine modesty, monogamy, faithfulness to one's spouse, honesty, right to own property, and capitalism. Mores and taboos are partially codified in our laws and religious teachings.

Parents and teachers spend a good deal of time instructing the young in our mores and reinforcing correct responses, though children and adolescents may learn more "unconsciously" than they do from the conscious efforts of their elders. Punishment for violation of the mores is harsh, ranging from gossip and shocked disapproval all the way to social ostracism and imprisonment.

Since mores are so strict and all-pervasive, we must pretend to conform, whether or not we actually do conform. Seldom does a person, particularly a woman, acknowledge to others premarital or extramarital sexual experiences, illegitimate babies, opposition to the capitalist system, or income obtained from bootlegging, gambling, or prostitution. When one transgresses the mores, his punishment is harsh, but less harsh than the punishment visited upon him who questions the validity of the mores. Every society, says Woodard, has its moods of forgiveness and reinstatement for violations, such as fines, penances, prayers, and purifications, so long as belief in the framework is professed. "But rejection of the fictional framework is the unpardonable sin in all societies. It was not for stealing or unchastity that the Inquisition tortured and killed its victims. It was for disbelief. It is not thieves, grafters, profiteers or prostitutes that are shot or put in concentration camps. . . . It is those who challenge the framework itself." [36] Another case in point is

34 *Ibid.*, p. 324.
35 W. G. Sumner, *Folkways* (Boston: Ginn & Co., 1906), p. 28.
36 J. W. Woodard, *op. cit.*, pp. 333-34.

the vituperation heaped on Judge Ben Lindsey a generation ago for his advocacy of the "companionate marriage."

Like mores, institutional roles exist in each culture—i.e., expected patterns of behavior for parents and children, for ministers, teachers, political and social leaders, doctors, and others. While not quite as binding generally as the mores, infractions of institutional roles are subject to strict sanctions, legal or otherwise. Consider how we react toward a mother who deserts or mistreats her children, a minister who is fond of liquor or burlesque shows, a young woman teacher found drinking or "necking" (especially in small towns), or a doctor who refuses to treat a sick patient.[37]

Thus the customs of a society, reflected in the social behavior of its members, serve as models for learning and are reinforced with varying degrees of reward and punishment.

Learning the "social norms." As the child learns the socially approved ways of behaving, he also acquires "social norms." The term "social norm" was introduced by Sherif to cover the accepted rules, customs, attitudes, values, and other standards found in every established social group.[38] The function of these norms is to provide anchorage points or *frames of reference,* which guide the feelings, judgments, and actions of group members. Thus individual liberty is an accepted (though sometimes violated) social norm in our country but not in a dictatorship. Humane treatment of children and animals is one of our accepted norms which is not found in certain primitive cultures.

Curiously enough, the social norms and values of a society are seldom codified. The laws represent a partial codification of mores and taboos, as do most religions. Handbooks of etiquette also present accepted practices in the area of conventions for at least part of a society—generally the upper classes. But laws, religious precepts, and etiquette are stated primarily in terms of behavior rather than attitude. Psychologists using scales and tests have had some success in discovering the outstanding attitudes and values of individuals and of groups—college students, businessmen, club members, etc. Sociologists and cultural anthropologists, using different methods, have sought to present the dominant values and attitudes found in a community or culture. The Lynds' chapter on the "Middletown spirit" is an example of this.[39]

How do these models or norms come about in the first place? Attempting to explain origins of the mores and values prevalent in

37 Roles will be discussed at length in Chapter 13.

38 M. Sherif, *The psychology of social norms* (New York: Harper & Bros., 1936).

39 R. S. and H. M. Lynd, *Middletown in transition* (New York: Harcourt, Brace & Co., Inc., 1937), chap. xii. See above, pp. 126-27.

any large social group is, of course, a complicated historical and anthropological as well as psychological matter. At least we have some good hypotheses, based upon both observation and experimentation.

Sherif demonstrated experimentally that when a person faces a new and "unstructured" (i.e., vague or unclear) situation, he sets up frames of reference.[40] His subjects were shown a pinpoint of light in a completely darkened room. The light was stationary, but seemed to move (the autokinetic phenomenon). Lacking standards of judgment for estimating the amount of movement, each subject established a range or norm for the movement he perceived (e.g., 3 inches; 8 inches), which remained quite consistent during subsequent trials. When two or three individuals who had each established different norms (e.g., 1 inch, 2 inches, 8 inches) were brought together into the dark room, a new *social norm* was established which remained consistent for that group or for the individuals of the group when tested separately. A group norm was also set up when the apparently moving light was observed by several individuals together for the first time. Often the individuals were not aware that they were being influenced in their formation of a norm by other members of the group.

Sherif's work thus indicates clearly that socially accepted and observed norms are set up in the course of social interaction. He describes a basic process operating in the formation of those commonly accepted standards of judgment and behavior which we call by such names as "values," "attitudes," and "mores."

The principle of *canalization* also aids us in suggesting why one kind of behavior rather than another becomes established as a norm. Canalization is simply the tendency to repeat and learn a first response which is satisfying in preference to other acts, no matter what caused the original response to occur.[41] Guthrie's ingenious experiment on cats is a good example of this principle.[42] He placed a cat in a problem box, with food outside. A door in the box could be opened if the cat moved an upright stick on the floor of the box. All the cats mastered the trick easily, but the interesting thing was that each cat continued to open the box in whichever way it *first* was successful—e.g., by pushing the pole with its nose, with a paw, brushing against it, backing into it, etc. The

---

[40] M. Sherif, A study of some social factors in perception, *Arch. Psychol.*, 1935, No. 187; M. Sherif, Group influences upon the formation of norms and attitudes, in Swanson *et al.*, *Readings* (2d ed.), pp. 249-62.

[41] See G. Murphy, *Personality* (New York: Harper & Bros., 1947), chap. viii.

[42] E. R. Guthrie and G. P. Horton, *Cats in a puzzle box* (New York: Rinehart & Co., Inc., 1946).

first chance act was perpetuated or "canalized," despite the fact that other more efficient ways of behaving might have been discovered with further experience. The first response, in other words, may be random, trial-and-error, or pure "chance." But if it brings reward, its particular pattern is reinforced and learned in preference to all other possible ways of responding.

It is more than likely that many of our mores and conventions originated in such random fashion—the food preferences found in any culture, for example. Indeed, the highly arbitrary and seemingly unreasonable food preferences of young children furnish a good illustration of canalization. Customs such as kinds of dress, forms of language used, and even many social relationships seem to stem from canalization.

However, it would be pushing the concept of canalization too far if we used it to explain all kinds of social interaction. Waller has elaborated on the same basic idea in his theory that mores and other sanctioned forms of social behavior arise out of the mutual adjustments or "accommodations" made necessary in our daily social living.[43] Newlyweds, in the process of learning to live together, work out a large variety of accommodations (some of them, at least, being haphazard in origin) which come to serve as "musts" in their household. In larger family units one can discover many local mores, centering about seating positions at the dining table, household chores to be performed, use of the bathroom, radio, and car, and many other matters. Mutually adjustive forms of behavior—"meshings of habits," to use Waller's term—evolve and come to be practiced and understood by all members of the family. Acceptance is rewarded and infractions are punished in various ways.

Here we have important evidence as to how mores, taboos, values, and other norms of social behavior are produced. Such products of social interaction and social learning, of course, are anything but static. Once established, they are immediately subject to change under the impact of technological progress and many other forces. Local mores generally change faster than national ones. Mores, as compared with usages and conventions, change slowly. We shall return to the subject when we discuss "social change" in a later chapter.

THE ROLE OF VALUES

Values are a type of norm and are closely related to attitudes. At the same time they are kinds of motives, since they represent

---

[43] W. W. Waller and R. Hill, *The family* (rev. ed.; New York: The Dryden Press, Inc., 1951).

orientation or striving toward a given goal. In the broadest sense, we may think of values as attitude-related attributes that are projected upon people, objects, and situations. Values have been defined as "desiderata, i.e., anything desired or chosen by someone sometime." [44] In polling behavior this would mean anything the individual wants as stated in a questionnaire is a value. Generally, however, we tend to think of values as the more enduring clusters of wants that a given individual or group works toward fairly consistently. With attitudes, they are basic to personality and yet may be distinguished from traits. They resemble attitudes, and differ from traits, in that they are more general reactions toward persons, situations, and objects in a positive and negative direction.

In philosophical literature there has been much speculation whether values are inherent in the universe or are the derivations and conceptualizations of man himself ("realism" versus "nominalism"). Does justice exist simply in the minds of men, or is it a "real" value in the Platonic sense? Although this is a philosophical argument and one that we cannot pursue in this context, we may accept the premise that whatever is demonstrated in human behavior is real in a social psychological sense. Consequently, if a sizable number of people are interested in justice, world peace, or even pioneering in the Klondike, these are values and may be empirically studied.

Some classifications of values. Values are subject to various classificatory systems. Philosophers have distinguished between higher and lower, mental and physical, permanent and transient. Also, they have differentiated the intrinsic—values that are an inseparable part of the object or situation—and extrinsic—values that are supplemental. Likewise, there is the distinction between instrumental and inherent values—those ideas and actions that are subordinate to certain goals or accomplishments. Familiarly, this is known as the distinction between means and ends—what is done in order to reach a given result. From a psychological viewpoint it is important to distinguish between implicit and explicit values.[45] Implicit values are those known only to the subject; explicit are sufficiently verbalized that the outside observer can make judgments about them. Naturally, this distinction is highly arbitrary.

44 S. C. Dodd, On classifying human values: a step in the prediction of human valuing, *Amer. sociol. Rev.*, XVI (1951), 645-53.

45 C. Kluckhohn, Values and value-orientations in the theory of action, in T. Parsons and E. A. Shils (eds.), *Toward a general theory of action* (Cambridge, Mass.: Harvard University Press, 1951), pp. 395-97.

One of the most comprehensive classifications of social values has been made by Kluckhohn.[46] He conceives of values in terms of *dimensions*, some of which are:

1. *Modality,* the positive-negative continuum, whether one is attracted or repulsed by the object, situation, or conceptualization
2. *Content,* the type of value, which falls into three classes: *Esthetic* (feeling aspects, art, etc.); *cognitive* (intellectual types of value, norms that rest more directly on logical thinking); *moral* (behavioral values, sanctions, laws, or ways of doing things)
3. *Generality* versus *specificity,* whether the value refers to a given situation in time or place, or covers the culture on a continual basis. The payment of a corporate tax as against taboo on stealing
4. *Intensity,* which has a number of tangents: (a) *Categorical* versus the *preferential*—values that are obligatory and those that are matters of choice. The "desire" to pay an income tax and the desire to buy a car. Various aspects of the preferential values are *hypothetical, traditionalistic,* or *utopian*— values that are now matters of choice and have possibly lost their effectiveness. (b) *Central* versus *peripheral,* whether the value has a dominant role, or is segmental to the major line of the culture

In contrast to the sociological and philosophical approach of classifying values, there is a psychological orientation. Personality and interest tests have attempted to arrive at a system of human motives, which may be identified as values; however, the single most influential classification of values has been made by Spranger, who proposed six basic value types: the theoretical, economic, esthetic, political, social, and religious.[47] Vernon and Allport prepared a scale of values, using Spranger's six types, to indicate which major areas of endeavor are most important to an individual.[48] Thus theological students are high on religious values and business students on economic values.

These values have proved to be of some predictability in the study of social behavior. It was found, for instance, that friendship patterns were correlated with value scores in a sample of college women. Friends were selected on the basis of corresponding values.[49] Value systems, based on the Allport-Vernon, proved to be

46 *Ibid.,* pp. 412-21.

47 E. Spranger, *Types of men,* trans. P. W. Pigors (Halle: Niemyer, 1928).

48 P. E. Vernon and G. W. Allport, A test for personal values, *J. abnorm. soc. Psychol.,* XXVI (1931), 231-48. In 1951 this test was revised by G. W. Allport, P. E. Vernon, and G. Lindzey; see their *Study of values* (Boston: Houghton Mifflin Co.).

49 Helen M. Richardson, Community of values as a factor in friendships of college and adult women, *J. soc. Psychol.,* XI (1940), 203-20.

useful in the analysis of certain social attitudes. An example is the negative relationship found between esthetic and social values and anti-Semitism, and positive relationship between political and economic values and anti-Semitism. The hypothesis that there would be positive relationship between the theoretical and religious values and anti-Semitism did not prove statistically valid, although there was a positive coefficient.[50]

Values in the culture pattern. In Chapter 3 we mentioned the significance of value orientations and the variations in goals that cultures and subcultures exhibit. In America there are a number of fairly well crystallized value-orientations; anthropologists have stressed the importance value-orientations may play in preliterate societies. For the Indians of northwest California certain ceremonial objects, such as white deerskins and flint blades, might be interiorized as a supreme value and might become the basis of achievement. With the Plains Indians the dominant value was bravery of warfare and the hunt.[51]

It may well be asked whether value orientations in our culture are measurable or whether it would be possible to determine by empirical test whether one national group preferred one set of values over another. In this connection an experiment was conducted in the search for culturally oriented goals. The subjects were Indian and Filipino nationals attending American universities and were administered a scale which elicited their responses to the culture pattern of a hypothetical foreign country as a means of obtaining international comparisons together with an American sample. There was much agreement between the Asian and the American responses on the value of education and equalitarian government, for example. It was found, however, that Filipinos, probably because of their Catholic background, disliked birth control; that Indians differed considerably from Americans in the kind of industrial system (technological versus handcraft) they preferred; that Filipinos slightly approved of censorship of mass media, which was slightly disapproved by the Indians and strongly disapproved by the Americans.[52]

[50] R. I. Evans, Personal values as factors in anti-Semitism, *J. abnorm. soc. Psychol.,* XLVII (1952), 749-56.

[51] W. Goldschmidt, Values and the field of comparative sociology, *Amer. sociol. Rev.,* XVIII (1953), 287-93.

[52] R. E. Carter, An experiment in value measurement, *Amer. sociol. Rev.,* XXI (1956), 156-63.

Besides the dominant values of any culture there are the more subsidiary or marginal values.[53] It will be of no surprise to the reader to learn that there is often a wide discrepancy between one's expressed values and his behavior, in the same way that a conflict frequently exists between behavior and verbalized attitudes. The businessman who never misses church on Sunday morning is not necessarily going to demonstrate on weekdays the essence of the Sermon on the Mount. The liberal who preaches humanitarianism may still prefer not to pay the prevailing wage to the Saturday morning cleaning girl. The student may aspire toward an "A"; however, the desire for social approval on the part of the opposite sex may be a stronger value. Conflicts in values are inevitable for both the individual, group, or even the whole society. One recalls that he has not infrequently been at a crossroads where it was a case of choosing one value over another. In fact, most of us have erected, both consciously and unconsciously, an organization of values—a value-hierarchy—by which we guide our lives in some degree by a not-altogether-consistent system of goals and norms.

SUMMARY

Attitude is a central concept in social psychology; it is a learned tendency to behave positively or negatively toward persons and situations. Attitudes are dynamic, with several dimensions or properties, and are basic ingredients of personality structure. Several types of scales have been devised for measuring attitudes, and these have been supplemented recently by more indirect techniques. Attitudes are culturally conditioned, and are particularly influenced by our membership and reference groups. They are most likely to be modified or changed through ego-involved group participation. Sometimes attitudes become stereotypes—a kind of standardized concept or pattern.

The customs and attitudes which a child absorbs from his social milieu constitute "social norms," which are strongly reinforced by the group. Values may also be considered social norms; they resemble attitudes but may be thought of as more generalized goal-symbols. Cultures and subcultures can be differentiated as to their value-orientations.

[53] It has been suggested that there are *dominant, variant* (choice-values), and *deviant* (rejected or antisocial) values. See F. Kluckhohn, Dominant and variant value orientations, in C. Kluckhohn, H. A. Murray, and D. M. Schneider (eds.), *Personality in nature society and culture* (2d ed.: New York: Alfred A. Knopf, Inc., 1953), pp. 342-57.

SUPPLEMENTARY READINGS

Books of Readings

MACCOBY, E. E., NEWCOMB, T. M., AND HARTLEY, E. L. (eds.). *Readings in social psychology,* 3d ed. New York: Henry Holt & Co., Inc., 1958.

Katz, D., and Braly, K. W., Verbal stereotypes and racial prejudice.

Sherif, M., Group influences upon the formation of norms and attitudes.

Asch, S., Effects of group pressure upon the modification and distortion of judgments.

Charters, W. W., Jr., and Newcomb, Theodore M., Some attitudinal effects of experimentally increased salience of a membership group.

Newcomb, Theodore M., Attitude development as a function of reference groups· the Bennington study.

Chapman, D. W., and Volkmann, J., A social determinant of the level of aspiration.

BRITT, S. H. (ed.). *Selected readings in social psychology.* New York: Rinehart & Co., Inc., 1950.

Sherif, M., and Cantril, H., The psychology of attitudes.

McGranhan, D. V., A comparison of social attitudes among American and German youth.

LINDZEY, G. (ed.). *Handbook of social psychology.* Reading, Mass.: Addison-Wesley Pub. Co., Inc., 1954. Vol. I.

Green, B. F., Attitude measurement.

Other References

ASCH, S. E. *Social psychology.* Englewood Cliffs, N. J.: Prentice-Hall, Inc., 1952.

This introductory text contains a good discussion of attitudes and values, especially chaps. xii, xviii, and xix.

BECKER, H. *Through values to social interpretation.* Durham, N.C.: Duke University Press, 1950.

A brilliant, though subjective, work on the role of values in social science and in Western society generally.

BONNER, H. *Social psychology.* New York: American Book Co., 1953.

An attractively written book; has illuminating material on attitudes, norms, and values in chaps. vii and ix.

EDWARDS, A. L. Techniques of attitude construction. New York: Appleton-Century-Crofts, Inc., 1956.

For the more advanced student with some knowledge of statistics.

KRECH, D., AND CRUTCHFIELD, R. S. *Theory and problems of social psychology.* New York: McGraw-Hill Book Co., Inc., 1948.

Chaps. v-viii contain a thorough discussion of the nature, development, and measurement of social attitudes.

NEWCOMB, T. M. *Social psychology.* New York: The Dryden Press, Inc., 1950.

Chaps. iv-viii are relevant to problems of attitudes and norms, especially in their relationship to motivation.

PARSONS, T., AND SHILS, E. A. (eds.). *Toward a general theory of action.* Cambridge, Mass.: Harvard University Press, 1951.

A brilliant but formidable investigation into, among other things, the role of values and value-orientations in social behavior.

SCHRAMM, W. *The process and effects of mass communication.* Urbana, Ill.: The University of Illinois Press, 1954.

There are reports of some attitude studies on pages 207-88.

SHERIF, M., AND SHERIF, C. W. *An outline of social psychology,* rev. ed. New York: Harper & Bros., 1956.

An analysis of norms and attitudes, particularly the problem of changes in attitude with reference to groups. Chaps. viii, xv, and xvi.

STOUFFER, S. A. *Communism, conformity, and civil liberties.* Garden City, N. Y.: Doubleday & Co., Inc., 1955.

The report of an attitude and public opinion survey on an enduring social issue.

YOUNG, K. *Social psychology,* 3d ed. New York: Appleton-Century-Crofts, Inc., 1956.

Chap. ix, on belief systems, and chap. xviii, on measurement, are most relevant.

9

The Ego and Self

Any treatment of personality or socialization would be incomplete without consideration of the ego or self. For however one defines it, the ego comes close to being the essence, the organizing principle, of personality. One's ego is involved in one's most intense motives and purposes, one's most poignant frustrations, one's most consistent attitudes and values. The ego also includes a person's estimate of himself and of his major roles in relation to others. Obviously, then, understanding and prediction of a person's social behavior require knowledge about his ego.

It is much easier for the psychologist to study motor abilities, language, memory, emotions, and intelligence than to deal with a complex synthesis like the ego. Between about 1910 and 1940 most psychologists preferred not to mention "ego" or "self" in their writings. When it became clear that the subject is one of their proper concerns, they found that certain early psychologists and sociologists had already worked out a number of productive ideas about the "self" and its development. Sigmund Freud, of course, had postulated the ego as an integral part of psychoanalytic theory. We shall review briefly these contributions before presenting our social psychological interpretation.

THE SELF AND ITS ORIGIN

Theories on the "social self." In his famous and widely used *Principles of Psychology*, William James devoted a long chapter to "The Consciousness of Self." [1]

[1] W. James, *Principles of psychology* (New York: Henry Holt & Co., Inc., 1890), Vol. I, pp. 291-401.

In its widest possible sense [wrote James], *a man's Self is the sum of all that he CAN call his,* not only his body and his psychic powers, but his clothes and his house, his wife and children, his ancestors and friends, his reputation and works, his lands and horses, and yacht and bank-account. All these things give him the same emotions. If they wax and prosper, he feels triumphant; if they dwindle and die away, he feels cast down,—not necessarily in the same degree for each thing, but in much the same way for all.[2]

One important constituent of the self, said James, is the social self. This is the recognition which he gets from his mates, since "we are not only gregarious animals, liking to be in sight of our fellows, but we have an innate propensity to get ourselves noticed, and noticed favorably, by our kind." [3] Furthermore,

. . . *a man has as many social selves as there are individuals who recognize him* . . . as there are distinct *groups* of persons about whose opinions he cares. He generally shows a different side of himself to each of these different groups. Many a youth who is demure enough before his parents and teachers, swears and swaggers like a pirate among his "tough" young friends. We do not show ourselves to our children as to our club-companions, to our customers as to the laborers we employ, to our own masters and employers as to our intimate friends. From this there results what practically is a division of the man into several selves; and this may be a discordant splitting, as where one is afraid to let one set of his acquaintances know him as he is elsewhere; or it may be a perfectly harmonious division of labor, as where one tender to his children is stern to the soldiers or prisoners under his command.[4]

To the philosopher and psychologist of the late nineteenth century, "self" was the closest approximation to what we now call "personality." James saw the significance of social components in the broad and complex self and realized the importance of what came to be called later "role-playing" or "role-taking." He did not, however, devote much attention to the origin and development of the self.

James Mark Baldwin, a pioneer developmental psychologist and contemporary of James, asserted emphatically that self is a social product. "My sense of myself grows by imitation of you," wrote Baldwin, "and my sense of yourself grows in terms of my sense of myself." [5] He concluded:

I do not see, in short, how the personality of this child can be expressed in any but social terms; nor how, on the other hand, social terms can get any content or value but from the understanding of the developing individual.[6]

2 *Ibid.*, pp. 291-92.

3 *Ibid.*, p. 293.

4 *Ibid.*, p. 294.

5 J. M. Baldwin, *Social and ethical interpretations* (New York: The Macmillan Co., 1913), p. 15. See F. B. Karpf, *American social psychology* (New York: McGraw-Hill Book Co., Inc., 1932), pp. 269 ff., for an excellent account of Baldwin's work.

6 Baldwin, *op. cit.*, p. 27.

A man is a social outcome rather than a social unit. He is always, in his greatest part, also someone else. Social acts of his—that is, acts which may not prove anti-social—are his *because they are society's first;* otherwise he would not have learned them nor have had any tendency to do them.[7]

Baldwin was one of the first to use terms like "social environment" and "culture" to designate the social milieu with which the child constantly interacts. He saw language, play, art, and inventions as necessary means for growth of the self. He felt that the main task of social psychology was the tracing out of this development of the individual in his constant give-and-take relation with his social surroundings. His views represent a fusion of contemporary tendencies in philosophical, evolutionary, psychological, and sociological thinking, and set the stage for the influential ideas of Cooley and Mead.

Charles Horton Cooley and George Herbert Mead were two early American sociologists whose contributions centered about the origin and development of the "social self." Though they had many ideas in common, we shall treat them separately.

Like James, Cooley interpreted the self as involving all that is included in the feeling of "self," i.e., all the persons, ideas, and activities with which the individual identifies himself. He agreed with Baldwin that self or personality is a social product which can arise only through social interaction.

In the process of social interaction, said Cooley, imagination plays a vital part. Each of us exists as a social person only in the minds of others; "the imaginations which people have of one another are the *solid facts* of society."[8] Furthermore, "any study of society that is not supported by a firm grasp of personal ideas is empty and dead —mere doctrine and not knowledge at all."[9]

For Cooley, the social self is a system of ideas, based on communication with others, which the mind cherishes as its own. Hence an individual's idea of self depends on the way others treat him. Cooley's famous theory of the *looking-glass self* describes succinctly how the self develops out of social interaction. The child gradually acquires the ability (1) to imagine how he appears to another person; (2) to imagine how the other person judges him; and (3) to have a resulting feeling such as pride or mortification.[10] Our self-estimates depend on interaction with others; we become socialized by understanding the reactions we produce in others.

[7] *Ibid.,* p. 97.

[8] C. H. Cooley, *Human nature and the social order* (New York: Charles Scribner's Sons, 1902), p. 87. (Reprinted by Free Press, Glencoe, Ill., 1956.)

[9] *Ibid.,* p. 89.

[10] *Ibid.,* pp. 151-52.

The most significant "others" for Cooley are the primary, intimate, face-to-face groups to which every child belongs: the family, play group, and neighborhood. These *primary groups* he regarded as the nursery of human nature and social life, in which are developed the fundamental virtues and ideals which are the real basis of human nature. Contacts with the more impersonal secondary groups, such as social institutions, are more casual and superficial, hence less significant to human development. In the primary groups, said Cooley, "human nature comes into existence. Man does not have it at birth; he cannot acquire it except through fellowship, and it decays in isolation." [11] Cooley's views on the significance of primary groups have been verified by many empirical studies, such as those mentioned in Chapters 4 and 5 above.

According to Mead, the birth and rise of the self depends upon the individual's ability to be an object to himself. Through communication with others, first by gestures and later by symbolic speech, the child learns what reactions his words produce in others. He learns to *introject* or imitate other people's responses to him; that is, he learns to take the role of others. He comes to see himself as others do; he perceives himself only after he has perceived others. [12]

Role-taking, for Mead, was an essential aspect of the child's development. He noted that the young child identifies himself with his mother, brother or sister, and others; soon he is playing at being "mama," "daddy," "big brother," "postman," "policeman," "Indian," and so on. He acts out the roles and talks out the parts imaginatively. As Kimball Young puts it, "In these dramas he develops multiple words of persons within his own activity" which "get organized into a wide range of separate roles, some actual, some imaginary, many related to his place in the family, in the schoolroom, on the playground and various other places." [13] This role-taking, with its internalized conversation, or "conversation in the inner forum," to use Mead's own term, is the essence of socialization, since the child is learning to make the speech, habits, attitudes, and behavior of others a part of himself.

The child learns roles, continues Mead, from his observation of the behavior of others, and also through control exercised by adults. He is told by his parents, teachers, and other adults what kind of behavior is expected of him—e.g., what a "good little boy" or "good

11 C. H. Cooley, *Social organization* (New York: Charles Scribner's Sons, 1909), p. 30.

12 G. H. Mead, *Mind, self and society* (Chicago: University of Chicago Press, 1934).

13 K. Young, *Personality and problems of adjustment* (2d ed.; New York: Appleton-Century-Crofts, Inc., 1952), p. 160.

little girl" should do. These learned patterns of expected behavior became integral parts of his personality. Out of a kind of
synthesis or distillation from all his role-taking experiences emerges
what Mead calls "the generalized other." This refers to the child's
own general role, which has arisen from his hundreds of social contacts. A significant part of this role is the child's conception of
himself or *self-image,* a concept on which several sociologists and
psychologists have placed great stress.

The self is not, however, merely an integration of roles the child
has learned from others. These make up the "me," according to
Mead; in addition the "I" develops, which is the self as actor and
which gives the personality its dynamic and unique character. The
"I" and "me" are always closely related. "Taken together they
constitute a personality as it appears in social experience. The self
is essentially a social process going on with these two distinguishable
phases. If it did not have these two phases there could not be conscious responsibility, and there would be nothing novel in experience." [14] The ever changing and unpredictable "I" is modified
by the "me." Much of the time they fuse and operate together,
especially in intense and interesting activity such as athletics. At
other times they are in some degree of opposition, as during mo-
ments of indecision and conflict.

Thus, according to Mead, the "I" and the "me" are both integral
parts of self or personality. The "me," based upon role-taking,
reflects social experience and represents the more permanent aspect
of the self. The more intangible and unpredictable "I" is the emergent factor which makes a person unique, which endows him with
"ego strength," to mention a term that developed later. Contrasted
with these dynamic, strong-willed persons are the conventional, the
timid Caspar Milquetoast type, in whom the "me" far outweighs the
"I."

As Young points out, Mead's theory of the "I" and the "me" is
subject to some criticism. The "actor phase" or "I" is constituted
of "previously derived 'me's' or 'others' dynamically in operation
plus the motives, emotions, and certain novel elements of the moment which come into play in overt action." [15] These elements may
be physiological, social, or personal variables, in addition to possible
chance events that occur at a given moment. In other words, the
self is something more than the roles we have derived from our
contacts with others.

14 G. H. Mead, *op. cit.,* p. 178.
15 Young, *op. cit.,* p. 166.

So much for a description of the "social self" theories of personality development. To experimentally minded psychologists and to many others, they seem speculative and intangible. In part, however, they draw upon common subjective experience such as conflict between different aspects of the self. In part they rest upon observed facts like role-playing.

These theories have to some extent been confirmed by empirical research. Consider, for example, Cooley's contention that, in social interaction, we react not to an objectively present person but rather to our imagined representation of his image of us. The developmental studies of Piaget have shown that the child's conception of himself is largely a reflection of social influences.[16]

Lois Murphy has in a sense been investigating concepts that developed out of the work of Cooley and Mead. She and her staff have focused on play activity of children as a means of understanding their personality growth. In addition to the development of emotions and of reactions to social situations, there is emergence of the self through role-taking, both in relation to the parent and in play with dolls. From his relation, the child "interiorizes" adult control, and his expressive behavior assumes several different forms: [17]

1. Child complies with adult's request, becomes submissive.
2. Child imitates adult expression, speech, habits, "consciously meeting adult expectations."
3. Child "unconsciously identifies with adult," and spontaneously acquires adult mannerisms, vocabulary, etc.
4. Child resists, defends himself from the parent, develops his own means of coping with the adult.
5. Child utilizes his childishness, humor, timidity, coyness, to appeal to sympathy on part of parent.
6. Child follows own ideas and impulses independently of the parent, develops autonomous expressive habits.

Thus the theories of Cooley, Mead, and other early social interactionists have furnished hypotheses which serve as a useful point of departure for investigations undertaken many years later.

Rediscovery of the ego. On the whole, however, the self was considered outside the pale of the experimentally oriented early twentieth-century psychology. Clinically minded psychologists began to get interested in Freud, but more for his therapy than for his theories about the ego. A few psychologists, particularly the Gestaltists Koffka and Lewin, did give the ego, or self, a place in their sys-

16 J. Piaget, *Moral judgment of the child* (New York: Harcourt Brace & Co., Inc., 1932).

17 L. B. Murphy, *Methods for the study of personality in young children.* Volume 1 of *Personality in young children* (New York: Basic Books, Inc., 1956), pp. 57-58.

tematic formulations. But by and large, from the time of James and
Baldwin until the late 1930's, "the ego (or self) became sidetracked
and lost to view," as Gordon Allport pointed out.[18]

The ego was "rediscovered" by psychologists chiefly because a concept of this sort became essential to help explain various experimental findings. Dembo, for example, coined the term "level of
aspiration" *(Anspruchsniveau)* for one's tendency to set for himself
certain goals-to-be-realized.[19] Hoppe found that success and failure
occurred according to whether or not one's aspiration-levels were
achieved. The adjusting of one's level of aspiration, Hoppe maintained, was governed by an effort to keep his self-esteem intact. He
found that some subjects set a low level of aspiration, hence were
"successful" in achieving their goals. Others set their goals too high
to be possible of achievement, thus giving themselves and others
the impression that they were superior persons, since they had such
high standards.[20] Summarizing several studies of level of aspiration,
Sherif and Cantril conclude that "unless and until there is some ego-
involvement no level of aspiration is set and the individual has no
concern about his own status." [21]

Another example showing how the concept of "ego-involvement"
aids in explaining behavior is furnished by an experiment of Klein
and Schoenfeld.[22] A group of subjects were given a number of tasks
to perform in the laboratory. After each task the subjects were
asked to rate their confidence in the accuracy of performance.
These ratings were found to depend upon the quality and difficulty
of the tasks, and they varied considerably for the different tasks a
person performed. Later, a similar series of problems was given to
the same subjects, but the whole psychological atmosphere was
changed; now they were told to try very hard, since their scores
would be sent to the personnel bureau of the college. Under these
conditions greater effort and anxiety appeared, and the confidence
ratings became much more consistent for each subject. As Sherif
and Cantril suggest, the subjects were now ego-involved because

---

[18] G. W. Allport, The ego in contemporary psychology, *Psychol. Rev.,* L (1943),
451-78. See also C. S. Hall and G. Lindzey, *Theories of personality* (New York: John
Wiley & Sons, Inc., 1957), pp. 257-95.

[19] See K. Lewin *et al.,* Level of aspiration, chap. x in J. McV. Hunt (ed.), *Personality
and the behavior disorders* (New York: The Ronald Press Co., 1944).

[20] *Ibid.* Also Allport, *op. cit.,* p. 471.

[21] M. Sherif and H. Cantril, *Psychology of ego-involvements* (New York: John Wiley
& Sons, Inc., 1947), p. 125.

[22] G. S. Klein and N. Schoenfeld, The influence of ego-involvement on confidence
J. abnorm. soc. Psychol., XXXVI (1941), 249-58.

their performance was related to their success and standing in college.[23]

The three psychologists most responsible for the revival of interest in the ego as a systematic concept are Sherif, Cantril, and Allport. In 1936 Sherif showed how we build up attitudes from our contacts with established social values or norms. These attitudes serve as frames of reference to guide our conduct. In fact, says Sherif, one's ego is made up chiefly of these interiorized social values derived from parents, teachers, and others close to the child. The ego is a genetic or developmental product which determines in large measure the goals for which one strives, the likes and dislikes one has, and the satisfactions one obtains. Thus Sherif interprets the ego as primarily an interiorized or learned constellation of social norms acquired from one's social environment.[24]

In his interpretation of social movements, Cantril agrees with Sherif's concept of the ego, though with minor modifications.[25] For example, Cantril stresses the *ego-drive*—a person's constant attempt to maintain or enhance his own feeling of self-regard. He maintains that the ego is not entirely bound by the surrounding culture, since some people rebel against dominant culture patterns. Ego or self-regard may be determined "by standards derived from a small minority group, from reading, from discussion or from their own creative intellectual activity." [26]

Gordon Allport reviewed both systematic and experimental contributions in a 1943 article entitled "The Ego in Contemporary Psychology." [27] He reports that, despite many differences, all writers agree that the ego designates only one portion of the personality— the one in closest relation to the external world. As it is the "contact-region" of the personality, it is also the conflict-region. The ego develops gradually "as the child comes to mark himself off from his environment and from other human beings." [28] The ego can be considered neither conscious nor unconscious. The "subjective sense of the ego" varies greatly from time to time; it contracts, expands, and changes in content. However, this does not deny to the ego a stable and recurring structure. "If you know a person well enough," says Allport, "you find that you are able to predict with

23 Sherif and Cantril, *op. cit.*, p. 125.
24 M. Sherif, *The psychology of social norms* (New York: Harper & Bros., 1936).
25 H. Cantril, *The psychology of social movements* (New York: John Wiley & Sons, Inc., 1941), pp. 154 ff.
26 *Ibid.*, pp. 44-45.
27 Allport, *op. cit.*
28 *Ibid.*, p. 473.

marked success what items will and what items will not be linked to his ego." [29] Also, there are degrees of ego-involvement, since a person may be intensely or only moderately partisan.

In 1947, Sherif and Cantril published the first book devoted to a psychological treatment of the ego.[30] They define the ego as a cluster or constellation of attitudes related to what the individual considers *me, I, my, mine.* These ego attitudes thus "determine the more or less enduring character of one's personal identity." [31] In a more recent formulation, the Sherifs define the ego or self as "a developmental formation (a subsystem) in the psychological make-up of the individual consisting of interrelated attitudes which are acquired in relation to his own body, to objects, family, persons, groups, social values, and institutions and which define and regulate his relatedness to them in concrete situations." [32] When ego attitudes are aroused, the individual's experience and behavior become *ego-involved.*

Ego-involved activity is goal directed, and, say the Sherifs, "characteristically reveals heightened selectivity, increased effectiveness of the person's perception, judgment, memory and action. In functional terms, the *consistency* revealed in ego-involved behavior is the outcome of this heightened selectivity and sensitized psychological processes concentrating on the relevant aspect of the stimulus field or on the ongoing psychological activity. This is why the more integrated, the more single-mindedly devoted of our fellow men, like Beethoven, Tolstoi, Van Gogh, and Gandhi, are those who become almost deaf and dumb to some of the ordinary details in their surroundings that are noticed by others not so intensely preoccupied." [33]

Social values and norms of many kinds enter into the formation of the ego. (These are the essence of the Freudian superego, which is thus included in the psychologists' conception of ego.) These values "serve the individual as frames of reference by means of which he makes those judgments that affect *him;* that define *for him* success and failure; that determine his loyalties and allegiances; that spell out what he conceives to be *his* role, *his* status, *his* class." [34] One's ego-involvements are significant in determining one's goals, loyalties,

29 *Ibid.*, p. 474.

30 M. Sherif and H. Cantril, *The psychology of ego-involvements* (New York: John Wiley & Sons, Inc., 1947).

31 *Ibid.*, p. 4.

32 M. Sherif and C. W. Sherif, *An outline of social psychology* (rev. ed.; New York: Harper & Bros., 1956), p. 581.

33 *Ibid.*, p. 583.

34 Sherif and Cantril, *op. cit.*, pp. 152-53.

responsibilities, identifications with persons and groups, and even enjoyment of reading, movies, and radio programs.

Sherif and Cantril emphasize that the ego develops gradually, its basic pattern being determined through the child's primary social contacts in the family, play group, school, and church. The ego is modified or re-formed at adolescence as the individual identifies himself with new groups and assimilates adult values and norms. As a result of environmental pressure or of certain organic disturbances, the ego may break down, as shown in studies of war neurosis and other pathological conditions.

By now the ego and the self are considered accepted if not essential aspects of personality. Lecky's little book *Self-Consistency* had much to do with stressing the significance of the self as a unity which gives purpose and continuity to living.[35] Stagner stresses the importance of the self-image, and, following William James, notes that a person has several self-images or *segmental selves,* depending upon the major groups with which he is affiliated. The self-image has much to do with security feelings and with self-esteem and functions to give control and stabilty to personality.[36] McClelland says: "Included among the ideas a person has about the world is one about the nature of himself. It is one of the most important ideas that he has . . ." [37]

Hilgard has dealt with defense mechanisms in relation to the self. "All the mechanisms," he said, "imply self-reference, . . . the mechanisms are not understandable unless we adopt a concept of the self." [38] Whether one views the mechanisms as defenses against anxiety and guilt or as processes bolstering self-esteem through self-deception, the existence of a self is implied. Hilgard commented, however, on the difficulty in arriving at an acceptable concept of the self. Since "problems of the self-concept are general problems of psychological science," he proposed that laboratories be established for the study of psychodynamics.[39]

Certainly psychologists are continuing to study the self and the ego by a variety of experimental and clinical techniques.[40] To show

[35] P. Lecky, *Self-consistency—a theory of personality* (New York: Island Press, 1945).

[36] R. Stagner, *Psychology of personality* (2d ed.; New York: McGraw-Hill Book Co., Inc., 1948).

[37] D. C. McClelland, *Personality* (New York: William Sloane Assocs., Inc., 1951), p. 529.

[38] E. R. Hilgard, Human motives and the concept of the self, *Amer. Psychologist,* IV (1949), 375.

[39] *Ibid.,* pp. 380-82.

[40] Sherif and Sherif, *op. cit.,* chaps. xvii and xviii, summarize a large number of experimental studies. A large-scale area of research, still in process, is concerned with involvement of the self in the moral situations of others. See R. H. Turner, Self and other in moral judgment, *Amer. sociol. Rev.,* XIX (1954), 249-59.

that the self-concept is now accepted as a matter-of-fact psychological variable, the following brief quotation is given from a recent work by two scientifically oriented clinical psychologists:

The self concept is a pattern of attitudes and is learned in the same way as other attitudes. . . . Like other attitudes, the self concept has an influence on perception and motivation in new situations. We have already seen that your attitude toward, say, the Chinese will determine to some extent what you will remember and believe about them. The self concept is no more mysterious and operates in the same way. A man who conceives himself as a humorist will take every opportunity to clown, and one who conceives himself as unappreciated and scorned will perceive rejection in many innocent acts of other people. Because the self concept shapes new experience to conform to its already established pattern, much behavior can be understood as a person's attempt to maintain the consistency of his self concept, a kind of homeostasis at a higher psychological level.[41]

EGO AND EGO DEVELOPMENT IN PSYCHOANALYSIS

A psychoanalytically inclined psychologist might say that, thus far, we have been more concerned with the self than with the ego. Symonds, for example, believes that the two terms should be kept distinct, since *ego* refers to the self as object, while *self* is subjective and "refers to the body and mind and to bodily and mental processes as they are observed and reacted to by the individual." Ego, on the other hand, denotes "that phase of personality which determines adjustments to the outside world in the interest of satisfying inner needs." It is in this sense that ego is used in psychoanalytic literature.[42]

The contribution of Freud. From the many years Sigmund Freud spent working with neurotic patients emerged not only his system of therapy but also his highly influential theories of personality.[43] Freud's system is a "psychic determinism"—that is, it stresses *psychological* factors rather than biological or social ones as the primal determinants of personality. He emphasized the necessity of going back to the earliest days of infancy to discover these causes.

A person's fundamental energy or drive Freud called the *libido*, which is pleasure-seeking and sexual in character. (Freud uses sex

41 L. F. Shaffer and E. J. Shoben, *Psychology of adjustment* (2d ed.; Boston: Houghton Mifflin Co., 1956), p. 94.

42 P. M. Symonds, *The ego and the self* (New York: Appleton-Century-Crofts, Inc., 1951), p. 4.

43 It is difficult to find a concise formulation of Freud's theories and therapeutic procedures in his own writings. Perhaps the most authoritative single reference is Otto Fenichel, *The psychoanalytic theory of neurosis* (New York: W. W. Norton & Co., Inc., 1945). More recent and less technical are Ruth L. Munroe, *Schools of psychoanalytic thought* (New York: The Dryden Press, Inc., 1955) and C. S. Hall, *A primer of Freudian psychology* (Cleveland: The World Publishing Co., 1954). The last has been reprinted in an inexpensive paperback edition.

in a broad rather than narrow sense in all his writings.) The libido originates in the unconscious, a deep reservoir of primitive impulses. Since the child's libido is constantly being frustrated by the demands of reality, the basis of conflict and maladjustment is found in childhood.

Freud noted three stages in the development of self or personality—the *infantile, latent,* and *adolescent* periods. During the first or infantile stage, which lasts until about five or six years of age, the child's libido is directed toward biological needs or immediate satisfactions. There are three distinguishable but overlapping substages during the period of infancy. The *oral* stage lasts until the end of the first or beginning of the second year. During this time the baby's activity centers about sucking, swallowing, and (later) teething, biting, and the onset of speech. Emotional difficulties occurring at this time arise from interference with these activities.

During the *anal* stage (in the second and part of the third year), the child is more active and responsive to the world about him. Major demands are made in the area of bowel and bladder training, with such associated activities as learning to keep clean, dress himself, and respond to his parents' wishes. The last stage of the infantile period is called the *phallic* or *genital* stage; it lasts from about age two or three to five or six. The child's oral gratifications are no longer predominant, and he has learned toilet habits. So his interests now go to the world beyond, and his growing curiosity centers about sex and reproduction. He discovers his genitalia and finds that stimulation is pleasurable, which leads to masturbation. He becomes interested in the origin of babies. His chief emotional problems at this time are produced by frustrations in the area of sex. During this stage he *introjects* or learns the prevailing ideas of shame and modesty.

About this time, at the end of the infancy period, according to psychoanalysis, the child experiences the *Oedipus complex.* The libido becomes attached to the parent of the opposite sex; the boy falls in love with his mother, and the girl with her father. Normally, says Freud, this attachment passes in a short time, and the child enters the latency period, which lasts from about age six to ten or twelve. Now sex interest is subordinated to intellectual and social activities. Hostility, or at least indifference, to the opposite sex develops. In this sense, the latency period is homosexual in character. The libido turns in such directions as seeking power. At the same time the superego comes on the scene; that is, conscience is born in terms of a knowledge of right and wrong, of what one ought and ought not to do.

When the child is about twelve, he enters the period of puberty or adolescence. Sex interest revives, and it is much stronger than in infancy because of the activity of the sexual glands. The changes caused by development of primary and secondary sexual characteristics make this an awkward age. The libido now proceeds in a definitely heterosexual direction, and the adolescent's major problems arise from his inability to obtain sexual satisfaction. Masturbation is revived and becomes a major source of conflict. Other problems center about school, preparation for vocation, and conflict with the wishes of parents. Normally the period of adolescence ends with passage to adulthood and with sexual adjustment in marriage.

Such is a rough sketch of Freud's schema of personality development. At any stage there may be, and usually are, conflicts which, if serious enough, predispose the child toward later neurosis. One common reaction to conflict is "fixation" or stoppage at one stage and failure to progress in a normal way. Another common reaction, as we have seen, is adoption of a "mechanism" such as repression, displacement, regression, or rationalization as an attempt to eliminate or reduce the conflict.

Good personality adjustment, according to Freud, consists in a harmonious relationship between the id, ego, and superego. The *id* is our primitive or animal nature, embodying our unconscious urges and desires which operate entirely according to the "pleasure principle." The *ego* is the rational self, which functions according to the "reality principle," a kind of rule of expediency, which permits some expression of id impulses if they are not morally or socially dangerous. The *superego* is a tyrannical agent, equivalent to conscience, which consists of moral ideas and prohibitions. It constantly acts to force the ego to repress all expression of id impulses, under penalty of strong feelings of guilt. Thus the ego is definitely "on the spot," having to mediate not only the insatiable desires of the id and the rigid requirements of the superego but the continuous demands and limitations of the environment as well. When the ego cracks under the strain, it must be built up and strengthened, which is precisely the goal of psychoanalytic therapy.

It is most difficult to evaluate accurately the Freudian contribution to our knowledge of the self and personality development. Freud's theories of the unconscious, of libido, of repression, and of other mechanisms and his whole dynamic approach have revolutionized our interpretation of personality and of abnormal behavior. It may indeed be, as some have suggested, that future generations will judge Freud's contribution to be even greater than Darwin's.[44]

Nevertheless, Freud has been criticized on many counts by psychologists and social scientists—among other things, for oversimplifying parent-child relationships in his "Oedipus complex," and for generally stressing instinctual forces to the neglect of social and cultural influences.[45] Without debating here the pros and cons of such criticisms, we can agree that Freud's followers, the contemporary psychoanalysts, can hardly be accused of overlooking culture and social forces.[46]

One psychoanalytic contribution which is relevant here is Erikson's formulation of a theory of libidinal development in which he cites the kinds of dilemmas or problems faced by the ego at each of the "eight stages of man." [47] Thus, at the "oral-sensory" stage early feeding experiences lead to basic trust or mistrust; at the "muscular-anal" stage bowel training may increase autonomy or develop feelings of shame and doubt." The latency period is concerned with the dilemma of industry versus inferiority, and puberty with strengthened identity versus role diffusion. Erikson sees these stages of ego-development as an orderly sequence but much affected by the child's social experience. He says:

The individual is not merely the sum total of his childhood identification. Children—perhaps more pronouncedly in a highly mobile society—are early aware of their parents' position in the community; of their reactions to friends, servants, superiors; of their behavior in pleasant, pious, angry, or alcoholized company; of Saturday nights in town and of mild enthusiasms and panics pervading neighborhoods, not to speak of lynchings and wars. If not impoverished too early by indifferent communities and selfish mothers, children early develop a nucleus of ego-identity . . . The patient, instead of blaming his parents or their conventions (i.e., turning his positive over-identifications into negative ones), should learn to understand the social forces responsible for the deficiencies of his childhood . . .[48]

Actually there are encouraging signs of integration today—of *rapprochement* between psychoanalytic and social-self theories and

[44] An excellent evaluation of Freud is given in C. S. Hall and G. Lindzey's Psychoanalytic theory and its applications to the social sciences, in G. Lindzey (ed.), *Handbook of social psychology* (Reading, Mass.: Addison-Wesley Pub. Co., Inc., 1954), Vol. I.

[45] See, e.g., R. R. Sears, Survey of objective studies of psychoanalytic concepts, *Soc. sci. Res. Council Bull.*, 1943, No. 51.

[46] Some of these, notably Kardiner, Horney, and Fromm, were discussed earlier in Chapter 3.

[47] E. H. Erikson, *Childhood and society* (New York: W. W. Norton & Co., Inc., 1950).

[48] E. H. Erikson, Childhood and tradition in two American Indian tribes, in C. Kluckhohn and H. A. Murray (eds.), *Personality in nature, society and culture* (New York: Alfred A. Knopf, Inc., 1948), p. 203.

of both with social science research—in many new volumes on psychotherapy and on personality.[49]

AN INTERPRETATION OF EGO AND SELF

We are now at the beginning rather than at the final stages of understanding the ego. It is agreed that the ego or self is a particularly dynamic aspect of personality, but disagreement exists as to its precise origin, structure, and function. The early self theorists stressed its development from social experience but were somewhat vague as to its content and over-all function in the life of the individual. Freud found the origins of the ego in modifications imposed by the external world upon the primal id and noted the important role of parental wishes and commands in the genesis of the superego. But he gave little attention to such social influences. He saw the motivational function of the ego as self-preservative, seeking to adjust the conflicting demands of the id, superego, and environment.

Recent psychological interpreters have drawn upon both earlier approaches. They agree that the ego develops slowly, largely in response to social experience. They find that it has an integrating and guiding function directed toward self-realization or self-enhancement. Psychologists differ somewhat on other aspects of the ego. Some emphasize the development of a self-image or concept of self whose fulfilment makes for self-esteem and happiness. Others emphasize "ego-involvement" rather than the "self-image," suggesting that one becomes ego-involved when ego-attitudes are evoked, whether or not a self-image exists.

We shall draw upon these contributions to describe and illustrate a concept of the ego which is meaningful and useful to the social psychologist. Our interpretation is admittedly oversimplified and tentative. Any depiction of the ego at the present time will need continual testing and reformulation.

The ego is a dynamic, patterned system within the personality, consisting of those attitudes, values, beliefs, and purposes which have become nearest and dearest to the individual through his life experience. The persons, things, and activities which satisfy him most completely come to have strong positive valence—the mother, a playmate, his tricycle, climbing trees, or playing baseball. The child soon comes to think of these as not only desirable but as defi-

---

49 E.g., D. Ausubel, *Ego development and personality disorders* (New York: Grune & Stratton, Inc., 1952); N. Cameron and A. Magaret, *Behavior pathology* (Boston: Houghton Mifflin Co., 1951); R. W. White, *Lives in progress* (New York: The Dryden Press, Inc., 1952); M. F. A. Montagu, *The direction of human development* (New York: Harper & Bros., 1955).

nitely "mine." The attitudes toward them get organized into an embryonic ego, and the child becomes ego-involved with respect to them.

The child's ego-structure changes rapidly as new experiences succeed one another. There are kaleidoscopic shifts in his enthusiasms —from one toy to another, from one playmate to another, from drawing to skating to hammering to radio thrillers to stamp-collecting to magic tricks to baseball. But as he grows older, his ego-structure becomes more patterned and more consistent. In large part this patterning is a function of his developing self-image.

The child learns gradually to distinguish between self and the world about him; physically, first, then in a more psychological sense. He slowly becomes aware of himself as a person—a person who is loved or rejected by his parents, who must be kind to a baby sister, who is a fast runner, who has two close friends, who is disliked by the lady next door, who must obey his parents or be punished, who is considered "cute" by his Aunt Mabel, and so on. Much of this self-image reflects the reactions of others toward him. He tends to see himself as others see him. The process is naturally facilitated if others refer to the child as a "nice boy," "a regular tomboy," "a good sport," and so on.

Normally there is fair consistency between the child's ego-involved activities and his self-image. When they are inconsistent, conflict and frustration occur. For example, a youngster who enjoys his school work, reading, piano-playing, and chess is called a "sissy" or "bookworm" by other children if not by adults. He resists incorporating such a concept into his self-image; frustration arises, followed by repression, fantasy, or compensatory behavior. Similarly a boy-gang member who plays hooky, smokes, swears, lies, and steals rejects the self-image of "bad boy," "young hoodlum," or "juvenile delinquent." His conflict leads frequently to aggressive behavior— which accentuates his difficulties.

Development of a self-image depends in large part upon the child's increasing command of language and ability to conceptualize. He becomes cognizant of his major social roles—that of child or adolescent, boy or girl, big brother or little sister, pupil, or perhaps athlete or leader. These are incorporated into his self-image and help to channel or pattern his interests and ego-involvements. The older child's desire for independence from his family leads to identification with "age-mate groups," giving him belongingness and status. As a result of increased understanding of his roles and acceptance of the dominant values and norms of the groups with which he is affiliated, the ego-structure of the older adolescent and young adult becomes more stable and consistent. The specific ego-structure and self-image, of course, are not solely a product of social influences. They are affected by his physique, temperament, and intelligence, reflected in interaction with his social milieu. Thus, a sensitive, intelligent, articulate boy becomes aware of himself as a good student and leader and identifies himself thoroughly with a high-school club in which he is accepted and given status. A less intelligent and articulate lad may have a poorly conceptualized self-image and may also be less completely accepted in the social groups to which he belongs.

Thus at any stage of a person's development a certain ego-structure exists. He has become identified or ego-involved with various persons, objects, activities, and goals. The corresponding needs and attitudes are organized into a more or less well-articulated pattern, the self-image. The individual strives toward ego-fulfilment or ego-enhancement. That which brings fulfilment of the ego-needs produces delight; that which threatens or is inconsistent with the ego-structure causes distress.

Ego-involvements obviously affect the course and intensity of much social behavior, at the level of the small group, of the community, and even of national and international affairs. Obvious examples are the boy who is wild about football, the teen-ager who adores a popular singer, the man who is dedicated to a cult or social movement. But so is ego-involvement exemplified in the social behavior of a new resident in a community who is bent on achieving membership in its most distinguished social club. Or in the sports fan who has so identified himself with the Yankees or Dodgers that he evades all social obligations in order to attend the World Series. Mrs. A., who is logical and dispassionate about most subjects, becomes defensive and emotional when a family friend hints that she has brought up her child improperly. On a larger scale, the country-wide grief occasioned by the death of Lincoln or of Franklin D. Roosevelt suggests the degree to which millions of Americans had become identified with their President.

The ego or self develops through all of our life experiences, and is a constantly dynamic process. Cultural, subcultural, and situational factors will determine the constant unfolding of the ego and its involvements. In traveling in different regions or in other countries, or in observing members of a different occupation from one's own, one is reminded of the various ways in which individuals project their egos into a situation. As illustration, the eagerness of Italians to be part of the tourist's photograph, compared to the "stand-offishness" of the Britisher; or the interest of an actor in a press report compared to that of a scientist, demonstrate some of the variables determining ego-involvements. Our contacts with other individuals will structure our definition of given events, and the kind of emotional involvements relevant to these events.

One's ego-involvements often have compensatory value; they are found in areas in which one feels inferior or insecure. An attractive but rather lazy-minded girl is not particularly flattered if one refers to her beauty. But she is elated if praised for her scholarly achievements. Professors occasionally become ego-involved with gardening or carpentry—a reaction against the stereotyped conception of the professor as an impractical theorist. Similarly, the enthusiastic loyalty of a not too-distinguished alumnus toward his alma mater seems to yield benefits of compensatory nature. The German people's intense and widespread identification with Hitler and the Nazi party rose, in part at least, from frustrations and inferiority reactions occasioned by defeat in 1918 and by subsequent inflation and depression.

SUMMARY

In Part II we have dealt with the processes and some of the products of socialization. We have described "dynamics" in the form of motives, frustrations, and defenses—tendencies which strongly orient the individual toward certain social stimuli and toward certain kinds of social behavior. We then turned to the cognitive processes of perceiving and learning, and to attitudes, values, and norms which are formed through socialization. We discussed the relationship of all these to mores, taboos, and other customs. Finally, we saw that the processes of socialization not only produce attitudes, habits, and the like, but they help bring about that system or synthesis within the personality which is called the self or the ego. Despite our difficulty in pinning down this elusive entity, its role in interpersonal relations is found to be of great significance.

SUPPLEMENTARY READINGS

Books of Readings

MACCOBY, E. E., NEWCOMB, T. M., AND HARTLEY, E. L. (eds.). *Readings in social psychology*, 3d ed. New York: Henry Holt & Co., Inc., 1958.
    Clark, K. B., and Clark, M. P., Racial identification and preference in Negro children.

LINDZEY, G. (ed.). *Handbook of social psychology*. Reading, Mass.: Addison-Wesley Pub. Co., Inc., 1954.
    Child, I. L., Socialization. Vol. II.
    Sarbin, T. R., Role theory. Vol. I.

Other References

ALLPORT, G. W. *Personality.* New York: Henry Holt & Co., Inc., 1937.
Chap. vi contains some significant material on the development of the self.

BECKER, H. *Man in reciprocity.* New York: Frederick A. Praeger, Inc., 1957.
An introduction to personality in society; chaps. vii and viii relate to self and society.

COUTU, W. *Emergent human nature.* New York: Alfred A. Knopf, Inc., 1949.
An advanced work on a variety of subjects, role-taking, ego-involvement, and the problem of meaning. Chaps. viii and ix are probably the most relevant.

FARIS, R. E. L. *Social psychology.* New York: The Ronald Press Co., 1952.
This textbook presents some stimulating discussions on the question of consciousness and the self. Chaps. v, vi, and vii.

FREUD, S. *The ego and the id.* London: Hogarth Press, Ltd., 1927.
This work set the pattern for the psychoanalytic theory of personality.

HALL, C. S., AND LINDZEY, G. *Theories of personality.* New York: John Wiley & Sons, Inc., 1957.
Includes the ideas of a number of theorists who have stressed the emergence of the self—from Freud and Jung to Carl Rogers and Gardner Murphy.

KARPF, F. B. *American social psychology.* New York: McGraw-Hill Book Co., Inc., 1932.
A superlative account of the theories of James, Baldwin, Mead, and Cooley.

LECKY, P. *Self-consistency—a theory of personality.* New York: Island Press, 1945.
A pioneering little volume which challenged mechanistic trends in personality and clinical psychology.

MEAD, G. H. *Mind, self and society.* Chicago: University of Chicago Press, 1934.
This philosophic work contained a number of insights and concepts that more recently have been supported by empirical testing.

MURPHY, G. *Personality.* New York: Harper & Bros., 1947.
A penetrating examination of the self and self-consciousness is found in chaps. xx-xxii.

NEWCOMB, T. M. *Social psychology.* New York: The Dryden Press, Inc., 1950.
A discussion of self-perception and its relation to the social group. Chaps. x and xi.

SHERIF, M. AND SHERIF, C. W. *An outline of social psychology,* rev. ed. New York: Harper & Bros., 1956.
Chaps. xvii and xviii present the subject of ego-involvements as does also Sherif and H. Cantril's work, *The psychology of ego-involvements* (New York: John Wiley & Sons, Inc., 1947).

SULLIVAN, H. S. *The interpersonal theory of psychiatry.* New York: W. W. Norton & Co., Inc., 1953.
This well-known psychiatrist gives his views in a thorough, readable manner.

SYMONDS, P. M. *The ego and the self.* New York: Appleton-Century-Crofts, Inc., 1951.
A neo-Freudian account, including many experimental findings.

YOUNG, K. *Personality and problems of adjustment,* 2d ed. New York: Appleton-Century-Crofts, Inc., 1952.
A rich summary of the literature on the self together with the author's own interpretations. Chaps. vii and viii.

Part III

INTERPERSONAL RELATIONS

In Part I of this book we described the leading social influences as they affect personality. Part II emphasized the dynamics of motives, perceptual and learning processes, attitudes and beliefs, and other personality components.

In Part III we deal first with the critical factor of language and speech as our primary means of communication, for culture is mediated to and from the individual by means of spoken and written words. The cognitive and attitudinal structures become conditioned by the language we acquire. In addition, since our social behavior is patterned in different categories of interpersonal relations, frequently known as social processes, we shall examine these modes of social interaction. And, most important, we shall discuss the role of the group, inasmuch as it is the group that conditions behavior. At all times, we are members of groups whether they are present or absent. Reward and punishment, goals and values, are determined by the groups of which we are a part, and these norms in turn determine group activity. Group life with all of its interpersonal relations provides socialization whether by the family in the early years or the more varied forms of group identification in later childhood, adolescence, and adulthood.

We shall also describe how behavior is channeled and patterned by sociocultural roles. And leadership, one of the complex roles in group life, will be analyzed. In conclusion, we shall synthesize our findings by a field interpretation of the individual in the social order, emphasizing the interoperation of the ego, cognition, attitudes, and roles.

10

Communicating and Symbolizing

Anthropologists agree that language is one of man's greatest achievements, if not the greatest of them all. For spoken and written language make communication possible, not only in face-to-face social situations, but across the world and through the centuries. A people's social heritage—their customs, laws, ethics, religion, philosophy, and science—is passed on to successive generations largely in linguistic form. Sociologists have noted that without language there is no true culture; moreover, language is fundamental to human nature as we know it. Only after a child has learned to talk does he enter into social life and become human in the full sense of the term. Feral or isolated children may seem human physically, but they are not psychologically, because they have not learned from and interacted with human beings.

In the unfolding of social psychology, the process of communication has moved to the center of the stage. The last decade has seen the inception of new research areas like psycholinguistics, metalinguistics, and information theory. These movements are highly technical and not related to the core of our subject. Consequently, we shall include only the more outstanding aspects. Certainly they signify the critical role that communication occupies in psychology and social science today. In this connection one recent social psychology text chooses communication as the principal social process and the major theme of the book. This orientation has partially grown out of the tendency to subsume under communication a number of other processes: perception, thinking, roles, public opinion. It is likely that with too broad an extension of its original meaning, the term may lose some of its serviceability. In this chapter we shall focus on communication as a means of symbolization between individuals and groups, leaving the more peripheral aspects to later chapters.

THE NATURE OF COMMUNICATION

There is little doubt that communication enjoys the central role in intergroup behavior. For instance, the primary problem in the world today is the inability to relieve international tensions. This impasse is, in large measure, due to failures in communication. Likewise, communication barriers may explain the inability to achieve harmony in labor and management; the difficulty for the therapist to reach the client; the teacher, his students; the minister, his congregation. In addition, there are frictions and barriers to communication in the primary group—the family, the work group, the neighborhood gang.

The communication process. Students of communication— whether of the communication of telegraphy and the electronic computer, of the artist and his public, or the conversation of Bill and John—have developed a technical jargon and diagramming to unfold their theory. Despite the multiplication in vocabulary that newer theory of communication involves, it has made possible some clarification of the communicative process. The relationship between speaker and hearer may be schematized as follows:

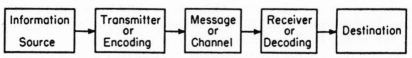

FIG. 7. The Communication Process.

Let us now examine this speaker-hearer relationship in its developmental sequence.[1]

1. *Source.* Psychologically speaking, this might be labeled as the "intentive behavior" of the individual. It refers to the cognitive material—i.e., perceptions, thoughts, feelings—that is to be communicated. There is neural activity of some variety prior to its being coded. In other words, information exists in some form.

2. *Transmitting* or *encoding.* This includes the decision to speak and the choice of words. The transmitter must decide in

[1] The analysis presented here is derived from a number of sources. Principally are: J. W. Gardner, Introduction to psycholinguistics, A survey of theory and research problems, *J. abnorm. soc. Psychol.*, XLIX (1954); J. B. Carroll, *The study of linguistics* (Cambridge, Mass.: Harvard University Press, 1953), pp. 89-94; and G. A. Miller, Psycholinguistics, in G. Lindzey (ed.), *Handbook of social psychology* (Reading, Mass.: Addison-Wesley Pub. Co., Inc., 1954), Vol. II, pp. 693-708.

what form he will communicate, whether by a gesture, by a musical composition, or by written or spoken word. There are almost infinite possibilities about the form the message will take. In some cases incipient responses will be inhibited, and no encoding will take place. The individual may communicate only to himself, and with only a few words. On the other hand, it might be an extremely elaborate encoding, as with a formal lecture.

3. *Message* or *channel* is the objective rendition of the communicative unit. The message has been defined as "that part of the total output (responses) of a source unit which simultaneously may be a part of the total input (stimuli) to a destination unit." [2] It is the link between the transmitter and the receiver. It may consist of a danger signal, a cave painting of prehistoric man (for which there has been intermittently a receiver for something over 25,000 years), or the words "I love you." Frequently, it is a composite, namely, speech accompanied by gestures. It is all the behavioral information that is observable to the receiver.

In the channel of communication, there are a number of barriers that may operate to reduce the effectiveness of the message. Anything that acts as a distraction or barrier is known as *noise.* To overcome this "noise," the transmitter is forced to use means of implementing his message. He may use repetition—"I love you, I love you"—or he may increase the size, volume, and/or color of the stimulus. Actually, in English, and probably all languages, there is a great deal of *redundancy,* or excess verbal material, to insure comprehension on the part of the receiver. For instance, "He goes to the end of the road to pick up the hat" could be rendered "goes end for hat." It has been estimated that perhaps 75 per cent or more of English is redundant.[3]

4. *Decoding* and *receiver.* The "hearer" makes discriminations and interpretations of what he has heard, seen, smelled, etc. There are a large number of details and cues to which he may respond. His whole background of experience may affect what he hears and reads. He may react to only certain parts of the message. The interpretation to "I love you" might be made in quite diverse respects, depending on the total situation. In some cases, owing to "noise," or some internal condition, the message may not reach the destination. Sometimes entirely false interpretations are made.

5. *Destination* or *output.* This might be considered the "interpretive behavior" that the receiver exhibits after receipt of the in-

2 J. W. Gardner, *op. cit.,* p. 2.

3 C. E. Shannon, Prediction and entropy of printed English, *Bell Syst. tech. J.,* XXX (1951), 50-64, as cited in Miller, *op. cit.,* p. 704.

formation. It is "information that is not linguistically coded." [4]
There is a multitude of possible behaviors at this stage—cognitions,
feelings, and the like. Overt behavior would include sitting down
to eat or opening the door or flying into a rage. Most likely, as in
the average conversation, there will be reciprocal activity on the
part of the hearer. He will answer the transmitter and the cycle will
be reopened.

One important factor in this cycle is the *feedback*—the reaction
of the receiver as interpreted by the transmitter. The term "feedback" has been used to refer to an autocorrective device in many
machines (including the electronic computer) as well as neural, sensory, and muscular mechanisms in the human being, such as the
semicircular canals. In the speaker-hearer relationship it is of crucial importance, to know whether one is "getting across." Generally, this is an automatic process of confirming by "yes" and "no"
reactions; at the same time it may lead to varied interpretations.
(For example, I may find my aunt's criticism deflating, although she
may mean it to be helpful.) There are a number of historical and
literary accounts of misinterpretation in the feedback—the interpretation the transmitter places on his destination. Hartley mentions
the case of Lincoln, who thought he had failed in his Gettysburg
Address. It was some time before he realized that the silence that
greeted him represented the highest level of appreciation. [5]

Communication among animals. It is language more than anything else which distinguishes man from the animals. This does
not mean that animals are unable to communicate with each other,
but rather that animals cannot develop symbolic language. Many
studies of animal communication have been made, showing that
certain animals, notably monkeys, can make and react to several
different sounds, with cries signifying fear, play, surprise, etc. Not
less interesting is the finding of von Frisch, who concluded after
years of study that bees have an elaborate system of communication.
Apparently they inform other bees of the location and direction of
a food supply by engaging in a type of dance. Dancing straight up
means toward the sun; downward, away from the sun; diagonal
movements indicate deviations in relation to the sun's position.
The number of dances per minute is in proportion to the distance
of the flowers. [6] It is customary to speak of animals as utilizing reflex

4 Carroll, *op. cit.*, p. 92.

5 E. L. Hartley and R. E. Hartley, *Fundamentals of social psychology* (New York:
Alfred A. Knopf, Inc., 1952), p. 45.

6 K. von Frisch, *The dancing bees* (New York: Harcourt, Brace & Co., Inc., 1955);
also *Bees: their vision, chemical senses and language* (Ithaca, N.Y.: Cornell University
Press, 1950).

cries or "signaling reflexes" rather than words or symbols. Klineberg notes that "the main difference between human language and that of all other animals seems to lie mainly in the fact that the language of animals can express only what is present at the time; it occurs mainly in response to an emotional situation; it may on occasions indicate desires or types of object or action.[7] As far as we can tell, however, it can have no abstract or symbolic meaning, nor can it to any extent describe what has happened in the past or what is to happen in the future."[8]

On the other hand, we do not have conclusive data to show that animals are incapable of learning symbolic speech.[9] The vocal apparatus of many animals is adequate, though their brain structure may not be sufficiently complex for the task. As mentioned earlier, the Kelloggs reared a young female chimpanzee for nine months with their infant son. At the close of the training period the animal was able to respond correctly to fifty-eight different phrases such as "Don't do that," "Hug Donald," or "Show me your nose." Her progress in this understanding of language was almost as good as that of the child, who responded to sixty-eight commands and questions, but who was two and a half months older. The Kelloggs did not carry on their experiment long enough to see whether their chimp could have mastered one meaningful vocal response comparable to the child's saying his first word.[10] However, two other investigators, the Hayeses, did manage to train another young chimpanzee to say three words, "mama," "papa," and "cup," more or less appropriately.[11] This is a great step ahead, but it hardly proves that animals are capable of symbolic communication.[12]

SPEECH AND LANGUAGE IN THE INFANT

In describing a child's language development, psychologists seem agreed on four stages.[13] First comes a *prelinguistic* stage of "ran-

[7] R. M. Yerkes and A. W. Yerkes, Social behavior in infrahuman primates, in C. Murchison (ed.), *Handbook of social psychology* (Worcester, Mass.: Clark University Press, 1935). (Reference from Klineberg.)

[8] O. Klineberg, *Social psychology* (rev. ed.; New York: Henry Holt & Co., Inc., 1954), p. 36.

[9] See Chapter 2, above.

[10] W. N. and L. A. Kellogg, *The ape and the child* (New York: McGraw-Hill Book Co., Inc., 1933).

[11] C. Hayes, *The ape in our house* (New York: Harper & Bros., 1951), pp. 66-67.

[12] However, some comparative psychologists believe that animals have sometimes demonstrated rather elaborate symbolic communication. See D. O. Hebb and W. R. Thompson, The social significance of animal studies, in G. Lindzey (ed.), *op. cit.*, Vol. I, pp. 537-40.

[13] See, e.g., K. Young, *Personality and problems of adjustment* (rev. ed.; New York: Appleton-Century-Crofts, Inc., 1952), chap. vi.

dom" vocalization when the newborn infant utters an undifferentiated series of cries, squeals, grunts, gurglings, and cooings. About the third or fourth month a period of babbling or *lalling* begins, marked by greater repetition of sounds. Apparently the baby responds to his own cries according to what has been called the "circular reflex": his own verbal response serves as the stimulus to evoke similar responses.[14]

This is followed, toward the end of the child's first year, by an *imitative* stage, or "echolalia," as some call it. "From the circular responses of the babbling stage," says Young, "it is but a step to the next, in which the self-starting, self-continuing neuromuscular vocal patterns of the child become associated with similar sounds uttered by another person." [15] The child imitates others in much the same way that, earlier, he imitated or responded to his own vocalizations. During this stage the variety of sounds made tends to be smaller; they are patterned according to the phonetics of the language spoken by the adults.

There is some disagreement as to when meaning emerges in the infant. Some authorities maintain that the child responds more to the adult's gestures than to his words. On the other hand, Lewis asserts that infants are not able to respond discriminantly to gestures before six months. Intonation appears to be the means by which the child acquires meaning. The infant responds to such expressive commands as "Don't fall," "Eat your food," etc. Movements, as well as intonation, play a role in these learnings.[16]

The last stage, that of real speech or *verbal comprehension,* begins when the ten- to eighteen-month-old child has mastered one or two words. When he consistently uses "da" for doll or daddy, "ma" or "mama" for his mother, "ta" for hot, "bye-bye" for good-by, and the like, he has begun true speech. In his first weeks of speaking, of course, the child uses words rather broadly, as Kimball Young points out.[17] "Mama" means the mother and all she does for the child. "Bath" stands for the tub, the water, the soap, and the splashing. Likewise "kitty" is used for a variety of small animals. The child's first words relate to whole situations; only as he grows older and learns more words does he differentiate and learn more specific meanings.

[14] F. H. Allport, *Social psychology* (Boston: Houghton Mifflin Co., 1924), p. 39.
[15] Young, *op. cit.,* p. 139.
[16] M. M. Lewis, *Infant speech* (New York: Harcourt, Brace & Co., Inc., 1936), as quoted in A. R. Lindesmith and A. L. Strauss, *Social psychology* (rev. ed.; New York: The Dryden Press, Inc., 1956), p. 172.
[17] *Op. cit.,* p. 143.

Keith J. Hayes

The chimpanzee is being socialized by imitating the actions of a doll, under the supervision of its "mother," Mrs. Keith J. Hayes. This and similar studies with animals indicate that a human social environment can produce significant effects even on creatures with a much narrower range of potentialities than a human child.

From the McGraw-Hill text-film *Social Development*

Along with family and school, peer groups account for a large share of the child's social, emotional, and attitudinal development.

The stereotype has a long history in Western culture, as indicated by this early nineteenth century Gillway cartoon of John Bull.

After the first few words, a child's vocabulary grows by leaps and bounds. One much-quoted study shows the following increase in words mastered: [18]

At age 1	3 words
2	272
3	896
4	1,540
5	2,072
6	2,562

Estimates furnished by Terman with the first Stanford-Binet test give figures for vocabulary size at later ages: [19]

At age 8	3,600 words
10	5,400
12	7,200
14	9,000
16	11,700
18	13,500

Vocabulary estimates vary greatly, however, depending on groups tested and methods of estimating. Another investigator, for example, found "recognition" vocabularies of about 23,000 words at age six (first grade) and of 80,000 words at age seventeen (twelfth grade).[20] All we can be sure of is that vocabulary increases very rapidly during the second, third, and fourth years, and more gradually thereafter.

Other criteria besides vocabulary indicate the child's linguistic progress. His sentences lengthen out; McCarthy found sentences averaging 1.2 words at eighteen months of age and 4.6 words at fifty-four months. She discovered also that only 26 per cent of the child's words are comprehensible at eighteen months, as compared with 99.8 per cent at fifty-four months.[21] Another study reveals how a child's loquacity progresses. Jersild and Ritzman counted the number of words spoken in three hours by nursery school children.[22] Their results are as follows:

Age	Mean number of words
24-29 months	402
30-35	763
36-41	1,296
42-47	1,772

[18] M. E. Smith, *An investigation of the development of the sentence and the extent of vocabulary in young children* (Univ. Ia. Stud. Child Welf., 1926, No. 5).

[19] L. M. Terman, *The measurement of intelligence* (Boston: Houghton Mifflin Co., 1916), p. 226.

[20] M. K. Smith, Measurement of the size of general English vocabulary through the elementary grades and high school, *Genet. Psychol. Monogr.*, XXIV (1941), 344.

[21] D. McCarthy, *The language development of the preschool child* (Univ. Minn. Inst. Child Welf. Monogr., 1930, No. 4).

[22] A. T. Jersild and R. Ritzman, Aspects of language development: the growth of loquacity and vocabulary, *Child Developm.*, IX (1938), 243-59.

Jean Piaget, the famous Swiss psychologist, distinguished between *egocentric* and *socialized* speech in the child.[23] Up to about age seven or eight, he found self-centered and self-assertive remarks predominate, after which the child's speech becomes more socialized. An American study of twenty-seven kindergarten children tended to confirm Piaget; 41 per cent of the remarks observed were self-assertive.[24] Others question the generality of Piaget's conclusions. McCarthy points out that the character of children's verbal responses varies according to the social situation.[25] She found egocentric speech common when children were playing with each other, but not when they talked with adults.

The process by which a child learns to speak has been referred to traditionally as "conditioning." One type of conditioning, the *circular reflex* "theory," is used widely to explain a young child's babbling and repetitive vocalization. Recently B. F. Skinner and his followers emphasized a different interpretation: [26] The infant learns to talk because he emits a variety of sounds, some of which are reinforced through rewards or satisfactions. As he matures during his first year, for example, certain vocalizations such as "da" or "ma" are rewarded and encouraged by the family. Others (e.g., "otch," "glug") are "extinguished" from lack of such reinforcement.

Skinner, however, is more interested in the function of language than in its precise form. He introduces two new terms to describe language functions—the *mand* and the *tact,* which parallel the imperative and declarative moods of syntax. The "mand," which develops early in the child's experience, functions to secure for the speaker specific reinforcements from the hearer. Commands, entreaties, and requests of all sorts fall into this category; they operate to satisfy drives on the part of the speaker. The "tact," on the other hand, has a declarative function; its form is determined by the names of particular objects or events which have stimulated the speaker. "Tacts" are learned through generalized reinforcement from hearers, such as smiles, rewards, and other signs of approval when the baby uses a word correctly.

Skinner's approach is behavioristic; it treats language as "verbal behavior" and focuses on the functions of verbal responses and on

[23] J. Piaget, *The language and thought of the child,* trans. M. Warden (New York: Harcourt, Brace & Co., Inc., 1926).

[24] H. Rugg, L. Krueger, and A. Sondergaard, A study of language in kindergarten children, *J. educ. Psychol.,* XX (1929), 1-18.

[25] D. McCarthy, A comparison of children's language in different situations . . . , *J. genet. Psychol.,* XXXVI (1929), 583-91.

[26] B. F. Skinner, *Verbal behavior* (New York: Appleton-Century-Crofts, Inc., 1957); also B. F. Skinner, *Science and human behavior* (New York: The Macmillan Co., 1955), pp. 210-16.

the conditions determining them. "Meaning" is not to be understood by introspection but simply by relating the act of speech to its controlling factors. Whether or not this new behavioristic, learning-centered approach will answer the major questions about symbolism and symbolic communication remains to be seen.

Conceptualization. The developing child learns from those about him the sound patterns and written words which make up the language of his group. As he learns the sounds, he acquires meanings; the words become symbols for particular persons, objects, situations, and activities which have furnished him with certain kinds of experience. At first, as already indicated above, the words do not have clearly differentiated meanings, but these become clearer as he gets older. He learns that "Mama" and "Daddy" are specific persons, and that "kitty" is a particular animal, to be distinguished from "doggie" and "birdie."

Later on he begins to understand the meaning of concepts—that is, more generalized ideas and symbols, abstracted from a number of experiences. A child of two may use correctly the words "kitty" and "doggie" or "papa" and "mama," but he cannot grasp the idea of "animal" or "man" and "woman" until he is older, say four or five. He knows what a chair or a ball is, but he cannot *define* either, even in simple terms like "to sit in" or "something you throw," until he is five or six years of age. Not until later still can he define "chair" as a "piece of furniture" or "ball" as a "plaything."

Learning meanings and concepts depends on both the child's mental development and his particular experiences. Many of these experiences are social; cultural norms have much to do with the way he perceives and conceptualizes his world. Sociologists refer to the socially transmitted meanings of things which are commonly understood and appreciated by members of the group. For example, if the cow is held sacred in a certain culture, the children will not consider the cow just another animal along with horses or sheep, as we do in our culture. Or again, color concepts differ from one culture to another. The Ashanti have names for black, red, and white. All dark colors such as blue, purple, and brown are called "black"; pink, orange, and yellow are considered "red." [27] One finds all kinds of interesting contrasts among cultures in the way numbers, weights, measures, and time relationships are conceptualized. [28]

[27] W. D. Wallis, *Introduction to anthropology* (New York: Harper & Bros., 1926), p. 421.

[28] For good examples, see O. Klineberg, *Social psychology* (rev. ed.; New York: Henry Holt & Co., Inc., 1954), chap. viii; M. Sherif and C. W. Sherif, *Outline of social psychology* (rev. ed.; New York: Harper & Bros., 1956), chap. ii.

These socially transmitted meanings are emotional as well as ideational. In each culture, and in smaller groups within the culture, many words and concepts arouse feeling-states consonant with the dominant values of the group. In the United States, for example, words like "home," "mother," "God," and "freedom" evoke favorable emotional reactions, while "liar," "sissy," "dictator," and "traitor" evoke unpleasant reactions.[29] We shall return to this subject later in dealing with propaganda and public opinion.

Thus our concepts and the language which symbolizes them reflect to a considerable degree the culture of which they are a part. Significant aspects of the culture, such as values and ways of thinking, are expressed in verbal concepts and communicated to the child, whose development is thereby patterned. Indeed, the "social norms" learned by the child influence what he perceives, what he learns and remembers, how he thinks, and what his attitudes will be.

LANGUAGE, CULTURE, AND THINKING

How symbolic communication originated in the course of human evolution is an interesting but highly speculative problem more in the province of the archeologist than of the social psychologist.[30] All we know is that language began somehow; it had utility and became the most essential part of man's cultural heritage. Anthropologists and philologists have investigated the basic forms and patterns of the languages of the world, both written and unwritten. Each one has become quite complex. As Kroeber says: "It may safely be estimated that every existing language, no matter how backward its speakers are in their general civilization, possesses a vocabulary of at least 5,000 to 10,000 words." [31]

We say that language is a form of symbolic communication because it consists of conventional cues or signs. A cue or sign serves "to control behavior in the way something else would exercise control if it were present." [32] Through usage, certain sounds and their written equivalents have come to represent persons, things, and activities. With very few exceptions, these words have no inherent or necessary connection with the items to which they refer. They are conventional substitutes or symbols in the sense that their mean-

[29] See, e.g., H. H. Briton, The function of emotions, Psychol. Rev., XXXIII (1926), 36-37.

[30] Klineberg, op. cit., chap. iii, gives a good brief review of the theories of language origin. See also E. L. Thorndike, The origin of language, Science, XCVIII (1943), 1-6.

[31] A. L. Kroeber, Anthropology (rev. ed.; New York: Harcourt, Brace & Co., Inc., 1948), p. 231.

[32] C. Morris, Signs, language and behavior (Englewood Cliffs, N. J.: Prentice-Hall, Inc., 1946), p. 95.

ing is understood and agreed upon by the members of the culture group. Before considering the significance of language in human social behavior, let us see how it is learned.

The function of gestures and nonverbal communication. Many authorities insist that symbolic speech derives from gestures. Floyd Allport called "gesture language" the earliest type of communication and the first stage in the child's linguistic development.[33] Charlotte Bühler noted that babies react to smiles, frowns, and threatening gestures before understanding words.[34] G. H. Mead attached great significance to the gesture; he considered it the basic element in communication.[35] For him a gesture is a "truncated" act, an act cut short, because it is responded to and does not need to be consummated. Indeed, Mead considered vocal responses under the head of gestures occurring in social interaction. "The fundamental importance of gesture," he adds, "lies in the development of the consciousness of meaning—in reflective consciousness. As long as one individual responds simply to the gesture of another by the appropriate response, there is no necessary consciousness of meaning. The situation is still on the level of that of two growling dogs walking around each other, with tense limbs, bristly hair, and uncovered teeth. It is not until an image arises of the response, which the gesture of the one form [36] will bring out in another, that a consciousness of meaning can attach to his own gesture. The meaning can appear only in imagining the consequence of the gesture." [37]

Whether or not speech and meaning arise from gestures still is a controversial issue. In any event gestures, like speech, are symbolic and play a significant part in human communication. Sometimes they are employed instead of speech; sometimes they serve to emphasize or clarify the spoken word, as in public speaking. Each culture pattern includes many commonly understood gestures. In our own culture we find the shake and nod of the head, shaking hands, waving the hand in greeting or parting, placing the finger to the lips to indicate silence, pointing directions with the finger and hand. Less polite gestures include holding the nose and thumbing the nose.

33 F. H. Allport, *Social psychology* (Boston: Houghton Mifflin Co., 1924), p. 178.

34 C. Bühler, The social behavior of children, in C. Murchison (ed.), *Handbook of child psychology* (Worcester, Mass.: Clark University Press, 1934).

35 G. H. Mead, *Mind, self and society* (Chicago: University of Chicago Press, 1934) pp. 42 ff.

36 Mead uses "form" here in the sense of "individual."

37 G. H. Mead, What social objects must psychology presuppose? *J. Phil., Psychol. sci. Meth.*, VII (1910), 178.

Anthropologists have studied the gesture language in many cultures; sometimes it is quite elaborate.[38] Comparison of different cultures shows tremendous variation in gestural expression of greeting, assent, dissent, beckoning, affection, dislike, and so on. Thus gestures cannot be considered a type of "natural" expression; their form is symbolic, the meaning being determined by historical and cultural influences. This cultural determination was brought out clearly in a study of the gestures of Italian and Jewish immigrants and their descendants.[39] Traditional Italian and Jewish gestures were found to disappear with the individual's assimilation into American life.

Gestures have been referred to as *sign language,* which ranges from the "monosyllabic" gesture of a railroad brakeman to the intricate "speech" of the deaf. Two other forms of nonverbal communication are *action language* and *object language.* The first refers to all movements that are not employed directly as signals. Smiling, eating, walking, closing a door, not only serve the individual's needs but are meaningful acts to those who perceive them. Object language includes all material things that communicate to the perceiver. A store display window, the type of dress one wears, debris scattered on a lawn—all make a statement for the observer. The statement may be intentional, as with the prearranged attractiveness of the store window, or may be nonintentional, as with the blond hair the wife discovers on her husband's suit! Object language may be very important in art, archaeology, or history, as it is possible to reconstruct a set of verbal relationships on the basis of certain remains.[40]

Nonverbal communication is particularly important where words fail to signify a given situation, as with spatial designs, for instance. It may, too, be used for emphasis; the arrow may make the road sign more meaningful, the gesture may amplify speech.

Language and culture. The early folk psychologists, as mentioned in Chapter 1, hoped to explain the "group mind" of primitive peoples by studying their language. They did not succeed, but clearly there is some relationship between material culture and language, and between a people's language and their thinking.

Anthropologists have shown that language reflects important aspects of a culture. For example, in English we have a few words

[38] See, for example, M. H. Krout, *Social psychology* (New York: Harper & Bros., 1942), chap. vi.

[39] D. Efron and J. P. Foley, Jr., Gestural behavior and social setting, in T. M. Newcomb and E. L. Hartley (eds.), *Readings in Social Psychology* (New York: Henry Holt and Co., 1947), pp. 33-40.

[40] J. Ruesch and W. Kees, *Nonverbal communication* (Berkeley: University of California Press, 1956), pp. 189-93.

for frozen water: ice, snow, sleet, hail, and slush. Boas pointed out that the Eskimos, in whose lives ice and snow are much more significant, have dozens of words to denote ice and snow in many different stages and conditions.[41] Even more striking is the evidence presented by Thomas; he finds several thousand words in Arabic connected with one important item, the camel.[42] Visitors to the United States are often impressed with the richness of our vocabulary in relation to mechanical and technical matters. When the Russians turned to industrialization, after the 1917 revolution, they borrowed technological terms from English and German. The Russian language now contains hundreds of words slightly modified from terms like "automobile" and "tractor."

It is interesting to note that under the National Socialist or Nazi regime in Germany, technical terms that were international cognates, like "Telefon" and "Munition," were nationalized and turned into "Fernsprecher" and "Rüstung." Language, then, reflects the culture in the size of vocabulary, and also in the interpretation given to classes of words—the feelings and needs that individuals in the cultures have toward the symbols and sounds themselves.

The extensiveness and imaginativeness expressed in vocabulary is nowhere better demonstrated in the United States than in the jargon surrounding a primary cultural trait, namely, money. Common words used to designate our currency include: lettuce, cabbage, green stuff, moola, lucre, shekels, jack, loot, dough, booly, mazuma, etc. Or, examine the overwhelming vocabulary that is associated with inebriation: pickled, high, plastered, potted, oiled, tight, crocked, soused, polluted, swacked, stinking, and the like. Undoubtedly the terms for money reflect the importance of that item in our culture. The richness of language referring to states of intoxication may be explained more by the ambivalent status of that particular physiological and psychological state: it both attracts and repels us.

LANGUAGE AND THOUGHT

Klineberg reviews evidence showing the interdependence of language and thought.[43] Where a concrete language, like Chinese, lacks hair-splitting distinctions, it is hardly strange to find the philosophy and literature similarly characterized. Also, Klineberg says, probably "an individual born into any particular culture will think in terms of the medium of expression current in his society, and . . . the nature of his thinking will be affected thereby." [44] Kluckhohn

41 See F. Boas, *General anthropology* (Boston: D. C. Heath and Co., 1938), p. 130.
42 W. I. Thomas, *Primitive behavior* (New York: McGraw-Hill Book Co., Inc., 1936).
43 Klineberg, *op. cit.*, chap. iii.
44 *Ibid.*, p. 49.

and Kelly note that language is a device for categorizing experience. A human being must select from his complex world. What he notices, what he thinks and talks about are partly a function of his linguistic patterns.[45] However, the relationship between language and thought is not simple. Lee reports that the Trobriand language has no words expressing causal relationship.[46] Does this mean that the language reflects—results from—the Trobrianders' lack of interest in motives, purposes, and causality in general, as Lee suggests? Or does it mean that the Trobrianders lack causal concepts because their language happens not to contain them? Or both?

It has been reasonably well established that thought structure is conditioned for the members of a specific culture by the language. Categories of space, time, movement, and various modes of perception are limited by language. Western languages are particularly disposed to time as a major category. When we say "the man is coming," the emphasis is on the present. Few students of foreign languages have failed to remark on the difficulty of learning the eight or ten verb conjugations expected of them in the course of the semester. On the other hand, the Kwakiutl may be more interested in whether the subject is visible or not visible rather than in any time considerations: "The visible man is coming." For other cultures the question is whether the noun is present or absent, animate or inanimate. Some suggestion of this is found in various Western languages in the use of gender; nouns are masculine, feminine, or neuter, although this distinction no longer has functional significance. The word or symbol *la constitution* does not lose its abstraction simply because it has a feminine article.

Apparently there is no close correlation between the structure of a language and the type of culture represented.[47] Primitive cultures may have as complex, or even more intricate, languages as the more advanced cultures. Undoubtedly, each language has certain advantages. If there is a superiority in the Western communication system, it is the ease of symbolizing certain kinds of abstractions.

---

45 C. Kluckhohn and W. H. Kelly, The concept of culture, in R. Linton (ed.), *Science of man in the world crisis* (New York: Columbia University Press, 1945), pp. 100-101.

46 D. D. Lee, A primitive system of values, *Phil. Sci.*, VII (1940), 7, 355-65. See also T. M. Newcomb and E. L. Hartley (eds.), *Readings in Social Psychology* (New York: Henry Holt and Co., 1947), pp. 219-24.

47 It is difficult to tell how much the language is affected by its morphology as opposed to its lexical or semantic nature. The former refers to syntax and grammar, whereas the latter is the vocabulary itself. In structure some languages are inflected, as with most European languages where suffixes and sometimes affixes are found in conjugation. Secondly, there are agglutinate languages, such as Finnish, where the words are added together. At the other extreme is the Oriental group, where words are strung together in what appears to Westerners an arbitrary fashion. In addition, there are various combinations of these types.

The Sapir-Whorf theory. The writings of the late Benjamin Whorf have stressed the viewpoint already enunciated by Edward Sapir [48] that our thought structure, as well as our general culture pattern, is conditioned by the vocabulary and syntax of the language we speak. Our whole mode of perceiving and thinking is conditioned by linguistic symbols:

... the linguistic system (in other words, the grammar) of each language is not merely a reproducing instrument for voicing ideas but rather is itself the shaper of ideas, the program and guide for the individual's mental activity, for his analysis of impressions, for his synthesis of his mental stock in trade. . . . We dissect nature along lines laid down by our native languages. The categories and types that we isolate from the world of phenomena we do not find there because they stare every observer in the face; on the contrary, the world is presented in a kaleidoscopic flux of impressions which has to be organized by our minds—and this means largely by the linguistic systems in our minds.[49]

Likewise, science largely developed in Western culture because of the possibility of abstractions, time-consciousness—which predisposed man toward record collecting with a meticulousness and curiosity that led to science, particularly in the Periclean age and the Renaissance. Scientific thinking itself is a kind of linguistic Gestalt. Science would unquestionably be more difficult for, say, the Hopi, whose concepts of mathematics and time are different from ours. Regarding spatial concepts, they perceive space forms as we do, "but they do not use spatial concepts as surrogates for nonspatial relationships such as time, intensity, and tendency." [50]

There is no conclusive agreement on the Sapir-Whorf hypothesis. Some writers believe that further investigation should be made to ascertain the relation of linguistic patterns to cognition. To what degree do the structural aspects (syntax, grammar) and the semantic or lexical aspects (vocabulary) limit the thinking of the member of a given language group? To cite an example, it appears that the Navaho have five color terms (two shades of black, white, red, blue, green) in comparison to our more varied terminology (although, in a sense we have a white-black-red-blue-green system). This is not to imply that the Navaho are unable to perceive our different shades, including the difference between blue and green, or that we are unable to distinguish his two shades of gray and black. In

48 E. Sapir, *Language, an introduction to the study of speech* (New York: Harcourt, Brace & Co., Inc., 1921).

49 B. L. Whorf, *Collected papers on metalinguistics* (Washington, D. C.: Department of State, Government Printing Office, 1952), p. 21. See also B. L. Whorf, *Language, thought and reality* (New York: John Wiley & Sons, Inc., 1956).

50 F. Fearing, An examination of the conceptions of Benjamin Whorf . . ., in H. Hoijer (ed.), *Language in culture* (Chicago: University of Chicago Press, 1954), p. 51. The present authors are indebted to Hoijer *et al.* for examples cited below.

other words, human beings may have ideas that are not symbonzed by a specific term. The French undoubtedly have the concept of "home" even though their language has traditionally been lacking in that specific word. Nor should we be too hasty in characterizing a certain language pattern. For instance, in Chinese there are two words for train: the first to be introduced was *hwoche,* meaning literally "firecart" (which is not unlike the appearance of early locomotives); the second term was *dyanli-hwoche* or "electric fire-cart." We must not infer that the Chinese are incapable of conceiving of trains as abstractly as we; they do not necessarily have an image of a locomotive belching fire. Linguistic patterns, then, require a great deal of investigation before we have a definite idea of their relationship to systems of thought, causality, and value orientation.

Many psychologists have insisted that thought goes on in linguistic form. The behavioristic sociologist G. H. Mead was one of the first to formulate such a view: thinking is "inner conversation." [51] Piaget's conclusions were similar, after he had studied the relation between the child's language development and his thinking. He wrote that "logical reasoning is an argument which we have with ourselves, and which reproduces internally the features of a real argument." [52] John B. Watson, the founder of behaviorism, emphasized from the first that thinking is subvocal speech.[53] He stated in 1930: "The behaviorist advances the view that *what the psychologists have hitherto called thought is in short nothing but talking to ourselves."* [54] The physical basis of thinking Watson found not so much in the tongue and larynx as in muscular responses of the cheek, tongue, throat, and chest. He presented a good deal of material in support of his theory but was unable to prove it experimentally.

The case for a linguistic influence upon thinking does not depend, however, upon demonstration of muscular movements. Our best psychological information indicates that thinking goes on in terms of some combination of words, concepts, images, gestures, attitudes, and feelings, without depending, *necessarily,* on any one of these.[55] All of them, whether basically verbal, visual, or emotional, have arisen in a context of social communication. Hence

[51] G. H. Mead, *Mind, self and society* (Chicago: University of Chicago Press, 1934), p. 141.

[52] J. Piaget, *et al., Judgment and reasoning in the child,* trans. Marjorie Warden (London: Kegan Paul, Trench, Trubner & Co., 1928), p. 204.

[53] J. B. Watson, *Behavior, an introduction to comparative psychology* (New York: Henry Holt & Co., Inc., 1914), p. 19.

[54] J. B. Watson, *Behaviorism* (New York: W. W. Norton & Co., Inc., 1930), p. 238.

[55] See H. L. Hollingworth, *The psychology of thought* (New York: Appleton-Century-Crofts, Inc., 1926).

the form or processes of thinking as well as its content are greatly influenced by language.

PITFALLS OF SYMBOLISM

We have seen that language makes possible the creation and transmission of a social heritage, which, in turn, gives us understanding of past and present and some ability to forecast the future. Language underlies our development of concepts and thinking and thus our command of the environment. Compared to the "signaling reflexes" of animals, symbolic language makes human social communication infinitely richer, more subtle, and more complete.

But along with the amazing advantages of linguistic communication there are dangers. These dangers have been stressed by Count Alfred Korzybski, the founder of "semantics," and his followers.[56] Semantics is concerned with critical examination of symbolic language.[57]

The province of semantics is well introduced by Hayakawa:

From the moment Mr. Smith switches on an early morning news broadcast to the time he falls asleep at night over a novel or a magazine, he is, like all other people living under modern civilized conditions, swimming in words. Newspaper editors, politicians, salesmen, radio comedians, columnists, luncheon club speakers and clergymen; colleagues at work, friends, relatives, wife and children; market reports, direct mail advertising, books, and billboards—all are assailing him with words all day long. And Mr. Smith himself is constantly contributing to that verbal Niagara every time he puts on an advertising campaign, delivers a speech, writes a letter, or even chats with his friends.

When things go wrong in Mr. Smith's life—when he is worried, perplexed, or nervous, when family, business, or national affairs are not going as he thinks they should, when he finds himself making blunder after blunder in personal or financial matters—he blames a number of things as responsible for his difficulties. Sometimes he blames the weather, sometimes his health or the state of his "nerves," sometimes his glands, or, if the problem is a larger one, he may blame his environment, the economic system he lives under, a foreign nation, or the cultural pattern of society. When he is pondering over the difficulties of other people, he may attribute their troubles too to causes such as these, and he may add still another, namely, "human nature." It rarely, if ever, occurs to him to investigate, among other things, the nature and constituents of that daily verbal Niagara as a possible cause of trouble. . . .

Whether he realizes it or not, however, Mr. Smith is affected every hour of his life not only by the words he hears and uses, *but also by his unconscious assump-*

56 A. Korzybski, *Science and sanity* (Lancaster, Pa.: Science Press, 1933); S. Chase, *The power of words* (New York: Harcourt, Brace & Co., Inc., 1953); S. I. Hayakawa, *Language in thought and action* (New York: Harcourt, Brace & Co., Inc., 1949); W. Johnson, *People in quandaries* (New York: Harper & Bros., 1946).
57 Charles Morris, author of *Signs, language and behavior* (Englewood Cliffs, N. J.: Prentice-Hall, Inc., 1946), suggests "semiotic" as a better name than "semantics" for a science of signs and symbols.

tions about language. These unconscious assumptions determine the way he takes words—which in turn determines the way he acts, whether wisely or foolishly. Words and the way he takes them determine his beliefs, his prejudices, his ideals, his aspirations—they constitute the moral and intellectual atmosphere in which he lives, in short, his semantic environment. If he is constantly absorbing false and lying words, or if his unconscious assumptions about language happen to be, as most of our notions are that have not been exposed to scientific influence, naïve, superstitious, or primitive, he may be constantly breathing a poisoned air without knowing it.[58]

Among other things, semanticists try to clarify the distinction between *extensional* and *intensional* meaning, i.e., between "denotation" and "connotation." [59] Extensional meaning is that which words stand for or denote; intensional meaning is that which is suggested or connoted "inside one's head." One of the greatest pitfalls of linguistic communication is mistaking intensional meanings for extensional ones; for example, assuming that words having strong pleasant or unpleasant connotations reflect objective reality rather than subjective feelings.

Another way of stating the point is to say that a word refers to some person, object, or event, which is called a "referent," much as a map symbolizes or represents a certain piece of territory. If the connotation of a word diverges greatly from its referent, the word is likely to be misleading or confusing. This is particularly true when words acquire strong emotional connotations. Stuart Chase gives some entertaining illustrations. A Nazi orator speaks:

The Aryan Fatherland which has nursed the souls of heroes calls upon you for the supreme sacrifice which you, in whom flows heroic blood, will not fail, and which will echo forever down the corridors of history.

Chase suggests substituting "blab" for each word which does not have a clear referent. The passage would then read:

The blab blab which has nursed the blabs of blabs, calls upon you for the blab blab which you, in whom flows blab blab, will not fail, and which will echo blab down the blabs of blab.[60]

Or again, we can find excellent examples in political party platforms. The effort of the platform drafter is to produce a document which will arouse favorable emotional reactions in as many people as possible and sound quite specific without actually being so. Consider the paragraph which follows, taken from the Republican platform of 1948.

[58] Hayakawa, *Language in action* (New York: Harcourt, Brace & Co., Inc., 1941), pp. vii-viii, xi-xii.

[59] *Ibid.,* pp. 61 ff.

[60] S. Chase, The tyranny of words, *Harper's Magazine,* CLXXV (1937), 567.

We shall erect our foreign policy on the basis of friendly firmness which welcomes cooperation but spurns appeasement. We shall pursue a consistent foreign policy which invites steadiness and reliance and which thus avoids the misunderstandings from which wars result. We shall protect the future against the errors of the Democrat administration, which has too often lacked clarity, competence or consistency in our vital international relationships and has too often abandoned justice.

Although political writing has shown some improvement in clarity in recent years, this selection from the Democratic Party platform of 1956 poses some semantic problems:

The Democratic Party is committed to support and advance the individual rights and liberties of all Americans. Our country is founded on the proposition that all men are created equal. This means that all citizens are equal before the law and should enjoy all political rights. . . .

This economy of ours, in the factory and on the farm, is blessed with ever increasing productive power. The Republicans have not permitted this potential abundance to be released for the mutual benefit of all. We reject this stunted Republican concept of America. We pledge ourselves to release the springs of abundance, to bring this abundance to all, and thus to fulfill the full promise of America.

Or from the 1956 Republican platform, there is no small number of undefined terms:

Every honorable means at our command has been exercised to alleviate the grievances and causes of armed conflict among nations. The advance of communism and its enslavement of people has been checked, and at key points thrown back. . . .

We firmly believe in the right of peoples everywhere to determine their form of government, their leaders, their destiny, in peace. Where needed, in order to promote peace and freedom throughout the world, we shall within the prudent limits of our resources, assist friendly countries in their determined effort to strengthen their economies.

Such statements, which are commonly found in the platforms of all political parties, make abundant use of words having pleasant and unpleasant connotations, e.g., "friendly firmness," "cooperation," "abundance," "appeasement," "enslavement," in the effort to win a following without making specific commitments. We should add in all fairness that political parties usually do make commitments on a few specific issues. An important part of propaganda analysis, or "communications" analysis, consists in identifying such extensionally meaningless items and in evaluating their effects upon people.[61]

On the other hand, language has certain functions besides the imparting of information. One is directive, as indicated above in

61 This will be discussed further in Chapter 17.

describing the "mand" compared with the "tact." Here language functions to control persons and events in accord with individual or social needs. Another use of language, particularly the spoken word, is expressive. Hayakawa calls this "presymbolic language," since it expresses feelings largely through loudness, tone, and other vocal qualities.[62] Cries of warning, exclamations, and insults are examples of expressive speech, as are many greetings, ritualistic utterances, and social conversations. The actual meaning of the words spoken is not important, but the manner of speaking is. As a young lady went through the receiving line at a formal reception, she shook hands, smiled, and said to each person, "I'm so glad I left my husband at home in the bathtub." No one paid any attention to the meaning of her words; they simply said, "So nice to meet you," and passed her along the line!

Other matters which concern students of semantics are "levels of abstraction" and definitions. Their approach is illustrated in the following example from Hayakawa:

[Definitions are useless, he says, if they mount] to higher levels of abstraction —the kind most of us tend to make automatically. Try the following experiment on an unsuspecting friend:

"What is meant by the word *red?*"

"It's a color."

"What's a *color?*"

"Why, it's a quality things have."

"What's a *quality?*"

"Say, what are you trying to do, anyway?"

You have pushed him into the clouds. He is lost.

If, on the other hand, we habitually go *down* the abstraction ladder to *lower* levels of abstraction when we are asked the meaning of a word, we are less likely to get lost in verbal mazes; we will tend to "have our feet on the ground" and know what we are talking about. This habit displays itself in an answer such as this:

"What is meant by the word *red?*"

"Well, the next time you see a bunch of cars stopped at an intersection, look at the traffic light facing them. Also, you might go to the fire department and see how their trucks are painted." [63]

Johnson, another semanticist, has elaborated Korzybski's thesis that semantic difficulties may lead to personal and social maladjustment.[64] Our quandaries, says Johnson, stem from our unfortunate subjective interpretations of failure, inferiority, and frustration. Difficulties arise, basically, because we introject from our culture ideas, values, and standards which are steeped in the language of

62 Hayakawa, *Language in action* (1941 ed.), pp. 74 ff.

63 *Ibid.*, p. 130.

64 Johnson, *op. cit.*

Aristotelian principles like the "law of the excluded middle." Maladjusted persons have notions of success and failure which are absolute and two-valued; "They tend to assume that they have 'failed' until they have *unquestionably* 'succeeded.' As a result, they feel driven to aim high, to be 'tops,' to break records, to do something 'bigger and better.' In this they are continually encouraged by many of the more obvious features of their semantic environment." [65] Furthermore, troubled individuals are more verbally inept than their normal brothers; hence they are very unclear about the nature of their difficulties. They cannot even frame good questions, much less work out the answers. More than anything else, concludes Johnson, mental hygiene demands clarity and accuracy, which comes through the study of language structure—that is, through semantics.

One recurrent answer to the problem of semantic barriers has been the search for a homogeneous language. If there are difficulties in communication between people speaking a relatively common language, the areas of misunderstanding are markedly greater when one involves entirely different languages. Differences of intelligence, class, and geography, as they affect speech, are minor compared to the problems of understanding between Englishmen and Germans, or Americans and Russians. We have already remarked on the gap that separates a Western and an Oriental language, a Western and a "primitive" language, or the entirely different linguistic structure of two preliterate groups, like Hopi and Navaho, which are more unlike than, say, English and Sanskrit.

Among the many attempts to establish a world language have been Esperanto, Interlingua, and most significant, Basic English, which Ogden presented in his book *The System of Basic English*.[66] Probably the reason that Basic English has been more successful in receiving attention is that a significantly large percentage of the world's population already has some knowledge of English. Also English appears to be more flexible, and by a statistical count, less redundant than other Indo-European languages. As illustration there are more monosyllabic words and fewer syllables in given selections of prose.[67] Basic English consists of 850 words, or "lexical units," in the jargon of psycholinguistics. Although it is hardly likely, and perhaps not desirable, that this medium should supplant other languages, it might prove to be a means of communication that will facilitate international understanding.

[65] *Ibid.*, p. 11.

[66] C. K. Ogden, *The system of Basic English* (New York: Harcourt, Brace & Co., Inc., 1934).

[67] G. A. Miller, *Language and communication* (New York: McGraw-Hill Book Co., Inc., 1951), p. 114.

SUMMARY

It is the ability to communicate symbolically, more than anything else, which differentiates man from animals. Through language the child becomes acquainted with his social heritage and is introduced to the concepts and norms of his social group. Both the form and context of human thought are, in large measure, functions of language, which, in turn, reflects basic features of the culture. Symbolic thinking and communication, however, are subject to various dangers, as students of semantics have indicated. Words may lose touch with their "referents" or may become so abstract they no longer convey meaning.

Having discussed language, the means by which most social interaction occurs, we now turn to inquire into the nature of social interaction.

SUPPLEMENTARY READINGS

Books of Readings

MACCOBY, E. E., NEWCOMB, T. M., AND HARTLEY, E. L. (eds.). *Readings in social psychology.* 3d ed. New York: Henry Holt & Co., Inc., 1958.

Brown, R. W., and Lenneberg, E. H., Studies in linguistic relativity.

Carroll, J. B., and Casegrande, J. B., The function of language classification in behavior.

Whorf, B., Science and linguistics.

Verplanck, W. S., The control of the content of conversation: reinforcement of statements of opinion.

BRITT, S. H. (ed.). *Selected readings in social psychology.* New York: Rinehart & Co., Inc., 1950.

Albig, W., Language and public opinion.

LINDZEY, G., *Handbook of social psychology.* Reading, Mass.: Addison-Wesley Pub. Co., Inc., 1954. Vol. II.

Miller, G. A., Psycholinguistics.

Other References

CARROLL, J. B. *The study of language.* Cambridge, Mass.: Harvard University Press, 1953.

    A good overview of linguistics, with its relationships to other fields.

CHASE, S. *The power of words.* New York: Harcourt, Brace & Co., Inc., 1953.

    As with his previous work, *The tyranny of words,* Chase popularizes the latest ideas in linguistics, communication, and semantics.

CHERRY, C. *On human communication: a review, a survey and a criticism.* New York: John Wiley & Sons, Inc., 1957.

    A well-documented study of the subject, including the history of research in the field. Later chapters are for the advanced student.

DOOB, L. W. *Social psychology.* New York: Henry Holt & Co., Inc., 1952.

    Chap. v contains significant material on language in reference to culture and semantics.

HARTLEY, E. L., AND HARTLEY, R. E. *Fundamentals of social psychology.* New York: Alfred A. Knopf, Inc., 1952.
This work, in Part I, provides an excellent theoretical framework of communication with experimental data.

HAYAKAWA, S. I. *Language in thought and action.* New York: Harcourt, Brace & Co., Inc., 1949.
An understandable presentation of semantics.

HOIJER, H. *Language in culture.* Chicago: University of Chicago Press, 1954.
A series of brilliant papers largely directed to the Sapir-Whorf hypothesis.

JOHNSON, W. *People in quandaries.* New York: Harper & Bros., 1946.
Presents in readable style the relationship of semantics to personal adjustment.

KORZYBSKI, A. *Science and sanity,* rev. ed. Lancaster, Pa.: Science Press, 1933.
A difficult but very influential book that initiated the semantics movement.

LINDESMITH, A. R., AND STRAUSS, A. L. *Social psychology,* rev. ed. New York: The Dryden Press, Inc., 1956.
An outstanding exposition of the development of language in the individual and its influence in our thinking. Chaps. ii-viii.

MILLER, G. A. *Language and communication.* New York: McGraw-Hill Book Co., Inc., 1951.
An advanced study of various aspects of linguistics and communication, from phonetics to semantics.

MORRIS, C. *Signs, language, and behavior.* Englewood Cliffs, N. J.: Prentice-Hall, Inc., 1946.
A philosophical and empirical introduction to the subject.

PIAGET, J. *Language and thought of the child.* New York: Harcourt, Brace & Co., Inc., 1926.
A deservedly much quoted study of development of language and its relationship to the self.

RUESCH, J., AND BATESON, G. *Communication, the social matrix of psychiatry.* New York: W. W. Norton & Co., Inc., 1951.
Information theory and the communicative process as part of the adjustment process.

RUESCH, J., AND KEES, W., *Nonverbal communication.* Berkeley: University of California Press, 1956.
Besides being an absorbing discussion, the book contains excellent pictorial material.

SAPIR, E. *Language; an introduction to the study of speech.* New York: Harcourt, Brace & Co., Inc., 1921.
A milestone in the history of linguistics.

WHORF, B. L. *Language, thought, and reality.* New York: John Wiley & Sons, Inc., 1956.
A brilliant work on linguistics by a scholar who met an untimely death.

II

Modes of Social Interaction

We began our study of interpersonal relations by describing communication—the means by which most social interaction takes place. Our focus enlarged to include two or more persons as they stimulate and respond to each other. In this chapter, we shall describe major forms or processes of social interaction, with their determinants and some of their effects. In the next chapter we shall discuss the interaction occurring within social groups.

Traditionally the subject of social interaction is a part of sociology; it has been treated as a group phenomenon more or less independent of the individuals composing the group. Social interaction may, however, be described as a function of the participating individuals, in which case it comes within the domain of social psychology. Thus instead of treating competition as a broad social process characterizing many whole cultures, we can describe it as a fairly specific way in which A and B interact—or as a way A behaves toward a whole group consisting of B, C, D, E, F, and G. Furthermore we may be able to account for the competition between A and B in terms of their respective personalities and may likewise trace the effects of the competition on each of them. Social interaction is a crucial matter for the social psychologist, as we shall see, from the standpoint both of theory and of application.

FACTORS IN SOCIAL INTERACTION
Social behavior is rooted in biological as well as social conditions. Due to the structure of mammals, for example, contact between mother and offspring is necessary if the latter are to survive. In primates, particularly in man, dependence on parents is prolonged

because the young do not come into the world prepared to fend for themselves through elaborate instinctive equipment. Obviously, too, social contact between male and female is implicit in the sexual differentiation found in humans as in all higher animal forms.

Climatic, geographical, and other environmental influences also play an important part. The struggle for survival (i.e., competition and conflict) noted by evolutionists arises chiefly because supplies of food, water, and shelter are insufficient for organisms living in a given area. Environmental conditions may likewise facilitate mutual aid and cooperation, as we shall see later. Social life, with its varieties of social interaction, is essential to man if he is to obtain the food, clothing, and shelter necessary for him to survive. Besides, out of the centuries of human existence has come culture—including fire-making, cooking, tool-using, clothing, and speech and also beliefs, values, institutions, and forms of social behavior. Just as a child learns to wear clothing, to use tools, and to speak, so he learns the beliefs and practices of his cultural group.

Since men are biologically alike the world over, knowledge of cultures may be enough to account for differences between peoples— between the placid, cooperative Arapesh, the suspicious Dobu, the schizoid Balinese, and the violently pugnacious Mundugumor.[1] But within a culture—our own or any other—the social psychologist must deal not only with the most prevalent forms of social interaction but also with the friendliness and sympathy of Mrs. A., the hostile competitiveness of Mr. B., the timid, unsocial behavior of Miss C. For this more complete interpretation of social behavior, we shall need to bring in the personality dynamics as well as the social experience of the persons participating.

Let us begin by asking what types or forms of social interaction are known to exist. There is, of course, a great variety, extending from the most loving sympathy and cooperation between husband and wife (at least some husbands and wives!) to murder and war between nations. It would be difficult to estimate accurately the total number of processes which society has developed. In this chapter we are selecting a few of the more recurrent ones for introductory analysis.

We have already surveyed certain social processes. For one, there is *communication,* which for some social scientists is the most basic type of social interaction, since it provides a medium in which other interpersonal relationships may take place. Its universality is evidenced in a variety of symbolizations, from the gestures made by

1 This point is emphasized by L. A. White in his *Science of culture* (New York: Farrar, Straus & Cudahy, Inc., 1949).

facial muscles to patterns of words on a printed page, from the signals of a railway brakeman to the canvas of a Leonardo da Vinci, from the infant's cry to the telegrapher's key. Another broad sweeping process is *socialization*—which includes the whole course of "humanization" of the infant and child. Another process, as we have seen, is *stratification*. This kind of patterning has left its mark on almost every society known, and apparently meets a universal need in that their different backgrounds, abilities, and roles lead men into different categories of status.

Even in a small community we can observe several clearly defined types of social interactional behavior.[2] We find an eccentric or recluse who refuses to have dealings with anyone. (This is zero-degree social interaction.) We see mutual aid and cooperation between members of a family and between neighbors, especially in time of trouble or crisis. We also note competition between the children in a family, between schoolmates, between athletic teams, between businessmen. Or we see dramatic conflicts, as in a fist fight or a lawsuit. Sometimes we find evidence for deeper, latent conflicts between employer and employee, landlord and tenant, farmer and townsman.

Interpersonal relationships show many qualitative and quantitative differences. In any community some people are mutually attracted; others repel each other. Some persons are dominant, others subordinate. A farmer exploits his hired man; an adolescent imitates his athletic hero; a wife controls her husband through subtle use of suggestion. One married couple used to scrap a lot and often were on the verge of separation; now they have become better adjusted to each other and conflicts are infrequent. Another couple started out harmoniously but have grown apart, and divorce is imminent. A businessman prospered, bought a big house, and began to act like "high society." Another businessman, newly arrived in the community, hated it at first, but has grown to like it and to feel "accepted."

How may one classify the many ways people behave toward each other? It has proved most difficult to categorize the major forms of social interaction. Park and Burgess proposed four basic proc-

[2] These are indicated in many community studies, e.g., R. S. and H. M. Lynd, *Middletown* (New York: Harcourt, Brace & Co., Inc., 1929); J. West, *Plainville, U.S.A.* (New York: Columbia University Press, 1945); S. T. Kimball and M. Pearsall, *The Talladega story: A study in community process* (University, Ala.: University of Alabama Press, 1954); R. G. Barker and H. F. Wright, *Midwest and its children* (Evanston, Ill.: Row, Peterson & Co., 1955). More dramatic treatment is found in Sherwood Anderson's *Winesburg, Ohio* and Edgar Lee Masters' *Spoon River Anthology*.

esses—competition, conflict, accommodation, and assimilation.[3] This classification, with the addition of cooperation, has been followed in many sociology textbooks.[4]

Other ways of framing the relationship of individuals have been suggested. First of all, there is the problem of proceeding from the individual to the group, or in one theorist's views:

Reference has already been made to the necessity of combining individual and social behavior into a single theoretical system. The reasons are obvious. In any social interaction, the interests, motives, habits, or other psychological properties of the acting individuals determine to some degree the kind of interaction that will occur. The shy youngster is likely to have less stimulating learning experiences with his teacher than is a bolder one; the traveler in a foreign land who knows the language forms different kinds of friendships than the traveler who uses an interpreter. Conversely, the social milieu, the interpersonal relationships, within which a person acts determine his psychological properties. A man in a subordinate role cannot act as a leader; a child reared as the younger of two develops differently from one reared as the elder of two. Whether the group's behavior is dealt with as antecedent and the individual's as consequent, or vice versa, the two kinds of events are interdependent.[5]

FIG. 8. Forms of Social Interaction.

SOURCE: Adopted from G. A. Lundberg, C. C. Schrag, and O. N. Larsen, *Sociology* (New York: Harper & Bros., 1954), p. 400.

[3] R. E. Park and E. W. Burgess, *Introduction to the science of sociology* (2d ed.; Chicago: University of Chicago Press, 1924).

[4] E.g., J. L. Gillin and J. P. Gillin, *Cultural sociology* (New York: The Macmillan Co., 1948); W. F. Ogburn and M. F. Nimkoff, *Sociology* (rev. ed.; Boston: Houghton Mifflin Co., 1950); F. E. Merrill, *Society and Culture* (rev. ed.; Englewood Cliffs, N.J.: Prentice-Hall, Inc., 1957). On the other hand, there are texts whose long lists of social processes rival the older classifications of instincts. See, e.g., L. von Wiese and H. Becker, *Systematic sociology* (New York: John Wiley & Sons, Inc., 1932).

[5] R. R. Sears, Social behavior and personality development, in T. Parsons, and E. A. Shils (eds.), *Toward a general theory of action* (Cambridge, Mass.: Harvard University Press, 1951), 468-69.

Actually the transition of individual to group involves a set of possible dyadic units.[6] These categories in Fig. 8 obviously are based on three types of relationships: attraction, repulsion, and indifference, which are probably the three most basic or unitary forms of social interaction.

THE PROCESSES OF SOCIAL INTERACTION

The traditional approach to social interaction is to study processes without much concern for the social situations in which they occur. The more recent trend, in social psychology at least, is to consider social behavior always within a group framework—as related to group structure and function. Both approaches have merit. We shall first follow the sociologists in studying major processes of social interaction, reserving until later the examination of social groups.

Isolation or avoidance of human contacts actually is not a form of social interaction, but rather the absence or negation of it. Complete isolation is very uncommon, partly because people's needs make them dependent on one another and partly because we are all brought up in a social milieu and acquire sociable or gregarious tendencies to some degree. The rare cases of feral and isolated children, as we have seen, avoid and fear human beings because they have no background of experience with them. With hermits and other voluntary isolates, traumatic social experiences always are discovered in the background. Very few individuals are complete isolates; generally at least one relative or friend is trusted and welcomed. Often a person who seems an isolate is merely avoiding contact with certain persons or groups—not with all of them. Complete and persistent isolation usually results in egocentrism, if not pronounced maladjustment, since many of man's needs—such as sex and recognition—require social contacts for their fulfilment. Enforced isolation of a normally socialized individual is intensely frustrating and sometimes results in suicide. Cases of solitary confinement show this, though this practice now is almost abandoned.

The patterning of interaction. The attraction-repulsion dimension probably is the most important criterion for social interaction. When mutual attraction exists, the stage is set for a variety of interpersonal relationships; with mutual dislike, social interaction approaches the zero point. The attraction-repulsion dimension is central to Moreno's sociometry, a method for studying intragroup

6 G. A. Lundberg, Some problems of group classification and measurement, *Amer. sociol. Rev.*, V (1940), 351-60. Also in G. A. Lundberg, C. C. Schrag, and O. N. Larsen, *Sociology* (New York: Harper & Bros., 1954), p. 400.

relations, which will be described more fully later.[7] While some individuals may be found who are attracted or repelled by people in general, likes and dislikes usually are personalized. A likes B, dislikes C, and feels neutral about D. Or, to be still more specific, A likes B but *loves* E; he dislikes C but *hates* F to the point of wanting to murder him.

Of course, the subtler nuances of interpersonal relationships are not revealed by discovering patterns of like and dislike; this dimension merely indicates the general framework. A and B may be attracted to each other because of common interests. C may like D because D laughs at his jokes; D may like C not because of his personality but simply because C makes D feel jolly. The mutual attraction of E and F may be fundamentally homosexual, and so on. The specific components entering into what we sum up as "attraction" or "repulsion" are almost infinite. Some are based on physiological factors—the growing attraction between boys and girls during adolescence, for example. Some likes and dislikes have irrational bases whose origins are obscure; for example, resemblance in appearance or voice to persons formerly liked or disliked. Probably the commonest basis for attraction is similarity of interests, ideas, and attitudes, and for dislike, dissimilarity. Group membership obviously is significant here, since persons belonging to the same or similar groups are more likely to have the same interests and attitudes.

Another broad type of social relationship is dominance-subordination. As with attraction-repulsion, it indicates a certain general pattern of interaction, not its specific content. X dominates Y because of superior intellect; Y dominates Z because of his social and financial position; and, indeed, Z may dominate X because Z was a major in the last war and X a lieutenant! Furthermore, as we shall see, the dominance-subordination relation often is situational. X is Y's superior in business and social situations, but X may defer to Y in the gymnasium or on a hunting trip. This question relates closely both to roles and to leadership, which will be discussed shortly.

MUTUAL SOCIAL INTERACTION

Much study has been given the more specific and goal-directed kinds of mutual social interaction such as competition, conflict, and cooperation. We shall describe each of these and report some of the research findings.

[7] J. L. Moreno, *Who shall survive?* (New York: Nervous & Mental Disease Publishing Co., 1934).

Competition. Competition is mutual rivalry or struggle between two or more persons for the purpose of obtaining a nondivisible goal.[8] It is the means of satisfying biogenic or sociogenic needs and proceeds according to some set of rules and regulations, stated or implicit. Contrary to older instinct theories, learning greatly affects competition. It is an approved form of social behavior in most cultures, though not in all. In Western cultures and among some primitive peoples, such as the Kwakiutl, competition not only is sanctioned but idealized. In some cultures, like the Zuñi, Dakota, and Bathonga, it is either absent or frowned upon.[9] In the United States, competitive behavior begins to appear in children at three or four years of age. Competitive patterns may be picked up from parents, siblings, members of the child's play group, or schoolmates.[10]

Psychologists have studied the origins of competition and its effectiveness compared with other types of social behavior. Maller found that the American children he studied worked harder and more effectively when they competed (either as individuals or members of a group competing with another group) than when they cooperated.[11] Several experiments showed that increased competition tends, on the whole, to increase output but to decrease quality.[12] Apparently competition is most effective when a spirit of rivalry exists, when the rivals are nearly equal, and when the competitors feel familiar with the task but are not too efficient at the start.

Many bad effects of competition also have been noted, particularly the arousing of frustration and anxiety. Karen Horney insisted that competition was a problem for everyone in our culture—an "unfailing center of neurotic conflicts." [13] The neurotic's anxiety and hostility result from exaggerated competitiveness. He measures himself against all others and seeks to defeat them; he seeks the impossible goal of being unique in every endeavor.

Various means are suggested to eliminate or reduce the bad effects of competition. One method is to compete with oneself instead of trying to outdo others, like the golfer who tries to improve his own

[8] Sociologists sometimes distinguish between rivalry and competition: rivalry implies a known competitor, whereas competition, the broader term, does not.

[9] See M. Mead (ed.), *Competition and cooperation among primitive peoples* (New York: McGraw-Hill Book Co., Inc., 1937).

[10] See G. Murphy, L. B. Murphy, and T. M. Newcomb, *Experimental social psychology* (New York: Harper & Bros., 1937), chap. vii, for a résumé of studies.

[11] J. B. Maller, *Cooperation and competition* (New York: Teachers College, Columbia University, 1929).

[12] See J. F. Dashiell, chap. xxiii in C. Murchison's *Handbook of social psychology* (Worcester, Mass.: Clark University Press, 1935).

[13] K. Horney, *The neurotic personality of our time* (New York: W. W. Norton & Co., Inc., 1937), p. 188.

score for the course. Better still is a changed set of standards. Instead of competing for grades, the student turns toward getting the most out of a course. Instead of striving to earn more than Mr. Jones, the professional man plans his work so he gets maximum enjoyment from it. From time to time colleges reduce the furious intercollegiate competition in sports in favor of more moderate intramural competition, in which many more students can participate and get the benefit of athletic exercise.

Though the forms of competition and the goals competed for are learned, competition may stem from the biological makeup of man—from the autonomic nervous system and the muscular and glandular systems which are mobilized for the expression of aggressive behavior. There is no conclusive evidence as to its over-all beneficial effects, compared with other forms of social interaction. However, many regard competition as a potent force in maintaining a high standard of living and continued aspiration for advanced status and as the most constructive form of conflict.

Cooperation. Cooperation is coordinated effort directed toward a sharable goal. It is most likely to occur in situations where an end cannot be attained by purely individual efforts. Kropotkin long ago,[14] and Allee more recently,[15] criticized overemphasis on the Darwinian theory of "survival of the fittest." They find much evidence of cooperation among animals, in connection with hunting, protection against danger, rearing the young, and establishing colonies with specialization of labor. Other studies show that cooperative behavior can be produced rather easily in chimpanzees and even in cats.[16]

Studies reveal that cooperative behavior appears in children at about the age of three. If anything, it occurs slightly later than competitive behavior in our culture, possibly because we emphasize the latter. It seems greatly affected by training. Nursery school and kindergarten teachers direct much of their effort toward encouraging cooperative behavior. The advantage of cooperative endeavor compared to individual effort shows up clearly in several studies.[17] However, it is difficult to assess the relative merits of competition and cooperation in general, since a given situation usually favors one or the other type of social behavior. For example, if one com-

14 P. Kropotkin, *Mutual aid in the animal world* (New York: Alfred A. Knopf, Inc., 1914).

15 W. C. Allee, *Animal aggregations* (Chicago: University of Chicago Press, 1931).

16 M. P. Crawford, *Cooperative solving of problems by young chimpanzees* (Comp. Psychol. Monogr., 1937, No. 68). C. N. Winslow, The social behavior of cats, *J. compar. Psychol.*, XXXVII (1944), 297-326.

17 See Murphy *et al., op. cit.*, pp. 709 ff.

pares individual and group efforts to solve a complicated problem, cooperative group activity nearly always succeeds better. But if the task is to see who among a number of individuals can get the solution first, the situation is slanted to favor competition.

Actually, much social activity is a subtle combination of competition and cooperation, often including other kinds of social behavior. A committee meeting contains elements of both, mainly emphasizing cooperative achievement. In a football game two teams compete, but the game is a poor one without good cooperation among the players on each team. In the classroom we stress individual achievement (and frown on cooperation as "cheating"). In a glee club or orchestra cooperation is the keynote; individual competition is minimized. Scientists and scholars seem to compete with each other, but we forget that each draws on the findings of his predecessors and contemporaries to the point that science and scholarship may more properly be considered cooperative enterprises.

Frequently the individual attempts some kind of competitive activity if the process of cooperation ceases to obtain his ends. This is particularly true of a crisis situation. For instance, a group waiting in line with relative discipline for a fire exit may bolt the line when it is severely threatened. Students who are afraid of flunking may resort to culturally nonacceptable forms of competition, including cheating, when they are convinced that "playing the rules" is not paying off. The classroom, we might add, is a competitive situation in which an honor system, whether "imposed" or "volunteered," generally prevails and elicits the cooperation of most of the students.

The conflict of cooperation and competition is well demonstrated in the "queueing up" before a "standing room only" sign where a limited number of tickets will be sold. If it is announced that only forty tickets will be sold, and the line reaches the fortieth man, future rivals are met by a constrained cooperation of solidarity on the part of the original group. The newcomers may express their variety of "cooperation" (however much it may be the result of hostility and individualism) by forming a rival line.[18]

Experiments continue to be inconclusive on the effects of cooperation and competition on problem solving. Generally speaking, recent research attributes greater significance to group sharing and solidarity than was true a generation ago. However, in one experiment the apparent superiority of the competitive process was exhibited. In a contest that involved a mechanical switching situation,

18 See R. W. Brown, Mass phenomena, in G. Lindzey (ed.), *Handbook of social psychology* (Reading, Mass.: Addison-Wesley Pub. Co., Inc., 1954), Vol. II, pp. 860-63, for a discussion of the cooperative aspects of a crisis-oriented situation.

and where there was considerable flexibility as to the degree of individual action as well as teamwork, superior results were obtained when one individual could control the entire panel. It may be, however, as the authors imply, that the more cooperative were frustrated from reaching maximum results because of the lack of cooperation on the part of one or two members.[19]

One of the most able studies in the area of cooperation and competition was made by Deutsch. In two general groups, one cooperative, the other competitive (each of which was divided into five teams), he provided rewards according to whether they worked as a unit or performed as individuals on various intellectual problems. The results clearly supported the efficiency of the cooperative process. According to this study, the cooperative members had several advantages: high motivation on the part of the members to complete the group task, consideration of the other members, division of labor that permitted variation in the volume of contribution, and more sensitive communication, with interstimulation, discussions, and friendliness.[20]

With cooperation, in contrast to competition, no frustrating or anxiety-producing effects are set up in the individual. However, in competitive cultures like our own, cooperative endeavors do not always produce results, as was discovered in many cooperative communities established in Europe and America during the nineteenth and early twentieth centuries. In a different cultural framework cooperative behavior seems more effective than competitive, judging by the highly cooperative social systems found in some other parts of the world.

Thus the question so often asked, "Isn't competition more effective than cooperation?" is meaningless unless we state our frame of reference. Competitive behavior is more effective than cooperative to produce *individual* achievement, which we value highly in our culture. In some cultures—Zuñi, for instance—competition is ineffective and useless because the Zuñi do not emphasize individual achievement. When *group* achievement is needed—in family, community, nation, or on a worldwide basis—cooperation is essential. The leading nations of the world have progressed largely by achieving a balance between competitive and cooperative activity within the nation. Civilization's future hinges on our ability to achieve cooperation on an international scale.

[19] H. G. McCurdy and W. E. Lambert, The efficiency of small human groups in the solution of problems requiring genuine cooperation, *J. Pers.*, XXVI (1952), pp. 478-94.

[20] M. Deutsch, An experimental study of the effects of cooperation and competition upon group process, *Human Relations,* II (1949), 199-231.

Conflict. Conflict (in the sense of interpersonal as compared with mental conflict) signifies mutual opposition or aggression, always with reference to an indivisible goal such as prestige or material reward. Conflict is intermittent rather than lasting and may emerge at any time from the quieter, more stable, ongoing processes of social interaction.

Park and Burgess noted that conflict arises typically out of competition; "The forces with which they are competing get identified with persons, and competition is converted into conflict." [21] Examples sometimes are found in athletic contests such as football games. When competition becomes intense, a minor incident may provoke a fight between two players.

While conflict develops most typically from competition, it may arise whenever a strongly motivated individual feels frustrated by another. Conflict is rooted in aggressive reactions to frustration and anger. If the individuals involved have learned to express their anger uninhibitedly, they may attempt to annihilate each other unless they perceive that they would be harshly punished for such behavior.[22]

Fortunately each society regulates the form of interpersonal conflicts. In our culture a fight, if permitted at all, must be conducted with fists, not kicks or brickbats. One must not hit below the belt, strike an opponent when he is down, and so on. When youngsters start to fight, adults often insist that they "put on the gloves." The duel is a strictly regulated form of expressing overt interpersonal conflict. Even international warfare is regulated to some extent, despite frequent transgressions; it is customary to spare the lives of prisoners and not to shoot someone bearing a flag of truce, for example.

Each culture also provides less violent means for settling conflicts. The whole mechanism of our court procedure, whose evolution can be traced back through several centuries, is a case in point. A newer and less clearly regulated instance is the strike. Other societies have interesting ways of regulating conflicts—for example the Eskimo "duel" in which each party sings sarcastic songs about the other and the spectators decide who is the winner. Or the Kwakiutl custom of shaming an opponent by outdoing him in giving away or destroying large quantities of blankets, horses, oil, and other property.[23]

[21] Park and Burgess, *op. cit.*, p. 509.

[22] See the discussion of reaction to frustration in Chapter 6.

[23] See O. Klineberg, *Social psychology* (rev. ed.; New York: Henry Holt & Co., Inc., 1954), pp. 94-95.

Why do interpersonal conflicts arise? Many persons argue that conflicts have a biological basis, presumably in the form of innate pugnacity or aggressiveness. Anthropological data cast doubt on these theories, as we already have seen. However, there does seem to be a biological basis for the evocation of anger and fear by frustration of dominant motives; these strong emotional reactions tend toward overt expression, one form of which is aggressive activity directed toward other persons. The intensity and the specific form of this aggressive behavior are affected, as we have seen, by a person's past experience (which includes cultural channeling) and the way he perceives the situation.

Besides regulating the form in which conflict is expressed, social factors have much to do with determining the frustrations that make conflict possible. For example, if the mores of a society or a subgroup within the society call for strict regulation and strong discipline of children, conflicts within the family are facilitated. If educational and legal restrictions are severe, the basis is laid for frustration and various aggressive reactions. In rapidly changing societies like our own, misunderstandings and conflicts between parents and children are almost inevitable—"conflict of the generations," as we say. Marriage, as Waller makes clear,[24] is bound to involve some disagreement and conflict in the process of establishing harmonious adjustments between two different personalities.

The broader problem of social conflicts—industrial, racial, political, and international—will be discussed later. These definitely relate to interpersonal conflicts, but are far more complex, as we shall see.

"ONE-WAY" INTERACTIONS

Competition, cooperation, and conflict we call "mutual interactions" because the persons involved behave in much the same way toward each other. Indeed, if they did not, the form of interaction would be different. If one person fights but the other does not, we can hardly refer to the situation as "conflict."

Coercion and exploitation. In other types of interaction the behavior of one person demands different responses from the other party. Coercion, for example, means that an individual enforces his wishes on others; their role is submissive or at least passive. In the case of exploitation, one or more persons utilize others to achieve certain desired goals. With imitation one person copies another; the latter plays a passive role in relation to the imitator.

24 W. W. Waller and R. Hill, *The family* (rev. ed.; New York: The Dryden Press, Inc., 1951), chaps. xiv, xv.

Similarly with suggestion: one person induces uncritical acceptance of ideas, or unconscious performance of acts, in others.

These one-way interactional processes have received much less direct study than the mutual types of interaction. Indirectly they have been examined in various ways. For example, historical study of feudalism and of modern dictatorships is concerned largely with the causes and the effects of coercive and exploitative government.[25] Some attention also has been given exploitation in the area of economics.[26] Many studies of the Negro in the United States are concerned in part with coercion and exploitation and their effects on the Negro's personality and on Negro-white relations.[27] Experiments of Kurt Lewin and his associates on the effects of authoritarian and democratic leadership open the way to understanding coercive and permissive social behavior.[28]

One thing already is clear: coercion and exploitation produce frustrations and tensions in their victims that are likely to lead, sooner or later, to hostility and aggressive behavior—that is, to interpersonal conflict. Apparently social relations based on coercion and authoritarian practices cannot remain stable. Tensions are produced that lead to conflict and social change and that ultimately are resolved only by social arrangements democratic and cooperative in form.

Imitation. Imitation and suggestion are also essentially one-way forms of interaction. The part played by imitation in social behavior often has been overestimated. Many social theorists have considered imitation an instinct and applied the term to all similarities in behavior, however produced. Psychologists have shown that many similarities in behavior are due simply to common constitutional factors, or to similar learning processes.[29] When two people say that a bell has rung, the second person to report is not imitating the first; they have had similar sensory experiences. Nor are motorists imitating each other when they all stop their cars at a red light; it is rather that they have been similarly conditioned. However, where one person models his behavior generally after that of another, or

25 See, e.g., F. L. Schuman, *The Nazi dictatorship* (New York: Alfred A. Knopf, Inc., 1936).

26 See, e.g., N. Thomas, *Human exploitation in the United States* (New York: Frederick A. Stokes Co., 1934).

27 See E. F. Frazier, *The Negro in the United States* (rev. ed.; New York: The Macmillan Co., 1957), and G. Myrdal, *An American dilemma* (New York: Harper & Bros., 1944); also A. Davis and J. Dollard, *Children of bondage* (1940) or other volumes in the series published by the American Council on Education. See Chapter 5.

28 See Swanson *et al.*, *Readings* (2d ed.), pp. 340-55.

29 N. E. Miller and J. Dollard, *Social learning and imitation* (New Haven, Conn.: Yale University Press, 1941).

where conscious copying exists, we may speak of imitation. Miller and Dollard insist that imitation, at least in the sense of copying, must be learned.[30] It is not found in animals or very young children, but develops with the child's increasing social experience. While "matched-dependent behavior" (Miller and Dollard's term for generalized modeling) plays a part in a child's learning and social development, the prevalence and significance of clear-cut imitation in social interaction is not nearly as great as was once thought.

Suggestion. Suggestion signifies inducing uncritical acceptance in others, or touching off responses in others almost automatically. However, only responses which previously have been learned can be produced in this automatic way. Thus suggestion evokes behavior by a kind of short-circuiting process. Of course, suggestion is two-way interaction in that one person does the suggesting and another reacts to it. But since the person receiving the suggestion behaves passively and uncritically, we classify it with one-way interactions. (The term "suggestion" refers to the whole process; "suggestible" and "suggestibility" indicate the state of the recipient.)

Many examples of suggestion can be given: the embarrassing epidemic of yawning that occurs in a social group in response to one person's yawn; the allergic individual who sneezes when presented with a beautiful but artificial rose; the children at a ventriloquist's show who are sure the dummy really talks; or the chemistry students, in a well-known experiment, who reported they smelled fumes from an odorless liquid ostentatiously uncorked at the front of the lecture hall.

Suggestion seems most effective when the recipient's attention is fixed elsewhere. Suggestibility is greatest during hypnosis, when the subject is in a dissociated state. There are tremendous individual differences in susceptibility to suggestion, for reasons not entirely clear. One investigator found that, in general, children at the age of seven or eight are more suggestible than at any other age.[31] Considerable controversy has centered about the question whether or not "suggestibility" should be considered a personality trait. Probably it should not be, since acceptance of suggestion seems to be affected by many temporary and situational influences. On some occasions everyone is suggestible; at other times, no one. A few individuals, though, do seem rather generally responsive or unresponsive to suggestion.

30 *Ibid.,* p. 92
31 R. Messerschmidt, Suggestibility of boys and girls . . . , *J. genet. Psychol.,* XLIII (1933), 405-37.

The part played by suggestion in human social behavior is hard to assess, but it is very significant. Parents know that subtle suggestion is a much better way to manage youngsters than commands or threats. Suggestion is a powerful means of social control, as is shown in advertising and propaganda. Rather than exhorting or even advising people to smoke "Puffos," an ad simply points out that the well-known society leader, Mrs. Reginald De Puyster, always has "Puffos" on hand for her exclusive gatherings. This is an example of "prestige" suggestion. At least one authority on propaganda, Doob, described propaganda as the attempt to control attitudes through suggestion.[32]

Historically, the suggestion-imitation hypothesis dominated social psychology at the turn of the century and for some time afterward.[33] Its first appearance was in the late eighteenth century with the work of Mesmer, the inventor of "animal magnetism." The most decisive expression of suggestion was that of Le Bon, who made it the basis of his "crowd mind." [34] Being a historian, he was fascinated by the excesses of the Parisian populace at the time of the French Revolution. He conceived of the crowd mind as an organic unity based on some synthesis of "collective nervous systems," all arising from the act of suggestion. Although later psychologists took issue with his extravagant version of suggestion, it still retained its pre-eminent position. Finally it was realized that suggestion had been a purely descriptive concept, and actually had explained nothing. It was hardly profound to note that one person could induce another person to take up the practice of smoking, but *how* and *why*, or *why* he was not able to influence another individual in the same direction was another question.

No more satisfactory was the process of imitation which was popularized by the French jurist Tarde, who presented a number of "laws," such as that the inferior tend to follow the superior. In the United States, Baldwin conceived of imitation as a universal tendency and stressed particularly its significance in socialization at the infancy level. As with the process of suggestion, neither the *how* nor the *why* was adequately answered.

[32] L. W. Doob, *Propaganda* (New York: Henry Holt & Co., Inc., 1935), p. 75. In his later *Public opinion and propaganda* (New York: Henry Holt & Co., Inc., 1948), Doob does not use suggestion in his definition of propaganda. See Chapter 17, for further discussion of propaganda.

[33] For a discussion of the background of this and related processes, see G. W. Allport, The historical background of modern social psychology, in G. Lindzey (ed.), *Handbook of social psychology* (Reading, Mass.: Addison-Wesley Pub. Co., Inc., 1954), Vol. I, pp. 3-56.

[34] See Chapter 1.

Latent conflict may become overt, as with this picket line.

Los Angeles Examiner

Cooperation or conflict? The college campus offers events that represent both processes simultaneously.

The term "social facilitation" for the interactional process by which one individual influenced another gradually replaced "imitation" and "suggestion." The most prominent name in this transition was Floyd Allport. In a number of experiments he demonstrated the intensification of experience that accompanied the presence of other people; there were higher scores for vowel cancellation, word associations, and analyses of excerpts from the reading of Marcus Aurelius in a group. Although there was an increase in the *quantity* of the performance, the *quality* suffered.[35] Unlike LeBon's mystical approach, which fused separate individuals into a group superconsciousness, Allport's perceived the group as simply the totality of a number of individuals. In fact, Allport has been criticized for emphasizing too sharply the separateness of individuals within the group. Although we cannot agree with the older viewpoint that somehow a group mind develops as a blending of separate nervous systems into one organic unity, the group does affect the thinking and behavior of individuals, so that an entirely different set of responses is possible in the group setting than was possible before. In other words, the group is something more than the sum of its members.

Whatever the theoretical and methodological arguments may be, there is ample evidence of the facilitating affects of other people. We have probably been aware of how much more we eat when others are around, how much more we may project into emotional experiences when there is a fellow participant. Few things seem as pathetic as a play acted in an almost empty theater. Facilitation remains a fundamental type of interaction and is undoubtedly related to cooperation, assimilation, and other processes of social adjustment.

INTERACTION BASED ON CHANGING RELATIONSHIPS

We now come to forms of social interaction which differ from those already discussed in that they represent changing relationships between the persons involved. As examples we mention accommodation, assimilation, alienation, and stratification.

Accommodation. Accommodation is a process of increasing mutual adaptation or adjustment. As sociologists use the term, it means establishing a working relationship between conflicting individuals or groups. Typically, accommodation is a kind of compromise by which conflict is halted, though often only temporarily.

[35] F. H. Allport, The influence of the group upon association and thought. *J. exp. Psychol.*, III (1920), 159-82. See also his *Social psychology* (Boston: Houghton Mifflin Co., 1924).

If the accommodation works, it may progress to complete mutual adjustment or "assimilation."

A nice example of accommodation is found in marriage. Normally, after the honeymoon is over, newlyweds have many misunderstandings and conflicts. They begin to reveal differing habits, attitudes, values, and interests. For example, each spouse may have certain friends the other cannot abide. After several arguments and emotional outbursts, they may evolve a plan whereby the husband goes out alone twice a month to see his friends, or perhaps he arranges not to be at home when the wife's friends call. Or again, after several stormy scenes, each comes to realize that there are certain subjects—politics, movie stars, hats, salad-making, or what not—which it is best not to discuss. Similar kinds of accommodations often are worked out between parents and children, between employer and employees, and between friends.

On a somewhat larger scale we may speak of accommodations in racial or industrial relations. Strikes and other industrial conflicts usually are settled by compromise, arbitration, or conciliation—all forms of accommodation. Establishing Negro-white caste lines in southern United States represents a kind of accommodation, though a less stable one than agreement or compromise between equals. Laws and political processes exist chiefly for the purpose of accommodating conflicts and incipient conflicts. Thus accommodation is a social interactional process, which moves from conflict toward mutual adjustment.

Assimilation. Assimilation was regarded by Park and Burgess as the final product of social interaction. "Assimilation is a process of interpenetration and fusion in which persons and groups acquire the memories, sentiments and attitudes of other persons and groups, and by sharing their experiences and history, are incorporated with them in a cultural life." [36] When an immigrant first arrives, his pattern of values and habits brings him into conflict with those having the values and habits of the new country. Accommodations are worked out; these represent the first phase of his acculturation. Slowly over the years, the immigrant's ways of thinking, feeling, and acting may be modified until they harmonize with those of the new environment. Many immigrants, however, particularly the older ones, never become very well assimilated. On the other hand, the assimilation of an immigrant youngster is remarkably rapid and complete; his main problem is not so much one of assimilation but one of adjusting to the conflict between his parents' ways and

[36] Park and Burgess, *op. cit.,* p. 735.

the mores and folkways of the new environment. Marriage provides another example of assimilation. After several years of married life, husband and wife often come to share each other's ideas, interests, attitudes, and purposes to a remarkable degree. By the time such assimilation has taken place, misunderstandings and conflicts are very unlikely.

Alienation. While accommodation and assimilation may best exemplify changing social interactions, they are by no means the only distinguishable processes. Alienation is the obverse of assimilation—the process by which individuals grow apart from each other and become less rather than more harmonious in their interaction. Alienation is illustrated in cases of immigrants who become increasingly less well adjusted to the new culture pattern or in the progressive worsening of relations between husband and wife which terminates in separation or divorce.[37]

Stratification. Stratification, as we saw in Chapter 5, is a process by which persons come to have "class, caste, rank or other fixed status—giving distinctions within a society." [38] Stratification develops out of other processes, notably competition and conflict. It represents a kind of accommodation, as in societies where rigid caste or class lines have developed to regulate many social relationships. Stratification seldom makes for mutual understanding and assimilation. It exemplifies rather an unstable equilibrium, as shown in class-stratified Czarist Russia or in societies having caste systems such as South Africa or the less progressive states in southern United States.

The forms of interaction involving changing relationships are two-way rather than one-way processes. Seldom is accommodation a matter of husband or wife adjusting without similar adjustments being made by the other. Even the immigrant's assimilation is a two-way process; the immigrant introduces linguistic, social, artistic, and other "culture traits" at the same time that he becomes assimilated to the American culture pattern. Similarly, alienation is mutual, though not necessarily to the same degree in each party. Stratification implies that when one person or group rises or falls in the social scale, others fall or rise correspondingly.

MAJOR DETERMINANTS OF SOCIAL INTERACTION

So much for a brief description of important social interactional processes. We consider now the causes of one or another type of

[37] See Waller and Hill, *op. cit.*, chap. 23.
[38] E. B. Reuter, *Sociology* (New York: The Dryden Press, Inc., 1941), p. 158.

social behavior. These determining factors overlap, but each is significant.

1. The first is the nature of the social situation. A given social situation does not necessarily produce, through its own composition or characteristics, a given type of behavior in its participants or observers. A street fight causes some persons to stop and watch, others to hurry by; one bystander cheers the fighters on, while another tries to separate them or calls the police. A drunk in the gutter may be shunned, laughed at, helped, or robbed, depending on who passes by.

Nonetheless, objective situational factors often predispose people toward one rather than another type of social behavior. Suppose a car is stuck in the snow on a narrow road, blocking the passage of other cars. Almost inevitably this will produce cooperative behavior from all the drivers and perhaps from some pedestrians as well, until the car can be moved. If two young men desire the same job or the same girl, the indivisibility of the goal almost assures competition between them.

Such situations, however, are not unaffected by cultural norms and individual differences. In some societies, for example, automobile drivers might refuse to push a car even if the alternative were to remain stuck in the snow; cultural norms might prescribe that both men withdraw if they find they are rivals in love. Or in any society an atypical individual might refuse to cooperate, or might withdraw rather than compete with a rival.

2. Secondly, the norms prevailing in any given social group—the traditional ways of behaving—have much to do with the form of social interaction. Competition not only is sanctioned but expected in our society, as compared with the Zuñi or Hopi. Coercive and exploitative behavior, however, is not. Norms vary greatly within any large cultural group. One finds aggressive behavior and conflict sanctioned in some communities of the United States, say a mining camp or a city slum, though not in others. At a Rotary Club meeting, behavior is expected to be friendly and sociable; an exclusive restaurant or a library calls for quite different behavior.

3. A person's social behavior at any moment depends also, in part, on his personality, which results from his heredity and experience. His basic motives and frustrations, his attitudes, values, and habits determine significantly his social behavior. A strong drive for prestige, a fear of women, a liking for parties, or a prejudice against foreigners obviously affects his reactions toward others. Such personality tendencies, unless extremely intense, never them-

selves determine social behavior; they are most compelling when the social situation is not strictly regulated or "structured." Compare, for example, the rather conventional behavior of a young man and woman at a college dance with their much less conventional behavior on a "date." In the former case their behavior reflects the standards operating in the college dance situation. In the latter, their own personality trends have greater scope in determining their behavior—whether they take a walk or read poetry together, whether they go to the opera, a movie thriller, or a tavern, whether they discuss the state of the world or make love to each other.

4. Another set of determinants centers about a person's more transitory tendencies such as emotional states, temporary drives and frustrations, mental sets, fatigue, boredom, euphoria, intoxication, sickness, and the like. These are not enduring characteristics of personality; yet their influence may be very significant. The part played by fatigue, illness, or intoxication in rude, boorish, or hilarious social behavior is obvious. Many romantic infatuations stem from transitory moods and frustrations rather than from basic and enduring personality traits.

5. Lastly, we mention the most subtle factor among those determining the pattern of social interaction—one that depends on all those previously described, yet which is not clearly predictable from them. This is the process of perceiving and interpreting a situation, to which we have referred before.

Most stimulus situations, notably social stimuli, do not produce behavior in automatic or reflex fashion. The situation, rather, is perceived or "defined" by a person before he makes overt response. That is to say, "meaning" is achieved, and this meaning becomes the most crucial determinant of behavior. Thus an oncoming car means "danger!" and we leap for safety. A red traffic light or a policeman's whistle means "stop," and we act accordingly. A large number of commonly understood "definitions of the situation" exist, in which are expressed the conventions, folkways, mores, taboos, laws, and practices of the group. In our culture, for example, we perceive as "bad" the beating of a woman or a child or public exposure of the naked body. We interpret as "good" the helping of blind and crippled persons, or maintenance of female chastity until marriage.

Uniform meanings, however, can hardly exist for the wide variety of complex social situations in which any individual participates. People perceive them differently. One person considers Mr. A. a bore and gives him a wide berth; another finds him pleasant or even interesting and seeks his friendship. Three people attend a revival meeting; one finds it amusing, another is deeply moved and becomes converted, while a third is upset enough that he writes an article exposing religious cults. When people interact, moreover, they are involved in a continuous process of perceiving, interpreting, and reacting in the light of new meanings obtained. Any conversation or argument furnishes a simple illustration. When "boy meets girl" each is alert to the impression apparently made on the other and guides his or her subsequent behavior accordingly. As was indicated earlier in discussing semantics, much misunderstanding stems from the differing meanings evoked in persons by a given situation.

How a situation is perceived, then, determines most significantly the social behavior of the persons in it. One reason is that perceiving depends upon and includes the other determinants mentioned earlier—characteristics of the situation, social norms, and both the underlying and transitory personality variables.

Recent psychological research demonstrates how social norms, motives, attitudes, and values influence what an individual perceives. Sherif's study of the autokinetic phenomenon, described in Chapters 7 and 8, showed how a person's perceptions depend upon standards operating among the members of his group. Several experiments have been performed demonstrating the effect of needs and values on perception. One involved showing hungry and satiated subjects ambiguous figures for them to identify. The hungry subjects perceived significantly more items of food among the figures than the satiated subjects.[39] Another study compared the accuracy of rich children and poor children in estimating the size of pennies, nickels, dimes, quarters, and half-dollars. The poor children overestimated the size of the coins much more than the rich ones, whether or not the coins were present while they made their judgments.[40] Still another found that persons recognize words most rapidly when the word's meaning is consonant with their own value-orientation. The experimenters proposed that people are perceptually sensitive to valued stimuli and set up perceptual defenses against inimical stimuli.[41]

Social psychologists have recently become extremely interested in perception as a crucial means to the understanding of social be-

[39] R. Levine, I. Chein, and G. Murphy, The relation of the intensity of a need to the amount of perceptual distortion, *J. Psychol.*, XIII (1942), 283-93.

[40] J. S. Bruner and C. C. Goodman, Value and need as organizing factors in perception, *J. abnorm. soc. Psychol.*, XLII (1947), 33-44.

[41] L. Postman, J. S. Bruner, and E. McGinnies, Personal values as selective factors in perception, *J. abnorm. soc. Psychol.*, XLIII (1948), 142-54. Reprinted in Swanson *et al.*, *Readings* (2d ed.), pp. 375-83.

havior.[42] Bruner and Postman describe three requisites for an adequate theory of social perception: [43] first, description of the physical stimulus and the environmental conditions; second, delineation of organismic factors such as prevailing dispositions, available response patterns, expectations, and the like; third, knowing the stimulus and the prevailing set of the organism, we need to describe the dimensions of the percept which results. "For it is this percept which constitutes the experience in terms of which the person responds and in terms of which people learn." [44] Unfortunately, Bruner and Postman note, accurate description of this perceptual component is extremely difficult and we do not yet have language or methods adequate for it.

SUMMARY

The forms or processes of social interaction are difficult to classify. Some processes, like attraction and repulsion, or dominance and subordination, provide a general interactional framework for more specific forms of social behavior. Cooperation, competition, and conflict represent mutual interactions, while coercion, exploitation, imitation, and suggestion exemplify one-way interactions. Other processes are marked by changing relationships; e.g., accommodation, assimilation, alienation, and stratification. Studies of social interactional processes tell us something of their nature, origins, and effects, but generalizations from such studies are dangerous, since interactional behavior always occurs within a particular sociocultural setting.

Five important determinants of social behavior can be noted: the nature of the social situation, the prevailing social norms, the individuals' basic personality trends, their more transitory states and conditions, and the way in which participants perceive and interpret the situation. The last of these is particularly significant, since it involves all the others.

SUPPLEMENTARY READINGS
See Chapter 12.

42 See especially R. R. Blake and G. V. Ramsay, *Perception—an approach to personality* (New York: The Ronald Press Co., 1951). Also H. Cantril, *Understanding man's social behavior; preliminary notes* (Princeton, N. J.: Office of Public Opinion Research, 1948).

43 J. S. Bruner and L. Postman, An approach to social perception, in W. Dennis (ed.), *Current trends in social psychology* (Pittsburgh, Pa.: University of Pittsburgh, 1948).

44 *Ibid.,* p. 74.

12

The Structure and Properties of Social Groups

Thus far in our treatment of social interaction we have focused on describing basic forms or processes and their determinants. We have said little about the groups within which so much of this social behavior actually takes place—the family, schoolroom, play group, gang, club, business office, committee, and so on. The structure and function of such groups affect powerfully the behavior of their members, as we shall see.

THE IMPORTANCE OF GROUPS

Earlier in the book it was said that social psychology might be called the "science of attitudes." If this statement were challenged, it would probably be on behalf of one other area—the small group— which has become a crucial research area for the social psychologist. Increasingly, social and industrial psychologists have maintained that the core of our discipline is found in the study of small groups. It is said that if we can solve the problem of the small group, then social psychological problems emerging from the "larger society" will not seem so formidable. If we can analyze and explain the behavior involved in the morale of a machine crew, the cohesiveness of a tribe, the motives of a delinquent neighborhood gang, the give-and-take process of the conference table, then it may not be so difficult to understand the causal relations within our large-scale organizations.

From another angle the importance of groups is clear. Our relations with other people occur, almost by definition, within a group.

The processes mentioned in the preceding chapter all take place in some variety of group setting. Study of the group is concerned with the problem of how "the behavior of an individual is altered by the actual presence of others." [1]

Definitions of what constitutes a group are widely varied; yet they all agree that some degree of interaction must be involved. A typical example is that of Sherif:

A group is a social unit which consists of a number of individuals who stand in (more or less) definite status and role relationships to one another and which possesses a set of values or norms of its own regulating the behavior of individual members, at least in matters of consequence to the group. [2]

Or we have, more briefly, Burgess's definition of the group as a "unity of interacting personalities." [3] Or somewhere intermediate between these two definitions is that of Newcomb: "A group consists of two or more persons *who share norms* about certain things with one another and *whose social roles are closely interlocking.*" [4] It is apparent from these definitions that concepts of personality, role, and status have no meaning apart from the group.

CLASSIFICATION OF GROUPS

Gestalt psychologists and semanticists have objected to classifications as being obstacles rather than aids to scientific thinking. [5] Yet as Brown points out, descriptive (as compared with explanatory) classifications are the starting point in science. [6] In describing social groups, we find they can be classified in many ways. For example, according to size—from the simple "dyad" of two persons to the complex nation of millions; according to permanence; according to how members are distributed geographically; according to determinants (e.g., blood relationship, similarity in bodily characteristics or in cultural interests, etc.).

It is a truism that there are different kinds of groups to which the individual may belong. The group to which we adhere fluctuates

[1] O. Klineberg, *Social psychology* (rev. ed.; New York: Henry Holt & Co., Inc., 1954), p. 437.

[2] M. Sherif and C. W. Sherif, *An outline of social psychology* (rev. ed.; New York: Harper & Bros., 1956), p. 144.

[3] E. W. Burgess (ed.), *Personality and the social group* (Chicago: University of Chicago Press, 1929), chap. x.

[4] T. M. Newcomb, *Social psychology* (New York: The Dryden Press, Inc., 1950), p. 492.

[5] See K. Lewin, *Dynamic theory of personality* (New York: McGraw-Hill Book Co., Inc., 1935); J. F. Brown, *Psychology and the social order* (New York: McGraw-Hill Book Co., Inc., 1936); S. I. Hayakawa, *Language in thought and action* (New York: Harcourt, Brace & Co., Inc., 1949); W. Johnson, *People in quandaries* (New York: Harper & Bros., 1946).

[6] Brown, *op. cit.*, p. 109.

many times during the course of the day.[7] Most influential is probably the family group, and it is apparent that this family group is
actually subdivided for various purposes into a husband-wife or, say,
a father-son relationship. Or the mother and daughter may constitute a private group which "gangs up" on the male contingent
of the family. There may be priority attached to a baseball-playing
group at the corner lot, or the Ladies Aid Society at the local church.
Or the group may for the moment be confined to one's bridge partner plotting how to triumph in the next tournament. In other
words, a group may emerge whenever two or more people are involved in a common activity. Even when an individual is not in a
group, he may be imagining himself in a group relationship: What
will my girl friend think of the roses I bought her? In other words,
we are constantly imagining or projecting ourselves into a group situation. The group then includes potential as well as overt interaction.

Group relations constitute a vast continuum, from the intimacy
of two people doing calculus, or making love, to the large-scale
group in a crowd situation buying war bonds. However, in this
chapter we are primarily concerned with small groups—i.e., those
groups which do not generally include more than one or two dozen
individuals.

A number of distinctions in groups is fundamental. These distinctions may pertain to either the structuring or organization of
the group or to the functions it may perform. We have already
pointed out the different purposes for which individuals enter into
groups. It must be remembered, too, that a group is something
more than a mere aggregate. In the group there is *interaction* between the individuals. Likewise, there is a difference, as Krech and
Crutchfield note, between groups, which are by nature psychological,
and social organizations. The criteria for the psychological group
are two: "(1) All the members must exist as a group in the psychological field of each individual, i.e., be perceived and reacted to as a
group; (2) the various members must be in dynamic interaction with
one another." [8] Social organizations, on the other hand, are groups
"characterized by the possession of the following: (1) cultural products (such as buildings, robes, prayers, magic formulas, songs); (2)

---

[7] This point is dramatically made in Goldschmidt's series of radio programs, now
recorded, made under the sponsorship of the Ford Foundation. See W. Goldschmidt,
Ways of mankind (Boston: Beacon Press, Inc., 1954).

[8] From *Theory and problems of social psychology* by D. Krech and R. S. Crutchfield
(copyright, 1948), p. 368. Courtesy McGraw-Hill Book Co., Inc., New York.

a collective name or symbol; (3) distinctive action patterns; (4) a common belief system; and (5) enforcing agents or techniques." [9]

Other social psychologists would categorize groups according to the more specific kinds of interpersonal relationships existing. Following the sociologist Park, Krout presents one such classification: [10]

1. Parasitism: a predatory relationship, without communication or cooperation (best examples found in animal societies)
2. Commensalism: association without contractual relationships, such as people who "eat at the same table," hotel residents, students in college class
3. Mutualism: a contractual relationship which is reciprocal and mutually beneficial, e.g., servant and master in a household; employer and employees in an office or factory (tends to be hierarchical rather than a completely social relationship)
4. Sociality: interdependence and intercommunication of equals, as in marriage, friendship, or a business partnership (the highest form of social grouping, and the one best manifesting consensus, *esprit de corps,* and morale)

Primary and secondary groups. Cooley made a distinction of tremendous significance when he contrasted "primary" with "secondary" groups. Primary groups refer to the intimate, face-to-face relationship found in the family, neighborhood, and play group.[11] Secondary groups denote those where contact is more impersonal, more indirect, less frequent, or removed in space or time, e.g., one's political party, state, or nation. Primary groups involve close physical proximity, but more important is the warm emotional tone. In the casual, fleeting contacts of modern urban culture, man has come to depend, increasingly, on secondary groups for his norms, his motivation, and the satisfaction of his affiliative needs. The great range of secondary group relationships has frequently prevented him from making the long-term type of friendship. Hence, man in the twentieth century appears to have developed a kind of *anomie* or "normlessness"—i.e., a personal disorientation or loneliness.[12] Although the contemporary American has been considered a professional joiner, his many associations are usually of a superficial

---

9 *Ibid.,* p. 369.

10 M. H. Krout, *Introduction to social psychology* (New York: Harper & Bros., 1942), pp. 226-28.

11 C. H. Cooley, *Social organization* (New York: Charles Scribner's Sons, 1909), chap. iii.

12 Erich Fromm recently commented that the major problems of modern man have become conformity and loneliness. See his *The sane society* (New York: Rinehart & Co., Inc., 1955). Much the same point is made by C. C. Bowman in Loneliness and social change, *Amer. J. Psychiat.* (1955), pp. 112, 194-98.

variety. It may be, too, that his diffuse secondary group contacts force the individual to make very rudimentary classifications of other people, which is a principal factor in the development of stereotypes and of prejudices.

The distinction between the primary and secondary group has been a recurrent one in modern sociology. Durkheim presented the thesis of *mechanistic society* as representing the blood group or primitive society with ties based on kinship, or on some other intimate basis. In the *organic society* there are the formalized aspects of the secondary group, and behavior is controlled by laws or standards that require more complex enforcement agencies. Where membership in the former is involuntary, the latter is more a matter of free choice.[13] This same type of categorization was made by Tönnies in his distinction between the *Gemeinschaft,* the folk community, and the *Gesellschaft,* the urbanized, rationalistic society in which one may pursue individual ends.[14] Respectively, these were called by Becker the *sacred* and the *secular* society, a distinction of importance to the sociologist.[15]

Formal and informal groups. Related to this concept of the primary and secondary group is the comparison of *formal* and *informal* groups. Although size is one determinant in the formalization of groups, it is more the type of relationship that signifies the need for rigidly defined roles and statutes. It has been found that with the bureaucratization of society and its accompanying tendency of formalizing group life, a counter tendency exists at the same time toward informal controls. In industry, government, and the military, there is the informal "chain of command" as well as the formal. Much of the decision process occurs at the coffee hour or the cocktail party, where primary groups can function on a less clumsy basis than through the formal "channels of communication."

In this connection one might distinguish between "real" and "ideal" groups. The groups as defined by the institutional framework, the factory hierarchy as shown on the organizational chart, for example, are cut across by more realistically oriented groups—the

---

[13] E. Durkheim, *The division of labor in society* (Glencoe, Ill.: Free Press, 1947). This is a translation of *De la division du travail social* (Paris: Alcan, 1893).

[14] F. Tönnies, *Gemeinschaft und Gesellschaft,* ed. by C. P. Loomis as *Fundamental concepts of sociology* (New York: American Book Co., 1940).

[15] H. Becker, *Through values to social interpretation* (Durham, N.C.: Duke University Press, 1949); also Sacred and secular societies, *Soc. Forces,* XXVIII (1950), 361-76, and *Man in reciprocity* (New York: Frederick A. Praeger, Inc., 1956), chaps. x-xiii. The concept of "sacred" and "secular," first presented by Robert E. Park, has received expanded analysis by Becker.

Up to the beginning of the twentieth century, primary group life dominated Western culture, as indicated by the intimacy of the general store.

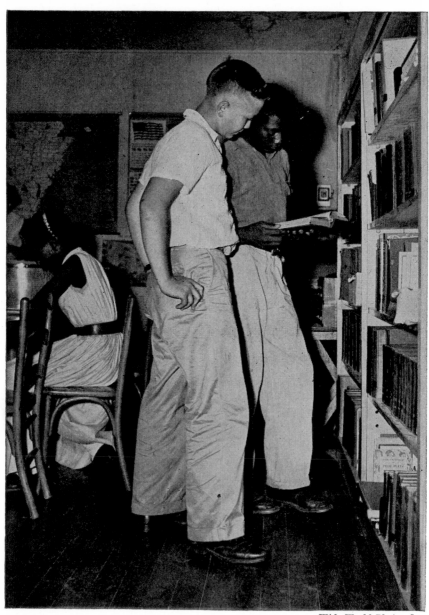

Racial attitudes develop early in life. In the South and border states, school integration is a new experience. The Supreme Court decision in 1954 called for a gradual end of segregated schools. This high school in Hoxie, Arkansas, was integrated the following year.

face-to-face relationship at the work bench or the assembly line.[16] In other words, it is not the ideal group, as conceived by the management, which reaches a certain production rate, accepts uncritically suggestions from above, and talks to his neighbor only during the coffee break. Studies of military personnel in the second world war, whether allied or German, showed the enormous importance of the informal primary group—the loyalty to one's "buddies" in contradistinction to the avowed purposes of higher echelons. In some cases the formal and informal group coincide, as when the machine-gun detail is also the primary group to which the "G.I." attaches his loyalties and derives his norms.

In-groups and out-groups. Another fundamental differentiation is that between in-groups and out-groups, i.e., majority and minority groups. The group that is socially accepted sets the dominant norms within a given society and tends to reject the marginal or "inferior" groups. What may be the in-group in one culture or subculture may be an out-group in another. The dominant Anglo-Saxon in the main stream of American culture may be an out-group in some portions of Chicago or the Bronx. Likewise, in-groups and out-groups may be very specific in that one team or squad may consider any adversary or deviant as the out-group. There is a kind of group ethnocentrism, whether it be the local lodge, or the infantry as opposed to the air force, or one particular battalion, squadron, or platoon.[17] The intensity with which in-groups and out-groups affect social life, and consequently mold the personality structure, has been of interest to both the social and clinical psychologist. Fortunately, society appears to be moving toward wider acceptance patterns on racial and ethnic lines so that the functioning of in-groups and out-groups does not enjoy the importance it had a generation ago.

Membership and reference groups. Recently a new distinction has been made, that between "membership" and "reference" groups.[18] For example, the child's ego or self has been defined as a

16 See F. J. Roethlisberger and W. J. Dickson, *Management and the worker* (Cambridge, Mass.: Harvard University Press, 1939), for examples. For instances in the military institution, see S. A. Stouffer and others, *The American soldier* (Princeton, N. J.; Princeton University Press, 1949).

17 For an interesting experimental study of group relations, including the formation of in-group and out-group attitudes, see M. Sherif and C. W. Sherif, *Groups in harmony and tension* (New York: Harper & Bros., 1953), chaps. ix, x; or summary in M. Sherif and C. W. Sherif, *An outline of social psychology* (rev. ed.; New York: Harper & Bros., 1956), chap. ix.

18 This distinction was first made by H. H. Hyman in *The psychology of status, Arch. Psychol.*, 1942, No. 269.

cluster of attitudes and values derived from identification with his membership and reference groups.[19] Membership groups are those to which he actually belongs, like the family, play group, gang, or school. Reference groups are those to which he aspires or "refers" himself, which may or may not be the same as the membership groups. Motivated by the desire to belong and to gain prestige among his peers, a child learns or "introjects" the group norms or standards. These, in large part, determine the structure of his ego and the nature of ego-involvements, which in turn affect his personality and his relationship to other persons and groups.

The fact that in our society status needs are so intense means that an individual frequently finds considerable conflict between the group to which he actually belongs and the group toward which he aspires. The expectancy on the part of both the individual and society regarding group roles leaves the individual with indecision about his group loyalties. In present day society this is what has been labeled as *multiple group membership*.[20] One may belong to the Presbyterian church, the Young Republican League, the Masons, the West End Bowling League, as well as the familiar primary group associations—family, neighborhood gang, and the golf trio on Saturday morning. Often group associations linger when there is no longer the attachment—school friends may in adulthood remain on the margin of one's social relationships although they have little to do with one's present life.

APPROACHES TO THE STUDY OF GROUPS

The small group was of interest even before empirical sociology was well established. Typical of early studies was one by Georg Simmel on the size of the group as a determinant of interpersonal relations: How is social interaction affected by the number and arrangements within the group? He was interested also in structural questions such as the implications of the small group to the larger social organization.[21] On the functional side, it was Cooley who, as we have seen, pioneered in distinguishing between primary and secondary groups, and in discussing the socializing aspects of the group, particularly the family.

[19] M. Sherif and H. Cantril, *The psychology of ego-involvements* (New York: John Wiley & Sons, Inc., 1947).

[20] See, e.g., E. L. Hartley, Psychological problems of multiple group membership, in J. H. Rohrer and M. Sherif (eds.), *Social psychology at the crossroads* (New York: Harper & Bros., 1951).

[21] See G. Simmel, *The sociology of Georg Simmel*, trans. and ed. by K. H. Wolff (Glencoe, Ill.: Free Press, 1950).

Sociometry. For over two decades, social psychologists have been concerned with quantitative techniques for investigating interpersonal relations. The pioneer in this movement was a socially oriented psychiatrist, J. L. Moreno, who coined the term "sociometry" for his technique.[22] The sociometrist is concerned primarily with obtaining choices in interpersonal relations, such as with whom one would like to live, work, play, etc. Using groups of girls at the Hudson Training School, Moreno mapped out the "spontaneous" likes and dislikes of each girl for her cottage mates. He then constructed a "sociogram" showing the pattern of attractions and repulsions. Such sociograms also reveal isolates and leaders, and subgroup networks of relationships. A simplified example is presented here in Figure 9.

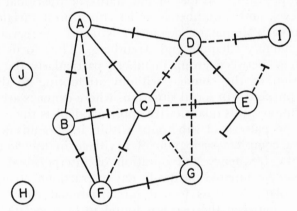

FIG. 9. Sociometric Diagram of a Small Group.

SOURCE: Adapted from Moreno.
　　　Mutual attractions: *AB, AC, AD, DE, BF, FG.*
　　　Mutual rejections: *CD, DG.*
　　　F accepts *A* but is rejected by him; similarly for *BC, CF,* and *ID.*
　　　Isolates: *H, J,* and *I.*

Moreno found the sociometric method valuable in many ways. For example, by its use individuals could be rearranged into congenial groups for purposes of living, eating, and working together. The technique has also proved useful for studying leadership and morale, as will be indicated later.

In offering choices to the individual, the requirements given in the following list are fundamental.[23]

22 J. L. Moreno, *Who shall survive?* (Washington, D. C.: Nervous and Mental Disease Publishing Co., 1934).

23 G. Lindzey and E. F. Borgatta, Sociometric measurement, in G. Lindzey (ed.), *Handbook of social psychology* (Reading, Mass.: Addison-Wesley Pub. Co., Inc., 1954), Vol. I, p. 407.

1. The individuals should make the choices privately and should make them in regard to specific criteria, namely, under what *conditions* will one person work with another?

2. The choices should be unlimited; as few or as many individuals should be chosen as the subject wishes.

3. Results of the test should be used to "restructure the group." New living arrangements or new incentives will grow out of choices made.

4. The items should be gauged to the level of understanding of the group. In some cases the questionnaire form may be used, in other cases interviews or some other form.

In the voluminous literature on sociometry, it is apparent that a number of variables have been found to correlate with choices, such as physical proximity, socioeconomic status, occupational roles, educational level, and a number of other subcultural variables.

An approach similar to sociometry is favored by certain anthropologists, notably Chapple and Arensberg. They focus simply on social contact between group members, particularly the frequency and duration of the contact, without attempting to describe its nature or purpose. In social situations where contacts are spontaneous or voluntary, this quantitative approach depicts the group structure and the pattern of subgroups within it. Loomis was able to construct a complete sociogram of a village in the Southwest by studying the frequency and duration of interpersonal contacts.[24] Another study compared the day-by-day interactional structure in an industrial plant with its formal (organizational chart) structure. Discrepancy between the two was found to be associated with low morale.[25]

Chapple finds that an individual shows quantitative consistency and regularity in the way he interacts with his fellows; hence measurements of the rate and duration of his interactions can be used to predict an individual's behavior.[26] Chapple devised an "interaction chronoscope" to measure accurately the frequency and duration of verbal behavior. He has reported characteristic interactional patterns not only for individuals in a given situation but also for certain types of psychotic patients, as compared to neurotic and normal persons.[27]

[24] C. P. Loomis, Informal grouping in a Spanish-American village, *Sociometry*, IV (1941), 36-51.

[25] C. M. Arensberg and D. McGregor, Determination of morale in an industrial company, *J. appl. Anthrop.*, I:2 (1942), 12-34.

[26] E. D. Chapple, Measuring human relations: an introduction to the study of the interaction of individuals, *Genet. Psychol. Monogr.*, 1940, No. 22, p. 48.

[27] E. D. Chapple and E. Lindeman, Clinical implications of measurements of interaction rates in psychiatric interviews, *J. appl. Anthrop.*, I:2 (1942), 1-11.

While Chapple's findings have not been completely accepted by other investigators, his technique is promising. It was used, for example, in studying verbal interaction within discussion groups. Results showed great inequality of participation from the various group members but at the same time high consistency in an individual's participation over a series of meetings.[28]

Group dynamics. Quantitative descriptions of group structure tell us little about the meaning of a group to its members. Social psychologists began to explore the effects of family, play group, gang, club, and other groups upon the needs, frustrations, attitudes, and values of their members, and upon their social behavior. For example, during the war Kurt Lewin studied how food consumption habits might be changed by group discussion, as opposed to the more traditional lecture method. Comparing experimental groups (group discussion) and control groups (lecture), it was found that ten times as many women in the former as in the latter changed their habits, on the basis of participation and discussion.[29] Or again, studying the unemployed man during the Depression, Koos was interested in the effect of unemployment upon the authority of the father within the family group, in the extent to which loss of employment lowered his status with his wife and children.[30]

Group dynamics developed out of Gestalt psychology, particularly through the work of Kurt Lewin. The difference between group dynamics and sociometry is somewhat arbitrary, and many empirical studies of interpersonal behavior have been influenced by both viewpoints. Group dynamics has introduced a number of new concepts for studying the functioning of groups, both as to changes within the group and relationships between groups.[31] We shall return to the topic later in connection with leadership, roles, and other aspects of human relations.

Interactional analysis. Bales has provided one of the most hopeful approaches to interaction within the group; he calls it *inter-* *action process analysis.*[32] After extensive experimentation with

p. 546

28 L. C. Hutchins, A study of certain aspects of participation in group discussion (Doctoral dissertation, Teachers College, Columbia University, 1949).

29 K. Lewin, Group decision and social change, in Swanson *et al.*, *Readings* (2d ed.), pp. 459-73.

30 E. L. Koos, *Families in trouble* (New York: King's Crown Press, 1946).

31 See D. Cartwright and A. Zander (eds.), *Group dynamics: research and theory* (Evanston, Ill.: Row, Peterson & Co., 1953).

32 R. F. Bales, *Interaction process analysis* (Reading, Mass.: Addison-Wesley Pub. Co., Inc., 1950). Also see R. W. Heyns and R. Lippitt, Systematic observational techniques, in G. Lindzey (ed.), *Handbook of social psychology* (Reading, Mass.: Addison-Wesley Pub. Co., Inc., 1954), Vol. I, pp. 376-81. The chapter contains various approaches to the study of group interaction.

observing and recording group behavior, he allowed for twelve categories or dimensions, as shown in Figure 10. They appeared to fit a range of interpersonal reactions at leadership training conferences, committee meetings, staff round tables, or many competitive situations, such as games. Each of these twelve dimensions is part of an "interaction system." Some of the problems involved in group discussion, accommodation, and cooperation are: (1) *orientation,* finding a common definition of a situation, which may be termed the orientation phase; (2) *evaluation,* finding some means of arriving at a common value system; (3) *control,* attempts of the par-

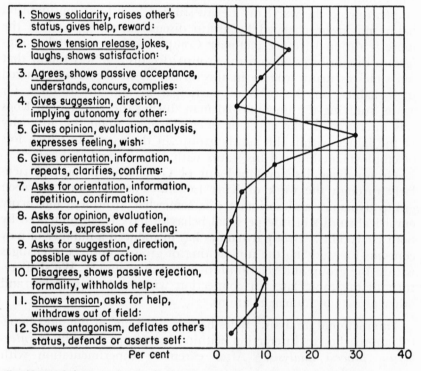

FIG. 10. Pooled Interaction Profile for Five Four-Person Groups of Ninth-Grade Boys.

SOURCE: R. F. Bales, *Interaction process analysis* (Reading, Mass.: Addison-Wesley Pub. Co., Inc., 1950), p. 23.

ticipants to influence each other; (4) reaching a final *decision;* (5) problems of interpersonal *tension;* and (6) *integration* and planning. In other words, interaction analysis is interested not in the content or results of group action and productivity but in the types and methods of interpersonal behavior: not in what is said but how it is said. Through use of the one-way screen the observer can be reasonably detached from the group itself; and after five or ten minutes it is reported that the group is unaware of the ubiquitous psychologist. This method of measuring interaction enables the observer to compare one group with another. Does one group exhibit more organization than another? What is the source of permissiveness in one group as compared with the rigidity of another? How does the leader emerge and what is his role? Do the members show passivity, or do they portray a dynamic involvement in the group?

FORMATION AND STRUCTURE OF GROUPS

As a group emerges (and again we are generally speaking of the primary group) it begins to assume organization or structure. There is a patterning of positions in the group. There are, as well, lines of communication (communication structure), arrangements as to how decisions are made, and the steps by which leadership may be assumed (power structure); specialization of tasks of the various members (occupational structure); relations of members to each other (sociometric structure); and the means by which individuals may move from one position to another (locomotion structure).[33] We have already referred to the formal as opposed to the informal group: the formal group has rules and regulations, fixed meeting places and obligations, whereas the informal group has more diffuse relationships—the poker-playing circle, the over-the-fence conversations, and the delinquent gang. These groups may be less ritualized but have subtle, though powerful, means of persuasion.

A group is always to some degree in a state of flux as concerns the interrelationships of the members, as they are constantly affecting each other within the group. However, there is in the formation of a group a reasonably stable framework of interpersonal relationships. Hand in hand with this is the emergence of norms by which the group members catalogue each other and their respective activities. For example, in the Hawthorne plant study, Roethlisberger and Dickson found that the men in the Bank Wiring Room (an equipment assembly section) had a socially derived code: the men who turned out too much work were "rate-busters"; those who pro-

---

[33] Cartwright and Zander, *op. cit.*, pp. 419-23. A distinction has been made between (1) *constitutional* determinants of the group (number of members, their age, sex, and other identifying characteristics) and (2) the *integrative* determinants of the group (recruitment or replacement of members, assignment of roles, communication system, and motivational factors). See J. P. Spiegel, Comparison of psychological and group foci, in R. R. Grinker (ed.), *Toward a unified theory of human behavior* (New York: Basic Books, Inc., 1956), p. 170.

duced too little were "chiselers"; negative remarks reported to the superviser made the individual a "squealer." Whether in the informal group, as with this face-to-face work team, or with the formal group, the existence and vitality of a group depends heavily on the effectiveness of its norms.[34]

The structure of the group is in large part the arrangement of roles and statuses. The emergence of a status hierarchy is well illustrated in the work of Whyte on an Italian neighborhood gang in Boston.[35] The hierarchy is indicated in Figure 11. Doc had become the official leader of the group—bowling scores being one of several criteria for leadership. In the channels of communication Doc might discuss a matter with Long John and it would go no further. Long John was on the periphery of the group structure, yet close to its leaders. On the other hand, a discussion with Nutsy

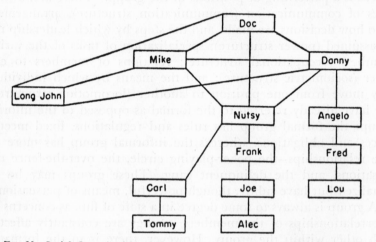

FIG. 11. Social Organization of the Norton Street Gang. (Position of Boxes Indicates Relative Rank.)

SOURCE: W. F. Whyte, *Street corner society* (Chicago: University of Chicago Press, 1943), reprinted in G. C. Homans, *The human group* (New York: Harcourt, Brace & Co., Inc., 1950), p. 161.

might filter down to Alec, or even to Carl or Tommy, who had a distinctly marginal position in the group. Probably, in all groups, there are the lieutenants, like Mike and Danny, who are closest to the leader and are frequently (although not in this case) jockeying for positions of power.

[34] Roethlisberger and Dickson, *op. cit.*, p. 522, also cited in G. C. Homans, *The human group* (New York: Harcourt, Brace & Co., Inc., 1950), p. 79.

[35] W. F. Whyte, *Street corner society* (Chicago: University of Chicago Press, 1943).

Age and sex roles differ from culture to culture, as shown by this aged Breton and his delicate embroidery work.

United States Information Service

The U.S.I.S. provides an important form of public relations. Both social scientists and representatives of foreign nations may call this "propaganda," but with a quite different connotation.

Wide World Photos, Inc.

Counterpropaganda. A University of Alabama group of students burn desegregation literature during the crisis of 1956 on whether a Negro might be enrolled as a student.

An introduction to in-group formation and emergence of a status structure is seen in the Sherifs' study of two rival sections of a boys' camp which may be summarized as follows: [36]

Stage 1. *Friendship clusters.* The boys attempted to establish attachment for other boys generally in groups of two to four over a three-day period. When the division of the camp into two rival groups occurred, these clusters were split up and a boy was placed in the group that held the fewest of his friendship choices, as shown by the sociogram.

Stage 2. *Experimental in-group formation—a transitional phase.* During the five-day period there was considerable repatterning of friendships, and the development of competitiveness between the two groups. Each group developed strong feelings of solidarity and loyalty. At the same time the power structure became evident. Out of each group developed a leader, although not necessarily the most popular boy.

Stage 3. *Tension and conflict.* Over this five-day period there was intense hostility. The norms of competitiveness developed in Stage 2 now began to pay off. In fact, the experiment had to be finally suspended, and some common activities were initiated so that there would not be excessive hostility as an aftermath. One boy who had been more or less accepted by the rival group for his athletic ability was encouraged to bridge the gap.

On a small scale, this two-week "quasi-primary" camp experience reflects the emergence of group solidarity and intergroup conflict found in many secondary group areas.

SOME DIMENSIONS OF GROUPS

Groups inevitably have a number of properties or dimensions. We have already mentioned some of these, such as structure, status patterning, in-group feeling, and role expectancy. In this concluding section, we shall present a few of the other salient characteristics of groups that are basic to their functioning.

Spatial and temporal relations. The effectiveness of a group is partially conditioned by the arrangement of participants. In one experiment with five individuals in a group the patterns used were: (1) circular; (2) chain or broken circle; (3) Y-pattern; and (4) wheel. The circular arrangement was generally conducive to equality and therefore harmony but was generally found not to be efficient. The

[36] M. Sherif and C. W. Sherif, *An outline of social psychology* (rev. ed.; New York: Harper & Bros., 1956); also M. Sherif, A preliminary experimental study of intergroup relations, in J. H. Rohrer and M. Sherif (eds.), *Social psychology at the crossroads* (New York: Harper & Bros., 1951), pp. 388-424.

individuals were given a task of locating symbols on a card, which made it necessary for the members to communicate with the others as to which symbols had appeared on their cards. While the group in the circular setting made more errors than the other groups, it also tended more to correct the errors. In other words, it was less likely that a gross error would be made. The chain and Y-pattern made for more efficiency by their "centrality," i.e., the fact that someone would act as leader or "go-between." The "Y" group made the least errors, and although leaving its members somewhat dissatisfied, this is the most familiar pattern in industry, the military, and other institutions.[37]

In a sense, time is always a determinant in group activity, since we are interested in changes in time. These temporal changes may affect control, attitudes, or any aspect of interpersonal relationships.[38] One of the questions that interested Moreno in his early research was the problem of time periods as affecting group relations.[39] How do frequency and duration of interaction influence choice of friends and, say, efficiency of group productivity? The problem of stages in Sherif's study is an example of this temporal problem.

Size. Undoubtedly the size of a group determines to a large degree the structure and functioning of a group. Historically speaking, one of the early researches in this area was by Simmel on the dyad (twosome) as opposed to the tryad (threesome).[40] It was Simmel's contention that the group of three was inherently unstable because of a tendency for two to combine their forces against a third party. Once this conflict commenced, the two would be held in still greater bond because of a common object of opposition. Mills made a recent test of this hypothesis when he arranged for groups of three to work on given intellectual processes. He found that there was a tendency for the triad to break down into a power structure with a dyad working against a third party.[41] In some cases the latter

---

37 H. J. Leavitt, Some effects of certain communication patterns on group performance, *J. abnorm. soc. Psychol.*, XLVI (1951), 38-50. Reprinted in Swanson, *et al., Readings* (2d ed.), pp. 108-25. Also see D. B. Hertz and S. L. Lesser, People in groups, *Scientific American,* 1951, 26-28.

38 H. W. Riecken and G. C. Homans, Psychological aspects of social structure, in G. Lindzey (ed.), *Handbook of social psychology* (Reading, Mass.: Addison-Wesley Pub. Co., Inc., 1954), Vol. II, pp. 816-29.

39 J. L. Moreno, *Who shall survive?* (Washington, D.C.: Nervous and Mental Disease Publishing Co., 1934), chap. iv.

40 G. Simmel, *The sociology of Georg Simmel,* trans. and ed. by K. H. Wolff (Glencoe, Ill.: Free Press, 1950), chap. iv.

41 T. M. Mills, Power relations in three-person groups, *Amer. sociol. Rev.,* XVIII (1953), 351-57. Reprinted in Cartwright and Zander, *op. cit.,* pp. 428-42.

might have an advantage in playing one against the other, or in forcing the others to appoint him as the neutral. It is not difficult to imagine the difficulty of the third person on a date, or on a vacation trip. At the same time the third party may be very useful as an arbitrator.[42]

It is significant that size can be related to the purpose or function of the group. James found that United States congressional subcommittees and certain governmental commissions (as in the state of Oregon) ranged from 5.7 to 7.8 members, this apparently being the number that work together effectively. It is significant that the mean size for action-taking groups was 6.5; for nonaction-taking, i.e., advisory groups, 14.0. In the case of informal groups—shopping, walking, conversing, working—the mean size was 2.4, indicating how much of our social life takes the form of the primary group.[43]

Cohesiveness. The most indispensable ingredient in group structure is cohesiveness, and the principal element in this unity is consensus among members. But cohesiveness is also a function of a number of factors, such as cooperativeness, affiliative needs, social facilitation, and other motives and processes. Another determinant is the degree to which the group may be useful to the individual in securing his goals. To some extent the determinants of cohesiveness may be physical ones, as in a housing project studied. It was found that the occupants formed friendships on the basis of (1) physical distance—with those living nearest them—and (2) functional distance—direction of the adjacent home, preference being for those living opposite rather than alongside.[44]

Another approach to cohesiveness is to study the tendency toward splintering or disruption in the group. French showed the results of a frustrating problem-solving situation. His task was so structured that interpersonal tension arose from the different interpretations of the problem by the group members. There was no universal agreement as to what the goal or solution might be. He found disruptive forces also in the competition for status, in interpersonal

[42] In this same connection it was found in another experiment on problem solving that groups were superior to individuals but groups of four were not qualitatively or quantitatively superior groups of two. See D. W. Taylor and W. L. Faust, Twenty questions: efficiency in problem solving as a function of size of group, *J. exp. Psychol.*, XLIV, 360-68. Reprinted in A. P. Hare, E. F. Borgatta, and R. F. Bales, *Small groups* (New York: Alfred A. Knopf, Inc., 1955), pp. 208-20.

[43] J. James, A preliminary study of the size determinant in small group interaction, *Amer. sociol. Rev.*, XVI (1951), 474-77.

[44] L. Festinger, S. Schachter, and K. Back, *Social pressures in informal groups* (New York: Harper & Bros., 1950), pp. 33-59. See also R. R. Blake, C. C. Rhead, B. Wedge, J. S. Mouton, Housing architecture and social interaction, *Sociometry*, XIX (1956), 133–39.

dislikes, and displaced aggression due to the frustrating situation.[45] In some cases, however, frustration may operate to encourage group solidarity, notably when aggression comes from outside the group in the form of attack or war.

Conformity. Conformity is a group problem that concerns all of us as individuals. All groups vary along a continuum from relatively complete freedom of behavior (as in an anarchistic society) to comparative rigidity (as under a dictatorship). In a democracy the individual feels threatened by any trends which demand political conformity, though he may accept pressures toward social conformity. It may be, of course, that conformity is a fundamental need, whether in manners and morals, food, esthetics, or politics. Klineberg suggests four main reasons for what he calls "customary" conformity:

> There is first the phenomenon of prestige suggestion . . . which in this case is associated with the fact that the group has power and importance, and ideas coming from it will therefore tend to be accepted. There is in the second place the fact that the individual often knows no other customs than those of his own community; this is of course true only of relatively small isolated groups, but among them it is highly probable that they act as they do because they are unfamiliar with any alternative. A third important factor is that the individual who does not practice the customary behavior related to the social and economic life of the group will soon be regarded as outside the system of reciprocal rights and duties upon which life in the community may depend; if there is a system of gift exchange, for example, and he fails to return an equivalent value, he will simply not be included in the next round of gifts, and will not be able to obtain what he wishes in exchange. Finally, and allied to this last, there may be punishment for transgression. This punishment may be violent and coercive in nature, but much more frequently in small communities it takes the form of ridicule. These four factors together make it possible to understand why individuals conform, without the necessity of assuming that custom in itself has power and authority.[46]

Newcomb's study of Bennington College students throws light upon the conformity-producing nature of group participation, in terms of individuals' attitudes.[47] Most students in this liberal arts women's college showed a marked increase in liberalism of socioeconomic viewpoint as they progressed from freshman to senior year. The general change Newcomb attributes partly to liberal attitudes on the part of faculty members, but even more to curricu-

---

[45] J. R. French, The disruption and cohesion of groups, *J. abnorm. soc. Psychol.,* XXXVI (1941), 361-77. Reprinted in Cartwright and Zander, *op. cit.,* pp. 121-34.

[46] O. Klineberg, *op. cit.,* pp. 457-58.

[47] T. M. Newcomb, *Personality and social change* (New York: The Dryden Press, Inc., 1943); or see partial summary by Newcomb in Swanson *et al., Readings* (2d ed.), pp. 420-30.

lar emphasis upon problems of the contemporary world. "Upper-classmen had learned more than freshmen about their world, and the forces and conditions making for social change. More than that," continues Newcomb, "those of the upperclassmen who participated most actively in discussions and in activities, in classes and outside of them, tended to be those who had most status and influence. In any community, presumably, those who participate most actively in approved activities are those who have most prestige." [48]

Studying the individuals whose attitudes changed little or not at all, Newcomb found them characterized by negativism, indifference, or divided allegiance toward the college community.[49] By and large those students identified themselves with outside "reference" groups, notably the family. In interviews they made such statements as, "The things I really care about are mostly outside the college," or "Every time I've tried to rebel against my family I've found out how terribly wrong I am, and so I've naturally kept to my parents' attitudes." [50]

Newcomb concludes that "in a community characterized by certain approved attitudes, the individual's attitude development is a function of the way in which he relates himself both to the total membership group and to the reference group or groups." [51]

It has long been known that an individual adopts the beliefs and attitudes current in the groups to which he belongs. This has been stressed in studies of folkways and mores since the days of Sumner,[52] and in discussions of "institutional ways," "group ideology," and the like. The studies of Sherif and Newcomb bring the individual into the picture as they show in which cases, under what circumstances, and to what extent he is affected by group norms.

Consensus. Closely related to conformity is consensus, which may be thought of as not only a "thinking together" but also a working together, a joint involvement on the part of members of a group.[53] Social psychologists have found that there is a strong need on the part of individuals to accede to group norms in forming their judgments. Asch, for example, gave subjects the perceptual task of matching a given line to one of three differing comparison lines.

48 Newcomb, *op. cit.*, p. 175.
49 *Ibid.*, p. 155.
50 Swanson *et al.*, *Readings* (2d ed.), pp. 424-25.
51 Newcomb, *op. cit.*, p. 155.
52 W. G. Sumner, *Folkways* (Boston: Ginn & Co., 1906).
53 See E. Gross, Symbiosis and consensus as integrative factors in small groups, *Amer. sociol. Rev.*, XXI (1956), 174-79.

Although the majority of persons remained independent of the judgments made by the remainder of the group, a considerable number were influenced by group performance. Some of those who remained independent did so because of their self-confidence, while others remained aloof because of seclusiveness or withdrawal. Those who yielded tended to do so because they lacked self-confidence or because they had a need not to appear different or inferior to their fellows.[54]

Group effectiveness. The degree to which a group attains its goal, however the latter may be defined, is an important consideration. Effectiveness may be defined in terms of a number of other criteria, such as productivity. Productivity often rises in a group setting because of social facilitation, as was indicated in the last chapter. Coch and French noted increased productivity and reduction of labor turnover when an experimental group was allowed wider participation in decision making—i.e., being consulted by management with respect to plant changes and policies.[55] In some cases, as with the Leavitt study (previously cited), the most productive process may not lead to the maximum satisfaction of group members, since their status or affiliative needs may not be satisfied. Consequently, if the goal of a group is the morale or psychological well-being of the members, effectiveness may be differently defined from the way it is when productivity is the end result. Very frequently, however, morale and productivity are positively related.[56]

Other variables. A number of empirical studies give further evidence of the complexity of group structure and functioning. One of these notes many dimensions along which group behavior may be measured: [57]

    1. *Autonomy*—the degree to which the group functions independently of other groups.

[54] S. E. Asch, Effects of group pressure upon the modification and distortion of judgments, in H. Guetzkow (ed.), *Groups, leadership and men* (Pittsburgh: Carnegie Press, 1951), pp. 177-90. Reprinted in Cartwright and Zander, *op. cit.*, pp. 151-62, and Swanson *et al.*, *Readings* (2d ed.), pp. 2-11.

[55] L. Coch and J. R. French, Overcoming resistance to change, *Hum. Relat.*, I (1948), 512-32. Also in Swanson *et al.*, *Readings* (2d ed.), pp. 474-91. See Chap. 21 below.

[56] One study found a close relationship between cohesiveness and productivity, the latter being a function of the success of the group in influencing the members to conform to given norms. See S. Schachter, N. Ellertson, D. McBride, and D. Gregory, An experimental study of cohesiveness and productivity, *Hum. Relat.*, IV (1951), 229-38. An outstanding study of morale is E. F. Gardner and G. G. Thompson, *Social relations and morale in small groups* (New York: Appleton-Century-Crofts, Inc., 1956).

[57] J. K. Hemphill and C. M. Westie, The measurement of group dimensions, *J. Psychol.*, XXIX (1950), 325-42.

2. *Control*—the tendency toward regulating the behavior of individual members.
3. *Flexibility*—the informality and freedom of the group.
4. *Hedonic tone*—group membership being accompanied by feelings of pleasantness.
5. *Homogeneity*—similarity in social and psychological characteristics among the members.
6. *Intimacy*—closeness of association as shown by depth of conversation and other variables.
7. *Participation*—application of time and effort to group duties and activities.
8. *Permeability*—readiness of the group to admit new members.
9. *Potency*—degree to which the group has meaning for its members.
10. *Polarization*—the working together toward a specific goal which has significance for all the members.
11. *Size*—number of members that constitute the group.
12. *Stability*—degree to which the group persists over a given period of time.
13. *Stratification*—development of status hierarchy within the group.
14. *Viscidity*—degree to which the group functions as a unit.

Another list suggests fifteen factors, varying along such continua as "vigorous unquestioned purposefulness vs. self-conscious unadaptedness," "democratic, explicit procedure orientation vs. horde urgency," and "intelligent role interaction vs. low morale." [58] Some would question the use of certain of these terms on the grounds that they are better applied to individual than to group performance. However, group behavior certainly derives from the intermeshing of the personalities of its members. Cattell has suggested the term "syntality" to distinguish the "personality structure" of the group from the personality correlates of the individual members.

A note of caution should be appended here in regard to the artificiality of some small groups experimented upon. In a recent critique it was pointed out that the family, as an example of a small group, operates under a different logic than experimental student groups, which have widely divergent roles and statuses.[59] Also the time factor is important; the laboratory group has a much briefer, more casual existence than the relatively continuous primary groups of daily life. On the other hand, there are similarities between what occurs before the one-way screen and what transpires within the

[58] R. B. Cattell, D. R. Saunders, and G. F. Stice, The dimension of syntality in small groups, *Hum. Relat.*, VI (1953), 331-56. See also the discussion in E. F. Borgatta, L. S. Cottrell, and H. J. Meyer, On the dimensions of group behavior, *Sociometry*, XIX, (1956), 223-40.

[59] E. F. Borgatta and L. S. Cottrell, Directions for research in group behavior, *Amer. J. Sociol.*, LXIII (1957), 42-48.

family gathered at the dinner table. In a word, it is hoped that future research can be done upon more permanent nuclear groups as well as upon the more transient laboratory groups.

It seems clear, in any event, that there are many measurable characteristics or dimensions of groups, and that the interrelationships among these factors are complex. Other research has been done in addition to that mentioned in this chapter; we shall return to it in a later discussion of human relations.

SUMMARY

Human beings are, from the nature of their social life, members of groups. Since social groups involve the interaction of personalities, it is not surprising that the group has become a primary concern of social psychologists. Historically speaking, the group was emphasized as a key concept by certain early social scientists, such as Cooley in America and Simmel in Germany. However, it is only since the close of World War II that the group has become, for a new generation of psychologists and sociologists, a research area of considerable magnitude. The interest is practical as well as theoretical, as we shall see in studying later various applications in industry, in clinical work, and in the armed services.

This chapter provided an introduction to a number of aspects of group functioning. After discussing some ways of classifying groups—primary versus secondary, in-groups and out-groups, membership and reference groups—some methods of studying groups were noted. Sociometry and group dynamics have spearheaded the major lines of research. These two approaches have now practically coalesced into one movement, "small group study," which is basic to the science of interpersonal relations. The formation and structure of groups were then discussed, and the chapter ended with an analysis of size, cohesiveness, and other group properties or dimensions.

SUPPLEMENTARY READINGS
Books of Readings

MACCOBY, E. E., NEWCOMB, T. M., AND HARTLEY, E. L. (eds.). *Readings in social psychology,* 3d ed. New York: Henry Holt & Co., Inc., 1958.

Back, K. W., Influence through social communication.

Leavitt, Harold J., Some effects of certain communication patterns on group performance.

Lippitt, R., Polansky, N. A., Redl, F., and Rosen, S., The dynamics of power: a field study of social influence in groups of children.

Shaw, M. E., A comparison of individuals and small groups in the rational solution of complex problems.

Zimmerman, C. and Bauer, R. A., The effect of an audience upon what is remembered.

BRITT, S. H. (ed.). *Selected readings in social psychology.* New York: Rinehart & Co., Inc., 1950.

Coffin, T. E., Situational conditions of suggestion: the Rorschach inkblot test.

Landis, J. T., Length of time required to achieve adjustment in marriage.

Postman, L., and Bruner, J. S., Perception under stress.

Withers, C., The folklore of a small town.

LINDZEY, G. (ed.). *Handbook of social psychology.* Reading, Mass.: Addison-Wesley Pub. Co., Inc., 1954.

Heyns, R. W. and Lippitt, R., Systematic observational techniques. Vol. I.

Kelley, H. H., and Thibaut, J. W., Experimental studies of group problem solving and process. Vol. II.

Lindzey, G., and Borgatta, E. F., Sociometric measurement. Vol. I.

Riecken, H. W., and Homans, G. C., Psychological aspects of social structure. Vol. II.

Other References

American Sociological Review, Special issue on small group research, Vol. XIX, No. 6, December, 1954.

A collection of articles on small group research.

BALES, R. F. *Interaction process analysis.* Reading, Mass.: Addison-Wesley Pub. Co., Inc., 1950.

This work is probably the most influential presentation of recent techniques of observing and measuring the group in interaction.

CARTWRIGHT, D., AND ZANDER, A. (eds.). *Group dynamics, research and theory.* Evanston, Ill.: Row, Peterson & Co., 1953.

A compilation of papers and articles on various problems relating to the group, particularly methodology, goals, standards, and structure.

FESTINGER, L., SCHACHTER, S., AND BACK, K. *Social pressures in informal groups.* New York: Harper & Bros., 1950.

An excellent monograph on interaction within the community, especially as it relates to a housing settlement.

GRECO, M. C. *Group life.* New York: Philosophical Library, Inc., 1950.

This is a study of emotional responses of the individual to the group, and the problem of conflict within the family and other sociocultural groups.

GRINKER, R. R. (ed.) *Toward a unified theory of human behavior.* New York: Basic Books, Inc., 1956.

Several important discussions of groups, the social system, and interpersonal behavior.

GUETZKOW, H. *Groups, leadership and men.* Pittsburgh: Carnegie Press, 1951.

The early selections are most pertinent to the problem of group interaction, but the whole book is relevant.

HARE, A. P., BORGATTA, E. F., AND BALES, R. F. (eds.). *Small groups: studies in social interaction.* New York: Alfred A. Knopf, Inc., 1955.

This is a methodological and theoretical work intended for the advanced student.

HOMANS, G. C. *The human group.* New York: Harcourt, Brace & Co., Inc., 1950.

The study of the primary group in several different settings, written in a most readable style.

KLEIN, J. *The study of groups.* New York: Humanities Press, Inc., 1956.

A review of the literature, with particular emphasis on the work of Bales and Homans.

LEARY, T. *Interpersonal diagnosis of personality: a functional theory and methodology for personality.* New York: The Ronald Press Co., 1957.
This book presents an interactional view of personality among a number of themes important to social psychology.

LEWIN, K. (ed. by D. Cartwright). *Resolving social conflicts.* New York: Harper & Bros., 1948.
The group dynamics approach to a variety of social problems.

MEAD, M. (ed.). *Competition and cooperation among primitive peoples.* New York: McGraw-Hill Book Co., Inc., 1937.
Description of the socioeconomic systems of a number of ethnic groups.

MORENO, J. L. *Who shall survive?* Washington, D.C.: Nervous and Mental Disease Publishing Co., 1934.
The classical introduction to sociometry by its founder.

MURPHY, G., MURPHY, L. B., AND NEWCOMB, T. M. *Experimental social psychology.* New York: Harper & Bros., 1937.
Contains a well-documented storehouse of material on cooperation, competition, and other types of social interaction.

PARK, R. E., AND BURGESS, E. W. *Introduction to the science of sociology,* 2d. ed. Chicago: University of Chicago Press, 1924. Chaps. vi-xi.
The Chicago school on social interaction, as influenced by Simmel.

SHERIF, M., AND SHERIF, C. W. *An outline of social psychology,* rev. ed. New York: Harper & Bros., 1956.
Part three is a discussion of the formation and structure of groups.

SHERIF, M., AND WILSON, M. O. (eds.). *Group relations at the crossroads.* New York: Harper & Bros., 1953.
A series of papers dealing with social psychological questions, focusing on the group.

WHYTE, W. F. *Street corner society.* Chicago: University of Chicago Press, 1943.
An engaging study of a neighborhood gang in the Italian section of Boston, written by a sociologist-participant.

13

Social Roles

By now "role" or "social role" has become a familiar term in social psychology, though there is some disagreement as to its definition, its function, and its scope. It is safe to say that role refers to the functioning of individuals in the group or the larger society and that it helps to explain the patterning of social behavior. At the same time role may be considered a phase of personality in the sense that a person learns his social roles as he does habits and various traits. Thus the concept of role has real possibilities for helping to bridge the gap between the individualistic and socially centered approaches.

THE IMPORTANCE OF ROLES

"Role," of course, derives from the theatre. According to Webster, a role is "a part, or character, performed by an actor in a drama; hence, a part or function taken or assumed by anyone; as, the role of philanthropist." The dramatic role, we note in passing, is fairly well specified, but involves enough latitude to permit individual interpretation by each actor.

Anthropologists speak of roles in describing the behavior of persons belonging to different age, sex, and occupational groups. Linton defines role as the dynamic aspect of status, i.e., of a special position in society. Thus role involves the performance of the rights and duties constituting a particular status.[1] He finds seven age-sex groupings in practically all societies: infant, boy, girl, adult man, adult woman, old man, old woman.[2] Many sociologists concep-

[1] R. Linton, *The study of man* (New York: D. Appleton-Century Co., Inc., 1936), pp. 113-14. Reprinted by permission of Appleton-Century-Crofts, Inc.
[2] R. Linton, Age and sex categories, *Amer. J. Sociol.*, VII (1942), 589-603.

tualize roles in a similar way. Wilson and Kolb, for example, define role as a "pattern of behavior corresponding to a system of rights and duties and associated with a particular position in a social group."[3] Parsons treats role from the standpoint of social structure. Role, he says, is the concept linking the actor or individual as a behaving entity to the social structure. Institutionalized roles (e.g., age, sex, occupational roles) are the means by which varied human potentialities "dovetail into a single integrated system capable of meeting the situational exigencies with which the society and its members are faced.[4] Thus Parsons sees society or the social system as a "pattern of roles."

This anthropological and sociological view of roles has brought out many important facets of the topic, such as the distinction between *ascribed* and *achieved* roles—between those assigned automatically by society and those which an individual fits into later because of his learning and experience. Ascribed roles, notably those pertaining to age and sex, are assigned largely on the basis of biological and physiological factors. Others, like that of nobleman or peasant, of upper- or lower-class status, are assigned on the basis of "social inheritance" or expected position in society. Intercultural similarities found in age and sex roles testify to the presence of biological factors. A child's role is typically one of active play and exploration; the adult's, one of dignity and less muscular movement—both of which agree with known physiological conditions. The woman's role centers about child-rearing and keeping up the home; the man's involves feats of strength and permits more overt aggressiveness. Again, biological factors are involved.

Of course, the intercultural variations in roles—even age and sex roles—are notable and suggest the influence of cultural factors. Ethnologists report that noisiness, rudeness, and disobedience of children are sanctioned or at least permitted in some societies. Margaret Mead discovered considerable variation in the sex roles of both men and women in three neighboring New Guinea tribes, as already noted.[5]

Achieved roles are attained through one's life experience and through selection among many roles which may be assumed. Thus one may become a self-made man, a lawyer, a laborer, an outlaw, a wife, a husband, a misogynist, a "grande dame," etc. Biological

---

[3] L. Wilson and W. L. Kolb, *Sociological analysis* (New York: Harcourt, Brace & Co., Inc., 1949), p. 208.

[4] T. Parsons, Systematic theory in sociology, in *Essays in sociological theory* (Glencoe, Ill.: Free Press, 1949), p. 35.

[5] M. Mead, *Sex and temperament in three primitive societies* (New York: William Morrow & Co., Inc., 1935). See Chapter 3 above.

factors play a smaller and more indirect part in the case of achieved roles. Consequently there are greater intercultural contrasts. Compare, for example, the doctor role in our society with that of the medicine man in many primitive cultures. Or compare the teacher role in the United States with that in old China or even in the Soviet Union.

We noted earlier, in discussing development of the self, G. H. Mead's theories of role-taking as the essence of the child's socialization.[6] In similar vein, Waller has noted that "the role is the means of social growth. Whenever we play the role of another, some part of him becomes a part of us. The young child reaches out into his family for his roles. . . . Later the child uses other and more distant models. . . ." [7]

Among psychologists Woodworth pioneered in 1934 by discussing *code* and *role* as two important social influences upon the child's personality development.[8] The individual "adopts the code of his group or at least builds up his personal code in living with the group; and he finds or makes a role for himself in the group." [9] But Woodworth emphasized that the available roles for a child are determined only in part by group organization. It may be more likely that "each individual gravitates toward a role that suits his own characteristics, and that he finds his role or makes it rather than having it thrust upon him by arbitrary group action." [10] Nevertheless, some roles, such as those of the spoiled or unwanted child, are given in the home and have an unfortunate effect upon personality characteristics.

Role-taking plays a crucial part in bringing about social adjustment. This is noted by Cameron when he says:

. . . by taking this role or that in fun, children learn incidentally to see things from something approaching the diverse standpoints of all the social persons whom they pretend to be. Each child finds out, in each role he plays, what he can look for in the behavior of children playing dominant, dependent or other reciprocal roles, and what he must do to meet, accept, resist or evade others' demands in those roles. In each role he gains experience in doing and saying things, in having things said and done to him, and in maintaining consistent and appropriate organized attitudes, none of which belongs to his real-life role of *the child of such-and-such a family*.[11]

6 G. H. Mead, *Mind, self and society* (Chicago: University of Chicago Press, 1934). See Chapter 9, above.

7 W. W. Waller, *The family* (New York: The Cordon Co., Inc., 1939), pp. 110-11.

8 R. S. Woodworth, *Psychology* (3d ed.; New York: Henry Holt & Co., Inc., 1934).

9 R. S. Woodworth and D. G. Marquis, *Psychology* (5th ed.; New York: Henry Holt & Co., Inc., 1947), p. 135.

10 *Ibid.*, p. 138.

11 N. Cameron, *The psychology of behavior disorders* (Boston: Houghton Mifflin Co., 1947), p. 92.

SEX ROLES

One of the most important role designations is that defined by sex, male versus female. Our clothes, occupation, tastes, values, hobbies, and speech, for instance, reflect this fundamental difference. Possibly because of the obvious biological differences between men and women, numerous assumptions about psychological differences have arisen. In our culture, for example, women are often said to be emotional, intuitive, and talkative, whereas men are logical and rational. A New York minister voiced some of these beliefs in a sermon attacking a proposal to ordain women to the Presbyterian ministry. "Women are not temperamentally fitted to be ministers," he said. They "are not especially good at keeping other folks' secrets, and . . . are apt to be influenced by their feelings in matters of belief rather than by sound judgment." [12] This kind of generalization is extremely common. Sometimes the women are given the advantage, but more often the men, possibly because men are more likely to be making speeches and writing books!

What evidence do we have relative to sex differences in psychological characteristics? Part of the role differentiation is in physical differences. In physical development boys are heavier and taller up to age ten, then girls to age fifteen or sixteen, after which boys forge ahead. In physical strength, the average male is far ahead of the average female. This is attested by the great superiority of men over women in athletic records, particularly in weight and jumping events.[13]

The occupational effects of sex differences—menstruation, for example—are less clear and subject to some dispute. Probably menstruation is not as much of a handicap as it was formerly because of our enlightened attitude toward it. Seward, indeed, finds that the menstrual cycle has little effect on the woman worker, though she notes that "the persistence of a code of menstrual invalidism, however, has contributed to industrial absenteeism." [14] The effects of pregnancy and child-bearing upon a woman's work are obvious. In practically every society, "primitive" or "civilized," provision is made for the lightening of occupational labors at this time.

Thus, the physiological differences between the sexes have something to do with occupational sex roles found in all cultures. But these undeniable sex differences are not *necessarily* or *entirely* the

12 See *New York Times*, February 17, 1947.

13 A. Scheinfeld, *Women and men* (New York: Harcourt, Brace & Co., Inc., 1944), chaps. iv and vi.

14 G. H. Seward, Psychological effects of the menstrual cycle on women workers, *Psychol. Bull.*, XLI (1944), 99.

reason for sexual differentiation with respect to activities like cooking, sewing, art and decoration, mechanical work, and the like, as is often alleged.

Let us turn, then, to abilities and aptitudes. The only significant sex difference in sensory acuity is in color vision, a sex-linked characteristic, in which women have a great advantage over men. Some 5 to 10 per cent of men have defective color vision, but less than 1 per cent of women suffer such handicap.[15]

In aptitudes there are certain small but significant differences between the sexes, judging by studies made in the United States. Boys and men are superior on mathematical, spatial, and mechanical tests; girls and women on verbal, memory, perception, and dexterity tests.[16] On some trade tests, where training plays a bigger part than with the aptitude tests, the differences are more striking. For example, in tests of clerical work, only about 20 per cent of males exceed the median of the females.[17]

Sex differences in general intelligence are negligible, partly because the test-makers endeavor to include items on which each sex excels. Actually the intelligence of girls tends to be slightly higher than that of boys up to about fourteen because the developmental rate of girls is faster. In tests which are largely verbal, the difference in favor of girls is greater.[18]

It is not in abilities, however, where sex differences are notable, but rather in the area of interests and attitudes and, to some extent, of personality. Several studies of spontaneous conversations agree that men are more likely to talk about business, money, sports, and politics, while women's interests run to men, clothes and decoration, and social relationships.[19] Other kinds of data bear out these differences. For example, use of the Allport-Vernon "study of values" test showed that men are higher on theoretical, economic,

15 See A. Anastasi and J. P. Foley, Jr., *Differential psychology* (rev. ed.; New York: The Macmillan Co., 1949), p. 647.

16 L. E. Tyler, *Psychology of human differences* (New York: Appleton-Century-Crofts, Inc., 1947), chap. iv; Anastasi and Foley, *op. cit.*, pp. 651-60. See also L. M. Terman and L. E. Tyler, Psychological sex differences, in L. Carmichael (ed.), *Manual of child psychology* (rev. ed.; New York: John Wiley & Sons, Inc., 1954), pp. 1067-75.

17 See G. G. Schneidler and D. G. Paterson, Sex differences in clerical aptitude, *J. educ. Psychol.*, XXXIII (1942), 303-9.

18 See G. H. Seward, *Sex and the social order* (New York: McGraw-Hill Book Co., Inc., 1946), pp. 234 ff.

19 See Anastasi and Foley, *op. cit.*, pp. 665-66. Likewise, when children were presented with a variety of play materials, the boys chose blocks, vehicles, and people in uniform, whereas the girls preferred furniture and people in everyday dress. See M. P. Honzig, Sex differences in the occurrence of materials in the play constructions of preadolescents, *Child Developm.*, XXII (1951), 14-35, as reported in Terman and Tyler, *op. cit.*, pp. 1077-78.

and political values, while women exceed the men on esthetic, social, and religious values.[20] Or again, a study of readership conducted by *Time* magazine showed that men are more interested in sports, business, science, international and national affairs, while women's interests run toward movies, the theater, books, and music, and (with very small differences) toward religion and people.[21]

Patterns of masculine and feminine interests, attitudes, and personality traits in our culture are well summarized by Terman and Miles, after their extensive research into "sex and personality." [22] Males, say these authors, are interested in adventure and strenuous occupations, in machinery and tools, science, invention, and business. Females turn toward domestic affairs and the arts; the occupations they prefer are more sedentary, ministrative, and charitable or humanitarian.

Terman and Miles also describe sex differences in "emotional disposition and direction." Males are more self-assertive, aggressive, hardy, and fearless, also rougher in manners, language, and sentiments. Females are more sympathetic, timid, and sensitive; they are more moralistic and emotional and admit more weakness in emotional control. Jones and Burks found that boys are more aggressive, "naughty," and unruly; girls are more nervous, shy, anxious, and jealous.[23] Personality test studies of adolescents and adults show women to be more submissive and neurotic and less self-confident than men.[24]

However, these differences between men and women are not always statistically significant. There is much overlapping between the distributions of the two groups. The range of individual differences within each group is almost always more striking than variations between the two groups.

The origin of sex differences. We have noted above the more striking sex differences in psychological characteristics found in our culture. What can we now say as to the causes of these differences?

Traditionally, sex differences have been considered innate, inherent—of the same order as male and female anatomical differences. This assumption was questioned by Margaret Mead, as we

20 G. W. Allport and P. E. Vernon, A test for personal values, *J. abnorm. soc. Psychol.*, XXVI (1931), 231-48.

21 Advertisement in *New York Times*, November 26, 1947.

22 L. M. Terman and C. C. Miles, *Sex and personality: studies in masculinity and femininity* (New York: McGraw-Hill Book Co., Inc., 1936), pp. 447-48.

23 M. C. Jones and B. S. Burks, *Personality development* (Monogr. Soc. Res. Child Developm., 1936, No. 4).

24 See Anastasi and Foley, *op. cit.*, pp. 671-78 for a good résumé of studies.

saw in Chapter 3. Mead's thesis, and that of several other social scientists, stresses the importance of cultural factors—notably the sex roles found in each culture.[25] Scheinfeld's book, *Women and Men,* swings the pendulum back toward constitutional and physiological determinants, though he is by no means unaware of cultural influences.[26] Possibly one difficulty in interpretation is that we have not always specified the aspects of personality or behavior with which we are concerned.

It is clear that differences in average height, weight, and strength of men and women are biological in origin; also their rates of childhood development and a few specific traits such as color-blindness. But as soon as we get to aptitude differences, training factors enter the picture. We have no evidence that boys are *inherently* better in mechanical and mathematical aptitude; in our culture, activities such as these are stressed for boys. Likewise with interests—our training of boys steers them toward business and politics, of girls toward the arts and domestic matters.

In other words, our society (like all societies) has different sex roles, different patterns of expected behavior for boys and girls, for men and women. We dress boys and girls differently even as very young children. We give the boys mechanical toys, Erector and Chemcraft sets and do not encourage girlish interest in them. We expect girls to be more polite, modest, and "lady-like"; we excuse various signs of exuberance and aggressiveness in their brothers by saying, "Just like a boy!" We teach the girls to play jacks and to skip rope, the boys to play marbles and baseball. We give the girls music lessons and the boys boxing lessons. This differential treatment of boys and girls extends to most areas of activity, in accordance with the sex roles of the culture, the social class, the region, and the community. It would be impossible for such differentiation not to affect the interests, attitudes, personality traits, and social behavior of men and women.

However, one must not overdo the cultural thesis. Boys and men are physiologically more muscular and energetic, which underlies their typical roles of athlete and warrior in all societies. Woman's child-bearing function and endocrinal postmaternal drive is basic to her child-caring role (found in all cultures) and is also related, more indirectly, to her domestic role. However, there is no necessary connection between motherhood and sewing, cooking, decoration, and

[25] Margaret Mead discusses sex roles at greater length in *Male and female* (New York: William Morrow & Co., Inc., 1949).

[26] A. Scheinfeld, *op. cit.*

the like. Indeed, we find several cultures where one or more of these duties are performed by the men.[27]

The relative weighting of physiological and cultural influences is still unclear. The question underlies many problems such as education and vocational training for women, to say nothing of the broader roles of men and women within any culture. Factual data of significance seem to be accumulating slowly. For example, after experimenting with sex equality for many years, the Soviet government modified its principles of equality by preventing women from doing work which might harm them or prevent them from bearing healthy children. Though women undoubtedly played a more important role in the military forces of the U.S.S.R. than in any other nation, they engaged in little actual combat.[28] As Scheinfeld concludes: "Thus, before long the Soviets had formally acknowledged that Nature, as well as social expediency, had to a certain extent ordained a division of labor for the sexes, and that there were many men's tasks which women could not and should not do." [29]

On the other hand, we are beginning to realize that many decisions as to division of labor between the sexes are dictated by other considerations than physiological ones. When it becomes part of a government's policy to employ men in preference to women and to keep women "in the home," the decision is usually based upon long-range plans such as increase of population or military strength. The Soviet decree of 1943 which abolished coeducation above the age of eight and specified that the boy should be prepared for the army and the girl for motherhood reflected Soviet national policy as much as it does the differing potentialities of men and women.[30]

The perennial problem of woman's role in a society such as ours will not be solved unless we face the underlying issues squarely. It is never as simple as the question of abilities: What can men do, and what can women do? Social values are always in the background. And these social values are of different kinds. Some people, for example, stress individual adjustment—e.g., each woman should have a chance to realize her desires and potentialities as a person. Others emphasize values such as population growth or national might. Only when these differing frames of reference are recognized can intelligent policies be formulated.

27 See G. P. Murdock, Comparative data on division of labor by sex, *Soc. Forces,* XV (1937), 551.

28 A. Scheinfeld, *op. cit.,* chap. xxviii.

29 *Ibid.,* p. 359.

30 *Ibid.,* pp. 140-41, 368-69.

CONFLICT IN ROLES

Guthrie was one of the first psychologists to discuss conflicts in roles as a source of maladjustment.[31] For example, he says:

The man who thinks of himself as an open-handed host loses his income and his social adjustment is thrown completely out of gear by his persistence in the rôle. He continues to be generous and spends more than he can afford. A small girl may play at housekeeping and her older sister may marry under the influence of the same rôle. To have a household means being married. If the marriage is a failure and the husband does not play the part that would be necessary for maintaining the rôle, the wife may continue to pretend in public that all is well, that she is happily married and has a pleasant home. She must keep the recognition of the true state of affairs from the public because she is keeping it from herself. She is still playing that she is happily married and doing her best to disregard the unpleasant interludes with the husband's non-cooperation. If the public becomes aware of the failure of the marriage it will be necessary for her also to recognize that failure or to withdraw from the public. Only in retreat or in an asylum can we be successful in maintaining a rôle against a public rejection of that rôle. Disgrace, which is often so intolerable as to lead to suicide, always consists in the public rejection of a character part which we have adopted. Disgrace seldom threatens physical harm or serious physical discomfort. An astonishing number of men in public life have failed to survive a public rejection of their rôle.[32]

Komarovsky has discovered a great deal of role conflict among college girls, especially the brighter and more serious students. The chief conflict she finds is between the "feminine" role and that of the career or professional woman.[33] One student's father, for example, wants her to get an *A* in every subject and to prepare for a profession. But her mother says, "That *A* in Philosophy is very nice, dear. But please don't become so deep that no man will be good enough for you." The student wonders how she is to pursue any course single-mindedly when those she loves and respects have such differing plans and expectations for her. Another closely related conflict faced by college women centers about whether to be oneself in relations with men or to play the expected feminine role, i.e., being dependent and inferior. Komarovsky found that nearly half her informants had occasionally "played dumb" on dates—concealed academic honors, pretended ignorance, or allowed the man the last word in discussion. But they felt unhappy at such hypocrisy, being only too aware of the counter-pressure upon the college girl to excel and to develop her skills to the utmost.

[31] E. R. Guthrie, *The psychology of human conflict* (New York: Harper & Bros., 1938).

[32] *Ibid.*, pp. 141-42.

[33] M. Komarovsky, Cultural contradictions and sex roles, *Amer. J. Sociol.*, LII (1946), 184-89.

A related kind of role conflict arises from the differing training of boys and girls in the parental family. Komarovsky found that the parents tended to speed up emancipation of the boy and retard it for his sister, to allow the boys more privacy and to hold the girls to a more exacting code of obligations.[34] One college girl wrote:

My mother is very hurt if I don't let her read the letters I receive. After a telephone call she expects me to tell her who called and what was said. My brother could say "a friend" and she would not feel insulted.

Or again:

My brother is 15, 3 years younger than I am. When he goes out after supper mother calls out: "Where are you going, Jimmy?" "Oh, out." Could I get away with this? Not on your life. I would have to tell in detail where to, with whom, and if I am half an hour late mother sits on the edge of the living-room sofa watching the door." [35]

A BIRD'S-EYE VIEW OF ROLES

Let us summarize and interpret a bit. A person's roles are to be understood in the light of his own pattern of hereditary and environmental influences. A youngster's first roles develop under the impacts from his family, his clique, his neighborhood, and his community. Biological forces play a part, though always refracted through the social milieu. A large, husky boy becomes a bully and gang leader; his size and strength are important, not per se, but in relation to the inferiority of his companions. A young lady of great "natural" beauty assumes her queenly role because she is admired by others and treated as their superior in pulchritude. A lad of high intelligence may become a scientific leader because in our society brains are, generally speaking, a prerequisite for professional eminence; the same may not be true in all societies.

Knowledge of the important roles in any society is communicated to the child by all his social contacts—in home, school, community; by parents, siblings, relatives, friends; in the movies, over the TV and radio, through the newspapers, magazines, and even the comics. Even more important, the child learns through his own observation. Naturally his knowledge of roles and of their functions differs according to his experience. His attitude toward various roles also depends on his social experience; one or another aspect of his personality orients him toward some roles and away from others. In

[34] M. Komarovsky, Functional analysis of sex roles, *Amer. sociol. Rev.*, XV (1950), 508-16.

[35] *Ibid.*, p. 511. For further discussion, see M. Komarovsky, *Women in the modern world* (Boston: Little, Brown & Co., 1953), chap. iii, and G. Seward, *Psychotherapy and culture conflict* (New York: The Ronald Press Co., 1956), chap. viii.

other words, study of an individual's major roles, like the study of personality variables, depends upon obtaining a good life history. Generally speaking, where abnormal or unusual inherited factors exist (deformity, disease, glandular imbalance, etc.), they will bulk large as role determinants. Where no unusual physical factors are present, the etiology of roles will be found predominantly in social experience.

Function of roles. Role-taking channels the various activities of group members so that they are mutually harmonious, and it enables us to predict the behavior of others. The reciprocal nature of many roles illustrates this nicely; husband and wife, teacher and student, parent and child, employer and employee, learn forms of interpersonal behavior which are supplementary and mutually beneficial. Much child training, education, and "social control" in general are devoted to instructing children, adolescents, and new group members in the sanctioned values and patterns of behavior. Mores or conventions and roles are normally taught simultaneously. Parents say: "Remember, Willie, *good* little boys wash their hands and wipe their noses on a handkerchief," or "A *nice* little girl doesn't *think* of biting her baby sister!"

At the same time, however, that roles make for predictability and harmony in social behavior and thus facilitate social adjustment, they may also contribute to individual frustration and conflict. This is particularly true when a person belongs to two or more groups which have different values. For example, a boy is brought up in a strict small-town home where card-playing, dancing, smoking, and drinking are taboo. His friends are from families whose attitudes are similar. When he goes away to college he may discover that the patterns of expected behavior are quite different; that a more sophisticated type of social behavior is called for if he wishes to be popular—or even just "accepted." A greater or lesser degree of emotional conflict is the usual consequence of two such incompatible patterns of behavior.

How roles differ. Furthermore, there are certain major ways in which roles differ; we may sketch several of these dimensions.

First, roles differ in *breadth or extensiveness*. A man of the cloth plays his ministerial role in all or practically all his social contacts, though many variations on the central theme are possible. A king or other important figure conforms in his public contacts to the culturally prescribed role. Other roles are more variable: a young man may be a leader in one group and a buffoon in another; a girl may act as a sophisticate in only one small circle of acquaintances; a man may be bossy and dominant only in his office, never in his home or club.

Second, roles differ in *specificity of patterning*. On "official occasions" or in ceremonial or ritualistic behavior such as a formal wedding, a college graduation, or a dramatic performance, the acts and words are quite rigidly predetermined. This is also true in highly organized hierarchical relationships such as military life. Of course, even here some latitude is permitted, which makes one President's inaugural different from another's, one officer's method of issuing orders quite distinctive, or one actor's performance of Hamlet outstanding. At the other extreme, in many roles there is little or no prescription of specific acts or words; the latitude is great, and conformity is demanded only within rather general categories of "musts" and "must nots." For example, a child must not be rude to or disobey his parents; a minister must not drink, swear, or go to burlesque shows; a doctor must treat all sick people to the best of his ability, and so on. Outside such broad limitations, behavior is left unregulated by the role. Perhaps the host-guest relationship already mentioned is an example that falls between these two extremes. The role defines the patterns of host-guest interaction, but does not specify the exact words to be spoken, the subjects of conversation, the food and drink to be served, or the hour at which the guests shall depart.

Again, roles vary in their *continuity* or *permanence*. The roles of man and woman, of prince and pariah, are permanent within a society, though they change as the culture changes. Occupational roles are permanent after one enters a calling. Age roles last over a period of years. On the other hand many roles are transitory; those of a debutante or eligible bachelor, for example, are of relatively short duration. Other roles are occasional and last but a few hours or minutes, though they may recur in comparable social situations.

Roles vary greatly in *importance and prestige*. The role of a friend entails far greater personal intimacy and evokes deeper emotional reactions than that of a casual acquaintance. The fulfilment of a family or professional role involves an enduring personality adjustment, as compared with such roles as those of visitor or neighbor. The importance of roles varies according to the estimate of individuals and groups. The role of worshiper may be deemed by some the central one in life. One woman regards her mother-wife role as her dominant theme; another woman does not. Peoples of the South Seas place little stress upon occupational roles; Americans value them highly. Within the United States, the relative ranking of roles varies greatly with the subcultural group. The Greenwich Village bohemian may consider it "corny" to work, marry, have children, attend church, and save for the future, while the resident of a midwestern small town values these activities and roles very highly.

In any culture some roles are idealized and the individuals playing them have high prestige, while others are deemed "respectable" or ordinary, and still others are disapproved, including both the tolerated and the outlawed. In our society, those eminently successful in business, athletics, or entertainment fall into highly honored roles. At the other extreme, left-wingers, bootleggers, and criminals are officially disapproved. Each subculture in a large and complex society has its own versions of honored and dishonored roles.

One finds much variation in the ease or difficulty of fulfilling roles. Some require a minimum of effort and adaptability, whereas others demand continuous activity. Thus a citizen of a community need only establish legal residence, pay taxes, and observe the mores to be considered a respectable citizen. Conversely, a scholar devotes his life to the tasks making up his role and may never achieve his goals.

In any institutional setting such as the home, school, or community, an individual usually plays several roles. A young woman may be a wife and mother, and perhaps a sister and daughter as well. The college boy functions as a student, fraternity brother, and campus leader. However, the number of roles a person actually plays is limited. Study of a sample group of midwestern college students shows that more than three roles are seldom played concomitantly.

Individuals vary greatly in the coherence or integration of their various roles, though most persons succeed in executing even divergent roles without becoming disorganized. Some persons have the capacity to reveal quite different aspects of their personality, each in its appropriate situation. If this is done skilfully, in accordance with situational demands, it may win approval, as with the gracious hostess of the adroit statesman. If, however, the changes in role are dramatized or are greater than the situations seem to warrant, the individual may be considered to have a chameleon-like personality or to be an insincere opportunist.

A SOCIAL PSYCHOLOGICAL INTERPRETATION OF ROLE

The social scientist's conception of role, as described above, would be more acceptable to the social psychologist if it were modified in certain respects. The following criticisms can be made of it.

First, it does not take into account the variations in role behavior which occur. In our culture, for example, modesty is expected of women, obedience of children, and self-restraint of clergymen. Yet, depending on the personality of a particular woman, child, or minister and on the specific situation involved, considerable variation in these themes is permitted.

Second, the orthodox conception of role does not include "situational roles"—that is, coherent patterns of social behavior appropriate to a particular situation. This kind of role typically occurs in new or "unstructured" situations where some selection is possible. Thus a person introduced into a new group may play the role of a sophisticate, a lady-killer, a "clinging vine," a man of learning, or a "very important person."

Third, despite Thomas' insistence on "defining the situation," [36] most treatments of role do not include a perceptual component. Actually, this is implied in the two points given above: individuals vary, so they perceive and interpret situations differently, which has much to do with determining the role behavior.[37]

Fourth, roles are more than interactional; they are reciprocal. The role of child has meaning only with reference to the role of parent, husband with reference to that of wife, employer with that of employee, student with teacher, and so on.

It is probably impossible for social psychologists to work out a comprehensive definition of role, which is satisfactory to all and which, at the same time, does justice to the complexities of the topic.[38] The interpretations they have offered, while not in close agreement, usually stress one or another of the four points just mentioned.

Cottrell, for example, notes that

A role [is] . . . an internally consistent series of conditioned responses by one member of a social situation which represents the stimulus pattern for a similarly internally consistent series of conditioned responses of the other(s) in that situation.[39]

A similar type of definition is offered by the clinical psychologists, Cameron and Magaret: A role is a "comprehensive and coherent

[36] W. I. Thomas, *The unadjusted girl* (Boston: Little, Brown & Co., 1923).

[37] A new treatment of role by Sarbin contains sections not only on "role perception" but on "role expectation" as well. See T. R. Sarbin, Role theory, in G. Lindzey (ed.), *Handbook of social psychology*, Vol. I (Reading, Mass.: Addison-Wesley Pub. Co., Inc., 1954).

[38] Two authors reviewed 80 conceptions of role and concluded it is "vague, nebulous and non-definitive." See L. J. Neiman and J. W. Hughes, The problem of the concept of role—a resurvey of the literature, *Soc. Forces*, XXX (1951), 141-49.

[39] L. S. Cottrell, The adjustment of the individual to his age and sex roles, *Amer. sociol. Rev.*, VII (1942), p. 617.

organization in behavior of functionally related, interlocking attitudes and responses." [40]

Sarbin gives a concise definition, and elaborates it in terms of perception and reciprocity:

A *role* is a patterned sequence of learned *actions* or deeds performed by a person in an interaction situation. The organizing of the individual actions is a product of the perceptual and cognitive behavior of person A upon observing person B. B performs one or a number of discrete acts which A observes and organizes into a concept, a role. On the basis of this conceptualization of the actions of B, A expects certain further actions from B. . . .[41]

Newcomb distinguishes between *role*, which characterizes all the occupants of any position, and *role behavior*, which refers to the actual behavior of specific individuals as they take roles.[42] Though role behaviors depend upon shared social norms, he sees them as unique to each individual. "Because role behaviors are personally motivated, and because they are in part determined by self-perceptions which are never fully shared, no two individuals ever take the same roles in identical ways. But these are not the only reasons for uniqueness in role taking. People differ in constitutional makeup, and in the previous experiences through which they have gone and in what they have learned from them. Inevitably, therefore, they behave in different ways, no matter how fully they share the same group norms." [43]

Endeavoring to cover the essential variables, one of the authors proposed the following definition:

A person's role is a pattern or type of social behavior which seems situationally appropriate to him in terms of the demands and expectations of those in his group.[44]

This conception suggests that roles are always enacted by individuals, though they are socially defined patterns or delimitations within which much variation is possible. "Situationally appropriate" brings in the function of perception in determining social behavior. One behaves in a way that seems appropriate to him, as he "sizes up" the situation. Thus an individual who perceives a party as "dying

40 N. Cameron and A. Magaret, *Behavior pathology* (Boston: Houghton Mifflin Co., 1951), p. 116.

41 T. R. Sarbin, *op. cit.*, p. 225.

42 T. M. Newcomb, *Social psychology* (New York: The Dryden Press, Inc., 1950), p. 330.

43 *Ibid.*, p. 333. Cf. Turner, who deals with role as a "set of norms" in our behavior. R. H. Turner, Role-taking, role standpoint, and reference-group behavior, *Amer. J. Sociol.* LXI (1956), 316-28.

44 S. S. Sargent, Conceptions of role and ego in contemporary psychology, in J. H. Rohrer and M. Sherif (eds.), *Social psychology at the crossroads* (New York: Harper & Bros., 1951), p. 360.

on its feet" endeavors to save it by becoming the "life of the party"
—whether or not this role is considered necessary or desirable by
others! Similarly, a woman perceives that conformity to the "feminine role" is more appropriate in the presence of a group of her
husband's business associates than when she is with several close
friends of her own sex.

The phrase *demands and expectations* connotes the function of
social experience in determining roles. We learn what kinds of behavior are sanctioned for what types of occasions, and this knowledge serves, more than anything else, to determine the character of
the role.

The term *group* signifies anything from a small, well-defined,
highly structured social unit like a family, gang, or fraternity to a
large and loosely structured collection of individuals such as those
found in a community, social class, region, or whole culture. Role
behavior is patterned according to the demands and expectations of
the members of one's group and occurs within one's group. When
the group changes, one's roles change, as we shall see.

A definition of *role* must be specific enough to have meaning yet
broad enough to cover what have been called *cultural* roles and
unique roles,[45] or in another formulation, "cultural," "personal,"
and "situational" roles.[46] The framework of cultural roles—the role
of woman, child, scholar, or priest, for example—is provided by
consensus in a society. Unique roles are shown by one or a very
few individuals. Personal roles are not in disagreement with cultural standards but involve more individual variation, as in the
reciprocal relations between a particular husband and wife or a
given teacher and his students. But cultural and personal roles are
often not sufficient to pattern behavior in a specific situation. So
situational roles emerge, in accordance with the individual's interpretation of the situation, e.g., the bully, flirt, man of the world,
helpless little woman, life of the party, etc.

However, roles often do not fall neatly into one or another
such category. Most examples of role behavior have elements of
both cultural and personal determination, often with temporary,
"situational" ingredients. Consider, for example, a guest at an
upper-middle-class dinner party. Without being particularly aware
of it, the guest arrives all "set" to manifest forms of behavior appro-

45 L. S. Cottrell, The adjustment of the individual to his age and sex roles, *Amer.
sociol. Rev.*, VII (1942), 617-20.

46 R. L. Warren, Cultural, personal, and situational roles, *Sociol. soc. Res.*, XXXIV:2
(1949), 104-11.

priate to the occasion. His past experience enables him to greet properly the host and hostess and the other guests, to wait for the ladies to be seated, to use the right fork, etc. But his behavior and conversation are not predetermined as would be that of a robot. It is delineated and guided by his knowledge of what is apropos and what is taboo in this kind of situation. He knows, if anyone asks him, that one does not discuss operations, sex perversions, or technical and highly controversial topics; but his role (as guest) is so "natural" he never even thinks of any of these matters.

Within the range of sanctioned topics, he selects certain subjects for conversation on the basis of his guess about the interests of his neighbors at the table. He can talk to anyone about the weather, current high prices, or the housing shortage. He may talk to the ladies about their children or the maid problem; to the men about business conditions or politics.

Our guest may, of course, be displaying other roles in addition to his central guest role. He may also take the role of a man of the world, a cynic, or a prophet. If so, his conversation will take a different direction and his behavior may change but will still remain within the bounds of the guest role. He will not insult or argue rudely with his host or another guest, as he might do in another situation—with a stranger he meets on a train, for example.

From a strictly psychological standpoint, role-taking is possible because the human organism can take and maintain a "mental set" which facilitates certain kinds of behavior and inhibits other responses. Such mental sets are illustrated in controlled association tests, where the individual is told to respond to stimulus words by giving the opposite, the synonym, or the superordinate. Much experimental evidence shows that behavior is effectively limited and channeled in this way, though no one has yet been able to describe this selectivity in neurological or physiological terms.

Normality and the J-curve. Roles have been found to be a source of neurosis and psychosis.[47] However, Cameron finds a greater source of trouble in the inability to communicate, to take roles, and thus to understand the values and perspectives of others. Only through social communication can a person share his anxieties with others and prevent isolation and domination by his fantasies. The paranoid's "pseudo-community" and the schizophrenic's "autistic community" result largely from this lack of skill in role-taking and in sharing the perspectives of others, says Cameron.

47 Cameron, *op. cit.,* pp. 95 ff.

The conformity behavior which Floyd Allport has studied is really one aspect of role behavior.[48] He and his students found that nearly all motorists stopped for a red traffic light, and that nearly all Catholics participated in the holy water ceremony on entering church. Each of these exemplifies expected behavior, with some degree of punishment for noncompliance. State and local laws define the motorist's role quite clearly in terms of "must" and "must nots." A good Catholic knows exactly what behavior is expected of him in church and, though it is less clearly prescribed, the proper behavior outside church as well. If conformity behavior is plotted on a curve, it resembles a reversed letter "J" (without the tail being turned up). Thus motorists' behavior at a corner, with red lights and a policeman, is depicted in Figure 12.

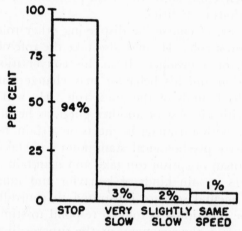

FIG. 12. Motorists' Behavior at a Corner.

SOURCE: After M. Dickens' study, reported in F. H. Allport, the J-curve hypothesis of conforming behavior, *J. soc. Psychol.*, V (1934), 141-83.

SOME UNSETTLED QUESTIONS

Consciousness of roles. Are people generally aware of their role-playing? On the whole a person seems to be unconscious of his role-playing, probably because he has learned, so gradually and so well, what is required of one in his position.

Teacher and student, employer and employee, husband and wife, seldom stop to think what is the appropriate interactional behavior. One never even *thinks* of smoking in church or of telling a ribald story at a polite dinner party. Such situations are clearly defined

[48] F. H. Allport, The J-curve hypothesis of conforming behavior, *J. soc. Psychol.*, V (1934), 141-83. Reprinted in Swanson, *et al.*, *Readings* (2d ed.), pp. 231-43.

by our past experience, and the behavior is performed without conscious decision.

In new and unusual circumstances, however, the situation must be interpreted or defined, and the role to be taken may be consciously considered. A recent recruit into the armed services is acutely aware of the requirements of his new role. When a young woman sees her ex-fiancé coming toward her in a restaurant, she decides rapidly (and more or less consciously) whether to ignore him, to be courteous but distant, to act like an old friend, to behave as if things were on the same old basis, or to choose some other alternative. Unfamiliar, unexpected situations, or personal-social crises, seem to heighten the level of role awareness.

In general, the higher the status or "visibility" and the greater the power associated with a given role, the more likely one is to be conscious of it. Thus a statesman, outstanding scholar, or corporation head is more likely to be aware of his role in the social order than a farmer, student, or housewife. One whose major role is considered unworthy or antisocial, such as a ward politician, vagrant, or criminal, is likely to repress awareness of his role and rationalize himself into a more favorable position in society. Aside from variations in situations and in status, people show great differences in self-awareness, including the ability to see themselves as others do and to be conscious of their roles. Of the many possible factors accounting for these differences, one of the most important is anxiety or insecurity. The neurotic is acutely concerned about the way others regard him, though his interpretations are frequently erroneous or exaggerated.[49]

An individual's self-image, whether or not it is fully conscious, undoubtedly includes his conceptions of his roles. As we saw earlier, the self develops in a social matrix.[50] Many of his social relationships—with parents, teachers, friends, club members, and so on—become crystallized into roles. His self-image is based in large part on such roles, especially if they are conceptualized—if he is considered "a good son," a "bright student," "a loyal friend," "one of our outstanding members," and the like.

One might add a semantic note: if it occurred to most people that they were "playing a role," the whole thing might smack of insincerity, of not being true to oneself; hence, they would unconsciously reject the notion.

[49] Cf. K. Horney, *The neurotic personality of our time* (New York: W. W. Norton & Co., Inc., 1937).
[50] See Chapter 9, above.

Perception of roles. Closely related to consciousness of roles is the question of their perception, where a few research studies have been done. Hartley and several associates showed that children of 6 or 7 years identify themselves with ethnic-group symbols and can distinguish between adult roles such as parent and worker. However, they had difficulty in perceiving multiple roles—for example, in seeing the same person as a mother and as a sales clerk.[51]

Sarbin and associates have used various techniques for studying role perception. Short sentences were presented on a record, such as "All right, boys, get in there and fight!" or a whining little girl who cried, "Somebody broke my dollie." Respondents were asked to indicate the role of the speaker. It was found that different middle-class groups perceived such role cues rather similarly, though there were noticeable individual differences.[52] Another study used stick figure drawings to give various kinds of postural cues. Certain of the postures were perceived, fairly consistently, as associated with acts or qualities of a person, such as impatience, resignation, shyness, and the like.[53] These experiments, though only a beginning, suggest the possibilities of studying how roles are identified.

Role-playing ability. A frequently raised question is, What kind of people are best at role-playing?[54] Dymond finds that role-playing depends upon *empathy*—i.e., the ability to transpose oneself into the thinking, feeling, and acting of another. Comparison of those high with those low in empathy gave the following picture:

. . . those whose empathy is high . . . [are] outgoing, optimistic, warm, emotional people, who have a strong interest in others. They are flexible people whose emotional relations with others, particularly their early family relations, have been sufficiently satisfying so that they find investing emotionally in others rewarding. . . .

Those low in empathy are rather rigid, introverted people who are subject to outbursts of uncontrolled emotionality . . . They are either self-centered and demanding in their emotional contacts or else lone wolves who prefer to get along without strong ties to other people. Their own early emotional relationships within the family seem to have been so disturbed and unsatisfying that

51 E. L. Hartley and D. C. Krugman, Note on children's role perception, *J. Psychol.*, XXVI (1948), 399-405; E. L. Hartley, M. Rosenbaum, and S. Schwartz, Children's use of ethnic frames of reference, *J. Psychol.*, XXVI (1948), 367-86; E. L. Hartley, M. Rosenbaum, and S. Schwartz, Children's perceptions of ethnic group membership, *J. Psychol.*, XXVI (1948), 387-98.

52 T. R. Sarbin, *op. cit.*, p. 230.

53 *Ibid.*, p. 231.

54 Coutu criticizes social psychologists for confusing the terms "role-taking" and "role-playing." Strictly speaking, we are here concerned with the former, but the latter term is used most frequently. See W. Coutu, Role-playing vs. role-taking, *Amer. sociol. Rev.*, XVI (1951), 180-87.

they feel they cannot afford to invest their love in others as they need it all for themselves. . . . They seem to compensate for their lack of emotional development by stressing the abstract intellectual approach to life as the safest. . . . It is unimportant to them to know what the other is thinking and feeling; it is their own thoughts and feelings that count.[55]

Thus we find that some people are much better than others at assuming roles, and we have some early evidence as to the personality factors involved. We shall describe later role-playing techniques used as a form of group therapy.

Multiple roles and role conflicts. Every child learns many roles as an essential part of his socialization. Furthermore, as Cameron and Magaret point out, having a number of well-practiced, realistic social roles at one's disposal is a great advantage if he is also adroit at shifting quickly from one to another.[56] This facility is aided by children's games, by parental instruction, and by fantasy and imagination. "The importance of imaginative role-taking becomes at once evident when we stop to consider how ordinary human beings operate in complex social situations. They commonly begin their organized behavior with an attempt to predict what will happen next, and after that, and what will then occur. The prediction is always a guess at how the other persons will react, and so we come once more to the question of anticipation—of being able to take the others' roles, to shift nimbly through probable perspectives and their probable consequences, and thus to be prepared for many developments and not for just one." [57]

At the same time, however, that a multiplicity of roles makes for adaptability it may also, as we noted earlier, be the occasion for conflict. Two conflicting student roles have been presented as follows: [58]

Role 1	Role 2
Expectations of one's college friends: good joe, parties, campus politics, fraternity affairs, dating, athletics, out with the boys, etc.	Parental expectations: good grades, conscientious study, writing home regularly, spending money carefully, preparing for future occupation, etc.

[55] R. F. Dymond, Personality and empathy, *J. consult. Psychol.,* XIV (1950), 349. See also W. A. McClelland, A preliminary test of role-playing ability, *J. consult. Psychol.,* XV (1951), 102-8.

[56] N. Cameron and A. Magaret, *op. cit.,* pp. 119-20.

[57] *Ibid.,* p. 121. A recent study found that ability to take another's role was one of the most striking differences between middle- and lower-class respondents. See L. Schatzman and A. Strauss, Social class and modes of communication, *Amer. J. Sociol.,* XL (1955), 329-38.

[58] A. R. Lindesmith and A. L. Strauss, *Social psychology* (rev. ed.; The Dryden Press, Inc., 1956), p. 616.

One is reminded of the disparate roles exemplified by George Apley in two letters he wrote home from Paris: [59]

Dear Mother: No sooner did we arrive at the hotel after a very rough channel crossing than I found again what a very small place the world is. There in the dining room were Dr. and Mrs. Jessup from Mt. Vernon Street, and Jane Silby and her aunt from Commonwealth Avenue, and the Morrows from Brookline. Aunt Brent says that the Hotel Metropole is one of the few hotels in Paris where one can be sure of meeting congenial people. We all made up a party for a drive this afternoon up the Champs Elysees. It is surprising how very much it is like Commonwealth Avenue. You will be glad to know that many of the waiters and cab drivers understand my French. Uncle Horatio and our driver had great difficulty over the fare, as Uncle Horatio does not believe in giving more than the usual ten per cent fee extra. We are going with Dr. and Mrs. Jessup through the Louvre tomorrow, where I am looking forward to seeing the Mona Lisa. . . .

(Letter to his classmate Walker)

Dear Mike: Well, here I am in Paris and I wish you were here too. I saw Wintie over in London and we split a bottle together in a Public House and talked about the Club. I have always heard how pretty the French girls were and I am disappointed. If you and I were to walk up Tremont Street we could see a dozen prettier ones. Uncle Horatio and Dr. Jessup and I have been out several evenings to "see the town." We have been to several shows. There is no doubt that the French are a very immoral lot, even when one does not understand everything that is said. They certainly seem to enjoy and thrive on immorality. Uncle Horatio is really quite a "sport" and once he has got Henrietta and Aunt Brent safely out of the way you would be surprised at some of his goings-on. Several evenings we have both of us been quite tight. He is very glad to have a vacation, he says, from Boston and so is Dr. Jessup. I am learning a great deal about the older generation. Again, I wish that you were here. . . .

It is hardly surprising that the more socially oriented clinicians are coming to construe "conflict" as basically a conflict in roles. Similarly the incongruity and inconsistency which is the essence of much of our humor is typically a disparity between roles. Some years ago *The New Yorker* reported on a well-dressed matron who came out of a Park Avenue apartment house and looked up and down the street for a doorman or a cab. Seeing none, she placed two fingers in her mouth and emitted a piercing whistle, which did the trick. Why is this amusing? Precisely because the lady was playing a role appropriate to an eight-year-old boy rather than a dignified matron. Likewise, inability to change or shift roles when a situation demands it often accounts for the humor of a cartoon or story.

Roles and personality traits. As already mentioned, one's personality enters into the selection of "achieved" roles. Furthermore nearly all of a person's role behavior is affected to some extent by

[59] J. P. Marquand, *The late George Apley* (Boston: Little, Brown & Co., 1937), pp. 81-82.

his personality traits. Contrariwise, much behavior attributed to personality traits is influenced by roles. We suggest that an understanding of roles helps explain the inadequacies of personality questionnaires and of personality theories which are built solely around traits.

Psychologists who construct personality questionnaires have utilized more or less specific items such as these:

Have you crossed the street to avoid meeting some person?
Have you found books more interesting than people?
Do you find it difficult to argue over prices with tradesmen?
Do you feel as if people are watching you? .

The scored answers to several dozen or hundreds of such questions are analyzed to show the degree to which a person is introverted or extroverted, dominant or submissive, sociable, self-sufficient, neurotic, and so on. The procedure rests upon the assumption that a person's traits may be described independently of the situations in which his behavior occurs.

Despite the fact that they have a certain degree of validity and predictability, such measuring devices are open to serious objections. One of them, the ease with which respondents may, consciously or unconsciously, select the socially preferred answers, need not concern us here. Another objection is more significant: The subject cannot answer the question accurately without having a specific situation in mind; he wants to know which person? which book? which tradesman? He tries to answer fairly, but finds it very difficult because he realizes, however dimly, that his behavior or role varies with the social situation.

This contrast between roles and personality traits is neatly demonstrated in an experiment conducted by the sociologist Leonard Cottrell.[60] Members of a class were asked to rate two youngsters on a simple personality scale, on the basis of case study data given them. One child was described as follows:

The parents complain that *A*, their eldest child, is a very difficult child at home. He is moody, sulks a lot, refuses to cooperate, does his work under protest, fights and bullies the younger children, and is frequently very cruel to them. He is always causing a quarrel or a fight and is stubborn and defiant in his attitude toward the parents . . . etc.

The students rated this child very high on aggressiveness, hostility, and stubbornness, low on passivity, cooperativeness, etc.

[60] L. S. Cottrell, An analysis of situational fields in social psychology, *Amer. sociol. Rev.*, VII (1942). 372-73.

Child B was described in the following way by the students.

When the teachers referred B to the clinic, he was described as a very isolated and shy child. He did what he was required to do in class work but was very timid and diffident about participating in discussions or volunteering to do anything. He was always on the sidelines in anything the class or play groups did. He was frequently bullied by children smaller and younger than himself, and never seemed to stand up for himself with his equals or superiors. He cried easily and seemed to have a general feeling of inferiority. He frequently daydreamed in class . . . etc.

The students rated this child low in aggressiveness, hostility, stubbornness, and self-confidence and high in passivity.

The experimenter then informed the raters that the two cases were one and the same child! He then asked them to rate his child on the basis of all they knew about him. This was a very difficult task; the ratings showed a great deal of scatter and no one was satisfied with his ratings.

Similarly, the chairman of the New York City Board of Examiners committee on personality testing reported dissatisfaction with such tests because "the sum of a man's personality qualities is apt to change with a change in position." [61] Specifically it was found that a teacher having goodwill, cooperativeness, a sense of humor, and a sense of democratic living often lost these qualities in favor of authoritarianism when he was moved up to an administrative post. The personality tests did not predict well when the social setting was materially changed.

The refusal of trait-minded psychologists to take seriously criticism of the sort implied in Cottrell's study may help account for the conflicting and not always meaningful lists of traits which emerge from factor analysis of personality questionnaires.[62] Part of the confusion, at least, arises from the fact that the data analyzed in such studies are obtained without reference to specific social situations. It is conceivable that a factor analysis of personality traits manifested in the home would differ from those manifested in the office, in school or college, in the club or other recreational group. In any event the psychologist would do well to see how much "personality" varies from one situation to another. We already know, from recent studies, that leadership (often treated in the past as a personality trait) varies with the situation and its demands.[63]

[61] Report on an interview with Dr. Harold Fields; see B. Fine, Uncertain tests for personality, New York Times, November, 1954.

[62] See, e.g., R. B. Cattell, Personality—a systematic theoretical and factual study (New York: McGraw-Hill Book Co., Inc., 1950) or H. J. Eysenck, The scientific study of personality (New York: The Macmillan Co., 1952).

[63] See Chapter 14.

A study using a newly constructed test of ascendance-submission asked questions involving each of six different social situations: classroom, group of friends, group of strangers, boy friend, girl friend, or salespeople and waiters. Some evidence was found for the effect of situations, though it was not conclusive.[64] More extensive data, however, using the same test and a similarly constructed one on introversion-extroversion, confirm the hypothesis that "personality traits" are significantly affected by situations. Thus respondents tend to be more ascendant in a group of friends than with strangers, or more extroverted with their own family or relatives than in a public meeting.[65]

Of course, a "situational" interpretation of personality is just as extreme as the psychologist's bias in favor of traits. Defining personality as "the subjective aspect of culture" or as an "emergent arising from the individual's main social roles" is by no means justified in the light of present knowledge. Until more research has been done, we shall do well to avoid both extremes of interpretation. In all probability some aspects of personality will turn out to be constant; others to vary according to the situation. Or again, some individuals will be found to change very little; others, like the chameleon, to adapt themselves adroitly to each new situation. We follow Murphy in insisting that personality must be interpreted in terms of organism-field interaction.[66] The role concept, we predict—whether it be called by this or by another name—will be an important vehicle in furthering this integration between enduring personality trends and changing situational demands.

VALUE OF THE ROLE CONCEPT

The concept of role is being adopted by psychologists, notably social psychologists, as is shown by examination of new books in the field. Among questions needing clarification is this: Since roles serve to pattern social interaction, how are they related to processes like competition, imitation, and accommodation? We suggest that a role involves one or more such forms of interaction but has to be described in other terms as well. The reciprocal roles of husband and wife include more than cooperation and accommodation, of employer and employee more than ascendance-submission. Roles must be delineated in terms of many kinds of interaction and of many specific duties and functions.

64 S. S. Sargent and K. Pease, Social roles and personality traits, *Amer. Psychol.*, V (1950), 302.

65 S. S. Sargent and K. P. Beardsley, unpublished manuscript.

66 G. Murphy, *Personality* (New York: Harper & Bros., 1947), chap. i.

The potential usefulness of the role concept may lead to over-enthusiasm on the part of social psychologists. After defining and describing roles, it is well to ask how much social behavior has role character and how much has not. Tentatively, we propose that while roles delimit and pattern to some degree much if not most social behavior, they are sometimes absent or minimal. For example, in emergency situations such as accident, fire, shipwreck, riot, or panic, the customary forms of social behavior break down in the face of individuals' strong emotions and self-preservative tendencies.[67]

Furthermore, some of our social behavior occurs in situations which are not highly structured—i.e., little regulated by established social norms or roles. Asking a stranger for a match or a street direction or making the acquaintance of one's seatmate in a train or plane might exemplify this, as may the interaction of passengers on a bus which is stalled for several hours during repairs. In the initial stages role factors are very unclear, but as time goes on they begin to emerge. One passenger comes to play the role of spokesman for the group, another becomes the "funny man" or the "life of the party," another the mechanical expert, and so on. Data on the emergence and change of roles in small groups is one of the major concerns of "group dynamics," a topic to which we shall return later.

We have already described several experimental or observational studies of roles. Many aspects of role behavior have research possibilities. For example, striking changes in roles often occur when situations change markedly: when the barracks door opens suddenly and the colonel appears; when the college girl stops gossiping with a group of classmates and goes to talk in dulcet tones to her one-and-only on the telephone; when the exasperated parent excuses himself politely from the guests and turns sternly to discipline his misbehaving child upstairs. Measurement of such role behavior is, of course, difficult, but it can at least be recorded and described in detail. The "Candid Mike" radio program of the late 1940's recorded the "pitch talks" of salesmen and other situationally linked verbal behavior without the knowledge of subjects. Qualitative if not quantitative analysis of words spoken, inflection, loudness, and the like would give us more accurate description of such roles.

Each culture has many dramatic and ceremonial roles, sometimes codified in a magazine like *Godey's Lady's Book* or a handbook of etiquette. Schlesinger has written a valuable and amusing historical

67 See M. Sherif and C. W. Sherif, *An outline of social psychology* (rev. ed.; New York: Harper & Bros., 1956), chap. xxi.

account of American etiquette books, depicting the changes in many of our roles over a period of two or three hundred years.[68] "Freshman week" and other initiation ceremonies are primarily devoted to establishing acceptable roles in novitiates; these offer good possibilities for research.

Another approach is to study the similarities in people's social behavior when placed in a given situation. Observing the guests' conversation and behavior at a social function helps us to map out a guest role, just as the common elements in the behavior of various hosts and hostesses suggest the pattern of the host's role. Using this technique, Waller has identified important elements of teacher and student roles in our society.[69]

One of the authors used a questionnaire to explore role behavior in a women's college.[70] Many specific items were clearly approved, e.g., having dates once or twice a week, reading the newspaper every morning, doing volunteer work in a settlement house. Others were definitely disapproved: carelessness about personal cleanliness, cheating on exams, or cultivating an English accent, for example.

That such patterns of expected behavior in their college community were not merely an expression of personal attitudes is shown in another part of the study. Here a comparison was made between qualities of student behavior most highly valued by the college community and those which the individual student herself admired. The three traits identified as most highly valued by the college community were "world-mindedness," "intellectuality," and "self-confidence"; those rating highest in the individual students' own preferences were "sense of humor," "tolerance," and "open-mindedness." There was, of course, considerable overlapping between the two scales, but enough differences to suggest that a pattern of institutionally accepted and expected behavior exists and can be distinguished from individual attitudes and values.

The role of the bureaucrat has come to the attention of social scientists.[71] Taking a somewhat different approach, another investigator used interviews to study the role of the civil servant, his subjects being administrative employees of a midwestern state gov-

---

68 A. M. Schlesinger, *Learning how to behave* (New York: The Macmillan Co., 1946).

69 W. W. Waller, *The sociology of teaching* (New York: John Wiley & Sons, Inc., 1932).

70 S. S. Sargent, unpublished study.

71 See e.g., R. K. Merton, Bureaucratic structure and personality, *Soc. Forces*, XVIII (1950), 560-68; also his *Social theory and social structure* (rev. ed. ; Glencoe, Ill.: Free Press, 1957), chaps. vi and vii; and G. Watson (ed.), Problems of bureaucracy, *J. soc. Issues*, I (1945), No. 4.

ernment.[72] He found these civil servants a congenial, efficient, secure group of middle-aged men. They did not feel themselves to be part of a governing class, identifying themselves rather with the professional group. They reported some conflict in that they were treated by the public as officials rather than as individuals. They rejected completely the idea that they were "bureaucrats," pointing out that bureaucracy is found only in the federal government! This type of study—disclosing how the members of a well-defined group conceive their role—has good possibilities.

Considerable interest has been aroused by studies of the role of the business executive—and of the executive's wife! One survey focused on one hundred executives, utilizing both interviews and tests.[73] A typical pattern was found, consisting of a high drive for prestige and achievement, a strong self-structure, aggressiveness, decisiveness, excellence at organization, identification with superiors, and impersonality with subordinates. The price paid for this included a degree of uncertainty, some fear of failure, constant activity and lack of introspection, and artificiality in social relations.

Since the executive's wife may account for the success or failure of her husband, she has also been studied. A consulting management firm sponsored a panel of executives, their wives, and management engineers which drew up a profile of the "ideal corporate wife." [74] She should be a college graduate or at least the "college type," with business experience; she should be a good homemaker, adept at social and community relations, able to keep up with and to plan for her husband and to be a symbol of everything he stands for. The study, unfortunately, did not indicate what proportion of executive wives were found to come up to these lofty standards!

SUMMARY

The concept of role, well established in sociology and anthropology, aids in describing and interpreting social interaction, especially within clearly defined groups. Role, as the social psychologist defines it, permits individual variation, stresses the perceptual factor and the reciprocal nature of the interaction, and includes "situational" roles. Most instances of role behavior involve both cultural and personal determinants, along with more temporary local ingredients. On the whole, people are unconscious of their roles,

---

[72] L. Reissman, The civil servant—a study of role conception in bureaucracy (Master's thesis, University of Wisconsin, 1947).

[73] W. E. Henry, The business executive: the psychodynamics of a social role. *Amer. J. Sociol.*, LIV (1949), 286-91.

[74] George Fry and Associates of Chicago, as described by columnist Sylvia Porter in the *New York Post*, October 25, 1954.

though everyone learns many roles in the course of his socialization. There can be conflict or at least incongruity among a person's various roles, which often occasions tension but may also be the basis for humor.

Roles provide a situationally oriented approach to personality which supplements and may help to correct the usual trait-oriented psychological approach. Much but not all social behavior has role character; role relationships are minimal in critical situations and in new and "unstructured" social groupings. Some fruitful research on roles has been done but much more is needed, and much more theorizing has to be done, before the advantages and also the limitations of the role concept in social psychology are understood.

SUPPLEMENTARY READINGS

Books of Readings

MACCOBY, E. E., NEWCOMB, T. M., AND HARTLEY, E. L. (eds.). *Readings in social psychology*, 3d ed. New York: Henry Holt & Co., Inc., 1958.
Bales, R. F., Task roles and social roles in problem-solving groups.
Gross, N., McEachern, A. W., and Mason, W., Role conflict and its resolution.
Janis, I. L., and King, B. T., The influence of role-playing on opinion change.
Sarbin, T. R., and Jones, D. S., An experimental analysis of role behavior.

LINDZEY, G. (ed.). *Handbook of social psychology*. Reading, Mass.: Addison-Wesley Pub. Co., Inc., 1954. Vol. I.
Sarbin, T. R., Role theory.

Other References

BERRIEN, F. K., AND BASH, W. H. *Human relations*, rev. ed. New York: Harper & Bros., 1957.
Interesting comments on problems of modern living well illustrated with some case material.

CAMERON, N., AND MAGARET, A. *Behavior pathology*. Boston: Houghton Mifflin Co., 1951.
This work discusses the problem of conflicts in role-taking, especially in reference to neurotic behavior.

DEWEY, R., AND HUMBER, W. J. *The development of human behavior*. New York: The Macmillan Co., 1951.
Chaps. ix-xiii contain significant data on roles of age groups.

EDITORS OF FORTUNE. *The executive life*. Garden City, N. Y.: Doubleday & Co., 1956.
What the executive is, what he does, and why he does it; a candid account of the executive role.

FARIS, R. E. *Social psychology*. New York: The Ronald Press Co., 1952.
Chaps. xi-xiii are an introduction to the subject of interaction and role, its variations, inconsistencies, and conflict.

GROSS, N., MASON, W., AND McEACHERN, A. W. *Explorations in role analysis*. New York: John Wiley & Sons, Inc., 1958.
The case study of a school superintendent as a portrait of the bureaucratic role.

HARTLEY, E. L., AND HARTLEY, R. E. *Fundamentals of social psychology.* New York: Alfred A. Knopf, Inc., 1952.
An excellent analysis of the origin, function, and patterning of roles, especially chaps. xvi and xvii.

KLUCKHOHN, C., MURRAY, H. A., AND SCHNEIDER, D. M. (eds.). *Personality in nature, society and culture.* New York: Alfred A. Knopf, Inc., 1953.
Section 5 contains three important contributions on role determinants.

LINDESMITH, A. R., AND STRAUSS, A. L. *Social psychology,* rev. ed. New York: The Dryden Press, Inc., 1956.
A very readable discussion of roles which has been influenced by Cooley and Mead as well as by some of the more recent viewpoints.

MAIER, N. F., SOLEM, A. R., AND MAIER, A. A. *Supervisory and executive development.* New York: John Wiley & Sons, Inc., 1957.
A manual for role-playing in executive development.

MEAD, M. *Sex and temperament in three primitive societies.* New York: William Morrow & Co., Inc., 1935.
A now classic picture of the variation in sex roles that makes a significant contrast to our own role patterns.

———. *Male and female.* New York: William Morrow & Co., Inc., 1949.
A discussion of sex roles in preliterate and complex societies.

MERTON, R. K. *Social theory and social structure,* rev. ed. Glencoe, Ill.: Free Press, 1957.
This collection of papers by a distinguished sociologist contains many references to the problem of role behavior.

NEWCOMB, T. M. *Social psychology.* New York: The Dryden Press, Inc., 1950.
Chaps. ix–xvii contain advanced social psychological thinking on roles.

YOUNG, K. *Personality and problems of adjustment,* rev. ed. New York: Appleton-Century-Crofts, Inc., 1952.
There are chapters on a number of age, sex, and institutional roles.

14

Leadership

Since leadership denotes a certain type of individual behavior with reference to a group, it is an excellent example of a role. Leadership—the leader-follower relationship—can be described and explained adequately only in terms of both individual characteristics and the nature of the social situation. Neither the "man" theory, emphasizing the leader's personality, nor the "times" theory, which stresses the situation, is alone sufficient. We need a field interpretation, involving "person-in-situation."

IDENTIFYING LEADERSHIP

Leadership suggests something more than mere control of a situation. The man with the machine gun who subdues an enemy squad may have perfect control of a situation; however, we would hesitate to call him a leader. A number of writers have made the distinction between "appointive" and "genuine" leadership. The former is identified with *headship;* for instance, hereditary rule, or advancement by seniority to the presidency of a board of directors. In contrast is the individual who obtains a position of leadership on the basis of a competitive election, or emerges spontaneously at the scene of an accident to solve an emergency and delegate the proper functions to other individuals, or acts as a kind of neighborhood coordinator in a slum clearance project. All of these would presumably have dynamic qualities of leadership lacking in more static headship. Then too, leadership, as defined in this chapter, implies a more specific concept than occupation of a leading role in arts, science, or some other intellectual realm. Freud, Einstein, and Frank Lloyd Wright are leaders in their respective orbits because of a set of integrated ideas that have been communicated to some extent to their colleagues and even to the public at large. However, that is not leadership in the context of personality and situational factors as utilized through the greater part of this chapter.

Some approaches to the problem. The question of what constitutes leadership qualities has intrigued philosophers, historians, political scientists, educators, psychologists, and sociologists since ancient times. Recent discussions have been oriented about certain fundamental approaches:

1. *Typology.* According to this approach, leaders are viewed as revealing a specific personality tendency that places them in a given classification, such as boss or theorist, conciliator or authoritarian.

2. *Traits.* Physical and mental characteristics are useful in identifying leaders, and all leaders must possess a number of these so-called leadership traits.

3. *Psychiatric.* According to this approach, leaders enjoy their rise to power because of certain neurotic needs and a background of infancy and childhood experiences. These may involve sibling rivalry or other competitive situations. The psychiatric orientation has generally been opposed to the trait approach in that it sees leadership as developing out of a maladjustment with the social environment rather than out of a set of optimum personality traits.

4. *Historical.* In the earlier literature it was very popular to conceive of the leader as a genius or as one in some respect endowed with almost superhuman abilities. This "great man" theory is well exemplified by Thomas Carlyle in his work, *Representative Men.* The lay public respects this approach as indicated by the decided preference given to one leader as against another, or by such remarks as: "He was born to be a leader," "He just doesn't have the touch," or "He has a spark of the divine." Certainly some leaders in the past have assumed a mythical significance. Whatever the limitations of the theory, there are individuals who have an ability at organizing persons and events that suggest more than commonplace capacities.

5. *Situational.* In contrast to the individualistic theory or theories is the situational approach, which perceives the leader as developing out of a group need. He fulfills the role that may be necessary in the realization of a task. Often it may be the breakdown of a social system, as with a war or severe depression, that precipitates the rise of a given leader. In other words, a Washington, Lincoln, or Franklin D. Roosevelt are outstanding because there was a far-reaching crisis with which they had to deal. It is the "times" rather than the "man" that made the leader.

In recent research on small groups, both group dynamics and sociometry have been oriented toward many different facets of the group and its leaders. One aspect of this has been the attempt to measure leadership in terms of the choices that followers may make and how the frame of reference or group norms may affect choices.

TYPES OF LEADERSHIP

Leadership **is a** broad and variously used term. Jesus, King George VI, Hitler, Einstein, William Lloyd Garrison, Robin Hood, Stalin, Henry Ford, Franklin D. Roosevelt—all are considered leaders. But what a varied group! About the only thing they have in common is fame—or notoriety.

Many types of leadership are suggested, in terms of origin, function, or other criteria.[1] No classification really is satisfactory. We present here a list of more or less distinguishable types of leadership, drawn from many sources. The distinctions are largely in terms of the kind of relationship existing between the leader and his group of followers.

The charismatic leader. This term, introduced by the German sociologist Max Weber, denotes leadership based on supposedly divine or supernatural power. Examples are Jesus, Mohammed, Joan of Arc, the Pope, and the Emperor of Japan before his postwar secularization. LaPiere suggests that charismatic leaders are like messiahs who emerge from movements that have taken on mystic, religious significance. Among recent charismatic leaders he places Freud, Hitler, Lenin, Sun Yat-sen, and Joseph Smith, the high priest of Mormonism.[2] Also might be added the charismatic leaders of more limited proportions like Father Divine.

The symbolic leader. A leader with prestige but little power may symbolize a nation or institution. The remaining European kings and queens have such symbolic value, as do certain other nominal heads of states, like the President of France. Grover Whalen, the official greeter for the city of New York, had a prominence largely symbolic.

The "head man." A "head man" is an institutional leader who fills a traditional position. Hereditary baronetcies and dukedoms are examples. Such positions may be filled by election or appoint-

[1] A good summary and discussion of the type approach are found in K. Young, *Social psychology* (3d ed.; New York: Appleton-Century-Crofts, Inc., 1956), pp. 270 ff.
[2] R. T. LaPiere, *Sociology* (New York: McGraw-Hill Book Co., Inc., 1946), pp. 523-24.

ment, like that of the Grand Sachem of Tammany Hall in New York City. Shortly after the recent war Winston Churchill was appointed "Warden of the Cinque Ports," an ancient and honorable post with little or no functional significance. Whatever authority a "head man" type of leader possesses derives from custom and tradition.

The expert. A Newton, Darwin, Einstein, Beethoven, Leonardo, or Shakespeare is a leader of a different sort—a creative genius in science or the arts. This leadership bases solely on achieved eminence in a certain field.

The intellectual leader or theorist. Related to the expert is the type of leader whose emphasis is in the world of ideas. Those leaders who have enormous influence on the philosophical climate of their times, like Galileo, Goethe, or Darwin, would belong to that classification. Likewise, it refers to political leaders like Jefferson and Lenin, who had definite aptitudes for government but were also concerned with ideology. Certainly, Woodrow Wilson and Adlai Stevenson reflected this theoretical approach in their writings and speeches. Not infrequently there is a problem of communication with the public. Hence, their success in reaching the group depends on a number of factors.

The administrative leader. Compared to the above types, executive leadership stems from the ability to manage, to get things done. This kind of leader is found in all societies and functions chiefly in business, government, and politics. He is necessary in social groupings of any sort; he is the man who gets people to work together to achieve the group purposes. Bismarck, Lincoln, Gladstone, and Franklin D. Roosevelt are outstanding examples. The executive leader may be democratic or authoritarian in his methods, as we shall see.

The bureaucrat. Related to the administrative leader is the bureaucrat. Max Weber suggested this type as a contrast to the charismatic.[3] However, Weber had a more flexible interpretation of the bureaucrat than the usual contemporary connotation of the term. Weber referred to the inevitable tendency toward the logic of efficiency within any large-scale organization—governmental, industrial, military, ecclesiastical, or within any institution. A bu-

---

[3] See, for a discussion of Max Weber's theory of leadership, A. W. Gouldner, *Studies in leadership* (New York: Harper & Bros., 1950), pp. 57-66. The administrative and bureaucratic leader is well presented in P. Selznick, *Leadership in administration* (Evanston, Ill.: Row, Peterson & Co., 1957).

reaucracy implies the division of tasks, services, and roles implementing production or the completion of the goal. Weber was hardly in error in predicting an increasing complexity of organization within Western society and consequently a growth of bureaucracy. Extending somewhat Weber's conception, the bureaucrat is one who stands in the chain of command and places rules and procedures above other values. If he is a leader, it is only in the upper echelons and as a kind of headship. To the point that he is a policymaker, he might be called an administrative leader rather than a bureaucrat.

The agitator or reformer. In this case leadership rests on persuasive and propagandistic ability rather than executive or administrative skill. Demosthenes, Tom Paine, William Jennings Bryan, Hitler, Huey Long, Father Coughlin, and Norman Thomas illustrate this type of leadership. Some persuasive and reformist leaders have also proved to be able administrators—Jefferson, Lincoln, Lenin, and Churchill, for example.

The authoritarian leader. Very similar to the coercive is the authoritarian leader, who is frequently contrasted to the democratic leader. These are leaders who have conscious or unconscious drives toward dogmatism, absolutism, and an inflexible exercise of power. They operate in a group or a social system that allows them autocratic control. This type of rigidity is best illustrated in totalitarian states and could hardly be better represented than by Hitler and Stalin; however different their personality dynamics, both of them exercised an arbitrary control over their followers. Likewise, the authoritarian leader is seen in the department head, the local union boss, and the industrial tycoon who jealously guard their power, make all the decisions, and hope by autocratic enforcement to hide their inner insecurity.

TRAITS OF THE LEADERS: THE TRADITIONAL VIEWPOINT

What kind of people are leaders? A number of psychologists and psychiatrists have tried to find the answer.

Mental traits. Bird has summarized twenty psychological studies designed to reveal the personality traits of leaders.[4] He found no less than seventy-nine traits mentioned, but only a third of them in more than one of the studies. Intelligence, initiative, extroversion, and sense of humor were found most characteristic of leadership.

[4] C. Bird, *Social psychology* (New York: Appleton-Century-Crofts, Inc., 1940), pp. 378-79.

A more recent survey by Stogdill covers over a hundred studies of "personal factors associated with leadership."[5] The investigators agree well in finding leaders above average in intelligence, scholarship, dependability, activity, social participation, and socioeconomic status. Stogdill found fair agreement that leaders possess initiative, persistence, self-confidence, insight, cooperativeness, adaptability, and verbal facility. As to age, height, weight, appearance, and dominance, leaders were only slightly superior to their followers. Disparity between the findings of different investigators results in part from variation in methods and terminology and in part from their use of different groups exemplifying different kinds of leadership.

Other psychologists have focused on a particular aspect of leader personality. Cox, collaborating with Terman in his *Genetic Studies of Genius,* estimated the I.Q.'s of some 300 outstanding persons by applying mental test standards to their childhood behavior as reported in history and biography.[6] She found a range of nearly a hundred points. Copernicus was placed at 105, Cromwell at 110, Lincoln and Washington at 125, Leonardo, Napoleon, and Darwin at 135, all the way to Goethe and John Stuart Mill, who were 180 and 190. Many persons would question the accuracy of these estimates, but in any event they suggest that leadership involves much more than intelligence. Another student of mental ability, Leta Hollingworth, believed a leader's intelligence is significant chiefly with reference to the level of his group.[7]

"To be a leader of his contemporaries," writes Hollingworth, "a child must be more intelligent, but *not too much more intelligent,* than those who are to be led. . . . Generally speaking, a leadership pattern will not form, or will break up, when a discrepancy of more than about 30 points of I.Q. comes to exist between the leader and the led."[8] She referred to an "optimum" I.Q. for leadership as one about 20–25 points above the average of the group.

Social factors. Several investigators studied the socioeconomic background of leaders. Cox found that 52 per cent of her eminent men and women came from noble or professional families, and another 29 per cent from semiprofessional higher business and gentry. Only 5 per cent came from families engaged in semiskilled or un-

[5] R. M. Stogdill, Personal factors associated with leadership: a survey of the literature, *J. Psychol.,* XXV (1948), 35-71.

[6] C. M. Cox, Early mental traits of 300 geniuses, in L. M. Terman *et al., Genetic studies of genius* (Stanford University, Calif.: Stanford University Press, 1926), Vol. II.

[7] L. S. Hollingworth, What we know about the early selection and training of leaders, *Teach. Coll. Rec.,* XL (1939), 575-92.

[8] *Ibid.,* p. 581.

skilled labor.[9] Laski analyzed the family background of 306 British cabinet ministers between 1801 and 1924; nearly 60 per cent came from aristocratic parentage.[10] Davis found much the same thing for 163 Communist leaders in the Soviet Union: most of them were from intellectual and professional families, while only 19 per cent came from the peasant families which made up 83 per cent of the population.[11]

Following up Cattell's studies of American scientists, Visher reported on the occupational background of the 800-odd most prominent American men of science.[12] He found the following proportions of parental occupations: professions, 46 per cent; business, 23 per cent; farming, 22 per cent; labor, 9 per cent. In an earlier study of 18,000 persons included in the 1922-23 edition of *Who's Who in America*, Visher found much the same distribution of occupational background: professional, 34 per cent; business, 35 per cent; farmers, 23 per cent; and labor, 7 per cent.[13]

Study of leader characteristics has provided some data about leaders, but it seems on the whole a rather sterile approach. Even where the findings of investigators agree, the differences between leaders and followers are small, with the possible exception of socioeconomic background. Two other approaches seem more fruitful: study of personality dynamics and of the interactional processes between the leader and his group.

PSYCHIATRIC INTERPRETATIONS OF LEADERSHIP

During World War I Sigmund Freud published a psychoanalytic study of Leonardo da Vinci, in which he stressed the great Florentine's maternal pampering and strong infantile sexual repression which "caused him to sublimate his libido into a thirst after knowledge, and thus determined his sexual inactivity for his entire later life." [14] Following this study, other psychoanalysts and many biographers applied Freudian concepts in interpreting Jesus, St. Francis, Luther, Henry VIII, Queen Elizabeth, Napoleon, Queen Victoria,

9 Cox, *op. cit.*, p. 37.

10 H. J. Laski, *Studies in law and politics* (New Haven, Conn.: Yale University Press, 1932), pp. 181-201.

11 J. Davis, A study of 163 outstanding Communist leaders, *Publ. Amer. Sociol. Soc.*, XXIV (1930), 42-55.

12 S. S. Visher, Scientists starred, 1903-1943, in *American Men of Science* (Baltimore: Johns Hopkins Press, 1947).

13 S. S. Visher, A study . . . of the fathers of subjects of sketches in "Who's Who in America," *Amer. J. Sociol.*, XXX (1925), 551-57.

14 S. Freud, *Leonardo da Vinci*, trans. A. A. Brill (New York: Moffat, Yard & Co., 1916), p. 126.

Woodrow Wilson, Lenin, and many great artists, writers, and thinkers.

Lasswell, a psychiatrically minded political scientist, used a psychopathological approach to study political leaders.[15] Seeking underlying dynamic forces, he traced many cases of political leadership to father- or brother-hatred, sex repression, feelings of guilt or inferiority, and the like. In a more recent volume Lasswell modified his earlier Freudian approach to leadership in favor of a power-seeking theme.[16] The drive for power which activates both administrators and agitators, he points out, arises from compensation for feelings of weakness and low estimates of the self.

Erich Fromm gives an interesting interpretation of Hitler and the authoritarian character structure in his *Escape From Freedom*.[17] As a result of various and continued frustrations men may come to love and crave those conditions that limit human freedom. They see life as determined by forces outside man's interests and wishes; they must submit to these forces—as personified in a leader. The authoritarian character, says Fromm, is marked by the presence of both sadistic and masochistic drives, "caused by the inability of the isolated individual to stand alone and his need for a symbiotic relationship that overcomes this aloneness." [18] Hitler personified these cravings in the German people; they felt attracted and excited by the teachings of a man who expressed what they felt. And in the Nazi state a hierarchy was created "in which everyone has somebody above him to submit to and somebody beneath him to feel power over; the man at the top, the leader, has Fate, History, Nature above him as the power in which to submerge himself." [19]

Various other psychiatric interpretations of leadership have been presented. Bluemel, for example, finds clear psychiatric syndromes in the case of various leaders. The obsessive-compulsive pattern is illustrated in Columbus, Peary, Lindbergh, Florence Nightingale, and Gandhi; this pattern typifies explorers and pioneers. It may or may not have an aggressive character; it does in such cases as those of Oliver Cromwell, John Brown, Anthony Comstock, Stalin, and James C. Petrillo. Joan of Arc and Hitler were schizophrenic; George III of England and Napoleon were manic-depressives; Mussolini was hypomanic, and Goering, a constitutional psychopath. Bluemel makes a strong plea for a "psychiatry of history":

[15] H. D. Lasswell, *Psychopathology and politics* (Chicago: University of Chicago Press, 1930).
[16] H. D. Lasswell, *Power and personality* (New York: W. W. Norton & Co., Inc., 1948).
[17] E. Fromm, *Escape from freedom* (New York: Rinehart & Co., Inc., 1941).
[18] *Ibid.*, p. 221.
[19] *Ibid.*, pp. 236-37.

It would be interesting to read a volume of history which dealt not so much with the masters of men and their feats of conquest as with the personality disorders which impelled them to their particular course of action. Such a history would deal with hypomania, schizophrenia, and similar topics, and it would mention wars and conquests only in connection with the psychoses which engendered them. In the appraisal of history hypomania is as important as gunpowder and schizophrenia may be as significant as the atomic bomb.[20]

Despite its great political value, the psychiatric approach is beset with many problems. It is very difficult to obtain data on leaders, especially those dead several hundred years, adequate enough to justify psychiatric diagnoses. The psychiatrist also is likely to select only leaders who fit plausibly into his categories. He takes Stalin, Hitler, and Gandhi; what about Eisenhower, Roosevelt, and Nehru? If psychiatric analysis does not help interpret some leaders, the psychiatrist should tell us so. The greatest danger of psychiatric interpretations is that preoccupation with personality dynamics can blind one to other aspects of the picture—especially the leader's social and cultural setting and his relationships with his followers.

THE HERO-LEADER IN HISTORY

Until fairly recently, historians, biographers, psychologists, psychiatrists, and social scientists have tended to take sides, favoring either the "man" or the "times" theory of leadership—the "hero" or the "history" interpretation. Those advocating the first theory stress the historical significance of a few great men, implying that their traits and qualities would have made them leaders whatever life situations they faced. (A few, following Galton in his early studies of genius, emphasize hereditary factors.[21] Most psychologists and psychiatrists recognize the interaction of heredity and environment in determining personality.) Brown believes the "man" theory dominates popular thinking and that of many biographers. In 1936 he wrote: "To account for the chief events of the last few decades, it is easier to attribute change to Wilson, Lloyd George, Clemenceau, the Kaiser, Lenin and others than to take into consideration all of the complex historical, economic, sociological, and psychological data involved.[22]

"Times" theorists, on the other hand, say the situation makes the man. A. G. Keller, the sociologist, puts it the following way.

20 C. S. Bluemel, *War, politics and insanity* (Denver: World Press, Inc., 1948), p. 65.

21 F. Galton, *Hereditary genius* (1869; American edition, New York: Appleton-Century-Crofts, Inc., 1870); L. M. Terman *et al.*, *Genetic studies of genius* (4 vols.; Stanford University, Calif.: Stanford University Press, 1925 *et seq.*).

22 J. F. Brown, *Psychology and the social order* (New York: McGraw-Hill Book Co., Inc., 1936), p. 330.

The great man is the product of his time and place, and his greatness consists in his insight, or luck, in producing a variation—in anticipating some massive movement that is about to take place anyhow. . . . The human agency . . . is always secondary and relatively incidental, and wholly ineffective by itself. . . . The effective cause lies in the unpremeditated movement of the masses of men. The great man interprets them to themselves.[23]

Clear cases that support this theory are war leaders. Churchill, Montgomery, MacArthur, and Eisenhower, for example, became world figures because of World War II. Or again, who would have heard of Theodore Roosevelt had not President McKinley been slain by an assassin's bullet?

History offers a number of examples of the interaction of the man and his times. Lenin for years was a dedicated revolutionary; he became a world figure only after the 1917 revolution demanded his return to Russia. Three years of depression in the United States provided a situation appropriate for the talents of Franklin D. Roosevelt. In Germany, defeat, inflation, and depression changed the setting so that the fanatically nationalist Hitler—a man long considered a mountebank—became an idol. Prewar Britain tolerated Winston Churchill, but the nation in 1940, defeated and threatened, turned to him as a peerless leader. When peace came the situation changed again, and Britain sought other leadership for her government during the postwar period. Again, the social and economic situation called him back into office in 1951.

Historical data do not furnish conclusive evidence. We cannot, of course, know whether Napoleon would have been a great leader if the French Revolution had not occurred, or whether Franklin D. Roosevelt would have become President had not depression struck us in 1929. Nor can we know whether these crucial events might have produced other leaders if a Napoleon or a Roosevelt had not been born.

THE SITUATION AS A FACTOR IN LEADERSHIP

Research is helping clarify the kind of interaction between a particular person and a particular situation which constitutes leadership. Studying boys' gangs, Thrasher showed that the characteristics necessary for leadership depend on the nature and function of the group.[24] Most gangs being action groups of some kind, the leaders are outstanding in "gameness," physical prowess, quickness and firmness of action, and persuasiveness. In sociometric studies, Jennings finds that the personality differences between leaders and other

[23] A. G. Keller, *Societal evolution* (rev. ed.; New York: The Macmillan Co., 1931), pp. 92-93.

[24] F. M. Thrasher, *The gang* (Chicago: University of Chicago Press, 1927).

group members lie not in age, intelligence, or emotional maturity but in the quality of their interactional behavior.[25] For example, leaders establish rapport with others and win their confidence; they insist on fairness and considerate behavior and take a definite stand on what they consider right. Jennings concludes:

> Leadership appears as a process in which no one individual has a major role but in which relatively many share. The superior capacity which one individual may have to recognize and respond to the needs of others does not show itself as a generalized capacity which may relate him to all other individuals. It appears in the special sensitivity between the individual and *specific* other persons, resulting in interaction between them.[26]

Gibb, interpreting the findings of the Australian Army Officer Selection Board, writes:

> These results mean that the characteristics which make for an individual's being propelled to leadership status in a group of which he is a member are any or all of his traits of personality, skill, and experience which enable him to make an interactional contribution toward the group's progress in the direction of its recognized goal.[27]

After reviewing seventy-five studies of leadership, Jenkins concludes:

> Leadership is specific to the particular situation under investigation. Who becomes the leader of a given group engaging in a particular activity and what the leadership characteristics are in the given case are a function of the specific situation including the measuring instruments employed. Related to this conclusion is the general finding of wide variations in the characteristics of individuals who become leaders in similar situations, and even greater divergence in leadership behavior in different situations.[28]

On the other hand, some studies find that the same persons emerge as leaders in different kinds of social situations. At the assessment center conducted during the recent war by the United States Office of Strategic Services, psychologists found that leadership as rated in one "field situation" correlated as highly (.41) with leadership in discussion and debate as it did with ratings in other field tests. Hence they concluded that "leadership is a relatively general trait." They noted, however, that the various situational tests may have been "sufficiently alike to elicit approximately the same be-

[25] H. H. Jennings, *Leadership and isolation* (2d ed.; New York: Longmans, Green & Co., Inc., 1947); summarized in Swanson *et al.*, *Readings* (2d ed.), pp. 312-18.

[26] Swanson *et al.*, *Readings* (2d ed.), p. 318.

[27] C. A. Gibb, The principles and traits of leadership, *J. abnorm. soc. Psychol.*, XLII (1947), 283.

[28] W. O. Jenkins, A review of leadership studies with particular reference to military problems, *Psychol. Bull.*, XLIV (1947), 75.

havior from each subject" and that staff members may have been influenced in their ratings by an over-all halo effect.[29]

Some slight tendency undoubtedly exists for those who are leaders in one situation to be leaders in others as well, depending on intelligence, insight, ability to deal with people, and the like. The more similar the two situations, the more likely an individual is to become leader in both. This conclusion is supported by an investigation by Carter and Nixon, who studied leadership among fifty pairs of boys in intellectual, clerical, and mechanical tasks. Between the fairly similar intellectual and clerical tasks, leadership correlated .64; between mechanical assembly and either of the other situations, the leadership correlation dropped to about .35.[30]

THE LEADER AND THE GROUP

The present tendency is to analyze the leader as a product of the group. In Chapter 12 it was evident that in-group formation inevitably would involve the emergence of a leader. To some degree all individuals in a group are potentially leaders. The development of a leader depends on the possession of certain skills, interpersonal relations within the group (as with all forms of behavior), and chance factors that operate to bring into focus a given individual under a specific set of circumstances. For instance, Bill Jones may be president of his high school class because his father is able to drive students to the local social functions, or Adlai Stevenson might have had a better prospect of becoming President had he not chosen to run in a period of Republican ascendency and against an adversary of almost charismatic proportions. In any case the leader cannot be understood apart from all the events that surround his accession to power and his maintenance of office once he has been installed. Whether within the small group or in the larger society, the group function and the varying reactions of members to the group function are uppermost in assessing leadership qualities, as Cartwright and Zander express it:

The "new view" of leadership stresses flexibility. Groups are (or should be) flexible in assigning leadership functions to various members as conditions change. Effective leaders are sensitive to the changing conditions of their groups and flexible in adapting their behavior to new requirements. Procedures for selecting and training leaders emphasize, accordingly, such characteristics as "sensitivity" and "readiness to take on or give up responsibilities in response to changing conditions." [31]

[29] OSS Assessment Staff, *Assessment of men* (New York: Rinehart & Co., Inc., 1948), p. 303.

[30] L. F. Carter and M. Nixon, Investigation of the relationship between four criteria of leadership ability for three different tasks, *J. Psychol.*, XXVII (1949), 245-61.

[31] D. Cartwright and A. Zander (eds.), *Group dynamics* (Evanston, Ill.: Row, Peterson & Co., 1953), pp. 537-38.

Leaders must demonstrate a versatility in handling group situations in order to be successful. In fact, an entirely different set of factors, both within the leader and his group, are involved in the achievement, as against the maintenance, of leadership. In the power structure one is aware of a constant tendency toward manipulation of events and situations for the leadership role. It may include a wide gamut of behaviors, from handshaking, throwing a succession of dinner parties, buying stock in subordinate companies, and, most important of all, effective execution of the appointed tasks.

Group structure as a factor in leadership. As with any group function, size may prove to be a determinant of how the leader performs and is accepted by the group. A study of clerical workers by Pelz found that in smaller groups, namely of ten members or less, the leader is best liked who appears to consider the individual members ahead of the organization. On the other hand, in the larger groups the leader or supervisor was preferred if he was interested in management goals as these might involve the interests of the individual workers.[32] Much the same results have been found by Hemphill in his extensive studies of leadership at the Ohio State University.[33] He found that the larger group permitted more dominance on the part of the leader. Certainly common sense observations would support this viewpoint. In the large-scale or bureaucratic type of group, the leader can make decisions with more independence than in the face-to-face groups. Leadership might be characterized as the successful attempt to retain a loyal distance.

A fundamental difference can likewise be made between leadership patterns in the *formal* versus the *informal* group. Harking back to change of attitudes and opinions, as presented in the last chapter, it was found that the small discussion group was a more effective means of opinion change than the larger group where an authority presented the subject in lecture fashion. It appears that there are markedly different problems in integration and leadership in the small informal group as compared to the large impersonal formalized organization. It was found in studies of military personnel that discussion groups led by admired and democratically chosen leaders were more successful than when the leader was not among the first choices of the group.[34]

[32] D. C. Pelz, Leadership within a hierarchical organization, *J. soc. Issues,* VII (1951), 49-55.

[33] J. K. Hemphill, Relations between the size of the group and the behavior of superior leaders, *J. soc. Psychol.,* XXXII (1950), 11-32.

[34] S. A. Stouffer and others, *The American soldier* (Princeton, N.J.: Princeton University Press, 1949), Vol. I, p. 471.

Effect of crisis. Undoubtedly an open threat to the survival of the group is an important factor in bringing out leadership tendencies. When the group's existence is in question, some member of the group is likely to assume the role of salvaging the group. A great many factors are involved, as, for example, goal potency (strength of the aims and plans of the group), interpersonal solidarity within the group, and magnitude of the threat to the group. Undoubtedly the most devoted followers are attached to leaders who have effectively solved a major crisis. Obvious examples are Franklin D. Roosevelt and Adolph Hitler, who enjoyed a charismatic role for having "solved" a depression within their respective nations. Despite the enormous differences in their personalities and in their socioeconomic reforms, both leaders were essentially products of a crisis. In the laboratory, findings are not very different; a group faced with a problem is the one most likely to choose a leader.[35]

By the same token, the leader who is unable to solve the basic problem or frustration of a group may become the scapegoat. Herbert Hoover at the time of the depression and Neville Chamberlain at the beginning of World War II were heaped with blame by their countrymen for lack of insight or failure to carry through a needed change. Bales found that in the equilibrium of discussion groups, as tension over disagreements in decision making mounted, there was a tendency to shift leaders. In the early phases of group formation there is a lack of specific role differentiation, but in the second meeting, leadership roles have emerged. The new structure may be upset in the third meeting:

Things go "from bad to worse," with a last meeting that breaks records for disagreement, antagonism, tension, perhaps tension release, and other signs of serious strains and an inability to achieve an equilibrated role structure. However, the stable structure is never, in our data, a "simply organized" one. It is rather one in which differentiated roles have appeared, in which one specialist "undoes" the disturbance to equilibrium created by another, and in turn is dependent upon another to remove the strains he himself creates—the total constellation of specialists being one which allows or aids the system to establish a full orbit in its dimensions of necessary movement.[36]

MOTIVATION OF LEADERS

One can scarcely overlook the factor of individual motivation on the part of the leader. There are ego-demands, dominance and

[35] C. A. Gibb, The principles and traits of leadership, *J. abnorm. soc. Psychol.*, XLII (1947), 267-84.

[36] R. F. Bales, The equilibrium problem in small groups in T. Parsons, R. F. Bales, and E. A. Shils, *Working papers in theory of action* (Glencoe, Ill.: Free Press, 1953), pp. 111-61. Reprinted in A. R. Hare, E. F. Borgatta, R. F. Bales, *Small groups* (New York: Alfred A. Knopf, Inc., 1955), pp. 454-55.

prestige interests, and creative needs that make leadership so rewarding. It is probable that all individuals in some sense are motivated by the desire for status, a primary basis of leadership. As fundamental as power needs are, however, there are undoubtedly limits. One experiment investigated the emergence of the leader and his enjoyment of power. On the first meeting of a given group, a leader was appointed who had practically a mean score on the leadership test. On the second and third meetings, the leader was given further support and apparently enjoyed his entrenched position. On the fourth, he was handed a disproportionately large amount of money at which point he began to recede, apparently out of embarrassment, from his leader role.[37] It appears that for most people, dominance and leadership are normal desires but only within moderation.

Whatever the needs may or may not be, the question remains whether leadership is an ability peculiar to some individuals. Although research has emphasized the situational explanation, this does not exclude the leader personality as a factor. A group of investigators explored this problem by submitting a number of Air Force men to a series of tests. One of each group satisfied a criterion that might be labeled as "greatness." The hypothesis was raised whether his choice early in the meetings was due to his own inherent superiority or whether it was due to interactional factors within the group. It was found that the leader continued in successive sessions to act as a mediator, namely, reducing interpersonal tensions. In addition he was first in "task ability" and in initiating action within the group.[38] What characteristics, then, may be identified with this leadership ability?

THE DIMENSIONS OF LEADERSHIP

Investigation continues to center on the problem of leadership traits; however, the emphasis has been in recent years on interactional or situational factors. As part of the Ohio State University studies, Halpin and Winer studied Hemphill's hypothesis of nine different dimensions of leadership:

1. *Initiation*—degree to which the leader originates new ideas or behaviors
2. *Membership*—frequency with which a leader interacts with members

37 B. Shriver, The behavioral effect of changes in ascribed leadership status in small groups. Unpublished doctoral dissertation, University of Rochester, 1952, as reported by L. F. Carter, Leadership and small-group behavior, in M. Sherif and M. O. Wilson (eds.), *Group relations at the crossroads* (New York: Harper & Bros., 1953), pp. 257-84.

38 E. F. Borgatta, A. S. Couch, and R. F. Bales, Some findings relevant to the great man theory of leadership, *Amer. sociol. Rev.*, XIX (1954), 755-59; also in A. R. Hare *et al., op. cit.,* pp. 568-74.

3. *Representation*—degree to which leader defends the group against attack and promotes the interest of the group
4. *Integration*—encouraging of pleasant group relations and reducing intra-group tensions
5. *Organization*—defining, planning, and structuring of his own and members' work
6. *Domination*—restricting behavior, opinions, and decisions of members
7. *Communication*—exchanging information with members
8. *Recognition*—engaging in behavior which expresses approval or disapproval of members
9. *Production*—setting levels and standards of achievement and encouragement of output

After extensive study of air crews, it was found that the nine qualities had to be reappraised, and four dimensions had the most validity:

1. *Consideration*—extent to which the leader had positive social relations and an understanding of the weaknesses of his men, although there was no implication of sentimentality in his relations with his followership.
2. *Initiating structure*—organizational ability, namely, "maintaining definite standards of performance," "making his attitudes clear to the crew," etc. Of the four, this appeared to be the most critical factor of leadership.
3. *Production emphasis*—stressing the meeting of schedules, extended work effort, and the like.
4. *Sensitiveness* or *social awareness*—insight into interactions between the crew and himself and within the crew members themselves—not blaming crew members for their mistakes and not making scapegoats of his subordinates.[39]

Using educational personnel, Seeman and Morris were particularly interested in status relationships in leadership. They defined leadership as that quality by which one affects others.[40] Four different dimensions by which the leader affected others were: (1) communication—the degree of upward or downward exchange of ideas, opinions, and standards within the group; (2) separatism—degree of leader's status within the group and the extent of interaction between him and the followers; (3) change—receptivity of the leader to new ideas and procedures; (4) domination—restriction of decision making and freedom of expression on part of members. It is significant that the respondents judged leadership to a large extent in terms of their own frame of reference. Respondents with higher status (principals and department chairmen) tended to rank their superiors more highly in leadership qualities than did the classroom teacher. There was marked difference of opinion regarding dom-

[39] A. W. Halpin and B. J. Winer, *The leadership behavior of the airplane commander* (Columbus, Ohio: Ohio State University Research Foundation, 1952).
[40] M. Seeman and R. T. Morris, *A status approach to leadership* (Columbus, Ohio: Ohio State University Research Foundation, 1950).

inance, namely, whether the superintendent should or should not be directive in his relations with subordinates.[41]

It appears that the search for leadership characteristics can hardly be detached from the situational approach. It is true, if pedestrian, to say that what determines the leader is the group. Within a complex culture pattern, particularly a democracy, a leader must function on a number of fronts: he must be the revered symbol and the scapegoat, the expert, and the handshaker (and at election time, the baby kisser). Nowhere is this better illustrated than in the intricate office that has become the Presidency of the United States.[42] In this case, leadership becomes by necessity a staff function—the White House staff numbers over two hundred, upon whom the executive is dependent. In addition, there is the problem of communication with the public, including the services of speech writers and coaching in television techniques. More significant, though, are the complex roles the leader must play in a wide variety of situations, peace or war, prosperity or depression. The Presidency of the United States seems to strengthen the viewpoint that leadership is more a function of the situation than of the individual personality itself.

FUNCTIONS OF THE LEADERSHIP ROLE

Leadership, then, is a form of social interaction between an individual and the members of his group. It might more properly be referred to as a "leader-follower" role. As Krout says in discussing "followership," "It is just as important to perceive how an individual becomes somebody's follower as it is to discover how one becomes somebody's leader."[43] The leader's role in a group is an interaction relationship which depends on his own personality and the needs, attitudes, and interests of his followers, always within a framework furnished by group norms. While a leader's role differs somewhat from group to group, we can describe its outstanding characteristics in terms of requirements for effective administration

[41] The empirical literature on leadership traits is steadily growing, and only the scantiest introduction to the subject has been presented in this discussion. One of the most recent studies is by Cattell and Stice, who, on the basis of results in problem-solving teams of air force and naval personnel, isolated four principal criteria of leadership: (1) *problem solving*, or intellectual ability; (2) *salient* or decisive; (3) *sociometric*, or having been chosen as a leader; (4) *elective*, actually elected as a leader. R. B. Cattell and G. F. Stice, Four formulae for selecting leaders on the basis of personality, *Hum. Relat.*, VII (1954), 493-507.

[42] L. G. Seligman, Developments in the presidency and the conception of political leadership, *Amer. sociol. Rev.*, XX (1955), 702-12.

[43] M. H. Krout, *Introduction to social psychology* (New York: Harper & Bros., 1942), p. 685.

and persuasion. The following generalizations are based on many sources, including Brown's "field-dynamical laws of leadership." [44]

1. A successful leader must have "membership-character" in the group. He cannot be an outsider; he must be regarded as one who has "the pattern of attitudes and reaction tendencies common to the group." [45] A newcomer seldom is accorded leadership. Nor is one whom the group members consider "different," as many teachers and social workers found when they sought leadership positions in the American labor movement. They were regarded as intellectuals or "white collar" professionals rather than real laboring men; officially they belonged to the group, but they lacked "membership-character" in it.

2. The leader, says Brown, "must represent a region of high potential in the social field. . . . Having high potential means that he symbolizes psychologically the ideals of all the members of the group." [46] He must have prestige and a background of achievement in the group's activities. It was no accident that the top leaders of the Communist party in Russia and of the Nazi party in Germany were persons who had suffered vituperation, imprisonment, and exile; this gave them prestige within their group. Similarly, the leaders in veterans' organizations are nearly always men who have seen combat service, not men who have "sat out the war" behind a desk in headquarters.

One important effect of prestige is to make possible members' identification with their leader, a significant emotional bond. Krout goes so far as to say, "Leaders can lead because followers identify themselves with the leaders, play their social roles through them, solve their problems with them." [47] The degree of identification with the leader probably varies widely among members of a group, depending on their needs and frustrations, but identification is an important ingredient of the relationship between follower and leader.

3. To be effective, the leader must understand his followers— their attitudes, values, fears, frustrations, ideals, and goals. This understanding may be unconscious or "intuitive," as with a gang leader. Often the leader of a large social movement, like Dr. Townsend, or of a national revolution, like Hitler, seems to have an essentially intuitive or emphatic understanding of his followers.

44 Brown, *op. cit.*, pp. 342 ff.
45 *Ibid.*, p. 342.
46 *Ibid.*, p. 344.
47 Krout, *op. cit.*, p. 687.

Leaders of large and varied groups like political parties probably
rely on reports from their field representatives or on public opinion
polls. Evidence shows that American political leaders take opinion
poll results seriously.[48]

4. A leader must formulate plans and policies in line with the
wishes and objectives of his group, yet consonant with realities of
the broad social, economic, and political situation. Hitler or Mussolini plots a war, a labor leader plans a strike, a congressman introduces a bill, or a college president announces a fund-raising
campaign, always guided by these two major considerations. In addition, the leader must be ready with alternative policies in case his
original plans do not succeed. Similarly, his efforts to win his
followers' support for a new course of action must be attuned both
to their needs and attitudes and to the broader social setting as he
understands it.

5. The leader must either be a good organizer and administrator
himself or have close associates skilled in these directions. Understanding and planning will come to nought unless machinery is
available to carry out decisions and plans. Trotsky's defeat after
Lenin's death probably resulted from his ineffectiveness as an organizer and administrator. Brilliant and dramatic, Trotsky was
no match for the methodical Stalin, who had quietly gained control
of the Communist party's machinery. Most leaders today must be
good administrators; the essence of good administration, as someone
said, is "analyze, deputize, and supervise."

6. A leader must be adaptable, able to retrench and shift his
course as emergencies arise. Unexpected events always occur; disputes and defections among followers are almost inevitable. A
successful leader foresees emergencies and prepares to deal with
them. The Nazi leaders, in their desperate game preceding the outbreak of World War II, seem to have been prepared for every possible diplomatic or military move by the other European powers.
Likewise the Soviet leaders have in recent years attempted to out-
maneuver the Western powers—with what degree of success is another question.

7. An effective leader must be adept at creating and maintaining
his group's morale in the sense of keeping individual purposes and
activities harmonious with the goals of the group. Many techniques
aid in maintaining morale. For example, constantly reiterating the
aims of the group and publicizing the progress made in achieving
them; promoting unity by stressing common dangers and devising

[48] We shall return to this subject in Chapter 16.

scapegoats; coining slogans and putting on dramatic "shows" of various sorts; providing opportunities for followers to participate and to gain prestige by holding offices, working on committees, and the like.

8. The leader should be able to reward and punish his followers as circumstances arise, and yet adhere to a consistent set of just principles. At the same time he must be prepared to play the same role in reference to himself. He must accept the judgment of the group, including the role of scapegoat, in case the group fails in some major undertaking. Kaiser Wilhelm II received most of the blame for World War I, although he happened to be on a yacht in the North Sea when the war was started. Herbert Hoover was held responsible for the Depression, even though the latter was largely to be ascribed to economic processes that had been accumulating through the decade prior to his election as President.

The above categories describe the most important features of the role of a successful executive or persuasive leader. While not all would be found in any particular case of leadership, they represent a typical or characteristic pattern.

Little has been said so far about democratic, authoritarian, or other forms of leadership. In our country, since we are a democracy, we favor democratic leadership. What advantages does it have over other forms? And how can we train democratic leaders?

AUTHORITARIAN AND DEMOCRATIC LEADERSHIP

Increasingly in recent history, there has developed a gulf between two types of leadership, namely, authoritarian and democratic. This distinction has grown out of the analysis of authoritarian personality structure and the observation of leadership in totalitarian governments. In addition, there have been the experimental studies of groups in which these two forms of social and administrative relations have been introduced. As we have seen, the authoritarian leader has been well documented: an inner lack of security frequently bolstered by an arbitrary display of strength. Characteristic of the personality are the projective and paranoid tendencies. Also, there is the tendency toward remoteness from the group, the demand to have activity and communication center on him. The stability that is seen in the group is artificial and fragile; it is maintained largely by the threat of violence. Since the eighteenth century, Western culture has not found this form of government acceptable. There have been exceptions. Among these are the German Reich under the National Socialists, Italy under the fascist corporate state of Mussolini, and Spain under Franco.[49]

One variation in the authoritarian regime as compared to the democratic is the type of manipulation that may occur in the authoritarian state.[50] Especially in the Communist regime or Marxist organization, there is a tight hierarchical structure by which any deviation or demonstration of irresponsibility or disloyalty is met with chastisement. Particularly serious is negative expression against the state or leader, although some "constructive" criticism of organizational practices is generally allowed. Elections are generally formalities.[51] That this type of control has some parallel to military leadership is not surprising. However, in a democratic framework, except for a war situation, there are administrative controls that supersede the military.

As Gibb points out, leadership is a means to an end rather than an end in itself, and democracy arrives at the problem of control under different methods, goals, and values.[52] One notes the adjustability and flexibility within a democracy. There is the more ready access to power, as the group, or the people, hold the power, and the leader acts as an agent. Locke and Rousseau, in quite different words, developed this concept in the seventeenth and eighteenth centuries. The kind of ego-involvement of a democratic leader is very different from that found in an authoritarian power. This is not to imply that there are not manipulative actions, nor occasional thrusts of arbitrary defense. However, there are checks which do not exist in the authoritarian frame of reference. At least in the democracy the leader is aware of the limits of his authority.

At the same time, it is evident that a democratic leader suffers from a lack of strength and the ability to accumulate power. Too, decision making must pass through more devious channels and hence be more time-consuming and more subject to change. The system of checks and balances and the varied interests of the group (especially in a time of crisis) make the democratic process very cumbersome, principally because of the representative nature of the leader. At the same time, the authoritarian type of leadership is exceedingly vulnerable because of the kind of crisis that may dis-

---

[49] Outside of Western culture, autocratic regimes do not have the same psychological basis. They are authoritarian, which is considered normal in their cultural milieu, though by our standards hardly desirable. Also, there is less threat to extinction, since they are not usually surrounded by democratic regimes.

[50] For a discussion of manipulation, see Gouldner, *op. cit.*, pp. 389-94.

[51] P. Selznick, *The organizational weapon* (New York: McGraw-Hill Book Co., Inc., 1952), pp. 29-36.

[52] Gibb, *op. cit.*, p. 910.

rupt the leader himself. The problem of succession, namely, who follows the leader into power, can be a major crisis in the authoritarian group.

Contrasts in systems. One of the more significant studies of authoritarian and democratic needs in leadership was made by Sanford.[53] On a scale devised to test orientation to this continuum, there were the following responses:

1. *Reaction to power, status, prestige.* Authoritarians generally preferred "status-laden leadership" and favored such "power-flavored attributes" as education, popularity, strength. The scale revealed that the nonauthoritarians were able to "take power or leave it alone." They are more likely to accept humanists and liberals as leaders.
2. *Emphasis on material support.* Interest is expressed in the relation of the leader position on vested interests of the respondent which might be termed "father-feed-me" attitude.
3. *Emphasis on love support.* Warmth and responsiveness did not appear in the value system of the authoritarians.
4. *Emphasis on in-group virtues.* There was an ethnocentric reaction; the leader must have "character" or be a "true American."
5. *Emphasis on the leader as a person.* Authoritarians look upon the leader as a special person, whereas the equalitarian responses were directed more to the social function the leader might perform. It might be expressed as a case of emotional involvement as compared to an objective appraisal.
6. *Need for cognitive structure.* There was a tendency for the authoritarian to depend on ready-made opinions, as against a freer attitude of finding things out for oneself.
7. *Relations with fellows.* There was relatively little concern with the fellow members on the part of the authoritarian's definition of leadership.
8. *Orientation to responsibility.* The authoritarian generally did not join groups, or become officers in groups they did join, and were comparatively indifferent to community interests.

Various advantages of democratic as compared with autocratic leadership patterns were demonstrated in several studies by Kurt Lewin and his associates.[54] Groups of boys functioning in a democratic "social climate" revealed, by and large, less irritability and aggressiveness and got more work done than groups of boys operat-

---

[53] F. H. Sanford, Leadership identification and acceptance, in H. Guetzkow (ed.), *Groups, leadership and men* (Pittsburgh: Carnegie Press, 1951), pp. 158-76.

[54] A good reference to these studies is R. Lippitt and R. K. White, An experimental study of leadership and group life, in Swanson, *et al., Readings* (2d ed.), pp. 340-55.

ing in an autocratic atmosphere. Autocratic leadership seemed to produce hostility toward the leader, which was displaced upon strangers or newcomers to the group. Moreover, in democratic groups the absence of the leader made little difference, while in the autocratic groups productive work dropped to a minimum when the leader was out of the room.

Such studies of eleven-year-old boys do not, of course, prove that a democratic government is superior to an authoritarian regime. Demonstration of comparative advantages and disadvantages of governmental forms on a national scale is a project to daunt even the boldest of investigators. But the studies of Lewin and his associates do indicate strikingly, in real-life situations, some of the benefits resulting from democratic leadership and some of the disadvantages of an autocratic "social climate."

SUMMARY

Leadership is a conspicuous instance of role behavior. The problem of leadership can be approached in a number of ways: by types, by traits, by psychoanalysis, by history, and by an analysis of the group or situation. The group-situational viewpoint is distinctly favored by recent empirical studies. Leader types range from the charismatic to the administrator, from the coercive to the intellectual. The type approach hardly offers explanatory concepts but does suggest an intriguing series of descriptions. Likewise, psychological studies of leader characteristics, in terms of physical makeup, intelligence, and personality traits, have disclosed few significant differences between leaders and their followers.

Psychiatric interpretations of personality dynamics help account for some but by no means all leaders and are likely to minimize influences of the social milieu. Also, there is little evidence that the critical factors or causes of leadership can be determined in that fashion. Neither the "man" nor the "times" theory, alone, explains leadership adequately; an interactional interpretation is necessary. A number of studies have been cited that indicate the relation of group structures and leadership variables. Shifts in the group, including crises, will determine the type of leadership that is acceptable to the members. All leadership qualities must be evaluated in a situational context.

Several aspects of successful leadership can be described: membership character, high potential or prestige within the group, understanding of group members' needs, formulation of appropriate plans, organizational skill, ability to create and maintain morale, and discrimination to promote intergroup harmony. Democratic leadership may be compared to authoritarian types of control by means of both historical and empirical studies.

SUPPLEMENTARY READINGS
Books of Readings

MACCOBY, E. E., NEWCOMB, T. M., AND HARTLEY, E. L. (eds.). *Readings in social psychology,* 3d ed. New York: Henry Holt & Co., Inc., 1958.
Haythorn, W. W., The effects of varying combinations of authoritarian and equalitarian leaders and followers.
Hollander, E. P., and Webb, W. B., Leadership, followership and friendship; an analysis of peer nominations.
Jennings, H. H., Leadership and sociometric choice.
Lippitt, R., and White, R. K., An experimental study of leadership and group life.
Merei, F., Group leadership and institutionalization.
BRITT, S. H. (ed.). *Selected readings in social psychology.* New York: Rinehart & Co., Inc., 1950.
Murray, H. A., and MacKinnon, D. W., Assessment of OSS personnel.
Williams, S. B., and Leavitt, H. J., Group opinion as a predictor of military leadership.
LINDZEY, G. (ed.). *Handbook of social psychology.* Reading, Mass.: Addison-Wesley Pub. Co., Inc., 1954. Vol. II.
Gibb, C. A., Leadership.

Other References

BROWN, J. F. *Psychology and the social order.* New York: McGraw-Hill Book Co., Inc., 1936.
The Lewinian field theory as applied to social science; chap. xvii presents his topological approach to leadership.
CARTWRIGHT, D., AND ZANDER, A. (eds.). *Group dynamics.* Evanston, Ill.: Row, Peterson & Co., 1953.
Part VI offers five empirical studies of leadership, preceded by a well-integrated introduction.
DOOB, L. *Social psychology.* New York: Henry Holt & Co., Inc., 1952.
Chap. xi has some interesting excerpts on leadership.
GILBERT, G. M. *The psychology of dictatorship.* New York: The Ronald Press Co., 1950.
The author presents some interesting hypotheses about the nature of the Nazi leaders on the basis of his experience with the Nuremberg trials.
GOULDNER, A. W. *Studies in leadership.* New York: Harper & Bros., 1950.
A series of readings on both the situational and personal factors, together with some excellent text material.
GORDON, T. *Group-centered leadership.* Boston: Houghton Mifflin Co., 1955.
A readable account on the "new" approach to leadership and leadership training.
GUETZKOW, H. (ed.). *Groups, leadership, and men.* Pittsburgh: Carnegie Press, 1951.
Several informative papers including studies of naval leadership.
JENNINGS, H. H. *Leadership and isolation,* 2d ed. New York: Longmans, Green & Co., Inc., 1950.
A stimulating presentation of research in the area by an outstanding sociometrist.

LaPiere, R. T. *A theory of social control.* New York: McGraw-Hill Book Co., Inc., 1954.
A study of status and power relationships of society with some remarks on the problem of leadership.

Lasswell, H. D. *Psychopathology and politics.* Chicago: University of Chicago Press, 1930.
An absorbing, if not altogether valid, account of the psychoanalytic approach.

Lindgren, H. C. *Effective leadership in human relations.* New York: Hermitage House, Inc., 1954.
A popular treatment of the subject.

O.S.S. Assessment Staff. *Assessment of men.* New York: Rinehart & Co., Inc., 1948.
The account of leadership tests during World War II.

Selznick, P. *Leadership in administration.* Evanston, Ill.: Row, Peterson & Co., 1957.
An exceptional presentation of leadership and bureaucracy, drawing from administrative practices in both government and industry.

Young, K. *Social psychology.* 3d ed. New York: Appleton-Century-Crofts, Inc., 1956.
Chap. xi is a most readable account on theories and types of leadership.

15

The Person and the Group

Before describing several social phenomena, it is appropriate to pause for a moment to evaluate our orientation in social psychology. It has been evident to this point that we have a discipline that is largely a fusion of psychology and sociology and that it provides a framework in which various social problems can be conceptualized.

We began by discussing major determinants of human social behavior in terms of cultural and social influences on personality. We saw that an individual learns, through his social experience, not only habits, but attitudes, values, and social norms. We discussed motives and frustration in relation to social behavior, and the central, directive aspect of personality known as the ego or self. We studied communication and social interaction as to both content and function, and the part played by social groups in patterning an individual's social behavior. We stressed the importance of roles in regulating interpersonal relationships and described an important example of role behavior—leadership—in some detail.

INTERPRETING SOCIAL BEHAVIOR

The field theory approach. How can these facts and theories be utilized in understanding social phenomena and in dealing with social problems? The answer, we believe, is a "field theory" interpretation. Field theory derives largely from Kurt Lewin's *topological psychology*, which represents all behavior as interaction between a person and his environmental situation. "Every psychological event," wrote Lewin, "depends upon the state of the person and at the same time on the environment, although their relative importance is different in different cases." [1] Lewin is not speaking of the physical or objective environment but rather the "psychological" or "behavioral" environment—the situation as a person perceives and understands it, as it is related to his needs. The person and his psychological environment make up his "life space" or "psychological field." [2] Interpersonal conflicts can be viewed in terms of topological concepts, such as "life space," "valences," "barriers," "permeability," "reality levels," and the like. [3] Lewin's field theory, despite certain criticisms, has made an enormous contribution to our understanding of the individual in the social order and of social problems in general.

Following Brown, who first applied the field concept to social psychology, [4] we find "field theory" valuable in that it brings into one conceptual framework individuals with their varying personalities, characteristics of the social situation, and depending on the above, each person's way of perceiving or interpreting the situation. Thus a social psychological analysis of, say, a dispute between two leaders in a social movement will involve knowledge about (1) the personality of each man, (2) their roles, and the norms of the group, and (3) the way each of them perceives the events leading up to the altercation.

The primary function of a scientist is to describe phenomena, but he is interested ultimately in their prediction and control. Essentially he is concerned with discovering their determinants or causes. The chemist or physicist is relatively successful in analyzing materials and events into their components or determinants. The psychologist or social scientist, however, works with more complex subject matter enbodying a bewildering number of variables. He must be content with identifying, describing, and measuring only the most potent or salient determinants—those whose effect is most significantly related to the behavior being studied, whose presence or absence makes a really big difference.

An example from clinical psychology may clarify the meaning of potent or salient determinants. When a clinician deals with a problem child, he studies the case history, which contains all rele-

[1] K. Lewin, *Principles of topological psychology* (New York: McGraw-Hill Book Co., Inc., 1936), p. 12.

[2] *Ibid.,* chaps. iii, iv.

[3] For a discussion of these concepts, in addition to Lewin's own writings, see M. Deutsch, Field theory in social psychology, in G. Lindzey (ed.), *Handbook of social psychology* (Reading, Mass.: Addison-Wesley Pub. Co., Inc., 1954), Vol. I, pp. 181-222. See also C. S. Hall and G. Lindzey, *Theories of personality* (New York: John Wiley & Sons, Inc., 1957), chap. vi.

[4] J. F. Brown, *Psychology and the social order* (New York: McGraw-Hill Book Co., Inc., 1936).

vant information about the child—his medical history, I.Q., school record, family background, and various other kinds of data. The clinician's aim is to discover, from the case history and from interviews with the child and his parents, the significant determining factors, after which a diagnosis is made and therapy prescribed.

He is aided in his analysis and diagnosis by his own experience and by knowledge of the findings of other workers in the field. Suppose, for example, the case is one of disobedient, aggressive, incorrigible behavior. The clinician hypothesizes "compensation for inferiority or insecurity" and looks for possible determinants such as physical weakness or ugliness, neglect or rejection by the parents, a broken home or one shattered by dissension between parents. He looks for these rather than for "bad instincts," a low I.Q., or inadequate religious training because research has shown that the former rather than the latter conditions are the more significant determiners of problem behavior. Actually, the clinician probably unearths a complex of causal or at least correlated factors, in which one or two stand out. Thus his problem child may wear glasses, masturbate, dislike his teacher, and hate his sister, but the really salient causal factors center about neglect or rejection by his parents. So the clinician attempts to deal with this basic feature of the problem rather than with symptoms or less relevant factors.

Our analysis of social behavior and social interaction has centered about the search for outstanding determinants. We find three broad categories: *personality,* the *social situation,* and the individual's *perception* of the situation. But we can be more specific. The aspects of the person most significantly related to social behavior are attitudes, values, habits, motives, frustrations, and ego-involvements. Crucial features of the social situation are the established roles and norms, including mores and sanctioned forms of social interaction. The way persons perceive a situation depends upon both personality and situation; it is the most immediate determiner of social behavior, as we have seen. This is not in any way to imply a lack of importance in hereditary factors; however, they are relatively less crucial in explaining the present social behavior than are situational factors.

Strictly speaking, of course, these three causal factors cannot be separated; they are highly interrelated. But it is frequently possible to distinguish between them in terms of relative potency or significance.

Consider, for example, social behavior which occurs outside clearly defined social groups. Here the situation is not highly "structured" in terms of prescribed roles and norms; personality variables have greater scope. In our relations with friends and acquaintances, with neighbors, with storekeepers and clerks, we may be cheery, loquacious, and sympathetic or serious and close-lipped. Either type of behavior is permissible; its form is determined largely by the personality trends of the participants. Or again, in any kind of social situation, extreme or unusual behavior usually reflects personality variables. Thus the singletracked conversation of a bore stems from his intense motivation or interest in a particular direction. A person's egocentric or dominating behavior derives in all probability from frustration and insecurity, just as noisy and bawdy behavior traces frequently to intoxication. In a word, when an individual has intense convictions, attitudes, or needs, they play an important part in determining the nature of his social behavior.

On the other hand, social situations may be highly structured or patterned as to expected and permissible behavior. When roles are rigidly prescribed and norms of conduct binding, little or no scope is provided for personal predilection. When the national anthem is played at a concert, everyone rises and stands at attention. The behavior of both hostess and guests at a reception is patterned chiefly in accordance with well-understood roles. Or again, at an indignation or protest meeting, each person's understanding of the feelings of the majority is usually sufficient to prevent any individual expression of critical or adverse reactions. In these cases the social norms are paramount and act as the real determinants of behavior.

Hanks has commented on a dilemma in interpreting social behavior.[5] "On the one hand," he says, "we receive accounts from psychologists of individuals in our culture whose reactions are clearly interpretable in terms of such psychological variables as weak ego formation, inadequate identification with the parent of like sex or inadequate development due to certain childhood traumas." On the other hand, continues Hanks, we get reports of primitive cultures "where life processes appear to be rigid and clearly predetermined by institutional patterns. . . . We have the psychologists' picture of personal flexibility, reaction against the established pattern, and choice governed by psychological motives. We have the ethnographer's picture of institutions mainly determined by geographical and sociohistorical factors, serving the needs of individuals yet alterable only at the peril of social collapse."[6]

[5] L. M. Hanks, Jr., The locus of individual differences in certain primitive cultures, in S. S. Sargent and M. W. Smith (eds.), *Culture and personality* (New York: Viking Fund, Inc., 1949).
[6] *Ibid.*, p. 107.

Hanks concludes that the raw data of anthropology and psychology are the same, and that behavior in a society falls along a continuum. "At one end all dimensions of behavior are invariable. At the other end all dimensions are variable. If the behavior of any society were itemized in such a manner and distributed along this line as a scale, it would probably fall in some kind of heap toward the middle." [7]

Our analysis harmonizes well with Hanks's. Somewhere between the extremes of the group-determined and the individually determined comes most social behavior. Consider, for example, the typical committee meeting. Such a group is structured as to its objective and its chairman, but the members' personalities also function significantly. One member is better equipped in knowledge, another more skilled in argument; one likes to make an impression, another plays the clown, while still another prefers to be an observer rather than a participant.[8] In most informal social gatherings the interests of those present determine whether they play games, dance, listen to music, or just talk. However, such social affairs are usually somewhat structured as to their general nature (e.g., polite social evening, a "gab-fest," or a convivial party) and as to host-guest or possibly other roles. The relationship between a young man and woman may follow a rigid pattern, as with the dating behavior found on some college campuses.[9] Or it may be relatively uncontrolled, as with an unattached male and female swallowed up in the anonymity of a big city. But usually it follows a general pattern sanctioned by the groups to which the parties belong, with considerable variation depending on the two personalities involved.

How does the perceptual factor—the *definition of the situation*—fit into our scheme? We repeat, it always is present and always operates as the final link in the chain of behavioral determinants. We tend to overlook it in situations where social norms are rigid, as at a church service, funeral, formal meeting, or ritual of any kind. In such cases conformity occurs because everyone perceives these situations in approximately the same way. But where social behavior is more variable, as in a new, informal, or "unstructured" situation, understanding of the participants' differing perceptions is necessary to an explanation of their behavior.[10]

7 *Ibid.*, p. 119.

8 Cf. discussion of the dynamics of the discussion group in Chapter 21 below.

9 W. W. Waller, The rating and dating complex, *Amer. sociol. Rev.*, II (1937), 727-34.

10 For the tendency to act in a given mode in a particular situation, Coutu has coined the term "tinsit" (*tendency in a situation*). Particularly important in his theory is the selective nature of behavior: "the situation is the immediate determinant of all behavior." W. Coutu, *Emergent human nature* (New York: Alfred A. Knopf, Inc., 1949), p. 16.

Suppose, for example, that a group of businessmen have met to set up a chamber of commerce for their community. To interpret the social behavior which occurs, we draw upon many kinds of data: the stated purpose of the meeting, the role of the chairman, the already established relationships among the members, their outstanding personality characteristics, and so on. But our analysis would not be complete without knowing which men construed the plan as a valuable civic enterprise or as a means to increase their own business profits or as a way to gain prestige in the community, or which men considered it a futile effort but put in an appearance lest they be criticized as noncooperative. The existence of such diverse individual interpretations exerts a most significant influence upon intragroup behavior, and their total pattern is reflected in the functioning of the whole organization.

The search for salient determinants. One of the social psychologist's major tasks is to discover the significant determinants of social behavior; many have already been disclosed. The studies of frustration and aggression, for example, showed that much of the behavior we call "aggressive" stems from certain dynamic tendencies in individuals. Sherif's experiment on the autokinetic phenomenon demonstrated that social norms exist and that they may influence behavior greatly. Lewin and his associates indicated how a democratic or autocratic "group atmosphere" could effect the interpersonal behavior of group members. The recent studies of ego-involvement seem to have identified another variable whose determining influence is great. We are just beginning to comprehend the nature and implications of social roles; research here is in its infancy. With this increasing knowledge of determining factors we can describe and interpret social behavior more accurately and progress further toward the prediction and control to which every scientist aspires.

The problem of perception presents grave difficulties, as mentioned earlier. Obviously a person's interpretations depend upon his own attitudes and needs and also upon the character of the "objective" social situation. At the present time, however, we are unable to describe such "definitions of the situation" at all accurately from our knowledge either of personality or of the social situation or of both together. It is very doubtful, for example, whether we could describe, in the illustration given above, the businessmen's private interpretations on the basis of what we knew about their attitudes, their experiences, their reputations, the stated purposes of the group, or the events occurring at the organizational meeting. Apparently many factors as yet unknown to us play a part.

Other instances can be given of the difficulty in predicting subjective reactions. The Joneses know Mr. A. and Miss B. and decide these two young people would like each other. So they arrange a meeting and are surprised and a little nettled to find that Mr. A. and Miss B. don't "click." That is to say, they do not manifest the expected favorable interpretations of each other. One might also ask why a large number of undecided voters finally cast their ballots for a given candidate. Why, for example, in 1948, contrary to the predictions of the pollsters, was Truman elected President? Or why did Negroes who voted Democratic in 1952 turn to Eisenhower in 1956? We simply do not know, though many plausible speculations have been advanced by those who studied the election carefully. Some day we hope to have more complete answers to these questions.

Direct attempts are sometimes made to discover a person's private interpretations, but their validity is affected by the individual's inability or unwillingness to disclose his thoughts and feelings. Rogers recently pointed out that one great advantage of nondirective therapy is the insight it gives the clinician into the private world of the patient.[11] "Client-centered therapy," he says, "has led us to try to adopt the client's perceptual field as the basis for genuine understanding. In trying to enter this internal world of perception, not by introspection, but by observation and direct inference, we find ourselves in a new vantage point for understanding personality dynamics. . . ."[12] Through clinical methods and through improved techniques for measuring attitudes and values, and for assessing motives, frustrations, ego-involvements, and conceptions of the self, along with greater knowledge of the processes of perception, we should make progress toward better descriptions and evaluations in this highly subjective but important area.

We have seen in the preceding chapters what a multitude of factors influence personality. Besides biological and temperamental forces, these include various sociocultural systems: family pattern, class structure, and other aspects of our institutional life. Yet crucial problems remain as to precisely how the individual acquires his motives, attitudes, and values, and how his perceptions and learnings are formed. Although we have presented earlier in the book a number of theories such as conditioning, canalization, and the like, fur-

---

[11] C. R. Rogers, Some observations on the organization of personality, *Amer. Psychologist*, II (1947), 358-68.

[12] *Ibid.*, p. 368.

ther research and interpretation are required. Certain recent studies, like James Olds' *The Growth and Structure of Motives*[13] and Herbert A. Simon's *Models of Man*,[14] offer considerable hope that some of the gaps in our understanding may be filled in.

We conclude that a "field" approach to social behavior, whatever its difficulties, is superior to either a personality-oriented or a situationally oriented approach. A case of youthful rebellion against parental authority cannot be explained solely on the basis of the personalities involved or solely in terms of family relationships and norms of behavior. Both kinds of data are essential, along with some understanding of how the parties concerned perceive the situation. Nor can we, shifting to a larger framework, account for the rise of Hitler *either* in terms of widespread frustration in Germany *or* in terms of German "character structure," though both of these played a part. So did the fanatical zeal of Hitler and the astute propaganda of Goebbels. Our best interpretation involves the interaction of all these potent variables of personality and social setting.

To what degree we will employ empirical methods and in what situations a more interpretive approach may be appropriate depend on the particular problem. Probably the understanding of most social phenomena involves both of these techniques—experimentalism or operationalism on one side and *Verstehen* (in the more recent jargon, i.e., *understanding*) on the other side. Certainly both orientations are found in the context of field theory.

SUPPLEMENTARY READINGS
Books of Readings

LINDZEY, G. (ed.). *Handbook of social psychology.* Reading, Mass.: Addison-Wesley Pub. Co., Inc., 1954.

Deutsch, M., Field theory in social psychology. Vol. I.

Other References

BERRIEN, F. K., AND BASH, W. H. *Human relations: comments and cases*, rev. ed. New York: Harper & Bros., 1957.

Part II contains a number of interesting case studies that portray the individual and his problems in a social setting.

COUTU, W. *Emergent human nature.* New York: Alfred A. Knopf, Inc., 1949.

An excellent presentation of the field approach regarding the self, roles, and other personality variables.

DIAMOND, S. *Personality and temperament.* New York: Harper & Bros., 1957.

The latter chapters of this study analyze some of the situational aspects of personality.

13 Glencoe, Ill.: Free Press, 1956.
14 New York: John Wiley & Sons, Inc., 1957.

GERTH, H., AND MILLS, C. W. *Character and social structure.* New York: Harcourt, Brace & Co., Inc., 1953.
Two sociologists have given a rich interpretation of the social factors in human behavior.

KRECH, D., AND CRUTCHFIELD, R. S. *Elements of psychology.* New York: Alfred A. Knopf, Inc., 1958.
Chapters viii (the self), x (motives), xi (frustration of motives), and xxv (the individual in society) present a field theory approach.

LEWIN, K. *Dynamic theory of personality.* New York: McGraw-Hill Book Co., Inc., 1935.
———. *Principles of topological psychology.* New York: McGraw-Hill Book Co., Inc., 1936.
———. *Field theory in social science* (ed. by D. Cartwright). New York: Harper & Bros., 1951.
Lewin is largely responsible for field theory; the first two books present the outline; the third book, which appeared posthumously, deals largely with applications.

LINDESMITH, A. R., AND STRAUSS, A. L. *Social psychology,* rev. ed. New York: The Dryden Press, Inc., 1956.
This text, as with certain other newer presentations in social psychology, has been influenced by G. H. Mead, Cooley, and Thomas, as well as later interactional viewpoints.

MURPHY, G. *Personality.* New York: Harper & Bros., 1947.
Still unsurpassed in its fusion of biological, psychological, and social influences. His chapter on "field theory" has been very influential in the viewpoint of the present volume.

Part IV

UNDERSTANDING SOCIAL PHENOMENA

Throughout this volume we have been interested in how the individual is socialized within a matrix of sociocultural influences. We have examined the problem of dynamics, particularly motives and perception, and social learning. We studied how social behavior is patterned through language, through sanctioned processes of social interaction, and through norms and roles deriving from group membership. We have seen that a field approach to social behavior is essential, including as it does personality factors, situational determinants, and the participating individuals' perceptions and interpretations.

In this section we shall discuss a broad range of social phenomena: public opinion, propaganda, crowd behavior, and, most important, the possibilities for change within our society. As Western society is generally caught in the web of a number of social movements and mass phenomena, these problems seem especially relevant to the social psychologist. In these areas social scientists hope to be able to make predictions and offer some possibilities of control. We shall describe each of the social phenomena in some detail, then attempt to interpret it in the light of both personality and situational determinants. Whenever data are available we shall discuss practical applications, i.e., efforts to predict social behavior and to solve social problems.

16

Public Opinion

Historically speaking, public opinion became an increasingly important social phenomenon as feudalism and monarchy gave way to democracy. With the invention of printing, later the movies and radio, and now television, means were at hand for influencing and crystallizing public opinion.

WHAT IS PUBLIC OPINION?

Everyone thinks he knows what is meant by "public opinion," yet few can define it satisfactorily. Sociologists give us a key when they speak of a "public" as a social group concerned with certain values or interests. Thus we may speak of the movie public, the sporting public, the baseball public, the racing public, and so on, each consisting of anywhere from a few hundred to several million individuals. A public can be very specific or quite general, depending on the number of individuals and interests that are involved. However, if we say *the* public, by itself, we usually mean a fairly inclusive group of publics in the community, state, or nation which are concerned with some issue. Though the members of a public have some common concerns, they may differ from each other in many ways—on political or social issues, or on matters artistic, athletic, scientific, or philosophical. Depiction of these differing reactions reveals public opinion, according to some social psychologists. Thus Doob says that "public opinion refers to people's attitudes on an issue when they are members of the same social group." [1] Others, particularly sociologists, noting that intragroup differences

[1] L. W. Doob, *Public opinion and propaganda* (New York: Henry Holt & Co., Inc., 1948), p. 35.

lead to discussion and often to "consensus" or agreement, stress interaction as the basis of public opinion. Reuter, for example, has defined public opinion as "a consensus or judgment arrived at through conflict and discussion on the basis of facts."[2] Still another view, somewhere between those expressed above, is advanced by Daniel Katz. He believes we should not speak of "public opinion" unless it has become somewhat crystallized. "Because a problem is of practical importance or possible political interest does not mean that there is a public opinion about it. Public opinion arises only after people have either lived through common experiences or have been subject to an educational or propaganda campaign. Only then are they ready to take a stand upon an issue."[3] One fairly simple way to test crystallization of public opinion is by the percentages of "no opinion" answers in polls. If this figure is high, there is doubt that the poll is really measuring public opinion.

Whether or not "public opinion" implies that consensus or crystallization has taken place, it is a very complicated phenomenon. We need to know what group is involved with respect to any given issue. Often the issue itself is complex and involves more than appears on the surface. Then, too, why do people respond to the issue? Many such relevant questions can be raised. In addition we may think of public opinion as expressed or unexpressed in terms of overt statements or behavior. When people are enthusiastic or indignant, their attitudes are more likely to be externalized, their behavior is more likely to be an expression of their attitudes. When institutional controls are strong, the expressed opinions may have little relation to the personalized or private opinions. A number of years ago Schanck managed to obtain both public and private expressions of opinion on certain issues such as baptism, card-playing, prohibition, and politics.[4] Many persons expressed one attitude in public (when with members of their own community) and quite another attitude in private (with only the experimenter). For the whole group of subjects, the privately expressed attitudes followed a more or less normal curve of distribution, whereas those publicly expressed concentrated at one position, resembling a "J-curve" of conformity.[5]

Doob also makes another distinction, between *actual* and *latent* public opinion, the latter referring to attitudes which are

[2] E. B. Reuter, *Handbook of sociology* (New York: The Dryden Press, Inc., 1941), p. 148.

[3] D. Katz, The interpretation of survey findings, *J. soc. Issues,* II:2 (1946), 37.

[4] R. L. Schanck, A study of a community and its groups and institutions conceived of as behavior of individuals, *Psychol. Monogr.,* XLIII:2 (1932).

[5] See Chapter 13.

dormant or which have not yet jelled. During peacetime, for example, public opinion about war may be considered latent, since the issue of war is not present or imminent.[6] The dormant attitudes are evoked if and when armed conflict occurs. This question of the contrast between existing surface attitudes and those which are deep and latent has been raised by others in criticizing opinion polls, as will be seen.

Opinions and attitudes. Opinions arise when the reactions of individuals to their world are differentiated or varied. One hardly has an opinion about mathematical data as they are too axiomatic and exact to allow for much variation. Nor is the term appropriate to a magnificent sunset or to knowledge of the deity; these experiences and concepts involve too deep an emotional involvement and are not amenable to scientific or logical proof. Again, there can hardly be differences of opinion about the mores; these are by definition sufficiently fixed that opinion appears irrelevant. Moreover, public opinion can exist only very tenuously in a totalitarian society, since power is not vested ultimately in the people.

There is danger, as Floyd Allport notes, in conceiving of public opinion as a thing; he speaks of the "fiction of an ideational entity." Nor is public opinion an entity above and beyond the individuals who express it.[7] Harking back to the discussion of the "crowd mind" in Chapter 11, it is apparent that public opinion is rooted in the reactions of individuals; it can have no real existence apart from the members of the group. It consists of attitudes and opinions which persons have learned.

These two concepts, attitude and opinion, are often used synonymously, although psychologists commonly make a distinction between them. Attitudes are treated as fairly consistent and lasting tendencies to behave in certain ways—primarily positively or negatively—toward persons, activities, events, and objects. Some would say they reflect the deeper, inner core of personality. Opinions are considered closer to the conscious level, more transient, and more likely to be verbalized than are attitudes. Some, indeed, consider opinions the verbal expressions of attitudes. Depending on his experience, one may have attitudes toward anything—airplanes, theosophy, swimming, Irishmen, or redheaded women. Opinions, however, center about controversial matters, possibly because these call forth decision and a statement of one's feelings and beliefs.

6 Doob, *op. cit.*, p. 40.

7 F. H. Allport, Toward a science of public opinion, *Pub. Opin. Quart.*, I (1937), 7-23. Reprinted in D. Katz, D. Cartwright, S. Eldersveld, and A. M. Lee (eds.), *Public opinion and propaganda* (New York: The Dryden Press, Inc., 1954), pp. 51-61.

While attitudes may be either general or specific, opinions tend to be specific. For this reason, as McNemar comments: "The typical attitude study involves a scale or battery of questions . . . whereas the typical opinion, particularly public opinion, study leans heavily on a single question for a given issue." [8]

Nevertheless, the distinction between attitudes and opinions is rather arbitrary. Usually the two go together. One's reaction to Mr. Tweedlehicks for mayor depends on how an individual feels toward people in general, his interest in politics, his feelings about this candidate's voice and appearance as well as his opinions about the candidate's party and voting record. And it is not inconceivable that the most important factor of all is how he felt, as a boy, toward an uncle whom Mr. T. resembles! More often than not, an individual's opinion that a certain political party is corrupt harmonizes with his unfavorable attitude toward it—and together they predispose him to vote against it. Sometimes, however, the opinion or belief is at variance with the attitude. A white girl sincerely believes Negroes are as good as whites and dislikes discrimination and segregation. Yet she cannot bring herself to dance with a Negro. Her more or less rational belief or opinion (which, incidentally, is probably a recent acquisition) conflicts with underlying attitudes, learned in her childhood, which are basically emotional.

Thus a person's opinions and attitudes develop within a social setting, namely his membership and reference groups—his family, gang, club, school, church, and community. His viewpoint, his frame of reference, his value system, and his philosophy of life all reflect the norms which he has learned in these groups. And, as noted earlier, attitudes and opinions tend to become standardized within the group, that is, to take the form of "stereotypes." [9]

FORMATION OF PUBLIC OPINION

Kimball Young notes four stages in the process by which public opinion evolves: [10]

1. There is an issue or problem which involves a considerable part of the community.
2. Next follow preliminary and exploratory discussions as to its seriousness, with exposition of the various facets of the problem.
3. Then comes a specifying of the solution to the problems, with groups taking sides, and often some appearance of crowd behavior.
4. Finally, consensus evolves, or at least a majority opinion is derived.

[8] Q. McNemar, Opinion-attitude methodology, *Psychol. Bull.*, XXIII (1946), 290.
[9] See Chapter 8.
[10] K. Young, *Social psychology* (3d ed.; New York: Appleton-Century-Crofts, Inc., 1956), pp. 334-35.

Often the process is interrupted and does not proceed to the final stage. Complete crystallization of public opinion depends upon many factors, some of them individual, and some of them subcultural, such as age, sex, social class, and related variables like education, intelligence, and occupation. But even more, in complex modern society, the quality and the development of public opinion depend upon the mass media: the press, radio, television, and motion pictures.

The press. For several centuries, the most decisive influence in the shaping of current opinion has been the press. Despite the inroads of other media, the newspaper, together with magazines and books, has been paramount. The influence of the newspaper is in part attributable to the variety of publics it reaches through its editorial page, fashion, society, sports, and financial sections, in addition to the more obvious news items. With its headlines and pictures, its cartoons and other features, not to mention its sometimes lively and emotionalized language, the press could hardly fail to evoke an intense degree of identification.[11]

Nevertheless, despite its great influence upon public opinion, the newspaper cannot prevail against strongly held views. This was emphatically true in the New Deal era when Roosevelt continued to be re-elected despite the opposition of some 80 per cent of the metropolitan press of the country. Of course, at the same time that editorials, cartoons, and columnists were castigating Roosevelt and the New Deal, the news columns had to present more or less accurate accounts of national news which kept people informed. No doubt it was this primary informational function which Thomas Jefferson had in mind when he maintained that "If left to decide whether we should have a government without newspapers, or newspapers without a government, I should not hesitate for a moment to prefer the latter." Since the time of Jefferson, newspaper and magazine publishing has become big business, and it is increasingly difficult for opposing views to find a channel of communication. With the decreasing number of dailies and weeklies in our country, one wonders whether the press is the solid bulwark of freedom our early leaders envisaged.

Radio and television. During the twenties, radio became an important force in public opinion, and despite the mushrooming of TV since 1950, it has remained a primary medium. For the housewife with her domestic chores, for the motorist, and for many

[11] See Edwin Emery and H. L. Smith, *The press and America* (Englewood Cliffs, N. J.: Prentice-Hall, Inc., 1954) for a good recent account.

manual workers on their jobs, the radio retains its influence. The fact that the number of radio channels was physically limited brought the issue of censorship to the fore, as did the fact that radio was listened to in the bosom of the family, by both adults and children. Codes were soon adopted by the producers to forestall direct action on the part of government. A Federal Radio Commission was instituted in 1927 to supervise the content of radio programs; it was followed in 1934 by the Federal Communications Commission, which was given licensing power. There was not only the problem of advertising and its effects on audiences, but the hotter issue of how to handle controversial topics. There was lengthy dispute over whether a radio broadcasting company (that is, the station or licensee) had the right to present issues from his own personal viewpoint. The Mayflower case upheld this prerogative on the part of the licensee. Generally speaking, however, radio has avoided the editorializing so common in journalism. Frequently, it appears to be impartial, as during recent political campaigns when relatively equal time has been granted to rival candidates. Undoubtedly, the pressure of the Federal Communications Commission is a relevant factor.

Social scientists have been greatly interested in the relative strength of radio versus newspapers in the determination of public opinion. It is significant that in the Erie County, Ohio, study made during the presidential campaign of 1940, those who listened most to radio also ranked highest in time spent reading newspapers. As to which medium had helped them to make their decision, 68 per cent of the interviewees responded "radio" while 66 per cent mentioned the newspaper. However, when they were asked for the "most important" source radio held a clear lead by 38 per cent to 23 per cent.[12] When vote decisions changed, going from Republican to Democratic, radio was more effective. while the reverse process (Democratic to Republican) was attributed more to the influence of the press. This may be explained by Roosevelt's magnetic radio personality and the pro-Willkie sentiment of the press.[13] For most individuals, however, there was little change in political preference during the June to November period of the campaign. In other words, it was only a minority whose opinions were determined or crystallized by mass media during the heat of the campaign. The public apparently chose newspapers and radio programs for the purpose of seeing and hearing their own ideas reflected. This

12 P. F. Lazarsfeld, B. Berelson, and H. Gaudet, *The people's choice* (2d ed.; New York: Columbia University Press, 1948), pp. 126-27.
13 *Ibid.,* pp. 129-33.

kind of reinforcement helps to explain the process of opinion formation and suggests that the relation of the individual to mass media is a reciprocal one.

The impact of television on our society is summarized by Coffin, who draws upon several dozen research studies.[14] In 1955 about two thirds of all homes in the United States had TV sets, and the figure was expected to reach 80 to 90 per cent within a few years. In general, according to this survey, TV homes tended to be of higher income and occupational status, and of larger family size. The average set, it found, was in use about five hours per day; radio listening and book and magazine reading were reduced. TV tended to keep the family together in a passive way. Attitudes of both parents and children toward TV were generally favorable. The lower status groups were more enthusiastic and showed greater effects of TV in their lives. Apparently the upper income group owned TV sets but chose in many instances to restrict their viewing time.

In another recent study, respondents reported less interest in hobbies on the part of TV viewers and a definite attachment to a variety of programs, especially those dealing with fantasy identifications. Although there seemed to be a minimum of TV interference with personal habit routine, frustration was found to occur between family members in the choice of a program.[15] (TV manufacturers are capitalizing on conflict between members of the family in their campaign to put second and third sets in the American home.)

To understand the effects of TV on politics, considerable research needs to be done. Both parties made use of TV in the election of 1952, when candidates and other key figures began to receive professional coaching in television techniques. A study of the effects of television on Ohio voters showed that panel members believed TV had influenced them considerably, although it was not proved that this influence had been decisive.[16] Apparently TV is more important with respect to the personalities of candidates than to the issues of the campaign.[17]

The educational possibilities of TV were signalized by the FCC's allotment, in 1952, of 258 TV channels for educational purposes. While relatively few of these have been put into operation, evidence

14 T. E. Coffin, Television's impact on society, *Amer. Psychologist*, X (1955), 630-41.

15 R. V. Hamilton and R. H. Lawless, Television within the social matrix, *Pub. Opin. Quart.*, XX (1956), 393-403.

16 J. C. Seibert *et al.*, *The influence of television on the election of 1952* (Oxford, Ohio: Oxford Research Associates, 1954).

17 *Ibid.* See also A. Campbell, G. Gurin, and W. E. Miller, Television and the election, *Scientific American*, CLXXXVIII (1953), 46-48.

exists as to the real teaching value of television.[18] This medium offers a tremendous range, both as to content and method, for extending classroom influence. In fact, its positive features—despite dangers of standardization, loss of spontaneity and of personal interaction—may help to meet the crisis caused by the teacher shortage.

Perhaps the best examples to date of opinion formation through TV are found in the Kefauver crime investigation committee of 1951 and the Army-McCarthy hearings of 1954. Probably the reason, as Wiebe notes, is that TV provides the viewer with an intimate and realistic frame of reference as compared with the printed page:

> Among the mass media, television, with sight, sound and now color, approaches the vividness of immediate reality. Radio, with its spoken language, while less vivid, still can create the illusion of experience within one's intimate world. Print, with its double system of symbols, tends to be perceived in the distant frame of reference.[19]

Whether the vividness and apparent reality of TV makes for greater *neutrality* or *objectivity* than the press, however, is open to question. A study of "MacArthur Day" in Chicago found that the TV camera indirectly structured the viewer's perceptions into the form which seemed appropriate to the communicating source. The individual sees the world through the TV screen which of necessity prevents a total perception. As the researchers comment:

> Above all, a more careful formulation of the relations among public opinion, the mass media, and the political process is vital for the understanding of many problems in the field of politics. The reports and telecasts of what purports to be spontaneous homage paid to a political figure assume added meaning within this context. The most important single media effect coming within the scope of the material relevant to the study of MacArthur Day was the dissemination of an image of overwhelming public sentiment in favor of the General. This effect gathered force as it was incorporated into political strategy, picked up by other media, entered into gossip, and thus came to overshadow immediate reality as it might have been recorded by an observer on the scene. We have labelled this the "landslide effect" because, in view of the wide-spread dissemination of a particular public welcoming ceremony the imputed unanimity gathered tremendous force. This "landslide effect" can, in large measure, be attributed to television.[20]

Motion pictures. Despite a sharp drop in movie attendance from 1949 to 1953, when the novelty and convenience of TV cap-

[18] See G. J. Wischner and I. H. Scheier, Some thoughts on television as an educational tool, *Amer. Psychologist*, X (1955), 611-14; also other articles in the same issue.

[19] G. D. Wiebe, A new dimension in journalism, *Journalism Quart.*, XXXI (1954), 414. See also G. D. Wiebe, Response to the televised Kefauver hearings; some social implications, *Pub. Opin. Quart.*, XVI (1952), 179-200.

[20] K. Lang and G. E. Lang, The unique perspective of television, *Amer. sociol. Rev.*, XVIII (1953), 11. See also their article, The inferential structure of political communications; a study in unwitting bias, *Pub. Opin. Quart.*, XIX (1955), 168-83.

tured the entertainment field, the movie audience has been partially recaptured. Approximately fifty million persons occupy theater seats every week. In addition, those who prefer, for one reason or another, the privacy of their automobile in approximately four thousand drive-in theaters, possibly comprise a new group equal in size to that which had fallen prey to television.[21] Middle-class individuals attend movies more often than those in the lower class, and persons under twenty-five attend three times as often as those over fifty.[22] The marked effect of motion pictures is due to the intensity of sight and sound, with their real life quality, plus the advantage of a live audience and the value of escaping from home and everyday affairs. With their enlarged screens, movies make the identification process easier than does the more limited screen of television. The impact is heightened by the presence and reciprocal influence of fellow spectators. Since the material of the movies is largely fictional it has a greater effect on values and attitudes than it does on specific social and political opinions. Nevertheless, in recent years there has been an increasing trend toward depicting broad social problems—from psychoanalysis to religion, from international relations to drug addiction. For example, in the years 1947 to 1949 a number of films on race relations appeared: *Pinky, Lost Boundaries,* and *Home of the Brave* on the Negro; *Gentlemen's Agreement* and *Crossfire* on the relations of Gentile and Jew. Although not all of these were box-office successes, Hollywood was not completely discouraged in its effort to produce more "serious" films. More recently, in 1956-57 several films were focused on social problems: *Edge of the City, Something of Value,* and *A Hatful of Rain.* Despite the continuing number of low-grade productions, several critics have commented on the gradual improvement in the quality of films since the end of World War II. This is probably due to the gradual rise in the educational level of our population, the competition from foreign films and from television, and more enlightened leadership in some quarters of Hollywood.[23]

Experiments have been directed to the problem of opinion change through the motion picture medium. Probably the most

21 See W. Albig, *Modern public opinion* (rev. ed.; New York: McGraw-Hill Book Co., Inc., 1956), p. 413.

22 L. A. Handel, *Hollywood looks at its audience* (Urbana, Ill.: University of Illinois Press, 1950), pp. 94-108.

23 "Television and other recent social changes have been causing major concern to movie producers," says Bosley Crowther in Communique from Hollywood and Vine, *New York Times Magazine,* Feb. 3, 1957. He notes a new sense of discrimination on the part of the public, which makes box office success hard to predict. Hence movie production has become more of a gamble, with fewer pictures made and a driving ambition to make "jackpot" films.

extensive research was done on the *Why We Fight* orientation films shown to our armed forces during the war. Many variables were found to affect the spectator's receptivity to the communicated message. The attitudinal base was important, that is, the attitudes deriving from his early life and from the lectures and other orientation materials he was receiving. Social background and intellectual differences were critical. Time factors were significant in changing attitude and opinion. Generally, films such as *The Battle of Britain* produced more increase in factual information than change in opinion.[24] When films dealing with Negro themes were played in the South, the audiences apparently saw in the pictures what their past experience had conditioned them to see; there was no basic change in their perception of the Negro and his problems. Of course, one should distinguish between short-term and long-term effects; it could be that no immediate change in attitude or opinion was elicited, but the viewing of these films might be one factor of many helping to produce a new outlook in the South. In any case, we need more empirical information on the effects of movies as well as of other mass media.

Mass media and public opinion. The causal relation between mass media and political opinions is not easy to establish. In the 1948 campaign, it was found that the more the "media exposure" (i.e. reading the paper or listening to the radio) the more likely a person was to vote for his traditional party and the more surely he went to the polls.[25] In the 1952 campaign, on the other hand, the picture was different: the more one was exposed to mass media, the more likely he was to vote Republican.[26] The reasons for this change are complex and not entirely clear.

An important factor in public opinion formation is the role of the *opinion leader*. This may be a well-known industrial, political, or social leader, but more frequently it is not. It is rather an informal leader who acts as a link or communicator between the media themselves and his associates in the neighborhood, club, or at the workbench. According to one sociological interpretation:

. . . the role of the media in influencing opinions does not end with direct exposure. In the relationship between the media of communication and personal conversation another arrangement facilitating opinion development has been noted. This relationship introduces the notion of the opinion leader who

24 C. I. Hovland, A. A. Lumsdaine, and F. D. Sheffield, *Experiments on mass communication* (Princeton, N. J.: Princeton University Press, 1949), pp. 247-83.

25 B. Berelson, P. F. Lazarsfeld, and W. N. McPhee, *Voting* (Chicago: University of Chicago Press, 1954), p. 244.

26 A. Campbell, G. Gurin, and W. E. Miller, *The voter decides* (Evanston, Ill.: Row, Peterson & Co., 1954), pp. 30-32.

upon being exposed to material from the formal media passes it on to associates who do not use the media so frequently in the particular area of content in question.

This "two-step flow of communication" describes the role in which the media of mass communication are perhaps most effective in the opinion-forming process. This effect is achieved through providing key people with symbol experience that may be stored and exploited in the right social situation. There are "opinion leaders" in all social groups and for all social topics, from politics to fashions and the weather. The conditions under which "opinion leaders" operate to select and pass on material from the mass media need to be clarified with further research. The "two-step" situation would seem, however, to provide the motivating ingredients for effective symbol transmission from the mass media since it involves personal contact and a social situation that readily permits of group identification or recognition.[27]

In an analysis of voting in Elmira, New York, it was found that these leaders, in comparison with those who were not leaders, were most interested in the election, had a higher score on the information index, and generally had more definite opinions on a variety of issues. Furthermore, the leaders were strategically located and were in a position to speak with individuals of various social ranks. It is not surprising that the voters "who talked politics the least agreed with their friends the most." [28] In their total effects, the opinion leaders at the informal levels seem to have far more influence than the less articulate and less available community leaders like the mayor, bank president, industrial director, or chairman of high status clubs.

POLLING PUBLIC OPINION

A person's opinions and attitudes do not, *ipso facto,* determine his behavior. As we have seen, social behavior is a function of individuals' personality variables operating within a framework of social norms and roles, always affected by their perception of the situation. However, it has been found that an understanding of people's opinions and attitudes often makes possible prediction of their behavior, particularly in situations like voting where they must choose between two or three alternatives. This discovery led psychologists and social scientists to become extremely interested in public opinion polls and attitude scales.

Historically, straw votes taken just before elections in the United States go back as far as 1824.[29] By the close of the last century many

27 G. A. Lundberg, C. C. Schrag, and O. N. Larsen, *Sociology* (New York: Harper & Bros., 1954), pp. 493-94.

28 Berelson *et al., op. cit.,* pp. 108-13.

29 See G. Gallup and S. F. Rae, *The pulse of democracy* (New York: Simon & Schuster, Inc., 1940), chap. iii, for a brief description of early polls. See also C. Robinson, *Straw votes* (New York: Columbia University Press, 1932).

newspapers were conducting polls, usually in connection with elections. In discussing methods used, Gallup and Rae comment wryly that, "Occasionally, early sponsors failed to appreciate the distinction between a public-opinion survey, a popularity contest, and a subscription-raising device." [30]

Soon magazines followed suit, notably the *Literary Digest*, which began in 1916 to do large-scale polling before each presidential election. Forecasts made on the basis of these polls were quite accurate. In 1928, for example, a Hoover victory was predicted with less than 5 percentage points of error in the estimated Republican popular vote.[31] In 1932 the *Digest* predicted the division of the popular vote within 1.4 percentage points.[32] The *Digest* kept increasing the size of its sample in order to improve the accuracy of its forecast.

In 1936 no less than two million ballots were returned, which gave the Republican candidate, Alfred Landon, a majority of 54 per cent and a victory in thirty-two states, with 370 electoral votes. But unfortunately for the *Literary Digest*, Roosevelt was re-elected with a popular majority of 62.5 per cent and a sweep of forty-six states with an electoral vote of 523 out of a 531 total! The blow was mortal; the *Digest* went out of business in a few months. What could have gone wrong?

The answer was given by George Gallup, Elmo Roper, Claude Robinson, and other statistically minded students of public opinion whose activities had expanded in the 1930's. These men had discovered that the key to successful polling is not large numbers of ballots, but careful sampling of the population. They saw that the *Digest's* techniques were erroneous, in that they relied far too heavily upon lists of telephone subscribers and automobile owners—in other words, upon people in higher income brackets. The controversial nature of the New Deal had produced a political alignment in which lower-income persons were strongly for Roosevelt and those with higher incomes were predominantly against him. Hence the old hit-or-miss sampling techniques, which had worked reasonably well through 1932, failed completely in 1936. The story goes that Gallup enraged the editor of the *Literary Digest* by stating in July, 1936, that its poll would select the wrong man, with a ma-

---

[30] Gallup and Rae, *op. cit.*, p. 37.

[31] *Ibid.*, pp. 40-41.

[32] L. Rogers, in *The pollsters* (New York: Alfred A. Knopf, Inc., 1949), chap. xii, has called attention to the distinction between "percentages" and "percentage points." If for example a certain vote of 40 per cent is predicted and the actual vote is 44 per cent, this is a *10 per cent error*, though it is only an error of *four percentage points*. It should not be called a "4 per cent error."

jority of about 56 per cent—a prediction which was within two percentage points of the *Digest's* final figures.[33]

Thus the scientific sampling procedures of opinion polling seemed dramatically validated by the middle 1930's.

PRINCIPLES OF SCIENTIFIC POLLING

Any scientific poll must be based upon a representative sample of the population, that is, a sample which corresponds closely to the total group being studied. Experience has shown that the sample must be representative primarily in respect to geographical and rural-urban distribution, race, and economic status. Account is also taken frequently of age and sex representation. Other variables, like religion, education, national background, and occupation, are usually not controlled, since it is assumed that they will approximate the census distribution if the first-mentioned factors are controlled. Actually, there has tended to be overrepresentation in most polls of the better educated and of those in professional and managerial occupations.[34]

The two common sampling procedures are the *quota* or "quota control" and the *area* method. In the first case interviewers are instructed as to the sex, age, occupational and other attributes of their selection of respondents. Thus an interviewer might be told to question thirty respondents, to select half from among persons under forty, to assure an equal sampling of men and women, and so on. This procedure has been criticized for permitting error through giving too much leeway to the interviewer. Under the area sampling or "specific assignment" method, representative localities within a city, state, or the whole country are chosen, and the interviewer is told, for example, to call at every fifth house, or to interview every tenth person. Thus possible bias or error of judgment in selection on the part of the interviewer is reduced. However, the method is relatively expensive as it may necessitate a number of visits to the home before the respondent is reached. Because of its somewhat higher validity, this method is preferred to the quota technique.

The second consideration in scientific polling is size of the sample. Interestingly enough, this does not have to be very large if the questions are asked of a really representative cross section. It has been found that a sample of five thousand is sufficient for correctness within an estimated error of about plus or minus 2 per cent.

---

[33] *Ibid.,* pp. 46-47.

[34] H. Cantril *et al., Gauging public opinion* (Princeton, N. J.: Princeton University Press, 1944), chap xi.

Tables have been drawn up by Wilks [35] to show the size of the sample necessary to achieve a certain degree of predictability.

For example, there are ninety-nine chances in one hundred that a sample of five hundred which yields 60 per cent "Yes" answers will be accurate between the limits of 54 and 66 per cent. When the breakdown of the vote is between 50–50 and 70–30, the margins of error for various sizes of the sample are approximately as follows:

Number Cases in Sample	Estimated Error
50	± 18%
100	± 13%
200	± 9%
500	± 6%
1,000	± 4%
3,000	± 2.5%
10,000	± 1.5%

If the distribution of the vote is still more uneven than 70–30, the margin of error becomes smaller than indicated above.

Several empirical studies have been done to test the validity of small samples. For example, it was found that carefully selected samples of about two hundred cases yielded an error of less than 5 per cent in predicting the results of a county, a state, and a national election.[36] However, samples of three hundred or less can be greatly affected by various unpredictable influences and are not generally trustworthy or useful to the investigator of public opinion.

Construction of the questionnaire. One important step in the polling process is the type of questionnaire and the kind of items that are selected. Generally, the procedure is not unlike that of measuring attitudes. In constructing a questionnaire the choice is generally made between two different types of responses: (1) the open-end question (the interviewee provides his own answer), and (2) the scaled or predetermined response (yes–no type of question). The advantage of open-end questions is that there is an opportunity for the respondent to express any nuance of opinion he may have. This technique is especially valuable in testing the climate of opinion. It allows the investigator to know the various facets of reactions to a given idea or fact. Hence it is a critical part of the pretesting phase. It is generally difficult to use in any large scale testing because of the problem of scoring and deriving any norms for purposes of comparison or correlation.

Scaling, or the polling type of question, may take a variety of forms, as pointed out in Chapter 8. These may range from yes-no

[35] S. S. Wilks, Confidence limits and critical differences between percentages, *Pub. Opin. Quart.*, IV (1940), 332-38.

[36] Cantril *et al., op. cit.*, chap. xii.

responses to more complex scales. Naturally the validity of these questions depends largely on the wording. It is essential to avoid "loaded" questions, that is, questions that suggest a certain answer to the respondent. It requires the utmost skill to devise items that are neutral and avoid eliciting a stereotype in the interviewee's interpretation.[37] For example, a study done by the American Institute of Public Opinion in mid-1941 demonstrates the prestige effect resulting in one case from the use of President Roosevelt's name:

(A form) So far as you, personally, are concerned, do you think President Roosevelt has gone too far in his policies of helping Britain, or not far enough?

Too far	20%
About right	57
Not far enough	17
No opinion	6

(B form) So far as you, personally, are concerned, do you think the United States has gone too far in helping Britain, or not far enough?

Too far	15%
About right	46
Not far enough	32
No opinion	7 [38]

While differences as great as this seldom occur as a result of using a prestige-bearing name, the use of emotionally toned stereotypes is almost sure to affect the results.

Interviewing. In certain areas of opinion measurement, particularly market research, a major problem has been the lack of training on the part of interviewers. First of all, the interviewer must be able to establish rapport and secure the cooperation of the respondent. An interviewer must be skilful in communicating effectively with the subject and must be able to rephrase an item so that it will be meaningful to the respondent, as the latter may have educational or other background deficiencies. Considerable skill is required in rephrasing so that the original meaning of the question is not altered. He must be able to record the responses accurately, and must, of course, be aware of the various scientific considerations: representativeness of the sample, and the ability to vary his interviewing techniques to whatever subcultural or practical situation that may appear, and yet retain their validity and reliability.[39]

37 For further discussion see M. Jahoda, M. Deutsch, and S. W. Cook, *Research methods in social relations* (New York: The Dryden Press, Inc., 1951), pp. 423-62.

38 Cantril *et al., op. cit.,* p. 39.

39 Jahoda *et al., op. cit.,* pp. 464-92. For further data, see L. Festinger and D. Katz, *Research methods in the behavioral sciences* (New York: The Dryden Press, Inc., 1953), chaps. v, vi, and vii.

In summary, the general procedure in conducting opinion research is (1) to make a pilot study of a small group or subsample, most likely with open-end questionnaires; (2) to interview a larger sample with poll or "fixed" response items, namely, with a standardized questionnaire; (3) to study a small subsample with open-end probing type of questions on some aspect or hypothesis of the larger study; and (4) to interpret the findings in view of other opinion surveys.

Gauging intensity of opinion. One possibility in polling techniques is to discover the intensity of opinions. As Katz puts it, "To interpret poll results adequately it is necessary to know whether an expressed attitude represents a superficially held view which may be discarded the next moment or whether it reflects a cherished conviction which will change only under unusual pressure." [40] Some experimentation has been done in investigating intensity, which suggests that the best method is merely to ask the subject how strongly he feels about the question—whether he feels very strongly, fairly strongly, or is indifferent. [41]

This is, of course, only a very rough way of determining the relative strength or intensity of attitudes. The self-rating method shows a slight relationship between strength of attitude on certain questions and type of response on others. For example, in a 1941 study respondents were asked whether they were willing to fight or have a member of the family fight. "Yes" responses among those rating themselves as strong isolationists were 28 per cent, moderate isolationists 35 per cent, and weak isolationists 39 per cent. Among those rating themselves as strong interventionists the "Yes" percentage was 82, moderate 64, and weak 60. [42] On other questions in the same study the relationships were not so clear. Such evidence, while interesting, hardly seems to justify the large-scale employment of intensity measures.

Panel studies. Another device to increase the effectiveness of opinion polling is the panel—a representative group which is interviewed repeatedly over a period of time in order to study the changes of opinion occurring. Despite obvious advantages, this technique has one danger, as Doob indicates: members of the panel become self-conscious and therefore unrepresentative as they anticipate being interviewed again. [43]

40 D. Katz, in Cantril et al., op. cit., p. 51.
41 Ibid., chap. iii.
42 Ibid., p. 58.
43 Doob, op. cit., pp. 176-77.

Lazarsfeld, Berelson, and Gaudet made the first widespread use of the panel method in their study of the 1940 presidential campaign in Erie County, Ohio.[44] They compared a panel of six hundred, who were interviewed once a month from May to November, with three equivalent groups each reinterviewed only once. They found that the distribution of Republican and Democratic votes was not affected by repeated interviews. (However, the interest of the panel members became greater than that of control group members and a higher proportion of them voted in the election.)[45]

The most striking use of the panel method was in the Elmira, New York, study in which *process analysis* was systematically followed in a sample of over one thousand cases. Opinion changes during the months before the election were studied, particularly those involving the choice of a candidate and the pressures and cross-pressures operating. Tradition was found to be important in determining stability of decisions; for example, a Republican vote intention held by a Protestant is more stable than one held by a Catholic because of the traditionally Republican heritage of the former group—in that particular part of the country, at least.[46] The panel technique seems well suited to probe into developments over a period of time with more sensitivity than ordinary polling shows.[47]

Panel studies, and polling in general, have been criticized by some psychologists, notably Asch, because they fail to offer a truly predictive science. Speaking of the Erie County study, he maintains that the researchers confuse psychological and sociological variables, at one time treating the individual, at another time focusing on the group:

> The studies examined fall short of the needs of psychological investigation in an essential way. They deal mainly with the statements of relation between sociological facts at a particular period of history. Their variables are not psychological processes or sociological constructs but specific historical events. The Republican and Democratic parties are not laws of nature; and the act of voting is a highly specific event embedded in numerous local conditions. Consequently the findings are valid only for a particular point of time.[48]

Furthermore, as voting decisions are always subject to change, he maintains, they cannot be the proper subject of scientific study;

[44] P. F. Lazarsfeld, B. Berelson, and H. Gaudet, *The people's choice* (New York: Duell, Sloan & Pearce, Inc., 1944).

[45] *Ibid.*, pp. 85-86.

[46] Berelson *et al., op. cit.*, especially chap. xiii.

[47] See also S. M. Lipset, P. F. Lazarsfeld, A. H. Barton, and J. Linz, The psychology of voting, in G. Lindzey (ed.), *Handbook of social psychology*, Vol. II (Reading, Mass.: Addison-Wesley Pub. Co., Inc., 1954), pp. 1124-76.

[48] S. E. Asch, *Social psychology* (Englewood Cliffs, N. J.: Prentice-Hall, Inc., 1952), p. 556.

forecasting in public opinion surveys is very different from true scientific prediction. Despite some sympathy with Asch's views, however, the present authors believe that historical events are not incapable of scientific treatment. At least, certain generalizations can be made that have predictive value within limits. As to the psychological, sociological, or other type of method employed, we revert to the theme in the first chapter that no one method is superior to others in the social sciences in attempting to explain behavioral events.

The depth interview. Can we conclude that opinion polls, even though they do not predict actual behavior, at least indicate people's opinions, attitudes, interests, values, and other *tendencies to behave* in certain ways? Some critics think not. Waller and Lee, for example, maintain that the polls tap only the conscious, verbalized, surface layer of the personality. They favor some type of "sentiment analysis" which would probe deeper and reveal the unconscious, unverbalized, and tabooed motives and other dynamic tendencies which underlie the surface attitudes and opinions.[49] Unfortunately, of course, any such procedure is difficult, expensive, and time-consuming; to do sentiment-analysis of a sizable representative group would be a Gargantuan undertaking. In many ways, the "depth interview" technique employed by Merton and others represents an attempt in this direction—a sort of compromise between opinion polling and a psychiatric interview.[50]

One variation of the depth interview was employed by Smith, Bruner, and White in a penetrating analysis of the attitude and opinion structure of ten young men.[51] Of primary interest was the development of their opinions toward the Soviet Union: what events in their psychological worlds had conditioned them toward or against the Soviet Union in the postwar years? A number of research techniques were used including projective tests and a "stress interview." A new device was the "Information Apperception Test," in which the subject was presented with a "fact" about Russia and asked to explain and interpret it. Several "strategies" were disclosed, such as denial, skepticism, isolation, and misunderstanding, which remind one of the clinician's defense mechanisms. A major conclusion is that the correlation between opinion and personality dynamics is not high. Two people may hold similar views of the Soviet Union, though their personalities are quite dissimilar.

[49] W. W. Waller and A. M. Lee, in a privately distributed paper.

[50] This technique is illustrated in R. K. Merton, *Mass persuasion: The social psychology of a war bond drive* (New York: Harper & Bros., 1946).

[51] M. B. Smith, J. S. Bruner, and R. W. White, *Opinion and personality* (New York: John Wiley & Sons, Inc., 1956), p. 251.

Sociological analysis. Anthropologists and sociologists have worked out various techniques for discovering the basic values and attitudes in the cultures and communities they study. For example, the Lynds, as was mentioned earlier, presented the dominant values of a fair-sized American community in a long chapter entitled "The Middletown Spirit." [52] Their methods included searching of records, arranging dozens of formal and informal interviews, analyzing newspaper files, and making hundreds of personal contacts in homes, stores, clubs, schools, churches, and other social situations. Many of the values and attitudes they report operate unconsciously, below the surface, and could not be readily studied by the polling technique. Two such items from their list are the belief that "American ways" are better than "foreign ways," and the suspicion or dislike of striking innovations in art, ideas, religion, education, and so forth. Direct questioning could hardly elicit these underlying attitudes because even if the subjects were aware of them, the admitting of such views seems intolerant or reactionary.

A related method of opinion study that appeared in Europe some decades ago is the geographical, or ecological, approach. Perhaps the first good example of this was Andre Siegfried's study of voting trends in parts of France on the eve of World War I.[53] The method has been adopted elsewhere, notably in the United States. Among others, Key has employed an ecological method in studying issues, voting trends, and sectional loyalties.[54] In the South he finds that public opinion and political solidarity are held together by the "Negro problem." The "solid South" was once united by economic issues and a common viewpoint on a number of issues; many compromises are made today but ideology remains rigid on the color front.

Whereas Key examines and analyzes election returns, other students use polling methods with ecological emphases. A good instance is Samuel Lubell, who used spontaneous interviewing in the home, the factory, on farms, and in front of churches. His "over-the-fence" type of approach enabled him to predict the Eisenhower victory in 1952. On the eve of the election, Lubell flatly declared:

Enough persons who voted for President Truman in 1948 have told me they intend to vote Republican this fall so that Gen. Eisenhower should win the election.[55]

[52] R. S. Lynd and H. M. Lynd, *Middletown in transition* (New York: Harcourt, Brace & Co., Inc., 1937), pp. 402-86.

[53] See R. Heberle, *Social movements* (New York: Appleton-Century-Crofts, Inc., 1951), pp. 218-22.

[54] V. O. Key, *Politics, parties, and pressure groups* (3d ed.; New York: The Thomas Crowell Co., 1952), pp. 261-70.

[55] *New York World-Telegram and Sun,* November 6, 1952.

He went on to say that most of the pollsters and forecasters were hedging; his house-to-house conversations with voters all over the country persuaded him that the swing against the Democrats took place long before the campaign started. His conversational framework allows a good deal more latitude than does the distinctly quantitative emphasis of the more conventional polls.[56]

Mass observation. At the beginning of World War II a new technique—"mass observation"—was tried out in England.[57] Harrisson, its leading proponent, believed that what people say to a poll interviewer may represent their "public" opinion, but not necessarily their "private" opinion. So he and his coworkers set about listening to conversations, observing people's reactions to movies and radio programs, noting the topics of sermons and newspaper and magazine articles, and even checking the writings and drawings on the walls of buildings!

Doob, who served in the Office of War Information, describes several mass observation techniques of public opinion study used in the United States during World War II.[58] A number of key individuals throughout the country served as a "correspondence panel" and reported to the OWI how people in their communities were reacting to major issues. Many government agencies analyzed the content of newspapers, radio programs, and other mass media. Elaborate studies were made of foreign radio broadcasts to determine public opinion trends in enemy, neutral, and allied countries. Attempts were made to study letters from abroad which had been intercepted by censors. At the same time that wartime rumors were being counteracted, they were also studied as indices of what people considered important yet about which they were confused.[59] Though these were pioneering attempts with little precedent, made under wartime conditions, they were considered of value in revealing the state of morale at home and in foreign countries.

RECENT HISTORY

The 1948 election. Because of their success in predicting election results, public opinion polls in the United States were widely considered, until November, 1948, reliable and valid indicators of public opinion. Critics of the polls were not lacking, however;

---

56 See S. Lubell, *The future of American politics* (New York: Harper & Bros., 1951); also his The politics of revenge, in *Harper's Magazine*, April, 1956.

57 T. Harrisson and C. Madge (eds.), *War begins at home* (London: Chatto & Windus, Ltd., 1940).

58 Doob, *op. cit.*, pp. 194 ff.

59 See Chapter 18 for further discussion of rumor.

Rogers and Borneman, among others, expressed their doubts that the polls really indicated the state of public opinion.[60] Notes of warning were also sounded by a few psychologists. Doob, for example, noted that "there is one pernicious error which must be avoided if the validity of polls is to be properly understood. That error consists of calling all polls valid because pollsters are able to predict election results. Polling during political campaigns is a very special and unique case of measuring public opinion. Polls, consequently, cannot coast along on the prestige they have acquired from this single instance." [61] But by and large, the polls were regarded as an accurate and sensitive measuring device which had achieved the status of a science.

When Gallup, Roper, and Crossley, heading our three largest polling organizations, agreed in predicting the victory of Dewey over Truman in 1948, the election was considered a foregone conclusion. Magazines ran pictures and articles about Dewey, "our next President," speculated about his cabinet, and sympathized with Truman. President Truman's prediction that the pollsters' faces would be red after the election merely evoked tolerant smiles. The election results were "amazing" and "incredible" precisely because everyone had placed so much faith in the poll predictions. The predictions and returns were as follows:

	Percentage of total presidential vote				
	Dewey	Truman	Thurmond	Wallace	Total *
National vote	45.1	49.5	2.4	2.4	99.4
Crossley	49.9	44.8	1.6	3.3	99.6
Gallup	49.5	44.5	2.0	4.0	100.0
Roper	52.2	37.1	5.2	4.3	98.8

* Exclusive of percentages for minor candidates. Gallup percentages calculated on total vote for four principal candidates.[62]

Immediately after the election, the Social Science Research Council appointed a committee of experts to inquire into the erroneous predictions made by the public opinion polls.[63] The committee's

60 L. Rogers, Do the Gallup polls measure opinion? *Harper's Magazine,* November, 1941, pp. 623-32; E. Borneman, The public opinion myth, *Harper's Magazine,* July, 1947, pp. 30-40.

61 L. W. Doob, *Public opinion and propaganda* (New York: Henry Holt & Co., Inc., 1948), p. 146.

62 See *Soc. sci. Res. Council Bull.,* LX (1949), 298.

63 Members of this committee were S. S. Wilks, Chairman, F. F. Stephan, J. P. Baxter, 3rd, P. M. Hauser, C. J. Hovland, V. O. Key, I. Lubin, F. Stanton, and S. A. Stouffer.

report was released December 27, 1948; its summary is worth quoting at some length:

> The committee has made a study of available data on the 1948 election forecasts and has come to the following conclusions:
>
> The pollsters overreached the capabilities of the public opinion poll as a predicting device in attempting to pick, without qualification, the winner of the 1948 presidential election. They had been led by false assumptions into believing their methods were much more accurate than in fact they are. The election was close. Dewey could have won by carrying Ohio, California, and Illinois which he lost by less than 1 per cent of the vote. In such a close election no polls, no advance information of any kind, could have predicted a Truman or Dewey victory with confidence. . . .
>
> The pollsters could have foreseen the possibility of a close contest had they looked more carefully at their data and past errors. They acted in good faith but showed poor judgment. . . .
>
> The evidence indicates that there were two major causes of errors: (a) errors of sampling and interviewing, and (b) errors of forecasting, involving failure to assess the future behavior of undecided voters and to detect shifts of voting intention near the end of the campaign. . . .
>
> The manner in which the pre-election polls were analyzed, presented and published for public consumption contributed materially to the widespread misinterpretation of the results of the polls and to the great public reaction to their failure to pick the winner. This led to a poor understanding of the lack of accuracy of the polls and of the nature of the errors residing in the polls, with the result that the public placed too much confidence in polls before the 1948 election and too much distrust in them afterwards.
>
> The public should draw no inferences from pre-election forecasts that would disparage the accuracy or usefulness of properly conducted sampling surveys in fields in which the response does not involve expression of opinion or intention to act. There are more appropriate methods to check the accuracy of such surveys.[64]

Increasingly, as the results of the 1948 election are analyzed, it appears that there also were problems peculiar to that campaign which made polling precarious.[65] For one thing, it was a choice between two candidates who were lacking in popular appeal for different reasons. Consequently, the voters, more apathetic and undecided than usual, fell back on party loyalties especially at the last minute. Lazarsfeld has called this *terminal horror*—a final revulsion at the idea of changing parties and a return to the fold on election eve. This was the case with individuals caught in *cross-pressures*, an ambivalent tendency to vote or hold an opinion in two different directions.[66] Examples are the wealthy Catholic or the isolationist New Dealer—individuals caught between the appeals of both parties.

---

[64] *Soc. sci. Res. Council Bull.*, 1949, No. 60, pp. 290-91.

[65] Berelson *et al., op. cit.*, pp. 19-34, 234-73.

[66] This term was suggested by Harold Lasswell; see Berelson *et al., op. cit.*, pp. 128-32.

While these cross-pressures operate in any campaign, they seem to be particularly evident when there is no enthusiasm toward the leading candidates. Analysis of the voting showed the following percentage changes in turnout at the polls between 1944 and 1948: [67]

Prosperous	— 7.7%
Upper-middle income	— 6.8
Lower-middle income	60.8
Poor	4.1

Thus the higher socioeconomic groups lost interest between the two elections. Lower socioeconomic groups, apparently feeling threatened, returned to the polls in large numbers, voting predominantly for the Democratic candidates.

The 1952 and 1956 polls. The pollsters felt relieved that their profession had not been dealt a death blow by the 1948 debacle. Their predictions in the 1950 congressional campaign proved heartening. For example, Gallup predicted 49 per cent for the Republicans; their popular vote was 49.7 per cent. He claimed to have checked on last-minute shifts by polling until three days before the election.[68]

This caution was continued into the 1952 campaign, along with more varied methods than had been used before. Gallup used quota samples and more probing questions. Roper explored more fully the attitudes of his respondents, and increased the size of his sample.[69] The caution in predicting in 1952 is shown by the following figures [70] (as well as by many qualifications and footnotes):

	Eisenhower	Stevenson	Others or undecided
Gallup	47.0%	40.0%	13.0%
Princeton Res. Serv.	50.8	48.8	.4
Crossley	47.4	42.3	9.9
N. Y. Daily News	52.1	46.9	1.0
Roper	No figures—Eisenhower ahead but Stevenson gaining.		

Gallup's final estimates gave Eisenhower 51 per cent and Stevenson 49 per cent. The actual vote gave Eisenhower 55.4 per cent and Stevenson 44.6 per cent—a more clearcut decision than any of the polls had indicated.

[67] *New York Herald-Tribune,* June 19, 1949, as cited in V. O. Key, *Politics, parties, and pressure groups* (New York: The Thomas Crowell Co., 1952), p. 576.

[68] W. Albig, *Modern public opinion* (rev. ed.; New York: McGraw-Hill Book Co., Inc., 1956), p. 226.

[69] *Ibid.,* pp. 226-29.

[70] *New York Herald-Tribune,* November 5, 1952.

Although some of the same cross-pressures were present as in 1948, the 1952 and 1956 elections became more a matter of personalities. Positive and negative reactions toward the candidates were more noticeable. After studying Eisenhower's political record, in 1952 two researchers concluded: "We consider it highly probable that Eisenhower could have been elected President on either major party ticket, in either 1948 or 1952. . . . If this analysis is correct, it is implied that the issues of Communism, corruption and Korea, over which the 1952 campaign was fought, were of decidedly less importance than was the simple candidacy of Dwight D. Eisenhower." [71]

In 1956 the pollsters predicted the election results quite accurately. Gallup's final figures, for example, were:

Eisenhower-Nixon	57%
Stevenson-Kefauver	39
Others	1
Undecided	3

Of those who had made up their minds, and excluding third party votes, the major party division became: [72]

Eisenhower-Nixon	59.5%
Stevenson-Kefauver	40.5%

The actual election results, called a "landslide" by some, gave Eisenhower 57.7 per cent and Stevenson 42.3 per cent—a plurality of about nine million. While this is a decisive victory, it does not compare with the magnitude of the eleven million plurality Roosevelt won over Landon in 1936, out of a smaller voting population. Furthermore, despite Eisenhower's triumph, the Democrats won both the House and Senate. Perhaps the voter is casting his ballot more specifically than in the past, voting for candidates rather than a party, possibly because of the growing similarity of the two parties since the days of the New Deal.

In summary, it may be said that, whatever their defects, the polls predict election results reasonably accurately, that is, within plus or minus four percentage points of error. Does this mean, then, that the polling technique is a valid indicator of behavior? Many investigators would answer in the negative. Hyman,[73] for example, found that questions involving prestige were answered unreliably; for example, 34 per cent of workers who had been absent from war plants denied that they had been absent. Doob suggests that the

[71] H. H. Hyman and P. B. Sheatsley, The political appeal of President Eisenhower, *Pub. Opin. Quart.*, XVII (1953), 460.

[72] Gallup Poll report, published in newspapers of November 5, 1956.

[73] H. Hyman., Do they tell the truth? *Pub. Opin. Quart.*, VIII (1944), 557-59.

validity of a poll as a guide to future behavior can be no higher
than the degree to which attitudes themselves determine such behavior.[74] Public opinion polls which happened to be taken just
prior to Pearl Harbor gave no indication that the United States
would declare war on Japan a few days later, on December 8, 1941.
Nor do the most careful studies of attitudes toward minority groups
predict actual behavior very reliably, since so many other factors
enter into the behavior occurring in a particular social situation.

LIMITATIONS OF POLLS

The need for better techniques. The most extensive suggestions
for increasing poll validity have come from those in or close to the
profession. We quote from the recommendations of the committee
of experts who studied the pre-election polls of 1948:

1. To improve the accuracy of polls, increased use should be made of the better techniques now available, particularly in sampling and interviewing. . . .

2. Increased attention should be paid to the development of research on each
step of the polling operation to attempt to improve methods used in opinion
research. This would include research on sampling methods, interviewer bias,
concealment of opinions, selection and training of interviewers, etc. . .

3. Research should be expanded on the basic sciences, particularly social psychology and political science, which underlie the analysis of voters' behavior.
Even if perfect sampling of individuals is employed, we now know too little
about voting intentions, factors affecting change in opinion, prestige effects, and
similar topics to predict who will translate his opinion into actual voting.

4. In view of the increasing amount of emphasis being placed on public
opinion polls, the committee considers it very important for the public to be
effectively informed about the limitations of poll results so it can interpret them
intelligently. It urges that polling organizations, newspapers and magazines, and
social scientists who work with poll results help provide the public with more
information about polls, their interpretation and limitations.

5. There should be more effective cooperation between research workers interested in opinion measurement on common problems of methodology, underlying theory, and research design, including more studies of validity and
reliability than have been made heretofore. . . .

6. More extensive training facilities and opportunities for practical experience under effective supervision should be provided for students who may be
interested in research careers in this field, which includes political behavior,
psychological research, and opinion measurement and statistical methods.[75]

It seems unfortunate that, in connection with point 3, the committee did not recommend research into techniques like "mass observation" or depth interviewing. Such techniques may be of great
value, as already indicated.

[74] Doob, *op. cit.*, p. 151.
[75] *Soc. sci. Res. Council Bull.*, LX (1949), 292-93.

Those interested in improving the validity of polls should not overlook the remarks of their critics. Foremost among these is Rogers, who insists that he is not so much against the polls as against the boasts that pollsters make. He says that "for the pollsters to maintain that percentages of 'yeses,' 'noes,' 'no opinion,' 'never heard of it' disclose public opinion on the policy that they have inquired about, and to which many respondents may not have given a moment's thought before they were interrogated, is to advertise a mouth-wash as a cure for anemia." [76] Rogers admits that polls give "the reading public data that it did not previously possess and that are sometimes worthy of analysis." [77] But the pollsters, he continues, are guilty of two great sins of omission: they have never attempted to define what they are measuring, and they do not give a "reasoned statement of premises concerning the nature of the political society in which public opinion should be the ruler." [78]

Judging the polls in terms of predictability, we conclude that they are least accurate in complex situations where unknown variables are operating, such as frustration and demands for conformity, or new and unexpected events such as those occurring in wartime or other periods of stress. On the other hand, polling techniques have improved to the point where they predict behavior reasonably well for situations not far removed in time and not affected by unexpected but significant influences, internal or external.

Another aspect of validity has to do with honesty and integrity. We now ask, How impartial are public opinion polls?

Biased questions. Questions are often raised as to the honesty and integrity of those conducting opinion surveys. Actually, with very few exceptions we may assume honest intent on the part of the "pollsters." Even if they wished to influence poll results in a certain direction, they would hesitate, because a serious error in their findings or an exposure of dishonest procedures would threaten their professional status.

Those who plan and conduct polls, however, are influenced by various kinds of bias which affect their findings. Several studies, for example, have revealed the presence of "interviewer bias"—that is, a more or less consistent tendency for interviewers to obtain high or low percentages in a given direction.[79] Comparing the re-

[76] L. Rogers, *The pollsters* (New York: Alfred A. Knopf, Inc., 1949), pp. 10-11.

[77] *Ibid.*, p. 10.

[78] *Ibid.*, p. 12.

[79] E.g., D. Katz, Do interviewers bias poll results? *Pub. Opin. Quart.*, VI (1942), 248-68. S. Shapiro and J. Eberhart, Interviewer differences in an intensive interview survey, *Int. J. Opin. and Attitude Res.*, I (1947), 1-17.

ports of different interviewers in the pre-election polls of 1948, Hyman found "that interviewer performance can and did in some instances affect the data obtained on presidential preferences." [80]

In a later volume, Hyman and others from the National Opinion Research Center reported on *interviewer effect*. Among other things they noted three kinds of interviewer expectations which might affect poll results: *attitude-structure expectations* (anticipated consistencies in response), *role expectations* (answers expected from people of a given category), and *probability expectations* (what the frequency distribution should look like).[81] Presumably such expectational errors can be corrected.

A less obvious kind of bias was disclosed in Kornhauser's study entitled "Are Public Opinion Polls Fair to Organized Labor?" [82]

Kornhauser examined all the poll material dealing with labor in the published reports of the leading opinion polling agencies between 1940 and 1945. Over half the 155 items revealed an anti-labor bias in subject matter (for example, "Westbrook Pegler, the newspaper writer, claims that many labor union leaders are racketeers. Do you agree or disagree with him?" "Do you think that the soldiers, when they come home, should have to join a union in order to get or hold a job?"). Furthermore, various kinds of bias against labor were discovered in the wording of questions. For example, "Would you like to see labor unions change their way of handling things?" is a question which implies an affirmative reply. Or "Which do you think is trying harder to help national defense production—labor union leaders or industrial leaders?" The question, Kornhauser pointed out, is hardly fair since it is the function of industrial leaders, but not of labor leaders, to get out production.

Anti-labor bias occurred also in the interpretations of poll findings. In 1942 the Gallup poll reported a two-to-one vote of disapproval of the government's policy with regard to labor union regulations. Actually the two-to-one majority did not represent the whole sample polled, but only the individuals in that part of it who had, in a previous question, expressed concern over the need for greater regulation of unions. Other misinterpretations were found, both in reports of poll results and in news headlines based on the reported results.

Kornhauser concluded that such anti-labor bias in polling can be corrected as far as technical problems are concerned. More difficult

80 *Soc. sci. Res. Council Bull.*, LX (1949), 133.

81 H. H. Hyman, with W. J. Cobb, J. J. Feldman, C. W. Hart, and C. H. Stember, *Interviewing in social research* (Chicago: University of Chicago Press, 1954).

82 *Pub. Opin. Quart.*, X (1946), 484-500.

and more subtle are the social-economic pressures upon the opinion polling agencies and the personal-social outlook of the agency staffs, which are generally anti-labor rather than pro-labor.

Kornhauser's study reveals some of the biases that may occur in an area where those conducting and those paying for the poll (for example, newspaper publishers) are pretty clearly united in either the pro- or anti-direction. The effects of this bias, be it noted, are probably unconscious, but this does not make them less dangerous. One way to correct such bias, as Kornhauser suggested, is to submit proposed questions for review by persons having opposite points of view, until a question satisfactory to both sides is formulated.

It should be emphasized again that the amount of bias found by Kornhauser is exceptional rather than typical; few questions have been as controversial as labor relations and labor policies. But such a study should put us on guard; many precautions are necessary in framing questions and interpreting responses in controversial areas such as sex, religion, and communism.

THE EFFECTS OF PUBLIC OPINION POLLS

The bandwagon psychology. Ever since polls began people have wondered what effect their findings have on behavior. The major hypothesis is summed up in the phrase "the bandwagon effect." According to this theory, people's opinions and actions (for example, votes) swing in the direction which poll results indicate to be the winning side. Is there evidence to show that polls produce a bandwagon effect?

The answer seems to be negative. We find that the thumping defeat predicted by the *Literary Digest* for Roosevelt in 1936 did not prevent a striking victory at the polls. The all but unanimous expectation of a Dewey victory in 1948 did not lead the majority of American voters to climb on his bandwagon. Gallup and Rae cite many other instances where publication of poll results was followed by a decline in the popularity of the leading candidate rather than the reverse.[83]

Such examples, however, do not prove that no bandwagon effect occurs. Perhaps the Roosevelt and Truman majorities would have been greater if the polls had forecast their victory. Another interesting hypothesis, heard frequently after the election of 1948, posits a "reverse bandwagon effect"—that is, increased efforts from those backing the candidate indicated as the loser.

On the other hand, existence of a bandwagon effect seems to be indicated in many experimental studies. When the members

[83] Gallup and Rae, *op. cit.*, chap. xx.

of a group are told what the majority thinks or feels, their reactions usually swing in that direction.[84] It should be noted, however, that a person's reaction to majority opinion in a small, closely knit group may be very different from a voter's reaction to what an opinion poll informs him is majority opinion in the nation. In the first case he is more likely to be identified with the group and therefore to be affected by the opinion of his peers. This kind of evidence is hardly relevant to the question of a bandwagon effect in elections.

Lazarsfeld and his colleagues studied the bandwagon effect in Erie County, Ohio, during the election of 1940, and reported evidence indicating its existence.[85] Many voters had not made up their minds in May; by October those who had decided were voting predominantly for the candidate they expected to win. Slightly over half of those who expected the Republicans to win had decided to vote for Willkie; slightly over two-thirds of those who expected the Democrats to win were supporting Roosevelt.

However, before we accept the conclusion of these authors that there is a definite bandwagon effect, several things should be mentioned. The number of voters included in the bandwagon study was less than one hundred, and nearly 40 per cent of them decided to vote for the candidate whom they expected to lose. Furthermore, factors other than expectation of being on the winning side undoubtedly influenced the decisions of the majority. Lastly, the part played by polls in determining expectation of the winner is not clear.

There may be a tendency for undecided voters to be influenced in the direction of the candidate that they expect will win. But no evidence has yet been adduced which shows that the "bandwagon effect" operates as a major determinant in an election. Compared with socioeconomic status, religious affiliation, geographic location, and other predisposing influences, it seems relatively minor. All in all, it must be concluded that the evidence for a bandwagon effect is too scanty to constitute a dangerous consequence of opinion polling.

As guidelines to government. Turning to the positive side, what are the major benefits of public opinion surveys? Perhaps their greatest value is to provide legislators and other leaders with rea-

[84] See Doob, *op. cit.*, pp. 167-68, for references.

[85] Lazarsfeld *et al.*, *op. cit.*, pp. 107-9, 167-68. In their later study in Elmira, Lazarsfeld and Berelson suggested that projection is as good an interpretation as the bandwagon effect; that is, an expectation that the candidate toward whom one feels favorable will win. After analyzing data from the 1940 and 1948 elections, they found that the bandwagon and projection effects were about equal in strength. See Berelson *et al.*, *op. cit.*, p. 299.

sonably accurate information about people's attitudes and opinions. Leaders who rely upon their personal impressions, upon the reports of special pleaders, or upon analysis of editorials or of their mail may easily go astray. Gallup cites a study of 30,000 letters received by fourteen United States senators during the summer of 1940.[86] Ninety per cent of these letters opposed the Selective Service Bill then before Congress. A national poll taken at the time showed that 68 per cent of the public actually favored the bill! The letters, of course, represented the views of an articulate minority; if the senators had followed the mandate of these correspondents, they would have gone counter to the wishes of the sizable but less articulate majority of the people.

This is not to imply, however, that our leaders should follow slavishly the opinion poll returns.[87] While they should know the attitudes and wishes of the majority, they are after all expected to *lead*. People in general are often ignorant of facts or poorly informed about them. They usually lack the experience and training necessary for devising solutions to complex problems and for describing the means by which solutions can be reached. As Cartwright concludes, an interest in poll results must not divest our leaders of their duties as experts and inventors.[88]

Such matters may seem theoretical unless we know whether our leaders pay attention to poll results. A 1940 study of United States senators and representatives revealed that nearly 40 per cent of them felt poll results have been of help in enabling them to know the desires of their constituents.[89] Hartmann circulated a questionnaire to members of the New York State legislature.[90] About a third of them replied; of these, 59 per cent stated that they studied (always or frequently) the published poll results on an issue before they voted on it. From such data it would appear that legislators do pay attention to the poll findings, though it is difficult to get a very accurate idea of the part played by polls in determining their voting behavior.

For government administrative leaders, on the other hand, the picture is more conclusive. After 1936, for example, the Depart-

---

[86] G. Gallup, *A guide to public opinion polls* (Princeton, N. J.: Princeton University Press, 1944), pp. 5-6.

[87] For a good discussion of this issue, see D. Cartwright, Public opinion polls and democratic leadership, *J. soc. Issues*, II (1946), 23-32.

[88] *Ibid.*, p. 32.

[89] G. F. Lewis, Jr., The congressmen look at the polls, *Pub. Opin. Quart.*, IV (1940), 229-31.

[90] G. W. Hartmann, Judgments of state legislators concerning public opinion, *J. soc. Psychol.*, XXI (1945), 105-14.

ment of Agriculture's use of "interview surveys" increased by leaps and bounds.[91] Some of this interest was stimulated by the necessities of wartime, when it was essential to plan rationing or war bond drives most effectively, and to know the state of civilian morale. By and large, administrative leaders are more enthusiastic about opinion surveys than are legislators, but it is too early to say whether systematic surveys will become a permanent part of government agency procedures.

Market research and other uses. In the area of commercial usage, opinion surveys have been widely acclaimed. Many industrial concerns have sounded out the tastes and preferences of consumers as to automobile design, packaging of products, and countless other matters. Recently the surveys have been extended to cover consumer preferences in movies, radio and TV programs, and reading matter—a policy which some people think may cause publishers and producers to stick to favored themes rather than try out new ones.

Polls have been used to indicate changes in public opinion caused by the impact of events. Cantril studied the changes in American reactions to the war in Europe between September, 1939, and December, 1941, when we entered the conflict.[92] Changing events caused changes in the issues as seen by Americans. In the fall of 1939 the main issue was, "Shall we sell war supplies to England and France?" A year later, after the defeat of France and the air raids on Britain, it was, "Shall we resist Hitler by aid to Britain short of war?" By November, 1941, after the Nazis had taken over most of Europe and attacked Russia, the question seemed to be, "When will we fight?" Many other studies done by the Office of Public Opinion Research and the National Opinion Research Center have been concerned with this relationship between events and public opinion.

Polls were used during the war and afterward as indicators of morale, though they are only one of many possible criteria.[93] After a careful study of the Detroit race riots of June, 1943, Lee and Humphrey recommended public opinion polls as an index of tenseness in interracial relations.[94] Along with other indicators, poll re-

---

[91] See A. Campbell, The uses of interview surveys in federal administration, *J. soc. Issues*, II:2 (1946), 14-22; also W. A. Neilson, Attitude research and government, *J. soc. Issues*, II:2 (1946), 2-13.

[92] H. Cantril, Public opinion flux, *Ann. Amer. Acad. pol. soc. Sci.*, CXX (1942), 136-52 (reprinted in *Readings*, pp. 591-605).

[93] See, e.g., D. Rugg, American morale when the war began, and J. and D. Belden, Student morale, in G. Watson (ed.), *Civilian morale* (Boston: Houghton Mifflin Co., 1942).

[94] A. M. Lee and N. D. Humphrey, *Race riot* (New York: The Dryden Press, Inc., 1943), pp. 127-28.

sults may act as storm signals to which alert community leaders can respond with preventive measures.

A CONCLUDING NOTE

Taking a broad view of public opinion, of course, one must distinguish between short-range and long-range variations. Every year issues, candidates, and political events fluctuate and consequently affect public opinion. At the other extreme there are the more basic, almost generational, trends. For example, there was the Republican "normalcy" of the twenties which lasted until the economic crash of 1929 ushered in the Democratic New Deal. The last embers of this era did not burn out for nearly twenty years; in fact many of the reforms instituted were taken over by the Republicans when they regained power in 1952. It has been noted that many of the Depression-decade children, who do not recall the dark period of the thirties when their parents were passionate supporters of Roosevelt, now occupy well-paid positions, have moved to the suburbs, and vote predominantly Republican, at least for the presidential candidates. A recent report from the Survey Research Center, for example, showed that in 1956 no less than 56 per cent of skilled and semiskilled workers voted for Eisenhower. On the other hand, in 1956 more voters than in 1952 split their tickets—43 per cent as compared with 33 per cent—indicating that many of these same voters probably voted for Democratic congressional candidates.[95]

There are interesting "cultural lags" of extreme traditionalism which can be found, such as the economically depressed Republicans of the southern Appalachian region who stick to the G.O.P. in the belief that it is still the liberal party as it was at certain times in the nineteenth century.[96] Perhaps a better example is the unchanging loyalty to the Democratic party which characterizes most of the South, particularly the Deep South. Even when southerners felt opposed to personalities and issues (for example, Al Smith and repeal of prohibition), many retained their allegiance to the Democratic party. Only in 1952 did a substantial rebellion take place, when a number of southern states voted for Eisenhower; and this pattern was continued in 1956. Similarly in the Deep North (Maine and Vermont) Republicans have won consistently for many decades; yet even here changes may take place as shown by the 1954 election of a Democratic governor in Maine.

[95] Reported in the *New York Times*, February 24, 1957.
[96] For further discussion, see Lipset, *op. cit.*, pp. 1164-67.

Analysis of election returns is a fruitful field for public opinion research, and there are many possibilities for future development here.[97] Many of the already established correlations seem to be giving way—e.g., that manual workers vote Democratic. The Survey Research Center finds that income and occupation, religion and education were less clearly related to voting behavior in the election of 1956 than previously.[98] But much may be learned from study of local voting, and of voting over a period of years. For example, Harris found that ethnic groups in New York City vote differently—more along cultural lines—in municipal elections than in national elections, where large issues tend to minimize national and religious differences.[99] Or again, to what extent does an occupational shift in a community change voting behavior? When individuals improve in social status, which issues become more and which less important? And what is the effect of sustained prosperity on traditional cleavages? More evidence, too, needs to be gathered on cycles of public opinion and on the factors that make it possible for one party to stay in power for a long period of time. No doubt the years to come will see more and better research in such areas of public opinion.

SUMMARY

Public opinion refers to the beliefs and attitudes held by the members of a sizable group with respect to a particular issue. It rests in considerable part upon background opinions and attitudes of individuals, crystallized through interaction with others and through communication via the mass media—press, movies, radio, and television.

Despite their shortcomings, public opinion polls seem to be the best indicators of public opinion we possess; the techniques of polling have been constantly improved, especially since their setback at the time of the 1948 election. Better interviewing methods have been developed and new research techniques devised, which make possible more accurate understanding and predicting of social behavior. It must be remembered, however, that no opinion or attitude measures can serve as infallible guides to future behavior. This is partly because of technical difficulties, partly because the measures can tap only surface layers of personality, but most of all

[97] L. Harris, Some observations on election behavior research, *Pub. Opin. Quart.*, XX (1956), 379-92.

[98] *New York Times*, February 24, 1957.

[99] Harris, *op. cit.*

because social behavior is influenced by conformity demands and by the impact of actual events as well as by people's attitudes and opinions.

SUPPLEMENTARY READINGS

Books of Readings

MACCOBY, E. E., NEWCOMB, T. M., AND HARTLEY, E. L. (eds.). *Readings in social psychology*, 3d ed. New York: Henry Holt & Co., Inc., 1958.

Berelson, B. R., Lazarsfeld, P. F., and McPhee, W. N., Political perception.

Hyman, H. H., and Sheatsley, P. B., Some reasons why information campaigns fail.

BRITT, S. H. (ed.). *Selected readings in social psychology*. New York: Rinehart & Co., Inc., 1950.

Farnsworth, P. R., Stereotypes.

Lazarsfeld, P. F., Berelson, B., and Gaudet, H., The people's choice.

Sherif, M., and Cantril, H., The psychology of "attitudes."

LINDZEY, G. (ed.). *Handbook of social psychology*. Reading, Mass.: Addison-Wesley Pub. Co., Inc., 1954.

Hovland, C. I., Effects of the mass media of communication, Vol. II.

Lipset, S. M., Lazarsfeld, P. F., Barton, A. H., and Linz, J., The psychology of voting, Vol. II.

Other References

ALBIG, W. *Modern public opinion,* rev. ed. New York: McGraw-Hill Book Co., Inc., 1956.

A readable and provocative text covering some of the basic problems of communication, attitude and opinion formation, polling, propaganda, censorship, and mass media.

BERELSON, B. R., LAZARSFELD, P. F., AND MCPHEE, W. N. *Voting.* Chicago: University of Chicago Press, 1954.

A study of the 1948 campaign in Elmira, this is probably the best social psychological analysis to date of factors in voting decision.

BOGART, L. *The age of television.* New York: Frederick Ungar Publishing Co., 1956.

An absorbing and well-documented study of America's new giant mass medium.

CAMPBELL, A., GURIN, G., AND MILLER, W. E. *The voter decides.* Evanston, Ill.: Row, Peterson & Co., 1954.

A study of voting decision in the 1952 election. Treats party identification, along with issue and candidate orientation, as a motivating factor.

CANTRIL, H. *Gauging public opinion.* Princeton, N. J.: Princeton University Press, 1944.

An understandable presentation of polling techniques and other types of measurement.

DOOB, L. W. *Public opinion and propaganda.* New York: Henry Holt & Co., Inc., 1948.

A deservedly classic study, including intensive psychological data, as well as discussion of the more conventional subjects.

HANDEL, L. A. *Hollywood looks at its audience.* Urbana, Ill.: University of Illinois Press, 1950.

Presents quantitative data on audience research, as well as other aspects of the industry.

KEY, V. O. *Politics, parties, and pressure groups,* 3d ed. New York: The Thomas Crowell Co., 1952.
A political scientist looks at voting trends.

LIPPMANN, W. *Public opinion.* New York: Harcourt, Brace & Co., Inc., 1922.
An early, subjective treatment that still reads as well as it did a generation ago.

LUBELL, S. *The future of American politics.* New York: Harper & Bros., 1951.
An example of perceptive political analysis using both sociological and psychological data.

MacDOUGALL, C. D. *Understanding public opinion.* New York: The Macmillan Co., 1952.
A pleasantly written journalistic account of cultural factors, especially the arts and mass media, in the formation of public opinion.

MOTT, F. L. *The news in America.* Cambridge, Mass.: Harvard University Press, 1952.
The social psychology of the newspaper, together with the problem of freedom and control.

OGLE, M. B. *Public opinion and political dynamics.* New York: Houghton Mifflin Co., 1950.
Although not a complete statement, political and other institutional aspects of the subject are presented.

POWDERMAKER, H. *Hollywood, the dream factory.* Boston: Little, Brown & Co., 1950.
An anthropologist's view of the industry, with analysis of the personnel, the product, and the mythology.

SCHRAMM, W. (ed.). *The process and effects of mass communication.* Urbana, Ill.: University of Illinois Press, 1954.
An outstanding collection of readings in public opinion and propaganda from the psychological viewpoint; also includes a section on international aspects.

SIEPMAN, C. A. *Radio, television, and society.* New York: Oxford University Press, 1950.
Although possibly premature on television, the book presents some history of the communications industry, with its problems of control.

YOUNG, K. *Social psychology,* 3d ed. New York: Appleton-Century-Crofts, Inc., 1956.
Chaps. xiv to xviii are a splendid exposition of opinion and the mass media.

17

Propaganda

Propaganda represents one of the major forms of social control. With the growth of democracy and the consequent importance of public opinion, propaganda became inevitable. With the rise of printing and other mass media of communication, it became possible on a gigantic scale.

THE MEANING OF "PROPAGANDA"

To most Americans the word "propaganda" has unpleasant connotations. One of the writers once asked the members of an adult forum audience to write on slips of paper their definition or conception of "propaganda." The responses followed a more or less normal curve of distribution. At one extreme were statements like "a kind of publicity" and "creating favorable public opinion." At the other extreme came "turning public opinion away from actual facts for selfish motives" and even "one way to lie"! The central tendency was typified by such statements as "the publication of statements, either true or false, to create thought and activities desired," and "information spread among the people for the purpose of influencing public opinion along special lines without appearing to do so." Slightly more than two thirds of the group of sixty-five respondents revealed their suspicion of "propaganda." They thought it was dangerous because it might warp facts or serve a special interest or both.[1]

As a result of this view, the word "propaganda" is typically used to describe the promotional efforts of our opponents—of those with whose policies we disagree. Democrats frequently accuse Repub-

[1] S. S. Sargent, Can adults be de-propagandized? *J. adult Educ.,* VI (1934), 440-43.

licans (and vice versa) of flooding the country with propaganda but seldom use the term to refer to their own publicity efforts. "Propaganda" is typically a term of opprobrium to be hurled at the heads of our enemies.

Curiously enough "propaganda" has different meanings in other countries. In Germany, as in much of Europe, the term has been roughly equivalent to "publicity" or "advertising"; the same is true of Latin America. In Nazi Germany, for example, Dr. Goebbels was named head of the "Ministry of Public Enlightenment and Propaganda." The personnel and policies of the propaganda ministry were described in many newspaper and magazine articles. "Propaganda" became such a favored concept it was even used as a brand name for such items as chocolate bars. In the United States prospective buyers would react approximately as they would to "Fake" or even "Poison." Somehow a strong negative reaction to propaganda developed in the Anglo-Saxon world, quite possibly through the many exposés of the propaganda campaigns of World War I.

The social psychologist in the United States, however, finds popular conceptions of propaganda highly unsatisfactory. For him propaganda is simply *an attempt to influence people's attitudes and opinions, and thereby their actions, in a desired direction.* Typically this is done through suggestion rather than by means of facts and logic.

Certain distinctions in emphasis can be drawn between propaganda and other forms of communication or interaction, such as news dissemination, entertainment, and education. The publisher, editor, and reporter collect and publish news for the primary purpose of informing people and not for the purpose of converting them to a particular doctrine. The playwright, artist, and script writer seek first and foremost to entertain people rather than to influence them in certain desired directions. The fact that many exceptions occur should not blind us to their primary purposes, which are different from that of the propagandist. The person who moans, "I can't believe a thing I see in the papers or on TV or hear on the radio—it's all propaganda!" is an extreme case of one who is confused as to these aims.

On the other hand, advertising and publicity are both forms of propaganda in the sense in which we use that term. Advertising is open and aboveboard in that we generally know who is responsible for it and what its purpose is—to sell goods. "Publicity" is a word which is free from the unpleasant connotations of "propaganda." But the publicity man (including the press agent and "public relations counsel") has a definite purpose—to create in people favorable attitudes toward the individual or group he represents. Neither the advertiser nor the publicity man is *ipso facto* dishonest; many if not most conform to high ethical standards. But he cannot be considered impartial in the sense that a scientific investigator is impartial; his function is to produce a certain type of attitude—i.e., a favorable one—and he must hew to this line, or lose his job!

The distinction between education and propaganda is somewhat harder to make, largely because each society sets about indoctrinating its youth in the accepted mores, values, and skills which make up its social heritage. Indeed, it is almost impossible for the educator to avoid imparting certain values to his students, however much he tries to be objective or impartial. For example, as Freeman pointed out years ago, even mathematics is not free of such indoctrination; problems in most arithmetic books deal with selling, buying, renting, working for wages, and interest on loans.[2] In other words, they reflect the capitalist culture in which the education takes place.

Doob suggests that various illustrations may be used for the problem "divide 60 by 80":

> A man wishes to borrow $80 but his friend lends him only $60. What percentage of the amount he wanted does he obtain?
> Medical and health authorities agree that a family of four requires a minimum wage of $80 per week. The John J. Jones Company in our town pays most of its workers only $60 per week. What percentage of a decent minimum wage do these workers receive? [3]

The first exercise could be used with impunity in our country. The second would probably get the teacher into trouble; in fact, he might well be accused of "propagandizing"!

Clearly there is much propaganda in education. But the fact remains that the goals of the educator and the propagandist are different, as are many of the techniques employed. Despite the indoctrinational aspects of elementary school and high school education, the college teacher and the teacher of adults in a democracy veer away from propaganda as they encourage students to think for themselves. Ideally at least, as Everett Dean Martin once said, the educator teaches people *how* to think rather than *what* to think; he seeks to open minds rather than close them.[4] While many teachers, for one reason or another, fall short of this ideal, we can still distinguish the essentially different goals of the educator and the propa-

---

[2] E. Freeman, *Social psychology* (New York: Henry Holt & Co., Inc., 1936), pp. 264-65.

[3] L. W. Doob, *Public opinion and propaganda* (New York: Henry Holt & Co., Inc., 1948), pp. 234-35.

[4] E. D. Martin, Our invisible masters, *Forum*, LXXXI (1929), 142-45.

gandist.[5] To put them into the same category is likely to produce more confusion than clarification.

Should one make a distinction between *intentional* and *unintentional* propaganda? Or should one use "propaganda" only when actual intent to influence people is present? This is a hard question to answer, since intent is almost impossible to prove. Often a propagandist is not fully aware of his intent, or he may achieve changes which were "unintended" on his part. If the term "propaganda" is applied to all types of interpersonal communication which bring about changed attitudes, it becomes far too unwieldy to deal with. Though he believes that a good deal of unintentional propaganda goes on, Doob concludes: "Ordinarily the term 'propagandist' refers only to an intentional propagandist whose efforts, when they are known, clearly represent an attempt to change people and their society." [6] We shall adhere to this usage of the term.

Thus propaganda is a concept covering all attempts to influence others' thoughts, feelings, and actions in directions desired by the propagandist. As a form of social control it is probably as old as human society, but it has come to the forefront as a natural outgrowth of democratic trends in government. When public opinion becomes important, efforts are made to influence and control it. And, as was pointed out in the previous chapter, the means are at hand—notably the press, radio and TV, and motion pictures. However, propaganda is neither necessarily "good" nor "bad," as we shall see.

PURVEYORS OF PROPAGANDA

How much propaganda plays upon us in our ordinary living? Obviously, this is a hard question to answer, since it depends on the person, time, and place. In a dictatorship, officially sponsored propaganda is the order of the day; it prohibits rival propaganda and discourages or completely eliminates information, education, and scientific findings which do not hew to the desired line. In a democracy, we are exposed to conflicting propaganda, along with more or less objective news and information. During an election campaign we live amid a welter of propaganda from all sides. In the newspapers we meet propaganda in the advertising and editorial sections, in the cartoons and columns—and for the most part we are aware of it. We are not so aware of propaganda in the news columns, such as the items inspired by press agents, or the distortions and omissions sometimes found in news reports or in the

5 See Doob, *op. cit.*, pp. 232-45, for a more extensive and rather different treatment of propaganda and education.
6 Doob, *op. cit.*, p. 264.

headlines above them which, in controversial areas, usually agree with the views of the publisher.

The last fifty years have seen the rise of whole professions dedicated to propaganda work, particularly advertising, press-agentry, publicity, public relations counseling, and lobbying. To these many thousands of professionals we must add the partial or occasional contributions of newspapermen, photographers, cartoonists, authors, artists, teachers, preachers, and many others. It is impossible to give an over-all estimate of the extent of their propaganda efforts. Opinion is influenced intentionally a good deal more than the naïve person assumes. He tends, in his naïveté, to say: "It must be true; I saw it in the paper." And there is a good deal less than imagined by the frantic soul who is reluctant to believe anything he reads, sees, or hears. Fortunately we know much more about propaganda than we used to, and we shall shortly describe some of the ways of identifying it.

The public relations man. Recent developments in the profession of publicity and public relations make a fascinating story. The old-fashioned press agent has largely been superseded by the more impersonal and systematic publicity man, who issues regular handouts to the press and radio. The cigar-passing, buttonhole-twisting lobbyist of the old days has given way to the publicity expert who operates in a more sophisticated way.[7] He keeps his organization informed about relevant legislative activities and brings pressure to bear upon legislators through getting the folks back home to send telegrams and letters which sometimes descend in an avalanche.

But the top man in the publicity field is the public relations counsel. He is far removed from the lowly work of giving handouts to the press or of urging clients to write their congressmen. His task is to devise ways of interpreting his clients favorably to the public. Frequently he succeeds in creating news which is so interesting the papers have to print it!

There are, indeed, many stories about two of our most noted public relations counsels, Ivy Lee and Edward L. Bernays.[8] Lee is

[7] In 1946 Congress passed a law requiring lobbyists to register and to itemize their sponsors, objectives, resources, and outlay. By the following year some 800 persons were registered. They represented business groups predominantly, with a sprinkling of labor and reform organizations. By 1956 over $4,000,000 a year was being spent to influence legislation on the part of some 250 organizations who filed reports with Congress. The largest spender was the Association of American Railroads and next was the AFL-CIO. (*New York Times*, December 1, 1956). For a comprehensive survey of lobbying, see Donald Blaisdell, *American democracy under pressure* (New York: The Ronald Press Co., 1957).

[8] A good brief account may be found in E. F. Goldman, *Two-way street: the emergence of the public relations counsel* (Boston: Bellman Publishing Co., Inc., 1948).

credited with revamping the old-time "public be damned" policies of the Pennsylvania Railroad and many other large corporations. Over a course of years he changed the stereotype of John D. Rockefeller from robber baron to philanthropic old gentleman who loved to play golf and hand out shiny dimes to youngsters. Bernays showed even more ability in the art of mass persuasion. One of his early achievements was to make possible the production of Brieux's *Damaged Goods,* a play about syphilis, by organizing a number of prominent persons into a "Sociological Fund" which backed the production and gave it an aura of respectability. Later he showed his inventiveness by publicizing the products of Proctor & Gamble (Ivory soap) in a national soap sculpture contest, and by organizing the Golden Jubilee of electric light on behalf of General Electric and Westinghouse.

Another example of astute and effective public relations work is furnished by the cigar makers, whose sales had been declining badly through the twenties and thirties.[9] They formed the Cigar Institute of America and hired a public relations counsel. The first move of the public relations counsel was to offer news photographers prizes for the best published photos of people smoking cigars. News pictures began to appear of the Duke of Windsor, Benny Goodman, and other notables with cigar in mouth. Later a handsome offer was made to movie producers: free advertising on 25,000 cigar counters for movies having a good "cigar scene." Heroes rather than villains began to puff at stogies. Within a couple of years the Cigar Institute could boast that forty major movies had good cigar scenes. The sales curve for cigars went steadily upward from the time the campaign began in 1940 until it more than doubled. Between 1952 and 1955 an estimated additional million and a half men became cigar smokers.

Bernays coined the term *public relations counsel* in 1923.[10] In a later publication he divided the periods of public relations into the following: [11]

"The public be damned"	(1865-1900)
"The public be informed"	(1900-1919)
"Public relations as an emerging profession"	(1919-1929)
"The coming of age"	(1929-1941)
"The era of integration"	(1941 to the present)

9 K. Monroe, They made the cigar respectable, *Harper's Magazine,* February, 1955, pp. 37-41.

10 E. L. Bernays, *Crystallizing public opinion* (New York: Liveright Publishing Corp., 1923).

11 E. L. Bernays, *Public relations* (Norman, Okla.: The University of Oklahoma Press, 1952), pp. 157-68.

He sees these changes as related to the basic transition which has been taking place in democracy—an extension of the consent of the governed so the individual is allowed to accept or reject aspects of his cultural environment. Thus public relations work might be termed the "engineering of consent." As Bernays suggests, a professional in this area must be thoroughly grounded in the principles of scientific social psychology. This implies an examination of the communication processes and extensive research in public opinion polling. The public relations analyst believes that practically any view can be disseminated provided sufficient planning, funds, and resources are available—a theory that is not accepted by all social scientists. However, ethical judgments may be involved in determining whether the end is worthwhile. The omission of this consideration is the critical difference, concludes Bernays, between the newer and older type of public relations.

IDENTIFYING PROPAGANDA

Even when certain persons are recognized and identified as propagandists, it is difficult to estimate the extent of their activities, since much of their work is done behind the scenes. But, one may ask, are there ways of identifying the propaganda itself—of distinguishing it from news, fact, entertainment, and other communicated material?

Many suggestions have been made for identifying propaganda—in terms of such factors as the source and motive, nature of the content, methods used, and social effects. Most of the "propaganda analysis" has implied that propaganda is dangerous; that is, it has been set in a framework of "protecting ourselves against bad propaganda." Actually it is impossible to draw a line between good and bad propaganda, since this implies certain value judgments on the part of the person doing the judging. If I am a Republican, I probably evaluate Democratic propaganda as bad, and vice versa. It is essential for the social psychologist to think of propaganda as an effort to influence people's attitudes in a desired direction. Identifying propaganda means simply discovering whether given communicated material falls into this category—as compared with other kinds of communication. If it does, it is propaganda, whether the desired end is to save the lives of more babies, make us vote for Mr. Smith rather than Mr. Jones, induce us to love or hate the Russians, or plunge us into another world war. If we are able to describe certain propaganda rather fully, it can be evaluated in certain ways. For example, is the end sought a desirable one from the standpoint of world peace, of the welfare of my country, my state, my organization, myself as an individual? Are the means used harmonious with the ethical norms accepted in my group? But note that such evaluations do not determine whether or not the material is propaganda; they merely help us to understand and interpret that which has already been identified as propaganda.

Can one tell whether a given news article, TV program, movie, editorial, poster, leaflet, cartoon, etc., is "propaganda"? To some extent, the problem is easier than we think. For example, posters and leaflets are put out by special interest groups whose aim, like that of the advertiser, is to influence and convince people. Editorials, cartoons, and the writings of columnists are separated from the news columns in the papers, since their functions are different. Almost every reader realizes that editorials seek to influence him. Most radio listeners are aware of the distinction between the news reporter, who brings the latest hourly headlines, and the commentator, who interprets the news as he sees it. Every voter realizes that the aim of all electioneering is to elect the candidates of a particular party, just as the advertiser's goal is to sell his own product.

Doob proposes as one classification of propaganda a division into the *revealed* and *concealed* types.[12] Propaganda is revealed when people are aware that propaganda is affecting them. Practically, this means when they know who is behind it and their intent. The propaganda that people fear is the concealed type—the kind that may be found in textbooks, in the news, in movie or radio programs, or in promotional campaigns in which the real sponsor and purpose are camouflaged.[13]

Most exposés of propaganda serve to turn concealed into revealed propaganda. Many years ago, for example, the Federal Trade Commission investigated the publicity activities of the old National Electric Light Association and showed how this group had influenced several newspaper publishers to print news favorable to the public utility interests and to suppress reports favoring municipally owned utilities.[14] It indicated how certain educational administra-

12 Doob, *op. cit.*, pp. 251-52.

13 On the concealed propaganda technique in advertising, see Vance Packard, *The hidden persuaders* (New York: David McKay Co., 1957). In this connection, we may note the recent development of "subliminal perception," utilized on the motion picture screen by introducing advertising or propaganda material for a fraction of a second. For instance, when an "invisible" message instructed the audience to eat popcorn, sales rose sharply without the victims being aware of what had been done to their unconscious. Will this technique be used on television? Norman Cousins has commented, "Nothing is more difficult in the modern world than to protect the privacy of the human soul. We live in an age where what we don't see and don't know can hurt us." From "Smudging the subconscious," *The Saturday Review*, October 5, 1957, p. 20.

14 See E. Gruening, *The public pays* (New York: Vanguard Press, Inc., 1931).

tors had been induced to choose and reject textbooks, how politicians, professors, and even preachers had been induced to speak and act favorably toward the public utilities. Similarly, case studies of propaganda analysis, whether concerned with big business, labor, or radical groups, are generally concerned with rending the veil of concealment and exposing the mechanism of propaganda, which seems to reduce its effectiveness—at least among the more literate public.

Can propaganda be identified by analyzing the content of specific communicated materials? To an extent, of course, it can be. If, for example, a message presents what purport to be facts and couples them with commands or suggestions (e.g., election campaign literature), the propaganda is fairly obvious. Generally speaking, the more a message appeals to emotions the more likely it is to be propaganda, particularly if the emotional responses are aroused in a consistent direction.

Some years ago one of the authors made a study of "emotional stereotypes" in the *Chicago Tribune,* a paper militantly opposed to President Roosevelt and his policies and to the newly organized CIO.[15] When referring to New Deal policies and practices and to organized labor in its news columns the *Tribune* used such terms as "Czarism," "dictatorship," "agitator," "communist," and the like, terms which it was possible to show arouse clearly unfavorable emotional responses in people. Similarly, when referring to Republican policies and practices or to workers who refuse to strike, the *Tribune* used such terms as "cooperation," "freedom," "recovery," "the right to work," etc., all terms which evoke favorable emotional reactions. This newspaper's adroit use of emotion-arousing terms was neatly illustrated in its identifying the disliked Senator LaFollette as "Radical, Wisconsin," instead of using the proper name of his party—"Progressive." ("Radical" had an unfavorable connotation, and "progressive" an extremely favorable one.) Several terms or phrases used by the *Tribune* were compared with parallel terms used in the same connection by the *New York Times:*

Chicago Tribune	*New York Times*
Government witch hunting	Senate investigation
Regimentation	Regulation
Communist CIO Leader	Maritime leader
Labor agitator	Labor organizer
The dole	Home relief
Farm dictatorship	Crop control

[15] S. S. Sargent, Emotional stereotypes in the Chicago Tribune, *Sociometry*, 1939, 2, 69-75. Reprinted in Swanson *et al., Readings* (2d ed.), pp. 103-6.

Inquisitor	Investigator
CIO dictator	CIO chieftain
Alien	Foreign
Mass picketing	Picketing

Typically the propagandist selects words, when possible, which have a desired emotion-arousing effect. Instead of "nonstrikers" (a relatively objective term) the *Tribune* used "loyal workers." Union labor calls them "scabs"! During the Spanish revolution it was possible to tell what side an American favored simply by asking him who was fighting. Those who opposed Franco called it a fight between the "loyalists" and the "rebels"; those supporting Franco said the "reds" and the "nationalists."

The effectiveness of emotionalized propaganda was demonstrated by Hartmann in a state election campaign.[16] In comparable wards of a fair-sized city rational appeals increased the Socialist vote by about 35 per cent, but highly emotional campaign propaganda increased it by 50 per cent, as compared with a "control" increase of only 24 per cent.

TECHNIQUES AND PRINCIPLES OF PROPAGANDA

The Institute for Propaganda Analysis was founded in 1937 to help the layman detect propaganda and thus protect himself against deception.[17] In its bulletins to subcribers, many contemporary campaigns were analyzed, and the "seven devices" of the propagandist were described:

1. *Name calling*—using a negative stereotype, like "fascist," "demagogue," or "radical"
2. *Glittering generality*—using a favorable sounding term, such as "Americanism," "democracy," or "justice"
3. *Transfer*—borrowing symbols with a strong value for use in a new way (e.g., showing one's political candidate with the American flag in the background)
4. *Testimonial*—utilizing supporting statements from persons having prestige

16 G. W. Hartmann, A field experiment on comparative effectiveness of "emotional" and "rational" political leaflets in determining election results, *J. abnorm. soc. Psychol.*, XXXI (1936), 99-114. Part of the effectiveness of emotional appeals in information campaigns can be traced to the fact that the primary group constitutes the network through which communication operates, as stated by Cooley and many writers since. See J. B. Ford, The primary group in mass communication, *Sociol. soc. Res.*, XXXVIII (1954), 152-58.

17 The Institute stopped functioning in January, 1942, just after the United States declared war.

5. *Plain folks*—stressing the simple, homey, grass-roots qualities (e.g., picturing a political candidate, in old clothes, digging in his garden)
6. *Card stacking*—selecting, distorting, or falsifying facts and figures
7. *Band wagon*—implying that "everybody's doing it—better come along" (e.g., each major party always predicts victory at the polls) [18]

The Institute also described other techniques used by the propagandist.[19] For example, "simplification," "reinforcement" (repetition), and "displacement" (blaming a scapegoat for one's troubles).

To show how propaganda analysis could be done in terms of the seven devices, two researchers analyzed a number of Father Coughlin's speeches, made during the 1930's.[20] They printed in full his radio talk of February 26, 1939, which seemed to them the best indication of similarity between his propaganda techniques and those of Adolf Hitler. The analysis was done by inserting pictorial symbols to represent the devices. Here is the peroration of Coughlin's talk, with the name of each device in parentheses:

> Ours *(Plain Folks)* must be a moral *(Glittering Generality)* platform from which there is preached *(Transfer)* a positive *(Glittering Generality)* policy based upon the principles of religion *(Glittering Generality, Transfer)* and of patriotism *(Glittering Generality)*. For God *(Transfer)* and country *(Transfer, Glittering Generality)*, for Christ *(Transfer)* and the flag *(Transfer, Glittering Generality)*—that is our motto as we prepare for action, for Christian American *(Transfer, Glittering Generality)* action, which is neither anti-German, anti-Italian, nor anti-Semitic *(Card Stacking)*. Any negative *(Name Calling)* policy is destined to failure. Only a positive policy *(Glittering Generality)* can hope to succeed. Unified *(Band Wagon)* action on a common *(Band Wagon)* program for God *(Transfer)* and country is more necessary now than at any other period in the history of our civilization *(Card Stacking)*.[21]

More recently Lee has grouped the propagandist's techniques as follows: (1) Techniques of basic procedure (including "selecting the issue," "case-making," and "simplification"); (2) Omnibus symbols (positive and negative symbols arousing emotions); (3) Techniques of identification ("Through these procedures, a proposal can be identified with a revered or detested institution (Transfer) or personality (Testimonial), with the masses of the Plain Folks, or with what those on the Band Wagon accept or reject.") [22]

[18] *Propaganda Analysis*, I:2 (1937).

[19] *Propaganda Analysis*, III:10 (1940).

[20] Alfred McClung Lee and Elizabeth Briant Lee, *The fine art of propaganda* (New York: Harcourt, Brace & Co., Inc., and the Institute for Propaganda Analysis, 1939).

[21] *Ibid.*, p. 131. Reprinted by permission of the authors, who are the copyright owners.

[22] A. M. Lee, *How to understand propaganda* (New York: Rinehart & Co., Inc., 1952), chap. iii.

Analysis of advertising techniques reveals similar devices. For example, one study specifies *humanization* by which advertisers create warm, agreeable pictures of themselves; typical stockholders and employees are introduced to show that they are "real folks." [23] *Denial* is to prove that certain unfavorable tendencies do not exist, and *conversion* transforms them into good qualities. The American Association of Railroads points out that soldiers on leave at Christmas may travel at two cents a mile, implying that the railroads are more concerned with patriotism, family, and religion than with profit. Furthermore, they use *identification:* "this is *your* railroad; it's like the Mississippi River, it's one of those things that makes America great."

Now let us turn to some of the principles which are involved in propaganda work. They may be summarized as follows.

1. The propagandist must consider the prevailing needs, frustrations, and anxieties of the individuals in the group to which he is appealing. This point is vividly exemplified in both wars where the German soldier was attracted by the promises of food and safe conduct he would receive on being taken prisoner. Senator McCarthy was particularly effective as a propagandist during the Korean war and at other low points in the "cold war" since the American people were disturbed by the threat of atomic destruction at home and the role that domestic Communists might play in an extended crisis. A Southern Congressman, no matter what his own personal views on "white supremacy," still finds it a required campaign slogan since it crystallizes the motives and anxieties of a large part of his constituency. Generally speaking, the propagandist finds a time of prosperity and psychological well-being an unpromising time in which to operate, since frustrations are minimal.

2. Not only must the propagandist understand the emotional and motivational character of his target group; he also must be sensitive to their values, attitudes, and social norms. Often propaganda fails because the communicator is naïve. For this reason the export of domestic propaganda is a problem. It came as a surprise to the Nazis that they were unable to conduct a successful anti-Semitic campaign among American troops, since the latter had very little feeling that our entry into the war was a Jewish plot. Likewise, the Soviets and Marxists have not been able to communicate successfully with others because of their rigid ideas and stereotyped language. A Soviet newspaper in Vienna failed to get results because of its use of unfamiliar terms like "overfulfilled the norm" or "the

23 L. I. Pearlin and M. Rosenberg, Propaganda techniques in institutional advertising, *Pub. Opin. Quart.,* XVI (1952), 5-26. Reprinted in Katz *et al., Public opinion and propaganda* (New York: The Dryden Press, Inc., 1954), pp. 478-90.

miasmas of capitalism"; the local Communist newspaper was more successful in its selection of topics and language.[24]

3. A related factor is ego-involvement; the individual must be identified with the cause, for status or other reasons. One sees this best, perhaps, in international conflict, where the persons on each side are convinced of the justice of their cause. Propaganda for racism or intolerant views often involves this principle: the recipient identifies with an anti-Negro or other antiminority viewpoint because it allows him to feel superior.

4. Propaganda must be adjusted to the target group in terms of age, intelligence, and education. Communication specialists find that the greatest success is with the more suggestible members of the population, such as younger people and those of lower socioeconomic status. Propaganda is most effective, by and large, when it is clear-cut, direct, and simple. Even in the most progressive states, the average adult has less than a twelfth-grade education; though this is not expected to be the case for long, in view of the increasing tendency to continue education beyond high school.

5. Other factors in propaganda work are gaining attention, particularly those of timing and repetition. A striking example is the front page news headline, which began its career with the sinking of the U.S.S. Maine in 1898. Various tricks and devices on the screen or in sound waves aid in attracting attention. Successful propaganda emphasizes urgency—"Do it now!"—and indicates the specific action to be taken. Repetition is important; some people, at least, will believe anything if they hear it often enough! Goebbels, one of the real professionals in propaganda work, maintained that a propaganda release must precede its competitors. Nazi defeats were therefore announced rapidly to the German people so as to counteract the effects of powerful foreign radio stations. He was convinced there is an optimum moment for a propaganda campaign. For example, he refrained from initiating a pro-German program in India because he felt anti-British feeling was not yet sufficiently strong.[25]

Since news releases are often an important function of government, especially at times of crisis, central facilitating agencies may be set up, as with the British or United States Information Services. In a totalitarian state, of course, the problem is more decisively resolved, through tight control by one central agency.

[24] M. F. Herz, Some psychological lessons from leaflet propaganda in World War II, *Pub. Opin. Quart.*, XIII (1949), 471-86. Reprinted in Katz *et al., op. cit.*, 543-53.

[25] See L. Doob, Goebbels' principles of propaganda (based on L. P. Lochner, *The Goebbels Diaries* [Garden City, N. Y.: Doubleday & Co., Inc., 1948]), in Schramm, *op. cit.*, pp. 517-36.

6. As already mentioned, propaganda is more effective when its origin is concealed. In psychological warfare this distinction separates "white" from "black" propaganda. The former refers to those materials that are clearly identified as information from the enemy. The latter is the hidden or camouflaged communication such as the World War II radio station occupied by Americans in Luxembourg which claimed to speak for, and as, Germans. There is also "gray" propaganda which avoids the whole problem of origin. Lee clarifies the distinction in terms of the Communist Party in the United States: [26]

The New York *Daily Worker,* so long as it is published openly and avowedly as a party organ, is white propaganda. Gray propaganda mediums would be the channels of front groups, or organizations recognized as controlled by Communists but not openly admitted to be so. The American Youth for Democracy, although the direct successor to the Young Communist League, was such a gray propaganda medium until it was destroyed by being effectively labeled for what it was. Black mediums are the utterances carried through many channels which are not identified as Communist but which accomplish Communist objectives.

7. Distortion is even more inevitable than concealment. It is questionable whether Hitler was right when he said that the big lie was easier to circulate than the small lie. Yet the world was astounded to discover what fantasies have been believed by a seemingly intelligent and mature people—the Nazi racial myth being a case in point. The propagandist aims to establish a particular viewpoint. Innuendo, rumor, and fabrication are almost sure to play a part in the process. Exaggeration or "card stacking" is much commoner than outright lies. Facts get restated and reinterpreted in more simplified form and in the direction desired by the propagandist.

8. Ideally, the propagandist manages to eliminate all competition. He seldom achieves this (except in a dictatorship) but many of his tactics are devoted to counteracting the statements of his opponents. In time of war counterpropaganda becomes an elaborate art with many opportunities for missteps; for example, denial of an event announced by the enemy helps call attention to the event, and may even serve to substantiate it. In advertising, business ethics generally forbids vilification of competing products, so the propagandist employs various devices to undermine his rival indirectly. When electric refrigerators first became a threat to ice manufacturers, the latter concentrated on the slogan "Ice never fails." Nowadays our youngsters see any number of "experiments" on TV, in which the

[26] A. M. Lee, *How to understand propaganda* (New York: Rinehart & Co., Inc., 1952), pp. 122-23.

advertised product wins out over "competing brands B, C and D" or over the "average" product.

THE EFFECTIVENESS OF PROPAGANDA

Probably the major error in most treatments of propaganda is to isolate it from its social context—to speak as if a particular leaflet, speech, article, poster, movie, etc., had certain inherent qualities of effectiveness apart from the persons and the social situation involved.

Evidence of this kind of thinking was neatly exemplified in the early days of World War II. Allied propaganda had been very effective in the closing days of World War I. Thousands of disillusioned, exhausted, and hungry German soldiers had been induced to surrender by the showers of leaflets from the air which described Wilson's fourteen points or which guaranteed safety and good food to prisoners of the Allies.[27] Because of this success at the end of the former war, the same techniques were used by both sides when the French and Germans faced each other during the period of the so-called "phony war" of 1939-40. Leaflets and loudspeakers called upon the enemy to give up, using a variety of appeals and arguments. And the propaganda had no effect whatsoever, because the situation was so utterly different from 1918. Now the Germans were confident of their military might, and the French felt secure behind their Maginot Line; the propaganda produced no response but ridicule. As Doob would put it, the *pre-action responses* (attitudes, opinions, etc.) were not of such drive strength that they could be reduced by the action suggested.[28]

Another illustration of the necessity for producing suitable attitudes before propaganda can be effective is found in the case of Mussolini's war upon Ethiopia. The Duce had planned the attack on Ethiopia as early as 1933, but felt that his people would not support a war at that time. So he spent the next two years publicizing the glories of a larger Italian empire and inflaming his people with tales of Ethiopian barbarities and atrocities. By 1935 the ground was prepared, and he launched his war.

Still another example, already mentioned, shows how the effectiveness of propaganda depends upon the broad social situation reflected in the needs and attitudes of people. Hitler and his followers subjected the German people to constant propaganda

[27] See H. D. Lasswell, *Propaganda techniques during the world war* (New York: Alfred A. Knopf, Inc., 1927).

[28] L. W. Doob, *Public opinion and propaganda* (New York: Henry Holt & Co., Inc., 1948), p. 398.

throughout the 1920's, with little or no effect, judging from party membership or number of deputies elected to the Reichstag. The situation was radically changed by the Depression; the people's confusion and frustration made them receptive to both Nazi and Communist propaganda. Both these parties grew greatly in influence between 1930 and 1933, when the Nazis finally took control of the government.

In appraising the effectiveness of propaganda, a distinction must be made between democracy and dictatorship—between the relatively rational and factual appeals on the one hand, and the predominantly emotional and "intuitive" on the other. For example, the National Socialist government in Germany may be said to have directed its propaganda toward the "superego," a kind of chauvinistic conscience. This type of communication was irrational and appealed to the fanatical élite. As the war entered its middle and late phases, a cleavage developed between the loyal guard and the mass of lukewarm followers. The propaganda machine was forced to rely on "ego orientations"—namely, the primary needs and anxiety. Hence our leaflet campaign was focused on food, shelter, and other ego-centered drives.[29]

In the ambiguity and unexpectedness of World War I both sides proclaimed the utter depravity of the enemy and the spotless purity of their own cause. The only communication medium of any consequence was the press, and the favorite device was the atrocity story. World War II offered a whole new dimension in thought control. The use of radio and motion pictures made possible an intensity and intimacy of contact with the war. Likewise, the ideological aspects of the conflict were clearer and more widely disseminated. There had already been considerable documentation of the regressive tendencies and antihumanitarian values of the Nazis, so a fervid hate and atrocity campaign was not used, except in Germany and the Soviet Union. The western alliance found subtler and more factual methods preferable. Churchill, for example, after being censured for employing the term "Hun," stopped using it.

At the same time, any nation fighting a war tends toward the form of the totalitarian state. Propaganda has to be effective. Here "Will it work?" is the criterion rather than "Is it true?" The United States introduced some arbitrary methods of "enlightenment," though the Office of War Information headed by Elmer Davis maintained generally high standards. And if our films did

---

[29] E. Kris and N. Leites, Trends in twentieth century propaganda, in Schramm, op. cit., pp. 489-500. See also K. Young, Social psychology (3d ed.; New York: Appleton-Century-Crofts, Inc., 1956), pp. 476-98.

portray Nazis as actual or potential sadists, or Russians as victimized idealists (between 1941 and 1945), it was in sharp contrast to the horrors attributed to the enemy in such masterpieces as *The Beast of Berlin*, produced in Hollywood a generation earlier.

Possibly the most impressive and most continuous propaganda campaign of all time has resulted from the ideological conflict between the United States and the Soviet Union. It began in earnest after the Second World War, and has encompassed most of the world. On one side is the powerful Voice of America; on the other, the Soviet Union offering its version of reality. In foreign capitals the America House confronts the Soviet Book Shop or the "People's Culture Palace." Any work of art, any scientific achievement (or failure) may become a *cause célèbre,* to say nothing of a Japanese fisherman who finds ten thousand square miles of the Pacific Ocean polluted by atomic tests, or a visiting African dignitary who is refused a malted milk in a Delaware drive-in! Even more exploited is the news of riots in Budapest, Berlin, or Warsaw— or in Little Rock, Arkansas. However effective these propaganda assaults have been, they have led to some reasonably healthy competition between the two power blocs, in the schoolroom, at the workbench, as well as in diplomatic interchanges. On the other hand, a more obvious result is the torturing of facts and the muddying of clear thinking that has accompanied the distortions over the air waves and in the press.

Thus propaganda may or may not be effective. Successful propaganda involves both receptive individuals and a well presented message. It depends upon people's needs and attitudes, upon the stimulus situation and the way they perceive the situation. While it is always difficult to predict which person will be affected by which bit of propaganda, certain principles and criteria such as those discussed enable us to assess the total picture.

PROTECTING OURSELVES FROM PROPAGANDA

For most people the practical question is this: Can I learn to recognize propaganda so I won't be influenced by it against my will? People might perceive something as propaganda—a community chest campaign, an appeal to aid starving children or to strengthen the UN, a campaign to abolish the income tax—and respond enthusiastically. Or they might identify the communicated material as propaganda and as a result fail to take any further interest in the subject. Or, again, they might know something is propaganda, be suspicious of it, and still be considerably influenced. What are the effects of teaching people to analyze and evaluate propaganda?

Following World War I Americans became tremendously interested in propaganda, which was interpreted as a rather sinister means of social control.[30] This interest is attested in an enormous number of books, articles, lectures, and psychological experiments during the 1920's and 1930's.[31] During its more than four years of existence, the Institute for Propaganda Analysis reached an audience of many thousands through its monthly bulletins and two books published under its sponsorship.[32] Its influence was probably greater than circulation figures suggest, since a large proportion of its subscribers were libraries, schools, teachers, editors, clergymen, and lecturers.

However, estimates differ as to the effectiveness of such efforts to train people in propaganda analysis; there is no clear evidence on the subject. It would seem that specific analyses of campaigns such as those done by the Institute (e.g., propaganda techniques of German fascism; Mr. Roosevelt's foreign policy; communist propaganda, U. S. A., 1939 model; the Great A. & P. Tea Co.) had an effect as far as these particular campaigns were concerned. A specific authoritative exposé—of an individual, a company, or a technique (whispering campaigns, or rumor-mongering in wartime)—makes an impression upon people.

The propaganda analyst has tried to interest people in answering questions such as these: [33]

Who is the propagandist? Who are the propagandists?
For what cause, organization, or person are they working?
How sure can we be of these matters?
What is the over-all point of view of the propaganda?
What is its apparent objective—immediate and long run?
Is its objective socially possible?
With what other objectives than its primary one is it identified?
The interests of what groups does the propagandist seek to advance?
  to oppose?
What techniques and appeals is he trying to use? How?
Stripped of techniques and appeals, how would this proposal look
  in terms of our own enlightened self-interest?

On the other hand, there is considerable doubt whether people who have learned to identify propaganda in certain situations can

[30] See pages 440-41 above.

[31] See the extensive bibliography in B. L. Smith, H. D. Lasswell, and R. D. Casey, *Propaganda, communication, and public opinion* (Princeton, N. J.: Princeton University Press, 1946).

[32] A. M. Lee and E. B. Lee, *op. cit.;* H. Lavine and J. Wechsler, *War propaganda and the United States* (New Haven, Conn.: Yale University Press, 1940).

[33] A. M. Lee, *How to understand propaganda* (New York: Rinehart & Co., Inc., 1952), p. 268.

extend their knowledge to propaganda in general. The two most extensive studies in this area indicate that resistance to propaganda cannot be inculcated by training. Using pupils in seventeen high schools, Osborn found that training in procedures of propaganda analysis had little or no effect.[34] He also discovered only a low correlation between intelligence or information and ability to resist propaganda. Collier gave a group of college students detailed instruction in propaganda devices, using as examples Nazi material exported to neutral countries in the early months of World War II.[35] After this debunking, the students studied Nazi propaganda, preparatory to writing a paper analyzing it. At the end of this period, surprisingly enough, these students showed a slight *decrease* in anti-Nazi attitudes, at the same time that comparison groups of students were showing a pronounced increase of anti-Nazi opinion!

The results of these experiments do not demonstrate that training in propaganda analysis can have no value. Indeed, other experiments (though generally less well-controlled ones) have arrived at different conclusions.[36] But they do warn us against credulous assumptions about the benefits of learning how to analyze propaganda.

While they admit that a knowledge of the techniques of propagandists has a certain limited value, Krech and Crutchfield note that "propaganda prophylaxis" encounters great obstacles. First of all comes the difficulty of generalizing or applying knowledge in a different area. "We might pick out one specific piece of material, label it propaganda, and then describe it in great detail. But that will by no means protect us against a piece of propaganda that might appear in the form of an arithmetic book, a lecture by a famous scientist, or a newspaper dispatch." There is, furthermore, a more dynamic factor: "as long as certain needs exist unsatisfied among people and certain belief systems are held and certain authorities remain the source for our facts, propaganda can be effective."[37]

These writers conclude that protection against propaganda involves not only knowledge of the tricks of the propagandist, but also aggressive counterpropaganda to induce beliefs and attitudes

34 W. W. Osborn, An experiment in teaching resistance to propaganda, *J. exp. Educ.*, VIII (1939), 1-17.

35 R. M. Collier, The effect of propaganda upon attitude following a critical examination of the propaganda itself, *J. soc. Psychol.*, XX (1944), 3-17.

36 E.g., W. W. Biddle, *Propaganda and education* (Teach. Coll. Contr. Educ., 1932, No. 531).

37 From *Theory and problems of social psychology,* by D. Krech and R. Crutchfield, 1948, pp. 352-53. Courtesy McGraw-Hill Book Co., Inc., New York.

contrary to those desired by the propagandist. Above all comes the necessity for doing something about the needs, demands, and beliefs which are responsible for making the "wrong propaganda" so acceptable.

COMMUNICATIONS ANALYSIS

One of the propaganda analyst's greatest difficulties is in deciding what is propaganda in the first place. This problem has led several students of public opinion to think of "communications analysis" or "content analysis" as a more satisfactory approach. Their efforts were stimulated by the outbreak of the war, with the great need for realistic study of mass communication, both domestic and foreign. Pioneers in this work were Lasswell, Lazarsfeld and Berelson.[38] Their methods of analyzing content agreed in identifying and counting selected symbols, in noting whether these are presented favorably or unfavorably, and in attempting to gauge their intensity, emphasis, or attention-value. However, they differed as to other procedures, and so far no one has been able to propose a comprehensive schema for content analysis.[39] Part of the difficulty, of course, lies in the variety of the media which are to be analyzed —such as a news column, editorial, short story, novel, radio drama, comic strip, or movie. Then, too, the analyst's purpose influences the techniques he uses. Berelson and Salter, for example, were interested in short story treatment of people with respect to ethnic background.[40] So they focused upon the characters' roles, status, ethnic origin, goals, and personality traits. With different purposes, the investigators might have analyzed speech, dress, age, humor, scene of the action, or various other matters.

Sometimes content analysis is focused on the relations of one group to another, or the comparison of cultures through investigating prevailing themes via the use of symbols, images, and concepts. Mass media offer rich possibilities for the more or less quantitative study of cultural values as expressed in art, literature and recrea-

---

[38] See H. D. Lasswell, Describing the contents of communications, in B. L. Smith, H. D. Lasswell, and R. Casey, *Propaganda, communication and public opinion* (Princeton, N. J.: Princeton University Press, 1946); P. F. Lazarsfeld and R. K. Merton, Studies in radio and film propaganda, *Trans. N. Y. Acad. Sci.*, VI:2 (1943), 58-79. The most comprehensive treatment is found in B. Berelson, *Content analysis in communication research* (Glencoe, Ill.: Free Press, 1952).

[39] An excellent example of content analysis is a study of treatment by the press of accusations of un-Americanism against Edward U. Condon, Director of the National Bureau of Standards, in J. T. Klapper and C. Y. Glock, Trial by newspaper, *Scientific American*, CLXXX:2 (1949), 16-21. Reprinted in S. H. Britt (ed.), *Selected Readings*, pp. 13-30, and in Katz *et al., op. cit.*, pp. 105-12.

[40] B. Berelson and P. J. Salter, Majority and minority Americans: An analysis of magazine fiction, *Pub. Opin. Quart.*, X (1946), 168-90.

tional activities. The literature of the Boy Scouts of America, compared with that of the Hitler Youth, showed widely different orientations. The reasons for recommending desirable action, for example, were as follows in the two organizations: [41]

	Hitler Youth	Boy Scouts
As member of national community	66%	25%
As member of face-to-face group	19	28
Essential for individual's own satisfaction or perfection	15	47

While both groups used propaganda, the kind of arguments and principles emphasized by the leaders in these two youth organizations are seen to be quite different. German and American cultural values have been compared in other studies, through noting the amount of space devoted to selected subjects in periodicals, through analyzing dominant themes of successful plays, or through identifying the types of music played on radio programs.[42]

Or again, the content analyst may investigate the positive or negative approaches to certain political, social, or economic issues. This may take the form of assessing "communication standards." For instance, treatment of the Taft-Hartley law restricting union activity was studied in fifty periodicals. Strikingly varied selection of news items was found; the percentages of items favoring and opposing the law were as follows: [43]

	Type of periodical (selected)			
	General	Financial	News	Opinion
Favor	90%	80%	31%	0%
Neutral	9	15	69	64
Oppose	1	5	0	36

His findings led the author to conclude: [44]

It is at least consistent with democratic theory to suppose that both employers and organized labor have an initial equal claim to the attention and support of the public . . . . The one-sided treatment of the Taft-Hartley law in the periodical press as a whole can scarcely be considered to accord with this aspect of democratic polity.

It is already fairly well agreed among communications analysts that a distinction must be made between *intent, content,* and *effect,*

[41] H. S. Lewin, Hitler youth and the Boy Scouts of America; a comparison of aims, *Hum. Relat.*, I (1947), 206-27.

[42] See chapter 3, pp. 80-82, on Germany.

[43] P. Ash, The periodical press and the Taft-Hartley Act, *Pub. Opin. Quart.*, XII (1948), 266-71 (as cited in Berelson, *op. cit.*, p. 48).

[44] *Ibid.*, p. 271.

or *response*, analysis. Content analysis is the heart of the matter, since without it neither intent nor response can be interpreted. For this reason, and also because the communicated materials are easily obtainable for study, most effort has gone into analysis of content. One suggestion may prove helpful as better methods of content analysis procedures are devised.[45] All content analysis procedures are not on the same level. Some stay close to the communicated content (e.g., counting symbols, noting prominence and relative emphasis, etc.). Another kind of analysis has a different frame of reference: relationship to objective data and conditions (e.g., judging content as to accuracy or distortion). A third level of analysis implies knowledge of the presumptive audience (e.g., stereotypes and mechanisms can be meaningfully identified only if we know the attitudes, frustrations, etc., of the persons to whom the material is directed). Thus, according to this interpretation, content analysis cannot be done solely by studying the communicated material per se. The analyst's frame of reference must include knowledge of outside events and conditions and of audience responses if the analysis is to be realistic and effective.

SUMMARY

For most Americans the word "propaganda" connotes something unpleasant and deceitful. The term is more likely to be applied to our opponents' than to our own persuasive efforts. Actually, propaganda is simply an attempt to influence people's attitudes and opinions in a particular direction, so that action desired by the propagandist will follow.

It is well to distinguish between propaganda on the one hand and news, entertainment, and education on the other; otherwise "propaganda" becomes so broad as to lose its essential meaning. Propaganda is all about us, due in part to the professional efforts of advertisers, publicity men, lobbyists, and public relations counselors.

Various techniques have been suggested for identifying propaganda, such as the "seven devices" proposed by the Institute for Propaganda Analysis. Principles involved in propaganda work include congruence with basic needs, attitudes, and other characteristics of the target group; simple and clear presentation of material; the concealment of its origin and stacking the cards favorably. In a word, successful propaganda involves both well-presented material and a receptive audience.

[45] S. S. Sargent and G. Saenger, Analyzing the content of mass media, *J. soc. Issues,* III:3 (1947), 33-38.

Since World War II social scientists have been developing and improving "content analysis," though a set formula for analyzing communicated material has not been discovered, and may never be. In regard to protection against propaganda, it seems that while people can learn to recognize certain specific kinds of propaganda, it is doubtful whether they can learn to protect themselves against propaganda in general.

SUPPLEMENTARY READINGS

Books of Readings

MACCOBY, E. E., NEWCOMB, T. M., AND HARTLEY, E. L. (eds.). *Readings in social psychology*, 3d ed. New York: Henry Holt & Co., Inc., 1958.
Hovland, C. I., The role of primacy and recency in persuasive communication.
Lumsdaine, A. A., and Janis, I. L., Resistance to "counter-propaganda" produced by one-sided and two-sided "propaganda" presentations.
Schein, E. H., The Chinese indoctrination program for prisoners of war: a study of attempted "brainwashing."
Weiss, W., and Fine, B. J., The effect of induced aggressiveness on opinion change.

BRITT, S. H. (ed.). *Selected readings in social psychology*. New York: Rinehart & Co., Inc., 1950.
Klapper, J. T., and Glock, C. Y., Trial by newspaper.
Linebarger, P. M. A., The British-German radio war.
Spitzer, H. M., Presenting America in American propaganda.

LINDZEY, G. (ed.). *Handbook of social psychology*. Reading, Mass.: Addison-Wesley Pub. Co., Inc., 1954.
Berelson, B., Content analysis, Vol. I.

Other References

ALBIG, W. *Modern public opinion*, rev. ed. New York: McGraw-Hill Book Co., Inc., 1956.
Part IV has worthwhile chapters on censorship and propaganda.

BERELSON, B. *Content analysis in communication research*. Glencoe, Ill.: Free Press, 1952.
Probably the best review of the purposes, methods, and results, as well as the literature of the subject.

BERNAYS, E. L. *Public relations*. Norman, Okla.: University of Oklahoma Press, 1952.
The history of the movement including applications in specific fields.

DOOB, L. *Public opinion and propaganda*. New York: Henry Holt & Co., Inc., 1948.
Still unsurpassed in its analysis of the problems in propaganda, especially chaps. xi to xvii.

KATZ, D., CARTWRIGHT, D., ELDERSVELD, S., AND LEE, A. M. (eds.). *Public opinion and propaganda*. New York: The Dryden Press, Inc., 1954.
A superlative set of readings, especially Part IV.

LASSWELL, H. D. *Propaganda technique during the World War*. New York: Alfred A. Knopf, Inc., 1927.
The classic study of the "fine art," 1914-1918.

LERNER, D. *Skywar: psychological warfare against Germany, D-Day to V-E Day*. New York: George W. Stewart, 1949.
The techniques as well as the effectiveness of propaganda in World War II.

Lee, A. M. *How to understand propaganda.* New York: Rinehart & Co., Inc., 1952.
A popularly written account of the field, with analysis of propagandists, their organizations, and the role of the mass media.

Merton, R. K. *Mass persuasion: the social psychology of a war bond drive.* New York: Harper & Bros., 1947.
A study of Kate Smith's successful attempt to sell war bonds. It deals with motivation and effectiveness in propaganda and morale.

Padover, S. K., and Lasswell, H. D. *Psychological warfare.* New York: Foreign Policy Association (Headline Series), 1951.
A brief review of war and foreign propaganda.

Smith, B. L., Lasswell, H. D., and Casey, R. D. (eds.). *Propaganda, communication, and public opinion.* Princeton: Princeton University Press, 1946.
An excellent bibliographic guide, in addition to some explanation of communication processes.

18

Mass Behavior

"Mass behavior" is a broad term often used to designate similar or common social behavior on the part of a large number of people, particularly when it is transitory or cyclical in nature and when it results from suggestion or some other irrational process. Sometimes persons showing "mass behavior" form a face-to-face group, as in a crowd, mob, lynching, riot, or panic. In other cases they do not, as with fashions, fads, crazes, "mass hysteria," or the circulation of rumors. Social movements will be treated separately in the next chapter, although they share many of the characteristics of mass behavior, because they have more permanent group structure and are related to major social changes.

After a description and illustration each form of mass behavior will be analyzed according to a field interpretation. First will be noted the more or less objective situational factors, such as the number of persons involved, their age, sex, socioeconomic and ethnic status, the leadership, and the propaganda, suggestion, or other type of communication. Then personality trends of participants will be discussed—their needs and frustrations, their attitudes, values, and interests—concluding with data on how they define or interpret the situation. The data in certain areas are scanty, and it therefore will be necessary to resort to hypotheses.

FASHION

Fashion has been defined as "relatively short-lived, socially approved, continuous variations in dress, furniture, music, art, speech and other areas of culture." [1] Kimball Young notes that "fashion

[1] H. P. Fairchild (ed.), *Dictionary of sociology* (New York: Philosophical Library, Inc., 1944), p. 117.

applies to the prevalent mode in those things in a culture which are subject to periodic change in form." [2]

Fashions are socially sanctioned norms which show continual change. In fact, fashions represent an accepted and expected kind of social change in certain areas. Sometimes the change is relatively rapid, as with dress, automobile design, or popular music. In other areas the changes are less rapid, as with art, architecture, interior decoration, manners, or philosophy. But fashion is cyclical; compared to the slowly changing mores, fashions are always in flux.[3] Furthermore, fashion seems to thrive in societies which show relatively rapid social change, notably the United States. One conception of fashion takes this feature into account by defining it as "a social ritual related to mobility, to upward striving in our modern society." [4] The presence of class lines, too, is reflected in fashions. As Young puts it: "There is often a sharp difference in the standards of beauty and attractiveness on the part of various classes. In our time, the lower and lower-middle-class groups are strongly attracted to the full-figured female with scantily covered bosom . . . On the other hand, the upper class . . . tends to regard the exposure of the bare bosom or the Varga and Petty type of girl display as being distinctly low-brow in character." [5]

"Being fashionable" means conforming to the newest of these sanctioned changes. In our country, current fashions are brought to the attention of everyone through window displays, advertising, and photographs in magazines, newspapers, and movies. Persons of high social and financial standing, and others in the public eye, act as pace-setters in introducing the new fashions, which spread fairly rapidly at first, then more slowly until they are succeeded by the fashions of the next season.

Once or more a year, the leading dress designers and manufacturers of Paris and New York meet to decide upon women's fashions for the coming season. New designs are agreed upon and samples made which are sent to leading stores, where they are displayed. Photographs and movies are made of the dresses worn by attractive models and sometimes by women prominent in social and artistic circles.

The new dresses are bought first by women of high socioeconomic status, who set the pace. Some of the designs are then manufac-

---

[2] K. Young, *Social psychology* (2d ed.; New York: Appleton-Century-Crofts, Inc., 1944), p. 411.

[3] *Ibid.*, p. 411.

[4] B. Barber and L. S. Lobel, Fashion in women's clothes and the American social system, *Soc. Forces*, XXXI (1952), 124-31.

[5] K. Young, *Social psychology* (3d ed.; New York: Appleton-Century-Crofts, Inc., 1956), p. 326.

tured more cheaply and sold in medium- and low-priced stores. This "sweep downward" of fashion, from higher- to lower-income groups, is neatly illustrated in the case of the "Wally" dress. On June 3, 1937, pictures of the Duchess of Windsor's $250 Mainbocher wedding gown appeared in several American newspapers. Ten days later Bonwit Teller, a fashionable New York store, advertised a version of this dress at $25. Early in July, Lord and Taylor had its copy of the "Wally" dress on display at $16.95. By the middle of July, Klein's cash-and-carry clothing store farther downtown had whole racks full of the same dress—price $8.90.[6]

The same percolation downward was noted in connection with the "new look." One of Dior's cocktail dresses, "Margrave," was put on the market by Bergdorf Goodman at $400. Other manufacturers then took it over with slight adaptations and changes in fabric and workmanship, to sell at $110, $45, and finally after three months, at $8.95.[7]

By the time a given fashion has spread into lower-income groups, the season has changed and the pace-setters at the top are wearing another kind of outfit. However, seasonal changes do not usually alter the major characteristics of a fashion. When a new fashion has really caught on, for example, it will be reflected in bathing suits and beach dresses.

It is difficult to overestimate the importance of status in determining fashion; the reward for adopting a new style early is the prestige that accompanies the accoutrements of status. "Rapidly changing fashion, therefore, depends upon a society in which upward mobility and prestige striving are favorably valued. The rapid succession of styles becomes necessary when the higher social strata are not able to maintain a monopoly of the symbols of high status." [8]

Most fashion changes represent minor rather than major variations in previous styles. In 1875 women's skirts swept the floor or were only an inch or two above it. From 1875 to 1887 they became shorter, but only to the point of exposing the shoes. Then they went down again until 1910. The shortening process gradually set in, until by 1927 knees were exposed. Skirts were generally longer in the 1930's, but became short again in 1940, until the days of the "new look" in 1947, which represented a most radical attempt to produce a change in style, as we shall see. (A style is a whole pattern, involving length, fulness, padding, etc.)

6 *Life*, August 9, 1937.

7 *Life*, March 1, 1948.

8 R. H. Turner and L. M. Killian, *Collective behavior* (Englewood Cliffs, N. J.: Prentice-Hall, Inc., 1957), p. 215.

Another characteristic of fashion is its cyclical nature. Superficially, fashions seem to run in cycles: skirts go up, then down, then up again; they become wide, then narrow, then full again. But this is an oversimplified description of fashion changes. For the most part the nature of new styles is unpredictable. Sometimes they duplicate the fashions of earlier periods, as with the return to the bustle in 1947, or to crinolines and hoopskirts in the mid-1950's. Often they are influenced by current events: for example, the Egyptian motif that followed the "King Tut" discoveries in the 1920's, or the various military styles that became popular during World War II.

If the design of next year's styles is unpredictable, one fact is certain: there will be *some kind of change*. The reason is partly that women have come to expect changes in fashion, but more basically that fashion has become big business. It is of utmost importance to a fair-sized army of designers, manufacturers, wholesalers, retailers, models, and advertising men that fashions change each season and that the changes be taken seriously, that is, that new dresses be purchased.

The story of the "new look" is an interesting case in point. During World War II fashion changes were slight, because of shortages and the need to conserve materials and manpower. Just after the war a little French designer, M. Christian Dior, worked out plans for what some have called "the third fashion revolution of the twentieth century." He studied the trends of the times, said *Life* magazine, then went against them.[9] With fabrics scarce and finances shaky in many countries, Dior launched a style "requiring extravagant yardage and luxurious fabrics." In February, 1947, he showed his long-skirted, bosom-exposing "new look" designs to a selected audience in his sumptuous salon. Everyone gasped—but followed his leadership. Dior's wide skirts were not only wide; "they stretched up to 45 yards. His narrow waists became as much as two inches narrower by means of specially installed corsets. His low necks were so low they barely stopped at the waist."[10]

Dior's daring and perfect timing made him a man on horseback for the clothing industry. Whether "radical" or "reactionary," the "new look" was a daring change. But could the industry make women like it and men accept or at least tolerate it?

First reactions from the public were unfavorable. A young Texas housewife founded the "Little Below the Knee Club" as a rebellion against longer skirts. Within a short time the revolt had spread to

9 *Life,* March 1, 1948.
10 *Ibid.*

many cities and the club had 300,000 members, according to *Life* magazine.[11] The men backed their wives for economic reasons and because they liked short skirts for other reasons. But the battle was short-lived; the "Little Below the Knee Club" succumbed before the united front of designers, manufacturers, merchants, and advertisers. By February, 1948, the revolt had failed. "The average woman's heart was not in it any more, and the average American woman's husband, long since resigned to footing the bill for the greatest feminine sartorial overhaul in a generation, had simply written it off as one of history's minor catastrophes. The women were agreeing that the parachute skirt and the padded hip did do something for the figure, and the men were marveling anew at the familiar fact that the most preposterous feminine rigging that a couturier's mind can conceive has a way of looking perfectly normal and natural a few months after women adopt it." [12]   The few strong-willed women who continued to resist were beaten as soon as they needed a new skirt; all they could buy was the "new look"! [13]

What about fashions for men? American males regard feminine fashions with amusement—and sometimes with alarm. The women consider men ultraconventional and conservative. They marvel at the way men cling to uncomfortable collars, at their adherence to coats in summer heat. One designer notes that a fully clothed man has seven layers of cloth around his waist, from undershirt to overcoat; he wears about seventy buttons, only thirty-three of which can be fastened to anything.

Many attempts have been made to introduce new fashions for men, with very little success. A fashion expert, Elizabeth Hawes, finally succeeded in introducing the slack suit for sport and recreation, but got nowhere with her suggested changes in business dress.[14] However, slow evolutionary changes have occurred, largely in the direction of greater casualness and comfort.[15] Vests and garters have all but disappeared, and shirts become continuously more colorful and informal. The *New York Times Magazine* could report on April 28, 1957, that "color in all men's apparel has become so commonplace that it is now worn with complete assurance by most of the male population, and has all but lost its value as news." Even in that most unchanging area of evening wear, men have come to

11 *Ibid.*

12 *Ibid.*

13 Ten years later—shortly before his death—Dior was still "dictator by demand" of French and of world fashion. See *Time*, March 4, 1957.

14 E. Hawes, *Men can take it* (New York: Random House, Inc., 1939).

15 S. Boal, For men only: The "old look," *New York Times Magazine,* December 19, 1948.

wear gaudy cummerbunds and, more radically still, scarlet jackets instead of the traditional black or white ones.

None the less, despite some exceptions, one is still tempted to conclude that American women are bound to follow any fashion, however bizarre, and American men are likely to resist any change, however sensible!

There are other fashion phenomena in our society besides clothing. Every year the automobile manufacturers put out one or more new designs. The new car differs in several respects from last year's model. Each company has a preview of its forthcoming models, with much publicity. Usually the new design involves minor improvements and changes; occasionally they are more radical, as with Ford's first Model A in 1928, or the streamlined Chrysler of the 1930's.[16] Of course conformity is not demanded here to the extent that it is with women's fashions, but the really stylish person feels he should not drive a car which is more than two years old.

Some would speak of fashions in popular music, referring both to general type and to specific songs. MacDougald describes the production of a song "hit."[17] Music publishers and record manufacturers seek out well-known writers to do the words and music of a new song. Their "song-pluggers" bring it to the attention of a prominent band or orchestra. If the band leader thinks the song has good possibilities and that the publisher or manufacturer will name and advertise his band, he "rides the song hard." If the song makes the "Hit Parade," as one of the leading songs of the week or month, its sales will boom. But its life as a hit is limited to about two months—compared with six months or more before radios became common.

Fashion motivation. Why does one conform to fashion? Actually, many people do not follow the dictates of fashion at all. Many elderly, rural, and lower-class women pay little attention to the latest styles. Many car owners are not impressed with the necessity of turning in a satisfactory older model for the sake of keeping up with the newest designs. Many fashions, as in music, dancing, or sports, are restricted to special groups such as adolescents or unmarried young adults.

However, most women do conform to current fashions in dress. Why?

16 Sometimes there is real doubt as to whether certain changes *are* improvements—for example, the accentuated tail fins of the 1957 models.

17 D. MacDougald, Jr., The popular music industry, in P. F. Lazarsfeld and F. N. Stanton (eds.), *Radio Research, 1941* (New York: Duell, Sloan & Pearce, Inc., 1941). See also J. Johnstone and E. Katz, Youth and popular music: a study in the sociology of taste, *Amer. J. Sociol.,* LXII (1957), 563–68.

Students of fashion seem to agree that two motives are paramount: the desire for conformity and the desire for recognition or prestige. But other motives are often mentioned, such as the wish for new experience, compensation for inferiority, and need for comfort or beauty. Psychoanalysts suggest that fashion serves women as a sublimated outlet for aggressive or exhibitionistic tendencies. Flugel, for example, notes signs of aggression in that one woman can hurt another by being more fashionably dressed.[18] Veblen's theory is also well known: a well-dressed woman symbolizes her husband's success and prestige, hence her fashionableness satisfies both husband and wife.[19] Sherif and Cantril find that one of the chief functions of clothes is to "extend the 'self' of the wearer, to enhance his ego, to display his status."[20] Thus many persons become strongly ego-involved in the process of keeping up with fashion.

Recent interpreters of fashion discount many once accepted theories such as sex attraction, economy, and utility. Young finds that sexual desires have little to do with determining the *content* of fashion, since whatever is accepted and worn by women soon comes to be thought attractive by the opposite sex.[21] (The male protest against the "new look" and eventual acceptance of it seems to bear out Young's interpretation.) It was discovered that economy is not a strong motive in determining acceptance of fashion, nor does modesty play a great part in resisting new fashions.[22]

Much controversy has taken place over utility as a determiner of fashions. Without doubt the broad trend over several generations is in the direction of greater utility. But comfort and convenience seem relatively unimportant as criteria for year-to-year changes in fashion. Young reports that his women students in 1925 assured him that bobbed hair and short skirts had come to stay. They were "so convenient, so sensible, that women would never give them up."[23] Five years later he found a third of his women students wearing their hair long; all but one had previously had bobbed hair. And the trend toward long hair continued into the 1940's. After 1925 skirts were lengthened, later shortened, and with the

---

18 J. C. Flugel, *The psychology of clothes* (London: Leonard and Virginia Woolf, 1930), p. 414.

19 T. Veblen, *Theory of the leisure class* (new ed.; New York: Viking Press, Inc., 1926).

20 M. Sherif and H. Cantril, *Psychology of ego-involvements* (New York: John Wiley & Sons, Inc., 1947), p. 349.

21 K. Young, *op. cit.*

22 E. Barr, *A psychological analysis of fashion motivation* (Arch. Psychol., 1934, No. 171).

23 K. Young, *op. cit.*, p. 327.

"new look" of 1947, considerably lengthened again. No wonder the students of fashion find it irrational!

We may, of course, have erred in overgeneralizing about the "whys" of fashion. A useful distinction might be made between pace-setters, followers, and "grumbling acquiescers." Pace-setters are women high on the socioeconomic ladder who gain prestige by introducing the new fashions. Those who follow closely after these leaders are conforming, yet they are also gaining some prestige by introducing the new styles into their community, club, or other social group. The "grumbling acquiescers" are the women who don't care for being stylish but at the same time don't wish to be considered queer or out of date. Their motivation is primarily conformity.

Without doubt, the groups to which a woman belongs and with which she identifies herself are of great importance in determining her attitudes and actions with respect to fashion. In some "society" groups it is essential to be up-to-the-minute on styles; in most bohemian groups it is important to be unconventional. In many adolescent and college groups it is essential to conform to local fashions, such as blue jeans, pedal-pushers, sweaters, and so on. What the psychologist might treat as individual motives seem to arise from group participation and identification with groups.

Here again, as with all social psychological phenomena, we require a field interpretation—data on personality variables, such as attitudes and motives; data on the social situation, which involves the way the fashion is presented, who has taken it up, and so on; and data as to how individuals interpret the situation—what they consider their role to be in view of their personality trends and the actualities of the social situation.

FADS

The term "fad" is used, typically, for a sporadic short-term kind of fashion, which sometimes borders upon the "cult." A fad may be local or national in scope but it is always temporary and unpredictable. Sometimes what begins as a fad may end up as a fashion, custom, or hobby. For example, bobbed hair, slacks, blue jeans, and bingo started as fads and have continued in more permanent form.

For convenience we may distinguish between the "cultist" and the spasmodic type of fad. The cultist type is illustrated by dietary practices such as Fletcherizing, eating roughage, the Hay diet, or vegetarianism, and by health cults such as sunbathing and nudism. In such cases there is an ideology centering about how one or another of these practices contributes to health, happiness, and better living. One example of such a fad was the "activationists," a group whose goal was uninhibited self-expression in athletics, dancing, art, and writing.[24]

Social psychologists have given more attention to the "spasmodic" type of fad—the practice which catches on and spreads like wildfire for a short time, then dies rapidly away. Some of these fads had quite general appeal, such as mah-jongg, jigsaw puzzles, miniature golf, "Confucius say," and "knock-knock." Others have appealed to more specialized groups. For example, in art and literature, we have had cubism, futurism, Dadaism, and surrealism, all within the first three or four decades of the twentieth century. The continuing interest in the art of Salvador Dali and the writings of Gertrude Stein suggests a more lasting interest—the tendency of a fad to become a fashion or a style.

Among adolescents, of course, fads are most prevalent. At various times American teen-agers have worn ten to twenty bangle bracelets, dog-collars around their ankles, slickers and sweatshirts inscribed with their friends' names, or shirt-tails outside their pants with one trouser leg rolled up to the knee. For several seasons they carried money in slits in their loafers. If "going steady," they have worn similar sweaters, or have had each other's initials carved in the soles of their shoes, or have walked along "handcuffed" by a chain of paperclips. As the president of the Youth Research Institute commented:

> If in the next few months the teen-age males of this country start wearing silk hats with their dungarees and the young females start wearing rubber boots to school proms, no one will be surprised.
> There is no sign of either trend right now. But who can say what bizarre and generally inexplicable mode of dress, style of speech or mass mannerism youthful faddists will adopt next? It has been going on for years, of course, but nowadays it goes on faster than ever before . . . .[25]

College fads have been generally less extreme than those of the teen-agers, but the term "collegiate" still carries a connotation of the raccoon coats and college-boy "rah-rah" behavior of the turbulent twenties. Various extreme forms of behavior, like goldfish-swallowing, flagpole-sitting, and marathon dancing have attracted attention out of all proportion to the small number of actual participants in such activities. In the 1950's, however, with the "panty-raid" fad or craze, college boys have managed to display enough

24 See *Life*, August 16, 1948.
25 Lester Rand, Kaleidoscope of teen-age fads, *New York Times Magazine*, October 17, 1954.

immaturity to convince many of their elders that they definitely were not grown up.

Unfortunately our knowledge of the nature and extent of fads is generally vague. Some research data, however, are available. For example, two Barnard College students studied high school fads and fashions in a suburb of New York and in a Southern city during the winter of 1945-46.[26] In the New York suburb all the teenage girls were wearing heavy wool plaid shirts with the tail flapping and dungarees, often with the pants legs rolled up to the knee. The boys were divided into three groups: a conventional or neatly dressed group, a sloppy pattern (plaid shirts and dungarees), and an athletic group, which wore T-shirts or "jocko-jackets," whose color identified the athletic team to which they belonged. In this community the girls tended more toward faddist behavior than the boys. In the Southern city, the prevalent fads and fashions of high school students were generally similar to those found in the North. However, dress was more conservative, on the whole, and was more influenced by parental wishes. In the South the boys, with their "peg" and "drape" trousers, showed more faddist behavior than the girls. The two studies suggest that fads and fashions operate within the framework of local and sectional mores. The Northern community manifested less conservatism, greater freedom for the girls, and less parental influence than the Southern community.

An interpretation of fads. Information as to the origin of fads is meager and unreliable. An attempt to discover the source of the "Kilroy" fad located no less than five widely separated persons, each of whom explained in detail how he had originated or witnessed the origin of the fad![27] Clothing fads sometimes percolate down from local style leaders or from magazine ads. Sometimes a businessman puts out bizarre products in the hope that they may catch on. For example, one manufacturer, after many tries, made a hit with his "windmill caps" for small fry in 1947 and 1948.

The Davy Crockett fad of 1955, sparked by Walt Disney's movie and TV shows, involved incredible commercial activity, starting with phonograph records, books, and coonskin caps. No one had an exclusive copyright on the name, hence many manufacturers and distributors tried to exploit it. No less than three thousand items glutted the shops, including Davy Crockett bath towels, telephone sets, ukuleles, ladies' panties, and plastic ice cream cones.[28] The

26 Unpublished study by A. Durant and E. McMillan.

27 See, Who is Kilroy?, *New York Times Magazine,* January 12, 1947, p. 30.

28 Peter T. White, Ex-king of the wild frontier, *New York Times Magazine,* December 11, 1955.

fad was short-lived, possibly because it became so intense, and dwindled to nothing by the end of the year.

However they may originate, why do fads catch on and spread? Many factors are undoubtedly involved, and those accounting for mah-jongg may be quite different from those operating to produce flagpole-sitting or enthusiasm for calypso or rock 'n roll music. Since adequate data are lacking, a few hypotheses may be considered:

1. To be successful, a fad must *seem novel and new*. Though variants of old fads do recur, they tend to be from a period before the memory of the participants—though often not of their parents!

2. Fads must be *broadly consistent with the times*. Jigsaw puzzles and miniature golf would hardly spread during wartime; on the other hand, adolescents' wearing of identification bracelets and service insignia, or putting pin-up girls on their walls, are consistent with wartime themes. The rise of miniature golf in the early thirties was consistent with the growth of automobiling, with people's wish for mild exercise, and with depression needs for reasonably priced recreation.

3. Fads must, of course, be *harmonious with widespread interest* and motive patterns, such as playing games, gambling, gaining attention, and the like. Pea-shooters, bubble-gum, cap-guns, water-pistols, and trading cards have tremendous appeal for preadolescents in our culture. A supply of these items in a store may start a local fad which runs a brief course. The Davy Crockett fad presumably derived from children's tendency to identify with national heroes. With adolescents the fad usually lasts longer—possibly a year or more. Apparently the strongest motive pattern here is a combination of attention-getting, asserting independence from adults, and conformity to the adolescent group. The director of the Youth Research Institute puts it as follows:

   "Broadly speaking, the teen-agers want acceptance by their contemporaries; "conformity" within the social group is a form of self-reassurance at an age when things can be pretty confusing. It is a period of natural resistance to—if not alienation from—the control of parents and teachers, so the youngsters find comfort in being like others of their own age. In doing this they nevertheless seek to express their individuality by wearing more and crazier charms or being the first to use a new bit of slang." He concludes on an optimistic note: "They are, all in all, pseudo-sophisticates teetering on the edge of growing up. And, while teetering, they are having a wonderful time." [29]

4. Despite the transience and unpredictability of fads, *publicity and advertising* may play a part in their dissemination. Pictures of

[29] Lester Rand, *op. cit.*

clothing fads, like fashions, sometimes carry the fad from one community to another. Some high-school students in the suburban New York community mentioned earlier got many of their ideas of dress and language from a widely circulated comic strip, whose creator seemed well versed in adolescent psychology. Several youngsters admitted picking up faddist ideas from magazines for adolescents. In 1956 and 1957, for example, teen-age magazines carried ads for "butch wax" hair control for "burrs, butches, and ducktails" (all faddist types of haircuts), for "Ivy League" clothes and for "sweetheart picture pumps"—girls' casual shoes with a toe slot for the boy friend's picture.

5. Our *rapidly changing American culture pattern* seems congenial to fads, as it is to fashions, crazes, social movements, and other mass phenomena. Whether this is a function of boredom and low morale, of prosperity, of "flaming youth," or of a pioneer spirit and freedom from regimentation, it is hard to say. In any event, fads seem indigenous to American culture, particularly in urban areas, and will probably continue to flourish intermittently. By the same token most fads do not last long; in a few months, in a season, they are forgotten, sometimes to be followed very soon be the next fad.

As already noted, the line is hard to draw between fads on the one hand and fashions, crazes, cults, and other phenomena of mass behavior on the other. What starts as a fad may remain as a fashion, hobby, sport, or custom. Bobbed hair, slacks, cosmetics, zippers, and no hats for men all started as fads. In the present state of our knowledge, prediction about fads seems shakier than in almost any other area of social psychology.

CRAZES

A craze is more intensive, more emotionally involved, and usually more extensive than a fad. Instead of centering about diet, clothing, or verbal expressions, crazes are feverish, all-consuming activities which spread like wildfire. The crusades of the twelfth and thirteenth centuries and the witchcraft mania of the sixteenth and seventeenth centuries are good examples of widespread crazes.[30] McCarthyism and the probing for communists and left-wingers during the early 1950's almost reached the proportions of a craze. Other examples are the chain-letter mania and the Frank Sinatra, Elvis Presley, and James Dean crazes which will be examined in some detail.

[30] See K. Young, *Source book for social psychology* (New York: Alfred A. Knopf, Inc., 1928), chap. xxiv, Mental epidemics.

The chain-letter craze. Early in 1935 people in Denver began to receive letters such as the following:

THE PROSPERITY CLUB

This chain was started in hopes of bringing you prosperity. Within three days make five copies of this letter, leaving off the top name and adding yours to the bottom, and mail or give it to five friends.

In omitting the top name send that person 10 cents. In turn as your name leaves the top, you will receive 15,625 letters with donations amounting to $1,562.50.

Now is this worth 10 cents to you? Have the faith your friend had, and this chain won't be broken.

Thousands of people fell for the appeal in all parts of the country. Mails were swamped with letters, and whole cities became convulsed. The "send-a-dime" letters were followed by "send-a-quarter" and "send-a-dollar" schemes. Racketeering was suspected but was difficult to prove. Rumors were rife and supported the schemes: somebody in town had just received $700; a woman was reported to have two quart milk bottles brim-full of dimes she had received. The mathematics was correct, so people refused to believe they could lose! It was months before the craze ran its course, through several variations of the original scheme. One commentator noted that a fool would have to be born every second to keep up with the geometric progression of the send-a-dime plan.[31] Another called the craze a fine example of the "economic cretinism" of the American people.[32]

Early in 1949 a lineal descendant of the chain-letter craze, the "pyramid friendship clubs," began in California and swept over the country.[33] According to the plan, a person invites two friends to a coffee-and-doughnut party at which a club is formed, and each guest puts a dollar or two into the kitty. Each of these invites two more for the next meeting, each of whom, in turn, invites two more, and so on. After a certain number of meetings the originator, whose name is at the top of the pyramid, gets the kitty. Then the next pair in line come to the top and are paid off next. Theoretically, as with the chain letters, everyone was to profit handsomely. Actually, of course, the chain was soon broken and only those in at the beginning reaped a reward. The pyramid plan, as compared with the chain letters, had the added attraction of friendship and refreshments. But it too soon ran its course.

[31] *The Nation,* June 12, 1935, p. 682.
[32] *New Republic,* May 22, 1935, pp. 43-44.
[33] See *The Nation,* February 12, 1949, p. 173; *New Republic,* March 7, 1949, p. 9; *Life,* March 7, 1949.

The Sinatra cult. In the latter part of 1944, the singer Frank Sinatra became the rage of young adolescent girls or "bobby-soxers." Thousands of them stormed the Paramount Theater in New York, where he was making personal appearances; they waited in line for hours and, once inside, stayed for several performances. As one fan remarked, the Paramount became "the home of swoon."

The foremost student of the Sinatra craze estimated in 1946 that "the Voice" had millions of fans, mostly young women in their middle teens.[34] The number of Sinatra clubs may have been as high as two thousand; their presidents were privileged to help open fan mail and paste clippings in the publicity office. Fan clubs were organized in many foreign countries as well. At the height of his popularity Sinatra was receiving some five thousand fan letters a week.

The antics of Sinatra's fans were unbelievable; the adulation reminds one of that accorded Rudolph Valentino almost a generation earlier. For example, a girl whose arm he had accidentally brushed wore a bandage over the spot for two weeks to prevent anyone else from touching it. Municipal health departments became concerned over the wholesale kissing of pictures of "Frankie" in theater lobbies. His appearance outside a hotel or theater was likely to provoke a near-riot in the course of which efforts were made to snatch his hat or buttons from his coat as souvenirs.

What was the secret of Frank Sinatra's powerful appeal to teenage girls? Perhaps the best interpretation is one compounded of publicity, suggestibility, and frustrated wishes for romance and understanding. Perhaps "Frankie" was both a father image and a dream-person with whom they could identify, as one editor suggested.[35] Or perhaps one essayist hit the nail on the head when she wrote, in a "Why I Like Frank Sinatra" contest: "I think he is one of the greatest things that ever happened to Teen Age America. We were the kids that never got much attention, but he's made us feel like we're something. He has given us understanding. Something we need. Most adults think we don't need any consideration. We're really human and Frank realizes that. He gives us sincerity in return for our faithfulness."[36]

The Presley craze. More intense and far-reaching, and far more commercial, was the 1956–57 Elvis Presley craze. A guitar-playing "rock 'n roll" singer, this 21-year-old former truck driver from

---

34 E. J. Kahn, Jr., *The Voice: The story of an American phenomenon* (New York: Harper & Bros., 1947).

35 B. Bliven, The Voice and the kids, *New Republic,* November 6, 1944.

36 Kahn, *op. cit.,* p. 49.

Memphis with his ducktail haircut and long sideburns became a national phenomenon. As *Life* put it: "Wherever the lean, 21-year-old Tennessean goes to howl out his combination of hillbilly and rock 'n roll, he is beset by teen-age girls yelling for him. They dote on his sideburns and pegged pants, cherish cups of water dipped from his swimming pool, covet strands of his hair, boycott disk jockeys who dislike his records (they have sold some six million copies)." An additional feature of Elvis Presley's appeal, adds *Life*, "has been deeply disturbing to civic leaders, clergymen, some parents. He does not just bounce to accent his heavy beat. He uses a bump and grind routine usually seen only in burlesque. His young audiences, unexposed to such goings-on, do not just shout their approval. They get set off by shock waves of hysteria, going into frenzies of screeching and wailing, winding up in tears."[37]

With the active aid of two astute businessmen, a line of Elvis Presley merchandise was developed including bracelets and belts, bobby socks, T-shirts, sneakers, green-stitched jeans, lipstick, and perfume, reportedly totaling almost $20,000,000 in business a year at the peak.

The James Dean phenomenon. A more unusual craze, because posthumous, centered about the talented young actor James Dean, who starred in *East of Eden, Rebel Without a Cause,* and *Giant.* Just after the filming of the last picture, Dean was killed in an automobile accident, in September, 1955. Letters poured in to the Warner Brothers office expressing regret, even resentment, for his untimely death. Instead of dwindling after a few months, however, the volume of mail increased. By the following July seven thousand letters a month were coming in, with money enclosed for photographs of Dean.[38] JIMMY DEAN IS NOT DEAD screamed the title of a feature story in a movie magazine. He had become a legend. Why?

One theory is that James Dean was the adolescents' idol in that he rebelled successfully against conformity, and got rich in the process. A related interpretation is the following:

. . . he had the intuitive talent for expressing the hopes and fears that are part of all young people . . . . In his personal life, he was continually struggling with a universal conflict. On the one hand, he wanted to experience all there was to life. Yet, he couldn't quite face life; he remained an adolescent to the day he died, unsure of the way others felt about him, afraid to form any lasting alliances, unwilling to accept tragedy without self-pity.

[37] *Life*, August 27, 1956.
[38] George Scullin, James Dean—the legend and the facts, *Look,* October 16, 1956.

James Dean didn't have time to find the answers to his problems. But he managed to dramatize brilliantly the questions that every young man and woman must resolve.[39]

BOOMS

A "boom" is much like a craze; it nearly always refers to a "get-rich-quick" scheme which expands like a bubble, then bursts. In other words, a boom might be described as an economic type of craze. Seventeenth-century Holland saw a boom, the so-called "tulip mania." Interest in these flowers became so great that prices skyrocketed and everyone began to speculate. Single bulbs of choice kinds sold for hundreds of dollars. Fortunes were made and people from all walks of life thronged to the tulip markets in the big cities of Holland. Notaries and clerks were appointed exclusively for the tulip trade. Foreigners became interested and money poured into the country; the cost of living rose. Within a few months, however, the bubble burst, and people "found themselves the possessors of a few bulbs which nobody would buy, even though they offered them at one quarter of the sums they had paid for them. The cry of distress resounded everywhere, and each man accused his neighbor. . . . Many who, for a brief season, had emerged from the humbler walks of life, were cast back into their original obscurity. Substantial merchants were reduced almost to beggary. . . ." [40]

Another notorious boom was the "Mississippi Scheme" concocted by John Law in Paris in 1717, for the exploitation of French territory in America. Shares were issued and sold with a promise of 100 per cent or more profits within a year. Crowds of eager speculators all but rioted to gain possession of the shares. The price of shares sometimes rose 10 to 20 per cent in the course of a few hours. Law was worshiped like a beloved ruler. But soon the "Mississippi Bubble" burst and thousands were disillusioned—until the next get-rich-quick scheme came along.

The United States had witnessed two major booms—the California gold rush of 1848–50 and the Florida land boom of the 1920's. News of the discovery of gold brought a migration to California which one historian called "so stupendous as to outrank in point of numbers anything of its kind in the nation's history, and to stand on an equal footing with some of the great world movements of population." [41] Few of the migrants, of course, struck it rich; many lost their homes, their fortunes, and even their lives. These "Forty-niners" were, however, an important factor in the development of

---

[39] Joe Hyams, James Dean, *Redbook*, September, 1956.

[40] K. Young, *Source book*, p. 704.

[41] R. G. Cleland, *A history of California: The American period* (New York: The Macmillan Co., 1922), pp. 226-39. See also Young, *Source book*, pp. 712-14.

the West, and many of them established families and businesses in our frontier territory.

In the postwar twenties word went around that Florida was beginning to boom, and that easy money could be made by investing in real estate. People began to flock to Florida—between three and ten million went there in 1925, according to various estimates. Land prices, already exorbitant, continued to rise; adventurous people were making money hand over fist. Speculation and optimism were the order of the day. One visitor was told, "The people who have made real fortunes check their brains before leaving home. Buy anywhere. You can't lose." [42] Few could resist the temptation to put down a few thousand dollars as a binder on an expensive lot with the hope of reselling it at a fabulous profit. The "bust" came in 1926.

Crazes and booms of the "get-rich-quick" sort are not, however, too difficult to explain. Acquisitive motives coupled with frustrations and hopes furnish the steam. A compound of facts, publicity, and rumors help people define the situation as a golden opportunity. They know that fantastic fortunes have been made in America; they forget, if they ever knew, that most speculators lose. Another factor in a craze or boom is its newness; the chain-letter craze or real estate boom is less likely to occur again than some new stunt with which we have not become disillusioned.

To analysts of mass behavior the distinction between fads, crazes, and booms becomes blurred. Certainly they have a number of properties in common: the suddenness of their appearance, some degree of emotional intensity, an ephemeral quality, some commercialization (in most cases), and considerable unpredictability. The adolescent, for whom the fad or craze is particularly attractive, is even more unpredictable than other age groups. As two observers remark:

> With perfect information, a normal distribution of tastes can be expected at most times and for most things. In certain industries, and among certain subgroups, the distribution is less likely to be normal, in part due to the pressures for new commodities, to the superficiality of the appeals themselves, to the publicity accompanying every product, and in the case of teenagers to their unstable moods.[43]

In fairness to the teenagers it should be added that the behavior of adults is sometimes just as bizarre; for example, in certain re-

42 G. M. Shelby, *Florida frenzy* (New York: Harper & Bros., 1926), pp. 172, 177-81. See also Young, *op. cit.*, pp. 714-17.

43 R. Meyersohn and E. Katz, Notes on a natural history of fads, *Amer. J. Sociol.*, LXII (1957), 594–601.

ligious cults, political splinter groups, and various get-rich-quick schemes.

RUMOR

Rumor is a kind of communication which is not only interesting in itself, but is also one of the means by which booms, crazes, panics, and other forms of mass behavior are produced. Before World War II social psychologists had paid little attention to the phenomenon of rumor. But as soon as the United States entered the war, rumors became rife and strenuous efforts were made to counteract them and to trace them to their sources. "Rumor clinics" were established in Boston and other centers to aid in this work. One of the leaders was Gordon Allport of Harvard; with Leo Postman he later undertook several experimental studies and published them under the title *The Psychology of Rumor*. A rumor, say these authors, is a specific proposition for belief, passed along from person to person, usually by word of mouth, without reference to secure standards of evidence. The essentials of rumor are importance and ambiguity. That is, "the amount of rumor in circulation will vary with the importance of the subject to the individuals concerned *times* the ambiguity of the evidence pertaining to the topic at issue." [44] For example, during the war many women repeated over their back fences such rumors as "I hear that out at Camp X they have so much meat that they throw whole sides of fresh beef into the garbage." The meat shortage was of great importance to these women, and they did not know the facts. The situation was ambiguous, and hence rumors circulated wildly.

Allport and Postman found that rumors serve to explain, justify, and provide meaning for the individual. Often the rumor is a projection of one's own motivational and emotional state, as is shown by Karl Menninger:

Mrs. Adams to Mrs. Beck: "Where is Mrs. King today? Is she ill?"

Mrs. Beck to Mrs. Clark: "Mrs. Adams wonders if Mrs. King may not be ill."

Mrs. Clark (who doesn't like Mrs. King) to Mrs. Davis (who does): "I hear Mrs. King is ill. Not seriously, I hope?"

Mrs. Davis to Mrs. Ellis: "Mrs. Clark is saying that Mrs. King is seriously sick. I must go right over and see her."

Mrs. Ellis to Mrs. French: "I guess Mrs. King is pretty sick. Mrs. Davis has just been called over."

Mrs. French to Mrs. Gregg: "They say Mrs. King isn't expected to live. The relatives have been called to her bedside."

Mrs. Gregg to Mrs. Hudson: "What's the latest news about Mrs. King? Is she dead?"

Mrs. Hudson to Mrs. Ingham: "What time did Mrs. King die?"

44 G. W. Allport and L. Postman, *The psychology of rumor* (New York: Henry Holt & Co., Inc., 1947), p. 34.

Mrs. Ingham to Mrs. Jones: "Are you going to Mrs. King's funeral? I hear she died yesterday."

Mrs. Jones to Mrs. King: "I just learned of your death and funeral. Now, who started that?"

Mrs. King: "There are several who would be glad if it were true." [45]

The transmission of rumor. Experimental studies were undertaken by Allport and Postman to discover the tendencies or processes influencing the content of rumor as it was communicated.[46] One person was asked to look at a picture and describe it to a second person, including a dozen or so details in his description. The second person then passed on the description to a third who had just entered the room; the latter told it to a fourth, and so on. The version of the last person (usually the sixth or seventh) was then compared with the original picture.

The findings showed clearly several tendencies involved in the transmission of rumor or testimony. One of these is *leveling*—an increasing brevity and loss of detail. Another is *sharpening* of certain details, such as retaining a certain word or idea through the whole series of communications. In one series the word "remonstrate" was passed on without change; in several series the detail of a flower pot falling from a window sill was emphasized.

A still more significant tendency influencing the communication of rumors is *assimilation,* that is, conformity to the habits, interests, wishes, and expectations of the subjects. A simple example is reporting as "Lucky Strikes" an advertisement which reads "Lucky Rakes." More significant was the interpretation of a Negro and white man facing each other and talking, with the white man holding an opened razor. More than half the time the razor had moved into the Negro's hand by the time of the terminal report—a clear instance of assimilation to stereotyped expectancy. Another example of assimilation had to do with interest. In a group of college women, the first report mentioned "three terrible-looking dresses" in a shop window and a sign marked "Bargains." These themes of unattractive clothes and bargains went through the whole series of reproductions; in male groups these items received less emphasis.

Allport and Postman use the term *embedding process* to cover the three-fold changes of leveling, sharpening, and assimilation.[47] Embedding means "an effort to reduce the stimulus to a simple and

---

[45] K. Menninger, *The human mind* (New York: Alfred A. Knopf, Inc., 1930), p. 282. (Quoted by Allport and Postman, *op. cit.,* pp. 39-40.)

[46] Allport and Postman, *op. cit.,* chap. iv.

[47] G. W. Allport and L. J. Postman, The basic psychology of rumor, *Trans. N.Y. Acad. Sci.,* VIII (1945), Ser. II, 61-81. Reprinted in Swanson *et al., Readings* (2d ed.), pp. 160-71.

meaningful structure that has adaptive significance for the individual in terms of his own interests and experience." In other words, the actual words a person hears "become so embedded into his own dynamic mental life that the product is chiefly one of projection." Rumor suffers such serious distortion through this embedding process, conclude the authors, that "it is never under any circumstances a valid guide for belief or conduct."

A practical application of the psychology of rumor has been called "cultivating the grapevine." Following the example of the wartime rumor clinics, employers have tried calling together small groups of employees to ask what rumors they have heard recently. Management can then verify the rumors, if true, or fill in missing details, or present the true situation. Another plan consists in actually "feeding the grapevine" by giving factual information to a group of leaders among the employees and encouraging them to disseminate it. According to a National Industrial Conference Board survey these methods help the processes of communication with employees and promote democracy in business.[48]

An intriguing example of rumor and mild hysteria, reminiscent of the earlier "Loch Ness monster" incident, occurred in the summer of 1947—the mystery of the flying saucers. Late in June an airplane pilot in Oregon reported seeing nine "flying saucers" in the sky, moving at a speed of 1,200 miles an hour in formation, and shifting in position like the tail of a kite. An Oklahoma flier immediately reported he had seen similar objects some weeks earlier, but fear of ridicule kept him from mentioning it. Other reports began to filter in about flying saucers, mostly from western states, but by the week-end of July 4th, flying disks had been "sighted" by persons in Michigan, Ohio, Quebec, New Brunswick, New Orleans, Pennsylvania, and New Jersey. In Idaho, 200 persons in one group and 60 in another reported seeing the saucers. A Coast Guard yeoman took a picture of what purported to be one of them—though it might have been a light splotch on the photographic plate. An air lines pilot, supported by his co-pilot and stewardess, reported seeing nine flat round disks, "bigger than aircraft" and flying in loose formation. Most observers agreed that the objects seen were bright, round, and traveling at high speed, though the reports varied greatly as to the number of disks and their altitude and velocity. To add to the confusion, a man in California said he saw four disks overhead, "changing shape as they flew." [49]

48 Harry C. Kenney, Cultivating the grapevine, *Christian Science Monitor,* November 8, 1954.

49 See *New York Times* and *New York Herald Tribune,* July 6, 1947, and *PM* for July 7, 1947, for extensive news summaries.

Though much skepticism greeted the reports, their frequency naturally led many people to suspect that *something* in the sky had actually been seen by at least *some* of the observers. But military and scientific authorities seemed mystified. A rumor attributed to a physicist declared that the phenomena were caused by "transmutation of atomic energy" experiments, that the saucers were twenty feet in width and controlled from the ground. But Dr. Harold Urey, the atomic scientist, called this "gibberish," and David Lilienthal, chairman of the Atomic Energy Commission, along with high Army and Navy officials, denied any connection between the flying saucers and atomic experiments. Various meteorological explanations, such as ice crystals or atmospheric reflections and distortions, were largely discounted by the experts, though some admitted that such phenomena might possibly have been involved.

Visual aberrations may have accounted for some reports, such as that of the New Jersey resident who looked upward after bending down to change a tire and saw shiny objects diving and fluttering in the air. Another explanation for certain of the reports was suggested by a weather bureau official who said the disks "sound like those things you see on New Year's Eve, except this was on the Fourth of July."

Without denying that some sort of physical explanation might account for some of the early observations, it seems likely, as one astronomer said, that the country-wide rash of flying saucer reports was brought on by a "mild case of meteorological jitters," induced by "mass hypnosis" or at least by suggestion and rumor.

THE CROWD

Most social scientists distinguish between an audience and a crowd. The audience is a highly structured group, with a fairly definite educational or recreational purpose. Its members are oriented toward the speaker or performers and only incidentally toward each other. Kimball Young notes that the chief characteristics of the audience are a specific purpose, a predetermined time and place of meeting, and a standard form of polarization and interaction.[50] Hence the audience is not an example of mass behavior as that term is commonly used.

The crowd is a less clearly organized group than the audience, though its members are in intimate contact. MacIver speaks of a crowd as "a physically compact aggregation of human beings brought

50 K. Young, *Social psychology* (3d ed.; New York: Appleton-Century-Crofts, Inc., 1956), p. 302. See also H. L. Hollingworth, *Psychology of the audience* (New York: American Book Co., 1935), for an extended discussion of the audience.

into direct, temporary, and unorganized contact, one with another." [51] Many sociologists and most social psychologists include common interests and attitudes in their definition. Thus Cantril defined a crowd as "a congregate group of individuals who have temporarily identified themselves with common values, and who are experiencing similar emotions." [52] For example, a street crowd may assemble around two young men having a fight, or a policeman arresting a drunk. The members of the crowd are interested in, or curious about, what is happening. They talk to each other, push forward to get a better view, offer comments and suggestions, make gestures, and generally register their approval or disapproval. In a word, the crowd situation is much more fluid than the audience, and the members interact far more with each other. This typical interstimulation often takes the form of what sociologists call "milling" before a stampede. [53] The remarks and gestures of some members stimulate similar behavior in others, which in turn facilitates further restless expression that may build up to a crescendo of excited action.

Blumer [54] classifies crowds into four types: (1) the *casual crowd*, like a street crowd watching a performance in a store window; (2) the *conventionalized crowd*, such as spectators at a baseball game; (3) the *acting crowd*, which is suggestive and oriented toward a particular objective; and (4) the *expressive crowd*, given to physical activity such as dancing, and found most commonly in religious sects.

Most treatments of crowd behavior are concerned with what Blumer calls the "acting" crowd, which is more likely to have a leader and which often turns to aggressive behavior—that is, becomes a mob. Brown categorizes things somewhat differently; he classifies *mobs* into four types: the *aggressive* (lynching, riot), *escape* (panic), *acquisitive* (for example, a run on a bank), and *expressive* (for instance, a revival). [55]

Often crowd behavior is facilitated by the presence of a leader, sometimes a self-appointed leader from the group. This leader focuses and expresses the sentiments of the group and may harangue

51 R. M. MacIver, *Society: A textbook of sociology* (New York: Rinehart & Co., Inc., 1937), p. 187.

52 H. Cantril, *Psychology of social movements* (New York: John Wiley & Sons, Inc., 1941), p. 80.

53 See R. E. Park and E. W. Burgess, *Introduction to the science of sociology* (Chicago: University of Chicago Press, 1924), pp. 788-89.

54 H. Blumer, Collective behavior, chaps. xix-xxi, in A. M. Lee (ed.), *New outline of the principles of sociology* (New York: Barnes & Noble, Inc., 1946).

55 R. W. Brown, Mass phenomena, in G. Lindzey (ed.), *Handbook of social psychology*, Vol. II (Reading, Mass.: Addison-Wesley Pub. Co., Inc., 1954), pp. 833-76.

his followers to the point where the crowd becomes a mob intent upon some kind of action such as tearing down the opponents' goal posts, staging a protest march, or storming the jail and lynching the suspect.

The mob and panic are later stages to which crowd behavior sometimes leads. A mob refers to a crowd engaging in excited, aggressive action, such as a lynching or riot. A panic is a rout, in which members of an audience or crowd, seized with fear, engage in frenzied efforts to escape, as during a theater fire, the sinking of a ship, or some other catastrophe.

Types of crowd behavior. Ordinarily a crowd does not turn into a mob. However, many exceptions have been noted. One of the authors happened to be present, as an observer, at a social event which began as an audience and turned into a crowd, then a mob, and ended in a panic—the Chicago "Memorial Day Massacre" of 1937.

The newly organized steel workers union (CIO) went on strike at the Republic Steel Plant in South Chicago. The strikers demanded the right to establish a picket line around the plant but were refused by the Chicago police. The Steel Workers Organizing Committee called a protest meeting for Sunday, May 30th, just outside a restaurant a few blocks away from the plant. A large group of strikers and their families attended the meeting, some of them carrying placards demanding the right to establish peaceful picketing. One or two of the speakers inflamed the audience and called upon them to march to the plant and assert their right to picket. The audience soon became a crowd, showing unrest, increased interstimulation, and milling behavior. Egged on by the organizers, they formed into a line of march which started across the fields toward the steel plant. Just outside the plant they were met by a line of a hundred or more policemen. Words were exchanged between leaders of the police and of the strikers; possibly insults and even stones were hurled, though there was no mob attack upon the police.

In any event, the police fired, and the strikers fled in a panic. Several persons were killed outright or died a few days later, and dozens more were wounded, including at least one small boy. Instead of dispersing the strikers with tear gas, the police used real bullets without warning, which accounted for the panic and the large number of casualties.

It is not unusual to find a crowd becoming a mob, since the structuring of these two situations is quite similar. Several accounts of mobs have been written, notably of lynching mobs.[56] Cantril calls a lynching mob *"a congregate group of individuals who feel strongly that certain of their values are threatened and whose attitudes direct them to kill or injure a human being."* [57] The typical lynching, Cantril found, occurred in the South, had a Negro for a victim, and was perpetrated by native white mob members, none of whom was arrested or punished for his actions.[58] Lynchings were commonest in rural and small-town areas where the cultural level was low, and where economic conditions were bad. According to one study, the frequency of lynchings varied inversely with the proportion of the colored population; counties with less than 25 per cent Negroes had nearly twice as many lynchings, proportionately, as counties having over 50 per cent Negro population.[59]

Exploring the psychological setting of lynching mobs, Cantril found strongly ingrained norms, notably the belief that the Negro was inferior and had to be kept in his place. Furthermore, the white southerner was strongly ego-involved with these beliefs or frames of reference and would act aggressively if he felt they were threatened. Violent behavior such as a lynching represented an attempt to defend his status; it was an aggressive response to frustration.[60] By 1940, lynchings were disappearing as a phenomenon of American social life, however.

While experimentation is practically impossible as a means of investigating mob behavior, Meier and two associates made an interesting attempt in this direction.[61] They distributed news bulletins to one large college group and a faked newspaper "extra" to another, each telling of a brutal kidnapping and murder. Then the investigators discovered which persons would join the mob as participants, which would go along to assist, which would not participate, and which would try to deter the mob from violence. Twelve per cent of the students wished to join the mob with the expectation of participating; 23 per cent chose to go along to see what happened. The would-be participants tended to be males, were younger, more

---

56 See, for example, A. F. Raper, *The tragedy of lynching* (Chapel Hill, N. C.: University of North Carolina Press, 1933); W. White, *Rope and faggot* (New York: Alfred A. Knopf, Inc., 1929); F. Shay, *Judge Lynch: his first hundred years* (New York: Ives Washburn, Inc., 1938).

57 H. Cantril, *op. cit.,* p. 80.

58 *Ibid.,* p. 83.

59 Southern Commission on the Study of Lynchings, *Lynchings and what they mean* (Atlanta, Ga.: 1931), p. 74.

60 Cantril, *op. cit.,* pp. 86-93, 110 ff.; see also Chapter 6 above.

61 N. C. Meier, G. H. Mennenga, and H. J. Stoltz, An experimental approach to the study of mob behavior, *J. abnorm. soc. Psychol.,* XXXVI (1941), 506-34.

extroverted, less self-sufficient, and less frequently associated with a church than the nonparticipants. (It is interesting to note that the great majority of the subjects thought the crime was genuine.) The investigators concluded that "in the crowd setting the individual will behave in accord with the dominance of previously established habits, attitudes, and behavior patterns, but that the action itself will be to some degree conditioned by the nature of the situation, since the response of participation or deterrence will be to some degree in accordance with the degree to which guilt is or is not completely established." [62]

Interpretations of crowd behavior. Attempts to explain crowd and mob behavior have been undertaken by many social psychologists. Le Bon, for example, noted that crowds are marked by increased suggestibility and loss of restraint. A collective mind is formed, via almost hypnotic contagion, which blots out the intellectual aptitudes and moral ideas of the individual.[63] Martin objected to the collective mind interpretation given by Le Bon.[64] In his *Behavior of Crowds,* Martin used a psychoanalytic interpretation: through suggestibility and social facilitation, the restraints of the superego are relaxed and primitive ego impulses come into play. Martin went so far as to state: *"A crowd is a device for indulging ourselves in a kind of temporary insanity by all going crazy together."* [65]

Perhaps, as one critic suggests, Le Bon regarded the crowd as feebleminded and Martin considered it psychopathic or at least abnormal.[66] Both these interpretations are extreme, though each contributes something to a comprehensive theory of crowd behavior.

A theory more acceptable to social psychologists was advanced by F. H. Allport.[67] Allport objected to earlier descriptions and interpretations of crowd behavior in that they directed attention to the crowd as a whole, overlooking or minimizing the significance of individual factors. All spontaneous, mob-like crowds, he insisted, have their driving forces in basic individual responses and not in the mere fact of aggregation or manipulation by a leader. "The individual in the crowd behaves just as he would behave alone, *only*

---

[62] *Ibid.,* p. 524.

[63] G. Le Bon, *The crowd* (London: George Allen & Unwin, Ltd., 1917), translation of *Psychologie des foules* (Paris, 1895).

[64] E. D. Martin, *The behavior of crowds* (New York: Harper & Bros., 1920).

[65] *Ibid.,* p. 37.

[66] M. H. Krout, *Introduction to social psychology* (New York: Harper & Bros., 1942), p. 702.

[67] F. H. Allport, *Social psychology* (Boston: Houghton Mifflin Co., 1924), chap. xii.

more so." [68] Again, he says, *"By the similarity of human nature, the individuals of the crowd are all set to react to their common object in the same manner, quite apart from any social influence. Stimulations from one another release and augment these responses; but they do not originate them."* [69]

The sociological approach to crowds emphasizes factors such as social unrest and interstimulation.[70] Social unrest grows out of interaction between persons who are tense, frustrated, and insecure. Their collective behavior is marked by milling, excitement, and social contagion. Blumer [71] outlines the steps in formation of an acting crowd, as follows: First, a striking event catches people's attention and interest. Then the milling process begins; they move around, talk to each other, and communicate their emotions, which facilitates general excitement and produces an intense common mood. It also increases responsiveness of the members to each other and facilitates later collective action. Next, a common focus of attention develops. Finally, says Blumer, impulses corresponding to the group objective are stimulated and fostered to the point where action occurs—that is, the crowd becomes a mob.

Cantril suggests these essential components of what has been called the "mob mind":

1. Confusion of causal relationships; jumping at oversimplified explanations
2. Restriction of the individual's "world," so that immediate action may occur in terms of temporary, limited values uninhibited by the usual cultural norms and values
3. Identification with the situation; the individual "loses himself" in the crowd or mob [72]

Sherif stresses the formation of new norms or values in "intense group situations"; being a part of the situation imposes conformity on the individual. This conformity often produces demoralizing effects, "in which the individual commits inhuman acts under the grip of a general outburst of mob fury." "On the other hand," says Sherif, "the group may produce the highest deeds of morality and self-sacrifice. A man whom we know to be stingy may surprise us by generous contributions in a group situation; heroism and stoical self-control are common experiences on the battlefield and in the great crises and revolutions of every era. In World War II, neighbors of mild-mannered, easygoing boys were surprised by their heroic deeds on the battlefields. Ordinarily they might have expected such

---

68 *Ibid.,* p. 295.
69 *Ibid.,* p. 299.
70 See Blumer, *op. cit.,* chaps. xx-xxi.
71 *Ibid.,* pp. 178 ff.
72 Cantril, *op. cit.,* pp. 118-19.

heroic deeds only from those who exhibited bravery in civilian life."[73]

Sherif's point that crowd action may be generous or heroic as well as hostile and destructive seems an important corrective to the generally held theories of crowd and mob behavior.

The foregoing interpretations of crowd and mob behavior suggest that neither a "situational" nor a "motivational" theory is, by itself, adequate. Crowd behavior has several essential components, all of which play a part in the outcome. Three interrelated influences may be mentioned:

1. *General "Atmosphere" or Setting.* Some social event has occurred—a child is injured by a car, a family has been evicted from their dwelling, an explosion or fire has taken place. Or an event *is alleged to have occurred*—a white woman raped by a Negro, a boy beaten by a policeman, a child left orphaned and destitute. Whether or not the event has occurred, the way it is reported determines the way the situation is perceived and interpreted, that is, provides the psychological atmosphere.

2. *Dynamic Tendencies.* According to how the situation is perceived, motives, emotions, and sentiments become important. When a Negro is accused of rape, relevant dynamic tendencies are hostility toward and fear of Negroes and economic and other frustrations which may easily lead to displacement or "scapegoating." Where the situation is very different—for instance, rescuing children from a fire— the salient dynamic tendencies of the members of the crowd are very different. A love of children may be manifested, or an urge to show physical prowess, and may lead to acts of great heroism and generosity. Conceivably the same individuals who call most loudly for the lynching of the Negro are among those most active, in another situation, in rescuing the children from the burning building!

3. *Conformity and Suggestibility.* Along with the general situation and the individuals' dynamic tendencies, group influences operate very significantly. Through interstimulation between the leader and followers, and between the members of the group, comes a change in the norms and values of those present. They become suggestible and identify themselves with the activity in progress— the lynching, the rescuing, or what not. Conformity or solidarity emerges. *Everyone* joins in to lynch the victim, to pull down the "enemy's" goal posts, to form a bucket brigade or a human chain, to empty his pocketbook for the support of the orphaned child. Many contributory factors have been mentioned in this connection:

[73] M. Sherif, *Outline of social psychology* (New York: Harper & Bros., 1948), p. 107.

conformity, suggestibility, identification, social facilitation, contagion, loss of critical abilities. The essential feature is that new attitudinal and behavioral norms emerge in a crowd situation and crystallize in a particular course of action.

All these features—situation, motivation, interstimulation—are essential to an interpretation of crowd and mob behavior. No lynching would take place without all three. The same type of alleged crime may lead to a lynching in backwoods Georgia or Mississippi but not in Minneapolis or New York City, because people's perceptions, motives, and emotions with respect to the Negro differ in the rural South and the urban North. Moreover, in the South an alleged rape seldom leads to a lynching unless a crowd gathers and becomes whipped up to aggressive action through interstimulation.

CRITICAL SOCIAL SITUATIONS

The term "critical social situation" is sometimes used to cover panics, disasters, crises, and various kinds of "mass hysteria." In all cases we can distinguish certain stimuli or situational factors, certain psychological or predisposing influences, and resulting ways of perceiving or defining the immediate situation.

Typical situations. In December, 1917, the city of Halifax in Nova Scotia was shaken by a tremendous explosion. Confused people ran in all directions—into cellars, into the streets, from their shops toward their homes. With the report that another explosion might occur, they headed south out of the city. Some carried babies or bundles, some were without clothes, as they fled from their homes and stores. Hundreds of acts of heroism and unselfishness as well as of stealing and profiteering were noted in the wake of the disaster.

The residents of Halifax had been expecting a German attack either by zeppelin or from the sea. Most of them were sure it had now happened—or perhaps that the end of the world had come. One man "saw" a zeppelin in the sky; another "heard" a shell pass over his head; another saw a German fleet in the distance. Rumor was rife and lent wings to the feet of those fleeing the city.[74]

We have a more complete account of the panic caused by the radio drama, the "Invasion from Mars." On October 30, 1938, the actor Orson Welles broadcast a drama which purported to be a realistic account of an invasion of Martians which threatened our

---

[74] See S. H. Prince, Catastrophe and social change—based upon a sociological study of the Halifax Disaster, *Columbia University Studies in History*, etc., XCIV (1920), 36-57. (Quoted in part in K. Young, *Source book*, pp. 84-94.)

whole nation. Hadley Cantril and associates did a follow-up study
to determine the extent of the resulting panic and its determinants.[75] In their words:

> Probably never before have so many people in all walks of life and in all parts
> of the country become so suddenly and so intensely disturbed as they did on this
> night. . . .[76] Long before the broadcast was ended, people all over the United
> States were praying, crying, fleeing frantically to escape death from the Martians.
> Some ran to rescue loved ones. Others telephoned farewells or warnings, hurried
> to inform neighbors, sought information from newspapers or radio stations, sum-
> moned ambulances and police cars. At least six million people heard the broad-
> cast. At least a million of them were frightened or disturbed.[77]

Drawing upon the data furnished by Cantril, we can distinguish
several salient factors both situational and personal. First, the
drama was done with great realism, not only in terms of vocal expression but by the use of actual place-names and of persons who
sounded authentic. Even more important was the fact that people
tuning in late on the program assumed, naturally enough, that it
was a news broadcast rather than fiction.

A significant general personality factor at the time was jitters
about war—the Munich settlement had occurred only a few weeks
before. There were also many more specific predisposing influences,
present in some but not all of the listeners. For example, some had
implicit faith in news heard over the radio. Of those who attempted
to check the validity of what they heard, some did it ineffectively,
for instance, by looking out of the window, seeing traffic going by,
and concluding "people were rushing away." A few were expecting
the end of the world and decided this was it. Some persons, more
unstable than the rest, became overly emotional and incapable of
any rational action.

It is hardly strange that such dramatic reports in the form of an
actual news broadcast, coupled with general and various specific
personality factors, led to panic reactions. Furthermore, people
lacked a frame of reference for dealing with such a weird event, as
compared with an accident or fire. Believing the event was real,
failing to verify it for various reasons, and knowing no means to
deal with it, many thousands of people turned to prayer or hysterical
flight.

When fire breaks out in a theater, or when bullets are fired at
a crowd, practically everyone shows a panic reaction. When knowl-

[75] H. Cantril, H. Gaudet, and H. Herzog, *The invasion from Mars* (Princeton, N. J.:
Princeton University Press, 1940). See also Swanson *et al.*, *Readings* (2d ed.), pp.
198-207.

[76] Cantril *et al.*, *op. cit.*, p. vii.

[77] *Ibid.*, p. 47.

edge of the precipitating situation comes from second- or third-hand evidence, as with the "Invasion from Mars," predisposing personality trends play a more salient determining role. Thus some who thought the broadcast was a news bulletin checked up to see whether it was genuine or not; others checked inadequately or became hysterical. In general, we may say that the more a stimulus situation fits into the category of rumor rather than direct evidence of the senses, the more a person's responses depend upon his underlying personality trends. We can see this illustrated further in the case of the Phantom Anesthetist.[78]

On September 1, 1944, a woman in Mattoon, Illinois, reported to police that someone opened her bedroom window and sprayed her with a sickish, sweet-smelling gas which made her ill and partially paralyzed her legs. Next day the local paper carried a front-page story under the headline "Anesthetic Prowler on Loose." Armed citizens lay in wait for the prowler, and rumors began to circulate. Several more cases were reported between September 3rd and September 12th, but no suspicious characters or evidence could be found. Donald Johnson, a psychologist from the University of Illinois, came to Mattoon and investigated the case carefully. He concluded it was entirely psychogenic—a matter of mass hysteria. The woman who first reported the case had a mild hysterical attack and her dramatic story made fine news copy. This led other suggestible people, of low educational and economic level, to report similar symptoms, which caused a rapid "snowballing" effect, though the lack of evidence soon caused the affair to subside. The degree to which hysteria is promoted by the press may be judged from one sensational example: On September 8th, Hearst's *Chicago Herald-American* ran a front-page story which opened as follows:

Groggy as Londoners under protracted aerial blitzing, this town's bewildered citizens reeled today under the repeated attacks of a mad anesthetist who has sprayed a deadly nerve gas into 13 homes and has knocked out 27 victims.

Seventy others dashing to the area in response to the alarm, fell under the influence of the gas last night.

All skepticism has vanished and Mattoon grimly concedes it must fight haphazardly against a demented phantom adversary who has been seen only fleetingly and so far has evaded traps laid by city and state police and posses of townsmen.

Did the whole town of Mattoon succumb to the "mental epidemic"? Johnson concludes not; there were many, perhaps a majority, who ignored the incident. However, many others than

78 D. M. Johnson, The "Phantom Anesthetist" of Mattoon: A field study of mass hysteria, *J. abnorm. soc. Psychol.*, XL (1945), 175-86. Reprinted in Swanson *et al.*, *Readings* (2d ed.), pp. 208-19.

those who reported actual gassings were affected. The police had a great increase in calls reporting prowlers; many citizens of Mattoon put off their evening stroll and locked their windows more carefully than usual. All of these represent persons with some degree of suggestibility. Here again, as with the Martian invasion, we find that a vague and poorly structured situation provides a setting within which underlying personality trends exert powerful influence.

In 1953 a team of social scientists was able to study a "miracle" —the supposed appearance of a Virgin Saint in Sabana Grande, Puerto Rico.[79] Between 100,000 and 150,000 people jammed into a small area to await the appearance of the saint, and despite their disappointment several thousand persons a week came for almost a year afterwards. What had led these people to anticipate a miracle? In their analysis the authors noted a number of predisposing conditions such as poverty, lack of education, hard daily labor, lack of recreation, and widespread illness. Several children had reported a vision of the Virgin; this had been taken up by the newspapers and radio stations. The mayor of a nearby town had acted as publicity agent and promoter. Thus almost everyone on the island had heard about the miracle and thousands had come to witness its recurrence, despite opposition from the Roman Catholic Church. Those who attended firmly believed in such miracles and in the reality of the supernatural; hence they were not daunted by the events of the day but experienced rather a reaffirmation of their faith.

Major factors involved. A comprehensive survey of the literature on panic behavior was made by Strauss, who noted agreement as to the following major factors causing panic:

1. Conditions which weaken individuals organically and thus are conducive to lessening of rational mental activity.
2. A state of lowered mental ability with lessened capacity to act rationally.
3. A state of high emotional tension and heightened imagination which disposes individuals to act impulsively rather than rationally.
4. Mechanisms of suggestion, mass imitation, and rapid mental contagion act to precipitate actual flight and panicked reactions. These mechanisms are brought about largely by lessened ability to act rationally, by high emotional tension, and by heightened imagination.

[79] M. M. Tumin and A. S. Feldman, The miracle at Sabana Grande, *Pub. Opin. Quart.*, XIX (1955), 125-39.

5. Loss of faith in the leader, which renders individuals more susceptible to suggestions from persons other than the leader of the
group.

6. As a dominant condition underlying all the above, there is the
awareness that one's life is in great danger.[80]

The first three factors, it is worth noting, refer to personality
trends in individuals, the fourth and fifth deal with social interaction, and the last refers to the stimulus situation as the individual
interprets it.

Strauss concludes by summarizing methods for preventing mass
panic as follows:

1. Creating intelligent leadership and faith in that leadership
2. Creation of group discipline
3. Fostering intelligent and conscious reactions
4. Avoiding or minimizing physically weakening factors such as sickness, intoxication, and exhaustion
5. Distracting attention from danger, especially through activities.[81]

SUMMARY

"Mass behavior" refers to standardized or similar patterns of
social behavior which are transitory in nature and due to suggestion. Some mass behavior occurs outside rather than within face-
to-face groups. Fashion, for example, is a sanctioned type of cyclical
change found in certain areas of social behavior, such as those involving dress and design. People who follow the dictates of fashion
seem to do so because of prestige and conformity motives. Fads
resemble short-term fashions and may be of the "cult" or sporadic
type. Though impossible to predict and difficult to interpret, a
successful fad is characterized by novelty, consistency with the times,
and harmony with widespread interests and needs. What starts as
a fad sometimes endures as a fashion or custom. Crazes and booms
are like intense fads, widely disseminated through rumor and publicity; the boom usually is stimulated by a "get-rich-quick" scheme.
Rumors are a form of mass behavior but serve also to facilitate
other kinds of mass behavior. They thrive where motivation and
emotion are strong and facts are scarce. Study of the course of
rumors reveals certain processes which direct and alter their content, notably *leveling, sharpening,* and *assimilation to expectancy.*

Crowds and mobs exemplify mass behavior in face-to-face
situations; they are marked by focalized attention, increasing inter-

[80] A. L. Strauss, The literature on panic, *J. abnorm. soc. Psychol.,* XXXIX (1944),
319. See also several preliminary studies in D. W. Chapman (ed.), Human behavior in
disaster: A new field of social research, *J. soc. Issues,* X:3 (1954).

[81] A. L. Straus, *op. cit.,* pp. 319-20.

stimulation of members, and identification of members with group norms and purposes. Though crowd and mob behavior tends to be aggressive, it may at times be highly moral or even heroic. Interpretation of such behavior requires data as to how the members perceive the situation, their personality dynamics, and the interactional processes occurring within the group. A *critical social situation* refers primarily to catastrophes and panics. Often the major determinant is not real danger but people's fears and emotional instabilities which lead them to misinterpret an event, or reported event, and to communicate their "hysterical" reactions to others.

SUPPLEMENTARY READINGS
Books of Readings

MACCOBY, E. E., NEWCOMB, T. M., AND HARTLEY, E. L., (eds.). *Readings in social psychology*, 3d ed. New York: Henry Holt & Co., Inc., 1958.
  Allport, G. W., and Postman, L. J., The basic psychology of rumor.
  Bettelheim, B., Individual and mass behavior in extreme situations.
  Cantril, H., The invasion from Mars.
  Killian, L. M., The significance of multiple group membership in disaster.
  Mintz, A., Nonadaptive group behavior.

BRITT, S. H. (ed.). *Selected readings in social psychology*. New York: Rinehart & Co., Inc., 1950.
  Allport, G. W., and Postman, L., Why rumors circulate.
  Cantril, H., *et al.*, Critical social situations.
  Hollingworth, H. L., Psychology of the audience.
  Janney, J. E., Fad and fashion leadership among undergraduate women.
  Meier, N. C., Mennenga, G. H., and Stoltz, H. J., An experimental approach to the study of mob behavior.

LINDZEY, G. (ed.). *Handbook of social psychology*. Reading, Mass.: Addison-Wesley Pub. Co., Inc., 1954.
  Brown, R. W., Mass phenomena. Vol. II.

Other References

ALLPORT, G. W., AND POSTMAN, L. J. *The psychology of rumor*. New York: Henry Holt & Co., Inc., 1947.
  The pioneer analysis of rumor.

American Journal of Sociology, Vol. LXII (May, 1957), No. 6.
  This issue is devoted to the "Uses of leisure," which, for the authors, means fashion and fad.

CANTRIL, H. *The psychology of social movements*. New York: John Wiley & Sons, Inc., 1941.
  Valuable for the interpretation of lynching.

CANTRIL, H., GAUDET, H., AND HERZOG, H. *The Invasion from Mars*. Princeton, N. J.: Princeton University Press, 1940.
  Field study of a remarkable example of mass hysteria.

FESTINGER, L., RIECKEN, H. W., AND SCHACHTER, S. *When prophecy fails*. Minneapolis: University of Minnesota Press, 1956.
  The authors investigate some interesting hypotheses regarding belief, opinion, and rumor.

HUNTER, E. *Brainwashing, the story of men who defied it*. New York: Farrar, Straus & Cudahy, Inc., 1956.
Although this popular book is not well documented, it does suggest some of the problems of the subject.

LE BON, GUSTAVE. *The crowd* (English trans.). London: George Allen & Unwin, Ltd., 1917.
The first psychological analysis of crowd behavior; still has a remarkably modern flavor, despite its biased viewpoint.

MARTIN, E. D. *The behavior of crowds*. New York: Harper & Bros., 1920.
An early psychoanalytic interpretation of crowds.

TURNER, R. H., AND KILLIAN, L. M. *Collective behavior*. Englewood Cliffs, N. J.: Prentice-Hall, Inc., 1957.
A comprehensive collection of readings, with interpretations, particularly relevant with respect to crowds.

YOUNG, K. *Social Psychology*, 3d ed. New York: Appleton-Century-Crofts, Inc., 1956.
Chapters ix (mythology), xii (crowds), and xiii (fashions) are excellent.

———. *Source book for social psychology*. New York: Alfred A. Knopf, Inc., 1928.
Contains several classic studies of "mental epidemics."

19

Social Change

Perhaps the most striking event or process in our present-day culture is *change*. Every culture pattern is continually being altered and, in turn, molds the personalities of its members. However, it is in the realm of material objects that this change is most drastic and noticeable. By contrast, the world of values, attitudes, ideas, and behavior is essentially conservative. Yet there are periods of crisis and revolution when change hurtles on in almost uncontrolled fashion and shapes both ideas and overt behavior. It is the job of social scientists—particularly anthropologists, sociologists, and social psychologists—to interpret this phenomenon of social change, which they proceed to do in a number of different ways.

The anthropologist's *cultural change* is a broad term which he applies to any significant alteration in a culture pattern—to changes in technology, architecture, food, clothing, or art forms, or to changes in values, customs, and social relationships. He is interested in the nature and extent of such changes and in the processes by which they occur.

The sociologist uses the term *social change* to designate primarily alterations in the nonmaterial culture—that is, in values, mores, institutions, and social behavior. Such changes, he finds, often follow technological and other innovations. Some sociologists focus upon short-term changes like fashions or political movements; others emphasize the changes which occur over decades or whole generations. Still others, notably Sorokin, conceptualize change even more broadly as social evolution and seek to account for the rise and fall of whole civilizations.[1]

[1] P. A. Sorokin, *Social and cultural dynamics*, 4 vols. (New York: American Book Co., 1937).

Historians have unearthed a vast array of changes, although their interest is generally in describing particular events rather than following long-range trends. However, in recent years they have been more aware of social history, that is, the large scale movements which reflect the less obvious but possibly more significant changes. Fortunately this trend does not deny the importance of certain single historical events; one can hardly overestimate, for example, the social significance of the Battle of Marathon, in which the Greeks defeated the Persians. This one event probably gave an indelible stamp to Western culture and is reflected in numerous aspects of our behavior today.

In any event the social scientist is concerned with the nature, causes, processes, and effects of changing social behavior, more or less apart from the individuals concerned. As noted frequently before, he is working at a different level from the psychologist. His major unit is the group rather than the individual, whereas the social psychologist deals always with the individual in his social relationships.

The utility of the social psychologist's approach depends in large part upon how he conceptualizes social change. He can contribute little to our understanding of the rise and fall of whole civilizations. Looking at so broad a canvas, it seems as if economic, geographical, political, and assorted historical factors bulk larger than the psychological as salient determinants. Indeed, one anthropologist, L. A. White, insists that psychological explanations are of no value in interpreting culture and culture change. In philology, says White, our explanatory concepts are linguistic laws and principles, not psychological ones. Similarly, he concludes, we need not psychology, but a new science of "culturology" to understand cultural phenomena.[2]

However, White's nonpsychological approach is not shared by those social scientists who interpret social change as an altering of social relationships *within* a more or less clearly defined culture group. They are concerned with describing the social processes and influences producing social change; the social psychologist's interpretation draws upon theirs and in turn supplements it, as we shall see.

ANTHROPOLOGISTS AND CULTURAL CHANGE

Anthropologists study culture patterns as a whole and make cross-cultural comparisons. They treat cultural change in terms of

[2] L. A. White, *The science of culture* (New York: Farrar, Straus & Cudahy, Inc., 1949).

processes involved, such as invention and discovery, diffusion, and acculturation.[3] Such processes, says Linton, increase the number of "alternatives" in a culture—that is, culture traits which are shared by many but which must be tested before they become fully accepted. Primitive societies have relatively few alternatives: two or three major pottery designs, for example, or two alternative ways of dressing leather, or travel by foot or horseback. In a society such as ours there are many alternatives, such as horses, bicycles, railroads, automobiles, or airplanes, for the single purpose of transportation.

In a sense all social change may be considered as innovation, which one writer defines as "any thought, behavior, or thing that is new because it is qualitatively different from existing forms." [4] Whether by intention or chance an individual or a group institutes a given change, however diffuse or specific, however significant or obscure, it in some way alters former practices. Although the social scientist may be more concerned with large-scale changes, such as variations in the birth rate or the shift to atomic power, we must not forget that a different hair style or the introduction of a new course at Saw Creek High School is equally an innovation.

Cultural changes, says Herskovits, are effected by innovations from within and from without.[5] The former may be either accidental or purposeful, in the form of discoveries or inventions. However, as Linton points out, the number of discoveries and inventions occurring in any one culture is relatively small; the comparatively rapid growth of human culture depends upon borrowing or diffusion.[6] He suggests the extent of this diffusion in a pointed illustration:

Our solid American citizens awaken in a bed built on a pattern which originated in the Near East but which was modified in Northern Europe before it was transmitted to America. He throws back covers made from cotton, domesticated in India, or linen, domesticated in the Near East, or wool from sheep, also domesticated in the Near East, or silk, the use of which was discovered in China. All of these materials have been spun and woven by processes invented in the Near East. He slips into his moccasins, invented by the Indians of the Eastern woodlands, and goes to the bathroom, whose fixtures are a mixture of European and American inventions, both of recent date. He takes off his pajamas, a garment invented in India, and washes with soap invented by the ancient Gauls. He then shaves, a masochistic rite which seems to have been derived from either Sumer or ancient Egypt.

3 R. Linton, *The study of man* (New York: Appleton-Century-Crofts, Inc.; copyright, 1936, by D. Appleton-Century Co., Inc.), chaps. xvi-xx; M. J. Herskovits, The processes of cultural change, in R. Linton (ed.), *Science of man in the world crisis* (New York: Columbia University Press, 1945).

4 H. G. Barnett, *Innovation* (New York: McGraw-Hill Book Co., Inc., 1953), p. 7.

5 Herskovits, *op. cit.*, pp. 150-51.

6 R. Linton, *The study of man*, p. 324.

Associated Press

The Ku Klux Klan represents a form of mass behavior and violent social control not entirely confined to racial matters.

French Government Tourist Office

Social change is not accepted by all, as demonstrated by this Parisian, who exhibits what might be called social change in reverse.

Returning to the bedroom, he removes his clothes from a chair of southern European type and proceeds to dress. He puts on garments whose form originally derived from the skin clothing of the nomads of the Asiatic steppes, puts on shoes made from skins tanned by a process invented in ancient Egypt and cut to a pattern derived from the classical civilizations of the Mediterranean, and ties around his neck a strip of bright-colored cloth which is a vestigial survival of the shoulder shawls worn by the seventeenth-century Croatians. Before going out for breakfast he glances through the window, made of glass invented in Egypt, and if it is raining puts on overshoes made of rubber discovered by the Central American Indians and takes an umbrella, invented in southeastern Asia. Upon his head he puts a hat made of felt, a material invented in the Asiatic steppes.

On his way to breakfast he stops to buy a paper, paying for it with coins, an ancient Lydian invention. At the restaurant a whole new series of borrowed elements confronts him. His plate is made of a form of pottery invented in China. His knife is of steel, an alloy first made in southern India, his fork a medieval Italian invention, and his spoon a derivative of a Roman original. He begins breakfast with an orange, from the eastern Mediterranean, a canteloupe from Persia, or perhaps a piece of African watermelon. With this he has coffee, an Abyssinian plant, with cream and sugar. Both the domestication of cows and the idea of milking them originated in the Near East, while sugar was first made in India. After his fruit and first coffee he goes on to waffles, cakes made by a Scandinavian technique from wheat domesticated in Asia Minor. Over these he pours maple syrup, invented by the Indians of the Eastern woodlands. As a side dish he may have the egg of a species of bird domesticated in Indo-China, or thin strips of the flesh of an animal domesticated in Eastern Asia which have been salted and smoked by a process developed in northern Europe.

When our friend has finished eating he settles back to smoke, an American Indian habit, consuming a plant domesticated in Brazil in either a pipe, derived from the Indians of Virginia, or a cigarette, derived from Mexico. If he is hardy enough he may even attempt a cigar, transmitted to us from the Antilles by way of Spain. While smoking he reads the news of the day, imprinted in characters invented by the ancient Semites upon a material invented in China by a process invented in Germany. As he absorbs the accounts of foreign troubles he will, if he is a good conservative citizen, thank a Hebrew deity in an Indo-European language that he is 100 per cent American.[7]

Diffusion refers to the transmission of "traits" from one culture to another. "Acculturation" and "assimilation" are terms designating broader and more intimate culture contacts. Gillin and Gillin define *acculturation* as "the processes whereby societies of different cultures are modified through fairly close and long-continued contact but without a complete blending of the two cultures." [8] *Assimilation* is the term used by sociologists and by some anthropologists to designate the process by which persons of unlike social heritages or cultures come to share the same body of sentiments, tra-

[7] *Ibid.*, pp. 326-27. Reprinted by permission of Appleton-Century-Crofts, Inc.

[8] J. L. Gillin and J. P. Gillin, *Cultural sociology* (New York: The Macmillan Co., 1948), p. 536. Cf. the discussion of socialization and social learning in Chapter 8 above, pp. 238-43.

ditions, and loyalties.[9] Assimilation is best exemplified by immigrants who have resided long enough in the new land to learn its language and customs and to become amalgamated through intermarriage and economic participation. Thus acculturation and assimilation account for considerable social and cultural change. And these are two-way changes, as compared with diffusion, which is fundamentally a one-way process. Our Indian tribes have taken over many American ways, but we have received from them many place names, foods, pottery, and other art forms. Likewise our assimilated immigrants have made linguistic, economic, artistic, and philosophical contributions to the American culture pattern.[10]

However, there is considerable variability among cultures as to the degree to which they will accept change. In Africa the resistant Dinka of the upper Nile contrast with certain of the Bantus who have accepted extensive Westernization. This variability is not easy to measure, because the pressures surrounding each group vary and hence affect vulnerability to change. Anthropologists and other social scientists generally have tended to study dynamics more than statics, partly to correct the stereotype that preliterate peoples are completely fixated in their cultural behavior.[11] As might be expected, material traits are more likely to change than are belief systems.

One of the most significant studies of change within a given society is Margaret Mead's report of her 1953 return visit to the Manus whom she had first known in 1928.[12] During her absence a number of innovations occurred: the advent of missionaries with a humanitarian message; a particularly effective local leader, Paliau; the Australian program of self-government; and the presence of American and other service personnel during the war period. From a harsh, rigid, suspicious group, the Manus had become an optimistic, cooperative, and friendly society. The implications are, she asserts, that rapid total change may be preferable to piecemeal transformation. The discontinuities and maladjustments are less when the total structure is altered than when constant reminders of the past continue to forestall adjustment to the new.[13] Further evidence

[9] E. B. Reuter, *Handbook of sociology* (New York: The Dryden Press, Inc., 1941). See also the discussion of assimilation as a form of social interaction in Chapter 11 above.

[10] See Gillin and Gillin, *op. cit.*, chap. xxii.

[11] See M. J. Herskovits, *Cultural anthropology* (New York: Alfred A. Knopf, Inc., 1955), pp. 447-52. For a recent empirical study of acculturation in an African tribe see L. W. Doob, An introduction to the psychology of acculturation, *J. soc. Psychol.*, XLV (1957), 143-60.

[12] M. Mead, *New lives for old* (New York: William Morrow & Co., Inc., 1956).

[13] *Ibid.*, pp. 445-58.

testing this hypothesis regarding rapid change would be welcome; one hopes it might help settle the thorny issue of gradual versus immediate integration of the Negro in our American South.

THE PROBLEM OF SOCIAL CAUSATION

The how and why of social change brings up the matter of cause and effect relationships, whether in sweeping historical events or in the less momentous occurrences such as an individual choosing to cross a street, the decision of a teen-ager to go to college, or the expansion of a city into the suburbs. Frequently, in attempting to explain the phenomenon of change, both laymen and social scientists tend to read causal relationships into mere correlation of events. Actually, the linkage of events in space or time, whether by intention or "chance," seldom, if ever, proves causation. A positive correlation between the number of automobiles and the extent of literacy in the countries of the world does not prove that one caused the other, since both events may have developed from a common factor or set of factors.

There are many causes of social change. Unicausal interpretations have been presented frequently—by Montesquieu, Malthus, Marx, and Freud, for example—and in each case the theory has had to be corrected subsequently or at least broadened. According to our multicausal approach, social events derive from a complex of variables, among which it is usually difficult to select one as more critical than another. Isolation of *the* crucial factor demands a controlled experiment, to which relatively few social phenomena lend themselves. Was the Hungarian revolt of 1956 due to long-repressed frustration and pent-up aggressiveness, to a liberal tradition growing out of the heritage of dissent in the Austro-Hungarian empire and the aftermath of World War I, to a militant anti-Soviet underground, to the restlessness and need for further professionalization on the part of the intelligentsia, to the Voice of America broadcasts urging self-liberation, to basic physical needs and a generally depressed standard of living, or to a deep-seated desire for change? All these factors, and others as well, seem to have been involved in this historic event. Then, too, in addition to these more general causes there were immediate precipitating factors during the critical days in late October: the immediate struggle for power by certain political and military leaders, and Russian indecision and retreat, followed by a new attack.

The recent revival of religion in America also lends itself to a multicausal interpretation. It may be traced to the breakdown of conventional values and moorings in World War I, which was followed by the materialistic 1920's with their over-expansion of credit that resulted in the economic cataclysm of the 1930's, which in turn might have caused the economic and political nationalism producing Hitler, who was the principal agent in precipitating World War II, which itself made possible atomic warfare, leading to a state of despair that brought about an increased interest in religion! This seems plausible, but obviously there would be great difficulty in proving the validity of such an oversimplified causal sequence.

The problem of causation is essentially the same problem that complicates analysis of motivation: no one has seen a cause or isolated one for inspection. Causes, like motives, are abstractions or, more accurately, a set of assumptions. The overlapping, non-discrete nature of social data makes the search for causes tremendously difficult, though new statistical techniques may help. For the immediate future we shall have to be content with describing, not clear determinants, but related situations or surrounding conditions whose precise causal relationships are not known.[14]

THE SOCIOLOGICAL APPROACH

The sociologist is interested in the pattern of change—the complex dynamics of change over a time period. He asks whether there is any universal tendency about social change. If so, what are its ingredients? How does the interrelationship of institutions affect change? Why is change more rapid at some periods than at others?

Fundamentally, sociologists approach these problems statistically, seeking quantitative data wherever possible. One example of such numerical findings is the sigmoid curve that appears among a number of phenomena. With many social inventions there is first a gradual acceptance, then a rapid rise in adoption, until a maximum is reached, followed by a tapering off. This is true for such diverse areas as motor vehicle registration and life expectancy tables on a long-term basis. It has also been demonstrated for more definitely social psychological problems, as experiments have shown regarding diffusion of messages in a limited time period.[15]

The sociologist deals with many aspects of change. The panel studies in public opinion surveys are one means of determining prin-

14 For further data on the problem of causation in the social sciences, see R. M. MacIver, *Social causation* (New York: Ginn & Co., 1942); W. F. Ogburn and M. F. Nimkoff, *Technology and the changing family* (Boston: Houghton Mifflin Co., 1955), chap. ii; A. W. Green, *Sociology* (rev. ed.; New York: McGraw-Hill Book Co., Inc., 1956), chap. xxv; and F. R. Allen *et al., Technology and social change* (New York: Appleton-Century-Crofts, Inc., 1957), Part I.

15 G. A. Lundberg, C. C. Schrag, and O. N. Larsen, *Sociology* (New York: Harper & Bros., 1954), pp. 693-98.

ciples of attitude change.[16] In interpreting the relation of events
to the underlying social system, two general theories have developed.[17] One is the *equilibrium theory,* which assumes that a social
system tends toward "a state of rest in which the conflicts and strains
among its component parts are reduced to a minimum." The
process theory, on the other hand, emphasizes evolutionary or cyclic
trends, illustrated by Sorokin as well as by Spengler and Toynbee
with their interest in the philosophy of history and the rise and fall
of civilizations. Or the two theories may be combined, as with the
Italian sociologist Pareto. Social dislocation or strain may in some
cases lead to revolution when one or more parts of the culture pattern are out of balance with the larger social order.[18]

Along with their theoretical interest and their studies of processes,
sociologists have tried to discover the major influences producing
change. Many of them believe that the greatest agent of social
change is the technology within a given society, since the material
substratum sets the pattern within which the culture may function.
Innovations like the discovery of fire, the invention of the wheel
and of agriculture, and the domestication of animals constituted a
revolution which made possible the advanced societies of the ancient
Near East. Since that time, with some fluctuations, there has been
progressive elaboration of the technology, which is the base on
which the remainder of the culture stands. Studies have documented the relationship of technology to the sociocultural pattern.
Webb, for example, pointed to the effect of the six-shooter, barbed
wire, and the windmill in making the Great Plains inhabitable.
Without these devices the farmer could never have subdued the
country that had belonged to the cattlemen.[19] In our present urban
order Ogburn notes that the invention of the elevator has made possible a lower birthrate because apartment houses encourage more
limited family size. In fact, technology has had many effects upon
family functions, of which the independence of women is only one
example.[20]

Many years ago Ogburn stressed the great significance of technological developments in producing the rapid social changes found in

16 See Chapter 16, pp. 420-21.

17 B. Moore, Jr., Sociological theory and contemporary politics, *Amer. J. Sociol.,* LXI
(1955), 107-15.

18 For an authoritative presentation of the equilibrium theory and the problem of
strain, see T. Parsons, *The social system* (Glencoe, Ill.: Free Press, 1951), pp. 491-535
especially.

19 W. P. Webb, *The great plains* (Boston: Houghton Mifflin Co., 1936).

20 W. F. Ogburn and M. F. Nimkoff, *op. cit.,* pp. 3-17.

Western European and American society.[21] Inventions and other technological changes have increased at an accelerated pace during the past few hundred years despite the many obstacles furnished by fear, tradition, conservatism, and vested interests.[22] The social effects of inventions like the automobile, radio, airplane, movies, X-ray, and so on are tremendous. Ogburn and Gilfillan have noted no less than 150 social changes due to radio; for example:

Standardization of diction
Greater enjoyment of music
Aid to ships at sea
Increased adult education
Prevention of crop loss through weather reports
Invalids being able to hear church services
Decline in phonograph sales
Employment for announcers, engineers, singers, etc.
Changed political campaigns
Increased irritation against excesses in advertising [23]

Perhaps the automobile has modified our way of living even more, with its far-flung effects upon business, recreation, crime, religion, family life, and even love-making! Effects of the airplane upon our lives in war and peace are already apparent. We are just beginning to learn something of the social changes to be expected from television.[24]

We shudder at the implications of the atomic and hydrogen bombs and hope fervently that their threat may be offset by beneficial consequences of the peaceful uses of atomic energy.

Ogburn coined the term "cultural lag" to designate our inability to develop new values and social arrangements which would make it possible to assimilate inventions and technological changes.[25] Cultural lag shows up in many areas, such as slowness in adopting effective means of traffic control, delay in installing safety devices in industry, failure to care adequately for those unemployed as a result

[21] See W. F. Ogburn, *Social change* (New York: The Viking Press, Inc., 1922); W. F. Ogburn and M. F. Nimkoff, *Sociology* (2d ed.; Boston: Houghton Mifflin Co., 1950), chaps. xxv-xxviii.

[22] See B. J. Stern, Resistances to the adoption of technological innovations, in *Technological trends and national policy* (Washington, D. C.: National Resources Committee, 1937).

[23] W. F. Ogburn and S. C. Gilfillan, chap. iii in President's Research Committee on Social Trends, *Recent social trends in the United States* (New York: McGraw-Hill Book Co., Inc., 1933). See also L. Morris, *Not so long ago* (New York: Random House, Inc., 1949), for a more popular account of social changes caused by the automobile, movies, and radio. F. L. Allen in *The big change* (New York: Harper & Bros., 1952) describes how American life has been transformed between 1900 and 1950.

[24] See pp. 411-12 above.

[25] W. F. Ogburn, *Social change*, Part IV.

of depression and technological change, or adherence to local governmental units and systems which have long since outlived their usefulness.

Another example of cultural lag is the slowness with which we apply scientific techniques, including psychiatric approaches, in the disposition and rehabilitation of delinquents and criminals. The jury system itself is beginning to come under scrutiny; some are asking whether an institution which was a real achievement in the thirteenth century has not become a questionable procedure in an age which emphasizes scientific method and utilization of trained personnel.

It may be that urbanization has become a kind of cultural lag. Cities were at one time a sign of progress. But it is doubtful whether the large metropolitan centers can still claim that distinction in view of the problems of urban living: distance from the land, traffic congestion, air pollution, and now vulnerability to atomic destruction. Planners are asking whether our cities should go underground or be dispersed into large constellations of small community centers. Probably the near future will see experiments of both kinds extensively undertaken.

Frequently the problem of cultural lag results from mechanical processes becoming outmoded. In one case the shift of railroads from steam to diesel engines threatened the survival of a number of communities which had served as railroad "shops." The entire community of Caliente, Nevada, for example, became obsolete through "dieselization" with accompanying social and personal disorganization in the lives of hundreds of people.[26]

Actually, however, it is in the acculturation problems of preliterate cultures that the role of technology is most forcibly presented. Sherif studied some of the effects of international contacts and modern technology on Turkish villages.[27] He found that the concepts of time, space and distance were westernized according to the degree of industrialization which had occurred. The individual's unit of measurement of distance depended upon the degree to which he used a vehicle or walked. For example, 50 kilometers might be expressed as: "You start early in the morning and reach there by sunset," or "You reach there (by the time) you work on crops of one *dönüm* (of land)."[28] It was found that the more a village changed the more possible was future change; that is, change

---

26 W. F. Cottrell, Death by dieselization: a case study in the reaction to technological change; *Amer. sociol. Rev.*, XVI (1951), 358-65.

27 M. Sherif and C. W. Sherif, *An outline of social psychology* (rev. ed.; New York: Harper & Bros., 1956), chap. xx.

28 *Ibid.*, pp. 693-94.

was positively accelerated. It is doubtful, according to another social scientist, that any so-called simple society can accept the machines of Euro-American culture and reject its basic social behavior.
For one thing, industrialization means that the individual must
orient his waking hours predominantly about a factory system, with
the consequent loss of time to his own family and village. Skills and
achievement become more important than personal gratification or
the retention of kinship ties. The best worker is chosen by the in-
dustrialist, and he must produce under given conditions and at a
specified time period.[29]

Africa offers many examples of acculturation and a changed way
of life as Western technology has transformed institutional behavior.
Cash economy has replaced the barter system in many areas; even the
bride price, or *lobola,* is paid in shillings instead of cattle. Also
there is the drift of men to the larger centers as laborers in mines
or industry, with consequent urbanization and further detribalizing
effects. Introduction of motor transportation has permitted the African more mobility in a year than he once knew in a lifetime.
Some of the results of this rapid transformation, of course, have
been less beneficial; for example, there has been an increase in
tuberculosis because of the wearing of Western clothing, which remains wet in a tropical climate.

Apparently cultural diffusion and social change have mixed effects, with many serious problems looming to counteract or at least
modify the undeniable benefits. Some writers believe that the problems are an inevitable part of a basic discontinuity—the disparity
between social science and natural science, the difficulty of keeping
up with technology in the fields of ethics, religion, social work, government, and other disciplines concerned with human relations.

PSYCHOLOGICAL FACTORS IN SOCIAL CHANGE

The anthropological and sociological analyses of social change
can be supplemented by psychological data, particularly in regard to
"attitudes toward social change" and a broad social psychological
interpretation of individual adjustment and resistance to social
change.

There are many variables determining the susceptibility of a
person's attitudes to change, as noted earlier with respect to the
modification of ethnic attitudes.[30] The relation between culture
patterns and the constellation of attitudes within the individual

[29] G. A. Theodorson, Acceptance of industrialization and its attendant consequences
for the social patterns of non-Western societies, *Amer. sociol. Rev.,* XVIII (1953),
477-83.

[30] See Chapter 8.

and among groups of individuals is a reciprocal one. That is, to change our social relationships people's attitudes must be altered; at the same time, changes in sociocultural arrangements modify the values and attitudes of the individual. For social scientists and for social reformers the problem is one of understanding resistance to change and, especially for the latter, one of knowing how to weaken that resistance.

Whether or not the members of a given society can adjust well to changing conditions depends in large part upon their attitudes toward change. In static societies, relatively few social changes will occur over a period of several generations. Here one discovers no awareness or expectation of change and therefore no attitude toward it. In Western Europe and America, on the other hand, technological, economic, and social changes have been accelerating in the last few hundred years. Attitudes toward change have naturally arisen in these cultures and tend to fall somewhere along a conservative-liberal continuum—somewhere between opposing and favoring change. Some would extend the scale to make it appear thus:

Reactionary	Conservative	Liberal	Radical

Here "reactionary" signifies one who would go back to the "good old days"; "conservative," one who stands for the status quo; "liberal" (or "progressive"), one who favors gradual social change; and "radical," one who favors rapid or even violent social change.

Such a schema is simple and roughly in harmony with common usage of the four terms employed, but several important questions arise. For example, should we speak as if generalized attitudes toward change exist? In the United States it would seem as if we have become used to technological changes and welcome them. (The fact that we expect rapid technological advance is illustrated by the often expressed surprise that television took so long to become perfected.) However, many of us who favor technical advances seem loath to advocate, and may indeed oppose, the social changes made necessary by technological change.

Or again, even if we limit "reactionary," "conservative," "liberal," and "radical" to attitudes toward *social* change, the generality of these attitudes may still be questioned. Some people welcome social security but abhor changes in manners and morals. Some who scent a danger of increasing socialization in government are found to favor simplified spelling, calendar reform, or compulsory teaching of Esperanto. Some who advocate the liberalizing of divorce laws oppose "United World Federalism." Obviously we need empirical evidence as to specificity or generality.

Fortunately, several studies have been made by social psychologists. Most of the investigators find that attitudes toward social change do have a fair degree of generality. Allport [31] and Vetter,[32] for example, found considerable generality or "internal consistency" in radicalism and conservatism. More recently, Stagner discovered that radical-conservative economic attitudes of college students act as a common factor or frame of reference underlying racial prejudice, nationalism, pro-fascist sentiment, and attitude toward forceful solution of problems.[33] Lentz [34] and others found that conservatism and radicalism can be reliably measured. Lentz's "C-R Opinionaire" studies the difference among persons "in degree of opposition or favor toward social change." [35] It contains such items as the following to elicit the individual's attitudes:

> Three meals a day will always be the best general rule.
> The proposal to change the present calendar to one having 13 months of 28 days is unsound.
> Socially-minded experts, rather than voters, should decide the policies of government.
> Criminals should be treated like sick persons.
> Cremation is the best method of burial.
> Preaching is one of the most effective ways of teaching people to lead better lives.

Thus it appears that positive correlations exist between conservative-radical attitudes in different areas, such as law, politics, social customs, religion, economics, and international relations. However, we must remember that these correlations are often low, which indicates that some people are not consistently "radical" or "conservative." Indeed, some investigators, focusing upon these inconsistencies, doubt the existence of generalized attitudes.[36] But the bulk of the evidence, to date, points toward some degree of generality.

31 G. W. Allport in *Amer. J. Sociol.*, XXXV (1929), 220-38. See also G. W. Allport, *Personality* (New York: Henry Holt & Co., Inc., 1937), pp. 430-31.

32 G. B. Vetter, Measurement of social and political attitudes . . . , *J. abnorm. soc. Psychol.*, XXV (1930), 26-39.

33 R. Stagner, Studies of aggressive social attitudes, *J. soc. Psychol.*, XX (1944), 109-20.

34 T. F. Lentz, Generality and specificity of conservatism-radicalism, *J. educ. Psychol.*, XXIX (1938), 540-46; G. W. Hartmann, Differential validity of items in a liberalism-conservatism test, *J. soc. Psychol.*, IX (1938), 67-78; R. Alpert and S. S. Sargent, Conservatism-radicalism measured by immediate emotional reactions, *J. soc. Psychol.*, XIV (1941), 181-86.

35 T. F. Lentz, *Manual for C-R Opinionaire* (St. Louis: Washington University, 1935).

36 E.g., L. W. Ferguson, Primary social attitudes, *J. Psychol.*, VIII (1939), 217-23.

A serious difficulty arises from defining conservatism and radicalism in terms of favoring or opposing the status quo. Anyone, whatever his dominant attitude may be, may seek to change existing affairs if they seem opposed to his own interests and values. Should the opponents of the Soviet-oriented governments of Eastern Europe, for example, be called "radicals" because they seek changes in the direction of capitalism? Should we label as reactionaries those Americans who, in the 1950's, tried to repeal the McCarran-Walter immigration act and go back to earlier types of less restrictive legislation? Or should we think of the Nazis as liberals or radicals when they brought in social changes such as racial purity laws and sterilization of citizens belonging to unfavored minority groups? Obviously, there are dangers in defining conservatism and radicalism solely in terms of attitude toward social change; the question of one's underlying goals and values is also important.

Despite these very real questions, however, we probably need terms like "reactionary," "conservative," "liberal," and "radical" to denote different patterns of attitude toward social change. Such concepts are real enough to be very useful in describing personality trends and in predicting the behavior of individuals and groups toward proposed social changes, or toward changes actually in process. When the Conservative party wins in England, we can predict fairly well the policies which will be followed; when the Labor party wins, we expect a different policy—one involving increased socialization of industry and other types of social change. In the United States the Republican party is generally considered conservative and the Democratic party liberal, but the lines are not very clearly drawn or the respective policies consistently oriented with respect to social change.

DETERMINANTS OF ATTITUDES TOWARD SOCIAL CHANGE

As we have seen, the social psychologist finds that in technologically advanced societies attitudes toward social change develop which play an important part in determining whether or not actual social changes will occur. However, in these societies, the prevalent attitudes are by no means uniform. With respect to a broad issue such as socialization of industry, we find attitudes ranging from wildest enthusiasm to deepest antipathy. And so we ask: What influences determine a person's attitudes toward social change?

First and foremost among the determiners of an individual's attitudes is the family in which he grew up, as already indicated in Chapter 4. Newcomb, for example, found that the attitudes of children in regard to religion, war, and communism correlated about

0.50 to 0.60 with their parents' attitudes.[37] Furthermore, he found that the parents' consistencies or inconsistencies of attitude tended to be reflected in their children. The study of voting behavior referred to in Chapter 16 revealed that parental political views had a great deal to do with the political preferences and later voting behavior of their progeny.[38]

The influence of the school upon pupils' attitudes is less significant than that of the family. This is true because the child's basic values and attitudes are in part already learned by the time he begins school. The teacher's influence is further limited, in the United States at least, by our objection to "propaganda" or "indoctrination" in the classroom.[39] As a result, our schools reflect and reinforce the prevalent attitudes of the community. The teaching of vigorous and aggressive "Americanism" is not considered propaganda, but teachers who have advanced views favoring social change usually get into trouble with the principal, the school board, or various community pressure groups. The attack upon "liberal" or "radical" teachers is commonest at the college level, where social issues are more likely to be treated, and where teachers tend to be more independent and outspoken. In times of economic and social strain, as in postwar periods or during depressions, college professors are under constant pressure. During the period of anti-Communist hysteria following World War II many professors were fired (along with government employees) on grounds of alleged sympathy for communism.[40]

Many educators have been concerned over our failure to prepare children for living in a changing world. Too often, they say, a child is prepared to live in a world that is already *passé* by the time he is old enough to vote. "Progressive" educators are endeavoring to teach the facts and implications of social change so that their pupils will not expect to live in a static world. But "education for a changing world" is hardly the watchword of most schools in the United States or, indeed, in other parts of the world.

Another influence affecting a child's attitudes is selection on the part of his parents. Mothers and fathers in higher income brackets typically choose private schools for their children in which values and attitudes held by the parents will be reinforced. Parental selec-

---

[37] T. M. Newcomb and G. Svehla, Intra-family relationships in attitude, *Sociometry*, I (1937), 180-205.

[38] P. Lazarsfeld *et al.*, *The people's choice* (rev. ed.; New York: Columbia University Press, 1948).

[39] See the discussion of education and propaganda in Chapter 17.

[40] See, e.g., H. S. Commager, The real danger—fear of ideas, *New York Times Magazine*, June 26, 1949. For sidelights on the period of "McCarthyism" see S. S. Sargent and T. Brameld (eds.), Anti-intellectualism in the United States, *J. soc. Issues*, XI: 3, (1955).

tion may influence, whether consciously or unconsciously, their children's choice of friends, clubs, social organizations, and leisure-time activities. Thus the well-to-do youngster's contacts in home, school, social organizations, and community may insulate him effectively from differing ideas and attitudes. If he goes to college, his value-system will probably be sufficiently rigid to protect him against the "dangerous" ideas of liberal professors.

Still another factor in the individual's attitudes toward social change is his intelligence and knowledge. Many studies of college students indicate that the more intelligent and better-informed students are also more liberal in their attitudes—though there are many exceptions.[41] The fact that students become more liberal in their attitudes as they go on through college seems related to their increased knowledge. However, many other factors are also at work, such as adaptation to the norms of the college community, as indicated in Newcomb's study of Bennington College.[42]

A positive correlation between conservatism and age is usually reported.[43] Radical political movements make their greatest appeal to those below middle age. Study disclosed that leaders in British reform governments were between thirty and forty-five years old; conservative leaders were between fifty-five and sixty-five.[44] Whether this correlation is due to increasing rigidity which is a part of the aging process is not clear. It may also be a function of disillusionment or of an increasing stake in the status quo as one becomes settled in his job, a parent, a home-owner, and a respected and conforming member of his community.

Certainly those who have a stake in the status quo—those who are well pleased with things as they are—have little desire to agitate for social change. Conversely, those advocating social reforms are drawn chiefly from the lower and lower-middle socioeconomic groups, who stand to benefit most by changes. These differing attitudes toward social change may or may not be reflected in political alignments. Before 1932 one could hardly say that either of our major parties was conservative or liberal. But after Roosevelt inaugurated the New Deal with its many reforms, a political realignment took place,

41 See P. H. Odegard, *The American public mind* (New York: Columbia University Press, 1931); D. Katz, F. H. Allport, and M. B. Jenness, *Students' attitudes* (Syracuse, N. Y.: W. E. Mosher, 1931).

42 T. M. Newcomb, *Personality and social change* (New York: The Dryden Press, Inc., 1943). See also Chapter 8, above.

43 An exception is the study by I. Lorge and K. Helfant, The independence of chronological age and sociopolitical attitudes. *J. abnorm. soc. Psychol.*, XLVIII (1953), 598.

44 See E. B. Gowin, *The executive and his control of men* (New York: The Macmillan Co., 1915), pp. 264-70.

with the Democratic party supported by liberals and some radicals (lower and lower-middle class) and the Republican party by conservatives (upper-middle and upper class). This alignment, however, seems to have been changed by the sweeping victories of Eisenhower in 1952 and 1956.[45]

In addition to the above-mentioned determinants of basic attitudes toward social change, a number of personality factors may be important. For example, a sensitive person, who perceives the ills of society, may become a strong proponent of social change, irrespective of his own personal stake in the matter. Another person may revere authority so much that he construes any suggested change as an attack upon organized society.

Sometimes rigidity of attitudes must be explained by unconscious motivational factors. The individual may resist an innovation because it is associated with his father, toward whom he feels hostile. The father might have favored changes the son could not accept, hence all change now becomes unattractive. A change in one area may suggest change in another area where the individual, unconsciously, feels very insecure.

Frustrated persons sometimes find, in either radical or reactionary movements, a means of sublimating their inner conflicts. The radical, for example, may be protesting parental authority or attempting to gain ego-enhancement by espousing unconventional ideas. Or the ultraconservative individual may be regressing, in an unconscious desire to return to his happy childhood or youth. In fact, the personality dynamics of the two extremes may be much alike, hence the swing from radical to reactionary is not too surprising. A number of cases have come to light where a Communist returns to the fold, which may be an authoritarian, ritualistic religion or the traditional socioeconomic attitudes of his parents. Such cases, however, are the exception rather than the rule; stability of attitudes is far commoner than extensive change.

As suggested earlier, attitudes with which we have become ego-involved are among the most difficult to change, since they seem to provide us with security and satisfaction. Furthermore, attitudes are most flexible where there has been little or no indoctrination— where they have not been strongly structured, either positively or negatively. Under these conditions there is less of a barrier to acquiring new viewpoints.[46] Also, change of attitude is more likely

45 See S. Lubell, *The future of American politics* (New York: Harper & Bros., 1952) for a description of trends which help to explain the election of 1952.

46 C. I. Hovland, A. A. Lumsdaine, and F. J. Sheffield, *Experiments on mass communication* (Princeton, N. J.: Princeton University Press, 1949).

to occur when only one side of an argument is presented. It is desirable to alter both the internal factors (cognition and experience) and external factors such as contact and communication at the same time.[47] The bank clerk may begin to see things differently and to vote differently from his manager when he marries, moves his place of residence, makes new friends and subscribes to a different newspaper, in addition to whatever thinking he has been doing.

THE PSYCHOLOGY OF THE INNOVATOR

One must remember that all social change is mediated by individuals. What are the motives of the minority which selects a new hair style, initiates a political slogan, or copies a foreign recipe, since diffusion, too, is a kind of innovation? In the psychology of invention an undeniable factor is chance—an inventor stumbling on his solution through comparatively random methods. Or in borrowing cultural elements the imitation is imperfect; mistakes occur and the altered copy becomes adopted. Creative needs are often responsible for innovation; dissatisfaction with unvarying ideas and activities may stimulate the individual to invent a new technique. Similarly, imagination and fantasy and the need for ego-expansion add to the urge to vary what is traditional. In all invention a complex of motives, conscious and unconscious, lies behind each innovation and its adoption. As Barnett points out, there is a convergence of wants involving a complex of motives, egoistic and altruistic, conscious and unconscious, adjusted and maladjusted.[48]

It is always the deviant individual in our culture, or in any culture, who is most likely to be the agent of social change. He may or may not be maladjusted, discontented with society, or driven by manic energy, neurotic anxiety, or obsessive-compulsive tendencies to change the world about him. But one thing stands out: he is certainly nonconformist and unorthodox, hence suspect and perhaps even hated by the great conforming majority. This is notably true for social as compared with technological changes; by the early twentieth century the value of technological progress—that is, change—was widely accepted if not idealized. We are much less sure about the value of social changes; in fact our attitudes toward social change are divided, as pointed out earlier, and are signalized by the conservative-liberal line-up which underlies much political and social activity.

[47] For further discussion of internal and external factors, see Sherif and Sherif, *op. cit.*, pp. 570-74.
[48] Barnett, *op. cit.*, p. 127.

FACTORS AIDING AND HINDERING SOCIAL CHANGE

Now let us examine social change further, especially at the level of the human individual who does the changing, or who fails to change. For ultimately, social change means modification of the behavior of a large number of differing individuals. We shall draw upon our earlier discussions of learning and of frustration.

Learning is, as we have seen, a vital part of living. The child, the adolescent, the young adult, or even the mature adult is constantly learning. That is, in terms of his needs and other dynamic tendencies he tries out responses to the new situations which confront him. If a given response is rewarded, it is reinforced and tends to persist. Much of the child's life consists of learning adaptive responses to the members of his family, his teachers, his classmates and friends. As noted earlier, these responses are not primarily simple verbal and motor habits, but rather roles—complex patterns or types of response. He also develops attitudes and values associated with these roles. When he becomes adolescent he learns the approved patterns of interaction with the opposite sex. Later still, he learns suitable vocational roles and his function as a citizen. By the time he reaches adulthood, his learning ordinarily fits him to be a more or less well-adjusted and productive member of society. His habits, interests, attitudes, and major roles are pretty well "set." But his learning has not ceased. He continues to learn on his job, in his courtship and marriage, in his role as parent, voter, neighbor, and member of his community. His learning never ceases, for he is constantly maturing, and his material and social environment is constantly changing.

Many innovations he takes in his stride—television and traveling by plane, for example. He adjusts to being a commuter, leaving at 8:06 and returning to Suburbia on the 5:22. He learns to be a handy man around the house and begins to take an interest in community affairs. After the children arrive, he gradually learns and accepts the role of, say, a firm but kindly father—though not without some strain on his nervous system!

In other words much of an individual's adjustment to change proceeds with only minor frustration if he is reasonably flexible and if the changes are not too great. If he has an insecure or rigid personality pattern, he may have great difficulty—in marriage, on the job, in his community. Or if the stress placed on him is too great; if his wife dies or becomes mentally ill, if he is fired from his job, or if he is drafted into the army, for example, he may be badly frustrated. How he reacts to frustration depends, as we have seen, upon many factors, notably his habits and the way he perceives the frustrating situation. He may compensate or sublimate in ways which are socially approved. He may develop aggressive types of response which are likely to interfere with his social adjustment. Or he may repress his anxiety and hostility to the extent that it becomes converted into neurotic symptoms.

Technological changes often produce major crises in a person's life—especially a middle-aged or older person. A man of fifty-seven who has been a streetcar motorman for 35 years is confronted by the introduction of buses and is too old to become a bus-driver. A bootmaker finally loses out in the competition with mass-produced shoes. An old-time bookkeeper cannot adjust to the introduction of business machines into the office he has run for a generation. These are cases of frustration that are real, even if not as dramatic as those cited in the writings of a Sherwood Anderson or an Arthur Miller.

The history of invention provides interesting examples of resistance to technological change, that is, aggressive reaction to frustration.[49] English spinners invaded Hargreaves' home and destroyed his spinning jennies in 1768. A few years later, workers sought to demolish Arkwright's machines for carding and spinning, which were forcing manufacturing out of the home into the factory. In the "Luddite riots" of 1811–12, knitters destroyed many newly invented weaving machines. About the same time French workers smashed Jacquard's looms for weaving brocaded silks.

While actual destruction of labor-saving machines became less frequent in the later nineteenth and the early twentieth century, opposition to technological innovations has often occurred on the part of manufacturers, workers, or both. Between 1911 and 1921, plumbers' unions and builders' associations jointly opposed the machine cutting and threading of iron pipe.[50] More recently still, attempts to introduce "prefabricated housing" have been fought by real-estate interests, banks, lumber companies, and labor unions. Outstanding among technological innovators are the Rust brothers, who have devoted a large part of the profits from their mechanical cotton-picker to the rehabilitation of displaced agricultural workers.

Technological innovations continue to cause distress in some quarters, though their main contribution is generally summed up under the head of "progress." They are said to have made possible the major changes occurring between 1900 and 1950: wider distribu-

---

[49] These examples are taken from B. J. Stern, Resistances to the adoption of technological innovations, in *Technological trends and national policy* (Washington, D. C.: National Resources Committee, 1937).

[50] Stern, *op. cit.*, p. 59.

tion of income; gradual disappearance of upper and lower classes, notably of domestic servants; movement to the suburbs; national migration to Florida and to the West and Southwest.[51]

Most of the changes mentioned above have come about more or less accidentally, because of technological changes. One might well ask: is it possible to bring about social change through rational planning? On the whole it seems very difficult to introduce changes of wide scope in areas sanctioned by usage and tradition. Consider, for example, the case for Monday holidays, which has been pleaded in the *Reader's Digest,* by columnist Sylvia Porter, by Frank Sullivan and many other writers. At present most holidays may fall on any day of the week, such as Tuesday, Wednesday, or Thursday, which causes considerable confusion and frustration (or on Saturday or Sunday, which means they may be overlooked). This could be changed by having several three-day week ends. We could have Memorial Day the last Monday in May, Independence Day the first Monday in July, and Thanksgiving Day the fourth Monday in November. In February, as things are now, Washington's birthday is observed in all states, Lincoln's in many, Jefferson's in four, Franklin D. Roosevelt's in two and Andrew Jackson's in his native Tennessee. This could be eliminated by designating the third Monday in February "President's Day."

Everyone seems to favor such a reform—transportation, hotel, and resort interests; labor, industry, and consumer alike. Monday holiday bills have been introduced many times into state legislatures, but very little happens. Why? "Laziness and habit" says Sylvia Porter, "these are the obstacles." [52] Frank Sullivan notes that the planners had better "gird their loins for the battle the traditionalists will give them. They will be hearing from those citizens who are sentimental about holidays and get their backs up at any proposal to tinker with them. You know, the man who says, 'The Fourth of July was good enough for my grandfather and it's good enough for *me.*'" The British, he adds, have four bank holidays, all but one of which are fixed on Mondays. "The British are more realistic about their holidays than we are. They go on the theory that the holiday was made for man, not man for the holiday. So they celebrate the birthday of Queen Elizabeth II on June 9, although she was born on April 21. This is not an accurate or logical thing to do but it is convenient." [53]

51 F. L. Allen, *The big change,* (New York: Harper & Bros., 1952).

52 Sylvia Porter in the *New York Post,* Dec. 1, 1952.

53 Frank Sullivan, The unlost week-end—three days, *New York Times Magazine,* May 28, 1955.

A similar situation—rational planning versus traditionalism—exists with reference to Interlingua, the new international language of science, and to the various plans for calendar reform, one of which is backed by both the United Nations and the Roman Catholic Church.

SOME CONCLUDING THOUGHTS

Many social scientists and all social reformers bemoan the slowness of change in our society. Sometimes they overlook important aspects of the total process. For example:

1. What appears to be an advantageous change to the innovator may not be so regarded by the society as a whole. The total frame of reference has to be considered; particularly, how the participants in the change are going to perceive the situation. Sometimes scientists, like laymen, suffer from a kind of ethnocentrism and forget to view the situation from the other fellow's standpoint.

2. Similarly, the change must be viewed not only with respect to the individual but as an element consistent with the total culture pattern. How does the change fit in with the sum total of the practices of a given people? As a recent UNESCO report indicated, it would be inappropriate to require all nurses in less advanced cultures to have an elementary school diploma, as that would be contrary to the tradition and would not solve the basic problem of securing a basic minimum of health conditions.[54] The value structure of a community or society must be examined before direct action is taken; change has to be considered a relative matter. Regarding integration in the South, it is necessary to allow a reasonable amount of time for adjustment, but this cannot be an invitation to indefinite delay. Evaluation of the total culture must be made in order to determine not only what changes are feasible but also how fast and by what means the changes may be furthered.

3. Undoubtedly cultural change is facilitated when a *minimum* of frustration is involved. However, it must be realized that some degree of frustration is always involved in change, along with the satisfactions, at least in certain quarters.

4. Success in introducing changes depends in part on a well-functioning system of rewards and punishments. As the UNESCO investigators put it: "The process of acceptance of change is more rapid, if simultaneously the old behaviors and attitudes provide less satisfaction, or no satisfaction, or meet with disapproval or other punishment."[55] The question of punishment must, of course, be

---

[54] M. Mead (ed.), *Cultural patterns and technical change* (Paris: UNESCO Tensions and Technology Series, 1953), p. 310. Reprinted in a paperback by Mentor Books, 1954.

[55] *Ibid.*, p. 292.

treated with special caution, and must be approved by a sizable minority, or preferably by a majority of the group. Acceptance of change is more rapid if the traditional behavior patterns are no longer rewarded and if the new practice is surrounded by reassuring experiences including a positive feeling tone.

5. Agents for change must be multidimensional in approach. As much as possible of the institutional framework should be employed. For a program of racial and ethnic integration, for example, one would have to operate on all fronts—legislation, formal education, mass media, churches, and so forth. Through these secondary channels information and the changed values and attitudes would then filter through to the grass roots—the family and other primary groups of individuals.

SUMMARY

Social change, meaning alteration of customs, values, institutions, and social behavior, has been the concern largely of sociologists and anthropologists. The most prominent sociological interpretation has emphasized the cultural lag between our rapid technological advances and the slower social changes which follow.

Social psychologists have been particularly interested in one aspect of the problem, attitude toward social change, and have devised reasonably valid instruments to measure it. Among the important determinants of a person's attitude toward social change are influences from his family, school, and community, his own intelligence and knowledge, his age and stake in the status quo, and certain personality variables such as sensitivity or reverence for authority. Most individuals adjust to social changes without great strain unless tremendous modification of behavior is called for, or unless they have become exceedingly rigid. However, technological and economic changes often produce a degree of insecurity and frustration along with material improvement. Bringing about considerable social changes through rational planning seems very difficult because of the forces of habit and tradition. Certain agencies are beginning to focus on the problem, to discover principles, and to work out practical techniques for producing change.

SUPPLEMENTARY READINGS

Books of Readings

MACCOBY, E. E., NEWCOMB, T. M., AND HARTLEY, E. L. (eds.). *Readings in social psychology*, 3d ed. New York: Henry Holt & Co., Inc., 1958.
Menzel, H., and Katz, E., Social relations and innovation in the medical profession: the epidemiology of a new drug.

BRITT, S. H. (ed.). *Selected readings in social psychology.* New York: Rinehart & Co., Inc., 1950.

Lynd, R. S. and H. M., The machinery of government.

Ogburn, W. F., and Nimkoff, M. F., The growth of culture.

Other References

ALLEN, F. L. *The big change.* New York: Harper & Bros., 1952.
A very readable account of the transformation of American life between 1900 and 1950.

ALLEN, F. R., *et al. Technology and social change.* New York: Appleton-Century-Crofts, Inc., 1957.
An up-to-date treatment by a number of authors on our contemporary culture, including atomic energy and the new warfare.

BARNETT, H. G. *Innovation.* New York: McGraw-Hill Book Co., Inc., 1953.
Probably the most penetrating analysis of the subject, largely from an anthropological and psychological viewpoint.

——. *Anthropology in administration.* Evanston, Ill.: Row, Peterson & Co., 1956.
Some of the problems in acculturation.

CHAPIN, F. S. *Cultural change.* New York: Appleton-Century-Crofts, Inc., 1928.
A classic study presenting the sociological approach.

GERTH, H. AND MILLS, C. W. *Character and social structure.* New York: Harcourt, Brace & Co., Inc., 1953.
Chaps. xiii–xvi revolve about the problem of historical change, the role of leadership, and collective behavior.

GITTLER, J. B. *Social dynamics.* New York: McGraw-Hill Book Co., Inc., 1952.
Part VI contains some interesting excerpts on the subject.

LEWIN, KURT. *Resolving social conflicts.* New York: Harper & Bros., 1948.
A social psychological approach to the problem of effecting change in groups and culture.

MACIVER, R. M. *Social causation.* New York: Ginn & Co., 1942.
Largely philosophical, this work presents some interesting questions regarding the interpretation of the "why?"

MALINOWSKI, B. *The dynamics of culture change.* New Haven: Yale University Press, 1945.
An anthropologist looks at cultural change from a functionalist viewpoint which has been very influential in a number of research studies.

MEAD, M. *New lives for old.* New York: William Morrow & Co., Inc., 1956.
A restudy of the Manus, and the drastic change in their culture over a generation.

—— (ed.). *Cultural patterns and technical change.* Paris: UNESCO Tensions and Technology Series, 1953.
A series of field studies on the problem of acculturation.

NEWCOMB, T. M. *Personality and social change,* 2d ed. New York: The Dryden Press, Inc., 1957.
A study of the factors producing attitude change in a college sample.

OGBURN, W. F. *Social change,* 2d ed. New York: The Viking Press, Inc., 1950.
Ogburn's original thesis on cultural lag and related topics, which has had world-wide repercussions.

SIMS, N. L. *The problem of social change.* New York: The Thomas Crowell Co., 1939.
A good survey of the philosophies of social change.

SPICER, E. H. (ed.). *Human problems in technological change.* New York: The Russell Sage Foundation, 1952.
A compilation of selected acculturation studies.

WASHBURNE, N. F. *Interpreting social change in America.* Garden City, N. Y.: Doubleday & Co., Inc., 1954.
A brief overview of some important changes.

20

The Psychology of Social
Movements

Technological and economic changes may produce considerable insecurity and frustration at the price of progress, as mentioned in the last chapter. Now we ask: How do people react to such frustrations? Like organized groups among labor, management, or veterans, they seek to improve their condition through collective action. Some of these collective efforts take the form of pressure groups, such as associations of tenants, with a very specific goal. Frequently, however, when the frustrations are broad and varied, collective action takes the form of a "social movement."

THE SCOPE OF SOCIAL MOVEMENTS

We may think of a social movement as a social group of a particular kind—a group which is "moving," dynamic, going somewhere. It is different from a club or professional association, or from an institutionalized group like the family, church, or school. The driving forces of a social movement are found in the needs and frustrations of the individuals composing it. As Blumer puts it: "Social movements can be viewed as collective enterprises to establish a new order of life. They have their inception in a condition of unrest, and derive their motive power on one hand from dissatisfaction with the current form of life, and on the other hand, from wishes and hopes for a new scheme or system of living." [1]

[1] H. Blumer, in A. M. Lee (ed.), *New outline of the principles of sociology* (New York: Barnes & Noble, Inc., 1946), p. 199.

As the term is commonly used, we may say that social movements have several characteristics:

1. They are relatively new groupings, not yet institutionalized and often amorphous in character.
2. The aim of a social movement is to achieve some change in the status quo, usually by orderly, evolutionary steps rather than by revolution.
3. The goals are broad rather than narrow and typically involve both humanitarian and self-seeking trends.
4. Proselytizing zeal and crusading spirit are shown by the members.

In the later years of the nineteenth and the early years of the twentieth century, the temperance crusade constituted a social movement. Spearheaded by the Woman's Christian Temperance Union and the Anti-Saloon League, tens of thousands of members expected that prohibition would be the dawn of a better day. To many religious people in small towns and on farms of the Midwest and South, the "demon rum" was the source of sin, poverty, and corruption. The Prohibitionists had able leaders and propagandists who made liquor a vital issue in many a local and state election. But after the prohibition amendment was passed toward the close of World War I, the "drys" were on the defensive. Their membership dwindled during the 1920's when it became obvious that prohibition had hardly ushered in the millennium.

There are a number of lines of classification that a movement may take. Green points out the difference between *inclusive* and *segmental* movements.[2] The former refer to the large-scale movements that may activate an entire nation like National Socialism in Germany. They generally are in the wake of vast social change, as, for example, a revolution. The segmental movements have more limited goals and appeal to a more restricted followership. The distinction might be labeled as general and specific movements. Instances of specific movements are old-age pensions, limitation of alcohol; even an interest in vitamin enriched foods could conceivably become a social movement. Frequently these movements direct their appeal to special-interest groups or some distinct part of the populations, like a given age or sex group. The temperance and suffrage movements were mainly confined to one sex. Class, geographic, or religious interests may also dictate the development of a movement. Christian Science is predominantly the expression of middle-class urban women who have found traditional Protestantism too confining for intellectual, health, and other reasons. The

[2] A. W. Green, *Sociology* (rev. ed.; New York: McGraw-Hill Book Co., Inc., 1956), p. 534.

Grange was largely the outgrowth of dissatisfaction on the part of small-scale farmers caught in the Panic of 1873.

Turner and Killian classify movements into three ideal types: *value-oriented, power-oriented,* and *participation-oriented.*[3] In the first type, issues, goals, and reform are all-important, as with the abolition movement prior to the Civil War or the World Federalists. Often such movements begin with widespread protest but no coherent organization. For instance, in California about 1950 there was general feeling, largely inspired by the press, for strong action in regard to "sex crimes"; eventually, specific groups emerged which called for effective legislative action. Power-oriented movements are preoccupied with force and aggressive tactics, as they are concerned with social control—i.e., changing the power structure of society. Frequently this type has a centralized form of leadership, and sometimes the leader personifies the movement, as with the Hitler movement or the Kingdom of Father Divine. In participation-oriented movements the members gain their greatest satisfactions from the participation itself, as in the later phases of the Townsend movement, described below. Probably all movements manifest these three orientations; yet one or another may dominate, depending on the developmental phase of the movement as well as on its structure and function.

CHARACTERISTICS AND STAGES OF SOCIAL MOVEMENTS

Most social movements have the following ingredients:

1. *Discontent with the status quo* that has become both intense and articulate
2. *Effective leadership,* frequently centered in one man who has charismatic properties, and consequently the followership can feel maximum identification
3. *A plan of action,* which includes a concrete and specific program for attainment of goals
4. *A set of symbols,* ideology, slogans, music, ritual, or other paraphernalia for implementing the program.

We shall illustrate these mechanisms in some typical movements. Movements that exhibit only a few of these characteristics are generally known as "incipient" social movements. Frequently they remain in this incomplete stage for a number of months or years before they assume the shape of a vigorous full-blown effort. The attempt of the American Negro to find equality, or at least to end some of the more obvious discriminatory practices, remained in the

[3] R. H. Turner and L. M. Killian, *Collective behavior* (Englewood Cliffs, N. J.: Prentice-Hall, Inc., 1957), pp. 327 ff.

incipient stage for over a generation. Since World War II, through the effort of the National Association for the Advancement of Colored People and the Urban League, antisegregation has become a major social movement. In this movement are mobilized a whole complex of facilities: the mass media, the church, and government institutions, including the legislature and the judiciary.

Developmental phases. King speaks of two general aspects in the development of movements: the *internal phase,* which refers to growth and articulation within the movement itself and the relations of leaders and followers; and the *external phase,* the reaction of society as a whole to the movement, namely, the problem of accepting the reform.[4]

From an internal viewpoint the three stages of the movement are known as *incipient, organizational,* and *stable.* The first phase refers to the process of crystallizing discontent and the question of focusing issues: in the second phase leadership and membership recruitment become more important, and the third stage refers to the more defensive, conservative period, when membership ebbs away and the movement is stabilized or even dormant. In other words, its petition granted, the interest is one of consolidating its gains or holding on to what it has achieved. Social movements might thus be labeled as *aggressive* or *defensive,* depending on whether they reject or accept the status quo.

On the external side, that is, the reaction of the public to the reform movement, King refers to the three stages as *innovation, selection,* and *integration.*[5] Social movements are, after all, agencies of social change. There is the adoption of the new idea by a relative few, the lengthy process of finding a receptive audience who accept the reform, and the enactment of the change itself. National Socialism had its inception in the early twenties; the selection process was slow and irregular during the middle and late twenties until the cataclysm of a depression, together with an extensive organizational network employing ruthless methods, brought success. After its accession to power in 1933 and the adoption of specific reforms, approval was signified on the part of most Germans by perhaps 1936. Yet the international situation, and finally war, meant that it attained stability only in a restricted sense. In all phases the success of the movement—or of any movement for that matter—depends on the historical configuration of the particular time. Regarding

---

[4] C. W. King, *Social movements in the United States* (New York: Random House, Inc., 1956), pp. 39-57.

[5] *Ibid.,* see also H. G. Barnett, *Innovation* (New York: McGraw-Hill Book Co., Inc., 1953), Parts III and IV.

the innovation period, it is remarkable that the National Socialist leaders were all born between 1885 and 1910, meaning that they were commencing their political careers at a period of considerable unrest in Germany, namely, the years following 1918, when democratic processes were hardly effective in resolving major economic and social crises. Hence, they had not become accustomed to utilizing consensus and compromise as a means of settling disputes.[6]

Again, it is the time factor that may spell the success of a movement. The Nazi movement might never have gained wide support if there had not been a depression, nor might Hitler's aggrandizement have been successful if France and Britain had been capable of joint action in the mid-thirties and forestalled his international aggression.

In-group solidarity and tactics. The question may be raised as to what degree a social movement is a group. Certainly, movements that involve thousands or millions of participants can hardly be of the nature of a primary group, but the degree of group cohesiveness and emotional tone is more marked than within a political party.[7] The emphasis is always on the role of the little man in this decisive movement. Much of the success of the leader is a function of the degree to which he can impart a genuine feeling of intimacy. Hitler stressed this approach in his speeches: "Du bist nichts, dein Volk ist alles" ("You are nothing, your people is everything"). At the same time he was seen petting animals, caressing the faces of children, and accepting bouquets from elderly women.

One factor that is important is the emphasis on the small group—the cell, the *Ortsgruppe,* the grassroots. In the local unit are practiced, often with more drama and feeling, the same rituals and ceremonies that make for solidarity in the larger group.

In strategy a movement must demonstrate a proselyting zeal; willingness to adjust tactics to social changes; ability to profit from, and at the same time, to exploit the mistakes of others; to emphasize felt needs, or to create them where they do not exist.[8] If any term may be relevant to effective tactics, it is realism. In fact, a number of movements have been a failure in the United States because they chose methods that were inappropriate to American mores: for example, curtailment of free speech, and control of communication

6 R. Heberle, *Social movements* (New York: Appleton-Century-Crofts, Inc., 1951), p. 251.

7 For some of the differences between movements and parties see R. Heberle, *op. cit.;* also his Observations on the sociology of social movements, *Amer. sociol. Rev.,* XIV (1949), 346-57.

8 King, *op. cit.,* especially pp. 79-84.

together with approval of violence. This weakness has been true of certain communist and fascist groups. On the other hand, one recalls the success of Reverend Martin Luther King's passive resistance movement that culminated in early 1957 with the ending of Jim Crowism on the transportation system of Montgomery, Alabama. The fact that he prevented his followers from meeting violence by violence impressed certain leading white citizens, particularly the clergy, that his cause could not be ignored.

EXAMPLES OF SOCIAL MOVEMENTS

Moral Rearmament. In 1910 a Lutheran minister, Dr. Frank N. Buchman, initiated what was called "The Oxford Group"; later it was known as "Buchmanism" and by the time of World War II, "Moral Rearmament." [9] Its basic idea was that men are sinners but can be changed and given access to God by confession. During the 1920's Buchman gained many followers in British and American universities, and by the 1930's he had a number of distinguished converts among clergymen, businessmen, and political leaders in several countries. Cantril estimated in 1941 that some 50,000 people throughout the world would acknowledge Buchman as the man who had shown them a new way of life. Leaders of the Oxford Group promised an end to personal, industrial, and international troubles if only enough individuals would give in to God, listen to His directions, confess their sins, and get straight with others.

In 1936 Buchman stated, "I thank God for a man like Adolf Hitler," apparently because he thought a dictator, if he listened to God, could bring about the millennium. However, the publicizing of this statement did not prevent the group from continuing its increase in membership, particularly among the well-to-do. A booklet, "Moral Re-Armament: The Battle for Peace," issued in England in 1938, contained endorsements from several dozen members of Parliament, peers, and baronets; also prominent athletes, journalists, industrialists, labor leaders, and academicians.

The Oxford Group has many interesting psychological angles. Basically its appeal stems from the individual's feelings of guilt and anxiety. Confession in the characteristic small group of followers brings relief and a feeling of unity with the group and with the larger movement, whose stated purposes are noble and uplifting. Cantril notes that Buchmanism flourished in the depression years of the 1930's and took a spurt in the fall of 1938 when war was impending. He concluded as follows: [10]

---

[9] See H. Cantril, *Psychology of social movements* (New York: John Wiley & Sons, Inc., 1941), chap. vi.

[10] *Op. cit.,* p. 168.

Buchmanism has gathered momentum, therefore, essentially because it shows certain bewildered people a way to interpret their personal troubles and the larger social problems of their world without endangering their status. It provides a psychological mechanism whereby they can escape the responsibility of dealing directly with conditions which they realize are not right and just. It attracts to itself people who want to improve these conditions without injuring their own positions and who want to avoid any alignment with existing institutions or ideologies which assume that individual problems cannot be solved without collective action.

Green describes three distinct stages in the Buchman movement. During the Depression phase the emphasis was on nearness to the deity, self-purity, and vitalization as a means of escaping material frustration. The second era was the prewar era, from approximately 1936 to 1941, when Moral Rearmament was directed to avoiding war, ostensibly at any cost. The third era was the postwar phase, during which interest has shifted toward the combatting of communism.[11] In this phase, Moral Rearmament continues as "big business" and as a socioreligious movement. It still appeals more to the middle and upper classes than the lower, although it attempts to bring all of society together. It remains a large-scale, but loosely consolidated, organization in western Europe and the United States. It boasts, for example, of converting a German communist labor leader to Christian renunciation and world peace, as one of its individual successes in promoting international understanding. In the United States there were some two hundred local groups, known as Christian Business Man's Committees, which performed a variety of services from solving labor disputes and providing training sessions for airline workers, to religious revival and confession meetings for the general public.[12] In the late fifties the Buchmanites appeared to be centering some of their attention on the "new" areas of the world, notably, Africa.

In all three phases the focus has centered on conversion and devotion to the four goals and duties: "absolute honesty, purity, unselfishness, love." The day is opened with a "quiet time," akin to the devotional time of the Quakers, although the diffuseness of the movement probably allows no definite control on religious practices. As a movement, it apparently appeals to a number of individuals who have lost their moorings or who need a strong emotional identification and yet do not find a spiritual home among the lower-class revivalist faiths. One of its most effective means of group sharing is with its confessionals which recall the methods of Alco-

[11] Green, op. cit., pp. 540-45.
[12] J. Ellison, The men who decided to do something, Saturday Evening Post, March 1, 1952.

holics Anonymous. Part of the program emphasizes ideological shifts, like a Frenchman who once suffered at the hands of the Germans being used to recruit members in Germany while preaching the basic unity of all peoples.

Much of the success of the movement is to be attributed to Buchman, who has retained his leadership despite advanced years. While his leadership can be labelled as only partially charismatic, there has not been sufficient bureaucratization to guarantee the movement's survival after his death. It is possible that the federation of local societies will provide a degree of institutionalization that may make the group relatively permanent.

A modern revivalist. The religious revivalism of the Reverend Billy Graham, starting about 1950, has some of the earmarks of a social movement. His biographer estimates that, as of 1956, Billy Graham had preached, face-to-face, to more people than anyone in all history—20 million. Another 20 million listened to his weekly "Hour of Decision" TV program. A million had been converted.[13] This "Barrymore of the Bible" made a triumphal tour of northern Europe, in the course of which he preached to no less than 120,000 at Wembley Stadium in England. In 1957 he and his team of co-workers, in the tradition of Billy Sunday, made a gigantic effort to convert "godless" New York City. On the whole, however, Billy Graham is a streamlined, modern-age revivalist rather than the founder of a new social movement.

The Townsend Plan. The background of the Townsend Plan, which flourished during the 1930's, was simply the increasing insecurity of our ever-growing number of older people. Retired on small pensions, or living on a dole or pittance from relatives, millions of aged people felt useless and unwanted, particularly during the years of the Depression. Dr. Francis E. Townsend, a retired rural physician living in California on his small savings, in 1934 proposed a scheme which spread like wildfire. According to the "Townsend Plan," all American citizens of sixty or over would receive a monthly pension of $200 which had to be spent within thirty days. (Such pensions would be paid for by a 2 per cent tax on business transactions.) This measure, it was claimed, would restore prosperity through the new purchasing power of our twenty to twenty-five million old people and their dependents. The fact that the plan was economically unsound and impractical in many ways did not stem from the enthusiasm aroused in older people. Before the end of 1935 there were some two million members en-

---

[13] Stanley High, *Billy Graham* (New York: McGraw-Hill Book Co., Inc., 1956).

rolled in several thousand clubs throughout the country, each paying twenty-five cents a year. Later a more select group was formed—
the Townsend National Legion, with dues of a dollar a month.
Spreading of the "word" was aided by various interested parties
such as chain-store operators. In 1935 and 1936, national conventions for the Townsend movement were attended by thousands of
members. In the election of 1936 they joined with followers of
Huey Long, Gerald L. K. Smith, and Father Coughlin in backing
Congressman Lemke's "Union Party," which disappointed its supporters by winning no electoral votes. As war in Europe approached, the movement declined, though it continued to maintain
some membership and influence, particularly in California, during
and even after the war.

The homey honesty of the leader, Dr. Townsend, was undoubtedly a factor in the growth of the movement. He was obviously one
of the struggling old folks, just like his followers. Townsend papers,
leaflets, buttons, slogans, and songs helped to dramatize the Plan
and to win converts.[14] One of the songs was sung to the music of
"Onward Christian Soldiers":

> Onward Townsend soldiers
> Marching as to war
> With the Townsend banner
> Going on before;
> Our devoted leaders
> Bid depression go,
> Join them in the battle
> Help them fight the foe.

In discussing why the Townsend movement flourished, Cantril
suggests four important reasons: [15]

1. It provided *satisfaction of needs* for food, clothing, shelter, for
medical and dental care, education, home improvements, and automobiles, radio, and travel. Poll results showed, significantly, that
people in lower economic brackets, irrespective of age, supported the
plan most vigorously. That is, it was seen as a remedy for general
economic insecurity.

2. The Plan was *simple to understand*. It avoided complicated
matters of banking, credit, taxation problems, administration, foreign trade, and the like. Its promises and its prospects were concrete and comprehensible.

3. The Plan *fitted old norms*. Its sponsors insisted that it was
democratic, American, Christian, and consistent with capitalism and

14 See Cantril, *op. cit.*, pp. 185 ff.
15 *Ibid.*, pp. 201 ff.

the profit motive. It was indigenous to America and disclaimed foreign or revolutionary ties. Americanism and Christianity were stressed in Townsend meetings and in their literature.

4. The Plan *enhanced self-regard.* Dr. Townsend gave old people a place and a status in the scheme of things; previously they had been disregarded in favor of youth and the middle-aged. This enhancement of self or ego may well have been the most important ingredient in the tremendous enthusiasm for the Townsend Plan and is a dynamic force to be reckoned with, politically and socially, in the years ahead.

In the two decades or more since Townsend presented his original appeal, the problem of the aged in our society has not been solved, even though pensions have been adopted by some of the more advanced states so as to provide the elderly with the bare essentials.[16] In a society that allows its older members so little status and encourages a minimum of activity, achievement, or feeling of creativity, the psychological adjustment is far from easy. Furthermore the postwar years have seen marked prosperity and inflation which has struck disastrously at many old people who had accumulated resources in years when the dollar had a much greater purchasing power.

As a social organization, the Townsend movement has shifted (beginning with the war period) to a purchase plan and advertising medium. Instead of recruiting new members, the group concentrated on sales and advertising. "Townsend Old Fashioned Horehound Drops," "Townsend Club Toilet Soap," and "Vitamins and Minerals by Francis E. Townsend, M.D." became the center of interest. *Townsend Club Manuals* referred to "sings," "pot-luck nights," and weekly dances, indicating that the movement had come to emphasize the social adjustment of the aged.[17] This is not unlike the transformation of another depression-born movement, Technocracy, whose newsletters, when last seen by the authors, referred predominantly to picnics and barbecues. It appears that the waning days of a social movement become mainly organizational, often with a nostalgic reflection on the past.

The Kingdom of Father Divine. A social movement of great significance among Negroes, though hardly of national or interna-

---

[16] A successor to the Townsend Plan, in California, George H. McLain's "Institute of Social Welfare," has backed various plans, in the 1950's, for increasing pensions for the aged. See also Joseph T. Drake, *The aged in American society* (New York: The Ronald Press Co., 1958) for a comprehensive discussion of society and its aged population.

[17] S. L. Messinger, Organizational transformation: a case study of a declining social movement, *Amer. sociol. Rev.*, XX (1955), 3-10.

Wide World Photos, Inc.

Moral Rearmament has been expressed as a social movement in various forms for almost half a century. It attained a certain mass appeal, even though it has attracted its supporters mainly from the middle and upper classes. In the postwar era, its interest has shifted toward the combatting of communism.

As it blossomed in the depression of the thirties, the Townsend movement and its leader, Dr. Francis E. Townsend (shown here), had a unique appeal, mainly, though not exclusively, among the lower classes. The economic problems of the aged in American society, which the Townsend Plan was designed to alleviate, remain as yet unsolved.

tional scope, was launched in Harlem about 1930 by the Reverend
M. J. Divine, known to his thousands of followers as "Father Divine." In many respects the kingdom is a cult and has earmarks
of old-time evangelism.[18] But it also has other goals, notably to
fight discrimination and achieve equal social and economic status
for Negroes.

The Saturday and Sunday meetings at Father Divine's "Peace
Missions" in New York and other centers are jolly affairs, with
music, singing, and abundance of good food. Testimonials and con-
fessions are frequent, pointing to the divine powers of the Father.
"Father Divine is God" is the message widely proclaimed on posters
and by word of mouth. A group of "Angels," sometimes including
white persons, wait upon the Father, having abjured their worldly
contacts and turned over their possessions to him. These angels
take names like "Crystal Star," "Heavenly Love," "Celestial Virgin,"
or "Wonderful Devotion." In return for their loyalty, the Father
provides for them and gives them spiritual nourishment. The
Father is a short, bald, pleasant-looking man, apparently in his sev-
enties. He mingles freely with his followers, blesses their food and
gives frequent inspirational talks. These messages sometimes defy
analysis and often contain newly created words, but they are always
greeted with enthusiasm by the "children." For example, the following paragraph appeared in one of Father's messages:

It is a privilege to realize GOD as INFINITE, EVERPRESENT and OM-
NIPOTENT, and yet INCARNATABLE and REPRODUCIBLE and RE-PER-
SONIFIABLE, as HE has been PERSONIFIED. GOD would not be the same
today, yesterday, and forever, if HE were not RE-PERSONIFIABLE. Now isn't
that wonderful? [19]

Some of the followers become alienated and leave, but others
take their places. The Father is continually buying property and
establishing new kingdoms. A few years ago he married an attractive young white woman, who is accepted as the new "Mother
Divine."

Many people outside the kingdom are impressed with the honesty and sincerity of the Father's followers. The "New Day," weekly
publication of the group, contains many endorsements and good
wishes from businessmen whose employees are followers.

Part of Father Divine's appeal, as with any Negro evangelist,
rests upon the tradition of old-time religion with its promise of
happy life in the hereafter. This is reinforced by the unemploy-

[18] See H. Cantril and M. Sherif, The kingdom of Father Divine, *J. abnorm. soc.
Psychol.*, XXXIII (1938), 147-67; also chap. v in Cantril, *op. cit.*
[19] *Ibid.*, p. 129.

ment and economic hardship found among Negro city populations. But the kingdom does more: it yields meaning, and hope for a better life in the world of today, along with sociability, recreation, and victuals. In addition, the followers can feel, as self-respecting Negroes, that they are improving their status by waging constant war upon discrimination and segregation. When one considers the Negro's cultural background and his contemporary frustrations, the success of Father Divine is not difficult to understand.

Father Divine represents par excellence charismatic leadership. Perhaps most certain proof of his divinity was in the early phase of the movement when he had been found guilty of disturbing the peace; the judge who had found him guilty conveniently died a few days later. His humble origin, his remoteness, and his elaborate regalia (including a $12,900 mink coat that two Chicago school teachers presented him for having healed a close relative) all equate him with the deity. Undoubtedly part of the appeal of the movement is the mythology and fantasy. The membership particularly attracts lower-class Negroes, but is not limited to them.[20]

Although the Father, being God, technically cannot die, it seems doubtful that the movement can survive his death. Indeed there are recurrent rumors of his death, which are promptly and vigorously denied by his staff. No individual is being readied to assume the leadership, which again indicates that it is a case of charismatic, as opposed to bureaucratic, command.

United World Federalists. A final example of a social movement is the postwar group, United World Federalists. It was formed early in 1947 by a merger of five organizations all interested in achieving world government. The first president chosen was Cord Meyer, Jr., a young war veteran and author of a hard-hitting book called *Peace or Anarchy*. In less than a year United World Federalists had 15,000 members in over 300 chapters; in two years (January, 1949) it had 40,000 members in some 650 chapters. It affiliated with the World Movement for World Federal Government in Geneva, with active organizations in England, France, Germany, and other countries.

UWF is a social movement whose leaders see world government as the only alternative to international anarchy and disaster. They see nothing but failure for the United Nations if it perpetuates national sovereignties and rivalries. The dynamic Cord Meyer and his associates have carried on a whirlwind campaign in the race against

[20] S. Harris, *Father Divine, holy husband* (Garden City, N. Y.: Doubleday & Co., Inc., 1953).

time, using every medium of publicity and persuasion. Before the election of 1948, for example, they polled all Congressional candidates on the following questions: [21]

1. Do you believe the United Nations should be transformed into a federal world government with powers adequate to keep world peace and with direct jurisdiction over individual persons in matters delegated to it?
2. If you become a member of the 81st Congress, will you support legislation to bring this about?

Of 275 candidates responding, 60 per cent were favorable, and nearly half of these won seats in the new Congress, forming a "potential world government bloc" of 66 Democrats and 21 Republicans.[22]

UWF also managed to have a referendum question on world government included on the election ballot in the state of Connecticut. Though the original statement had to be cut down to "strengthening the United Nations," and though only about 20 per cent of the voters participated, their reaction was 12 to 1 in favor of world government.

The Berlin blockade and especially the Korean War of 1950-53 marked the end of the United World Federalists as a vigorous social movement. It appeared to most members and neutral observers that if member nations were restive and only partially cooperative within the United Nations Organization, the problem would still be more difficult in a world state. Also a number of the World Federalists broke up into rival camps.[23] The division of the world into two major power groups seemed too great a barrier for any strong world federation. While the number of World Federalists has markedly declined, the organization has not altogether disappeared. The official position has shifted to one of securing more interest in the United Nations, improving its operation, including abolition of the veto power, and inviting more nations into the organization as members. However, most Federalists regard the United Nations as a transitional form until a closer federation can be effected.

CONCLUDING INTERPRETATION

What causes social movements, such as those described above, to flourish? First, considerable discontent and frustration exists.

21 Where they stand, *World Government News,* October, 1948.
22 *World Government News,* December, 1948, p. 4.
23 H. L. Pendleton, Another look at World Federation, *American Mercury,* June, 1952, pp. 56-74.

Basically this results from social changes such as war, depression, or the cultural lags resulting from technological change. However, some movements such as woman suffrage or prohibition may stem from long-standing injustices and evils which have become intolerable in an age of increasing democracy and scientific progress.

Second, the general social atmosphere must be propitious. Though old people were insecure and frustrated in 1930 and 1931, the Townsend Plan could hardly have developed at that time. We still thought of the Depression as a temporary recession and still had faith in Republican leadership to get us out of it. But depression got worse; the banks closed. Roosevelt inaugurated the New Deal, with increased regulation of banking and industry, with home and work relief—in a word, with an emphasis upon the importance of the "forgotten man." By 1935 the social psychological atmosphere was changed, and forgotten men were ready to rise up and do something for themselves.

Or again, Buchman's appeal was largely a function of the post-war twenties, with their jazziness and disillusionment. Youth had discovered Freud but was uncomfortable over the loss of faith. The Oxford Movement combined psychoanalysis and religion and promised to solve not only the personal but also the industrial and international problems of the day. Hence its great appeal in America and Europe.

In any social movement, leadership plays a great part. Frustrations may abound and the atmosphere be favorable, but without leadership a social movement fails to crystallize. The central role of Father Divine, Dr. Buchman, and Dr. Townsend in their respective groups is obvious. With prohibition, woman suffrage, and world government, however, no single leader stands out as prominently. In any event, leadership is essential, either as a great figure about whom members can rally and with whom they can identify, or as the administering and propagandizing source which gives the movement its direction.

SUMMARY

Social movements are new and dynamic groupings of people who seek a change in the status quo. Their goals are both humanitarian and self-seeking, are usually broad in scope, and are proclaimed fervently by the crusading members. Recent examples of American social movements are the temperance movement, the Oxford Group, the Townsend Plan, the Kingdom of Father Divine, and United World Federalists. Though widely different in their aims, membership, and methods, all of these groups can be traced to discontent and frustration arising from some kind of cultural lag. Furthermore all of them manifest dynamic leadership and owe their popular support to the fact that their programs harmonize with the dominant values and attitudes which make up the prevailing social psychological atmosphere.

SUPPLEMENTARY READINGS

BLUMER, H. Collective behavior in Lee, A. M. (ed.), *New outline of the principles of sociology*. New York: Barnes & Noble, Inc., 1946.
Some important classifications and generalizations about social movements.

CANTRIL, H. *Psychology of social movements*. New York: John Wiley & Sons, Inc., 1941.
Although now somewhat outdated, this study of four social movements (The Kingdom of Father Divine, the Townsend movement, Buchmanism, the Nazi Party) remains unsurpassed.

CARR, L. J. *Analytical sociology*. New York: Harper & Bros., 1955.
The author examines many facets of the contemporary order, the prospects and means for social change, and potential social movements.

DAWSON, C. A., AND GETTYS, W. E. *An introduction to sociology*, 3d ed. New York: The Ronald Press Co., 1948.
Chap. xxv presents an examination of the sociological aspects of movements.

GILBERT, G. M. *The psychology of dictatorship*. New York: The Ronald Press Co., 1950.
The motives and personalities of the Nazi leaders as seen by the psychologist of the Nuremberg trials.

GREER, T. H. *American social reform movements*. Englewood Cliffs, N. J.: Prentice-Hall, Inc., 1949.
A historical and sociological examination of some leading movements of the latter part of the nineteenth century and early twentieth century.

GREEN, A. W. *Sociology*, 2d ed. New York: McGraw-Hill Book Co., Inc., 1956.
Chaps. xxv and xxvi present psychological aspects of social change and an analysis of the Buchman and Townsend movements.

HEBERLE, R. *Social movements*. New York: Appleton-Century-Crofts, Inc., 1951.
A penetrating study of politico-economic movements, both in the United States and abroad, from a number of viewpoints, including the ecological.

KING, W. *Social movements in the United States*. New York: Random House, Inc., 1956.
A brief but illuminating analysis of movements, their organization, leadership, and progress.

NORDSKOG, J. E. *Contemporary social reform movements*. New York: Charles Scribners' Sons, 1954.
Selected readings on politico-economic movements of the past and present.

TURNER, R. H., AND KILLIAN, L. M. *Collective behavior*. Englewood Cliffs, N. J.: Prentice-Hall, Inc., 1957.
Part IV is an excellent account of social movements with selected readings.

Part V

IMPROVING HUMAN RELATIONS

In Part IV we presented an analysis of some of the critical social phenomena in a complex society. Both sociologists and social psychologists attempt to work with these problems; however, the social psychologist is especially interested in analyzing social phenomena in terms of the underlying mechanisms. Particularly, the psychologist is concerned with the role of the individual in these tension areas.

In Part V we return to the significance of the group for industry and other aspects of practical living. We are interested in what the social psychologist can contribute to solving industrial conflicts. Next we turn to ethnic or racial prejudice, which is certainly one of the most important problems facing the United States today. Likewise, the psychologist has become interested in international tensions and offers some explanations of nationalism and some proposals to reduce conflicts among nations. Applying scientific findings from psychology and sociology to problem areas such as these is sometimes termed "improving human relations."

21

Group Dynamics and Its Applications

Throughout this volume we have dealt, directly or indirectly, with many applications of social psychology. The findings on effects of cultural and social influences on personality have significance for parents, teachers, legislators, and administrators of schools and institutions. Data on the effects of frustration on social behavior, likewise, have tremendous implications for intergroup relations on a local, national, or even international scale. Our increasing knowledge of propaganda can be applied either to perfecting techniques for influencing others or to protecting ourselves from such influences. Understanding social change can lead to more intelligent educational procedures and to better social planning by public officials. Public opinion polls can be used not only to predict election results (more or less accurately!) but to discover areas of intergroup tension and thereby prepare to cope with the problems involved. As we shall mention below, only social psychological research can indicate the relative effectiveness of various methods for reducing intergroup prejudices and hostilities. We turn now to consider more direct applications of social psychology in crucial areas of human relations.

At the outset we note certain grave difficulties in the path of the social psychologist who would make practical application of his techniques and findings. His field is a relatively new one, which overlaps both psychology and the social sciences. It is tremendously complex; it involves all the variables which beset the psychologist

541

and psychiatrist plus those which plague the sociologist and anthropologist! Because of the newness of his specialty and the lack of quantified data in many areas, the social psychologist often hesitates to offer his services. In addition, he may suffer from the cautiousness and timidity that often characterize the academic man and scientist.

Furthermore, the social psychologist is concerned with broad areas of human relationship that are ridden with tradition and in which many vested interests operate strongly to oppose new ideas. Then, too, he may find that the very persons who stand to benefit most from a proposed social change are the same ones who oppose it most vigorously. So the social psychologist has the added task of studying ways and means of convincing people that his proposals are desirable and feasible. Truly, the applied social psychologist faces a world that is far from friendly to his best efforts!

The study of social issues, which is basic to an applied social psychology, was greatly facilitated by the founding in 1936 of the Society for Psychological Study of Social Issues, more commonly known as "SPSSI." This group consists largely of social psychologists, with a fair-sized minority of educators, sociologists, and other social scientists. Its viewpoint is well described in a booklet issued in 1939:

It has long been recognized that every social question, such as war, depression, crime, race prejudice, the conflict between "capital" and "labor," etc., has its roots in the mental processes of human beings. The leaders of social reform, as well as the opponents of social progress, have been "practical" psychologists. Fundamentally, a nation accepts certain ends and means and rejects others because of the influence of factors which are commonly agreed to be psychological in nature.

Unfortunately, professional psychologists as a group have neglected the field of inquiry presented by this situation. They have been concerned with simpler though equally legitimate problems—preferably such as were not matters of serious social controversy. . . .[1]

World events such as the rise of dictatorship in Europe and the Depression in America, continues the booklet, underscore the need for scientific attack upon social problems and social issues. Basic objectives of SPSSI, as stated more recently, are:

. . . to achieve greater effectiveness and freedom for psychology in its efforts to make society intelligible, to advance scientific knowledge regarding social change and other social processes, and to encourage the application of the findings of psychology to the problems of society.[2]

[1] SPSSI, the Society for Psychological Study of Social Issues (New York: The Society, 1939), p. 1.

[2] SPSSI, The Society for Psychological Study of Social Issues (New York: The Society, 1954).

In 1951 a group of sociologists and kindred spirits formed the Society for the Study of Social Problems (SSSP). It is described as:

. . . an association of pure and applied social scientists, including sociologists, psychologists, anthropologists, social workers and other specialists, who are concerned with the following objectives: (1) advancement of the study of social problems; (2) application of social science research to the formulation of social policies; (3) improvement of the opportunities and working conditions of social scientists; (4) protection of freedom of teaching, research and publication; and (5) interdisciplinary cooperation in social science research.[3]

These two organizations are doing much to focus and systematize the practical and theoretical interests of social scientists in such areas as social change, intergroup relations, and human relations in general. We turn now to some of these applications of social psychology.

Increasingly in the last twenty years, social psychologists have turned to the study of groups as the primary means for improving human relations. We mentioned group dynamics and sociometry earlier, in Chapter 12; together these have provided a new tool for understanding and for improving social relationships. The use of scientific methods in solving group problems—in business, industry, and the community—is implied in the term "human relations," which encompasses most of the applications of social psychology.

THE DEVELOPMENT OF GROUP DYNAMICS

It will be recalled that psychiatrist J. L. Moreno devised sociometry as a technique for bettering interpersonal relations. He asked each girl at the Hudson Training School to name the girls she preferred to eat with, work with, and live with, and which ones she wished to avoid.[4] From these data he constructed "sociograms," or patterns of intragroup relationships; he was then able to group the girls according to their preferences and found that morale improved greatly. Several psychologists and social scientists have applied Moreno's technique to the study and improvement of social relations within groups.[5] The more recent "psychodrama" and "sociodrama," which developed from sociometry, are essentially

---

3 From the masthead of *Social Problems,* the official journal of the Society for the Study of Social Problems.

4 J. L. Moreno, *Who shall survive?* (Washington, D.C.: Nervous & Mental Disease Publishing Co., 1934). Reissued, 1953, by Beacon House, Inc.

5 See symposium in *Sociometry,* VI:3 (1943); also C. P. Loomis and H. B. Pepinsky, Sociometry, 1937-1947: Theory and methods, *Sociometry,* XI (1948), 262-86. The technique is described fully in Lindzey and Borgatta, Sociometric Measurement, in G. Lindzey (ed.), *op. cit.,* Vol. I; and in H. H. Jennings, Sociometric structure, in M. Sherif and M. O. Wilson, *Group relations at the crossroads* (New York: Harper & Bros., 1953).

techniques for depicting maladjustive roles and for producing better types of intragroup relationships.[6]

Group dynamics has become a full-grown movement; it has been primarily the work of psychologists, whereas sociometry has been more the province of the sociologist.[7] Traditionally, group dynamics has stressed the social psychological forces within the group; sociometry has more generally emphasized interpersonal relations within the group setting. Though the distinction between the two viewpoints is rapidly disappearing, the terminology differs somewhat. Group dynamics, deriving from field theory, uses such terms as "tension" and "force." Following Lewin, these are used in a psychological rather than a physical or mathematical sense.[8] Another concept is the interdependence of parts, or the holistic nature of the social situation. Since group dynamics was an outgrowth of Gestalt psychology, the wholeness of the group and the interdependence of its individual members are naturally emphasized.

The studies of Kurt Lewin and his students include a variety of social settings. The experiments on different group atmospheres showed the superiority of democratic leadership over other types in increasing productivity and reducing interpersonal tensions within the group.[9] Bavelas showed that group workers could be trained in democratic leadership to an extent which was reflected in improved efficiency and morale.[10] Other studies dealt with group discussion as an alternative to lecturing or individual instruction. Lewin found, during the war, that group discussion and "group decision" were much more effective than other methods in bringing about changed food habits, such as utilizing sweetbreads and kidneys or giving cod-liver oil and orange juice to babies.[11] The same phenomenon occurred in industry; group decision on the part of a group of sewing-machine operators in a factory raised their level of

[6] See J. L. Moreno, *Psychodrama,* Vol. I (New York: Beacon House, Inc., 1946) and the journal *Sociatry*.

[7] Beginning with 1956, the quarterly journal *Sociometry* was broadened and subtitled *A Journal of Research in Social Psychology*. It had been founded in 1937 by Moreno and for nearly twenty years served as the official journal for the sociometrists. Apparently Moreno felt it might serve a broader base. It is now published by the American Sociological Society. Its editor is L. S. Cottrell, Jr.

[8] For further discussion of this point, see M. Deutsch, Field theory in social psychology, in G. Lindzey (ed.), *Handbook of social psychology* (Reading, Mass.: Addison-Wesley Pub. Co., Inc., 1954), Vol. I, pp. 183-85. In addition, Lewin's own viewpoint is presented in K. Lewin, *Field theory in social science* (New York: Harper & Bros., 1951), pp. 130-54.

[9] See Chapter 14 and below in the present chapter.

[10] A. Bavelas, Morale and the training of leaders, in G. Watson (ed.), *Civilian morale* (Boston: Houghton Mifflin Co., 1942), pp. 143-65.

[11] K. Lewin, Group decision and social change, in Swanson *et al., Readings* (2d ed.), pp. 330-44.

production from an index of 75 to one of 87. As Lewin says, "experience in leadership training, in changing of food habits, work production, criminality, alcoholism, prejudices, all indicate that it is usually easier to change individuals formed into a group than to change any one of them separately." [12]

Both of these problems illustrate Lewin's conception of group decision and social change. He believed that life by its nature was dynamic and "flows on but still keeps a recognizable form." [13] He employed a term in physics, "quasi-stationary equilibria," to the tendency of a person or a group to maintain a variety of homeostasis by which processes are kept at their respective levels. Deutsch states:

The field of forces in the neighborhood of the level of equilibrium presupposes that the forces against going higher than the equilibrium level increase with the amount of raising and that the forces against lowering increase (or remain constant) with the lowering. Thus, if we assume that a group standard is operating to determine the level of worker productivity in a factory, any attempt upon the part of the worker to deviate from the standard by higher productivity will only result in stronger forces being induced upon him by his co-workers to push him back into line. That is, as the Festinger experiments have demonstrated, the deviant will be exposed to stronger forces the more he deviates. However, as Lewin points out, the gradient of forces may change at a distance from the equilibrium level so that after an individual has gone a certain distance from the equilibrium level, the forces may push him away rather than pull him toward the group standard.[14]

The Research Center for Group Dynamics was established in 1945 by Kurt Lewin at the Massachusetts Institute of Technology; a few years later it moved to the University of Michigan. Its aim is to discover the laws of group behavior, and to study committees, clubs, and other small groups with a view to increasing their efficiency and productivity. Intergroup relations is another subject of interest at the center and at its summer institutes in Bethel, Maine.[15]

Other research in group relations. Inspired both by sociometry and group dynamics, a great deal of interest has developed in "group relations" [16] and "small group research." [17] As mentioned

12 *Ibid.,* p. 343. See also Lewin's *Resolving social conflicts* (New York: Harper & Bros., 1948).

13 Deutsch, *op. cit.,* p. 217.

14 *Ibid.*

15 For the scope of group dynamics, see D. Cartwright and A. Zander (eds.), *Group dynamics; research and theory* (Chicago: Row, Peterson & Co., 1953).

16 M. Sherif and M. O. Wilson (eds.), *Group relations at the crossroads* (New York: Harper & Bros., 1953).

17 A. P. Hare, E. F. Borgatta, and R. F. Bales, *Small groups: studies in social interaction* (New York: Alfred A. Knopf, Inc., 1955).

p. 325

earlier, Bales at Harvard has developed an *interaction process analysis*—a set of roles for describing interpersonal behavior within the group. To recapitulate, these categories are as follows: [18]

1. *Shows solidarity,* raises other's status, gives help;
2. *Shows tension release,* jokes, laughs, shows satisfaction;
3. *Agrees,* shows passive acceptance, understands, concurs;
4. *Gives suggestion;* direction, implying autonomy for others;
5. *Gives opinion,* evaluation, analysis, expresses feeling;
6. *Gives orientation,* information, repeats, clarifies;
7. *Asks for orientation,* information, repetition, confirmation;
8. *Asks for opinion,* evaluation, analysis, expression of feeling;
9. *Asks for suggestion,* direction, possible ways of action;
10. *Disagrees,* shows passive rejection, withholds help;
11. *Shows tension,* asks for help, withdraws from field;
12. *Shows antagonism,* deflates other's status, defends or asserts self.

Some students, of course, would find these categories too cumbersome for actual field work. One of the authors, for example, modified them into more workable form, with the help of a graduate seminar: task-setting (what do we do?); means-discovering (how do we do it?); orienting (where are we now?); information- and opinion-seeking; information- and opinion-giving; supporting and agreeing; opposing and disagreeing; summarizing; nonproblem directed or irrelevant.

Group and social therapy. As a part of improving intragroup relations, we might mention several types of "social therapy"—that is, therapy accomplished via the social group.

Perhaps the best-known example is Alcoholics Anonymous, which seems to be the most successful approach to alcoholism or "compulsive drinking." [19] The alcoholic is accepted into a group with problems just like his own; he feels he is among friends who understand him. He achieves catharsis, gains friendship, and comes to identify himself strongly with the group. He learns that he is "allergic" to alcohol and that he must avoid the first drink. Sometimes religion is a great aid. Through solidarity with his group comes a new self-respect and a process of re-education which have rehabilitated thousands of alcoholics. The same kind of group therapeutic technique has been used with recently divorced persons and with others sharing a major problem. Perhaps the most colorful

---

[18] R. F. Bales, *Interaction process analysis* (Reading, Mass.: Addison-Wesley Pub. Co., Inc., 1950). See pp. 325-27 above.

[19] See R. F. Bales, Social therapy for a social disorder—compulsive drinking, *J. soc. Issues,* I:3 (1945), 14-22. See also the publications of Alcoholics Anonymous.

example was "Overweights Anonymous," which was started in New York about 1951.

Group psychotherapy has been coming to the fore in recent years as a supplement, or even as an alternative, to individual therapy.[20] While there are many types of group therapy, the purpose of all is to effect change in the personalities of the participants through open discussion of their problems and the establishing of new interpersonal relationships.[21] Probably group therapy has been influenced more by psychoanalysis than by group dynamics or sociometry; yet it shows the imprint of both psychiatry and social psychology. From a practical standpoint group therapy is more economical in cost than individual treatment. From a social psychological viewpoint, this approach introduces the patient to a number of role situations and provides a practice area for role flexibility—for social reality testing. It increases the participant's communicability and prepares him to verbalize with more appropriate emotional tone than formerly. In a way, group therapy offers the client a substitute family setting, with the guidance and interpretation of the therapist.[22] As we shall see later, group psychotherapy has had its influence in many settings, including industry and personnel work.

Just after World War II, the Tavistock Institute of Human Relations was founded in England. It is an organization of psychiatrists and social scientists dedicated to the diagnosis and treatment of various community problems.[23] The keynote is that "group problems can only be treated by a group." It is important to do things *with* people rather than to do things *to* people. The social therapist, taking a neutral role, provides social science knowledge and techniques for the school, recreational, or industrial group. His function is to get the members of the group launched upon the study of their own problems; then he withdraws as rapidly as possible. Hostility toward the social therapist arises, as in individual therapy, but the processes of group decision may overcome such resistance. If it does not, the resistance can be brought into the open and worked through as with any other part of the problem of change. The Tavistock Institute has already aided the democratization of

20 S. R. Slavson, *An introduction to group therapy* (New York: Commonwealth Fund, Division of Publications, 1943); H. E. Durkin, Theory and practice of group psychotherapy, *Ann. N. Y. Acad. Sci.*, XLIX (1948), 889-901. F. B. Powdermaker and J. D. Frank, *Group psychotherapy* (Cambridge, Mass.: Harvard University Press, 1953).

21 See H. S. Sullivan, *Conceptions of modern psychiatry* (Washington, D. C.: W. A. White Foundation, 1947).

22 G. R. Bach, *Intensive group psychotherapy* (New York: The Ronald Press Co., 1954), pp. 322-26.

23 See E. Jaques (ed.), Social therapy, *J. soc. Issues*, III:2 (1947).

schools, has worked at the improving of morale in industrial plants, and has extended its services in other directions as well.

THE SOCIAL PSYCHOLOGY OF INDUSTRY

Industrial social psychology and industrial sociology are fairly new developments. Although such problems as work efficiency and fatigue measurement have interested the experimental psychologist almost since the beginning of the century it is only since the late thirties that group problems in the office or factory have occupied the social scientists. As Hughes indicates, work experience is a critical part of one's life; consequently, it is not surprising that increasing attention is directed toward that area.[24] In fact, certain psychologists and sociologists are so completely identified with the subject that they have become known as "industrial experts." Along with this technical competence has developed a jargon that in some cases makes the work communicable only to a limited public.[25] In contrast to the professional scientists, popularizers have diffused the information through a large public. Examples are Stuart Chase's *Roads to Agreement* [26] and *The Proper Study of Mankind* [27] or Donald and Eleanor Laird's *The New Psychology for Leadership*.[28] The testing programs and the many training courses for foremen, supervisors, union representatives (and even the general worker) testify to the importance of a human relations program.

The industrial setting. Undoubtedly the outstanding point of departure of industrial social psychology was the series of studies performed in the Hawthorne plant of the Western Electric Company, starting in 1927. These were conducted by three Harvard professors, Elton Mayo, F. J. Roethlisberger, and T. N. Whitehead, and by W. J. Dickson of Western Electric.[29] The original aim of the studies was to obtain concrete data on the effects of illumination, temperature, rest periods, hours of work, wage rate, etc., upon production. A group of six girls, average workers, were chosen for the experiment; their task was the assembly of telephone relays. Almost from the beginning, unexpected results appeared: the pro-

[24] E. C. Hughes, The sociological study of work: an editorial foreword, *Amer. J. Sociol.*, LVII (1952), 423-26.

[25] E. C. Hughes, The relation of industrial to general sociology, *Sociol. soc. Res.*, XLI (1957), 251-56.

[26] New York: Harper & Bros., 1951.

[27] New York: Harper & Bros., 1956.

[28] New York: McGraw-Hill Book Co., Inc., 1956.

[29] Perhaps the best single reference is F. J. Roethlisberger and W. J. Dickson, *Management and the worker* (Cambridge, Mass.: Harvard University Press, 1939). A good summary is provided by G. C. Homans in Swanson *et al.*, *Readings* (2d ed.), pp. 637-49.

duction rate kept going up whether rest periods and hours were increased or decreased! In each experimental period, whatever its conditions, output was higher than in the preceding one. The answer seemed to lie in a number of subtle social factors.

First of all, the girls felt honored to be chosen for the experiment, and they enjoyed working in the test room. Second, they felt differently—less anxious—about their supervision; for example, they were permitted to converse freely. More important still, they developed a strong group or team spirit, to the extent that if one of the girls felt sick or tired the others would work harder to make up for her low output. Also one of the girls became a self-appointed leader and focalized their spirit of doing their best to increase production—a goal which they adopted more or less unconsciously. As Homans summarizes it, the increase in the girls' output rate "could not be related to any change in their conditions of work, whether experimentally induced or not. It could, however, be related to what can only be spoken of as the development of an organized social group in a peculiar and effective relation with its supervisors." [30]

What, then, was wrong with "human relations" in the regular shop departments? Interviewing showed several types of discontent with respect to wages, supervision, and chances of promotion, and a fear of "speed-up." As a result, the workers had adopted various restrictive practices to prevent output from going above a certain level; an informal sort of leadership had grown up to enforce these production norms. The investigators found there was a generally accepted notion of what constituted a good day's work, hence output was kept quite constant and had no relation to intelligence or skill of the workers. Anxiety about rate reduction and speed-up was common, even though few of the workers had ever experienced them.

In other words, the remarkable point of the Hawthorne studies was that they approached the problem of industrial morale and efficiency from the perspective of the worker rather than from a purely management orientation. The researchers, states one author,

. . . . do not try to define a response as the result of the introduction of change; they recognize that it is a result of the specific change *plus* the employee's attitudes, his social situation on the job, and his previous attitudes as determined by his personal history and background.[31]

One of the difficult problems is the depersonalization of the individual worker because of the growth of technology and the bu-

[30] G. C. Homans, in Swanson *et al.*, *Readings* (2d ed.), p. 641.
[31] M. L. Blum, *Industrial psychology and its social foundations* (rev. ed.; New York: Harper & Bros., 1956), p. 49.

reaucratization of industry. As Merton has suggested, technological changes often cause the loss of the worker's job status, of initiative, and of identity with the job. They also increase stratification within industry, and depersonalize contacts between worker and managers, all of which accentuates personal and social tensions.[32]

Nowhere are some of the social psychological problems of status and size better illustrated than in Whyte's study of the restaurant industry. For one thing, he found that there were certain stages of growth in the restaurant business. Problems of coordination and relations with customers are comparatively manageable when the organization is small, but when it is a large, often multi-floored restaurant, problems are magnified. In the smaller establishment, employees become classifiable as service employees, kitchen employees, and dishwashers. On the more advanced level, there is the manager, supervisor, checker, cost control supervisor, waitress, bartender, pantry worker, kitchen worker, runner, and dishwasher. And most important, there are the customers. Besides, there is the general complexity of relating the functions of one individual with the needs of other individuals. One factor that complicates inter-employee contacts is the relation of sex roles and status. In an ideal sense employees initiating orders, namely, the waitresses, should have higher status than those receiving them; however, conventionally there is no clearly defined relationship between the dining room and the kitchen. The problem is that the male orderman or cook takes his orders from a female, a reversal of the usual sex roles in our society. This problem may be partially resolved by a skillful dining-room supervisor, who may act as mediator when tension mounts, or by some mechanical system of communication (written orders, telephone, public address system, or telautograph) so that face-to-face conflicts are avoided. Much of the group conflict in any large-scale situation is a result of the problem of communication. The industrial world is no exception.[33]

Motivation and work. One of the important problems in industrial psychology is the disentangling of motives that underlie the worker's reward system. Motivation is always a complex process, and "homeostatic pressures" may operate in a variety of directions to account for industrial morale and productivity. In the foregoing

32 R. K. Merton, The machine, the worker and the engineer, *Science*, CV (1947), 79-84.

33 W. F. Whyte, *Human relations in the restaurant industry* (New York: McGraw-Hill Book Co., Inc., 1948). Also his article, Social structure of the organization, *Amer. J. Sociol.*, LIV (1949), 302-8.

discussion the importance of the employee-employee and employer-employee relationships was noted. Certainly the Western Electric study drew attention to the importance of primary-group relations and the satisfaction of ego-needs of the workers when they are a target group of an experiment. Whyte's study of the restaurant industry showed how status needs become especially complicated in a quasi-bureaucratic structure.

In regard to motivational analysis, Tumin maintains that men find their reward in differentiated amounts of "scarce and desired goods," whether of income or status. The worker inevitably has a calculating attitude when he does not consider his reward to have been based on his true value, and he realizes the sharply differentiated status and role structure that industry represents. In other words, the average worker is too remote to feel complete ego-identification. Tumin asserts that "blue collar" workers particularly tend to learn to refer themselves to their work-group peers for the appropriate model of the on-the-job behavior. There is, as was found in the Hawthorne study, little incentive for producing beyond the norm, since upward mobility for the manual worker is distinctly limited. Moreover, blue collar work activity allows little creativity and decision-making. The employee is less likely to work efficiently at a process over which he has so little control. The role of the worker may be contrasted to his role as a parent, where he is in full charge of the "project"; the child's upbringing is his own responsibility, for better or for worse. Unless this situation of parental conscientiousness and identification can be to some extent duplicated in the work area, no reward system can be completely effective. Certainly monetary reward is restricted in its capacity for motivating the worker.[34]

Productivity and employee-employer relationship. Undoubtedly the most important variable in determining industrial morale is the type of supervision involved. Evidence has been increasingly apparent that broadening the basis of authority and decision-making has been followed by increased productivity, as well as reduced turnover, absenteeism, and transfer requests. The Coch and French study hypothesized that productivity is partially a function of employee-employer communication; that is, when management invites a worker group to share in policy making, production does not necessarily suffer, but will possibly increase. Their study pertained to piece-time work in a garment factory, where workers who were

[34] M. M. Tumin, Rewards and task-orientations, *Amer. sociol. Rev.*, XX (1955), 419-23.

transferred to a new section were slower in acquiring the new skill than original learners. It was assumed that this delay might be due to the frustration of transfer, including status problems, resistance to the new job, along with the likelihood of reaching the standard rate, and the unpleasantness of leaving one's work group.

In view of this situation, the management decided to reduce the resistance to change by introducing a more satisfactory orientation program by which workers would be briefed on their new assignment. The supervisors explained to them the new piece rates. As the orientation sessions were in the nature of a group discussion, there was ample opportunity to investigate and accept psychologically the new assignment and its production code. The new behavior became accepted at the ego level, supported by group approval. In other words, participation becomes the key to new methods of production and job transfer. In the various experimental groups, it was seen that the smaller and more intensively participating a group was, the higher its production rate. The groups accepted the management's quota of 60 units per hour; once on the job, they considered this norm as their level of aspiration. The closer the level of achievement approached this figure, the stronger the force (amounting to a steep gradient) to meet the quota. This force was met by an opposite force, namely, the difficulty of the new job, and the difficulty of accelerating one's output beyond what is already a high level.

This illustrates the concept mentioned earlier as the "quasi-stationary equilibria." Behavior is the result of opposing tendencies. The difficulty of relearning appears to be largely a product of hostility toward management for transferring the worker. Further, the attainment of the new skill is dependent on a consensus that is dynamically achieved within the group.[35]

Not only does the Coch and French experiment provide a brilliant example of Lewin's group dynamics approach, but it offers an experimental model of methodology as applied in the industrial setting. A hypothesis is formulated that offers some solution to an industrial problem such as a decline in morale or productivity. The next step is selection of several groups to test the hypothesis or competing hypotheses. These groups would represent a preponderance of constant variables, one of which could be studied as the inde-

[35] L. Coch and J. R. P. French, Jr., Overcoming resistance to change, Hum. Relat., I (1948), 512-32. Also, J. R. P. French Jr., Field experiments: changing group productivity, in J. G. Miller, Experiments in social process (New York: McGraw-Hill Book Co., Inc., 1950), pp. 81-96. For a discussion of the Lewinian aspects of the study see M. Haire, Industrial social psychology, in G. Lindzey (ed.), op. cit., Vol. II, pp. 1109-10.

pendent variable. There would be one or more control groups to offer some satisfactory means of comparison.[36]

Much of the research in group dynamics conforms to this general experimental design: a given function or variable is studied in several groups over a period of time. The difference between this technique and, for example, "process analysis" in public opinion research (mentioned in Chapter 16) is that group dynamics is primarily interested in motivational and behavioral change within the *small* group.

The basic problem that concerned Coch and French has been the point of departure for a number of studies: that is, the amount and quality of policy making on the part of the group as opposed to its supervisors. It is related to what has been known as the newer "employee-centered" boss versus the more traditional "production-centered" boss. Actually, productivity is found to be higher with the former orientation.

In examining the problem of productivity in studies of a sample of office workers and of railroad workers, Haire points out that the following generalizations can be made about the supervisor's role: (1) The successful supervisor associated with highly productive groups tends to view his role as a leader rather than a production worker. In other words, more time is devoted to leadership functions. (2) The successful supervisor works through groups; or, as stated above, supervisors are employee-centered. In some situations, this function might include a variety of roles, among them that of an industrial counselor who needs to understand some of the problems of his workers. (3) The supervisor should be nonpunitive. When censure is necessary it should develop from the group situation, rather than from his own lead position.[37]

One principal aspect of the employee-centered supervision is the sharing of decision-making. Tannenbaum and Massarik report that participation has a number of advantages such as (1) a higher rate of output and, particularly, an increase in quality of the product; (2) a reduction of turnover, absenteeism, and tardiness; (3) reduction in the number of grievances and more cooperative relations along the line of the manager-worker hierarchy; (4) greater willingness on the

---

[36] A readable discussion of the experimental aspects of the Coch and French study is L. Broom and P. Selznick, *Sociology* (Evanston, Ill.: Row, Peterson & Co., 1955), pp. 536-39.

[37] Haire, *op. cit.*, p. 1116, as adopted from D. Katz, N. Maccoby, and N. Morse, *Productivity, supervision and morale in an office situation* (Ann Arbor, Mich.: Institute for Social Research, 1950); and D. Katz, N. Maccoby, G. Gurin, and L. Floor, *Productivity, supervision and morale among railroad workers* (Ann Arbor, Mich.: Institute for Social Research, 1951).

part of the workers to accept change; (5) more facility in the management of subordinates—fewer managers may be necessary; (6) higher quality of managerial decisions. The upward flow of information is given a broader channel. In fact, in less efficient bureaucracies a great deal of information never rises above the lower echelons and consequently cannot be used by management.[38]

The degree to which shared decision-making can be employed depends on a number of factors. For one thing, there is the question of time; some critical decisions cannot wait long enough for the democratic process. Also, there is the question of cost. Decision-making may have to be performed on a purely administrative basis.[39]

In employer-employee relations a wide repertory of techniques is employed today. For one thing, there is role-playing in the context of group therapy, sociodrama, "gripe" sessions, and the like. The problem of communication is so intricate that a highly efficient plant may utilize a number of these techniques. The ability of the worker to identify with the manager, as well as the reverse process, depends on a skilful application of group dynamics.

DEMOCRATIC LEADERSHIP AND ITS TRAINING

The "new" leadership. It will be recalled from Chapter 14 that the prevailing definition of leadership is in terms of a field approach —a fusion of personality and situation. In fact, group dynamics is partly responsible for rejection of the notion that leadership is inherent in a personality type, a genius, or in the genes. Whatever the lay definition of leadership may be, personnel divisions of industry, government, and the military establishment are at present utilizing group dynamics approaches in their leadership selection and training programs. The roles of the leader are sufficiently varied that an individual might be notably successful in one situation and yet fail to command any attention as a leader, even within the same group, when another set of circumstances occurs.

In this group-centered approach there are questions that can appropriately be raised by research in the area of leadership. Perhaps the list of items suggested by Gordon is representative:

What are the personality variables that inhibit the free expression of an individual's capacities?

What are the chief factors in an individual's environment that tend to suppress and restrict spontaneous expression?

38 R. Tannenbaum and F. Massarik, Sharing decision-making with subordinates, in R. Dubin, *Human relations in administration* (Englewood Cliffs, N. J.: Prentice-Hall, Inc., 1951), pp. 223-28.
39 *Ibid.*

How do individuals learn to be constructive and productive members of a group?

What are the main factors that predispose individuals to submissive dependence upon authority figures?

What are the effects of various kinds of leader behavior on the spontaneity and freedom of expression of group members?

How can a formal leader create the conditions most conducive to the development of self-directing and mature groups? [40]

In selecting leaders, military authorities have found it necessary to employ a situational outlook, although their methods do not meet the criteria of group dynamics. The British army experimented with what have been called "leaderless-group" tests. Problems were given to groups of seven or eight individuals. One might include the building of a bridge over a ravine within a specified time. A candidate would be judged as to how he reacted toward others, or whether he seemed interested in showing off his own ability.[41] Likewise, the Office of Strategic Services in World War II employed an elaborate appraisal system, including a number of tests among which were the ability to stand up in stress, frustration tolerance, and acuity of perception.[42]

Leadership training. As already implied, increasing attention is being given to the selection, recruitment, and training of leaders. The distinction between democratic and autocratic leadership has already been discussed, at the close of Chapter 14, including the studies of Kurt Lewin and his associates.[43] Advantages of the democratic over the autocratic leader role have been shown, for pre-adolescent boys at least, in greater productivity during the absence of the leader, less dependence upon the leader, more socialized expression of aggression, and the like. Each group developed a fairly consistent pattern of relationships between members and the leader. This pattern was found to change markedly when a new leadership role or "social climate" was introduced.

Perhaps of greater interest, in regard to the training of leaders, is the fact that each of the three major roles—democratic, autocratic and laissez-faire (do-nothing)—could be played realistically and convincingly by each of the leaders participating in the experiment.

---

[40] T. Gordon, *Group-centered leadership* (Boston: Houghton Mifflin Co., 1955), p. 43.

[41] J. W. Eaton, Is scientific leadership selection possible? in A. W. Gouldner (ed.), *Studies in leadership* (New York: Harper & Bros., 1950), pp. 615-43.

[42] OSS Assessment Staff, *Assessment of men* (New York: Rinehart & Co., Inc., 1948), pp. 392-435.

[43] The best single reference to these studies is R. Lippitt and R. K. White, An experimental study of leadership and group life, in Swanson *et al.*, *Readings* (2d ed.), pp. 340-55.

This does not necessarily mean that *any* leadership role can be taken by *any* person in *any* group, but the experiment does show that consistent leadership roles may be learned and enacted.

Bavelas, another colleague of Lewin, showed that recreational leaders could be trained in democratic methods and found that the change bore fruit.[44] The customary method used by his leaders was that of direct command. Dividing them into two equated halves, he spent three weeks training one half in democratic procedures. This training involved discussion of the fundamentals of group work and of the leader's role in it, as well as the realistic teaching of techniques through example and actual participation. When these leaders put their newly acquired "group method" into practice, Bavelas found, it created an atmosphere of productivity and cooperation. Its success "was evidenced in various ways: (a) a doubling of the number of children attracted to participate, (b) the enthusiasm and persistence of the group, (c) the holding power of the group for the individuals, (d) the efficiency of the work organization, (e) the high degree of self-discipline, and (f) the quality and output of the work."[45] In comparison, the untrained leaders continued their customary procedures with mediocre results.

Lippitt and others have found role-playing an effective method for leadership training and have used this technique in a variety of situations.[46] The trainee is asked to act out, spontaneously, a role which is called for in his own group. For example, he may be asked to take the part of a foreman or supervisor, while others play the role of subordinates; later, he may be shifted to the role of a subordinate. He also observes other trainees playing similar roles and is encouraged to discuss them and evaluate their effectiveness. Those using the role-playing technique find that it gives a trainee insight into problems of leadership and facilitates his adoption of better methods. With larger groups, such as a conference of leaders in community relations, role-playing demonstrations have been used to "break the ice" and to help the delegates focus on their major tasks and difficulties.[47]

---

[44] A. Bavelas, Morale and the training of leaders, chap. viii in G. Watson (ed.), *Civilian morale* (Boston: Houghton Mifflin Co., 1942).

[45] *Ibid.*, p. 155.

[46] R. Lippitt, The psychodrama in leadership training, *Sociometry*, VI (1943), 286-92; L. P. Bradford and R. Lippitt, *Supervising training for group leadership* (Ann Arbor, Mich.: Research Center for Group Dynamics, 1945); A. Bavelas, Role-playing and management training, *Sociatry*, I (1947), 183-91; A. F. Zander, Role-playing; a technique for training the necessarily dominating leader, *Sociatry*, I (1947), 225-35.

[47] R. Lippitt, L. P. Bradford, and K. D. Benne, Sociodramatic clarification of leader and group roles . . . , *Sociatry*, I (1947), 82-91; R. Lippitt, *Training in community relations* (New York: Harper & Bros., 1949).

Gordon describes some of the problems and functions involved in training leaders toward the group-centered approach. A whole new set of roles is relevant. Members of his leadership workshop maintained that the following characteristics would be important in the democratic leader: developing in the group the capacity to solve its own problems, willingness to have members take over leadership of the group, acceptance of attacks on his leadership, ability to abide by the majority decision, and regarding his task as one of reducing dependency of members upon himself. Important functions for the leader include listening to the problems of his group, conveying acceptance, "linking" (i.e., interpretation of the separate remarks into a coherent and synthesized statement). This new leadership role was sufficiently bizarre that the first contact was somewhat anxiety-producing. However, increasing self-confidence came with successive meetings. In some respects the group-centered leader is not unlike the functioning of the clinician in client-centered therapy.[48]

SUMMARY

Despite many obstacles social psychologists are applying their findings in several important problem areas of social behavior. Aided by sociometry and group dynamics much has been discovered about the working of groups, and means have been devised for improving morale and interpersonal relationships. Some of these developments fall under the head of social therapy, notably group therapy. Others are more definitely in the area of industrial social psychology, following the lead of the Western Electric studies or breaking new ground via experimental research. One overall finding in all the research is the significance of democratic participation and decision making. Similarly, the new emphasis in leadership training is on group-centered or democratic methods as the most effective, generally speaking.

SUPPLEMENTARY READINGS

Books of Readings

MACCOBY, E. E., NEWCOMB, T. M., AND HARTLEY, E. L. (eds.). *Readings in social psychology*, 3d ed. New York: Henry Holt & Co., Inc., 1958.
Bennett, E. B., Some factors in group decision.
Coch, L., and French, J. R., Overcoming resistance to change.
Homans, G. C., Group factors in worker productivity.
Lewin, K., Group decision and social change.

48 Gordon, *op. cit.*, pp. 162-200.

BRITT, S. H. (ed.). *Selected readings in social psychology.* New York: Rinehart & Co., Inc., 1950.
Lewin, K., The practicality of democracy.
Lippitt, R., Group functioning and productivity.
Stagner, R., Psychological aspects of industrial conflict: perception.
Twentieth Century Fund (Labor Committee), More dignity in the job.

LINDZEY, G. (ed.). *Handbook of social psychology.* Reading, Mass.: Addison-Wesley Pub. Co., Inc., 1954.
Deutsch, M., Field theory in social psychology. Vol. I.
Haire, M., Industrial social psychology. Vol. II.

Other References

BACH, G. R. *Intensive group psychotherapy.* New York: The Ronald Press Co., 1954.
A comprehensive study of group therapy with attention to both theory and practice.

BLAU, P. M. *The dynamics of bureaucracy.* Chicago: The University of Chicago Press, 1955.
One of several works dealing with the bureaucratic personality and its relevance to human relations.

BLUM, M. L. *Industrial psychology and its social foundation,* rev. ed. New York: Harper & Bros., 1956.
The first half of the work contains relevant material in the problem of motivation and allied areas. There is competent review of the Hawthorne studies.

CARTWRIGHT, D., AND ZANDER, A. (eds.). *Group dynamics, research and theory.* Evanston, Ill.: Row, Peterson & Co., 1953.
A compilation of papers on group properties and leadership.

COOK, L. A. (ed.). *Toward better human relations.* Detroit, Mich.: Wayne University Press, 1952.
Contains five very readable essays on group dynamics and human relations.

DUBIN, R. (ed.). *Human relations in administration: the sociology of organization.* Englewood Cliffs, N. J.: Prentice-Hall, Inc., 1951.
A series of papers, mainly from the sociological viewpoint, of management and the lower echelons.

GORDON, T. *Group-centered leadership.* Boston: Houghton Mifflin Co., 1955.
A valuable description of democratic leadership in the workshop.

HAIMAN, F. S. *Group leadership and democratic action.* Boston: Houghton Mifflin Co., 1950.
Group dynamics and leadership effectively presented by a professor of speech.

HOMANS, G. C. *The human group.* New York: Harcourt, Brace & Co., 1950.
The formation and structure of several different types of groups.

JAQUES, E. *The changing culture of a factory.* New York: The Dryden Press, Inc., 1952.
An intensive study of a business and industrial organization.

KLEIN, A. F. *Role playing in leadership training and group problem solving,* New York: Association Press, 1956.
A Y.M.C.A. book for a lay public; it contains some useful generalizations on human relations.

LEWIN, K. *Resolving social conflicts.* New York: Harper & Bros., 1948.
———. *Field theory in social science* (ed. by D. Cartwright). New York: Harper & Bros., 1951.
These two works present the essence of group dynamics and its applications by its founder.

MORENO, J. L. *Who shall survive?* Washington, D.C.: Nervous and Mental Disease Publishing Co., 1934.
The comprehensive outline of sociometry by its founder.

POWDERMAKER, F., AND FRANK, J. D. *Group psychotherapy.* Cambridge, Mass.: Harvard University Press, 1953.
A methodological study of an extensive project with the Veterans Administration.

ROETHLISBERGER, F. J., AND DICKSON, W. J. *Management and the worker.* Cambridge, Mass.: Harvard University Press, 1939.
The classic study of the Hawthorne Western Electric plant, which initiated industrial social psychology as we know it today.

WHYTE, W. F. (ed.). *Industry and society.* New York: McGraw-Hill Book Co., Inc., 1946.
A number of papers that developed out of the Committee on Human Relations in Industry at the University of Chicago.

WHYTE, W. H., JR. *The organization man.* New York: Simon & Schuster, Inc., 1956.
The ideology of the manager; his training, problems, and social relationships.

22

Ethnic Relations and Prejudice

No other areas of attitude have been the subject of more research than ethnic prejudice. Of all group differences—race, age, sex, occupational, etc.,—the problem of race and ethnic differences remains the most disturbing. Much of the world is engulfed in nationalism and religious antagonisms, and wide areas of Asia and Africa seek liberation from colonial domination. In our own country nearly a third of the citizenry has minority ethnic status, whether on racial, national background, or religious lines. The role of these out-group members in private and public life has been frequently challenged. Especially for our largest single minority racial group, the Negro, there has been a far-reaching struggle for social, political, and economic equality. Discriminations of various types, especially in certain regions, are thrust upon the Mexican, the Oriental, and our first citizens, the American Indian. Even a large and well entrenched minority religious group, the Roman Catholic, is subject to disadvantage in certain social areas, particularly in access of its members to political office. Consequently, next to the troubled area of international relations, ethnic prejudice is the most important social problem confronting the social psychologist. In fact, there is an inescapable relationship between ethnic relations and international tensions.

In this chapter we shall examine some of the viewpoints on race and ethnic differences, the bases and formation of stereotypes and prejudice, and the means of combatting prejudice. Much of our success in establishing satisfactory relations abroad depends on the degree to which we can effect better intergroup relations in our own country.

The matter of "group differences" is of great significance to social psychologists. This term implies comparison or contrast between modal characteristics or behavior of various social groups. We have already touched upon the subject earlier in connection with "culture and personality" studies; we return to it now with particular reference to differences found among ethnic subgroups in a culture and the implications of these variations.

The phenomenon of subcultural variation has been treated somewhat differently by sociologists and psychologists. The former have typically called it "social differentiation," indicating the processes by which individuals and groups of individuals develop differing roles. Kimball Young, for example, discusses causative factors such as biological differences, age and sex roles, specialization, leadership, stratification, and class structure.[1] Psychologists have emphasized in their studies the amounts of individual and group differences in intelligence, attitudes, and personality traits; they have paid less attention to the processes by which the variations come about.

In studying the extent of such differences, psychologists have used quantitative measures which, whatever their drawbacks, permit us to discover whether or not differences between groups are statistically significant. Often the differences between averaged measurements of two groups are small; we need to know whether the difference is real and meaningful or just due to chance.[2]

The social psychologist sees merit in both the psychological and sociological approaches. He is interested, on the one hand, in the nature and extent of group differences and, on the other, in the processes by which they occur. These are related matters, but they are best treated separately. They are frequently confused, as when someone discovers a difference, then assumes—quite gratuitously—that it is due to innate factors. Our task is, first, to discover what group differences actually exist, then to search out the evidence for determinants. This chapter deals with ethnic differences.

RACE AND ETHNIC GROUP DIFFERENCES

Race is a statistical concept that refers largely, if not exclusively, to physical differences. These would include skin color (which is probably one of the most arbitrary criteria of physical differences),

[1] K. Young, *Sociology* (rev. ed.; New York: American Book Co., 1949), chaps. xxv-xxviii.

[2] This computation, called the "*t*-test," is based upon the size of the actual difference, the number of individuals in each group and the variability within each group, i.e., the tendency of each measure to cluster about the mean (average). See H. E. Garrett, *Statistics in psychology and education* (4th ed.; New York: Longmans, Green & Co., Inc., 1954) or other standard texts in statistics.

head shape (broad skulled or narrow skulled), hair texture, and a number of other complex physical traits, such as blood typology, facial features, and distribution of body hair. It might be more accurate to speak of overlapping normal probability curves rather than of distinct races. While it is popular to refer to the three dominant racial groups, namely, Caucasoid, Mongoloid, and Negroid, there is no universal agreement among anthropologists on the matter. Since a number of racial myths are often accepted by laymen and scientists alike, it is important to bear the following facts in mind:

1. There is no pure race. In fact, some of the racial stocks that have most prided themselves on their purity and achievements appear to be the result of considerable admixture. This is true for the Nordic "subrace," (or racial "stocks," as Nordic, Alpine, and Mediterranean—variations of the Caucasoid—have been labeled). The same is true for Polynesians or the American Negro.[3]
2. Differences between the individuals within a race often exceed the differences between races. There are individual Norwegians darker than some Sicilians. There are occasional Mediterraneans darker than some of the *average* of certain Negroid groups in Africa.
3. Racial differences can apply only to bodily traits. All of our knowledge to date confirms further the physical definition of race. What mental differences have appeared seem to be the result of environment.[4]
4. A system of racial superiority and inferiority based on evolutionary concepts with allusion to nearness or remoteness to animal forms is a recurring but preposterous notion. If the flat nose and relatively long arm length of the Negro suggest primate ancestry, the Caucasoid has by far a hairier skin. The Caucasoid may have a less protruding jaw than the Negroid race, but the Mongoloid has the least of all.
5. Race must not be confused with a nationality (e.g., "the British race"), a religion ("the Jewish race"), a language ("the Aryan race"), or a culture ("the Chinese race"). The cultural fallacy in these various forms has been frequently used to prove the inherent superiority of Western civilization. Any careful analysis would only backfire when one recalls that European culture was confined to a fairly primitive level of behavior during the early Middle Ages when the Arabs were a highly cultivated people; another example might be the general retardation of our ancestors at the

[3] Coon, C. S., *The races of Europe* (New York: The Macmillan Co., 1939), as abridged in Count, E. W., *This is race* (New York: Henry Schuman, 1950), pp. 576-92.
[4] For a brief review of these studies, see O. Klineberg, *Social psychology* (2d ed.; New York: Henry Holt & Co., Inc., 1954), pp. 291-324.

time of the high advance of China and the Near East five thousand years ago. Reversals of this type do not appear impossible in view of the uncertainty of bringing atomic weapons under control. It is possible that the "civilization" of the contemporary leading powers may suffer some future eclipse.

The whole problem of "racial" characteristics has become so confused that it is now more popular to speak of "ethnic" differences. These refer to variations among groups which differ in race, religion, language, culture, or some combination of these. In other words, except for a few physical differences, ethnic variations are cultural phenomena. The behavioral aspects of these variations are expressed in such factors as intelligence, attitude, personality, and language. The social psychologist is interested in what differences actually exist and what may account for the differences that do appear.

Ethnic differences in intelligence. Most studies undertaken by psychologists have centered about intelligence. Several dozen comparisons of I.Q.'s of white and Negro school children have been made, with the Negro mean usually found to be 10—15 points lower than the white.[5] Results on the Army Alpha and Beta tests in World War I showed considerable superiority of white over Negro in average intelligence. They also revealed noticeable differences between Northern and Southern Negroes and showed that the intelligence means of Negro recruits from some Northern states were greater than the means for white persons from some Southern states.[6] Furthermore, the differences between whites and Negroes in Army Beta (the nonverbal test) score were considerably less than in the verbal Alpha test.[7] Studies of American Indian children have shown them to average about 70 or 80 I.Q. on linguistic tests, but to be between 90 and 100 or even above 100 on performance tests.[8] Chinese and Japanese children in the United States were found to average about 90 in I.Q. on verbal tests and slightly over 100 on performance tests.[9]

[5] For a good summary, see O. Klineberg, *op. cit.*, pp. 304-12; also L. E. Tyler, *Psychology of human differences* (New York: Appleton-Century-Crofts, Inc., 1947); and A. Anastasi and J. P. Foley, *Differential psychology* (rev. ed.; New York: The Macmillan Co., 1949).

[6] R. M. Yerkes (ed.), *Psychological examining in the United States Army* (Mem. Nat. Acad. Sci., 1921).

[7] *Ibid.*, p. 764.

[8] O. Klineberg, *Race differences* (New York: Harper & Bros., 1935), p. 172; also W. Dennis, The performance of Hopi children in the Goodenough Draw-a-Man test, *J. comp. Psychol.*, XXXIV (1942), 341-48.

[9] Klineberg, *Race differences*, p. 171.

Study of ethnic differences in personality is exceedingly difficult, as we already noted in Chapter 3, partly because reliable and valid personality tests are so hard to find. Some believe the Rorschach test offers the greatest opportunities in this area; it is being used in intercultural study.

We are more likely, however, to find ethnic differences in attitudes and values and, of course, in social behavior, than in the area of temperament or personality "traits." Several anthropological studies have highlighted such differences between cultures, and social psychologists have made recent efforts in the same direction.[10] On the whole, however, we lack scientific evidence, though it is accumulating slowly.

The clearest quantitative evidence of the effects of cultural influences as compared with innate or strictly "racial" factors is found in the area of intelligence. In 1931 Klineberg reported a study of racial groups in Europe.[11] He tested 100 boys between ten and twelve years of age in each of three large cities and seven rural districts, using the Pintner-Paterson Performance Scale. His urban subjects were mixed racially, but his rural subjects were relatively pure Nordic, Alpine, and Mediterranean types. The means and medians were as follows:

	Group	Average	Median
Urban	Paris	219.0	218.9
	Hamburg	216.4	218.3
	Rome	211.8	213.6
Rural	German Nordic	198.2	197.6
	French Mediterranean	197.4	204.4
	German Alpine	193.6	199.0
	Italian Alpine	188.8	186.3
	French Alpine	180.2	185.3
	French Nordic	178.8	183.3
	Italian Mediterranean	173.0	172.7

The strictly racial differences are insignificant and inconsistent. The Nordics average 188.5, Alpines 187.5, and Mediterraneans 185.2. One Nordic and one Mediterranean group is high, while the others are low; the Alpines are in the middle. The only consistent difference is a superiority of all city groups over the rural groups—a difference explainable in terms of educational and other environmental advantages.

[10] See, for example, D. V. McGranahan, A comparison of social attitudes among American and German youth, *J. abnorm. soc. Psychol.*, XLI (1946), 245-57.

[11] O. Klineberg, *A study of psychological differences between "racial" and national groups in Europe* (Arch. Psychol., 1931, No. 132).

In other studies Klineberg showed that when Negro children came from the South to New York, their average I.Q.'s rose perceptibly, for at least the first five or six years. He was also able to show that the children leaving the South were of the same average intelligence as those who stayed; there was no perceptible "selective migration." Thus the gain in I.Q. is clearly a function of the new environment.[12]

It was noted in the preceding section that the I.Q.'s of children in other ethnic categories than white Americans often averaged less than 100. Considerable research has shown that the tests are unfair to non-Americans on a number of counts. For example, unless a child is motivated to make a good showing on a test, he does not reveal his actual ability. Many Indian children are quite noncompetitive, or are taught that it is bad form to answer a question in the presence of someone who does not know the answer. Or again, a visiting white tester may not get the rapport from Negro, Indian, or foreign children which is essential for valid test results. Even when the groups tested constitute a respresentative sample of their race or nation (which seldom happens), cultural factors such as language, education, or social status would influence the differences found. True "racial" or "national" differences can be estimated only when all other factors are constant.

McGraw made an attempt to get at racial differences before social and cultural factors had a chance to operate.[13] She administered the Bühler "baby tests" to sixty-eight white and sixty Negro infants between two and eleven months old and found the white babies superior mentally. However, the white babies were also superior in height and weight, suggesting they had an advantage in nutrition; this physical condition might well influence mental performance. Pasamanick studied the behavioral development of Negro and white babies in New Haven, during World War II when rationing made nutrition more constant for the two groups. He found Negro and white development practically identical up to the age of one year but noted that unfavorable environmental conditions began to operate adversely upon Negro infants during the third half-year of life.[14]

Reasons for the differences found. Our evidence points to a variety of cultural and social, rather than strictly racial, factors as

[12] O. Klineberg, *Negro intelligence and selective migration* (New York: Columbia University Press, 1935).

[13] M. B. McGraw, A comparative study of a group of Southern white and Negro infants, *Genet. Psychol. Monogr.*, X (1931), 1-105.

[14] B. Pasamanick, A comparative study of the behavioral development of Negro infants, *Genet. Psychol. Monogr.*, LXIX (1946), 3-44.

the determinants of group differences in intelligence. However, we do not yet possess irrefutable evidence that innate racial differences in intelligence are lacking. We shall have such proof only when we can get large groups of babies, of two or more distinct racial strains, and rear them in a common culture pattern with equal participation for all groups. The difficulty of achieving this is apparent when we consider the impossibility, *anywhere in the United States,* of rearing a group of Negro, Oriental, or Indian children with social, economic, and educational opportunities equal to those of white children. In some parts of the world, such as Brazil and certain islands of the West Indies, Negroes have more equal opportunity than in the United States, but it cannot be considered real equality. However, where discrimination is reduced, mental differences become smaller. Davenport and Steggerda, for example, compared Negro and white test performance in Jamaica, using Negroes and whites living on much the same plane.[15] Using Army Alpha, they found the whites superior on half of the subtests and the Negroes on half. The slight superiority of the whites on mean score was not statistically significant. We may conclude with Klineberg that "as the environment of the Negro approximates more and more closely that of the white, his inferiority tends to disappear." [16]

Much of the present discussion regarding school integration revolves about the supposed and actual difference in mental ability between the white and colored races. An article appeared in a national weekly reporting "scientific" evidence that whites had superior I.Q.'s to Negroes.[17] There were, of course, a number of refutations to this misstatement, most notable of which was the reply of the Society for the Psychological Study of Social Issues.[18] It repeated the statement drawn up by 32 outstanding social scientists that had been submitted three years earlier to the Supreme Court at the time it was conducting its hearings regarding segregation:

The available scientific evidence indicates that much, perhaps all, of the observable differences among various racial and national groups may be adequately explained in terms of environmental differences. . . . It seems clear, therefore, that fears based on the assumption of innate racial differences in intelligence are not well founded.

15 C. B. Davenport and M. Steggerda, *Race crossing in Jamaica* (Carnegie Instn. Publ. 1929, No. 395).

16 O. Klineberg, *Race differences* (New York: Harper & Bros., 1935), p. 189.

17 F. C. McGurk, A scientist's report on race differences, *U. S. News and World Report,* September 21, 1956.

18 Social scientists call innate differences theories scientifically unjustified, *SPSSI Newsletter,* November, 1956.

In view of the evidence presented, it may be concluded that little support is given to those who would explain psychological differences between ethnic groups on the basis of inherent racial or constitutional factors. Clearly they have the burden of proof to establish their case.

AREAS OF PREJUDICE

The reaction of the in-group to the out-group, or the ethnic majority to the minority group member, is known as prejudice. Gordon Allport defines prejudice as: "an avertive or hostile attitude toward a person who belongs to a group, simply because he belongs to that group, and is therefore presumed to have the objectionable qualities ascribed to the group."[19] Briefly, a prejudice is an unfavorable attitude toward an individual, group, or activity. Furthermore, it is an attitude formed without knowledge of all the relevant facts —a persisting "prejudgment" or snap judgment. Prejudice is conspicuously present in the case of the individual who exhibits rigidity toward changing his attitude when he is presented with further information about the subject.

Some understanding of the scope of the problem may be derived by examining the history of prejudice as it has affected some of the major ethnic groups in the United States:

Negroes. Of the nearly sixteen million Negroes in the United States, over 70 per cent of them still live in the southern states. However, in both the South and North the Negro is treated with discrimination. Undoubtedly the long history of the Negro as a slave plays no small role in his unfavorable position.[20] Racial prejudice is less practiced in Brazil, where slavery, which existed nearly twenty years later than in the United States, was not identified exclusively with one racial group. In addition to historical factors are the causes relating to economic, psychological, and social advantage that the white enjoys as a result of a dual society.

In the South the situation of the Negro after 1865 may have been worse than before the Civil War and the end of slavery. Under the antebellum social order the Negro possibly enjoyed more security and personal identification than he has with "freedom"—especially when the freedom is ridden with anxiety and is associated with wide-scale differentiation of social status and economic dependency. Periodically the Negro has been subject to mass violence beginning

19 G. W. Allport, *The nature of prejudice* (Reading, Mass.: Addison-Wesley Pub. Co., Inc., 1954), p. 7.

20 See Naomi Friedman Goldstein, *The roots of prejudice against the Negro in the United States* (Boston: Boston University Press, 1948).

with the Ku Klux Klan movement after the Civil War, which had a revival in the 1920's. One finds a counterpart to the Klan in the present activities of White Citizens Councils that came into being following the Supreme Court decision of May 17, 1954, regarding school segregation.[21]

At least five types of segregation exist in varying force in the South: residential, political, occupational, educational, and transportational. In addition, there are discriminative practices in the courts and the disenfranchisement at the polling booth. Health facilities are distinctly limited; segregation is practiced in hospitals and even in morgues. It was not until 1946 that a Negro veteran could be buried at Arlington National Cemetery. More recently in Washington, D.C. (which is on the border of the South) the management of a cemetery for pets stated they would accept only animals belonging to whites. "In announcing this policy, the owner stated he assumed the dogs would not object, but he was afraid his white customers would." [22]

In the North restrictions are less far reaching. In fact, state laws regarding interracial marriage remain as almost the only form of legal segregation. Yet less formal means of discrimination keep the Negro "in his place." In one New England town of 10,000 with less than 2 per cent of the population colored, according to a recent study, separation is most acute in housing, and, in decreasing order, in more desirable types of employment, in social and religious activities, politics, and lastly in education.[23] As with the South, change in the North is apparent particularly since World War II, in the mobility and more permissive relationships of Negroes. Nonetheless, subtle and not-so-subtle varieties of discrimination are still practiced. It has often been stated that the Negro experiences more anxiety and personality conflict in the North than in the South because of the vagueness and unpredictability of specific social situations that may confront him. The mores and folkways are more precise in the South, whereas the lack of specificity in Chicago or Cornerville may elicit vacillation and uneasiness. The rural Negro who migrates to urban centers may in some cases be so conditioned

[21] For an early appraisal of the effects of the Court's decision, see K. B. Clark (ed.), Desegregation in the public schools, *Soc. Problems*, II, April, 1955. More recent accounts are: J. D. Grambs, *A guide to school integration* (New York: Public Affairs Pamphlets and SPSSI, 1957); and D. Shoemaker (ed.), *With all deliberate speed—segregation-desegregation in southern schools* (New York: Harper & Bros., 1957).

[22] K. M. Landis, *Segregation in Washington* (Chicago: The National Committee on Segregation in the Nation's Capitol, 1948), as reported in A. W. Green, *Sociology* (rev. ed.; New York: McGraw-Hill Book Co., Inc., 1956), p. 233.

[23] F. F. Lee, The race relations pattern by areas of behavior in a small New England town, *Amer. sociol. Rev.*, XIX (1954), 138-43.

Desegregation has fought a long battle in the sports of the North and the West; in the South it must apparently await integration in a number of other areas of society.

Discrimination in employment was abolished by law in some of the northeastern states as early as 1945.

to terror that he never feels at ease. Although Cayton's remarks do not have the same pertinence they may have had a decade or two ago, they portray the plight of a Negro caught in the bewildering life of the Northern city:

But how, one might ask, even if that fear characterizes the people of the South, would people in Northern cities such as New York, Chicago, Detroit, and Cleveland be affected by it? My hypothesis is that Negroes are so conditioned by this and other forms of violence (and their defenselessness before such terror) that there has developed in the group what might be called an oppression phobia. . . . The collective experience of the Negro people has been such that even when they are in the North they fear the violence which they or their parents experienced in Mississippi.

It is difficult, without this concept, to explain why, in a state which has a civil rights law, an eminent Negro lawyer, perhaps even one employed by the Court, will shamefacedly leave a restaurant when told by a slip of an illiterate white waitress that he will not be served. The law is on his side. He knows that cases have been won on such issues. He may be, as I have indicated, an officer of the Court itself. But the fear he experienced in Mississippi when a Negro was burned alive for talking back to a white girl dissolves his manhood.[24]

The toll of discrimination as shown in personality manifestations has been partially told in Chapter 5. Seward reports a number of illnesses; for example, vitiligo, a rare skin disease, and peptic ulcers. It is notable that both of these occur mainly among Northern Negroes.[25] Neurotic and even psychotic symptoms, along with a relatively high incidence of delinquency and economic dependency, signify an unhealthy and unhappy Negro population. In addition, discrimination means a loss of human resources, as segregation prevents the Negro community from making its full contribution to the national employment market.

At present the gradual emergence of the Negro from his traditional caste status anticipates a fuller development of his capacity. A number of recent reports indicate that even within the South the Negro is enjoying more occupational mobility than was true a generation, or even a decade ago. White employers are now more interested in developing technical skills.[26] The future of this development depends not only on attitudinal maturity of the American public and its government, but on the level of economic prosperity and on the solution of international tensions.

[24] H. Cayton, The psychology of the Negro under discrimination, in A. M. Rose (ed.), *Race discrimination and prejudice* (New York: Alfred A. Knopf, Inc., 1951), p. 277.

[25] G. Seward, *Psychotherapy and culture conflict* (New York: The Ronald Press Co., 1956), pp. 149-50.

[26] H. A. Bullock, Urbanism and race relations, in R. B. Vance and N. J. Demerath (eds.), *The urban South* (Chapel Hill: The University of North Carolina Press, 1954), pp. 207-29.

Jews. In the United States there are over five million Jews, or approximately half of the world's Jewish population. Despite the enormous contribution the Jews have made to Western culture, discrimination has existed throughout much of history. During the Middle Ages the Jew was confined to the ghetto. Later, Pope Innocent III decreed a badge to be worn so there would be no mistaking Gentiles and nonbelievers. Here again is represented the basic fallacy of the stereotype: errors can be made despite the "obvious" physical and mental signs. Without the badges intermarriage might have occurred and the "pure Christian race" might have become impure.

In contemporary American society, the Jew has been exposed to more subtle forms of discrimination: quotas in the "Ivy League" colleges, biases in employment interviews, restrictions in clubs, resort hotels, and the like.[27] Often the Anglo-American may happily work alongside the Jew, or other minority group member, but at the end of the day prefer to go with his own friends, who, somehow, are "nicer" people. In contrast to certain other ethnic groups, the Jew is blamed for his efficiency and superior achievement. Since fear is at the basis of anti-Semitism, it must be rationalized in other terms; hence, the "race" is clannish, grasping, aggressive, etc.

Perhaps the outstanding study of anti-Semitism is Bettelheim and Janowitz's investigation of 150 veterans in the Chicago area. From the veterans, all of whom had been randomly selected and formerly of enlisted rank, four general reactions were noted: (1) *tolerant,* those who felt no overt prejudice against the Jew, constituting 41 per cent of the sample; (2) *stereotyped anti-Semitic,* expressing epithets such as "materialistic" and "aggressive," but felt that these qualities were not sufficient reasons for discrimination, 28 per cent; (3) *outspokenly anti-Semitic,* rationalizing restrictions, as employed in Nazi Germany, but not necessarily advocating them for the United States, 28 per cent; (4) *intensely anti-Semitic,* maintaining that the Jews are dangerous and must be constantly limited in their activities, 4 per cent. The difference between categories 2, 3, and 4 is largely a matter of "controls," both external and internal. Some of the stereotyped anti-Semitic might have been more intense had they not felt it undignified to express such hostile remarks in regard to an ethnic group. The intense anti-Semite might have advocated restrictions if it were not opposed to his democratic ideology. More significant were the security needs of the individual—

27 See S. Marcson (ed.), Segregation and integration in college fraternities, *Soc. Problems,* II, January, 1955.

namely, the role of frustration and emotional conflict as they affected the degree and pattern of anti-Semitism.[28]

It hardly needs to be repeated that the Jews actually meet none of the criteria of race. They cannot be distinguished in any reliable fashion from other groups. Nor is it possible to label them as a religious group, since approximately half of the Jews in America have no active religious participation. Also, they have been incorrectly referred to as a nationality. Except for the million and a half Jews in Israel, they are identified completely with their respective national groups. It would be difficult to consider the Jews a distinct cultural entity since there is almost as much heterogeneity in Jewish culture as in the total American pattern. It would be difficult to find any valid demarcation of the group, although a kind of loyalty or identification generally exists among people who call themselves Jews. In some cases the members of this aggregate refer to themselves as Jews simply because they have ancestors who carried this label. In any case, Jews are not a race.

As a target of discrimination, and constantly exposed to cultural conflict, the Jew experiences considerable ambivalence. Self-hatred among Jews is probably less intense than among Negroes, yet there are studies indicating pronounced self- and group-devaluation.[29] In some cases this leads to a rejection of both the traditional Jewish group and the dominant Anglo-Saxon pattern.[30] A Los Angeles study showed that 46 per cent of petitions for change of name came from Jews, although they constituted only 6 per cent of the population. The desire for changing one's name is probably due to a number of factors beyond anti-Semitism. Yet it is remarkable that Polish and Russian names of non-Jewish persons were not changed. Here changing implies some rejection of one's own group.[31]

Orientals. Both the Chinese and Japanese have been subject to marked discrimination, if not persecution. Both groups have been severely regulated by legal action, especially as concerns their entry into and residence in the United States. From the 1880's to the present there have been a number of exclusion acts. Most notable of these was the act of 1924, which ended for all practical purposes Asiatic immigration to the United States. Undoubtedly the passage

28 B. Bettelheim and M. Janowitz, Dynamics of prejudice: a psychological and sociological study of veterans (New York: Harper & Bros., 1950).

29 K. Lewin, Self-hatred among Jews, in Rose, op. cit., pp. 321-32.

30 Seward, op. cit., p. 255.

31 The authors suggest that the desire for change of name may result from status mobility and possibly suggests the final act of assimilation. See L. Broom, H. P. Beem, and V. Harris, Petitions for change of name, Amer. sociol. Rev., XX (1955), 33-39.

and retention of this act had no small part in fanning anti-American feeling in Japan prior to World War II.

Orientals, who number about two hundred thousand for the entire country, have been concentrated on the West Coast, especially in California. Individuals and organizations in that area became through the decades fairly expert in identifying the "racial type." Although differing somewhat for Japanese and Chinese, the Oriental was considered by nature to be "inscrutable," "non-Westernizable," and "subhuman" in his living standard. Whatever correspondence the stereotype may have had to reality was due to the social and economic forces that prevented the Oriental from developing Western ways.

The Chinese were first brought here in sizable numbers as railway labor following the Civil War. When the need for this cheap labor supply was removed, discrimination appeared in the form of both stereotypes and legal sanctions. Confinement to urban centers was largely based on the adoption of trades that encouraged survival, as, for example, restaurant and laundry establishments. One complication in the adjustment of the Chinese was the fact that migration to the United States was for lengthy periods almost exclusively male. The custom of bringing in "mail-order" or "picture-postcard" brides was prohibited from time to time by the Chinese or United States governments. By the 1930's Chinese Americans were finding their status somewhat less unsatisfying because of the sympathy of the American people for the plight of the Chinese caught in the Japanese invasion. Various factors, including gradual reduction of prejudice in the United States, has favored partial assimilation of the Chinese. It is noticeable that the number and importance of "Chinatowns," so characteristic of several American metropolises, has declined.[32] As with other minority groups, civil service and liberalization of hiring practices have permitted the Chinese new and more varied occupational roles.

The Japanese-American community has been larger in number and subject to even harsher condemnation than the American Chinese. The concentration on the West Coast in such activities as farming, fishing, and merchandising was resented by white competitors. As with the Jew, their hard work and efficiency called forth projection and displacement on the part of the in-group. The Japanese attack on Pearl Harbor on December 7, 1941, provided the excuse. At the urging of a number of organizations and of certain journalists, including Westbrook Pegler, the government (with the

---

[32] R. H. Lee, The decline of Chinatowns in the United States, *Amer. J. Sociol.*, LIV (1949), 422-32. Reprinted in Rose, *op. cit.*, pp. 146-60.

hearty recommendation of General John DeWitt of the Western Defense Command) forced the evacuation of practically all west coast Japanese to relocation centers deep in the interior of the country. This was all the more significant in that the Japanese in Hawaii were not involved in a similar exile. It may be added that no act of sabotage, as far as is known, was perpetrated by American Japanese either on the mainland or in Hawaii. The fact that the removal fell on *Issei,* first generation, and *Nisei,* second generation, alike testifies to the "scapegoating" nature of the forced exile.[33]

The return from relocation centers was aggravated by loss of property and employment and, most of all, by the demoralizing experiences of detention. However, the Japanese Americans have made an impressive recovery. For one thing, their resettlement has been less concentrated geographically, which makes the group less vulnerable to future discrimination. For instance, many of them are now located in the Midwest, a movement that commenced in the late war period. Consequently, more Americans have an opportunity to become acquainted with them. The postwar prosperity has allowed them remunerative employment and more occupational mobility than was possible before the war. As a third generation of Japanese are now coming of age, the assimilation process is nearing completion. Undoubtedly, too, the guilt feelings on the part of "true" Americans for the relocation episode have made them more accepting of the Oriental.

Other minorities. The history of successful and not-so-successful accommodation and assimilation could be repeated for other non-European groups. There is the paradox of the American Indians who number over three hundred thousand and experience discrimination when they attempt to participate in full citizenship. In Chapter 3 were discussed some of the conflicts of this group as members of two cultural worlds. Besides the social and economic disadvantage they have suffered, severe psychological dislocations are present as well. It is significant that though the larger society rejected this minority group, in wartime these individuals were expected to fulfil their military obligations. The returning veteran experienced considerable frustration in making the transition to his tribal setting.[34]

33 D. S. Thomas and R. S. Nishimoto, *The spoilage, Japanese relocation and resettlement* (Berkeley, Calif.: University of California Press, 1946).

34 The readjustment was only partially successful and was differentially received. In the Hopi culture the returning veteran was expected to overcome the detribalizing effects; among the Navahos he was celebrated as having had experience in the outside world. See J. Adair and E. Vogt, Navaho and Zuñi veterans: a study of contrasting modes of culture change, *Amer. Anthropol.* LI (1949), 547-62.

On the whole, however, since 1933 when John Collier was appointed as Commissioner of Indian Affairs, there has been a notable betterment of white-Indian relations. The present policy of integration may culminate in the abolition of reservations, a transitional and generally unsatisfactory form of protecting the Indian against discriminative practices. As with the Negro, fuller absorption into American life should find these "first Americans" achieving and contributing equally if they are treated as equals.

The Mexicans, who number something over two and a half million, are concentrated largely in the Southwestern States within a few hundred miles of the border, though there has been in recent years some movement of this group into other parts of the country, notably the Midwest. Incapacitated in the eyes of the "Anglos" (the in-group) by economic, moral, religious, and linguistic inferiority, it has been a struggle for this group to find genuine identity. Most acute discrimination has been experienced in Texas. On the labor front, they have had even less success than other minority groups in finding adequate employment, in many areas being largely confined to the role of seasonal agricultural labor. Their status has been further complicated by the problem of legal entry into the United States. A more liberal policy on the part of the United States government has partially resolved the situation, but illegal entry by the "wetbacks" continues due to attraction of the American economy and the surreptitious cooperation of industrial agriculturists hungry for a cheap labor supply. The Mexican's relegation to this role has only served to strengthen the stereotype of dirtiness, ignorance, and laziness. In certain agricultural areas of southern California his low status is equalled only by the Negro, although the latter is less favored as a field worker.[35]

How much intergroup prejudice exists in the United States? The amount is great, though figures are somewhat elusive. Opinion and attitude research has given approximations; the figures found by Bettelheim and Janowitz have already been mentioned. Campbell, for example, found in 1942 that about 40 per cent of his national sample made unfavorable comments about Jews.[36] Gordon Allport, in 1944, gave the following over-all summary of prejudice in the United States:

Drawing our evidence chiefly from published and unpublished public opinion polls, we may estimate roughly that one-fifth of our people are implacable Anglophobes; five to ten percent are violently anti-Semitic, while perhaps forty-five

[35] E. C. McDonagh, Attitudes toward ethnic farm workers, *Sociol. soc. Res.*, XL (1955), 10-18.

[36] A. A. Campbell, Factors associated with attitudes toward Jews, in Swanson *et al.*, *Readings* (2d ed.), pp. 603-12.

percent more are mildly bigoted in the same direction. At least forty percent express prejudice against the Negro. The numbers that are anti-Catholic, anti-Russian, anti-labor, anti-Protestant vary, but in all cases the proportion is fairly high.[37]

Any such summary, however, fails to indicate the ramifications of prejudice in our country. Many sectional and local patterns are overlooked. Prejudice against French Canadians is observable in some of New England and northern New York, as is anti-Oriental feeling in the Far West and prejudice against Spanish-Americans in the Southwest. At one time, cities like Buffalo and Detroit manifested anti-Polish sentiment; anti-Italian attitudes have been common in many localities. Add to all this the less intense prejudices found in any community—the disapproval of those with foreign names or with accents, of those who dress badly, of those who live on the wrong side of the tracks—and a staggering total results. Probably well over half our population have felt the sting of prejudice— perhaps everyone except the minority of native-born Anglo-Saxon Protestants!

THE FUNCTIONING OF PREJUDICE

The formation of ethnic attitudes. Ethnic attitudes were at one time regarded as instinctive: one somehow knew intuitively that he belonged to a superior group. According to the Hartleys this belief still is prevalent in the South.[38] When asked how children acquired their race attitudes, the parents reported "by instinct"; after all, race differences are "inborn." On a more intellectual basis, certain authorities have argued that since physical differences, such as skin color and hair texture, are organic, preferences must also be innate, or at least learned on a very primitive and deep-seated basis.

In reality, *all* prejudice is a result of environmental influences, whether through chance events or deliberate instruction. The major social institutions (family, school, etc.) structure the individual's cognition to form positive or negative attitudes along given variables: economic status, hereditary privilege, categories of color, or other physical disposition. Undoubtedly historical factors, as has already been implied, play a major role in this process. For instance, not least important in the present low status of Negroes is the fact that his ancestors were slaves, and slavery as an institution in this country was identified with the Negro. In contrast, Brazil has had less discrimination against the Negro, which may be related

37 G. W. Allport, The bigot in our midst, *The Commonweal*, October 6, 1944.

38 E. L. Horowitz, The development of attitude toward the Negro, *Archives of Psychology*, No. 194, 1936, as reported in E. L. Hartley and R. E. Hartley, *Fundamentals of social psychology* (New York: Alfred A. Knopf, Inc., 1952), pp. 701-6.

to the different historical development in that country whereby slavery was not confined to any single racial group.

A fundamental question for the psychologist is to determine the precise means by which the individual acquires prejudice. One important consideration is the early age at which prejudice is evident, according to the surveys made in this area. For example, the Clarks found in an experiment involving the choice of white and colored dolls, that children as young as three years were able to select the doll that looked "like the white or colored child." [39] Apparently by five years these choices represented actual preferences on the part of the child.[40]

The Hartleys point to three stages in the development of ethnic attitudes of children, namely, *differentiation, identification,* and *evaluation.*[41] *Differentiation,* the first stage, refers to the ability of the child to distinguish between two or more racial groups on a recognition test, as with the Clark experiment. *Identification,* the second stage, might be described as a type of ego-involvement with one's own group. Tests, such as the Hartleys' "Show me the one that looks like you," is an indication of a growing race awareness that utilizes the self as a frame of reference. The third phase, *evaluation,* is the emergence of reactions of superiority and inferiority. Goodman, in an extensive study, found that the majority of a white and Negro sample of children were able to identify racial characteristics by the age of five, although there was considerable variation in the accuracy of their judgments. There was little racial hostility in making the identifications but reticence or embarrassment appeared on the part of some Negro subjects.[42]

As the child goes through elementary school, the adult attitudes are further introduced and crystallized in his experience. In fact, it is the parents who play the dominant role in developing prejudice. This parental conditioning is not only through direct indoctrination, but is implemented by innuendo, negative gestures, tone of voice, as the parents talk about the people next door or who should be chosen as a playmate.[43] Allport and Kramer found that 69 per cent of a college-student sample stated that they were influ-

[39] K. B. and M. P. Clark, Racial identification and preference in Negro children in Swanson *et. al., Readings* (2d ed.), pp. 551-60.

[40] Horowitz, *op. cit.*

[41] Hartley and Hartley, *op. cit.*

[42] M. E. Goodman, *Race awareness in young children* (Reading, Mass.: Addison-Wesley Pub. Co., Inc., 1952).

[43] G. W. Allport, *The nature of prejudice* (Reading, Mass.: Addison-Wesley Pub. Co., Inc., 1954), pp. 293-294.

enced by their parents in the formation of their ethnic attitudes.[44] In addition to the parents, the role of siblings and neighborhood play groups are instrumental in this selective process.

There are a number of institutional groupings that are critical in the structuring of ethnic attitudes. Both positive and negative findings have been reported in regard to the effect of education on the formation of race attitudes. For one, Campbell found a positive relationship between education and anti-Semitism.[45] In other words, through the school years the child and adolescent are deriving their ethnic biases. Generally speaking, however, most studies have indicated that higher education is favorable toward the reduction of prejudice. This is particularly true in the South, where college students have shown more liberalism in the area of integration than have their parents.[46] In one study it was found that a college sample was more tolerant of both Jews and Negroes than was an adult middle-class sample, largely without higher education. In Chapter 8, it was noted that the type of education and the selection of course material is the determinant in the success of changing attitudes. Much depends on significant variables: the personality of the teacher, the particular motivation of the students, and the home background.

Religion appears to be another conditioning agent. Again, the findings are not altogether consistent. In certain studies the Catholics were the least tolerant, the Protestants next, the Jews the most tolerant. Some studies have not revealed religion to be a significant factor in explaining prejudice, as in the study of anti-Semitism among veterans, where scores were the same for Catholics and Protestants.[47] Perhaps it is the degree of religious intensity that may be crucial. In an investigation of southern Catholic college students it was found that those reporting stricter religious practices were the least accepting of Jews and Negroes and, in addition, supported segregated schools. Those whose Catholicism appeared nominal were more tolerant.[48] In still another study, involving southern subjects, Catholics were more friendly than Protestants toward Negroes.[49] It is noteworthy that in the South, Catholic churches

[44] G. W. Allport and B. M. Kramer, *Some roots of prejudice, J. Psychol.,* XXII (1946), 9-39.

[45] A. A. Campbell, Factors associated with attitudes toward Jews, in Swanson *et al., Readings* (2d ed.), pp. 603-12.

[46] E. T. Prothro and O. K. Miles, *J. soc. Psychol.,* XXXVI (1952), 53-58.

[47] Bettelheim and Janowitz, *op. cit.,* pp. 50-52.

[48] C. T. O'Reilly and E. J. O'Reilly, Religious beliefs of Catholic college students and their attitudes toward minorities, *J. abnorm. soc. Psychol.,* XLIX (1954), 378-80.

[49] D. T. Spoerl, Some aspects of prejudice as affected by religion and education, *J. soc. Psychol.,* XXXIII (1951), 69-76.

are less likely to be segregated than are Protestant churches. Also, it may be that in the studies where Catholicism has been correlated with prejudice, the critical factor is nonreligious, such as low social rank or lack of formal education. We cannot say at this point precisely which are the most predictive factors in ethnic attitudes; we can merely present some relative correlations.

The problem of differential status. Fundamentally, as with all behavior, prejudice involves the definition of the self in the continuity of experience. The individual must impose meaning on the events that surround him. We have seen how in early life stimuli are structured so that the child realizes that individuals and groups about him are assigned positions of deference according to the color of his skin, the language he speaks, where he goes to church, and what kind of employment he secures. This area of attitudes was explored in Chapter 8 and some consideration was made of the problem of measuring social distance. In this discussion we are interested in the phenomenon of prejudice in its structure and patterning, rather than the methodology.

It was the early work on social distance that provided insight into the differential responses in regard to ethnic groups. In fact it was Bogardus who, in the 1920's, devised a social distance test by which individuals indicated their attitudes toward various national, racial, and religious groups, in these terms:

1. Would admit to close kinship by marriage
2. Would admit to my club as personal chums
3. Would admit to my street as neighbors
4. Would admit to employment in my occupation
5. Would admit to citizenship in my country
6. Would admit as visitors only to my country
7. Would exclude from my country [50]

Bogardus found very consistent tendencies to rank English, Scotch, and other North Europeans high in the list, South Europeans near the middle, and Negroes, Orientals, Turks, and Hindus at the bottom.

Later studies confirm Bogardus' findings.[51] When the test is taken by members of a particular racial or nationality group, the rankings differ only with respect to the position of their own group on the scale. Hartley's study demonstrates this neatly. He found

[50] E. S. Bogardus, Measuring social distance, *J. appl. Sociol.*, IX (1925), 299-308.

[51] E.g., J. P. Guilford, Racial preferences of a thousand American university students, *J. soc. Psychol.*, II (1931), 179-204; H. Meltzer, Group differences in nationality and race preferences of children, *Sociometry*, II (1939), 86-105; E. L. Hartley, *Problems in prejudice* (New York: King's Crown Press, 1946).

very high correlation coefficients (.68 to .95) in the rankings made by students at Princeton University, Howard University (Negro), two unidentified teachers colleges, City College of New York (with many Jewish students), Columbia University, and Bennington College (a progressive liberal arts college for women). Furthermore, Hartley found that the rankings he obtained about 1940 differed very little ($r=.78$) from those reported by Bogardus in studies made ten to fifteen years earlier. Apparently the prevalent American attitudinal patterns toward ethnic groups are remarkably consistent. Not only is the pattern of ranking consistent, but so is the content of the ideas or "stereotypes" about ethnic groups. G. B. Johnson surveyed books written about the American Negro over a period of nearly a hundred years.[52] He found fair agreement among the white authors; "on the whole there is a tendency for most of the current common stereotypes about Negro traits to appear over and over—laziness, improvidence, rowdiness, sexual looseness, superstition, love of music, and so on." [53] Also, though with some exceptions, the traits Negro writers assign to themselves are very similar to those assigned to them by white people.[54]

Katz and Braly found that Princeton University students showed great consistency in the assignment of traits characterizing ethnic groups.[55] Thus 84 per cent called Negroes superstitious and 75 per cent, lazy; 79 per cent called Jews shrewd; 78 per cent considered Germans scientifically minded. However, as noted earlier, the definiteness of the stereotype was not related to the degree of prejudice manifested. For example, great prejudice was expressed against Negroes and little against Germans, though a quite definite stereotype existed in both cases.

Almost twenty years after the last study, Gilbert repeated it on Princeton students to see if changes had occurred during the years of depression and world war.[56] Except for greater prejudice against the Germans and Japanese, he found the ethnic stereotypes much the same. However he did find that his college students in 1950 were more unhappy about making racial and national generalizations. Gilbert concluded that "college students today make fewer generalizations about ethnic character, but those they do make tend

52 G. B. Johnson, The stereotype of the American Negro, in O. Klineberg (ed.), *Characteristics of the American Negro* (New York: Harper & Bros., 1944).

53 *Ibid.*, p. 15.

54 *Ibid.*, p. 16.

55 D. Katz and K. W. Braly, Racial stereotypes of 100 college students, *J. abnorm. soc. Psychol.*, XXVIII (1933), 280-90 and Racial prejudice and stereotypes, *J. abnorm. soc. Psychol.*, XXX (1935), 175-93. See also Swanson *et al.*, *Readings* (2d ed.), pp. 67-73.

56 G. M. Gilbert, Stereotype persistence and change among college students, *J. abnorm. soc. Psychol.*, XLVI (1951), 245-54.

to be based more on cultural and historical realities and less on fictitious caricatures or the prejudices of their parents." [57] In other words, stereotypes continue, but they are somewhat less distorted than they were a generation ago.

Similarly, Bogardus obtained practically the same results on his scale in 1946 as he had in 1926. There were a few changes; for example, the Chinese gained, whereas the Japanese lost in prestige.[58] It was found in another study that the opinion toward the Russians was not favorable in 1938, high in 1942 during our wartime alliance, but again low in 1950 during the cold war.[59] Inevitably, attitudes toward ethnic groups are influenced by the political and social climate. One has only to reflect on the changes in feelings toward the Germans at the time we were fighting them and of the high status they enjoy today when we regard them as partners in the Western defense.

In this matter of ascribing status to minority groups, it is conspicuous that among lower socioeconomic classes more prejudice is elicited. The necessity for ego-expansion is felt most keenly by those who experience frustration of lower status. A number of studies have found that expressed attitudes follow this pattern. For instance, in an area of racial change in Chicago it appeared that integration, residential and otherwise, was less favored by lower class than by middle-class respondents.[60] In this connection, anti-Semitism bears a close relationship to failure to achieve upward mobility on the part of the individual and particularly a sudden sharp downgrading in status mobility.[61] Briefly, the ranking of ethnic groups depends on the position of the individual in the in-group.

The status of the minority group member determines, in all probability, the amount of social distance he feels toward the in-group. For example, Westie and Howard found that on the basis of interviews held with a sample of Indianapolis Negroes, the higher the status of the Negro, the less the distance expressed toward the white. Also, least distance was voiced toward high status whites, and most distance was expressed toward low status whites. In addition, there

[57] Ibid., p. 252.

[58] E. S. Bogardus, Changes in racial distances, Int. J. Opin. and Attitude Res., I (1947), 58-64.

[59] J. E. Marsh and M. E. Smith, Judgments of prejudice before, during, and after World War II, J. soc. Psychol., XXXVIII (1953), 31-37.

[60] A. E. Winder, White attitudes toward Negro-white interaction in an area of changing racial composition, J. soc. Psychol., XLI (1955), 85-102.

[61] Bettelheim and Janowitz, op. cit., pp. 55-61. See also, W. C. Kaufman, Status, authoritarianism, and anti-Semitism, Amer. J. Sociol., LXII (1957), 379-82.

was more flexibility and reserve in the judgments of the upper status Negroes.[62]

The foregoing evidence indicates that a "scale of social distance" or prejudice exists as a part of the culture pattern. The developing child learns this scale from his "membership" and "reference" groups,[63] which reflect the cultural norms, though with some variations. These patterns of prejudice, with their stereotyped conceptions, show great consistency and persistence even though the individual encounters many exceptions. Thus, one can be very friendly or even intimate with individual Jews or Negroes, yet maintain intact the unfavorable stereotype and the prejudice. It can be true that some of a person's "best friends are Jews" and that at the same time he is definitely anti-Semitic.

The role of perception. One can hardly escape the judgment that the expression of prejudice is largely a matter of perceptual relativity. In other words, one perceives the behavior of other individuals according to certain social and cultural norms. The world about one either makes sense or it does not. Certainly to a Southerner, and perhaps to a Northerner, it seems appropriate for a Negro to be a bootblack but hardly a diner at one's favorite restaurant. We have already stated that status relationships are the basis of prejudice. It is the perception and definition of the situation that determines the individual's responses and the impression of prejudice. A sample of college students was shown a number of rearranged photographs of the Negro in a stereotyped situation (a Negro walking in a slum) and then in a nonstereotyped situation (a Negro as a passenger on a yacht). The investigators found (1) that their subjects tended to perceive the picture more in terms of the situation, i.e., what the Negro or white might be doing, rather than in facial characteristic or the like. (2) When the Negro was seen in a stereotyped situation he was described more unfavorably than in the nonstereotyped settings—"a situation in which the mass media generally portray white persons." (3) Prejudiced persons (as measured on an attitude scale) tended to explain the meeting or association of Negroes and whites in nonstereotyped situations as unplanned or coincidental, whereas the nonprejudiced ascribed the juxtaposition to something more than a casual meeting, such as the action of friends. (4) In comparison to the unprejudiced, the

62 F. R. Westie and D. H. Howard, Social status differentials and the race attitudes of Negroes, *Amer. sociol. Rev.,* XIX (1954), 584-91.

63 See M. Sherif and C. W. Sherif, *An outline of social psychology* (rev. ed.; New York: Harper & Bros., 1956), chaps. xviii and xix.

prejudiced respondents judged the Negroes as inferior to the whites in both stereotyped and unstereotyped situations.[64]

The problem of perception as affecting race relations is well demonstrated in Philadelphia, where the number of arrests of Negroes by policemen was studied.[65] The rate of arrests varied in different parts of Philadelphia, and within a given area the higher the arrest rate, the higher the policemen's estimation of the rate. In addition, those officers who overestimated Negro crime also exaggerated the number of Negroes on the police force. Hence, it appears that perception is a differential phenomenon depending on the individual's total need system. One perceives a minority group member in terms of the minority group. Findings that the estimation of the crime rate functioned on an exponential principle (geometric progression as opposed to arithmetic progression) imply that prejudice became progressively greater as white policemen effected arrests in Negro areas. The more they made arrests, the more they felt there was need for arrests and the more inferior the outgroup appeared to them. What we have learned of selective perception might lead us to believe that the policemen actually "witnessed" more delinquencies committed by Negroes, and somehow classified the dubious behavior of white adolescents and adults as simply momentary infractions not necessarily requiring attention.

This same problem of differential perception was studied on a sample of school children, in a projective test dealing with situations involving both a "white" individual, a light-skinned Negress, and a dark-skinned Negress, each functioning as a mother figure. When the children were tested by a white experimenter, they preferred the white mother and light-skinned mother. When tested by a Negro, they selected the light or dark-skinned figure. Thus, though many variables are present, the existing social situation is shown to be important in determining the perception of ethnic differences.[66]

Earlier we mentioned the term *perceptual defense* to indicate how perception may protect or support one's inner needs and security. In one experiment subjects were classified as to their degree of prejudice, then asked to judge the Negroidness of a series of faces differing from mulatto to definitely Negro characteristics. The more prejudiced subjects, in contrast to the neutral ones, perceived even the more Caucasian portraits as having relatively strong Negro

[64] A. B. Riddleberger and A. B. Motz, Prejudice and perception, *Amer. J. Sociol.*, XLII (1957), 498-503.

[65] W. M. Kephart, Negro visibility, *Amer. sociol. Rev.*, XIX (1954), 462-67.

[66] R. D. Treat, The color of the investigator as a variable in experimental research with Negro subjects, *J. soc. Psychol.*, XL (1954), 281-87.

traits. In other words, the anti-Negro individual intensifies the stereotyped features of the Negro.[67] The stereotype becomes an important part of perceptual defense. Thus prejudice functions to protect the ego amid the continuous barrage of perceptual stimuli.

Consistency and change. Perhaps one of the more hopeful aspects of ethnic relations is the lack of consistency, or specificity, of behavior. We have already mentioned the tendency to accept minority group members in certain situations (e.g., on the job) but within the same day to reject social relations with them in other situations (e.g., after hours, at the club, over the fence). In a study of race relations in the coal fields Minard reports the relatively equal status that Negro and white Southern coal mine workers demonstrate on the job and in work-oriented activities: union meetings, transportation to the mines. Yet off-the-job behavior is of a quasi-caste nature.[68] Somewhat similar reactions were encountered in Winder's interviews of a Chicago group. Negroes, although rejected by lower-class whites, were accepted within limitations among the middle class. Some housewives mentioned, for instance, that they would accept certain roles for the Negro, such as that of pastor providing he were "otherwise" qualified. Some of the factors that apparently influenced white attitudes toward acceptance of interaction were: favorable experiences in the past with Negro domestics and other help; situations that would not follow traditional lines of social distance, as with interaction among adolescents (due to some fear about intermarriage); and lack of strong competition between Negroes and whites for jobs and housing. There was particular anxiety among those individuals involved with a recently "invaded" neighborhood. In other words, the patterning of attitudes toward the Negro depended on the totality of experiences that had operated on the individual.[69]

Saenger and Gilbert found that there was little, if any, discrimination against Negro sales people in a sample of department stores in New York. In their hypothesis that prejudiced, as well as non-prejudiced clients, fail to reject Negro clerks, they maintain that the motives for accepting this service are greater than those for withdrawing, namely, the desire for quick service, democratic humani-

[67] P. F. Secord, W. Bevan, and B. Katz, The Negro stereotype and perceptual accentuation, *J. abnorm. soc. Psychol.*, LIII (1956), 78-83.

[68] R. D. Minard, Race relations in the Pocahontas coal field, *J. soc. Issues*, VIII (1952), 29-44.

[69] A. E. Winder, *op. cit.*, and White attitudes towards Negro-white interaction in a number of community situations, *J. soc. Psychol.*, XLIV (1956), 15-32.

tarian ideology, and the inappropriateness of nonconforming behavior.[70]

As implied in the preceding pages, reactions to minority groups vary enormously for groups and individuals and the particular situation confronting them. Likewise, reactions vary over a period of time, because of changed conditions: acquisition of new friends and the influence of their attitudes, frustrations of various types, and their changing Gestalt of motives and values. In other words, social norms function to determine how minority group members are regarded. The Sims and Patrick study is significant in this connection. They employed the Hinckley attitude scale with three populations: 97 Northern students at Ohio University, 115 Northern students at the University of Alabama and 156 Southerners at the latter institution. The mean score for the Northern students was 6.7; for the Southerners, 5.0. The Northerners in the South were midway between, and demonstrated consistently an increase in prejudice from their freshman to senior year.[71] Again, the frame of reference is a changing norm. Broadly speaking, it is this mutability of attitudes that makes possible the advances in race relations that are now occurring in many parts of our country.

PSYCHODYNAMICS OF PREJUDICE

The authors attribute prejudice to a set of cultural causes operating on a need system of the individual. The cultural factors include, among others, historical traditions and economic pressures. These sociocultural frames of reference are rationalized by the individual in his perceptual and cognitive processes, as explained in the last few pages. Beneath this conscious superstructure lies a set of unconscious, dynamic causes of prejudice. In fact, it is difficult to distinguish adequately between what are the more conscious and "rational" processes underlying ethnocentrism, and what are the unconscious and frequently neurotic needs and stresses.

Satisfying strong motives. From this point of view, prejudices persist because they satisfy certain needs or motivational tendencies. Some of these are economic. It is advantageous to Southern whites, for example, to have a lower stratum of Negroes to act as their servants and laborers. While this motivation is probably unconscious, for the most part, it sometimes comes near to the sur-

[70] G. Saenger and E. Gilbert, Customer reactions to the integration of Negro sales personnel, *Int. J. Opin. and Attitude Res.*, IV (1950), 57-76, as reported in G. Saenger, *The social psychology of prejudice* (New York: Harper & Bros., 1953).

[71] V. M. Sims and J. R. Patrick, Attitude toward the Negro of Northern and Southern college students, *J. soc. Psychol.*, VII (1936), 192-204.

face. For example, the school board in a Southern community is considering a proposal to build a fine new high school for its Negroes. Two or three members are uneasy; they wonder whether more education for Negroes won't make them "uppity" and dissatisfied with their lot. The question may even be raised whether Negroes won't refuse to do labor and domestic work if they have "too much education." Likewise, the discrimination faced by Jewish students seeking to enter medical and other professional schools traces, in part at least, to economic motives on the part of the dominant Gentile group.

Other needs served by prejudice are in the area of prestige and recognition. Prestige involves being superior to someone; prejudice helps keep some groups in an inferior status to whom other persons and groups can feel superior. Perhaps this type of dynamic tendency is shown most clearly in parts of the rural South where both whites and Negroes are depressed economically. The only superiority "poor whites" have is with respect to Negroes, hence their higher caste status satisfies a very strong need. Infraction of caste lines by Negroes is a very serious offense in the rural South, as suggested by the fact that the great majority of lynchings have occurred in small towns and rural sections.

Other needs of a more specific sort might be mentioned as possible bases for prejudice. Dollard, for example, stressed the wish of Southern white men to have sexual access to Negro women as a factor in the preservation of caste lines.[72]

A host of striking dynamic tendencies grow out of frustration. As we saw in Chapter 6 above, frustration leads to emotional reactions which press toward behavioral expression, often of aggressive character. Perhaps the clearest of the defense mechanisms making for prejudice is displacement. In the form of "scapegoating," it is responsible for much hostile and aggressive behavior directed against minority groups.[73] Nazi treatment of Jews, lynchings, and the programs and practices of ultranationalistic groups in the United States are examples, predominantly, of displacement growing out of economic and other frustrations.

Another reaction to frustration and insecurity is projection—the attribution to others of one's own tendencies and acts about which one feels guilty. Gordon Allport describes the mechanism in the following quotation.

[72] J. Dollard, *Caste and class in a southern town* (New Haven, Conn.: Yale University Press, 1937).

[73] See G. W. Allport, *The ABC's of scapegoating* (New York: Anti-Defamation League, 1948).

In the mental dynamics of bigotry one further twist is involved. It is, I think, the weirdest twist of which the human mind is capable. Besides venting our fury upon scapegoats for their alleged vices, we go still further and blame them specifically for our *own* sins and shortcomings. The term psychologists give this mental twist is *projection*. Though the label is new, the process is as old as humanity itself. Am I secretly ashamed of my wastefulness? Let my conscience be at rest, for behold, the army wastes "whole sides of beef." Do my fantasies wander a bit in lascivious directions? I should not feel sinful, for I ponder (and gossip about) the moral laxity of others. Does my conscience plague me for the low wages that I pay my Negro employees? I can be at rest, for *they* would only grow "biggety" if they had more money. After all, what a small thing my own greed is, for the Jew will skin you alive if he gets a chance. In the catalogue of indictments drawn by the Nazi against the Jews we find a faithful listing of the Nazi's own monstrous sins.

In short, we evade feelings of personal guilt by accusing others of the evils we ourselves practice. It was Goethe who said, "We never feel so free from blame as when we expatiate on our own faults in other people." The worst of it is that this mechanism of self deception is shielded from our own view. Though we may suspect its operation in others, we will almost certainly deny it in ourselves.[74]

If displacement and projection help to focus and direct our prejudices, another mechanism, rationalization, aids in making them stick. As we noted earlier, rationalizing is a process which justifies, to ourselves and others, attitudes and actions which are essentially irrational. Thus, to justify prejudice and discrimination against Negroes, we say they are unintelligent and naturally prefer menial work. We excuse anti-Semitic real estate covenants by stating that Jews are clannish by nature and prefer to be by themselves. One is reminded of the gigantic rationalization used by imperialist powers to justify their exploitation of colonial peoples—the "White Man's Burden." According to this, the "civilized" peoples have the duty to improve and care for the backward, inferior peoples of the world. Such rationalizations provide comforting justification for acts ranging from the mildly prejudicial to the definitely exploitative, and they prevent an honest appraisal of the facts.

The unconscious need system. At the basis of rationalization, projection, and displacement are many psychological dynamisms that are pressing toward conscious expression. One of these is a deep-seated hostility toward the self and the world. Frequently, self-hate is the basis of projection, as indicated above. One form of this is the "mote-beam mechanism," which may be defined as the tendency to exaggerate traits in others that we ourselves also have.[75]

[74] G. W. Allport, The bigot in our midst, *The Commonweal*, October 6, 1944.

[75] G. Ichheiser, Projection and the mote-beam mechanism, *J. abnorm soc. Psychol.*, XLII (1947), 131-33.

As Allport points out, Hitler very likely developed his intense hatred against Jews for a number of reasons. One of them was that he frequently was asked whether or not he was a Jew because of his own darker-than-average hair.[76] The Texan may hate the Mexican, or the Manhattanite may hate the Puerto Rican, because the immigrant is less tidy than the Anglo-American. Our native American dislikes his own lack of tidiness so he prefers to see this fault in another rather than face his own incompetence. Yet he might like to be more unrestrained and thus unconsciously envy the more carefree Latin attitude. Hostility is a dynamic and often inconsistent emotion. The concept of ambivalence poses this alternation between love and hate. Consequently self-hatred and self-love are in a sense interchangeable and become attached to some other individual or out-group. Frequently reference has been made to the Southern pattern, where both affection and rejection are demonstrated in white-Negro relationships.

Hostility may readily pass into aggression. Free-floating aggression is ready to spring into action on the part of many individuals. To some degree it is channelized into violence or quasi-violence, as indicated by the popularity of boxing matches (or in another culture, bullfights). Yet, for many individuals, the culturally approved outlets are not sufficient and some victimization must be directed toward a minority group. Hence, displaced hostility becomes a major cause of discrimination.[77]

Another aspect of this psychiatric approach to prejudice is the problem of guilt and anxiety. Much of self-hatred and fear is related to the existence of internal guilt. The individual feels guilty for what he has done, or for what he has not done, or even for what he would like to do but for some internal or external reason is blocked from direct expression. The man whose mother never treated him like a growing adult may have interiorized guilt and a feeling of rejection of both the mother and himself but is forced to find some one else guilty—a Jew, a Negro, or perhaps a Republican or Democrat. Any strong feeling, if repressed, may lead to guilt and anxiety. The Freudians and neo-Freudians have pointed to repressed homosexuality, for example, as a cause of deep-seated projections. The unconscious mind cannot permit the conscious expression of this antisocial urge either in thought, fantasy, or be-

[76] G. W. Allport, *The nature of prejudice* (Reading, Mass.: Addison-Wesley Pub. Co., Inc., 1954), pp. 388-89.

[77] For a more complete discussion of displaced hostility see J. Harding, B. Kutner, H. Proshansky, and I. Chein, Prejudice and ethnic relations, in G. Lindzey (ed.), *Handbook of social psychology* (Reading, Mass.: Addison-Wesley Pub. Co., Inc., 1954), Vol. II, pp. 1042-44.

havior. Consequently, the individual may indulge in protective ritualized thinking at the conscious level.

Prejudice and mental illness. In addition to the operation of mechanisms on the part of more or less normal people, we find prejudice playing a role in the lives of mentally ill persons, notably those with paranoid trends or obsessions. The paranoid individual suffers from delusions, notably of grandeur and of persecution; in many cases he attributes sinister motives to minority groups. The paranoid is impervious to self-criticism and rational argument; he represents closed-mindedness to the utmost degree. Allport finds a strong paranoid component in the psychology of a bigot, a peculiar proneness to projection and scapegoating. In similar vein the neurologist Wechsler interprets racial and religious hatred as a kind of group neurosis.[78] Prejudice and discrimination serve as a vicarious outlet and a flight from conflicts and frustrations. The emotional basis of a prejudice, says Wechsler, is illustrated by the contradictions which are involved in anti-Semitic and anti-Negro propaganda. For example, the Jew is accused as a capitalist exploiter and financial slave-driver, and also as a radical seeking to destroy capitalism.

Obviously, when an individual with paranoid or obsessional trends becomes a leader, he is in a position to share his irrationalities widely and to produce widespread misunderstanding and social conflict. The essentially psychopathic nature of Hitler and many of his lieutenants (e.g., Streicher, who directed the anti-Semitic campaign) has been brought out in practically all psychiatric and psychological interpretations of National Socialism.[79]

Some attempt to evaluate these theories of the relationship of mental illness and neurotic tendencies to prejudice was made in a number of surveys. Possibly the most far-reaching was *The Authoritarian Personality* by Adorno and his collaborators. The study dealt mainly with the personality correlates of a sample of California men and women. Specifically, it related the authoritarian personality structure with ethnocentrism. On the basis of Minnesota Multiphasic, Rorschach, and T.A.T. (Thematic Apperception Test) scores, neurotic tendencies were found to be relatively prevalent on the part of the prejudiced subjects. In fact, anxiety states, particularly among the women, were found to be identified with prejudice.[80]

[78] I. S. Wechsler, *The neurologist's point of view* (New York: L. B. Fischer Publishing Corp., 1945).

[79] E.g., R. Brickner, *Is Germany incurable?* (Philadelphia: J. B. Lippincott Co., 1943); E. Fromm, *Escape from freedom* (New York: Rinehart & Co., Inc., 1941).

[80] T. W. Adorno, E. Frenkel-Brunswik, D. J. Levinson, and R. N. Sanford, *The authoritarian personality* (New York: Harper & Bros., 1950), p. 909.

For instance, on the T.A.T., ethnocentric, as opposed to the non-prejudiced, subjects attributed to the protagonists in the pictures less enjoyment of sensual pleasures, less creativity, and less congenial relations with other individuals. Aggression was expressed in more direct form, and the individual was caught up with impersonal forces over which he had a minimum of control. On the other hand, the less prejudiced sublimated aggression into more constructive channels and were more likely to favor "inner rational decision" on the part of the heroes in the pictures.[81]

To summarize: we have been describing two types of approach to prejudice, the *socio-cultural* and the *psychodynamic*. Unfortunately some interpreters have a way of cleaving to one *or* the other, when obviously both the situational *and* the personality determinants are important. The Handlins expressed it well:

> In one sense, the causes of prejudice lie in the nature of the personality of the man who holds the prejudice. But they are also socially determined. Whether the impulses that result in prejudiced behavior shall find expression or not, the form in which they will show themselves, and the object upon which they will fix are the products of the time and place in which the individual lives.[82]

Perhaps the interpretation can be enlarged as follows. Historical-cultural influences clearly determine attitudes and prejudices toward ethnic groups, as shown by many social distance studies. However, these data do not indicate at all clearly which groups will suffer discrimination and scapegoating at a given time. Nor does a social distance test show which prejudiced persons will engage in discriminatory behavior. The potential scapegoats are disclosed, but actual discrimination and scapegoating depend upon the dynamic tendencies found in individuals. An insecure, frustrated, possibly paranoid person is primed for scapegoating—and it will probably take an anti-Semitic or anti-Negro direction because of our American frames of reference. (In an Irishman, however, it is more likely to be anti-British, or in a Texan, anti-Mexican.) In times of national stress, as during depression, during postwar readjustment, or during periods of "jitters," fears and insecurity are widespread and the stage is set for large-scale intolerance. During the 1930's, as noted earlier, membership in nationalist "hate" groups fluctuated up or down depending on whether economic conditions worsened or improved.

Thus cultural tradition furnishes the potential scapegoats, but actual scapegoating occurs only when frustration and insecurity enter the picture.

[81] *Ibid.*, p. 543.
[82] O. Handlin and M. F. Handlin, *Danger in discord* (New York: Anti-Defamation League, 1948), p. 7.

CHANGING ETHNIC ATTITUDES

During the past generation an increasing number of Americans have become concerned over the problem of prejudice in our country. The reasons for this interest are various. Partly it is a function of fear—fear that riots, lynchings, and other violence may increase—and of shame that the rest of the world will see the shortcomings of our democracy. More significantly, perhaps, it results from increasing knowledge about ethnic differences and their causes and realization of their relative insignificance compared to the ways in which groups are similar or equal. Then too, as we evaluate our democracy in the face of increasing authoritarianism, we realize more forcefully the inconsistency between democracy and ethnic prejudice. We are more aware than before of the irreconcilability of prejudice and the Golden Rule. And we seem more cognizant of the destructive effects of prejudice upon personality and the utter unfairness of judging a person according to an ethnic category rather than upon his merits as an individual.

Organizing against prejudice. During and since World War II, the number of organizations devoted to tolerance and the improvement of intergroup relations has grown tremendously. The 1945 Directory of Agencies in Race Relations listed 123 national organizations, excluding federal agencies. Hundreds of local and state organizations are also working on problems of intergroup relations.[83] Some of the larger groups represent ethnic minorities, such as the American Jewish Committee, Anti-Defamation League, National Association for the Advancement of Colored People, and the Urban League. Others are more inclusive, like the Council Against Intolerance in America, or the National Conference of Christians and Jews. Some have the scope of coordinating agencies, such as the National Community Relations Advisory Council, or clearing houses like the American Council on Race Relations.[84]

Despite a common goal, the many organizations devoted to improving intergroup relations manifest considerable diversity of specific aims and techniques. Studying seventy-five national organizations, Johnson found some primarily engaged in action and community organization, some concerned with education, some promoting cultural and recreational activities, others engaged in promoting legislation or securing legal redress, and a few undertaking

[83] See G. Watson, *Action for unity* (New York: Harper & Bros., 1947), chap. ii, for an account of the types of organizations in the field.

[84] See R. M. Williams, Jr., *The reduction of intergroup tensions* (Soc. sci. Res. Council Bull., 1947, No. 57).

research.[85] While this variety in activity may be worth while, it may also reflect lack of knowledge about the most effective ways to cope with the problem. As Williams says:

> It is clear that organized attempts to improve intergroup relations are numerous and significant. Considering the seriousness of the problems, the possibly dangerous results of inappropriate action, and the very great amount of time and money involved, it might be anticipated that these agencies of social engineering would systematically check the effectiveness of their efforts by appropriate research. With only a few exceptions, however, this has not been done until very recently. Such agencies as the Commission on Community Interrelations have begun to operate on the principle, "no action without research, no research without action." [86]

Commenting further, Williams notes several differing goals for programs of intergroup relations. A few groups are working toward complete "Americanization" or assimilation of different ethnic groups to one fairly homogeneous set of beliefs and behavior patterns. Other groups envisage the retaining of traditional culture patterns by ethnic groups, as they live together harmoniously and with tolerance in a mosaic type of society. Somewhere between these extremes comes *cultural pluralism,* in which distinctive cultural characteristics will be retained within a framework of shared American values and traditions. The doctrine of cultural pluralism represents a compromise position and is the viewpoint taken, although sometimes unconsciously, by most of the agencies in the field of intergroup relations.[87]

As to the means by which these groups seek to promote intercultural understanding and reduction of tensions, Watson has distinguished seven basic patterns, which he calls "exhortation," "education," "participation," "revelation," "negotiation," "contention," and "prevention." [88] Williams is somewhat more detailed, specifying political and legal pressures, organization of intergroup contacts, public commendations and awards, psychotherapy, and fact-finding.[89]

However, after careful examination of some fifty research studies of factors producing changes in intergroup attitudes, Williams comments that "the findings are largely inadequate as aids in matters of everyday decision and practice in action programs," though we know that some kinds of communication and contact are accom-

85 C. S. Johnson, National organizations in the field of race relations, *Ann. Amer. Acad. pol. soc. Sci.,* CCXLIV (1946), 117-27.
86 Williams, *op. cit.,* p. 8.
87 *Ibid.,* p. 11.
88 Watson, *op. cit.,* pp. 25 ff.
89 Williams, *op. cit.,* pp. 20 ff.

panied by a lessening of prejudice.[90] He proposes, therefore, a number of propositions for strategic research in the areas of hostility (its origin, types, and incidence), reactions of minority groups, and techniques or approaches for reducing intergroup tensions.[91]

TECHNIQUES FOR TOLERANCE

On the basis of our present knowledge, which are the most promising ways of reducing prejudice?

Let us start by mentioning several frequently used techniques which seem largely ineffective. First, it is clear that knowledge or information does not, per se, lead to increased tolerance. Years ago Donald Young found that a whole course on American race problems did little or nothing to reduce the prejudices of 450 college students.[92] More recently, Samelson showed that persons with a great deal of education may be more prejudiced than those with little.[93] She found that southern college graduates are just as well (or better) informed about the facts of racial differences and discrimination as are northerners with less education. But the southerners do not see that Negroes are being treated unfairly; regardless of their educational level, they are more prejudiced in their fundamental attitudes, because of conformity pressures from the community. While she found some evidence among northerners for a positive correlation between education and lack of prejudice, attitudes toward the rights of Negroes were not much affected by general education.

With respect to argument, also, there is no evidence that it is effective in reducing prejudice, probably because a person's ego-defenses are called into play. Yet argument remains the chief stock in trade of many well-meaning promoters of better intergroup relations.

Intergroup contacts. On the other hand, increasing contacts between different ethnic groups may reduce prejudice. One such experiment, Smith's study of the visit of a group of white graduate students to Harlem, the Negro section of New York, was mentioned in Chapter 8. MacKenzie made an extensive survey of changes in attitude toward Negroes as a result of contacts in war industries.[94]

90 *Ibid.,* p. 32.

91 *Ibid.,* chap. iii.

92 D. Young, Some effects of a course in American race problems . . . , *J. abnorm. soc. Psychol.,* XXII (1927), 235-42.

93 B. Samelson, Does education diminish prejudice? *J. soc. Issues,* I:3 (1945), 11-13.

94 B. MacKenzie, The importance of contact in determining attitudes toward Negroes, *J. abnorm. soc. Psychol.,* XLIII (1948), 417-41.

She found a notable improvement where white persons had met and worked with higher-status Negroes, especially if they had had a variety of contacts. She also discovered that willingness to associate with Negroes in one situation is closely related to willingness to associate with Negroes in other situations (e.g., working with, riding with, eating with, and living near Negroes).

Similar findings were also reported in a survey conducted by the Information and Education Division of the War Department.[95] Interviews were held with 250 white officers and platoon sergeants in twenty-four companies containing Negro platoons. Sixty-four per cent said they were relatively unfavorable at first about serving in a company with some Negro platoons. However, after serving in a unit with colored soldiers, 77 per cent said their attitudes had become more favorable toward them. Over 80 per cent stated that the colored soldiers in their company performed "very well" as compared with 16 per cent who said "fairly well." To the question "With the same Army training and experience, how do you think colored troops compare with white troops as infantry soldiers?" 69 per cent of the white officers and 83 per cent of the sergeants responded, "Just the same as white troops." Further evidence indicated that white and colored soldiers got along best together in the units which had the heaviest combat duty. Apparently the contacts induced by army service, especially being under fire together, brought about a marked increase in favorable attitudes of whites toward Negroes.

Deutsch and Collins compared prejudices found in integrated interracial housing projects with those in segregated bi-racial projects. The former were characterized by more friendly, neighborly contacts between Negroes and whites and by less prejudice in general. These results were due chiefly to the greater proximity of Negro and white families in the integrated project and to the new social norms favorable to friendly interracial relations.[96] Very likely, too, the residents were initially more liberal since they had chosen to live in an interracial area. The importance of entering a new group with different standards is underscored in a study of persons who had experienced marked changes in their attitudes. (Taking a job, going to college, entering the armed forces were the commonest situational changes.) Even more important for the stimulation

95 Report No. B-157 Information and Education Division. Army Service Forces, U.S. War Department, 1945. See Swanson *et al., Readings* (2d ed.), pp. 502-6.

96 M. Deutsch and M. E. Collins, *Interracial housing* (Minneapolis: University of Minnesota Press, 1951), pp. 122-23.

of more favorable attitudes was close personal contact with an equal status member of the minority group in question.[97]

Despite considerable casual and unsystematic use of clinical methods for reducing prejudice, their value is by no means clear. Apparently self-analyses may reveal the irrational origins of prejudice and initiate processes which eventuate in greater tolerance. Allport makes a good case for the necessity of catharsis as a part of the process of re-education, based upon his experience in teaching an extensive course in race relations to a group of officials.[98] Some evidence from clinicians indicates that the processes of therapy, especially group therapy with children, may bring about a diminishing of prejudicial attitudes.[99]

Intercultural education. Almost therapeutic, too, is the kind of group retraining which comes to those who participate in a community self-survey. The processes of planning the survey, collecting the facts, making interpretations, and the like, causes people to become identified with the undertaking and thus experience a diminution of their own prejudices.[100]

A great deal of current effort is directed toward intercultural education. The central theme is not to initiate courses on tolerance, but rather to make whole school programs intercultural, in the sense of increasing the student's understanding of cultural differences.[101] The youngsters become interested in Jewish holidays, Scandinavian cooking, Hungarian dances, and Slovak art. They visit the communities and homes of minority group members and come to know them as people and as Americans with distinctive cultural contributions. The school system of Springfield, Massachusetts, was one of the first to be organized on an intercultural basis.[102] There is some evidence, though not entirely conclusive, that children brought up under the Springfield Plan show less ethnic prejudice, as measured by the Bogardus Scale, than does a control group.[103]

[97] J. Watson, Some social and psychological situations related to change in attitude, *Hum. Relat.*, III (1950), 15-56.

[98] G. W. Allport, Catharsis and the reduction of prejudice, *J. soc. Issues* I:3 (1945), 3-10.

[99] See G. Konopka, Group therapy in overcoming racial and cultural tensions, *Am. J. Orthopsych.*, XVII (1947), 693-99; V. M. Axline, Play therapy and race conflict in young children, *J. abnorm. soc. Psychol.*, XLIII (1948), 300-310.

[100] M. H. Wormser and C. Selltiz, *How to conduct a community self-survey of civil rights* (New York: Association Press, 1951).

[101] See, e.g., W. H. Kilpatrick and W. Van Til (eds.), *Intercultural attitudes in the making* (New York: Harper & Bros., 1947).

[102] See C. I. Chatto and A. L. Halligan, *Story of the Springfield Plan* (New York: Barnes & Noble, Inc., 1945).

[103] D. T. Spoerl, Some aspects of prejudice as affected by religion and education, *J. soc. Psychol.*, XXXIII (1951), 69-76.

Trager and Yarrow conducted an experiment on intercultural education methods with first-grade children. One group was taught according to a carefully planned cultural pluralism approach—to show the part played by each ethnic group. A second group was taught by orthodox methods which did nothing to correct existing stereotypes. A third group had no intercultural training at all but engaged in craft work. Results showed a decrease in prejudice in the first group, an increase in the second, and no significant change in the third.[104]

Kagan compared the effectiveness of direct and indirect educative methods in reducing the prejudice of Christians against Jews.[105] The experimenter, a rabbi, was asked to teach the Old Testament in two summer seminars, one for Episcopal and one for Methodist students. In one seminar, conducted by the indirect method, no reference was made to anti-Jewish prejudices, nor were the students encouraged to speak of their attitudes toward Jews or of their experiences with them. The direct method included group discussion of anti-Jewish attitudes by the students and their Jewish instructor. Kagan found that "before" and "after" attitude tests revealed no change as a result of the indirect method. However, the direct discussion method did bring about a significant decrease in anti-Jewish prejudice, a change which was maintained eight months later.

Much of the effort spent by groups engaged in improving intergroup relations takes the form of propaganda and advertising pamphlets, leaflets, car-cards, radio talks, and even matchcovers. To date, the effectiveness of these efforts has not been gauged with any degree of accuracy.[106] We know that movies, radio talks, and the like *can* be effective in changing attitudes, and we know that emotional appeals are probably more effective than nonemotional ones.[107] But whether any particular campaigns and messages conducted by the antiprejudice groups are achieving their ends is uncertain. The same is true of novels like Lillian Smith's *Strange Fruit,* Richard Wright's *Native Son* and *Black Boy,* and Laura Hobson's *Gentle-*

104 H. G. Trager and M. R. Yarrow, *They learn what they live* (New York: Harper & Bros., 1952).

105 H. E. Kagan, *Changing the attitudes of Christian toward Jew* (New York: Columbia University Press, 1952).

106 Cf., however, the study of Mr. Biggott, cited in Chapter 10 above.

107 See, e.g., R. C. Peterson and L. L. Thurstone, *Motion pictures and the social attitudes of children* (New York: The Macmillan Co., 1933); W. H. Wilke, *An experimental comparison of the speech, the radio and the printed page as propaganda devices* (Arch. Psychol., 1934, No. 169); G. W. Hartmann, A field experiment on the comparative effectiveness of "emotional" and "rational" political leaflets in determining election results, *J. abnorm. soc. Psychol.,* XXXI (1936), 99-114.

men's Agreement. It would indeed be surprising if these had no effect upon prejudice, but the evidence is not yet at hand.

Tolerance by fiat. Legislation in the area of intergroup relations is aimed primarily at eliminating discriminatory behavior. Prejudices, being attitudes, cannot be changed by legal fiat. The FEPC during the war was instrumental in removing barriers to employment in the case of Negroes and members of other minority groups. New laws in Massachusetts, New York, New Jersey, and many other states prohibit the refusal of jobs to a qualified person for reasons of racial, religious, or other ethnic affiliation. Such legislation, of course, being contrary to the local mores in certain parts of the country, notably the South, is opposed vigorously. However, as Allport notes, folkways are changeable; in fact, the Jim Crow laws in the South created folkways.[108] Nondiscriminatory state legislation has established new folkways in factories and department stores.

The Supreme Court decision of May, 1954, outlawing segregation in public schools has become the center of tremendous controversy.[109] The fact that school integration is proceeding, however slowly, indicates the effectiveness of court action in changing the environmental supports of discrimination. In the border states some progress is being made toward ending educational Jim Crowism, although the Deep South offers tremendous opposition to integration. Reports from some of the areas where integration has been attempted, notably, Washington, D.C., testify to the ill-founded nature of the predictions that educational standards would be lowered.

In the same way it had been predicted that integration within the armed forces was impossible. Moreover, the South only reluctantly accepted the requirement that industrial plants producing defense materials subsidized by the Federal government be integrated. Yet, success with this kind of interracial experience has made it possible to reduce other barriers. Once Negroes and whites had bunked together in a common barracks, and worked together on a factory work bench, such symbols as separate entrances, drinking fountains, and bowling alleys become the more ridiculous; they continue to be supported in some cases only because of legal action or some other coercive measure. In fact, it was specifically found that within the defense plants of the South, integration on the job was followed by indifference to a number of separate facilities.[110]

108 Allport, *The nature of prejudice,* p. 471.
109 The decision was described in Chapter 5.
110 For a more complete study of these changes in the South, see L. Nichols, *Breakthrough on the color front* (New York: Random House, Inc., 1954). Also, The South vs. the Supreme Court, *Look,* April 3, 1956.

However, in some southern states there were trends in the opposite direction after the 1954 Supreme Court decision. State laws, for example, have been enacted to prevent bi-racial employment.[111]

A beginning has also been made in discovering effective techniques for counteracting prejudicial remarks. For example, in one study over 1,000 adults, in small groups, were presented with a dramatization of an incident involving an anti-Semitic remark, which was answered in two different ways.[112] One response emphasized the American tradition of fair play and equal treatment for all groups. The other stressed individual differences and the inaccuracy of generalizing about Jews as a group. Each answer was presented either calmly and quietly or in an excited, militant manner. Results showed the "American tradition" answer was effective in modifying attitudes; the other answer was not. The manner in which the answer was presented did not affect attitudes.

We should mention, in conclusion, what may be the most effective though the most difficult of all methods for reducing prejudice—social betterment. In so far as prejudice and discrimination arise from anxieties and frustrations, any reduction of the latter will be reflected in increasing tolerance and improved intergroup relations. As our nation, or any nation, progresses toward more widespread security, both economic and psychological, we may be confident that the problem of prejudice will diminish.

SUMMARY

Psychologists and social scientists are both interested in group differences, but the two groups have somewhat different approaches. The psychologist seeks to measure the amount of the difference and

111 While the United States and other nations are moving gradually toward desegregation and integration, South Africa has chosen the opposite direction. *Apartheid* (segregation) has become national policy, and the separation of the white minority and non-white majority is implemented by far-reaching legislation, with the ultimate goal of separate nations for "Europeans" and "natives." Most observers believe such policies will have serious consequences, certainly demoralization of both groups if not civil war and revolution. Among the considerable social psychological literature on South Africa are I. D. MacCrone, *Race attitudes in South Africa* (London: Oxford University Press, 1937); S. Patterson, *Colour and Culture in South Africa* (London: Routledge and Kegan Paul, Ltd., 1953): and A. H. Richmond, *The colour problem* (Edinburgh: Pelican Books, 1955.) For the position of one of the authors, see R. C. Williamson, Race relations in South Africa, *Sociol. soc. Res.*, XXXIX (1955), 165-70; and Crime in South Africa, some aspects of causes and treatment, *J. crim. law, criminol., and pol. sci.*, XLVIII (1957), 185-92.

112 A. F. Citron, I. Chein, and J. Harding, Anti-minority remarks; a problem for action research, *J. abnorm. soc. Psychol.*, XLV (1950), 99-126. C. Selltiz *et al.*, The acceptability of answers to anti-semitic remarks, *Int. J. Opin. and Attitude Res.*, IV (1950), 389.

test whether or not it is statistically significant. The social scientist is more interested in discovering the factors producing social differentiation. The social psychologist sees merit in both approaches; he searches first for significant differences, then tries to discover their determinants.

Studies of ethnic differences indicate that psychologically significant variations among groups are of cultural origin. The case is not entirely proved, however, because of the difficulty encountered in studying racial or constitutional factors apart from nationality, language, and other cultural influences.

Prejudice is a negative attitude toward an individual, group, or activity. Ethnic prejudices which, in varying degrees, are widespread in the United States spring from a belief that other groups are different and therefore inferior. Prejudices, like other attitudes, are definitely learned and are passed on from one generation to the next. Historical and cultural factors are responsible for a hierarchical scale of social distance which is remarkably constant within the United States. This scale establishes the relative ranking of ethnic groups, but people's needs and frustrations largely determine the timing and the intensity of prejudice and discrimination. Anti-Negro and anti-Semitic prejudices are latent in America; they pass over into actual intolerance during periods of economic stress and personal insecurity.

Much time and energy is being devoted to combating ethnic prejudice and intolerance in our country. We are only beginning to understand the most effective means to achieve this end. The best methods seem to be the increasing favorable intergroup contacts, intercultural education, and reduction of prejudice through psychotherapy and through gradual improvement in economic and social welfare.

SUPPLEMENTARY READINGS

Books of Readings

MACCOBY, E. E., NEWCOMB, T. M., AND HARTLEY, E. L. (eds.). *Readings in social psychology,* 3d ed. New York: Henry Holt & Co., Inc., 1958.
Deutsch, M., and Collins, M. E., The effect of public policy in housing projects upon interracial attitudes.
Frenkel-Brunswik, Levinson, D. J., and Sanford, R. N., The antidemocratic personality.
Star, S. A., Williams, R. M., and Stouffer, S. A., Negro infantry platoons in white companies.
Williams, R. M., Religion, value orientations, and inter-group conflict.
Yarrow, L. J., *et al.,* Interpersonal dynamics in racial integration.

BRITT, S. H. (ed.). *Selected readings in social psychology.* New York: Rinehart & Co., Inc., 1950.
  Anastasi, A., Major group differences.
  Klineberg, O., Race.
  Murphy, G., Murphy, L. B., and Newcomb, T. M., Attitudes of white children toward Negroes.

LINDZEY, G. (ed.). *Handbook of social psychology.* Reading, Mass.: Addison-Wesley Pub. Co., Inc., 1954.
  Harding, J., Kutner, B., Proshansky, H., and Chein, I., Prejudice and ethnic relations. Vol. II.

Other References

ALLPORT, G. W. *The nature of prejudice.* Reading, Mass.: Addison-Wesley Pub. Co., Inc., 1954.
  Unexcelled for its historical and particularly its psychological treatment of the subject, including a section on remedial aspects.

BARRON, M. L. (ed.). *American minorities: a textbook of readings in intergroup relations.* New York: Alfred A. Knopf, Inc., 1957.
  One of several excellent compilations of articles on ethnic problems.

BERRY, B. *Race relations.* Boston: Houghton Mifflin Co., 1951.
  Outstanding on the processes of group interaction—conflict, assimilation, segregation, and others.

BETTELHEIM, B., AND JANOWITZ, M. *Dynamics of prejudice.* New York: Harper & Bros., 1950.
  A study of veterans and anti-Semitism with both psychological and social approaches.

BROWN, F. J., AND ROUCEK, J. S. (eds.). *One America.* Englewood Cliffs, N. J.: Prentice-Hall, Inc., 1952.
  A compilation of essays on the history, contributions, and problems of ethnic minorities.

DAVIE, M. R. *Negroes in American society.* New York: McGraw-Hill Book Co., Inc., 1949.
  A relatively complete study of the history and processes of America's largest minority group, including the institutional aspects.

DOLLARD, J. *Caste and class in a southern town.* New Haven, Conn.: Yale University Press, 1937.
  An analysis of patterns of prejudice in the Deep South.

DUNN, L. C., AND DOBZHANSKY, T. *Heredity, race and society,* rev. ed. New York: New American Library of World Literature, Inc., 1952.
  A summary of the genetic theories of race presented in a thoroughly objective fashion.

FRAZIER, E. F. *Black bourgeoisie.* Glencoe, Ill.: Free Press, 1957.
  The middle class of the American Negro as seen by an outstanding Negro sociologist.

———. *The Negro in the United States,* rev. ed. New York: The Macmillan Co., 1957.
  A comprehensive history, with treatment of demography, institutional problems, and questions of adjustment.

GOODMAN, M. E. *Race awareness in young children.* Reading, Mass.: Addison-Wesley Pub. Co., Inc., 1952.
  An insightful approach to the formation of race attitudes among the youngest part of the population of an Eastern city.

HARTLEY, E. L., AND HARTLEY, R. E. *Fundamentals of social psychology.* New York: Alfred A. Knopf, Inc., 1952.
Chaps. xxi and xxii present an analysis of ethnic attitudes and their modification.

HUGHES, E. C., AND HUGHES, H. M. *When peoples meet.* Glencoe, Ill.: Free Press, 1952.
A delightfully written account of prejudice and ethnic groups from French Canada to South Africa.

KARDINER, A., AND OVESEY, L. *The mark of oppression.* New York: W. W. Norton & Co., Inc., 1951.
A profound study by two psychiatrists of the psychological bases and results of discrimination on the American Negro, well documentd with case studies.

KLINEBERG, O. *Race differences.* New York: Harper & Bros., 1935.
This classic work deals with the results of mental testing in different ethnic groups.

MACIVER, R. M. (ed.). *Discrimination and national welfare.* New York: Institute for Religious and Social Studies, 1949.
A committee of distinguished social scientists study the problem in its many aspects, with special reference to the problem of reducing ethnic discrimination.

McDONAGH, E. C., AND RICHARDS, E. S. *Ethnic relations in the United States.* New York: Appleton-Century-Crofts, Inc., 1953.
A readable text with sociological emphasis on the intergroup approach.

McWILLIAMS, C. *A mask for privilege.* Boston: Little, Brown & Co., 1948.
McWilliams has written extensively on most of our ethnic minorities. This one examines the antecedents of anti-Semitism.

ROSE, A. M. (ed.). *Race prejudice and discrimination.* New York: Alfred A. Knopf, Inc., 1951.
Some excellent readings in this general area.

SAENGER, G. *The social psychology of prejudice.* New York: Harper & Bros., 1953.
Theories and experiments on the psychology of prejudice.

SEWARD, G. *Psychotherapy and culture conflict.* New York: The Ronald Press Co., 1956.
The marginal role of minority group members as analyzed in a number of case studies.

SIMPSON, G. E., AND YINGER, J. M. *Racial and cultural minorities.* New York: Harper & Bros., 1953.
One of the most complete statements including historical, educational, economic, legal, and other institutional aspects of the problem.

WILLIAMS, R. M. The reduction of intergroup tensions, *Soc. sci. Res. Council Bull.,* LVII (1947).
A most adequate statement on the combating of prejudice.

23

Social Psychology and International Relations

For many years social psychologists have been interested in international relations and have been working in relevant areas of research and application. Several of these have been described already—culture and personality, especially, national character (Chapter 3), attitudes and attitude change (Chapter 8), public opinion and propaganda (Chapters 16 and 17), and ethnic relations (Chapter 22). The plan of the present chapter is to describe several more specific contributions to the study of international relations and the furthering of international cooperation.

CONTRIBUTIONS TO PEACE

The "inevitability" theory of war. It seems easier for scientists to cooperate in helping win a war than in helping prevent one. However, many social psychologists in the 1930's turned their efforts toward research and education in the areas of war and peace. Collaborative efforts by a number of SPSSI members over a period of years finally bore fruit in a yearbook, *Human Nature and Enduring Peace,* published just before the close of the war in Europe.[1]

This volume included a section entitled "The Psychologists' Manifesto," a series of forthright statements about war and peace signed by over 2,000 members of the American Psychological Association. The first of these statements answered the question: Is war inevitable—is man "instinctively" warlike?

[1] G. Murphy (ed.), *Human nature and enduring peace* (Boston: Houghton Mifflin Co., 1945).

War can be avoided: War is not born in men; it is built into men. No race, nation, or social group is inevitably warlike. The frustrations and conflicting interests which lie at the root of aggressive wars can be reduced and redirected by social engineering. Men can realize their ambitions within the framework of human cooperation and can direct their aggressions against those natural obstacles that thwart them in the attainment of their goals.[2]

In July, 1948, a group of eight internationally famous social scientists from six countries was brought together by the United Nations Economic and Social Council to consider the causes of nationalistic aggression and the conditions conducive to international understanding. Their statement began with this sentence: "To the best of our knowledge, there is no evidence to indicate that wars are necessary and inevitable consequences of 'human nature' as such." [3]

These statements express the views of the experts: war is not inevitable from the standpoint of "human nature." Perhaps a more important question is: Do people generally, over the world, accept these conclusions? Unfortunately, we do not know. But we do have evidence that they expect another war. For example, the National Opinion Research Center asked this question at intervals from 1945 to 1947: "Do you expect the United States to fight in another war within the next 25 years?" Just after V-J Day, about 40 per cent of the sample questioned expected a war, and 40 per cent did not. By March, 1946, the per cent expecting war had risen to over 65, and almost the same proportion continued into 1947.[4] Since then the proportions have varied depending on our relations with the Soviet Union, existence of tension spots in the world (Korea, Israel and the Near East, Hungary, Formosa, etc.), experiments with nuclear weapons, and the like. We can be sure that a substantial percentage deplore war but expect it to continue. And, as Allport says, *what people expect determines their behavior*.[5] This expectancy is an indispensable condition for war and obviously must be replaced by an expectancy of peace if war is to be avoided.

Understanding nationalism and its causes. Social psychologists and other social scientists continue to explore the obstacles to peace, of which one of the greatest is nationalism, or nationalistic prejudice. Sumner, many years ago, coined the term *ethnocentrism* for the view that one's group is the center of everything, that it is superior,

2 *Ibid.*, p. 455.

3 Tensions affecting international understanding, *Bull. Amer. Assn. Univ. Professors,* XXXIV (1948), 546.

4 See E. Maccoby and B. Willerman (eds.), Citizen participation in world affairs, *J. soc. Issues,* IV:1 (1948), 23.

5 G. W. Allport, The role of expectancy, in H. Cantril (ed.), *Tensions that cause wars* (Urbana: University of Illinois Press, 1950).

and that its folkways are the only right ones.[6] Patriotism he considered a kind of ethnocentrism, and chauvinism, "boastful and truculent group self-assertion," an extreme form of it.[7] More recently, scholars have used "nationalism" to express the same idea.[8] Numerous historical and anthropological studies have revealed that nearly every tribe, state, or nation, primitive or modern, gives evidence of considering its people and its culture superior to all others.

As the cause of war is, to a considerable extent, aggressive nationalism, one may well ask what causes nationalism. For one thing, there is a deep-seated ethnocentrism among the various peoples of the world, even in a primitive society. In fact, for a number of tribes the name for "man" is also the name of the tribe. Within the larger context of Western history, ethnocentrism has referred to one's locality—the village, or at most, the province. One was a Burgundian or a Norman; the concept of Frenchman was hardly current before the fifteenth century. The term "German" referred to a language until the nineteenth century; in fact, Bismarck gave the definitive mark to German national unity only in 1870. Likewise, Italians were actually Tuscans, Lombards, and the like until approximately the same period. However, increasingly since the Napoleonic period overt nationalism has gone hand in hand with the Industrial Revolution, military defense and expansion, educational institutionalization, and other aspects of a mobile, dynamic, urbanized society. More than one authority has implied that nationalism has replaced religion as a driving force in our modern world. No other concept or institution has been able to place a large segment of the population in uniform within the modern state, whether democratic or totalitarian.

Undoubtedly, one of the causes of nationalism is the deliberately cultivated stereotype by which one society judges others. We have already referred to stereotypes as the attitudinal identification of ethnic minorities or, for that matter, any out-group. One psychiatrist refers to national stereotypes as related to "anxiety fraught, eidetic or 'imaginary' people." [9] Undoubtedly, a stereotype does have the character of an eidetic image. Certainly the Katz and Braly and the Bogardus studies with their "follow-ups," cited earlier in the text, demonstrated that these responses to individuals of a national

[6] W. G. Sumner, *Folkways* (Boston: Ginn & Co., 1906), p. 13.

[7] *Ibid.*, p. 15.

[8] See, e.g., C. J. H. Hayes, *Essays on nationalism* (New York: The Macmillan Co., 1926).

[9] H. S. Sullivan, Tensions interpersonal and international: a psychiatrist's view, in H. Cantril (ed.), *Tensions that cause wars* (Urbana: University of Illinois Press, 1950), p. 108.

group remained relatively constant over a long period. In a recent survey of the stereotypes of an eight-country sample regarding members of several different national groups (Americans, British, Chinese, French, and Russians), it was found that four different generalizations could be made:

1. that there exists in all eight countries surveyed a tendency to ascribe certain characteristics to certain people;
2. that there is a uniform tendency of respondents of all countries, taken as a whole, to describe the Russians in the same terms, and somewhat less agreement on the Americans;
3. that stereotypes of one's own countrymen are invariably in flattering terms;
4. that the prevalence of complimentary over derogatory terms in a national stereotype is a good index of friendliness between nations.[10]

Although the stereotype is comparatively fixed, there are variations depending on historical events and the economic and psychological pressures that occur within a given nation or group. One recalls that Americans changed their stereotypes of Germans, Russians, and Japanese before, during, and after World War II.

Related to the problem of attitudes and stereotypes as a cause of nationalism and international tensions is the effect of cultural conditioning, whether in the form of parental remarks, formal education, or the information transmitted by the mass media (newspapers, radio, television, and motion pictures). Negative attitudes toward the out-group are reinforced by any number of cultural stimuli. In this connection it is amusing, or perhaps tragic, to observe that the South Korean Ministry of Education was forced to place a ban on "movies showing mistreatment of American Indians and reflecting colonialist thinking." It was pointed out that the Soviet Union could make political capital out of such Hollywood products, as Communists had already created a stereotype of Americans as attempting to enslave non-white racial groups.[11]

Another factor in the implementation of nationalism is the fact that a number of individuals profit from nationalism. It has become a vested interest, whether to a certain political columnist, a brigadier general who wants to become a major general, or, as was true in the days before World War I (and possibly since), a munitions manu-

[10] W. Buchanan and H. Cantril, *How nations see each other* (Urbana: University of Illinois Press, 1953), as reprinted in W. Schramm (ed.), *The process and effects of mass communication* (Urbana: University of Illinois Press, 1954), p. 204.

[11] *Time,* June 3, 1957.

facturer who may want to sell both newspapers and guns. It would appear that during the present cold war, it is safer, career-wise, for an atomic physicist to voice nationalist rather than internationalist ideas.

The latter point brings up still another factor. From the beginning of history it has appeared that the only defense is some kind of nationalism. To admit the equality of another nation has been to invite disaster. In wartime this is further implemented by the sacrifices of those fallen on the battlefield, calling for greater sacrifices from those still living. A national group becomes a shibboleth with all the cultural props of literature, religion, and political history. To give up American sovereignty would be a direct insult to all those who played a role in its making, from Washington, Webster, and Whitman to everyone who participated in at least one war. Although most individuals are aware of the luxury of sovereignty, it would be difficult to relinquish even if it were not for an enemy totalitarian communist state. In other words, the very condition that makes us aware of the need of world organization, namely, fear of Soviet Russia, prevents us from any far-reaching cooperation with at least a third of the world. This is not the place to delve into historical, philosophical, or moral theorizing, but these factors are all relevant to a psychological treatment of nationalism and the means of waging effective peace.

Still another factor in nationalism, as so ably demonstrated by Karl Deutsch in his *Nationalism and Social Communication*,[12] is the lack of effective communication between the peoples of the world and their governments. Although the present authors do not regard with enthusiasm the claims of semanticists that the world's problems are largely verbal, the lack of an international language and the vagueness of many abstractions in most languages have made for a minimum of common definitions. Again, vested interests have frequently prevented the diffusion of information. The "iron curtain" countries are particularly famous for this penchant; however, it is relevant to mention that the third largest city of the United States had for several years a public school board that frowned on the teaching of UNESCO ideas or use of its literature. One may well wish that in such a highly mobile society as the middle of the twentieth century represents there might be more opportunity for people, especially the young, to visit different parts of the world and

[12] Published jointly by the Technology Press of the Massachusetts Institute of Technology and John Wiley & Sons, Inc., 1953.

become personally acquainted with a larger number of "foreigners," their institutions, and outlook on the world.

In addition to nationalistic attitudes, cultural differences engender different values and ways of looking at the world. With their varying backgrounds, it is impossible for Americans, Russians, Germans, Englishmen, or Frenchmen to view the international situation similarly, as Emery Reves made clear in the opening chapter of his *Anatomy of Peace*.[13] Even if a given set of facts is objectively established, the peoples of different nations cannot perceive and interpret them in the same way. It was naïve to assume, for example, that the defeated Germans after World War I would perceive the Versailles Treaty as did the victorious Allies. Similarly, a good part of the misunderstanding and bad feeling after World War II has resulted from opposing interpretations of the Russian occupation of Eastern Europe, the administration of Berlin, the Atlantic Pact, the Marshall Plan, NATO, and so on.[14]

Cultural exchange programs. Since World War II, international exchange of students has boomed (there were 34,000 foreign students in the U.S. in 1954); several studies have sought to survey the effects of such cross-cultural education.[15] For example, an extensive study was done by John and Ruth Useem of western-educated students in India.[16] Extensive interviews were held with Indians educated in America or Britain. Most of the group had been changed by their experience: a gain in self-confidence, a new philosophy of life, different methods of working, or a more democratic social approach were some of the major changes noted. Those trained in the U.S. seemed more optimistic and willing to gamble, and had more exaggerated ideas of their own economic worth than those educated in Britain. Most of the returnees admired the British or American people; the authors noted that "a moderate gain in international understanding has been achieved through foreign training." [17] At the same time, the Indian students were greatly disturbed by the racial discrimina-

13 E. Reves, *The anatomy of peace* (New York: Harper & Bros., 1946).

14 Behanan finds a similar threat to peace in the contrasting roles and aims of Hindus and Moslems. See K. T. Behanan, Cultural diversity and world peace, in W. Dennis (ed.), *Current trends in social psychology* (Pittsburgh: University of Pittsburgh Press, 1948).

15 See M. B. Smith (ed.), Attitudes and adjustment in cross-cultural contact, *J. soc. Issues*, I (1956), 12. In, America through foreign eyes, *Ann. Amer. Acad. pol. soc. Sci.*, 1954, p. 295, R. D. Lambert (ed.) tells how the United States is seen by Indian, Japanese, Mexican, and Scandinavian students.

16 J. Useem and R. H. Useem, *The western-educated man in India,—a study of his social roles and influence* (New York: The Dryden Press, Inc., 1955).

17 *Ibid.*, pp. 134-35.

Attitudes in the schoolroom may be developed in different directions—ethnocentrism on one side and internationalism on the other side. In both cases the teacher is eliciting behavior that may change attitudes in both the present and the future.

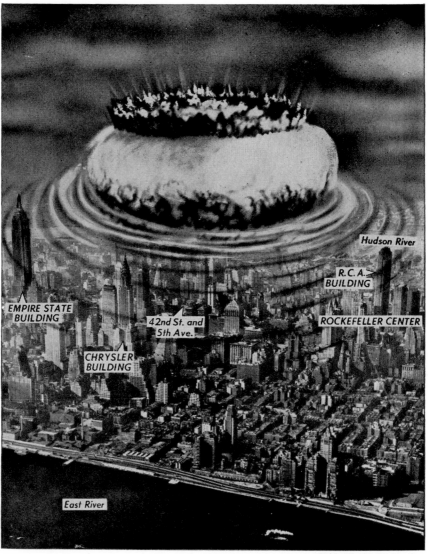

Hudson River

R.C.A.
BUILDING

EMPIRE STATE
BUILDING

42nd St. and
5th Ave.

ROCKEFELLER CENTER

CHRYSLER
BUILDING

East River

Wide World Photos, Inc.

Atomic destruction would be most acute in the highly urbanized areas, and each decade the potential effects of the bomb become deadlier as physicists and engineers perfect their research and technology. This composite drawing indicates the devastation possible in a skyscraper city—New York. Of course, the holocaust resulting would destroy much of the surrounding area as well.

tion they observed in both America and Britain. At home, the returnees enjoyed some prestige but had difficulty finding employment. One of the Useems' recommendations is that foundation funds be used to help the foreign-educated Indian obtain a position commensurate with his training.

It is not easy to sum up briefly the effects of exchange programs. Certainly they are not *necessarily* productive of more favorable attitudes. One study, for example, found that Belgian exchangees were not lastingly more favorable to United States policies and behavior as a result of their experience. Nor did they seem to have much influence on the attitudes of the Belgian population in general.[18] One reason generalizations are difficult to make is that students differ so much among themselves in their role as exchangees. They may act as detached observers, promoters, or salesmen for their homeland, enthusiastic participants in American life, or prospective settlers in the United States.[19] Obviously the meaning of the experience to the student and the long-range effects on his behavior will be greatly affected by the attitude and role which he adopts.

Another level of international cooperation is furnished by collaboration of scientists from different countries. While international scientific meetings are fairly common, it is unusual to find scientists from different countries working together on the same project. A pioneering piece of cross-national, social psychological research was participated in by more than thirty European social scientists and six American colleagues in Europe on Fulbright grants.[20] The problem investigated was the effect on group processes of perceived threat to the group; that is, does external threat make for greater or less group solidarity, and does it or does it not make for intolerance and curtailment of civil rights? Considerable similarity was found in interview results from Belgium, the United Kingdom, France, the Netherlands, Norway, Sweden, and Western Germany. For example, in the preliminary findings the acceptability of war relative to other solutions of international problems is related consistently to which of the major powers is seen as the source of danger in the world.[21]

18 O. W. Riegel, Residual effects of exchange of persons, *Pub. Opin. Quart.*, XVII (1953), 319-27.

19 W. H. Sewell and O. M. Davidsen, The adjustment of Scandinavian students, *J. soc. Issues*, XII (1956), 9-19.

20 E. Jacobson and S. Schachter (eds.), Cross-national research: a case study, *J. soc. Issues*, IV (1954), 10.

21 V. Aubert, B. R. Fisher, and S. Rokkan, A comparative study of teachers' attitudes to international problems and policies, *J. soc. Issues*, X (1954), 25-39.

UNDERSTANDING WAR AND ITS CAUSES

More dynamic interpretations of international misunderstandings and hostilities can be made.[22]   When the people of a nation are economically insecure or seriously frustrated, their tensions can easily be directed into aggressive action. Nearly all students of Germany, Italy, and Japan during the years preceding World War II noted much frustration, which was capitalized on by the dictators in power and funneled into preparation for war. Possibly the most basic of these frustrations is economic. The group of social scientists mentioned above stated in their 1948 declaration: "If we are to avoid the kind of aggression that leads to armed conflict, we must, among other things, so plan and arrange the use of productive power and resources that there will be maximum social justice. Economic inequalities, insecurities, and frustrations create group and national conflicts." [23]

However, we must not make the mistake of assuming that widespread frustrations automatically lead to war. As we saw earlier, the thesis that "frustration leads to aggression" is best considered a tendency rather than an absolute law. Many primitive peoples, and whole nations like China and India, may suffer decades if not centuries of deprivation and frustration without attacking their neighbors. Furthermore, Allport points out a difficulty in the aggression and scapegoating interpretations of war:

The fallacy of this purely personal explanation lies in the fact that howsoever pugnacious or frustrated an individual may be, he himself lacks the capacity to make organized warfare. He is capable of temper tantrums, also of chronic nagging, biting sarcasm, or personal cruelty; but he alone cannot invade an alien land or drop bombs upon a distant enemy to give vent to his own emotions. Furthermore, whereas national aggressiveness is total—all citizens being involved in offensive and defensive efforts—relatively few of the citizens feel personally hostile toward the enemy. Studies of soldiers in combat show that hate and aggression are less commonly felt than fear, homesickness and boredom. Few citizens, in an aggressive nation, actually feel *aggressive*. Thus their warlike activity cannot be due solely to their personal motivations.[24]

On the other hand, widespread frustrations give rise to strong emotions which may be channeled into war by such means as skilful propaganda. Given the frustrations of the Italian and German people after World War I, their dictators were able, after several years of astute propagandizing, to evoke considerable enthusiasm for war.

[22] See, e.g., G. W. Kisker (ed.), *World tension—the psychopathology of international relations.* (Englewood Cliffs, N. J.: Prentice-Hall, Inc., 1951); and M. L. Farber, Psychoanalytic hypotheses in the study of war, *J. soc. Issues,* XI (1955), 29-35.

[23] Tensions affecting international understanding, *Bull. Amer. Assn. Univ. Professors,* XXXIV (1948), 547.

[24] H. Cantril (ed.), *op. cit.,* pp. 44-45.

Hence the parts played by national leaders and the techniques they use form an important ingredient in the brew of war. One may argue, of course, that another leader instead of Hitler would have led Germany down the road to war just as Hitler did. However, no two leaders would have acted in just the same way nor would they have had equally efficient party organizations and propaganda machines, nor would they have played their cards in the same way. Another leader might have struck in 1937 instead of 1939—or might have waited until 1941. Or another leader might have played the diplomatic game more astutely than Hitler, or might have been much less efficient in his domestic propaganda. In any event the personality equation of powerful leaders is not to be omitted from the list of influences determining war or peace.

Some interpreters, of course, insist that man is by nature aggressive. But whether aggressiveness is inborn or acquired, the tendency is sufficiently deep-seated and universal that some provision must be made for its expression. Thus William James wrote of the "moral equivalent of war," meaning the attempt to discover constructive activities offering excitement and challenge such as those furnished by military exploits. Apparently aggressiveness can be sublimated through creative projects, in medicine or sports, in art or exploration. Can we find outlets so that aggressiveness and hostility will not smolder and fester at a deep unconscious level? One example is furnished by the many projects of the American Friends Service Committee, including summer work camps for draining swamps in Mexico, rebuilding devastated towns in Finland, or constructing a cable car line to replace a dynamited bridge in Italy.[25]

More specifically, what contributions can or might the social psychologist make toward maintaining peace?

First of all, he can help people to understand that war is not an inherent part of human nature. He can implement and explain the preamble of UNESCO's constitution, which reads: "Since wars begin in the minds of men, it is in the minds of men that the defences of peace must be constructed." War is not an aspect of human life in the sense hunger and sex are, nor is it an inevitable end result of living like old age and death. Wide realization of this fact is the first step toward intelligent action.

Second, the psychologist can join the educator in pointing the way toward reduction of nationalistic attitudes and development of worldmindedness. As the Psychologists' Manifesto puts it: "In planning for permanent peace, the coming generation should be the

25 See C. E. Pickett, *For more than bread* (Boston: Little, Brown, & Co., 1953), especially Part IV, The moral equivalent.

primary focus of attention. Children are plastic; they will readily accept symbols of unity and an international way of thinking in which imperialism, prejudice, insecurity, and ignorance are minimized." [26]

Furthermore, "Racial, national and group hatreds can, to a considerable degree, be controlled . . . people can learn that their prejudiced ideas about the English, the Russians, the Japanese, Catholics, Jews, Negroes, are misleading . . . that members of one racial, national, or cultural group are basically similar to those of other groups, and have similar problems, hopes, aspirations, and needs." [27] The psychologist can call attention to specific tasks like the revision of nationalistic textbooks and the value of travel and exchange of students and professors. Likewise he can stress the importance of mass communication "to encourage adequate understanding of the people in other countries. This must always be a two-way traffic. It will aid the cause of peace if nations are enabled to see themselves as others see them!" [28]

Again the social psychologist has a most significant job to do in making people realize the danger to peace which comes from frustration, emotion, and hysteria. This has broad implications—from exposing chauvinistic, rabble-rousing journalism all the way to underlining the need for progressive social changes in the direction of wider economic and emotional security for all peoples. Also, he can stress the guiding reality of the basic needs and cravings of human personality the world over—the bodily demands and security for their satisfaction; the needs for friendship and love, for freedom from fear, constraint, and frustration; the desire to realize one's potentialities and achieve some degree of status and recognition; the need for meaning and a philosophy of life. As the two thousand psychologists noted: "The root-desires of the common people of all lands are the safest guide to framing a peace. Disrespect for the common man is a characteristic of fascism and all forms of tyranny. The man in the street does not claim to understand all the complexities of economics and politics, but he is clear as to the general directions in which he wishes to progress." [29]

The social psychologist can join the historian and political scientist in informing people that man has shown he is capable of achieving ever larger and more inclusive loyalties. To quote again the Psychologists' Manifesto: "The trend of human relationships is

[26] Murphy, *op. cit.*, p. 455.

[27] *Ibid.*, pp. 455-56.

[28] Tensions affecting international understanding, *Bull. Amer. Assn. Univ. Professors,* XXXIV (1948), 547.

[29] Murphy, *op. cit.*, pp. 456-57.

toward ever wider units of collective security. From the caveman to the twentieth century, human beings have formed larger and larger working and living groups. Families merged into clans, clans into states, and states into nations. The United States are not forty-eight threats to each other's safety; they work together. At the present moment the majority of our people regard the time as ripe for regional and world organization, and believe that the initiative should be taken by the United States of America." [30]

But the social psychologist's task does not end with recommendations for action, based upon his knowledge and research. At least two other tasks remain for him—research into techniques by which people can learn to modify their nationalistic attitudes and enlarge their loyalties, and actual participation in international cooperation at the professional level.

Work has already begun in both these areas. Some twenty social psychologists, for example, participated in the preparation of a publication devoted to discussion of citizen participation in world affairs.[31] Their contributions were concerned with reasons for public apathy, techniques for getting people interested, ways of reducing hysterical and irrational public reactions, ways of getting relevant information to the public, and ways of making the public's views known to policy-makers.

An active group of social scientists, chiefly social psychologists, set up the Research Exchange for Prevention of War in 1952, which has greatly stimulated research in this whole area.[32] Its Bulletin was succeeded in 1957 by a new quarterly, the Journal of Conflict Resolution, with a large group of outstanding social scientists participating.

UNESCO, the educational and cultural branch of the United Nations, has pioneered in bringing social scientists together as a necessary step in the broader plan of furthering international cooperation at the intellectual and artistic levels. Otto Klineberg, one of the first directors of the International Tensions project of UNESCO and later director of the Division of Applied Social Sciences, has discussed the role of the psychologist in international affairs. He notes several activities of UNESCO which are psychological in nature: [33]

[30] Murphy, op. cit., p. 457.

[31] E. Maccoby and B. Willerman (eds.), Citizen participation in world affairs; problems and possibilities, J. soc. Issues, IV:1 (1948).

[32] See also H. C. Kelman, W. Barth, and R. Hefner (eds.), Research approaches to the study of war and peace, Jour. soc. Issues, I (1955), 11; and T. Lentz, Towards a science of peace (St. Louis: Attitude Research Lab., 1955).

[33] O. Klineberg, The role of the psychologist in international affairs, J. soc. Issues, Sup. series, IX (1956).

1. Research studies on stereotypes and national cultures;
2. Disseminating research findings, notably a series of booklets on race questions in modern science;
3. Sponsorship of research requested by member states, such as the Murphy study of intergroup tensions in India; [34]
4. Evaluation, through research, of UNESCO programs on international cooperation;
5. Stimulation of international developments in psychology—e.g., aiding in the establishment of the International Union of Scientific Psychology.

In addition, Klineberg calls attention to the activites of psychologists in the World Health Organization, the International Labour Organization, the World Federation for Mental Health, and the European Productivity Agency. One of the projects is concerned with studying the techniques of international cooperation, along the lines of group dynamics research.[35]

Let it not be thought, however, that social psychologists are starry-eyed about the possibilities of achieving world organization and lasting peace. They realize the task is tremendous and theirs but one contribution among many. Miller suggests, for example, that in preventing war "a mass religious conversion, a mass intellectual movement to develop a world-wide value system, or the intensive research in physics and biological warfare that is going on now—are more promising in the short range than anything offered by social psychology." [36] He sees greater hope in social psychological contributions over a longer period of years, in terms of communications research, study of group functioning, of attitude change, of personality dynamics, of group therapy, and of effective educational methods. Watson calls on social psychologists to approach the problems of world understanding with humility. The points made in the Psychologists' Manifesto, while true, he suggests, "do not come to grips with the problem of peace as we face it today." [37] Reexamination of such principles shows the need for a wider grasp of social sciences, for research on the power problems of society, for practical "know-how" through action research, and for an effective world-wide organization of psychologists.

Realistically speaking, of course, the social psychologist's contribution in this tremendous area of international relations, of war

[34] G. Murphy, *In the minds of men* (New York: Basic Books, Inc., 1953).

[35] See *Intl. soc. Sci. Bull.*, V (1953), 278 ff.

[36] J. G. Miller, Psychological approaches to the prevention of war, in W. Dennis (ed.), *Current trends in social psychology* (Pittsburgh: University of Pittsburgh Press, 1948).

[37] G. Watson, Psychological contributions to world understanding, *Amer. Psychologist*, IV (1949), 65.

and peace, is only a drop in the bucket. But there are hopeful aspects too. One is suggested by Gunnar Myrdal:

> In spite of all their very apparent weaknesses as organs for interstate cooperation, international organizations, when once established, and no matter how ineffective they are in carrying out their terms of reference, show an amazing resistance to death which contrasts sharply with the frequent instability of public opinion in international questions.[38]

Research and applications in the thorny field of international relations, it would seem, are extremely difficult but by no means impossible, even though the nations of the world are lining up in two rival camps. The intensity of present-day antagonisms is a luxury that we cannot indefinitely afford. Social psychologists, along with fellow-scientists in other fields, have made a small beginning and are determined to carry on their work.

SUMMARY

Since World War II the social scientist's interest in international relations has increased; social psychologists are cooperating with other specialists to study the causes of international tension and to explore ways by which more lasting peace may be achieved. Among other things, they are seeking techniques for changing nationalistic attitudes, for reducing and channeling aggressiveness, and for encouraging international cooperation of students, and of social scientists. Only a small beginning has been made but we have reason to expect greater achievement in the future.

SUPPLEMENTARY READINGS

Book of Readings

BRITT, S. H. (ed.). *Selected readings in social psychology.* New York: Rinehart & Co., Inc., 1950.
 Cantril, H., Psychology working for peace.
 Cottrell, L. S., and Eberhart, S., Are the people concerned?

Other References

CANTRIL, H. (ed.). *Tensions that cause wars.* Urbana, Ill.: The University of Illinois Press, 1950.
 A series of articles by international social scientists brought together by UNESCO. "The role of expectancy" by Gordon Allport is particularly worth reading.

CARR, L. J. *Analytical sociology.* New York: Harper & Bros., 1955.
 Although the book treats the problem of social change and planning in general, there are some pages specifically concerned with international relations.

38 G. Myrdal, Psychological impediments to effective international cooperation, *J. soc. Issues,* Sup. series, VI (1952), 29.

DEUTSCH, K. W. *Nationalism and social communication.* New York: John Wiley & Sons, Inc., 1953.
A scholarly work on the roots of nationalism and its economic aspects, and the role of communication.

JANIS, I. L. *Air war and emotional stress.* New York: McGraw-Hill Book Co., Inc., 1951.
A psychological study of the effects of bombing as demonstrated in surveys in Germany and Japan during World War II.

KELMAN, H. C., BARTH, W., AND HEFNER, R. (eds.). Research approaches to the study of war and peace, *J. soc. Issues*, XI:1 (1955).
In addition, material on citizen participation in world affairs is found in Vol. IV, No. 1, (1948).

KLINEBERG, O. Tensions affecting international understanding: a survey of research, *Soc. sci. Res. Council Bull.*, LXII (1950).
———. The role of the psychologist in international affairs. *J. soc. Issues*, Supplement Series, IX (1956).
Klineberg, probably more than any other psychologist, has occupied himself with international tensions and UNESCO projects.

KRECH, D., AND CRUTCHFIELD, R. S. *Theories and principles of social psychology.* New York: McGraw-Hill Book Co., Inc., 1948.
Chapter 15 still stands as a brief but penetrating analysis of the problem of securing peace.

MAY, M. A. *A social psychology of war and peace.* New Haven: Yale University Press, 1943.
The problem of aggression analyzed in terms of learning and motivation theory.

MURPHY, G. (ed.). *Human nature and enduring peace.* Boston: Houghton Mifflin Co., 1945.
An interdisciplinary approach reflecting more optimism than some of the authors might express today.

SHILS, E. A. *The torment of secrecy.* Glencoe, Ill.: Free Press, 1956.
American security policies, the problem of intellectual integrity and of scientific communication and their relevance to present world peace.

SPEIER, H. *Social order and the risks of war.* New York: George W. Stewart, Inc., 1952.
A number of essays on war, especially with reference to German politics and ideology.

STOUFFER, S. A., *et al. Studies in social psychology in World War II.* Princeton: Princeton University Press, 1949.
The psychology of war as intensively studied in attitudinal surveys of the American soldier in World War II.

24

The Present and the Future
of Social Psychology

This text has been an introduction to an exciting area of social science. In the quantity of theory and research, printed literature, and number of college classes and students, it appears that the field has been growing even faster than some of its neighboring disciplines. Hundreds of books, monographs, and articles in this field appear every year in the United States. It is significant, too, that social psychology has become a vital subject to foreign countries in recent years. The reason for this growth, both here and abroad, is clear: the need to discover the psychological basis for a number of critical social problems.

Social psychology has come a long way in the half century since the texts of Ross and McDougall appeared in 1908. Progress in theory, in methodology, and in applications has been great, although there is still far to go before social psychologists reach a satisfying state of agreement. The attempt has been made in this book to advance a fairly systematic theoretical framework and to describe some major areas of application. It may be well to summarize and discuss these briefly here.

Psychologists and psychiatrists are primarily interested in the individual; sociologists and anthropologists concentrate upon the group. The social psychologist overlaps all of these and also provides links between them; he studies the individual-in-the-group—the individual as he stimulates and responds to others. For research he utilizes the best methods available, preferring experimentation and controlled observation but refusing to limit himself exclusively to these if the data do not lend themselves to such treatment.

After a clarification of the hereditary-environmental relationships the socialization of the individual was investigated in order to discover what cultural and social influences affect the development of personality and social behavior. Both preliterate and more advanced cultures were discussed to discover what generalizations could be made about the individual personality in the cultural milieu. The differences between an American, a German, a Japanese, and a Russian must be explained in the social pressures that operate on him. It must be constantly kept in mind that individual differences generally transcend cultural differences. Regarding the conditioning of cultures and subcultures in the early years, further evidence is necessary before any reliable generalizations can be derived. However, we found that there are some significant, though tentative, empirical regularities regarding the effects of family, school, peer group, and such broader influences as the community, social class, and ethnic background. There appears to be a complex relationship between heredity and environment, including social learning and cultural conditioning.

It was concluded that these cultural and social influences are most significant with respect to attitudes, interests, values, and habits rather than with respect to temperament, intelligence, or even personality "traits." Through the processes of learning, one's social experiences fill in the details or furnish the content of personality. Hence, a child endowed by heredity with certain physical, temperamental, and intellectual potentialities may come to be liberal or conservative, sociable or nonsociable, tolerant or bigoted, selfish or altruistic, devoted to sports, music, gardening, or politics, an insecure dilettante or a productive professional man, a minister, lawyer, businessman, embezzler, or drunkard, largely depending on the complex of social and cultural influences operating upon him from the moment of his birth. However, this interpretation by no means relegates hereditary and physiological influences to a position of insignificance. The range of one's performance or achievement is to a large degree limited by hereditary endowment. But within that range lies an almost infinite variety of possibilities, whose specific outcomes are chiefly a function of social experience.

Motivation of the human being remains a tantalizing area of investigation because of the impossibility of observing these elusive variables. An outline of social motives was suggested with utmost caution and tentativeness. Drives, motives, needs, urges, and the like are sets or predispositions of complex nature, almost impossible to classify meaningfully. They involve directed energies of the organism and are normally set off by incentives—that is, related environmental stimuli. Some motives are clearly physiological in origin—the tissue needs or drives—while others depend upon social experience. The question whether, and to what degree, sociogenic motives become autonomous has not been settled. In any event, motives represent directed energies of the individual and are affected by a complex of physiological and social determinants.

When strong motives are blocked, frustration occurs. The sign of frustration is strong emotion, notably anger or fear, which impels the individual to action. The specific behavior occurring, however, is no simple function of the dominant emotion. It is determined primarily by two factors: learned mechanisms or modes of reaction to frustration, and the way in which the individual perceives the situation. Most persons, for example, have learned how to displace, to regress, to project, to rationalize, to repress. Which of these mechanisms will be employed to channel the anger or fear aroused by frustration depends in large measure on the way the individual interprets his immediate social environment.

Equally important in understanding the behavior of the individual are his cognitive processes, perception and learning. The individual is oriented toward the world by his sense organs operating together with a complex set of symbols. Through this perceptual process he imposes meaning on his environment. All socially relevant stimuli are fitted into perceptually derived frames of reference.

We did not become deeply involved in learning theories, as it appears that further research and integration will be necessary before a learning theory may be applicable to social phenomena. Probably most hopeful is the schema of Miller and Dollard describing major factors in the learning process: drive, cue, response, and reward. "Drive" refers to any tension on the part of the person which impels him toward action. "Cue" signifies the stimulus situation, as perceived and interpreted by the individual. "Response" is the reaction made as a result of the joint effects of the drive and the cue. But this response, once made, is not thereby learned; it is learned (or eliminated) as a result of reward (or punishment)—i.e., of "reinforcement." Mores, taboos, conventions, attitudes, values, concepts, roles, and social norms are among the products of social learning having great significance for social behavior.

Attitudes occupy a central role in social psychology and follow logically from a Gestalt of motivation, learning, and perception.

Attitudes constitute the focal area for many social psychologists. They are relatively permanent cognitive dispositions, marked by feeling tone, impelling the individual toward or away from certain persons or situations. Related to attitudes are social norms and values as determinants of cognition and behavior.

Closely related to motives, cognitions, and attitudes are other dynamic aspects of the individual, notably the "ego" or self. It was indicated that older theories of the self or ego are being revived, as "that which is peculiarly one's own"—the ideas, objects, persons, and activities with which one identifies himself. Likewise one's self-image or idea of self develops from his social experience and comes to occupy a central and directive position in his personality. According to Sherif and Cantril, the ego is a constellation of attitudes and norms built up through one's contacts with his major membership and reference groups. One becomes "ego-involved" when persons, objects, and events become related to that which he considers peculiarly *his own* or *himself*. Ego-involvement can be observed when ego-attitudes are aroused, as when an acquaintance makes fun of an activity or group which is very dear to a person. Interpreters of the ego, despite differences, agree that it is a central, dynamic core of personality which cannot be overlooked if we are to understand an individual's social behavior.

A survey of interpersonal relations was begun with an examination of language and communication. It was observed that symbolic language is distinctively human and that any language reflects the culture from which it springs. As the infant learns to speak and thereby acquires the most significant means of communicating with others, he also assimilates important social concepts and values. However, any symbolic medium contains pitfalls; words break away from their referents and acquire connotations, emotional and otherwise, which lead to errors in communication and thus to disturbed interpersonal relations.

Descriptions of social interaction are various. Most social scientists list a few basic forms such as conflict, competition, and cooperation. Others refuse to classify forms but focus on the frequency and intensity of interpersonal responses, irrespective of their nature.

If social psychologists are attracted to the study of attitudes, it might be said that they equally regard the investigation of the group, particularly the small group, as their logical niche in the domain of social science. No other area of social psychology has been more the subject of research than group processes. It was noted that there are some distinctions in types of groups. The difference between the primary and the secondary group is fundamental, whether in the neighborhood, school, factory, or in a military encampment or battleline. It is equally important to understand the formation and structure of the group, as well as dimensions like consensus, cohesion, and conformity.

To describe the specific pattern of interaction existing between a given person and another person or group, the concept of role is valuable. A role is defined as a type or pattern of social behavior which seems situationally appropriate to the individual in terms of the demands and expectations of those in his group. A role such as that of teacher or student, employer or employee, parent or child, host or guest, channels and delimits the social behavior occurring. Some roles may be called cultural, in the sense that their characteristics are determined largely by cultural norms; others depend more upon particular personal-social relationships, while still others, more temporary in character, are evoked by specific social situations. Roles can be contrasted with personality traits; the former operate largely as situational determinants and the latter as enduring habitual tendencies of the individual. In some social situations, such as those where conformity is demanded, a person's perceived role is the major determinant of his social behavior. In a less structured social situation, such as a meeting of strangers, social interaction depends more upon the interacting personalities of the individuals.

Leadership is a good example of role behavior; each leader plays a fairly well-defined role in his group. Neither the "man" (personality) nor the "times" (situation) theory alone accounts for leadership. The most complete interpretation of a leader depends upon the interrelationship of his personality dynamics and his role in relation to his followers. One important aspect of leadership is the contrast between democratic and authoritarian roles. Whether in business, education, or politics, this distinction has enormous implications for our society.

Thus, ours is a field-theory approach to social psychology, by which we study the outstanding or "salient" personal and situational influences operating. Sometimes, as with psychotic or highly frustrated individuals, the salient determinants of a given bit of social behavior are found in personality dynamics. At the other extreme, as in highly structured situations such as ceremonies or rituals, prevailing social norms and roles are the outstanding factors. Most social behavior, however, is somewhere between these extremes; it can be interpreted, predicted, and controlled only through a knowledge of the participants' personality trends *and* the social structure.

Research in social psychology is directed largely toward discovering, in the whole field of interacting forces, the important personal and situational determinants of social behavior. In experimental studies, the investigator seeks to study the effects of one significant variable at a time. The oftener he finds it operating in various social situations, the more certain he can be of its general importance. It is difficult, of course, to make accurate quantitative estimates of the strength of major variables in any given situation. But, as more and more research is done, we acquire better methods for identifying and measuring the salient influences which operate. We must deal with the whole pattern of important variables in a given social situation, however, whether or not it is possible to quantify them accurately. To limit oneself to the factors which are measurable is questionable procedure. In social psychology today, oversimplification is a greater danger than underquantification.

In Part IV we undertook to analyze and interpret selected social phenomena which are particularly challenging to the social scientist—public opinion, propaganda, mass behavior, social change, social movements, prejudice, and social conflicts. We found that the social psychologist can measure opinions and attitudes fairly accurately but is less successful in predicting future behavior on the basis of these measures, although predictions are becoming more valid with every decade. The nature of propaganda is understood, but it is difficult to identify. Though it is possible to formulate general rules for effectiveness of propaganda, it is doubtful that people can learn to protect themselves against propaganda in general.

The social psychologist is reasonably familiar with the characteristics and determinants of crowd and mob behavior, of panics, fashions, fads, crazes, booms, rumors, and mass hysteria, though he has little to report with respect to their prediction and control. He supplements sociological and anthropological approaches by studying attitudes toward social change and personal adjustment to change. Likewise he has contributed to an understanding of social movements—those active groups seeking to bring about gradual but extensive changes in the status quo.

The last part of the text revolved about the problem of bettering human relations. First, we discussed the nature of group dynamics and its applications to industry. This type of applied social psychology appears to be the essence of human relations programs. In addition, problems of morale, productivity, and employee-employer relations in general have been investigated by research methods developed by Lewin and his students and colleagues. Group dynamics, moreover, is important in investigating democratic leadership and its training.

Another critical area in applied social psychology is ethnic relations. Race differences are generally discussed under the heading "ethnic differences," as there is considerable mythology attached to the word "race." Ethnic prejudice is acquired with perceptual and motivational processes playing a major role. Status needs are very important in the formation of prejudice, especially when driven by personality mechanisms, such as conflicts, frustration, and projection. Being learned, ethnic prejudice can be unlearned, or at least reduced, by appropriate methods.

International problems represent perhaps the most crucial area in social psychology with the survival of mankind itself at stake. Some of the psychological mechanisms of aggressive nationalism were described, as well as some preventative and ameliorative aspects as revealed in action research.

In applied, as in theoretical studies, the social psychologist needs to use a field approach. Persons are always involved—individuals with certain attitudes, needs, and habits. And every case is a social situation, large or small, structured or unstructured as to prevalent norms and roles. Personality and situational influences both enter into people's perceptions and interpretations, which serve as the immediate determinants of their social behavior. Sometimes personality trends clearly predominate, as when people's needs and frustrations drive them to engage in prejudice or discrimination or prevent them from adjusting to social change. Conversely, compelling social norms and rigidly prescribed roles may weigh the more heavily, resulting, for example, in stereotyped opinions and attitudes or in crowd behavior. Most frequently, of course, personality and situational determinants operate more equally, as was noted in the discussion of propaganda and of social movements.

If our interpretations lean too far in one or the other direction, efforts to make applications are likely to be lacking in effectiveness. We shall not eliminate prejudice, for example, by changing traditional attitudes toward minority groups if deep-seated frustrations abound. Nor, conversely, will prejudice vanish in those persons whose frustrations are alleviated, since they have learned the traditional attitudes. Granting, of course, that either change would probably *reduce* prejudices, the most effective tolerance program will address itself both to the modification of traditional attitudes and to the removal of personal tensions.

CONTEMPORARY ISSUES IN SOCIAL PSYCHOLOGY

In this treatment of social psychology, the authors have insisted that a scientific approach must be the first consideration. We agree with Sherif when he speaks of three primary considerations in social psychology: (1) the use of scientific methods and techniques, (2) checks against the investigator's own ethnocentrism, and (3) the study of social behavior within a framework of interacting influences of the individual and the group.[1] In applying the scientific method the social psychologist must consider wherever possible the operational definition of his concepts. That is to say, all terms must be defined, quantitatively if possible, in terms of their function, i.e., what they actually do. This would be true whether the orientation is that of pure theory or in applied action research.

Methods and theories. Undoubtedly, the prerequisite to the advancement of a social science is a satisfactory methodology. In the preface to the *Handbook of Social Psychology*,[2] Lindzey asks whether social psychology as a science has developed on the basis of a well integrated combination of theory and methods. He concludes that the discipline has actually grown piecemeal without much empirical sophistication, but it is likely that future advances will rest increasingly on the development of explicit methods. It is improbable that social psychology, either in its theory or in its methods, will ever reach the precision of physics or chemistry. At the same time, it has been demonstrated that casual observation in its various forms is hardly adequate to establish a science in any contemporary sense. Throughout the text some of the major methods were indicated, such as field and case studies, controlled experiments, and naturalistic observation. In recent years these have been multiplied to include panel analyses and prediction studies, especially to observe the behavior of a group through time.

Hand in hand with the development of methodology has been the advance of theory. In this volume some of the major theoretical constructs have been outlined, whether cultural relativism, or symbolic interaction, or any number of other concepts. As with methodology, the task is not simple. The variables are sufficiently complex so that the derivation of a theory accounting for all relevant events frequently eludes the investigator. Repeatedly, the authors have pointed out the problems involved in "explaining" individual and social behavior. Why a young man chooses to be a professional lawyer rather than a high-level embezzler depends on

[1] M. Sherif and C. W. Sherif, *An outline of social psychology* (rev. ed.; New York: Harper & Bros., 1956), p. 758.

[2] G. Lindzey (ed.), *Handbook of social psychology* (Reading, Mass.: Addison-Wesley Pub. Co., Inc., 1954), Vol. I, p. viii. See also A. W. Gouldner, Theoretical requirements of applied social sciences, *Amer. sociol. Rev.*, XXII (1957), 92–102. Gouldner believes some of the "pure" theories should be revamped in the light of newly developing applied fields.

the interaction of many events. A valid theoretical explanation of why Russians are likely to retain a military police state, although Czechoslovakians may not, would require considerably more research, and certainly a more far-reaching set of constructs of national character than we have at present, despite the impressive progress made in recent years in that field of inquiry.

Biases, goals, and values. In regard to Sherif's caution about the problem of ethnocentrism and the role of the social scientist, it cannot be overemphasized that the social scientist is subject to biases that are highly distracting. These biases may or may not be conscious: the desire for promotion in academic rank, or a position with the Federal government (which may necessitate a security clearance). Then one must not offend his dean, who might be a bridge player, a Christian Scientist, or a conservative Republican. His own more latent value orientations, too, may act to influence his predisposition to investigate social events, in terms of what problems he chooses to study and how he looks at them.

Furthermore, the social scientist can hardly avoid the very basic question of how great a devotion he is prepared to pay for his professional responsibility as a scientist. This dilemma is not confined to our discipline. After all, the physicist must decide whether he is, or is not, going to aid in the fabrication of nuclear and hydrogen bombs. But the social psychologist is potentially interfering with a number of crucial issues most of the time. Vested interests may conspire to make the role of social scientist particularly vulnerable. During the early fifties when the cold war was at its height, for example, it became less than healthy for a social psychologist to voice conceptualizations that might be interpreted as having a "leftish" tinge. Writing of the individuals who refused to sign the loyalty oath at the University of California at a time when a certain Wisconsin senator was excessively active, Tolman stated:

It may well be that the McCarthy psychology is going to win out in the end over our non-signing psychology in determining the future course of this country's social institutions. If it does, we psychologists and sociologists must be prepared to close up shop right then and there just as our confreres had to do in Nazi Germany and have done in Communist Russia.[3]

The attempt to exclude human values from science has been challenged by many writers, among them Robert S. Lynd.[4] It is futile for the social scientist, says Lynd, to cloister himself in a cita-

---

3 E. C. Tolman, A theoretical analysis of the relations between sociology and psychology, *J. abnorm. soc. Psychol.*, XLVII (1952), 291-98.

4 R. S. Lynd, *Knowledge for what?* (Princeton, N. J.: Princeton University Press, 1939).

del of "objectivity" while the world cries for aid in the solution of its social problems. Furthermore, he adds, the scientist is deluding himself if he thinks he is free of value concepts, for "a science is itself but a bit of culture. And every going culture, even our own 'free' culture, actually operates as a selective screen that tends to set the scientist to work on certain problems and to distract his gaze gently but coercively from others." [5] He goes on to say:

A social scientist has no place, *qua* scientist, as a party to power-politics. When he works within the constricting power curbs of a Republican or of a Communist "party line," or when he pulls his scientific punch by pocketing more important problems and accepting a retainer to work as an expert for the partisan ends of a bank or an advertising agency, he is something less than a scientist. In a positive sense, when he does such things he is actively inviting the Hitler-type of open control over science by whittling away the crucial claim of science that it is objective and cannot be bought for the use of unscientifically defined versions of the public interest. But, also, when the social scientist hides behind the aloof "spirit of science and scholarship" for fear of possible contamination, he is likewise something less than a scientist. We social scientists need to be more candid about ourselves and our motivations. We should be more sensitive and realistic about what our evasions do to ourselves and to our science. [6]

The same view has been expressed by social psychologists. Objectivity and impartiality are unattainable ideals. Cultural and personal values affect the social scientist's selection of subjects for research and the interpretations he makes of his findings, if not the methods he employs. This being the case, runs this argument, he would do best to throw his weight in a direction which will count in a real world, where problems are many and where time is short.

Can these conflicting viewpoints be reconciled? Lynd and others are certainly correct in insisting that even the most objective social scientist operates according to value concepts, whether or not he is aware of them. They make a trenchant observation in pointing out that many social scientists are little concerned with the real problems facing the world today. But what are the implications of these views? Surely it would be short-sighted to insist that the scientist's value concepts be determined exclusively by current social needs and problems. The major contributions of G. H. Mead, Cooley, Dewey, Boas, Malinowski, Linton, Lewin, Sherif, and Lynd himself were made chiefly within a value framework of pure rather than applied science.

It would seem that the distinction between theory and application is valid if one considers it a difference in degree rather than in kind. Seldom is the "pure" scientist oblivious of the potential ap-

5 *Ibid.*, p. 177.
6 *Ibid.*, p. 178.

plications of his findings, or the engineer and practitioner uninterested in possible theoretical implications of his work. If we make a sharp distinction, we may forget that both emphases are frequently found in the same person. One thinks of Dewey in philosophy and education, of Boas in anthropology, of Merriam in political science, of Thorndike in psychology, as figures whose contribution is great in both theory and application.

In social psychology, particularly in recent years, we find that the outstanding persons have contributed both to theory and to practice; examples are Gordon Allport, Gardner Murphy, Kurt Lewin, Otto Klineberg, Theodore Newcomb, Hadley Cantril, and Paul Lazarsfeld.

By and large, social psychologists refuse to make a forced choice between theory and application. They do not wish to be classified as *either* pure *or* applied scientists. They exemplify the dictum well expressed by Lewin in the words: "No research without action; no action without research."

When one looks about him at the amount and variety of social psychological research now taking place, one may be reminded of the daring horseman who mounted his steed and "rode off in all directions." He will see social psychologists studying perceptual processes, propaganda, frustration, industrial relations, language, cooperation among animals, public opinion polls, effects of class membership on personality, fads and fashions, social roles, acquired drives, international attitudes, and all kinds of small group behavior. But if the observer looks more closely he will find order and system. He will note that many of the "theorists" are also interested in practical social problems. Conversely a number of those primarily concerned with applications are contributing likewise to psychological theory. Many students of social perception are equally interested in international relations. Several social psychologists engaged professionally in opinion and attitude measurement are also doing research on topics of theoretical import. By and large, social psychologists believe that worth-while applications cannot be made unless supported by sound theory, much of which will derive from research in practical areas. The most highly developed curricula for training in social psychology, such as those at Michigan, Harvard, and Columbia, stress both theory and practice. This unitary approach seems an encouraging sign for the future.

Another hopeful note is the increasing collaboration among psychologists, psychiatrists, sociologists, anthropologists, and other specialists in attacking a variety of problems. Fruitful cooperation has already been shown in such areas as "culture and personality," frustration and its effects, social roles, leadership, "group dynamics," public opinion polling, prejudice, and industrial and international problems. Psychologists, psychiatrists, and social scientists are demonstrating that they can collaborate productively without losing their professional identities. It is true that increased proximity sometimes generates misunderstanding and even intolerance, but the general trend is definitely toward greater interdisciplinary cooperation. The newly developed graduate training programs in "human relations" and "social relations" at Yale, Harvard, Michigan, and many other universities and colleges suggest that this tendency will continue. And, as indicated earlier, social psychology is close to the focal center of *rapprochement* of the psychological and social sciences. Certainly when one considers some of the excitingly "new" areas of social psychology, like psycholinguistics, national character studies, and medical psychosociology, one finds a number of disciplines are involved.

Undoubtedly social psychology could have a more useful function if, along with other social sciences, it received more social support. It is almost pedestrian to point out that considerably more prestige is assigned to researchers in the physical sciences than is given to the behavioral sciences. Certainly, business and industrial organizations perceive more advantage in the concrete explorations of chemistry and petroleum geology than in, say, psychology or cultural anthropology. Consequently, private and public funds are likely to be allotted to the more practical fields of endeavor. To cite an example, one reflects how difficult it has been to obtain funds from the United States Congress for the social sciences as compared to the physical disciplines. Although there has been improvement in recent years, the problem still remains.

Social psychology, we conclude, is being increasingly accepted as a valuable field of study. Its methods and techniques and its theoretical and practical contributions to problems of human social behavior are recognized, although they are but a beginning. Perhaps the greatest task facing social psychologists is to synthesize the personality-oriented interpretations of psychologists and psychiatrists with the situational emphases of social scientists. The outline of such a synthesis has emerged in the field approach already described, but continuing clarification and refinement are needed.

The progress of social psychology since 1900 gives us reason to believe that it will play an important role in the world of tomorrow. Behavioral scientists are directing their energies toward developing not only more systematic theory but also more useful applications. Every decade brings increasing public demand for improved techniques of human relations, which are, after all, the applications of social psychology and closely related disciplines. If communication and understanding between the social scientist and the public continue, only beneficial results can follow.

SUPPLEMENTARY READINGS

BARBER, B. *Science and the social order.* Glencoe, Ill.: Free Press, 1952.
The sociology of science and the nature of research, comparing the social and natural sciences.

GILLIN, J. (ed.). *For a science of social man.* New York: The Macmillan Co., 1954.
An interdisciplinary approach especially in regard to the role of anthropologist, psychologist, and sociologist.

GRINKER, R. R. (ed.) *Toward a unified theory of human behavior.* New York: Basic Books, Inc., 1956.
A number of behavioral scientists discuss the prospects for integration between their disciplines.

HULETT, J. E., AND STAGNER, R. (eds.). *Problems in social psychology: an interdisciplinary inquiry.* Urbana, Ill.: University of Illinois Press, 1952.
Some provocative questions are raised regarding the methods and goals of the discipline.

LEIGHTON, A. H. *Human relations in a changing world.* New York: E. P. Dutton Co., Inc., 1949.
The role of the social scientist in world affairs, as reflected in the author's experience in World War II.

LUNDBERG, G. A. *Can science save us?* New York: Longmans, Green & Co., Inc., 1947.
An empiricist demonstrates that science can find the answers for some of our problems and is the only secure method for the improvement of society.

LYND, R. S. *Knowledge for what?* Princeton, N. J.: Princeton University Press, 1939.
The adequacies and inadequacies in values and aims of the social science research.

SARGENT, S. S., AND BRAMELD, T. (eds.). Anti-intellectualism in the United States, *J. soc. Issues,* XI:3 (1955).
A number of studies analyzing anti-intellectualist tendencies found in government, business, education, and other institutions.

SHERIF, M., AND SHERIF, C. W. *An outline of social psychology,* rev. ed. New York: Harper & Bros., 1956.
The final chapter summarizes some of the tendencies and problems of contemporary social psychology.

Name Index

Subject Index